Derek Walcott

Derek Walcott: A Caribbean Life

by Bruce King

Also by Bruce King

Derek Walcott and West Indian Drama: Not Only a Playwright But a Company:
   The Trinidad Theatre Workshop 1959–1993
V. S. Naipaul
Three Indian Poets: Ezekiel, Ramanujan and Moraes
Coriolanus
Modern Indian Poetry in English
The New English Literatures: Cultural Nationalism in a Changing World
History of Seventeenth-Century English Literature
Marvell's Allegorical Poetry
Dryden's Major Plays

Books edited by Bruce King

New National and Post-colonial Literatures: An Introduction
West Indian Literature
The Later Fiction of Nadine Gordimer
Post-Colonial English Drama: Commonwealth Drama since 1960
The Commonwealth Novel since 1960
Contemporary American Theatre
A Celebration of Black and African Writing
Literatures of the World in English
Introduction to Nigerian Literature
Dryden's Mind and Art
Twentieth Century Interpretations of 'All for Love'

Series edited by Bruce King

Modern Dramatists
English Dramatists
Literature, Culture, and Identity

Derek Walcott
A Caribbean Life

Bruce King

'no writer knows what direction his work will take, for his work is his life, and whatever happens to his life, however radical or subtle its changes, such changes will appear in his writing'

Derek Walcott, 'Is V. S. Naipaul An Angry Young Man?', *Sunday Guardian Magazine*, 6 August 1967, 8–9

OXFORD
UNIVERSITY PRESS

OXFORD
UNIVERSITY PRESS

Great Clarendon Street, Oxford OX2 6DP

Oxford University Press is a department of the University of Oxford.
It furthers the University's objective of excellence in research, scholarship,
and education by publishing worldwide in

Oxford New York

Athens Auckland Bangkok Bogotá Buenos Aires Calcutta
Cape Town Chennai Dar es Salaam Delhi Florence Hong Kong Istanbul
Karachi Kuala Lumpur Madrid Melbourne Mexico City Mumbai
Nairobi Paris São Paulo Singapore Taipei Tokyo Toronto Warsaw

and associated companies in Berlin Ibadan

Oxford is a registered trade mark of Oxford University Press
in the UK and certain other countries

Published in the United States
by Oxford University Press Inc., New York

British Library Cataloguing in Publication Data

Data available

Library of Congress Cataloging in Publication Data

Data available

ISBN 0-19-871131-X

1 3 5 7 9 10 8 6 4 2

Typeset by Graphicraft Limited, Hong Kong
Printed in Great Britain
on acid-free paper by
T.J. International Ltd.
Padstow, Cornwall

To Adele King and in memory of Nicole King

Preface

DEREK WALCOTT had answered a Marxist political polemic by saying that a writer's ultimate duty is to his God. When a friend remarked that West Indians are very religious, I realized that although I had written about Walcott's poems and plays I knew little about his personal beliefs or West Indian culture beyond the clichés that circulated among literary critics. By chance I ran into Walcott shortly afterwards and this led to my spending the next four years on *Derek Walcott and West Indian Drama: 'Not Only a Playwright But a Company': The Trinidad Theatre Workshop 1959–1993*, a study of a part of his life little known outside Trinidad. I was stunned that I had previously paid so little attention to the actual contexts of writers in the former colonies, how they earned their living, how they discovered their literary market, and how their thought might or might not change over the years.

I decided to start again by building on what I had learned about Walcott who months earlier had been awarded the Nobel Prize for Literature. Walcott was reluctant, but I received his permission to research and write a biography provided that I focused on what was relevant to his work and avoided unnecessary private and family matters. An old friend of his remarked 'but Derek's private life is in his work, that is what he writes about'. I can see that now. This is a book about a poet, dramatist, theatre director, painter, journalist, critic, teacher, intellectual, artist, what made him, what he made or tried to make, not who he made.

It is a long haul, and could have been twice as long, but afterwards some readers will look differently at Walcott, the West Indies, the arts, especially the arts in former colonies, and even parts of modern American culture. I do not include laundry lists, especially lists of stained laundry, but I do include some financial details and many dates. Even the reader who skips them will get an idea of a modern literary career, how much hard work and promotion goes into it, and how difficult it is to have one if living far from the world of publishing networks, a world uninterested in foreign cultures except as exotica and politics.

One of Walcott's favourite personae is Robinson Crusoe, and I came to see him as a new Robinson Crusoe, a Castaway who survived by creating a Caribbean culture for himself in a British colony from imported and local materials, who brought this culture of the Caribbean to the United States and Europe, who had to earn a living by making use of a talent which his religious training taught him it was death to hide. The more he felt fallen the more he wanted to write hymns and sermons. Being human he had fantasies of riches, and his personal life could at times be messy. His Friday and Muse was a woman, but which one?

One of three children of a widowed Methodist infant school teacher in St Lucia during the Great Depression, Derek Walcott had a long journey to the Nobel Prize for Literature in 1992. This book is about that journey and its contexts. It is also indirectly about cultural decolonization, the growth of New National literatures, the role of the United States in the creation of an international cultural market, even the changing basis of American and British literature.

Although best known as a poet, Walcott is a productive artist in many different fields. He has also been a teacher during most of his life, a teacher of poetry, painting, and theatre. His life and career are international. To understand why, what he was doing, what he created, how he earned his living, how he seized opportunities, who became his friends and whom he worked with, means following him from St Lucia to Jamaica, Grenada, Trinidad, St Croix, New York, Boston, London, Spain, not as distinct phases of a life but as a continually expanding map of places between which he is constantly commuting, almost criss-crossing, as much as any global businessman or diplomat. It is a story about important moments of West Indian culture, but also about American and recent international culture. His is a very modern life, a life that needs to be recorded partly in admiration of energy divine, but also because of what it reveals about art and a literary career at present.

I thought of organizing his life by topics, a chapter here on poetry, a chapter there on painting, another chapter on New York, still another about Walcott and Alan Ross, or Joseph Brodsky, or Paul Simon. The next biography can have the privilege of such simplicity, selectivity, and clarity, but it will be misleading. Lives are not clear unless you take the blood out of them and reduce them to ideas and illustrations. Walcott usually works on several projects at once. I wanted to show his ambitions, dreams, false directions, continual struggles, achievements, jokes, emotional outbursts, hard work, contradictions, even his leadership, emotional need, and use of others; how his life consists of many stories simultaneously in process, like the many metaphors, many punning words, many relationships between sounds in his poetry.

There was a strong Cubist influence by way of Eliot and early Auden on his own early poetry, and his life at times reminds me of a work by Duchamp or perhaps an Italian Futurist, fractured, moving on various planes in different directions at once. There is the Walcott trying to get advertising to pay for programmes for his theatre company in Trinidad, who sometimes reviewed their productions in local newspapers because no one else would, and whose posters for his plays will in future be collected as works of art. There is the Walcott who earned an Obie for the off-Broadway *Dream on Monkey Mountain*, who was awarded the 1992 Nobel Laureateship for Literature, and a few years later co-wrote *The Capeman* with Paul Simon, the biggest flop in Broadway history. At a time when critics were saying he is perhaps the best poet writing in English, Walcott was flat broke, had to start his life over again, and moved to the United States looking for a job and security.

Walcott could be a character in an eighteenth-century novel by Defoe, the epic of the early colonial period, the transition from aristocratic romance to the bourgeois capitalist epic of provincial origins, exploration, self-creation, accumulation, achievements, and making a place for oneself and family in the world, especially the New World. Such comparisons enlighten, but, as Walcott warns, reduce. Walcott's many obsesssions, interests, abilities, and careers have their genesis in his family, youth, and St Lucia. This is a West Indian story and therefore both universal and unlike others. My admiration for Walcott's poetry and plays will be obvious, but usually I have let the facts speak for themselves.

B. K.

Contents

List of Illustrations

The author and publisher gratefully acknowledge the following for permission to reproduce the illustrations:

Nancy Atkinson: plate 38
Mats Bäcker / Kungliga Dramatiska, Stockholm: plates 58, 59, 60, 61
Robert Benson: plates 41, 49, 50
Cadet Photos, St Lucia: plate 2
Helen Camps (photo: Chester Williams): plates 27, 28
Caribbean Quarterly: plates 9, 10
Centre for Caribbean Studies, University of Warwick: plate 64
Faye Chin: plates 4, 5, 6, 7
The Crusader, St Lucia: plate 8
Bill Grant: plate 62
Robert Hamner: plate 29
Peter Ireson: plates 15, 16, 17, 18, 21, 22, 51, 52, 53
Horace James: plate 11
Albert Laveau: plate 19
Mark Lyndersay: plates 42, 43, 44, 45, 46, 47, 48, 63
Richard Montgomery (photo: Sally Montgomery): plates 30, 31
Signa Nama: plate 39
PhoTOBIAS, Castries, St Lucia: plates 54, 55, 56, 57
A. Vincent Scarano: plates 13, 14
University of West the Indies, Trinidad (Special Collection): plates 32, 33, 34, 35, 36, 37

All other illustrations are from Bruce King's collection.

Part I

St Lucia Formation and Early Writings

I

〜〜〜〜〜〜〜〜〜〜〜〜〜〜〜〜〜〜

1930–1937 The Walcotts of St Lucia

DEREK WALCOTT has often written in a very New World way against the burden of History. For Walcott it is entangled with claims that the West Indies has no history or that it has no major events and achievements upon which to build, or that its events and achievements have mostly to do with, or build upon, slavery, racism, and violent conquest. Faced with such discourses it is better to begin afresh, to see life and history as an ocean which washes away the past and brings renewal with each wave and change in the tide. Better to be Adam, Crusoe, or Makak at the conclusion of *Dream on Monkey Mountain* who returns to his green mountain after a nightmare of black self-hatred and attempted purgation through visions of revenge. Walcott sees himself, his work, and the West Indies as a new start, but he also sees life and art as a series of imitations, like a child learning from the example of parents or an artist copying the work of an older master. Life imitates the past as Derek had to complete his father's work as an artist, as all loves imitate a person's first love, as cultures build upon previous cultures. Art and life survive by the memories of the elders, by example.

There is the Walcott who regards biography as about the dead, who reluctantly gave permission for this book, and there is the Walcott who throughout his life has filled his works with personal allusions and who has himself written several autobiographical works, some published, others unpublished. The latter Walcott has at times carefully preserved diaries, dated drafts of his work, made certain that future scholars have materials for research, and wants to be remembered. The wish for life as a continual new start, the American Dream of perpetual youth and creativity, coexists with the desire for permanence, for monuments, and *Remembrance*, the title of another Walcott play. Monuments are not only of the Self and its works, but also of its passions, time, and place, of the events and even non-achievements that are history as well as what they have come to symbolize.

Walcott is one, perhaps the best, of a generation of writers born around 1930 who rapidly created new national literatures, brought their cultures to international attention, and who are viewed as the cultural side of decolonization and the new nationalism which in turn led to 'post-colonialism'. While Walcott's life could be seen as that of any successful artist who moves from the provinces to the metropolis where by a combination of talent, luck, and opportunities, he becomes a success, it could be seen as representative of many of the great cultural changes of our time. It could also be seen as an epic of leaving home, explorations, battles abroad, conquests, the return home, the founding of a lineage. Walcott's life is like that of the epic hero of unusual abilities, of great strength, intelligence, and cunning, who falls into temptation, has rages, but is driven by his fate, by a seemingly God-given gift and purpose. There is even a bit of romantic epic when the low origins of the hero really disguise high connections. I like that story, it is a true one, but we live in a non-heroic age that deconstructs myths and heroes and claims that there are no agents.

Perhaps the bourgeois hero of the eighteenth- and nineteenth-century novel is more appropriate? Someone not only from the provinces, not only from the colonies, but someone who is 'red', 'high brown', someone who as a child was raised to think of himself as much more like the 'whites' than those darker and lower on the social scale, until in his teens he discovers the history of slavery, becomes conscious that his grandmothers were descended from slaves, that there is illegitimacy in his family, and who himself experiences the discriminations of racial prejudice. It would take a decade to recover, learn to see that most people have at one time been conquered, sold, or enslaved, but he would now have a sense of the relationship between colour and social distinctions which would often be present in his poetry through puns although seldom the central topic:

> their verandahs
> shuttered at both corners by half-cranked jalousies
> through which pale cousins peered or a half-cracked aunt . . .
>
> .   .   .   .
>
> . . . or with a white head dipping in a rocker
> while the black town walked barefoot . . .
>
> .   .   .   .
>
> they looked on their high-brown life[1]

This is from a section of *Omeros* primarily about Derek's father, Warwick Walcott, and the social texture of life in Castries, St Lucia. It alludes to the role of Christianity in the creation of a brown middle class, contrasts the changing local flowers (here) with the 'dried East palm' (traditions and symbols from elsewhere), distinguishes between the Methodist Church and the Roman (and Anglo-)Catholic celebration of Easter (the family was Methodist but Warwick was Anglican), and leads on to a miniature portrait of Warwick's relation to an agnostic barber, a Marcus Garveyite. The passage is rich in social history and is related to another poem, 'Verandas', also about Derek's colonial inheritance through his father.

'They' and 'their', however, suggest difference. There is not only the imprisoning notion of group identity to be avoided, but there is a modern sense of the self as isolated, alienated, distinct, the artist as a Castaway whether in society, or from God. Much of Walcott's writing has been concerned with such paradoxes as being 'black' when raised culturally 'white', of writing 'English' literature on a largely French Creole-speaking Caribbean island, of being a nationalist poet outside the majority culture of the island, of being a West Indian writer long after the West Indian Federation fragmented into many micro-nations, of being held up as a model of the one major West Indian writer who remained at home while in fact he had become economically dependent on his earnings from North America.

To think of Walcott as black or West Indian can be as much a misleading generalization as that of New World poet or any broad category that ignores the social specificity of a life, its many identities, and their relationships to their contexts. For most of his life Walcott has had a British passport. When he speaks of himself as a colonial he is being accurate. He is also a Methodist, a native English speaker on a Francophone island, and bilingual in also speaking Creole. He might be thought of as a second-generation immigrant, his light-brown father being born in St Lucia but raised as a Bajan, his light-brown mother being born in Dutch St Maarten. If he is part 'black', he is more than half 'white'.

St Lucia, where Derek Walcott was born and lives, is one of a belt of French-speaking islands—Martinique is only 20 nautical miles to the north—which share a similar French Creole. Culturally and linguistically the island was, and until recently remained, French or French Creole, a mixture of African survivals and French. It was settled by the Arawaks 2,000 years ago; around 1350 they were conquered by the Caribs who evicted the men and kept their women and children. Because of its magnificent harbour, supposedly the twenty-seventh best in the world, it changed hands more than a dozen times as it was fought over by the British and the French. The French usually governed the island from the mid-seventeenth to the early nineteenth century. There were still some Caribs until the eighteenth century, and it remained without European settlement until after the Treaty of Choc (1724) when the French and English agreed to share the harbours to take in wood and water; a decade later St Lucia was divided into districts and some Irish and French from Martinique settled. After

St Lucia was given back to France in fulfilment of the Treaty of Paris (1763), sugar and a large number of slaves were introduced. A civil government took office in 1774.

St Lucia then consisted mostly of small estates owned by the French or Free Coloured with black slaves. Soufriere was the French capital, an area rich in plantations and soon famous as a tourist attraction due to its smoking sulphur holes and two lovely mountain peaks, Gros Piton and Petit Piton, which often figure in Walcott's poetry. When the British ruled they used Castries and the north of St Lucia as a military and naval base and hardly bothered with the estates, which continued to be French. The French Revolution of 1789 brought St Lucia a revolutionary government with its guillotine, abolition of slavery, abandoned estates, and fleeing white owners.

From 1803 the British ruled. They brutally attempted to reimpose slavery and were strongly resisted; soon the slave trade ended and by the 1830s there was complete emancipation. The population was still small, perhaps 20,000. St Lucia was poor, especially after the collapse of the sugar market; it was a garrisoned naval station with Castries a coaling station which was rebuilt in the late nineteenth century and began attracting people from the plantations. The plantations went into decline, but the Castries merchants, few of whom were black, became wealthy. The population of St Lucia by 1900 was still under 50,000 and now included Asian Indians originally brought as indentured plantation labour to replace the slaves, and who in St Lucia became Methodists (unlike Trinidad where they remained in Hindu or Muslim communities). By the 1930s, during Walcott's youth, the population was perhaps 80,000, of whom at most 2 per cent were white, mostly civil servants, a few owners of large estates, and old French families; fewer than half the population spoke any English, although, with the decline of French power, English became the language of the élite, the civil service, the educated, and Castries—where over a third of the population now lived. Creole had become the language of rural areas and of the illiterate, but was known by everyone.

During the years when the French and English competed for the harbour of 'Fair Helen', they depended on the co-operation of the Africans, French law prevailed, and a local culture developed of French and African origins. Many of the 'national' traditions of St Lucia have their obscure origins in this period. English was not widely used until well into the twentieth century and then mostly in Castries. There are several religious rituals thought to be African survivals and in a few inland villages African drumming and dance traditions survive.

St Lucia is beautiful, green, mountainous, rainy, and a difficult place in which to travel except along the coast; areas still remain inaccessible during bad weather. Like Ireland and Barbados, it was for a long time somewhat feudal—agricultural with owners of large estates who had minor titles, a peasantry that spoke differently, and a small class in between to which Derek Walcott and his family belong. The whites owned the large estates and cane fields which were the primary source of wealth before sugar was replaced by bananas. A few families owned perhaps two-thirds of the land. The children who resulted from the union of white estate owners and black women were often given a good education, even sent abroad for further education, but not legitimized. In the 1930s coaling remained the main business and source of employment in Castries.

A military base until early in the twentieth century, St Lucia is socially and racially complex. Many from the regiments stayed on or intermarried with St Lucians. During the First World War there was also a camp in St Lucia. So there was mixing and whitening. A small but distinctive group was white, near white, or high brown, and British, along with the older French families. Between 1924 and 1951 in St Lucia there was steady progress from a limited franchise to general adult suffrage; it had a local administrator with little power, shared a Governor with St Vincent and Grenada, and had an elected local council. In the 1950s the population was 85,000 of which 26,000 lived in Castries. St Lucia joined the West Indian Federation in 1958. When that collapsed the island, feeling too small to stand alone, remained British for several decades.

Leadership was often Protestant, especially Methodist, and by graduates of St Mary's College, a small élite of various backgrounds that, until the mid-1950s, attended the only secondary school for males on the island. Many of the politicians were mulattos whose local family history began outside marriage two or three generations earlier, as was the case with the St Lucian Walcotts. Legitimacy was and remains a sensitive matter. One of the laws passed by the brown political élite forbids giving birth and marriage records to any except the lawyers for those involved.

Barbados was from the start a British colony with English settlers, and it was from Barbados that the English layer of language and culture came to the eastern part of the West Indies. Barbados created a myth of itself as England in the Caribbean, it was Bimshire, a place of seventeenth-century Anglican churches, eighteenth-century country houses, neat lawns, and public schools that taught Latin and Greek. It has a large white population and was long ruled by a plantocracy. To be Bajan was to be more British than the British. By the late nineteenth century Barbados with its large estates was becoming crowded for those hoping for land of their own. Derek's paternal grandfather, Charles Walcott, came to St Lucia to purchase a plantation near Choiseul (on the south-west coast of the island) which had a Barbadian Anglican community. He was white, one of the Walcotts of Barbados, an old and still important family, which had almost died off before receiving a fresh infusion from England during the nineteenth century.

Charles was part of that infusion, and in Derek's poetry is said to be a 'bastard'. He had a family of five children by Christiana Wardrope (1866–1947) a local woman from River Doré near Choiseul. She was dark brown, long haired, strong willed, highly regarded, and had two sisters, Sidone Wardrope (at whose house Derek would learn local legends), Paulina (an eccentric aunt who had a crush on a white clergyman), and a brother, Maxwell Wardrope, who worked on a sugar plantation as an overseer. The eldest of the children, and Derek's father, was Warwick (1897–1931). Derek imagined that his grandfather's origins were in Shakespeare's county, which would make Derek spiritually an heir of the great tradition of English literature:

> His name was Warwick Walcott. I sometimes believe
> that his father, in love or bitter benediction,
> named him for Warwickshire.[2]

> 'I was raised in this obscure Caribbean port,
> where my bastard father christened me for his shire,
> Warwick. The Bard's county.'[3]

The second child, Henry, was among those West Indians who left home to work on the Panama Canal and died abroad; his sister Mildred married Leonard Charles. She later died in Trinidad. William was the youngest brother and is buried at the Anglican cemetery along with Warwick and Christiana. Emma married Herbert Bernez, a light-skinned wealthy government official with a Spanish-sounding name who claimed to be from an aristocratic Creole French family that lost its title as a result of the Revolution.

Although he treated his relationship to Christiana with seriousness and eventually married her, Charles had other women. She took the children to Castries for their education and stayed in a house she owned while refusing to live with him on his estates. He eventually died in a fire that was thought to be suicide brought about by mental instability; Warwick who was in his twenties at the time buried him.

> 'A ghost steps from you, my grandfather's ghost!
> Uprooted from some rainy English shire,
> you sought your Roman

> End in suicide by fire.
> Your mixed son gathered your charred, blackened bones,
> in a child's coffin.

> And buried them himself on a strange coast.
> Sire,
> why do I raise you up? Because

> Your house has voices, your burnt house,
> shrills with unguessed, lovely inheritors,
> your genealogical roof tree, fallen survives,
> like seasoned timber through green, little lives.'[4]

A plantation that after his death went to another of Charles's families became one of those Caribbean stories about what might have been. Christiana continued living in Castries, dying during 1947 when Derek was 17.

Warwick, Derek's father, was born at La Fargue, Choiseul, had light skin, wavy hair, the Walcott large ears, and as a child was sent to Barbados in the hope that the family would accept Charles's marrying a brown woman and regard the children as legitimate. They did not. This and other details of family history were to worry Derek over the decades as in St Lucia to be born out of wedlock was both usual and a disgrace. In Derek's youth girls at St Joseph's school wore different uniforms according to whether they were 'legitimate'. Walcott's later criticism of defining the Caribbean by its past had a psychological as well as a logical basis.

Warwick was bright and at an early age, when 9, won one of the first scholarships to St Mary's College. Due to ill health he did not complete his studies, but an inspector of education helped him find employment as a 'Copyist' at the Education Office. He was later appointed to the Registry Department in Castries where he worked for J. E. M. Salmon the Attorney-General and Acting Chief Justice.

Warwick was thought a perfect English Barbadian, helpful, socially impeccable, quiet. He listened to recordings of opera, loved gardening, and was a gifted amateur in many arts. He had a library including a set of the complete works of Dickens, read English classics and modern novels, wrote verse, was a draughtsman and a watercolourist. He ordered books for the Castries Carnegie Library which his children would later consult. In 1959 Mabel Rawlins, whom Walcott remembered for the 'small, buttoned boots' she wore to church on Sundays, wrote in 'Letter from Brooklyn':

> 'Your father was a dutiful, honest,
> Faithful and useful person.'
>
> .   .   .   .   .   .
>
> 'A horn-painter, he painted delicately on horn.
> He used to sit around the table and paint pictures.'[5]

He was part of a small group concerned about culture and the arts. Warwick started The Star Literary Club and he and his friends staged 'concerts' at the Methodist school, including scenes from *The Merchant of Venice*. Alix, his wife, played Portia and Emmanuel 'Man' Auguste, a friend of Warwick, played Shylock. 'Man' during his travels had seen John Barrymore's *Hamlet*, earned his living as a druggist, and was later a town clerk. Everyone in St Lucia had a nickname; 'Man' was renamed 'Liege' after a long poem he recited. Derek was present in the late 1940s when 'Liege' attempted to recite the long Robert Service poem 'The Life Boat' in Columbus (now Walcott) Square on St Lucia's day, an incident that was treated with bored superiority by Patrick Lee Fermor in *The Traveller's Tree.*[6]

The Walcotts lived at 17 Chaussée Road on the eastern edge of Castries, in a small, compact, two-storey wooden house with gothic gables. The front and back porches were covered with vines of red and lilac bougainvillea and alamanda flowers. There was a small front bedroom and an upstairs bedroom. The parlour had a bookcase and Warwick's paintings. The house though small was charming with balconies, fretwork, decorated by a grape vine and various plants including roses. Socially the area was middle class, with some houses of the well-off, but was bordered by rougher social terrain. The house still stands and has been used in recent decades by a printer:

> 'Our house with its bougainvillea trellises,
> the front porch gone, was a printery. In its noise
> I was led up the cramped stair to its offices.
>
> I saw the small window near which we slept as boys,
> how close the roof was. The heat of the galvanize.
> A desk in my mother's room, not that bed, sunlit,
>
> with its rose quilt where we were forbidden to sit.'[7]

Castries was small, a large town rather than a city; it was possible to walk the town's circumference in a half-hour. The Walcotts were a short walk from the Methodist school and church as well as St Mary's College and Columbus Square (around which the white and rich had homes). Until the 1948 fire, many of the buildings were wooden in an older, provincial French tropical style that still survives in a few streets and towns of St Lucia.

Warwick and Alix had three children. Pamela Avril was born 14 August 1928, sixteen months before Derek and Roderick (23 January 1930) for whom Alix stylishly obtained one of the first twin prams seen in St Lucia. With Warwick soon to be promoted from Clerk to Acting Deputy Registrar, and Alix teaching at the Methodist Infant School they were on the verge of becoming economically secure, upper middle class, and moving to a larger house in Vigie, a better area, when Warwick Walcott died 23 April 1931, at the age of 34. He was operated upon at Victoria Hospital on Thursday, 16 April, for mastoiditis, a second operation was performed the next week, and he died in much pain. It was as a well-bred English colonial gentleman that he was loved, praised, and expired. Warwick was too much a gentleman to borrow money from relatives to jump the queue for the special operation he needed in Barbados.

The *Voice of St Lucia* described Warwick as charming, obliging, and helpful, a gifted self-taught painter and penman, fond of classical music and cricket. The last rites were performed by Canon R. Laurie, and the Anglican church was filled to its limits with many people outside. He was 'immensely popular with all classes of the community', and there was a large cortège to Holy Trinity Churchyard where he was buried. Another article was headed 'Moving Tribute to Late W. Walcott: One of Nature's Gentlemen'. It mentioned that Warwick was a Clerk at a District Court who, on the day of his death, was to become Acting Deputy Registrar. J. E. M. Salmon spoke movingly about Warwick Walcott with whom he had been closely associated as well as being a friend, 'he was one of Nature's gentlemen'. During the May 1927 fire which levelled much of Castries, Warwick helped Salmon, took charge of his things, and then went to the office to see if help were needed there. 'He was quiet, reserved, of an artistic temperament and always ready to use his pen or pencil for the good of others.' Garnet H. Gordon, whose family started the Methodist school and the *Voice of St Lucia*, spoke about Warwick's genial manner and agreed with Salmon's praise.[8]

Warwick was buried in the Anglican cemetery in a plot for immediate members of Christiana's family, 'my father's grave from the blackened Anglican headstones in Castries . . .'. Alix, because of a quarrel with Emma, would later be excluded from the plot which, as recalled in *The Bounty*, would require Derek finding another cemetery in which to bury his mother, 'near the white beach stones'.[9]

Derek's mother Alix (1894–1990) was born from the union of a Johannes van Romondt, a large estate owner in St Maarten—'The Dutch blood in me'[10]—and a brown woman, Caroline Maarlin, from a family still found on the island. The first van Romondt came to St Maarten in 1801, and was Governor 1820–40. He was a Methodist and argued for the need to teach the slaves the Bible. Until his arrival the Methodists of St Maarten were usually slaves, now the white élite joined the church. Diederik Johannes van Romondt (1781–1849) had eight sons including August Alexander (1823–1900) who started a tradition of his branch of the family using an A as a middle initial, a tradition carried on by Louis Alexander, who became owner of many of the best estates on the island, and founder of L. A. van Romondt and Sons, a leading import–export firm in the region. He travelled in a fancy coach with six horses and imported the first auto-mobile. The sons and grandsons of Diederik Johannes increased, multiplied, and were often appointed Governor in the various colonies of the Dutch West Indies. It is now difficult to tell them apart as they often had similar names and held many offices. Diederik Charles van Romondt (1835–1904), or someone with similar initials, was Governor 1864–5, 1874–7, 1893, 1898–1900. His son Diederik Christian van Romondt (1871–1948) decided to grow cotton on the uninhabited island of Tintamarre off the north-east of St Maarten, where he settled 1902–32 with hundreds of servants, 65 cows, 540 sheep, and was called the uncrowned king of Tintamarre. Diederik Christian never married but had several black mis-tresses and a common-law wife. He shocked local society by bringing his black common-law wife to gatherings of white society. Although at one time the largest estate owners in St Maarten, the van Romondts no longer exist there. For generations they had been trading with the United States, arguing for St Maarten to join the United States, marrying Americans, studying in the United States, acting as American Consul, and moving north or to other islands; Diederik Christian was the last. Derek's grandmother Caroline Maarlin bore other children, including Derek's uncles Osford and Eric, by other men. There was a trading link between St Maarten and St Lucia, and Caroline went to Castries where she married and had little contact with Alix when she arrived later.

As a young girl Alix was brought to St Lucia to finish her schooling by a Dutch trader for whom Arundel Hill outside Castries is named and who was part of a small group of people from St Maarten who helped form the St Lucian Methodist church. She was conscious of the high social position of her father's family. In a colonial society where 'shade' influenced social position she bragged of the blond hair and blue eyes of her father and the light skin of her children; her daughter Pamela is fair with grey eyes. Derek would be embarrassed by such assertions, but they were part of the time and might be thought to have influenced his own complicated relationship to 'blackness'. Alix made several trips back to St Maarten and told friends how a carriage would be sent to meet her. In St Lucia she attended the Methodist primary school and upon graduation was trained to teach in the Methodist infant school, beginning in 1910, of which she became the first head teacher, in 1918, until she retired in 1958.[11]

For decades the Methodist school was the centre of English-language teaching in Castries, a place where French Creole-speaking Roman Catholics would risk excommunication to educate their children alongside the English-speaking Protestant minority. 'Teacher Alix' with her large classes and strict discipline was a well-known, highly respected figure in the community. She was welcomed in the highest circles, and has her own place in the development of St Lucian culture.

Alix was an attractive energetic woman with light skin and long hair who in her younger days had an aura in keeping with her gubernatorial blood. She had a strong personality and knew what she thought and wanted. She married Warwick Walcott while in her thirties and was a few years older than he was. After his death, she was dedicated to her husband's memory and her children. Her financial situation was perilous; her survival and that of her children depended on her abilities, judgement, and work.

During the Great Depression teachers without degrees were paid very poorly, teachers in church schools were paid worse, and salaries in St Lucia were among the lowest in the English Caribbean. Teacher Alix sewed to earn extra money; as soon as the school day ended she would return home to sew. She sewed for the élite, for wealthy neighbours, for the Governor's wife, at times for charity. She spoke English with an impeccable British accent, played the piano, sang Methodist hymns and quoted Shakespeare and other poets while working, and was one of a group of cultured Creoles, mulattos, and near-whites who were invited to the Governor's cultural events. An extrovert, she had a sharp tongue, said what was on her mind, and could be terrifying in her directness. Derek early developed an equally sharp tongue and would answer her with a similar sense of assurance.

In later years Derek would at times joke about Alix taking in more washing when she had to earn money, but that is an exaggeration. The Walcotts were part of an English-speaking high-brown élite in a society in which education, colour, position, property, propriety, and family counted. They had little money, but their washing was done by Creole-speaking servants, and a servant looked after the children while Alix worked. Besides earning extra money as a seamstress, Alix used her sewing machine to make costumes for the children's Carnival and for the Arts Guild plays. At the time of her death in 1990, George Odlum recalled how her position behind the Singer sewing machine 'became the seat of power, authority and comfort in the Walcott household'. 'The machine was not only a machine it was the repository of all authority in the home. It was a consulting room. It was a parliament where important decisions were taken. It was a throne which errant school-children could approach. It was a fitting-room for carnival and concert costuming. It was a confessional . . . a social focal point.' She sewed every night except Sunday.[12]

Alix could speak Creole and took an interest in local culture. Carnival in St Lucia, now a national event, was originally one of Teacher Alix's projects for children. She, Warwick, and their friends had been involved with Carnival around 1927, and she, along with her wealthier neighbour and friend Frances Clauzel, revived Carnival in St Lucia, persuading children to dress up, masquerade, and make music. She 'was quite passionate about the French Creole traditional dress of *douillette* and *madras*, and her own musical composition, "Belles of Helen of the West". All these elements appeared in her school concerts.'[13] She was often Acting Principal of the Methodist's primary school, once for three years, as well as Principal of the infant school. Being a woman and lacking paper qualifications, her advancement was blocked. Eventually the Principal of the primary school, who was on secondment to the government, was replaced by a man with a university degree. She may also have been held back by a continuing dispute between the Methodists and Roman Catholics over education, culture, and the future in St Lucia.

Besides being a teacher, administrator, seamstress, head of a family of three children, Alix was one of a group of active women who were becoming visible in the 1940s, secretary of a women's athletic group, and later the 'mother' of the St Lucia Arts Guild. Grace Augustin, one of Warwick's friends, was the first woman in St Lucia to qualify for the bar, but when she returned from England to St Lucia she was prevented from working as a lawyer although she was on many local government committees. Alix remained attractive and independent even when old. She was conscious of her social position and the respect with which she and the family were held. She was cultured and self-supporting in a community where poverty and lack of schooling were the norm. She knew the Governor, the Administrator, and the important families, whether white or black. She taught her children the importance of the Bible, discipline, work, the arts, self-respect, position, and earning a living.

Teacher Alix was complex. She has been described as a 'saint' who devoted her life to her work, children, and charity. She had to bring up three children on an insufficient salary, and everyone agrees that she was highly practical, which means knowing about scholarships, how to earn money, knowing useful people, knowing how to survive, while remaining respected. It is said that Derek learned the ways of the world from her. She never remarried and claimed that was because no one could compare to her deceased husband, but for a time she had a lover, a fact that still hurts Derek. She had pride in her work and wanted her children to be independent. When the marriage between Derek and Faye broke up, Alix raised their son Peter for a while. Later she lived briefly in Trinidad with Derek and Margaret, his second wife, and for a period lived in Barbados with her daughter Pamela, but she did not want to leave St Lucia and would not go to Boston with Derek. She died in a Catholic old people's home in St Lucia. In *Omeros* there is a touching portrait of her shortly before her death, no longer able to remember Derek and her family. She raised and made Derek, encouraged him to be a poet and dedicate himself to the arts, gave him a strong Protestant sense of guilt, the need for achievement, awareness of life as a divine gift to be repaid, and is often said to have 'spoiled' him in the sense of being expected to be waited upon and praised, especially by women; several of his books are dedicated to her. He was raised to fulfil and complete the cultural ideals of his dead father.

Warwick's books and paintings remained in the house after his death. He had painted a small oil portrait of Alix, a self-portrait, a watercolour miniature of Pam in a late impressionistic style, a watercolour of the Coconut Walk on Vigie peninsula, a backcloth of a moonlight scene for some 'concert' performance; there were pencil studies including one of a cow. Warwick made copies of paintings by Millais and Turner. Alix kept his copy of Millais's *The Gleaners* in the living room. Warwick had a little book of Dürer's drawings and engravings. Instead of Dürer's signature D, under an A Derek created his own emblem. In *Another Life* Derek mentions a book containing reproductions of Boucher and Fragonard. Warwick also had *The English Topographical Draughtsmen* in which Derek would love the monochromes of Paul Sandby, Peter de Witt, and John Sell Cotman. Besides being an amateur painter, actor, and director, Warwick wrote some poems in the manner of Rossetti and some comic American dialect verses.

Warwick's interests and methods were passed on to Derek who has continued to regard Art as imitation, a copy, in which the work of others is a model, and part of a tradition. Derek has often written of life in similar terms, life as imitation, with one's first love being a model for all future love. Warwick's own drawings were concerned with detail, a practice continued by Derek who when young would draw detailed close-ups. That Derek's own paintings and poems can still give equal emphasis to all parts of a scene is derived from this way of seeing and working. The size of the land or object does not matter. One concentrates on a part of the object, the light, the texture, the metaphor. Everything is both naturalistic and made of equal significance. Such a view of the world transfers over to the religious, with all things being equal, and helps to explain Derek's interest in the poetry of John Clare. The cover of Walcott's *Collected Poems* (1986) is a detail from a larger painting and yet it seems self-sufficient as a work of art; the plays are more like scenes than stories with plots; many Walcott poems are made up of parts and sequences that can stand on their own. The title poem of *The Bounty* (1997) self-consciously makes a principle of giving everything equal attention, with no hierarchy between the ants and the dead body of Alix Walcott.

Derek Alton Walcott, born 23 January 1930 at the Victoria Hospital, Castries, was the elder of the twins, the first to see the world, as he would often remind his brother Roderick Alden. (It was later often noted that William Arthur Lewis (1915–91), St Lucia's 1979 Nobel Laureate in Economics, was also born on 23 January.) The names Derek and Roderick derive from Diederik. Alton and Alden continue a family tradition of middle names beginning with the letter A. Although in interviews and his published prose Walcott creates an impression of isolation, his poetry alludes to being raised in a Castries populated with family. Both are true. The actual family was Alix, Christiana, Mildred, and sometimes Emma, although Emma and Alix did not get along. There were many aunts and uncles of various distances and shades, including the 'mad aunt' Paulina. Some were from Christiana's mother's other children, from Christiana's half-sisters, from Alix's side of the family. Relatives passed for periods through Derek's childhood. Besides Alix's St Maarten connection, Derek was related to others through his grandfather Charles's children, names were mentioned, at times people lived with them, there were relatives on the other islands and in the United States, but in general Derek and Roddy kept to themselves and were not conscious of or admitted to the adult world. Alix's brother Osford ('Ossie') arrived from St Maarten, sat listlessly or whittled in a favourite chair, was not spoken to, screamed loudly in his room, and eventually was moved to a mental asylum: 'I see a childhood uncle, mad, now dead, | sweating to whittle a cane stalk'.[14] Most relatives did not share their interests; one still complains at Derek saying that she was badly raised and ill-behaved.

Otherwise the immediate family was small. Alix and the children would visit Christiana, with whom Warwick's youngest sister Emma was living, and his elder sister Mildred. Christiana lived on Jeremie Street, then a smelly area overlooking the wharves, where Derek would see women carrying heavy baskets of coal on their head, African style, on and off ships. The carriers, all women, sang, climbed the ramp like slaves building pyramids. The coal baskets were filled with a 'hundred weight'. Their Aunt Anna, a St Maarten connection, who lived on Edgecombe Avenue in Harlem, would send them clothes and comic strips she cut from Sunday newspapers. She wanted Alix to emigrate to the United States with her three children. Uncle Eric, tall and 'red', stayed with Alix, then went to the United States. Eric was himself a printer, a writer of essays, another 'writer' in the family. He quarrelled with Anna and lived and, to Alix's distress, died alone, an illustration of the isolation of life in the United States. Alix's friends included the Clauzels, Belmars, Phillips, Augiers. The Augiers were friends of Warwick as well as Alix, a link which would continue through several generations as Roy Augier was still at St Mary's when Derek entered, and later he would teach at the University College of the West Indies when Derek was in Jamaica. Catholics, the Augiers are an illustration that religion was not usually as divisive as it was sometimes made to appear in St Lucia.

Walcott family history is fairly representative of the region where many emigrated to seek employment and betterment elsewhere, whether to build the Panama Canal or work in Harlem during the 1920s. Outside the West Indies, however, there was then racial prejudice of a kind different from the discriminations and silent barriers of the Caribbean; even a light-skinned well-educated mulatto would be expected to know his place.

> from the dunes of coal
> Near my grandmother's barracks on the wharves,
> I saw the sallow faces of those men
> Who sighed as if they spoke into their graves
> About the negro in America. That was when
> The Sunday comics, sprawled out on her floor,
> Sent from the States, had a particular odour;
> Dry smell of money mingled with man's sweat.'

Some returned with money, stylish clothes, sophistication, and experience of racial prejudice.

> the bowed heads of lean, compliant men
> Back from the States in their funeral serge
> Black, rusty Homburgs and limp waiters' ties,
> Slow, honey accents and lard-coloured eyes'[15]

America was a place of jazz, spirituals, relatives, much money, work, famous black actors and singers, and the humiliation of being Negro.

Although there were a few wealthy black merchants and some black land-owners, advancement in the West Indies for those not white was mostly through education. Those who could read and write were at first mostly teachers and preachers; many were wanderers educated in schools in Jamaica, Barbados, or Antigua, who found employment in Trinidad, Grenada, or St Lucia. Other possibilities opened in government, journalism, politics, and the professions, but, as qualifications could not be earned in the colonies, the height of achievement was to go to a university abroad and return as one of the few local professionals or senior civil servants, a leader of the community. West Indians migrate as much from lack of mobility, opportunities, and adventure as for economic reasons. Colonial society remained Victorian, at least on the surface. The arts were respected as a gentlemanly attainment, and there was a common culture shared by the small middle class and those who aspired to the middle class: they read Dickens, Scott, the World Classics, the better English weeklies; they performed at 'concerts' consisting of scenes from plays, poetry recitations, and skits; they listened to classical music on the victrola, then the gramophone. Walcott, like V. S. Naipaul, was among the first who aspired to a living through creative writing. Walcott and Naipaul were preceded about a decade earlier by Edgar Mittelholzer, Sam Selvon, Andrew Salkey, and John Hearne.

The Walcotts were Anglophone Protestant immigrants on a Francophone Roman Catholic island. The Roman Catholics formed well over 90 per cent of the population. Protestants, especially the Methodists, usually came to St Lucia from the northern islands. The parents of the other future St Lucian Nobel Laureate, the economist Arthur Lewis, were Anglican school teachers from Antigua. There is a feeling sometimes expressed by St Lucians that those, such as Warwick Walcott, whose parents come from Barbados or from the Anglophone islands are alien. This view was stronger in the past, when the Protestant–Catholic division accentuated the English–French language divide. The argument later found in Derek Walcott's writings, especially in his play *Franklin*, that one earns a place in society through love and commitment, and that West Indians are all immigrants, might be seen as influenced by his own and his family's place in St Lucia. *Franklin*, which has never been produced outside the West Indies, is an example of how Walcott's works derive from a specific social context that is likely to be missed by those beyond the Eastern Caribbean. The 'alien' whiteman in the earliest version was a mulatto. *Pantomime* and *Omeros* also in part are concerned with how alien whites become part of the community in small 'black' islands. The many times Walcott would ask himself whether he had Jewish blood (an occurrence more common than one might think in the Caribbean where many 'Spanish' and 'Portuguese' are descended from Spanish Jews) was in the hope that he was less black, but there are obvious ways in which the St Lucian Methodists were like the Jews, an energetic, talented, immigrant minority with a belief in education and work. The Methodist community was small, in Walcott's youth probably no more than 200 in Castries, and the families all knew each other. Even the Anglicans were only about 500.

The role of the Methodists in the region was important from the days of slavery; whereas the Bajan Anglican Church denied Christianity to the black slaves as a way of enforcing authority and denying consideration, other denominations, such as the Quakers and Moravians, encouraged slaves to join. The Methodists were especially active and regarded as anti-slavery agitators. Attempts were made to outlaw Methodism and in 1823 the Methodist Chapel in Bridgetown was destroyed by a mob. The Methodists often were preacher educators bringing schooling to the ex-slaves. Derek Walcott in his late twenties still saw his options as a pulpit or pedagogy if he were not a writer; most of the West Indian poets at the time were teachers.

While there was some schooling in French in the eighteenth century, education in St Lucia is usually said to have begun with the 1838 Mico schools, based on an endowment from Lady Mico, established to redeem Christian slaves from 'Barbary'. There were soon Mico Teachers' Colleges in Antigua and Jamaica. The first Mico Trust school in St Lucia was established in 1838, and a small brown Protestant élite that had an enormous role in modern St Lucian history derives from the school. Such schools existed until 1891 when they became Government Schools. They were soon passed on to the churches or sold. At the end of the century the schools of St Lucia divided by denomination were Catholic 19, East Indian Mission 16, Methodist 2, Anglican 2. The East Indian Mission schools eventually closed apart from one which became Methodist. Education was still rare, perhaps only 13 per cent of the population were enrolled in primary school and average attendance was under 7 per cent. Over the years in Castries, the Methodists were to become the leading educators, and as education became important in society the Methodists, although a minority within the Protestant English-speaking minority, had a major role in the cultural politics of St Lucia.

The history of the Methodists in St Lucia also begins with the Mico schools. During the 1880s T. D. Gordon (grandfather of the Sir Garnet Gordon, CBE, QC, who figured prominently in the St Lucia of Walcott's youth), a Congregationalist from Jamaica, took charge of the Mico school in St Lucia and brought together Free Church people including some Methodists from St Maarten. One result was the appointment of the first Methodist Missionary in 1888. When the Methodist Church took over one of the schools relinquished by the Mico Charity in 1891, Gordon became headmaster of a mixed age school of 170 pupils ranging from 4 to 16 years. At first Methodist services were limited to the Mico school, but after the appointment of a minister they purchased a site on Chisel Street where in 1903 a school-chapel was erected—the building is still used for the Methodist infant school. In 1910 the building stopped being used as a church and a partition began to separate the primary from the infant school at around the time Alix Walcott joined the school.

To escape from menial and rural labour, survive in the capital, obtain government employment, have access to the legal system and to the professions, it was necessary to use English. The best way to do this was to attend the Methodist school and this meant—unless one were born into a rich family and could obtain private English lessons—starting with Alix Walcott's infant school, eventually following local events from the English language press, usually the *Voice of St Lucia* (owned by the Gordons), or the smaller, Garveyite, also Protestant *West Indian Crusader*. The importance of studying at the Methodist school can be seen from the scholarship examinations for secondary schools in 1944. Students from Castries Methodist school won five of six scholarships awarded, including the two better-paying government scholarships. Others attending secondary school had to pay fees. By 1947 there were 200 boys and girls in the Methodist infant school and 245 in the primary school. The Roman Catholic boys and girls infant and primary schools had about 1,100 pupils, so the Methodist 2 per cent of the population was educating and influencing nearly half the number of students the Catholic schools were. Anglican figures are not known. Secondary education required boys going to St Mary's College or girls attending St Joseph's Convent, run by Sisters of St Joseph of Cluny. As late as 1954 there was no government secondary school.

Strong willed, hard-working, socially active, knowing that the future of her children depended on more than bare economic survival, Alix made certain that they had time to pursue intellectual and artistic interests. She believed in her religion and that the talents of her children were God given and meant for the glory of God, a belief that Derek inherited and which to him is the ultimate significance of his work. He early developed a sense of himself as someone unique with a talent he had to use. At times this was a feeling that he was meant to lead, was elect, something that can be seen in 'What the Twilight Says', written during a period of estrangement from his Trinidad Theatre Workshop. His Methodism, along with his sense of being raised in genteel poverty while belonging to an élite, meant dedication to hard work, self-improvement, and the ambition to become financially comfortable. Derek wanted to regain what had been lost through his father's death, and, consciously or not, had to create a new legitimacy which would transcend that to which he had been denied. As in those old romances, he, the one of seemingly humble origins, would turn out to be the real prince, the one at the end to inherit the empire.

Throughout most of his life Derek would get up at 5 a.m. to start writing, nothing would stop him; unlike most people he seemed never to avoid work. He seemed to feel that if he stopped working he would die. He is driven by the need to work, by setting continually further goals (a joke among Walcott observers after he was awarded the Nobel Prize was that he would now start working even harder towards being the first writer to win it twice). During perhaps the first conversation I had with him, I understood him to say that he would not be his mother's son if he did not know how to get the best financially for his work. This would suggest a hard-hearted, practical view of the world. Walcott can be that way, but much of what he has earned has gone into domestic and other family responsibilities, matters of status and immediate comfort (using a taxi rather than learning to drive a car, flying first class), and supporting or investing in the arts. There has always been in Walcott's personality an aristocrat's mixture of personal haughtiness along with an egalitarianism towards those he respects. In speaking of his early days in Trinidad he will mention the high social circles in which he moved and found many of his supporters and actors, but he was also proud to have brought talented if barely literate actors into his group.

Although Alix proffered Warwick as a model for her children to imitate, Derek was ambivalent about his father. Warwick was the absent father who died instead of taking care of his young. If Alix had not worked hard and insisted on her status the Walcotts could have plummeted socially as well as economically during the Great Depression. Warwick presented other problems as well as dying. He was a model for white, British, gentlemanly behaviour, culture, and amateur accomplishment. The three children were expected to become poets like their father: 'no heaven is ruled as neat | as those blue copybooks in which he wrote'.[16]

Derek was expected to fulfil his father's aborted artistry; his works are filled with references to how he had become his father. While the death of his father gave him a purpose to continue and surpass Warwick's early flame by himself becoming famous, Walcott often felt he were reporting his progress to his father and he would meet his father around some corner. Walcott had his own Oedipal vision. As might be expected he at times hated his father as too white, too much the gentleman, too timid, too cultured, too amateur, not man enough. Derek would often think of himself as Hamlet, the Hamlet who needed to be more than his father to complete his father's work and free himself. In places he is Hamlet aware that someone replaced his father in his mother's affections:

> Something more than love
> my father lacked which God will not approve:
> a savage, sundering sword, vile to the touch
> breeding fidelity by its debauch.[17]

As Warwick died from an infected ear the Hamlet parallel seemed especially appropriate. That Warwick died on Shakespeare's birthday was another reason for Derek to see himself as heir of his father's 'Will'.

2

1938–1943 Making an Artist, Harold Simmons, Dunstan St Omer

WRITERS usually know at an early age they are going to be writers. Walcott had the poet's instinct for words, their meanings, the sound and texture of language. His ability to memorize poetry, familiarity with the classics of Palgrave's *Golden Treasury of English Poetry*, as well as knowledge and command of traditional forms, have their origins in his youth when he was raised around people who enjoyed and recited poetry. Growing up in the midst of Alix, his teachers, and his dead father's circle of friends, he knew before his teens that he was extremely talented with language and that he was meant to be a writer. He was told and felt he had a gift as a poet, that he would take his place among the poets, that he would be another Marlowe or Milton. He wanted to be admired and to hear his verses recited the way famous writers were by his mother and teachers. Early in life he assumed that he would some day be awarded the Nobel Prize in Literature and in his forties already felt it was getting late.

Something of his mother's Methodism went into his single-minded dedication of his life to his gift as an artist; he had a talent that must be used before he met his Maker. No matter what else you do, what sins you commit, you must use that talent. Walcott joined the other children swinging on the vines which hung from the large banyan trees near the mostly white Vigie Country Club, he had friends and later girl friends, loved movies, followed cricket, but there was never any doubt that he was an artist and that he was to devote his life to art, books, and the creative world. His mother had shaped him. Other children might imagine themselves artists, but few had such continuous encouragement as he received including at the Methodist school from his teachers Ira Simmons and George French.

His habits as a writer were formed early. His mother gave him an exercise book in which to write his poetry, and he dated his poems like a diary. He usually wrote a poem or two a day; for years he did not write drafts or revise. For inspiration he would go for walks so that he returned as the sun was setting; if he found nothing to write a poem about the day seemed wasted. He at first wrote without models and with a distant respect for metre. He thought of poetry as prayer which should be immediate and spontaneous. Alix would later give him a poem each night to copy and imitate before going to bed. He altered poems, learning their shape, using them as models. The method with which he began, consciously modelling his poetry on earlier works, was similar to that of painters who have traditionally copied, imitated, modelled their work on others. This had a lasting importance to him which can be seen in his respect for stanzaic form, care with rhyme and prosody, echoes of and allusions to great poems. Walcott is always the craftsman aware of technique, of working in the traditions of a craft. Modern culture values originality, sees the authentic as unique; Walcott came to feel the opposite, that in art originality is a vice. Echoes, influences, traditions, are liberating; his imagination was influenced by everything—English poetry, Japanese art, movies, local folk tales. While books were scarce in St Lucia those available were selective; he read good writers, the classics, serious writers. His world was Arnoldian, not Third.

The tradition of choir singing in the Methodist Church contributed to his being a poet. Poems by George Herbert, John Bunyan, and Wesley were sung at services. When he was 8 years old, inspired by such hymns, he decided to be a poet; he thought he would be a preacher writing hymns. Hearing hymns sung in quatrains contributed to his sense of form. Methodist hymns also offered him a language that was Elizabethan and Victorian. The Methodist service, with its hymns, biblical oratory, and sermons, uses words in formal designs and metre. Walcott's poetry still often echoes the canon of English religious verse.[1] While Walcott has spoken of the formal influences of the hymns on his poetry, the inheritance is more than craft and diction. Many of his poems, while secular, are meditative, have biblical analogies, might be thought psalms considering and praising the divinity of the creation, and conclude with blessings and prayers. They are infused with a sense of sin, guilt, retribution, and desires for forgiveness along with praise for the created world.

Walcott and the Methodists continually ran into trouble with the Catholic Church. To avoid unrest the British long allowed Catholic authorities to dominate the island's life. The Church controlled education and tried to control culture. The priests were French, themselves usually from rural backgrounds, intolerant, and resistant to the modernizing secular culture of the English-speaking Protestants who were regarded as dangerous heretics. The St Lucia of Walcott's childhood had many of the characteristics of a Catholic country in the past, such as Spain, with a public communal religious life marked by saints' days and other celebrations. In contrast to the large stone Catholic Cathedral, the Methodist church was a small grey wood chapel with a banner over the altar. Unlike the Catholic processions, the Methodists once a year celebrated Harvest Sunday by bringing fresh fruit and preserves which would be auctioned on Harvest Monday at the Methodist school alongside the chapel. Walcott sang hymns by Watts and Wesley, which he thought then and still thinks good poetry. He loved the Jacobean style of the King James Bible with its colourful language. To him Methodism and Protestantism were the modern world, even the New World, while Catholicism was the past, the Old World, but had the splendour of Renaissance art and the dark secrets rumoured of Renaissance popes.[2]

While still a youth he was treated as a writer; a group of older people read his poetry. There was a feeling of continuity between generations, a small community of those with cultural interests. Derek was expected to follow in their path. H. D. Boxill, Derek's godfather, who came to St Lucia from Barbados when he was 17, was a friend of Warwick and was along with Harry Simmons, Father Jesse, and B. H. Easter, an amateur archaeologist who sought Indian remains. Boxill brought him books. Easter was a pioneer in adult education and created the Extra Mural Department on St Lucia in which Derek would be one of the first lecturers. A convert to Catholicism, Boxill taught Latin and French at St Mary's College. He was interested in French Creole, and after the Second World War earned a first-class degree in French externally from the University of London, and then became Head of Education in St Lucia before returning to Barbados. Boxill would recite Francis Thompson's 'The Hound of Heaven', Swinburne's 'Dolores', and lyrics by Verlaine to Derek. Derek would for a few years be a junior master at St Mary's.

Derek and Roderick first went to the Methodist infant school where their mother was the teacher, and then to the Methodist primary school. The infant school was a room which included children who spoke English along with those who only knew Creole but who had to use English at the school. The class was large and divided by a partition from the primary school in which all grades were in the same room, and students were expected to keep quiet and work while others in a different grade were being instructed. Discipline was essential. The Walcotts were model students, who were at times asked to explain lessons to their class.

While in the Methodist primary school Walcott was already conscious of paintings and the names of painters. The school reader had a reproduction of G. F. Watts's *Hope*, a sad Hope which sat despairingly with a lyre on a globe of the world. There was also a dull reddish-brown reproduction of a painting of a bored abandoned Robinson Crusoe searching the sea without hope of rescue. Similar images of a bored observer watching an unchanging watery horizon without a sail in sight, or without interest in the sail, would appear in Walcott's poetry as would the mask of the poet as Crusoe, the castaway, whose abandonment on his tropical island was Walcott's own image of alienation from the surroundings he would need to master as an artist. Walcott wanted to be Crusoe the craftsman, the superior master, rather than an abandoned Crusoe of madness, fearing the night, a threat he often found within himself which, although sharpened by social and cultural isolation, was a fear he had inherited as a result of several 'mad' relatives. The Crusoe image became in Walcott's imagination mixed with that of Adam in Eden, with civilization as well as sex being the fruit of knowledge offered by the serpent.

Standards were high in primary school and Roderick can still remember George French carefully, patiently, explaining Coleridge's 'Rime of the Ancient Mariner'. When he was 10 Derek wrote some verses at Christmas which Oscar A. Walker, headmaster of the school, thought distinctive; he asked him to recite his poetry to the school. Walker, a Bajan who came to St Lucia to head the Methodist primary school—he later became Head of the Education Department and Inspector of Schools—was another of the teachers Walcott has credited with encouraging him.

He was encouraged further by Grace Augustin, another friend of Warwick. When he stayed with her he would write a poem or two a day which he would show her. She introduced him to the poetry of Whitman and mysteriously warned him against it, presumably for its homosexuality. At her estate house, when he was 11, Derek took an oath to live longer and be a better poet than his father. The estate would be recalled in several poems:

> Ten or eleven; heaven
> was nearer; the yellowing, old estate house crumbled like cake,
> stencilled with fern-prints, veiled mosquito nets[3]

The same year in a national competition, at the age of 11, Derek won one of the two St Lucia government scholarships to St Mary's College, Castries, for the years 1941–7. The examinations were British, highly competitive, marked in England, and there were very few scholarships to the secondary school. The two best scholarships were the national ones, but there were a few others, offered by Castries, one of which Roderick, who through illness had fallen behind Derek, won the next year. Although primary education could be had at various schools, the only secondary school for boys was St Mary's College. Arthur Lewis attended on a scholarship 1925–9 before winning the biennial St Lucia scholarship; he received the highest marks ever given at the London School of Economics, was appointed the first black lecturer at the School, and eventually was awarded the Nobel Prize for Economics.

St Mary's College is a British-style public school meant to produce an élite. There was no science, only the Arts (Humanities) at that time. St Mary's was competitive, very demanding, formidable, exciting. It was also the way up for those without money. In the sixth form, there was the Oxford or Cambridge entrance examination, and one scholarship every two years to pay for education at a British or Commonwealth university. The students were really being trained for Oxford or Cambridge, but most students attended St Mary's for five years, from the age of 11 until 16, and only a few stayed on the extra two years to prepare for the advanced examinations which might gain them entry to a British university.

St Mary's College for boys had been opened by Father Tapon in 1890 with twenty-seven students ranging from 6 to 15 years of age. Whereas the Catholic clergy in St Lucia would long remain French, Tapon decided to follow the model of a British public school. He went to England for a year to improve his English and to learn how English schools were run. In 1903 St Mary's College's grant from the government was doubled provided that ten scholarships be awarded each year on the basis of a competitive examination. The first scholarships to primary school followed in 1906. Warwick Walcott earned one. In 1918 Island Scholarships (which Derek would later win) were introduced. In 1946 St Mary's College was handed over to the (Irish) Presentation Brothers.

Patrick Leigh Fermor's *The Traveller's Tree: A Journey through the Caribbean Islands* (1950) reports a visit on Speech Day to St Mary's, 'a school justly famous throughout the Antilles'. He saw

a completely English atmosphere ... The Inter-House trophies came next: Rodney had won the cricket and football, Abercromby the aquatics ... the island fashions had remained faithful to Oxford bags. Those obsolete trousers were especially noticeable ... When the last of the colours and prizes had been carried away, the curtain came down and after a minute or two, rose again on the Forum scene in *Julius Caesar* ... A loudspeaker announced His Honour the Administrator, and Mr. Stow, an elegantly dinner-jacketed figure in the blinding spotlight, rose, and made an excellent speech, which was answered by the Head Prefect in words ... far better than any head prefect's speech I had ever heard at school. After a series of hip-hoorays, the stage was filled by the school choir.[4]

Walcott would himself a few years later be a junior master and direct scenes from *Macbeth*.

There was a hierarchy including headmaster, assistant headmaster, prefect, and monitor. The courses were French, Latin, English Literature, English Language, History, Geography, Religion, Arithmetic, Geometry, and Algebra with few options. Students were disciplined by being detained after school; those sent by their teachers to have their names in the principal's black book were caned after a number of listings. They were taught British history which Walcott found boring, the British refighting their battles with the French. There were no texts for West Indian history. Walcott studied Latin, Shakespeare, English poetry, Dickens. On

Barbados he would have learned Greek. The students sat Cambridge examinations, London matriculation, and other British-devised, administered, and graded competitive tests used throughout the Empire. It did not feel incongruous. Walcott was excited by what he learned at school and by the life around him.

St Mary's was divided into four houses, Derek was in Abercromby House. George Odlum (later a representative to the United Nations) and Vincent Floissac (Chief Justice of OECS) were both in Abercromby. Derek, although a year behind Floissac, thought of him as his friend and rival. Derek was a promising bowler at cricket, but after a year at St Mary's he gave up sports. Once as a wicket keeper he felt that the bat had barely missed his Adam's apple; angered he played dead until everyone had gathered around him, after which he would not play cricket again. He was already thought a prodigy as a poet; he would concentrate on his writing and school work. From an early age Derek had participated in some Methodist shows, including a pantomime when he was 11, and he continued acting and then writing scripts at St Mary's for the weekly college speech night shows from which his early plays evolved.

Shortly after entering St Mary's College, Walcott met Dunstan St Omer who was from a black Catholic family. Dunstan's father was a soldier in the First World War who fought in Egypt, and who later became a customs inspector limited to a low rank by the lack of a secondary education. The family decided that Dunstan and his older brother would not be limited to primary school; they paid Dunstan's fees at St Mary's where he stayed until 1946. Dunstan was a few years older than Derek. He was born in Castries (24 October 1927) and early showed a natural talent for drawing. He began drawing by imitating advertisements and illustrations in newspapers. His aunt showed Dunstan's paintings to Harold Simmons. There was no academic training possible for a painter in St Lucia, but Simmons (1914–66), a friend of Warwick Walcott, and himself a remarkable person, was to guide Derek and Dunstan towards making a St Lucian art and proclaim their coming to others.

Simmons, brother of Ira Simmons (one of Derek's teachers and later Governor), was born in Castries, educated at the Methodist elementary school, and then at St Mary's College until 1934. He studied for some diplomas in art and by 1940 he had devoted himself to painting. Six years later, in 1946, he became a civil servant as Officer for the Co-operative Societies. He was for a time a District Officer, on many local committees including the Library Committee and the advisory committee for the Extra-Mural Department. He was a founder member of the Arts and Crafts Society and the Archaeological and Historical Society, a correspondent for Reuters and the *Trinidad Guardian*, and 1957–9 editor of the *Voice of St Lucia*. His favourite poets were Dylan Thomas and Derek Walcott. After some decades of community leadership, however, Simmons died, a drunk, rejected by local society, an illustration to Walcott of what happened to West Indian artists who remained at home.

During 1942 Simmons began giving art lessons to Derek, Dunstan, and a few others at his studio. Simmons, who exhibited abroad and sold his work, was the only professional painter in St Lucia. He wanted to use local subjects and designs, but he also understood the need for basic instruction, materials, and encouragement. Whereas Warwick Walcott was conventional in style and a competent watercolourist, Simmons was the first important St Lucian painter, a local Gauguin who moved local painting into the modern period, but not really a Modernist. He painted peasants rather than imitations of European landscape scenes, he used vivid tropical colours. Instead of black shadows he used pure colour, emerald seas, and cobalt. Simmons loved the island; Walcott and St Omer became the heirs of a landscape he invented.

Simmons saw beauty in black bodies, and made paintings of local people which caught the muscles, shapes, and colours of St Lucians with the kind of exciting exactitude that the Renaissance had with European bodies. In Simmons's studio, besides the usual statuette of the Venus de Milo, there was a head of a black woman based on a head by Delacroix. Walcott had been brought up by his mother to value whiteness. Alix had American Sears and Roebuck catalogues she used for patterns. Derek wanted to be white, American, and marry a blonde wife with long hair. At Simmons's studio he saw that black women could be beautiful, a subject for art. He decided he wanted to be a painter, that he wanted to make that his career. Simmons also told him about the poverty of most St Lucians and would take him for drives around the island to see rural areas and how people lived.

Derek and Dunstan used Simmons's studio on Saturdays to paint, listen to classical music, read, and borrow books. He gave the young people a place, his veranda, and equipment with which to paint. He taught them some techniques, such as watering the paper, how to circle it, how to do a sky, how to draw, but basically his influence was as a model of a professional artist. Derek would also use the typewriter and, eventually, the liquor cabinet.

Derek and Dunstan painted together and became friends. As Dunstan had gone to the Catholic Boys School he would have been unlikely to move in the élite 'red' Methodist circle frequented by the Walcotts. Walcott only once visited the St Omer house, and Dunstan later claimed it was to have ice-cream. One of Dunstan's relatives told me of the excitement in the family that a St Omer was accepted by the Walcotts. As both Dunstan and Derek had an unusually strong interest in art, a subject not then taught at St Mary's, they were allowed to prepare for and take the 1944 Cambridge Junior Certificate on their own and passed with distinction. This was the first time Art was taken as a Cambridge examination subject at St Mary's. A year later the two of them took the exam at the next level and Dunstan received a better grade than Derek.

Walcott thought he could be a poet while having a career as a painter, but he was learning that Dunstan was naturally a better painter; that painting was in

Dunstan's wrist in a way it never would be in his own. Walcott would need to earn his living as a writer; he would continue painting while wishing that he had the same natural talent for it that he had for words. His interest in painting would strongly influence his poetry and theatre; the poems would be filled with descriptions, colours, perspectives, distinctions between foreground, background, and middle distance, and adapt such painterly genres as the still life. He would imagine his plays as paintings, in colours and period styles, his characters as character types in costume. He would himself draw costumes, paint scenery. His manuscripts would be filled with illustrations and visual notes. The plays he directed would be filled with painterly scenes and allusions to paintings; as a director he would be praised for the visual interest and beauty of his tableaux, and faulted for how long the plays took on stage.

In 1946 Dunstan went to work in the Curaçao oil fields, a common way for St Lucians to earn money; after a few years he returned to St Lucia. He and Derek became young rebels together, drinking and singing in the streets at night with Dunstan talking about his genius and always doing something mad, making the first underwater painting, squeezing lime into the sea to make a punch bowl, singing Italian opera. Dunstan was darker and assertively black. In 1950 he painted some murals in a club with a black Neptune and mermaids. His *Rape of Castries* in the style of Rubens has a black Vulcan and Cupid. He was influenced by the murals of Diego de Rivera, but he would soon create his own prismatic style of Modernism.

Walcott soon became a Cubist, he enjoyed Braque, and was influenced by Cézanne whose orange, brown, and greens might be St Lucia in the dry season. Walcott has claimed that, when looking from his roof, what he saw, the roofs, road, brickwork, cliff, the colours and shapes, although vertical, looked flat, even in cubes, like a painting by Cézanne. Many of Walcott's early landscapes and still lifes are a simplified cubism, more a flattened Cézanne than a Picasso.

Reading Derek's poetry about St Lucia is to have an impression of a self-enclosed world of himself, his friends, the landscape, the sea, peasants in the distance, tourists on the fringe. That is part of its achievement, to see, accept, and make the West Indies a self-sufficient concern for an artist and reader. To do this, part of the reality was ignored, although some of it was written about in early works. The West Indies were still feudal, ruled by the white estate owners and the Church. The region was impoverished, without jobs, a place to leave in search of work, qualifications, adventure. West Indians were migrants, travelling from island to island, and when possible abroad to North America or England seeking better conditions and opportunities. Life was elsewhere. Culture was elsewhere. History was elsewhere.

It was to be the achievement of Derek and Roderick Walcott, Dunstan St Omer, and Dunstan's cousin, the novelist Garth St Omer, to see that life, culture, and history could be in St Lucia. No one had really done it before them, although Harry Simmons made a start. To achieve such a focus on local life meant excluding other contexts. The relation of the new St Lucian art to England and Europe remains obvious; no one could then begin to write well in English without being indebted to Shakespeare, Milton, Wordsworth, or begin to paint without learning from the masters of Renaissance Italy or nineteenth-century France. Besides seeing his father's copies of European art and art reproduced in books, Walcott often picked up and returned his mother's sewing to the rich in their large houses with European paintings, even tapestries! European art and culture was around him.

One of the books of his youth was Thomas Craven's *A Treasury of Arts Masterpieces: From the Renaissance to the Present Day* (1939), which offered a canon of great paintings from Giotto and Duccio to Reginald Marsh and Grant Wood and from which he would copy in watercolour paintings by Turner and Goya. This was his museum, a history of European and American art on which his imagination built. He would in future refer to such works as Velásquez's *Meninas* or Watteau's *The Embarkation for Cythera*. He could imagine himself in St Lucia a Cézanne, Van Gogh, or Gauguin, find Caribbean echoes in Diego Rivera, or later use Winslow Homer as a model for a Caribbean watercolourist. Craven's book remained an influence on his work, in his poetry and plays. The attention he gives Pinkie in *Another Life* may have more to do with a painting by that title by Sir Thomas Lawrence in Craven's *Treasury* than with Derek's own emotions concerning the pale-skinned child of his aunt.[5]

His belief that he would be a landscape painter meant that his vision was filled with the bays, forests, people, and villages of St Lucia; they were a new race. He went on painting expeditions. There was the intense light, the broken shadows, the canoes, the coconut palms, colours far different from the dull industrial colours of Auden and Eliot. The attention Walcott's poetry gives to the natural world, especially to describing St Lucia, derives from his paintings. In his poetry he used his pen as a brush, but the world and colour of tropical St Lucia contrasted significantly with the depressed greys of postwar England. Although his paintings treated St Lucian landscape through Cézanne and Gauguin, he learned the difference between a tropical sky and the shades of France, just as Creole was different from metropolitan French studied in school.

Walcott did need to think through his relationship to English as a language and English literature. English was his language, but not the spoken English of England, he could not use that for poetry. In the colonies the accent taught in schools was not how people spoke English. Too often mastery of accent became the object of education and alienated people. Awareness of the difference between good local speech and trying to copy British diction and tones became a starting-point for many of Walcott's ideas. Walcott never thought of himself as a 'young English poet' entering a tradition awaiting him. Walcott learned to read poetry in his own voice, naturally. Older English, Jacobean forms and accents still survived in the West Indies, especially in Barbados. Whether painting or training actors, Walcott aimed at using the tonal colours around him, attempting to become neither British nor a romantic primitivist.

The Walcott children were often observers of a lively street culture including forms of street theatre which they watched through jalousies. On Boxing Day there was a troupe of devils led by Flavier Dab (Flavier the Devil), a Lucifer-like lieutenant devil, and a man playing a she-devil. Flavier's costume was a mixture of Santa Claus, the devil, and African with 'an exaggerated pair of comically large balls'.[6] He would lead people through the city, and children would chant Creole responses to him. At times he would charge the children, and they would flee. The town was thought of as belonging to him and the bourgeoisie avoided involvement. At every crossroad the troupe reached, the devils put down a sisal bag and portrayed their own version of Lucifer's fall. Seewo, this equivalent of Lucifer, would challenge authority, in this case the rule of the main devil. There was also a kind of resurrection. Various kinds of cultural myths were mixed together in a drama which was highly codified and rigid.

There had been laws against folk customs, including a law against drumming at night and dancing to drums. It is said that as late as 1943 a summons was issued to a former Governor of the West Indies for dancing to drums at the Castries Social Club. Derek and his brother, however, spent time with his Aunt Sidone, an Anglican who lived at Choiseul, listening to folk tales:

> Sunset would threaten us as we climbed closer
> to her house up the asphalt hill road . . .
>
> .   .   .   .
>
> She began to remember at the minute of the fireflies,
>
> .   .   .   .
>
> stories she told to my brother and myself.
> Her leaves were the libraries of the Caribbean.[7]

Walcott would remember the folk tales and magical rural vision of nature with talking animals and insects told him by his Aunt Sidone, he would remember the strange creolized folk customs that developed in St Lucia, and the eccentrics found in Castries. The talking animals and folk tales would later find expression in such a play as *Ti-Jean and his Brothers*.

It was at St Mary's College that he first heard the story of Ti-Jean and his brothers. A boy told a story about three boys whom the devil challenges; the devil will eat them if they lose their temper. This version of the story is based on word play on three degrees of anger—*fâché, enragé, désolé*. The first and second brothers are tested, admit to becoming annoyed, and are eaten, but the third brother tricks the devil into saying 'Moi fâche tout seul, moi désolé' (I am enraged, I am desolated). Years later Walcott would work the pattern into his *Ti-Jean* play.[8] Not all folk traditions were good. People could remember that during the early part of the century there was a ritual murder, an event mentioned in 'Tales of the Island' and *Another Life*.

The more Walcott studied the peasants the more unlike them he felt. He was part-white, part of the urban, educated, middle-class, Protestant, English-speaking minority, everything they were not. As he came to understand their apathy, he became angry with God and the Church. The Catholic Church was all powerful both in the town and the villages; there was always the Church year, the saints' days, religious societies, festivals, St Peter's for fishermen. St Lucia itself was named after Santa Lucia. Roderick and Derek as Protestants were excluded from processions and retreats that formed part of the life of the community; they stayed at home during Church holidays, withdrawn, aware of mysteries being celebrated outside.

People spoke English and French Creole. Alix could speak Creole, but Derek and his friends spoke good English at home, at school, or with equals: Creole or Caribbean English was used when speaking with servants, maids, joking on the street, and at the market. Unlike Jamaica, St Lucia did not have a separate local English. The local language was French Creole. French Creole was the language of the poor and the rural. Derek spent time talking to local winos and others outside his social class. His plays *Jourmard* and *Dream on Monkey Mountain* would be based on local characters, the eccentrics of his youth, different from, but the equivalents of, the characters who populate V. S. Naipaul's *Miguel Street*. The Walcotts grew up with two languages, English and French Creole, but these two included another 'language', the creolized-accented English spoken in St Lucia. French Creole would remain important to Derek's imagination. St Lucia was the setting of several of his early plays—*Sea at Dauphin, Ione, Wine of the Country, Dream*. In *Dream* the characters often have French- or Patois-derived names—Souris, Makak, Lestrade, Tigre. In many of his plays he would use the frame of a *conteur*, as in *Ti-Jean* or in *Dream*; the *conteur* is the chorus which works as narrator.

Derek Walcott and his family may appear unique. They are not. Mulattos related to Governors and rich estate owners are part of Caribbean history. As a group such mulattos belonged to an élite below the whites and replaced them before themselves being challenged by black nationalism and those representing the poor. For decades West Indian politicians, professionals, editors, journalists, teachers, writers, estate managers, nationalists, and agitators were likely to be mulattos. Nor was it just a matter of colour. Those who could obtain educational or other qualifications became honorary browns or whites, there were good jobs for them. As brown history is overtaken by black history and now the new multiracial history of the Caribbean, it is useful to recall that the mulattos were the ones who had the education, language, training, and social contacts, and that for perhaps three-quarters of a century much of the significant cultural and political history of the region is mulatto. Although mulattos used black folk culture as part of their own nationalism, they were as a group near-white, culturally and physically.

Walcott was brought up culturally as a European, reading Hawthorne's 'Tanglewood Tales' and Charles Kingsley's 'The Heroes'. He wrote Greek-styled epics in unrhymed pentameters, using as a model Kingsley's myth of Perseus. He was reciting verse in school, drawing and painting about the European world he read about. He drew comic strips with white faces and accepted what he was told about American Indians, Japanese, Germans. He saw the world in terms of Europe, then the United States. In his teens he read American novels by Steinbeck, Faulkner, Hemingway, and Sinclair Lewis.

For many years he could not believe his skin and hair; he fantasized that they would change. How could he be a poet and not be white? The heir of Marlowe and Milton should have their hair. The situation was intensified by his mother's concern for whiteness, and the whiteness of his family. Derek was light, but somewhat negroid in features and a shade darker than his family. Such distinctions as straightness of hair were carefully observed and could form the basis of marriage and jobs. The British would marry brown, local whites did not. Those who married darker skins were likely to be excluded socially, the subject of his poem 'Country Club Romance'. Qualified blacks were appointed to the Civil Service and held high positions in government, bank employees were always fair-skinned. Derek blamed the white God for making what was valued white. In St Lucia and England there was no legal racial discrimination such as found in the American South, but people were conscious of distinctions of shade and the newspapers carried stories of lynchings, of American servicemen in England demanding the exclusion of blacks, and of the first postwar racial incidents. Roderick in his teens did not know many whites; Derek due to his interest in the arts moved among them, made friends, at times felt patronized, at times was hurt. It is a topic to which he still only refers in generalities. Such seeming racial and cultural contradictions and paradoxes became a source of creative tensions central to his art in which there is a continual unresolved arguing, shifting, nuancing, and balancing about matters of race, history, and culture.

Whereas he was aware of colour he did not feel he was conflicted by ideas of two cultures until his teens, until he began writing. How could he be a poet writing in 'white' English when he was in part a descendant of African slaves like the Creole-speaking Catholic rural peasants? Where was his culture, his language, his religion? Self-division began with writing and remained central to it, producing more sophistications like a growing dialectic; power came from the creative use of seeming contradictions. It was not until middle age that he began to feel that such self-divisions were false, that life is universal, and that St Lucia and his youth embodied the universal.

Shades of colour were, however, less important in St Lucia than in, say, Barbados with its large white population and ruling white plantocracy. Alix Walcott owned her house in a middle-class area, and carried herself well with pride and dignity. There were servants to do the cleaning and laundry. Dunstan St Omer was from a family lower on the social scale, and Dunstan's father was known to drink. For Dunstan to be a friend of a Walcott was a step up. The excitement that Simmons, Derek, and Dunstan felt during the 1940s and early 1950s was in breaking through class manners and boundaries to be artists living like artists for art rather than striving for financial and social security.

Walcott, Simmons, and St Omer, using local subject-matter and incorporating local arts within European forms, were the St Lucian equivalent of the cultural decolonization, nationalism, and racial assertion apparent in other colonies during the 1940s. The revolution was not only in racial and cultural politics; just as important was breaking through older inhibiting social conventions with their acceptances of limitations and trying to create and live as fully as such great artists of the late nineteenth century as Van Gogh.

During their teens Derek and Roderick drifted apart; Roderick was more interested in sports and mischief than books. Derek was moving among the élite. Then when they were about 16 it began to change. Both Roderick and Derek were in love with the cinema; if they could they would have been at Clarke's Theatre watching movies every night. They liked films, pretended that they had movie studios, and drew comic strips in imitation of films using their friends as the characters. Roderick's version of *Casablanca* was 'Leipzig'. When in the 1960s Derek started writing a film script, it continued this older dream. Derek still wants to be a film maker, still wants to write for Hollywood. Derek and Roddy turned to the theatre as a substitute for the movies. There was a veranda on the house where they made a toy theatre from sticks and would gather with friends to talk, sing, recite poetry, and perform Derek's plays. The St Lucia Arts Guild really began there, a development of the Junior Wesley Guild. Discussions ranged from religion and philosophy to songs from recent American films and Broadway musicals. Derek's cultural background consisted not only of Shakespeare, T. S. Eliot, and the discovery of Creole tales, it included songs from *South Pacific* and Bob Hope jokes.

Although Roderick had a reputation at school as the class clown, Derek was the more assertive of the two brothers and was favoured by Alix. Derek already seemed to know his way through life; by contrast Roddy was less resourceful, fell ill, and was behind Derek at school. Both were talented, but Derek was the one who first wrote poetry and plays, first published, started the Arts Guild, and it was Derek who taught at St Mary's College while awaiting going to university.

After Derek left for Jamaica, Roddy became a dramatist, director, and leader of the St Lucia Arts Guild, but significantly this only happened after Derek left. Derek would move on from Jamaica to Trinidad, whereas Roddy remained in St Lucia. Derek would aim towards an international career and fame, whereas Roddy would for almost two decades be central to the creation of culture within St Lucia. Derek was gifted, but so was Roderick. Early on some critics thought Roderick the better dramatist. Derek, however, had more a sense of career, personal destiny, and the ways of the world. He was tougher, less conventional, better able to use his talents and contacts.

During Walcott's youth the West Indies lacked money and the cultural abundance to which we are accustomed. There was, for example, no bookshop in Kingston, Jamaica, during the 1930s. There was, however, a common culture shared by the English-speaking élite, the small middle class, and the aspiring. There were concerts at which people entertained themselves and others with scenes from plays, recitations of poetry, music, and jokes. People listened to opera and 'classical' music. There were a few good libraries with standard texts in good editions. Derek has often observed that there were classics and comic books, but without the masses of commercial reading materials that have now become common. Besides the Castries public library funded by the Andrew Carnegie Foundation, Walcott had his father's small library at home in which he read Dickens, Sir Walter Scott, and Sabatini, 'the adventurous Italian novelist'. He was growing up during a time when the West Indies was moving towards independence, preparing for self-government. The notion of the British Empire became elegiac for him, and he was aware of writing during its 'twilight' as it withdrew and faded. St Lucia was not a place of radical politics, of armed nationalist movements, or armed white police. There were unarmed black constables. Although the ultimate power was white British, for Walcott, like many West Indians of his generation, British rule of law still represents an idea of the government as a service to the public that has since been lost in the Caribbean.[9]

While the Walcotts were part of a new local English-language culture, they, along with Harold Simmons and Dunstan St Omer, also helped make local customs and Creole culturally respectable. The position of Walcott in his society had a lasting effect on his sensibility, his imagination, and his writing, which would be characterized by use or consciousness of such opposites as white/black; English/French; written/oral; standard English/dialect; Old World/New World; North/South; classical/folk; exile/home; European/Caribbean. His life and work were to be marked by the creative coexistence of antagonistic opposites. There were to be attempts to heal division, but resolution would probably have meant the end to creativity. Because Walcott makes use of overlapping levels of diction, analogy, metaphor, perspectives, and traditions, his work naturally accommodates and uses puns, paradoxes, contrasts, and contradictions. In Walcott's work Modernism with its many voices, its revolt against history, its inconclusive conclusions, becomes mulatto, representative of the coexistence of cultural pluralities in the Creole, the artist expressing the meetings between cultures in the last third of the twentieth century.

As Derek learned more about the world, history, his family history, and experienced racial hurts, he became angry at slavery and social prejudices, but later in life he was to view this as another reason to see the New World as a new start, a new culture. 'Think about illegitimacy in the Caribbean! Few people can claim to find their ancestry in the linear way. The whole situation in the Caribbean is an illegitimate situation. If we admit that from the beginning that there is no shame in that historical bastardy, then we can be friends.' This might be regarded as a basis of Walcott's dislike of history as tradition, lineage, sequence. The New World is like the sea, ever changing, a place of bastards and new beginnings.[10]

Many of the hurts of Walcott's childhood would, however, continue to haunt him. In his own broken marriages he would wonder if he was re-enacting the lover who abused his mother; there was Pam's first son left illegitimate when the young father denied paternity, 'O child as guiltless as the grass'.[11] There was much in Walcott's childhood and youth to forget; it was self-destructive to dwell on it, better to mock psychology and create a new myth in which the hurts were ignored or referred to in generalities about the regional past. The hurts are still there, as they must be for any artist, but like grains of sand encrusted with pearls—the pearls of art and of a vision of the New World.

There is the Walcott who is more than half-white, who sees his whiteness mostly as language and culture, but who shows little interest in his actual family lineage and England. Walcott knows that the countries to the north regard him as black and that they treat blacks differently, sometimes violently, sometimes patronizingly, but whether they see you as inferior or victim they do not see you as a St Lucian, a Methodist, a shabine or red, a product of a religious, highly respected, hard-working élite in the colonial world. They incorporate you into their history, not knowing that you have your own story.

3

1944−1947 From Pantheist to
Modernist, James Rodway

St Lucia recovering from the Great Depression was largely an isolated colonial backwater of the Empire where Britain's entry into the Second World War is said to have been announced by the bugler of the volunteer fire brigade slowly bicycling from town to town announcing in patois 'C'est la guerre'. The war brought shortages, refugees from Vichyite Martinique, a German submarine in the harbour, and volunteers to fight for England—including airmen. The plunder of a wrecked boat brought many children their first commercial ice-cream. There were American soldiers, an American airbase, American roads, and American money. During the war the Coconut Walk and Country Club golf links on Vigie Peninsula became an airfield which now reaches the cemetery and new roads were built. The silent colour bar which had limited non-whites to a few professions such as law and medicine crumbled as locals replaced the British in positions of administrative responsibility. Although the Americans withdrew from the islands after the war, their presence remained; the British Empire was coming to an end, and the United States and Canada would now become more influential. The first election in Jamaica under universal suffrage was in 1944 and limited self-government followed.

Walcott was already becoming known as a poet; whereas others might be asked to sing at school assembly, he was expected to recite his poems. When he was 14, he spent the summer at the country hotel of Grace Augustin. There while walking along on a hill he had a vision, a trance, his mind floated, he felt pity for the world. He began to cry, knelt, and felt changed. The pattern was that of a mystical experience leading to conversion. He saw the beauty of the world, saw the presence of God in it, and he christened and confirmed himself a poet. He made the experience into '1944', his first published poem, at the age of 14, when in the fourth form at St Mary's. It has forty-four lines, imitating the blank verse at the opening of *Paradise Lost* and appeared in the *Voice of Saint Lucia*, the newspaper owned by Garnet Gordon, the Methodist friend of his father and mother.[1]

> Oh! in what happy state I would then be
> As an acknowle'ged friend to bird or beast
> As our first father was—alive and free.
> And who, would not, happy in that condition
> Rejoice he lived? yet, fearing to pray out,
> That by his speech the wrong name he would call
> And bring strong retribution from his Benefactor,
> Each peaceful night, as sure as death after this life,
> His happy soul he would to Him commend
> And what his lips would fear to undertake,
> His pounding heart not hesitate to make
> A joyous full confession . . .
>
> .   .   .   .
>
> Ah! that such happy state would e'er exist.

Derek's youthful prodigy attracted hostility; the animosity was religious. Father Jesse, an Englishman who had converted to Roman Catholicism, was the most articulate and argumentative of the local priests. An historian and anthropologist, he belonged to the same societies as Harold Simmons and others who regarded Derek as continuing his father's place among the local artists. Jesse, however, had a convert's zeal and was offended by such a young man being praised for a poem which argued for the superiority of learning God through the study of Nature rather than 'By moral mouth, or men's dry means of lesson'. While drawing upon Traherne, Vaughan, and Wordsworth, Walcott's notion of the innocent child's communion with Nature and discovery of God through his Creation was thought close to deism or a romantic transcendentalism. It was certainly Protestant in an otherwise religiously observant Roman Catholic St Lucia.

Although Christianity has long made analogies between pre-fallen Adam and the innocence of childhood, between the direct knowledge of God in Eden and the use of nature as a source of meditation, Walcott's poem might be read as rejecting Christian revelation as a source of anxiety and confusion. The iconography of Christian meditation in Andrew Marvell's 'The Garden' had been transformed into symbols of sceptical doubt for someone in the process of losing his faith, unable to feel Divine Love, and who blamed it on the consequences of being raised a Christian. As the poem has the reputation of being a Wordsworthian meditation on Nature, it should be noted that the argument claims that teaching supposed religious truths results in fear and trembling of error, in contrast to the peaceful nights and faith produced by a natural religion.

'1944' foreshadows many of Walcott's later characteristics as a poet: the embedding of small phrases from other poets; the irregular and varied mixing of kinds of rhymes with other, less obvious, forms of harmonization at line ends; the strong argumentative structure within what is really a meditative lyric with unresolved contradictions which suggest despair while the pitch goes 'up' and seems happy at the end; the formal structure of two halves each of twenty-two lines; long compressed sentences which change direction and have a loose, confusing, syntax which results in some obscurity; the cadenced phrases and lines with their own movement that are a sign of a master poet. While the poem is written within the conventions of English religious, nature, and mystical poetry, it might be read as an attack on priests, sects, and those who claim to know God's word from other sources than a personal study of the Book of Nature:

> Then in the silence of that shady dell
> Far beyond knowledge man could tell of well
> I should desire to learn, and, having learned prove
> Myself to be, also an object of The Maker's love

Instead he is filled with fears of retribution, sleepless nights, and he questions what he has been taught.

Walcott's later troubled relationship to Christianity and God seems present here, and St Lucians recognized that it was a poem of doubt in which formal religion was being blamed for loss of faith. Derek attended St Mary's College, a school run by Roman Catholics; he could be a dangerous influence.

Three days later Father Jesse, FMI, replied with 'Reflections on Reading the Poem "1944"'. The reply is in five stanzas each rhymed ababcc and might be said to parody as well as answer Walcott's work. It is tightly rhymed whereas Walcott's poem uses rhyme sparingly. Walcott's poem is Wordsworthian in the way the movement of thought appears to flow: Jesse's poem is tightly argued and the points reply to those raised by Walcott. In contrast to Walcott's Trahernean and Wordsworthian diction, Jesse uses a plain diction with sarcastic Augustan touches.[2]

Jesse's reply is framed in terms of such opposites as Walcott's youth and Jesse's age, poetry and the Bible, Nature and Revelation, individual interpretation contrasted to God's Church. The basic argument is the received tradition, handed down from Moses through the Prophets, Christ, Paul, and the Roman Catholic Church, which requires faith. Jesse's second and third stanza were, however, more than doctrinal, they were insulting:

> Dim thoughts do not a poem make,
> Nor far sought words a youthful chime ...

> But quite apart from outward form
> The lines of our young poet fail
> To take this critic's heart by storm—
> They've poison in the head and tail!
> Youth would have none to speak of God,
> Except the tree, the ant, the sod!

The 'dim thoughts', 'far sought words', 'poison', and ambiguity of 'the sod' were far from the encouragement that a 14-year-old poet might expect from an elder; indeed Jesse's 'Reflections' reeked of malice and intolerance. They were a declaration of war. It hurt. This was a criminal attempt to crush Walcott's youthful love of nature.

A letter to the editor answering Jesse said that 'A. Seeker' thought Walcott's poem beautiful and filled with 'depth of soul, a longing to find God, an honest simple desire to be an object of His love' rarely found at present. Father Jesse's reply was neither beautiful nor correct in finding 'poison' in the sentiments. There were many ways to find God, in a mother's love, in the beauty of the sky, in the majesty of the deep seas, or the silence of the cloister. The letter urged Walcott not to be discouraged; he should keep up the search and find God in his own way.[3]

Father Jesse would continue his war with the Walcotts and the Methodists for more than a decade. One area of contention was education. As the government wanted more influence concerning what was taught and by whom, Catholic control of education was increasingly challenged by the Protestants and especially by the Methodists. During September 1944 Father Jesse published a poem in the *Voice of St Lucia* concerning 'The Agreed Syllabus' which complained that it failed to teach 'Doctrine': 'True Religion is dogmatic | Neither fluid nor erratic— | So your Syllabus my favour ne'er will find!' The issue also carried a letter to the editor complaining about Father Jesse's attack on Mr H. H. Pilgrim, ex-Inspector of Schools in Grenada.[4]

In his sixties Walcott still remembered with anger the hurts that Jesse and other priests had inflicted on his family and himself. To be from a minority and then accused of heresy when attending a Church school was like being singled out for trouble. His classmates shunned him or told him that he was doomed to Hell or Limbo. Walcott was shocked by Jesse claiming that love of nature was heresy (and by Jesse's ease with metres that took him effort). Father Jesse was accusing Walcott of straying from Christianity through youthful pride and wrong intellectual influences. In a highly religious community, where Catholics were the overwhelming majority and the Church was powerful, such accusations were serious. There are rumours about threats to the family. Alix felt her own advancement was blocked. Such an atmosphere had a lasting effect on

Walcott, making him conscious of his distance from the Catholics, making him aware of what he considered to be his loss of faith (although by most modern intellectual standards, Walcott may be one of the few remaining religious poets), making him feel part of a threatened progressive, rational Methodist community, making him feel an outsider within the national community.

Jesse had detected something in Walcott's poem or in the Walcotts, an aspect of Protestantism which to a Catholic can be heretical. It is the Augustinian inner light, the voice of God within. Walcott already believed that God spoke to and through him. As a child he thought he had been sent to redeem all the sinners of the world. He had a private religion, it would remain with him. There would always be that sense of being one of the elect, of having a gift, of being set apart, yet a leader. Walcott never was an atheist or agnostic. He believed in a personal God, the spiritual, but did not believe in the resurrection, heaven, and hell; something happened after death, but like Hamlet he did not, and still does not, know what.

Many of the older priests were intolerant white French peasants sent to a poor agricultural island to speak French to black peasants. Father Jesse (1897–1985) by contrast was well read, a scholar, intelligent, later the author of the standard *Outlines of St Lucia's History*.[5] Walcott was being used by Jesse to attack the Methodist community and especially the Methodist school. Here was the fountain of heresy, in the teaching of such poets as Wordsworth!

Walcott as a minority Methodist attending an overwhelmingly Catholic school was already different, but after the attack by Jesse in the newspaper, he began to experience mockery and persecution. At St Mary's College he had arguments with classmates who would tell him that as a non-Catholic he could never understand. Curiously Walcott began using AMGD, his version of 'Ad Majorem Dei Gloriam', to the Greater Glory of God, to indicate when he was satisfied with his writing. Walcott thought and thinks of his talents as God-given, to be used for God. He thought of himself as a Protestant who rebels against the Church, like Luther, and later, like the Stephen Dedalus of Joyce's *Portrait of the Artist*, as someone who quarrels with God and loses his faith. There remained, however, a sense of the religious which would variously assert itself in his writing as a personal relationship to God. Although Walcott appreciated the symbolism of Catholic art, he was a Methodist; he detested the cult of Mary and its popular iconography.

The small world in which Walcott lived can be seen from the size of St Mary's College. Twenty-five students were admitted during 1944 making eighty-five in all. For the 1943 Junior School Certificate thirteen from St Mary's entered, eleven passed, including Derek Walcott, Dunstan St Omer, Derek King, Kenneth and O. Monplaisir, and C. Theobalds. At St Joseph Convent four entered and passed, including Ruth Theobalds. The same names come up later with the Arts Guild. The next year those who passed School Certificate examination included the two Augiers, Michael Beaubrun, Vincent Floissac. Only about one-third of those who entered for the examinations passed and almost all of that third were from St Mary's or St Joseph.

While food was still minimal and even such imports as low quality red butter in tins still sporadic, St Lucia by late 1944 was moving towards a postwar society with a renewed interest in the arts, increased opportunities for education, public festivities, and governmental plans for development. The people the Walcotts knew were centrally involved in making a postwar St Lucia, even a postwar West Indies. In 1943 the Trinidad and Tobago Art Society was founded; Harold Simmons was among the first exhibitors, the only one from outside Trinidad. In December 1944 Simmons had his second one-man showing in St Lucia. It was held at the Castries Social Club. The paintings included *U Boat attack in Castries Harbour, March 1942, Prelude in C Sharp Minor, Mother and Child, Surrealistic Landscape, Choiseul,* and *Her Daily Bread* and demonstrated his versatility.[6]

To celebrate St Lucia Day, 12 December, there was a Costume Ball given at Government House attended by 200 guests from several islands together with representatives of the US Army and Coast Guard. The judges included the Woodings; he was a King's Councillor and a leading Methodist from Trinidad. Quadrilles were organized by Mrs A. Beaubrun from Castries. Mrs E. O. Plunkett was awarded first prize for her Lavinia. First prize for men went to the Hon. Garnet H. Gordon who was dressed as an eighteenth-century gentleman. Second prize for men went to Major E. O. Plunkett, who had served in various colonial police forces, dressed as Claude (c.1870).[7] The Woodings would later help Derek's entry into Trinidad. The Beaubrun family, although Catholic, sent their children to take private English lessons with Walker, the Methodist teacher. A wealthy black merchant family, the Beaubruns would often be part of the Walcott circle; Stella Beaubrun (who married into the family) was co-owner of the art gallery in which Derek would exhibit in Trinidad and a sponsor of at least one of his plays. Plunkett would give his name to the white English couple in *Omeros,* and Mrs Lucille Plunkett, who was co-founder with Harold Simmons of the Arts and Crafts Society, had some of the interests of Maude Plunkett in *Omeros,* including the use of local motifs in sewing quilts.

Harold Simmons was the leader of the group which in 1945 founded an Arts and Crafts Society. Such societies were being formed at that time throughout the colonies, a postwar Labour version of the William Morris and Ruskin handicraft tradition. Although by comparison high brow, Modernist, and mostly brown and black, the St Lucia Arts Guild, the Trinidad Theatre Workshop, and the other groups Walcott would form might be seen as building upon ideas and aspirations that Simmons and Mrs Plunkett had in starting the Arts and Crafts Society. A central assumption is that art and creativity are more natural to being human than politics. Indeed creativity is a form of politics in that art is not divorced from life, does not exist in a sacred realm of its own, but is of this world, like choosing a meal, clothing, or furnishing. Simmons argued that Man is happier if he creates something, something that is of himself. Anticipating the Mrs Plunkett of *Omeros*, Simmons and Mrs Plunkett claimed that a dressmaker, a woman with a needle, would be happier doing her own design rather than copying others. She would be happier if once she learned how to create stylistic patterns she could make designs using the world around her, the paw-paw or breadfruit, rather than 'white bears and log-cabins weary with snow'. 'The majority of West Indians are unfortunately preconditioned to accept certain standards of culture, the influence of Western civilization . . . Art in itself could not be called art unless it springs from the people unless it records those things felt and experienced . . . A picture of the dirty squalor of a house or room in the slums is beautiful, because it is truth.'[8]

The St Lucia Arts and Crafts Society was officially started in April 1945 by the usual suspects, Mrs E. O. Plunkett, the Hon. Garnet Gordon, A. M. Lewis, F. J. Carasco (a labour leader), J. A. Rodway, and Harold Simmons. Harold Simmons was the initiator, organizer, and Secretary; the first President was Mrs Plunkett. The Society began with a membership of over 100 and aimed to encourage and give recognition to music, painting, sculpture, drama, dance, and hand crafts. Simmons argued for the need for a local cultural centre, a state-funded building in which to meet for lectures, readings, and to listen to recordings of Beethoven, with artist studios, a stage for performances, and various amenities needed for the arts including annual visits by theatre companies.

Walcott would over the years similarly campaign to persuade St Lucia and Trinidad to build a sensible cultural centre which could be used as a little theatre, by a dance company, and for the training of artists. Derek himself had listened intensely over and over to phonograph recordings of Beethoven's symphonies. He learned from Simmons that the English watercolour was the epitome of graceful art with the subtlety of its dissolving line. It was evanescence in a frame. He would need to adjust his youthful education within the English tradition to the still undescribed world of St Lucia with its different seasons, strong primary colours, tropical culture, and muscular semi-nude black bodies.

Instead of the English countryside and thatched cottages, there were beaches, swimmers, black fishermen, palm trees, months of never-ending sun, tropical storms, brightly coloured parrots, flame trees, breadfruits, mountains, women earning their living by carrying coal in baskets on their head. There was the nationalist task of avoiding the European prejudices that nothing of value really existed in the New World. This was partly a matter of what Walcott would later describe as naming, the giving of the local landscape a value as authentic and worthy as that of Europe, so that the breadtree or a black fisherman would be as suitable a subject as a rose or white seafarer. Beyond the general categories of naming are the more nuanced shades that are necessary for art and a genuine, as contrasted to ideological, habitation; there were the many variations in the rainy season, the colouring of the blue skies, the shades of water, the social and cultural differences in the West Indians. It was not enough to replace an apple with a breadfruit; the shape, colours, uses, users, and associations of the breadfruit had to be described. He would need to learn how to describe this in the art forms and language of Europe while finding his own voice and vision. The vision and understanding of its politics would come early, the remainder of his life would require steady practice and thought to master and refine and vary ways of presentation until eventually some colonial offshoots of English art and poetry became St Lucian, West Indian, Commonwealth, and then took their place in that international museum of the world's culture. Then there was the problem of how to make a living, support a family, build a home, while creating such an art in a society which because of poverty, snobbery, and a colonial education had no tradition of supporting artists, especially local artists.

Around 1946 Walcott realized he would be a poet rather than a painter. Dunstan was the one with natural talent as a painter, the loose movement of the arm and wrist, whereas Derek approached painting as something to be analysed. He had the technique but lacked the talent. Dunstan left for Curaçao where after the war there was a shortage of labour and wages were high. This was Dunstan's introduction into the adult world of money and whores, and allowed him to purchase his own oil paint set which was then an expensive rarity in St Lucia. The young were known as the Turks, young Turks, and Roderick, who was behind Derek at St Mary's, formed a Turks steel band. This got Roddy into trouble with the Church by way of the College, which threatened to expel band members. Another Walcott in trouble!

During March 1946 Harold Simmons reviewed *First Poems* by George Campbell in the *Voice of St Lucia*. Campbell, a relative of Norman Manley (the leading Jamaican politician and future Prime Minister), had moved from Jamaica to Harlem and published a book of poems, many of which concerned blacks. According to Simmons art has added value when it chooses to mirror the life and thought of the present, and to speak with the prophecies and aspirations and hope of a people. When art speaks of feelings, the more violent the changes, whether political or mental, the more likely a chosen few will express the destiny of a race. All artists feel beauty, shabbiness, false hopes, irony, strivings, failure. The artists are trying to touch each other and understand each other's cultures. Simmons claimed that Campbell's *First Poems* are the best poems published from the West Indies, along with those of Collymore and Arthur Seymour. Campbell is the artist as seer, he uses a free style without modern extremism. The poems are the fresh singing of a race, not as bitterness and segregation but springing from mixing blood, tolerance, and understanding. 'It is poetry expressing the beauty of Negro, European, Indian, Chinese, all ethnic groups who have fallen into the various melting-pots.' It is no use comparing Campbell's poetry with that of others. The art of each race has a different purpose. Campbell speaks for all West Indians.[9] Simmons introduced Walcott to Campbell's poetry, read him poems with such lines as 'Holy be the white head of a Negro'. For Walcott this was a breakthrough; here were poems actually written by a West Indian about black West Indians.

Walcott's poetry, that had been Miltonic, Jacobean, Wordsworthian, began to change during 1946, when he discovered modern poetry, especially Eliot, Auden, Spender, Pound, and Thomas. He began writing original poems, very knotty and compact. Simmons had recordings of Eliot reading *Four Quartets*, the Dent edition of Dylan Thomas's *Death and Entrances*, but it was James Rodway who made him feel he was a modern poet.

James Rodway (BA, London) from British Guyana, had taught at St Vincent Grammar School during 1940–3, and in December 1944 became Inspector of Schools in St Lucia, then acting Education Officer. Rodway's poetry was published in Guyanese magazines; years later Walcott would recall 'The Telephone', a terse modern free verse dismissal of a love affair in a modest style. Rodway wanted to share with Walcott his own interest in poetry and writing it. Rodway would read poems to Walcott, read Walcott's poems, encourage him to write more, discuss literature with him; he introduced him to modern poetry and lent him various books of Faber poets, which influenced his views of modern poetry. Rodway and Simmons made modern poetry part of his life.

He mostly read anthologies, such as Michael Roberts's *Faber Book of Modern Poetry*. The first complete volume of modern verse Walcott remembers reading was Joseph Auslander's *Cyclops Eye* (1926). Auslander (1897–1965), an American, wrote over a dozen books, beginning with *Sunrise Trumpets* (1924) and concluding with *Islanders* (1951). Walcott recalls the banal toughness of such rhymes as 'What is life, Is it the stale | smell of water in a pail?' Although Auslander is not complex and not really an influence, his 'Cyclops Eye', the title poem, with its mixture of Modernist and biblical apocalypse imagery, religiosity and cynicism, and alienated narrator with a taste for horror effects, has some characteristics of Walcott's poetry in his later teens:

> I heard a thousand wheels wince
> Under the throttle of brakes: I saw
> Men and motors crash—the splints
> Of Windshield glass, the bleeding skull, the raw
> Horror of a sagging jaw;

Auslander was a living poet. Walcott was determined that he too would write his own book.[10]

Modern poetry excited him with its different tone and immediacy, but all of English literature, whether Shakespeare or Dylan Thomas, was an influence. Walcott now had two exercise books filled with imitations of poems by others, usually following their shape or form. Each day he would model poems directly on what he read, the way an apprentice painter would copy a head by Leonardo. He would model a poem on one by Spender, Hopkins, MacNeice, Eliot, Pound, Auden, or Thomas, using the same rhyme scheme or structure but with different rhymes to learn the shapes of poetry, even if the tone and manner was different from his own. He was a craftsman learning from masters out of the standard anthologies by Oscar Williams and Selden Rodman. The variety of what he imitated was exciting. His subject-matter was new; no one had written about it before, but he had to learn how to shape it. Walcott still feels that you cannot learn to write without learning 'the shapes'.[11]

Walcott felt a greater immediacy in Auden's lines than Eliot's and often wrote poems modelled on Auden and other 'Pylon' poets such as MacNeice, Spender, and Day Lewis. He liked the freshness, wit, intelligence, excitement, and vigour. There were strange words, Anglo-Saxon derivatives, the casually astonishing descriptions and landscapes. He was learning the use of telegraphese, the attractions of a landscape of ruins and rust, and such mannerisms as dropping definite articles and capitalizing abstract nouns. His familiarity with Methodist hymns made him appreciative of, and at home with, Auden's formal structures, clear metrics and language, emphasis on words, lack of ornamentation, and pastorlike quality. He would later speak of Auden as the great poet of the century who created a new vocabulary about the ordinary and contemporary, in contrast to Eliot's more jaded, wary way of regarding life. Where Eliot appeared nostalgic, Auden seemed vigorous and more technically daring.[12]

From early on Walcott's poetry was regarded as a phenomenon to be brought to the attention of other West Indians by those interested in literature. John Figueroa, the poet and a future teacher of Walcott, first heard of Walcott's poetry in 1946 from Rodway on SS *Jamaica Producer*, when Rodway and Figueroa were sailing to England on British Council scholarships. They discussed George Campbell's poetry and Rodway said Walcott was potentially better.[13]

In November 1946, Harold Simmons brought together a group of 'ladies and gentlemen' to study the work of West Indian authors. 'Mr. Keith Alleyne gave an interesting lecture on the compositions of two St Lucian poets at the Circle's last fortnightly meeting.' The probability is that Derek Walcott was one of the poets. To understand Walcott's sense of vocation, his quest for fame, his sense of superiority, there is not only the influence of his family and the Church; Walcott was moving in a world where his elders were expecting great poetry from him. The West Indies wanted a poet.[14]

During 1946 Walcott appeared in print again. In September 1946, the *Voice of St Lucia* published two poems by 'D.W.' ('Pardon me Muse, I am a humble man, ...'

and 'Once, long ago I made two worlds be one, . . .'), rare examples of Walcott's pre-Modernist poetry. 'Pardon me Muse . . .' suggests that the neurotic spiders he was later to be accused of were already there by 1946, as the poem rejects them. The poems are written in extremely simple, strict ten-syllable pentameters, the first of sixteen lines, the second of twelve. Although often alternating or consecutive, the rhymes are unpredictable. The style, tone, and manner are that of the often monosyllabic seventeenth-century religious poetry of George Herbert or maybe Vaughan or Quarles and are influenced by Methodist hymns. The first poem, 'Pardon me Muse, I am a humble man', has a Herbertian imagined bare setting and concerns worldly vanity, 'I pay for fame, t'is an old, old thing'. As in the older poems disillusion follows (his heart screams 'fear | Of mediocrities') and his 'soul' becomes angry and fearful until 'Hope' calms the poet 'and my pen | Works wonders then, with never sound or sight | Of grotesque shadows flitting over light.' The argumentative and allegorical structure of an older religious poem has been imitated while being applied to Walcott's own fears, ambitions, and experience as a young poet. He desires fame, hates the second rate and imitative, is aware of death, is filled with painful anxieties about himself and his work ('Can find me tightening fingers round my hair . . .'), until Hope works its wonders and he writes clearly without grotesque imagery.

The second poem ('Once, long ago I made two worlds be one,') is also in the manner of Herbert, Vaughan, or Traherne, and appears to be a religious rejection of the worldly, but there is a pessimism or fatalism:

> That world is crumbling now, yes, so it seems
> I do not think there is one thing of Man's
> Even made by God lasts on its own . . .

Even within the clarity of such poems there is a puzzling confusedness about syntax and reference. Walcott wants the tangled syntax, the piling up of possibilities, ambiguities, and analogies.[15]

In December 1946, Walcott's 'Epitaph for the Young' was published in the *Voice of St Lucia*. This poem is unlike the volume of poems published a few years later with that title, but has narrative ideas and other motifs that anticipate it. Walcott was to date *Epitaph for the Young* as having been started in December 1946, so while the poem in the newspaper is not an early draft, it was a starting place. Suddenly the poetry has a different pitch and manner; it is fresher and modern in diction, the cadences of the voice swing over the steady iambic pentameter, as if this were a prose story and the speaker were addressing the reader in a colloquial voice, that of Hemingway or Steinbeck. The use of abstract terms is Audenesque; in places the poem is Eliotic mock-Victorian in manner as Walcott experiments with different voices and tones. The poem tells a similar story to many other Walcott poems of this period; he suffers anxieties, knows that life will be a painful journey from home as he searches for himself, and that death eventually awaits him who 'Never had time, nor place, nor guts to pray'. It is not clear whether this is a nightmare of the present or an allegory of the future as the journey motif and use of time are selectively alluded to rather than sustained. One thinks of a similar ambiguity in some of T. S. Eliot's poems in which time passes while events or significant non-events occur in the speaker's mind. One peculiarity about the poem is that the speaker calls himself 'I, the unmaimed but manacled quadroon'.

This marks the change into a modern poet expressing Victorian nightmares and lost faith in a twentieth-century vocabulary of irony, impersonation, fragmentation, impersonality, of images rather than symbols. It seems in places like that original Modernist nightmare that Auslander was attempting to imitate!

> In that noiseless womb of terror you can find
> Hard terror shattering the imprisoned mind
> I dreamt I saw a hundred horses
> Running wild, hunted by mounted formes.
> Heard their hoofs pound the drum-skin of the plain
> Til in my throat I felt like stone again.
>
> Had the time then come to visit some new land?
> In fresh verdure, thinking, seeing the old novelties
> The desert, the unending caravan
> The cement tower Jamaican, hills, the ocean
> Boundless and heaving blue,
> Signs like the unhurried motion
> Of yourself questing the inscrutable anew,
> To know when such is such and you are you[16]

Walcott would learn during 1947–9 the modern diction of the 1930s. He was especially attracted towards Auden's use of traditional metres, terse vocabulary, dropping of definite articles to create a sense of urgency, a sense of malaise, of a dying Europe, revolutionary excitement, and heroic doom. Auden's ruined industrial England of tractors and iron pylons was in contrast to the exotic, tropical, flowery, precious language of West Indian poetry. This is a long way from the Wordsworthian, Miltonic '1944' and the Herbertian and Vaughanian poems.

Although Walcott's evaluation of T. S. Eliot as a poet wavered over the years, he respected Eliot as a critic and the echoes of older poets in Eliot's poetry made Walcott read the earlier corpus of English-language poets and learn from them. Craft and technique were Walcott's concerns and would continue to set his work aside from, and make it far superior to, those who assumed that something supposedly essentially West Indian—such as being 'black', using dialect, or as a kind of political slogan—was the heart of poetry and art. Walcott's views would become more subtle, more inclusive, but fifty years later he would still hold the basic aesthetic position that the joy of painting is in painting, the joy of poetry is in words. If you want to be an English-language poet (which is different from an English poet) you need to master the English language and the craft of poetry. One begins as an apprentice.

During June 1947 Walcott published 'One Poem' in the *Voice of St Lucia*; basic-ally a sonnet with a 4–6–4 stanzaic structure, it speaks of 'the heart's drought, desire' and fear of sudden death, 'senile sighs', 'prayer and palsey', and towards its conclusion 'Heresies pinion my flight. | Yet let my words recall | Healed wings … | The journey to the sudden time of birth.' A bit of seventeenth-century religious poetry mixed with early Dylan Thomas, 'One Poem' proclaims that he has lost his faith, he is already near death; the writing of poetry is a record of his inner state and a possible way towards salvation. The poem feels con-trived, an unfortunate characteristic of many of Walcott's poems into his early thirties. In the few years from '1944' to 'Epitaph for the Young' and 'One Poem', Walcott had travelled from a youthful pantheistic romanticism to an increasingly neurotic-appearing manner of Modernist verse proclaiming pain, loss of faith, and fear of death. Nature, in the form of descriptions of St Lucia, would rescue him.[17]

One of the earliest poems Walcott has continued to publish is 'As John to Patmos', written when he was 17 as a result of looking at the channel between Vigie and Martinique. It is modelled even in its triple rhymes on G. M. Hopkins's 'Dun Scotus Oxford' and on a memory of a sermon on John's vision on Patmos:

> This island is heaven—away from the dustblown blood of cities;
> See the curve of bay, watch the straggling flower, pretty is
> The wing's sound of trees, the sparse-powered sky, when lit is
> The night. For beauty has surrounded
> Its black children, and freed them of homeless ditties.[18]

The poem textually owes much to Hopkins, but the subject, the landscape with 'black children', owes nothing to him. This is a typical Walcottian distinction between a borrowed or imitated form and the subject (and emotion). Over the years Walcott has often mentioned the excitement of this period and how he felt his writing was part of the local landscape. He was feverish, elated, intense, finding parallels. He had a vocation, like John, but his was to hymn St Lucia. The placement of the poem towards the start of *25 Poems*, and in his later *Collected Poems*, is thematic as well as chronological, an announcement of purpose.

He also was nervous, priggish, shy, lonely, saw ruins, and was afraid of death. He had times of visions, times when he felt he was aware of his soul; he feared madness, and the world seemed wondrously beautiful.

During his teens he became conscious of the history of slavery, of parts of his family history, of the treatment of blacks in America, felt insulted by some whites, realized that he was unlikely to marry a white St Lucian, and was annoyed by an American who raised pigs or kept a pig on his yacht. As his talents brought him into contact with rich foreigners, he envied them and contrasted their wealth and comforts to the poor blacks who served them. He went through a period of hating whites as oppressors while secretly wishing he were white. He was also a College Prefect at St Mary's along with Michael Beaubrun, Kenneth Monplaisir, and three others. Desmond Mason and Vincent Floissac, recent Old Boys, were appointed junior masters.

4

$\sim\!\!\sim\!\!\sim\!\!\sim\!\!\sim\!\!\sim\!\!\sim\!\!\sim\!\!\sim\!\!\sim\!\!\sim\!\!\sim\!\!\sim$

1948–1949 *25 Poems, Epitaph for the Young,* Frank Collymore

BESIDES becoming a Modernist, Walcott was learning how to be a nationalist. This was far from a straightforward affirmation of roots, folk traditions, orality, and the past. The culture of Walcott's parents, friends, teachers, to which he looks back with nostalgia in *Remembrance* and *Omeros*, was highly literate and British although, perhaps because, schooling was scarce. The *West Indian Crusader* in April 1948 reported under Club News that the Soufriere Literary League was meeting to discuss Word Building, Hyde Park, and Shakespeare Criticism. A paper was read showing that Shakespeare created unheroic characters like himself, but compared with those of Sir Walter Scott his women characters were lifeless abstractions. Shakespeare was said to have paid tribute to his mother, was too dull to be humorous, and hated dogs. The same issue contained a long letter concerning 'An appreciation of literature' by a teacher addressed to other primary school teachers. It would be difficult to find primary school teachers at present who quote at length from the poems of Matthew Arnold, allude to Shakespeare's *Julius Caesar* and Sheridan's *School for Scandal* as part of what might be taught, and quote Aristotle in Latin.[1]

By contrast, on 11 February 1948, the *West Indian Crusader* mentioned that yesterday evening the steel bands at Carnival kept going until late and drew large crowds 'more from novelty than from musical entertainment'. Steel band had been created a few years earlier, during the war, in Trinidad, when tuned oil drums started to be used to play Carnival songs. Soon the musicians turned their attention to European melodies and more complex harmonies. What began as imitation became a new orchestral form with its own distinctive sound and, sixty years later, its own traditions, taught in Trinidadian schools and exported as authentic Caribbean culture. While not a precise analogy to Walcott's art, it shows some of the complications in the ways a culture develops and cross-breeds from various sources.

Writers might use ballads or other supposed folk forms, but most literary forms are equally 'foreign'. The method with which Walcott began, consciously modelling his poetry on earlier works, was similar to that of painters who have traditionally copied, imitated, and modelled their work on others, as steel band musicians used European melodies and harmonies. This had a lasting importance to him. Walcott upset those trying to build a West Indian literature upon political sentiments, free verse, supposed African survivals, and bits of dialect and folk culture, by proclaiming in 'I With Legs Crossed Along the Daylight Watch':

> And my life, too early of course for the profound cigarette,
> The turned doorhandle, the knife turning
> In the bowels of the hours, must not be made public
> Until I have learnt to suffer
> In accurate iambics.[2]

This would later be revised as 'Prelude', a poetic preface to *In a Green Night*, and still later to his *Collected Poems*.

Another context of Walcott's work was the movement towards decoloniza-tion and independence and the discussion concerning the form they should take.[3] Each part of the West Indies had a different mixture of ethnicities, reli-gions, national origins, colours, and social classes. The small islands feared domin-ance by the large islands, the Catholic islands by the Protestants, the labour movement by the middle classes. There were even a few islands populated only by whites. There were two newspapers in St Lucia at the time. The *Voice of St Lucia*, modelled on British newspapers, was started and owned by the Gordons and continues to publish. The *West Indian Crusader*, considered black and milit-ant, has a sporadic history. The *West Indian Crusader* was concerned with the 'Negro' world. From his childhood Walcott was aware of older 'Negroes' who were Garveyites and talked of returning to Africa, a theme of his poems and plays. In contrast to the mythological past there was the present and future. The appointment of the St Lucian William Arthur Lewis as Professor of Economics at the University of Manchester was headlined as 'Britain's First Negro Professor'. Others had political ideas and thought in terms of racial communities. Walcott could not avoid such topics, they were part of his world and come into his poetry, but his subject-matter would be himself, his situation, the landscape, language, poetry, his relationship to the world, especially St Lucia, and the indi-viduals he observed, such as the local drunks, the peasant, the landowner, the foreigner.

Walcott would often recall his awareness when 18 years old that he would be the first to write about local places, people, scenes. Until then West Indian poetry could have been taken from postcards in its descriptions; it was literary, not based on actual observation and experience. It did not name. It was easy and lacked difficulty. Classical and English literature did not, however, seem out of place to Walcott. The villas on the hillsides were the terraces of the Roman pastoral poets, local boats with sails could be Greeks sailing with Odysseus through the islands of the Aegean archipelago, French Creole could be the demotic in the ballads of Villon. Much later, in *Omeros*, Walcott would claim he was wrong, but only in the sense that the world of the classics was like St Lucia rather than St Lucia like the classics. He was becoming aware that poetry is not solely a craft; words and phrases must feel as if they were written for the first time, and their meaning discovered. Later Walcott would speak of the New World poet as a kind of Adam naming the creatures.

There was then no usable literary language for St Lucia and its people, so how could he write about it? He read literature for references to black people. He could not at first use local names and the names of villages; they seemed too raw, lacking stature. There was no literature then about guava, breadfruit, cassava. He would take a bus, and as he looked out the window he fantasized about the countryside, the fishing villages, and the hills. He populated them with drama, African scenes, metaphysical questions. He and Roddy often travelled on the *Jewel II*, a boat which three times a week took mail, priests, pigs, lumber, and charcoal around the island. Early characteristics of a national, ethnic, or regional literature are claims of equality, of a history, of a religion and mythology. Walcott was learning and creating his own nationalist folk tradition which soon would be the subject of some of his plays.

He was also a rebel. A well-read Modernist rebel. Several of the great Modernist rebels also had unusual relationships to nationalist movements, opposing backward-looking and separatist traditionalism. Indeed the learning of a Modernist vocabulary and manner, the joining of the contemporary world, was often a necessary step from colonial provincialism to creating a national culture; the model was Ireland earlier in the century. During 1948 Walcott read James Joyce's *Portrait of the Artist* and *Ulysses*. He wanted to be Stephen Dedalus, intelligent, wounded. In *Ulysses* he liked the humour, the fresh detailed treatment of the ordinary, and the theme of the wandering Jew. Walcott had read an article in the special issue on Jamaica of the English *Life and Letters* (November 1948) predicting a new Ulysses emerging from the Caribbean and, in another of his imaginings of fame and destiny, he was certain it meant him. The epic analogies in his poetry over the decades were not solely the result of reading James Joyce. As of 1946 there were new Irish priests, from the Christian Brotherhood, the same brotherhood who had taught and against whom James Joyce had rebelled, thus providing Walcott with a surprising insight into, and link with, Joyce and the Irish Renaissance.

He never liked the French priests, but he liked the Irish Brotherhood of Presentation from Cork who replaced them. He liked the way they spoke, shared their contempt of the British, liked their bawdy humour. At College Walcott now heard Irish accents, heard about Synge, Yeats, the Abbey Theatre, Ireland, and the Irish Renaissance. Brother Liam was a poet who taught maths and who would recite Clarence Mangan's 'My Dark Rosaleen'.

When Walcott was painting with Dunstan the latter would cross himself and so at times would Walcott when going to swim. Living and educated with Roman Catholics, Walcott was influenced by their ways. He picked up the vocabulary, the assumptions, attitudes, and gestures. He felt Irish, like the new brothers, because of Joyce, because he liked drink. He felt like Joyce, a proud rebel opposing the Church. Walcott's pride then, and even now, is not to be underestimated. It could be strong, contemptuous, but it kept him going in the face of continual opposition to being his kind of poet and dramatist. The 14 year old who survived the ironies of Father Jesse would be strengthened by being condemned by the Archbishop; university professors, corrupt politicians, racial critics, the weight of marriages, and continual travel as part of an international career, would not break that sense of the self as right, someone with a destiny in spite of a hostile society. He was Stephen Dedalus.[4]

On 19–20 June 1948, a disastrous fire ravaged two-thirds of Castries, which until then was architecturally a colonial small French town of tallish, two-storeyed wooden houses, 'pillared balconies with fretwork eaves', and 'curled bonnets of mansard roofs'. The fire is believed to have been caused by a tailor who left a coal pot (used for ironing) smouldering when he closed for the night. The Walcott house was on the edge of town and not touched, but Alix woke her children, told them to dress, while she packed. The fire, devastation, and rebuilding of Castries became a symbol to Walcott of a lost childhood, the loss of the world he knew, including many mementos of his father which were lost that night.[5]

Poems about the Castries fire almost immediately became a new literary sub-genre. The *West Indian Crusader* of Saturday, 10 July, carried poems from Barbados, St Vincent, and Tobago, but no poem from St Lucia. 'Is the Muse of Hewanorra asleep? Or is our Muse still weeping over dear little Castries which is no more. Let the Muse of Hewanorra Arise!' A year later the *Voice of St Lucia* was still publishing such poems as 'Castries Fire 1948' by P.J.M.S. (probably Philip Sherlock):

> 'Twas Saturday the nineteenth day of June
> The year of grace nineteen Forty-eight
> Aurora dawned with its beaming light
> Giving signs of a pleasant day . . .[6]

Walcott waited to publish his *25 Poems* before revealing his Modernist sonnet 'A City's Death By Fire':

> After that hot gospeller had levelled all but the churched sky,
> I wrote the tale by tallow of a city's death by fire;
> Under a candle's eye, that smoked in tears, I
> Wanted to tell, in more than wax, of faiths that were snapped
>   like wire.[7]

The poem attracted comment due to its manner, line lengths, striking imagery, clearly articulated structure, complex sound patterns, unusual near rhymes, and compound meanings which, as the poem develops, contrast the failed 'wooden world' of Castries with the renewal of faith offered by the green nature of its hills, thus, while celebrating the city Walcott loved, finding hope once more in nature rather than human institutions including religion. St Lucia had its first 'classic', a literary work now taught in its schools, which defines an important moment in national history, symbolizing the end of an era.

After the fire, a new Castries was built with a boulevard and main streets which to Walcott seemed too large and impersonal, too steel and concrete modern, in contrast to the surviving parts of the old town with their embellished wooden buildings. The late colonial world of his childhood was coming to an end. The rebuilding of Castries seemed to be the start of Americanization, a new imperialism of music by Nat King Cole and Doris Day, of American drinks and night clubs. Walcott became restless, discontented, more self-conscious about his life.

In Trinidad there was a competition each year for four scholarships to study at a university, which meant going abroad. St Lucia was a smaller, less wealthy island and one scholarship was given every other year. It was necessary to apply before September of the previous year for the January London Matriculation examination. To qualify for the scholarship it was necessary to pass in the first division and to produce a certificate of moral character and general conduct from teachers. The scholarship was tenable for three to six years at any university in the British Empire or the United States. Derek did poorly in Mathematics and the scholarship went to Derek King who wanted to study dentistry. Michael Beaubrun, Kenneth Monplaisir, and Derek Walcott were in the second division. Roderick passed the Cambridge School Certificate in December 1948, with credits in Geography, Latin, and French. Derek Walcott was not going to London or, as Alix wished, to Oxford.

After graduating, starting in October, he was a junior master for two years at St Mary's College. During part of that time Simmons was in England, Dunstan was in Curaçao, but the promising young writer, Dunstan's relative, Garth St Omer was a student in the sixth form. Derek taught Latin and Art and is remembered as a serious teacher, dignified, never frivolous, but also modest, who expected and received the respect of his students. That he was already known as a published poet and a practising painter helped. He also fell in love.

> 'I failed Matriculation
> in Maths; passed it; after that,
> I taught Love's basic Latin:
> *Amo, amas, amat.*
>
> In tweed jacket and tie
> a master at my college
> I watched the old words dry
> like seaweed on the page.
>
> I'd muse from the roofed harbour
> back to my desk, the boys'
> heads plunged in paper
> softly as porpoises.
>
> The discipline I preached
> made me a hypocrite;
> their lithe black bodies, bleached,
> would die in dialect;'[8]

Andreuille Alcée was a blonde, very light-skinned St Lucian whose father had a bar near the waterfront which attracted sailors. After the fire they had moved to a converted warehouse at Lunar Park on Vigie peninsula, where the father had a restaurant. The father liked Walcott and allowed his children to make a fuss over the young poet, but thought him an unlikely son-in-law. Girls of Andreuille's complexion expected to marry white and go to England: Andreuille herself would eventually become a nurse, marry an Englishman, and live in England. Walcott paid an oarsman, who was black, a shilling to be rowed across the harbour to where Andreuille lived. He was welcome, liked; he and Andreuille would be allowed by the others to withdraw into their own emotional circle. Walcott mentions in 'Brise Marine' 'Andreuille all gold' and the Sundays on the small inlet where everyone would gather to picnic and play games.[9]

His love of Andreuille, which he treats in his poetry as his first great love, was to become a central theme of *Another Life*, where, following his theory of imitation, she is not only the model of every later love, but he even sees her as an imitation from a Renoir painting or Bergman film. She is a model for his tortured relationship to whiteness, the white muse which he passionately desires and which in his early poems reciprocates his feelings, but which he feels rejects him because he is not-white. Andreuille is an innocent young girl, the women he reads about in literature, the Muse, the White Goddess in her many incarnations, a symbol of the desired. Everything is an imitation, substitute.

Such puppy love would not be Walcott's only knowledge of women during his late teens; others were easily available, and he felt conflicted between his various emotions.

Like other writers Walcott has presented himself in as positive a light as possible, leaving out digressive or complicating details. If some of his poems appear to contradict the general ideas Walcott offers the reader, there is often some fact in those poems. Besides prostitutes there were other women in his youth including, it is said, a white Trinidadian, who was part of a drama group around 1946 when they were working on *Another World for the Lost*, a play he wrote when he was 16. Her father made certain they were not alone together. Derek's early poems will often refer to the attraction between those of different colours and how they are separated by society. Some poems allude to a local blonde daughter from a wealthy family who acted superior. Later, in 1949, there was Margaret whom he met while taking his St Mary's students to Grenada, and to whom he wrote at least one poem.

Two of Walcott's early poems, 'A Letter to a Sailor' and 'The New Jerusalem', are dedicated to Alan Landsman, a New Yorker with literary interests with whom he became friends. Landsman was the first Jew Walcott met and interested him because of the history of Jews as outsiders, victims, and because the Jews as well as New World blacks were a diaspora. The Jews, however, were fighting for their state, Israel, against the British as well as the Arabs. Landsman could choose between two 'homes', but was a wanderer. There were further complications. Although the horror of the extermination of the Jews in Europe was still fresh, there were rich Jews soaking up the sun and service alongside the rich blondes that Walcott desired. One of the continuing themes of Walcott's first three books of poetry is the colour ladder in which shade was part of class and upward mobility from black to white. Despite his talent, the women he wanted seemed beyond his reach, at least for marriage.

During 1948 Walcott decided that he had enough poems for a volume of his own work. He had over a hundred and selected twenty-five. Those he chose were often modernistic, influenced by his reading of Eliot, Pound, Thomas, and especially Auden. Earlier ones not included were more Miltonic, more Jacobean. As there was not a local printer used to producing works of literature, the volume would need to be printed in Port of Spain, where the *Trinidad Guardian* printery took outside jobs. Walcott's mother gave him the $200; Walcott in 1991 estimated that it was about $8,000 at current rates.

Such small, private, limited editions were common in the West Indies until the 1960s. V. S. Naipaul's father had similarly self-published a small book of his stories in Trinidad during the 1940s. There were no commercial publishing houses for local writing, few readers interested in such writing, and none of the support, patronage, and promotion the arts have in metropolitan centres. To be a

West Indian writer could be thought a humiliation; if you were good you moved to London or New York and were published by real publishers. Mittelholzer, C. L. R. James, Roger Mais, and John Hearne had already gone to London; Sam Selvon, George Lamming, and V. S. Naipaul soon followed.

25 Poems is dedicated to Alix and the memory of Warwick. While the first edition is dated 1948, the second printing corrects this to January 1949. It begins with 'Inspire Modesty By Means of Nightly Verses', which, while referring directly to Walcott's own exercises, is an Audenesque sonnet moving between various kinds of significance, in which some clear statements unexpectedly leap forward:

> Our ultimate disaster make circumspect,
> Strengthen the fraud that white and black are brothers,
> Give us the wisdom that does not expect
> More from ourselves than we expect of others.[10]

The second poem, 'The Gay Plague', is an oblique, highly compressed allegorical journey through life, but with autobiographical allusions to Walcott's ambition, writing, sexual experience, white–black relations, and the role of art in preserving 'wisdom's rare disease'. 'Words we correct all the night . . . White pairs and black are holding hands | In prologues that sex understands.' Experience leads to 'nervous souls' and 'neurotic dance'.

'As John to Patmos' concludes with Walcott promising to devote himself 'To praise lovelong the living and the brown dead', which is followed by the Audenesque 'Letter to a Painter in England' (Harold Simmons):

> Where you rot under the strict grey industry
> Of cities of fog and winter fevers, I
> Send this to remind you of personal islands
> For which Gauguins sicken, and to explain
> How I have grown to know your passionate
> Talent and this wild love of landscape.[11]

Many of the characteristics of Walcott's later poetry are already present—the mastery of the pentameter line, the use of, and experimentation with, traditional forms, the loose connecting of poems throughout a volume by recurring words, phrases, and motifs, the building of poems from the phrases of other poets, the obscurity which is often the result of extreme compression and unusual grammar, the leaps between levels of significance, the making of sequences of poems, the revealing yet puzzling autobiographical allusions.

'A Letter to a Sailor' (dedicated to Alan Landsman) is concerned with the complexities of black–Jewish relations when a New York Jew is both part of a class of victims, exiled from a homeland, and part of white American privilege:

Here as in Brooklyn, the mixed living mingle

Whose only truth is the belief in terror,
Whose single faith is the rule by complexion.
Here the pink are most secure and pattern
The exile-by-race or-faith their thoughtless living.
The fabled rich retire to holiday islands,
Continuing the culture of the exclusive club;
On Sundays you can see them, supine on beaches,
The couples in gold, the brown hair in the aristocracy of seas,
There the wave kowtows, one may not pass
Through the suave snarl of accents without thinking

That they are doing us away from what is ours.

In 'The New Jerusalem' (also addressed to Alan Landsman) Walcott contrasts the Israel that the Jews have fought to retain as a home with the conditions of blacks; 'never shall | my people, being black and natural slave gather | Under the violent flag in a skeptic world . . . Where one is born is not always home'.

The thirty-five pages of 25 Poems were an anthology of influences applied to local subject-matter, but where as others only saw hunger and deprivation in the West Indies he, like Stephen Dedalus, saw a whole race to write about. He saw the making of a book, which he was pioneering locally, as opening new paths. (Two others, Hunter Francois and Howick Elcock, would soon follow his example.) It was exhilarating. To have a book in print, no matter how, was a joy; he expected everyone to be astonished. And they were.[12]

Over forty years later, when Walcott had been awarded the Nobel Prize, the Trinidadian poet Wayne Brown would explicate some of the word play in 'Private Journal' to explain why 25 Poems was recognized as a totally new voice in the region of someone with an extraordinary gift and determination, perhaps genius. Brown quoted a few lines from 'Private Journal':

We started from places that saw no gay carracks wrecked,
And where our green solitude did not look deciduous,
And afternoons after school, well our aunt Sorrow came,
Disciplined, erect,

To teach us writing.

Brown asks the reader to note 'the precocious recognition of sorrow as Muse, the pun on "started" (began, startled), the multiplying meanings of "green", (bushbound, immature, fecund), the serpent's hiss in "deciduous", the aural interplay and darkening vowels between "green soli" (tude) and "aunt Sorrow", which is an interplay of sense and meaning as well; and above all, perhaps, at the tone of high seriousness (despite that mock-blasé "well")—so startling in a kid of seventeen!'[13]

A painter, Walcott was concerned about the physical appearance of books. Books for him are treasured objects, part of the arts, of value beyond their words. When he first began to see novels by West Indian writers, he would regard them with awe; abroad it was possible to be published in good bindings, with carefully chosen type, on good paper, and with cover designs. Naipaul, however, would often satirize the difficulties of publishing a book in the West Indies, and how shoddy they appeared due to lack of such essentials as a wide range of types and good paper. Over the years, Walcott's publications would use some of his own drawing or paintings. Pat Strachan, who was for many years Walcott's editor, remembers his continuing interest in the production of his books. The manuscripts would arrive prefaced with drawings, Walcott would be concerned with the type, the cover, suggesting which photographs of himself he wanted used, offering his own paintings as possible covers; he would heavily revise his manuscripts at all stages, paying for going over the limits allowed by publishers for revisions in proof. When in New York he would take the production staff to a meal or for a drink. The physical production of a book was part of the arts, something which took effort, care, and should be celebrated; it required artisans as well as writers. The production of a book was similar to the production of a play; the script only came to full potential through the aid of others that made the production possible. The full realization of a book depended on everyone from the editors, designers, and typesetters to the publicity.[14] Walcott used a Faber volume of Auden as the typographical model of *25 Poems*. He wanted a typeface that looked like one of the Faber volumes. He would be D. A. Walcott, like T. S. Eliot and W. H. Auden.

25 Poems arrived from Trinidad early in 1949 and copies were sold by Walcott and his friends for a dollar. Walcott had not shown Simmons the proofs, and Simmons was disappointed by what the *Guardian* printers had done; he felt that the format of the book, the paper cover, and the binding should have been better.

During the 1940s the West Indies saw the founding of several journals that had a significant role in bringing local writers to attention. Before then there was no regional literary community, no way that a reader in Antigua would know of a writer in St Vincent, and little chance that writers would know of each other. The few anthologies were limited to a specific colony, Jamaica, or British Guyana. *Bim*, the major literary magazine in the region, was started in Barbados in 1941, *Kyk-over-al* in Guyana in 1945. Between these journals and the new BBC *Caribbean Voices*, a literary community and local publishing network was being formed. On 17 January, Simmons sent his friend Frank Collymore, editor of *Bim*, twenty-four copies of *25 Poems* to sell in Barbados. Collymore had already heard of Walcott. While Walcott was still a schoolboy some of his poems were shown to Collymore by James Rodway. Simmons said he was impressed by Walcott's work, especially the maturity of the contents for someone not yet 19 (he would be in a week), and hoped that Collymore could review the book in a newspaper.

Collymore did more than that. He read his 'An Introduction to the Poetry of Derek Walcott' to the Literary Society, Barbados; Alan Steward of the British Council read the passages from the poems themselves. Collymore's talk was then printed in the Barbados *Advocate* and republished in *Bim* in June along with the reproduction of a charcoal sketch of Walcott by Harold Simmons. The talk remains a good introduction to Walcott's work, perceptive of its characteristics and the personality behind it. Collymore praised in 'A City's Death by Fire' the 'swarming imagery, the deft turn of phrase, the religious motif—above all, the high poetic fervour'. In 'Elegies' he mentions 'the unusual flood of imagery', the echo of Keats in the last couplet. This led Collymore to mention the various influences on Walcott, including Auden's use of generalizations, half-rhyme, and assonance. Besides echoes of G. M. Hopkins and Dylan Thomas, he noticed much religious imagery and use of Christian myths along with the geography and sociology of the region. The poems were different from each other, the manner astringent, harsh, and disillusioned, as in 'Travelogue'. There was a strong religious strain in the poems which created a tension between the conflicts of life, the indifferent harshness of nature, and the spiritual. Human efforts were felt to be futile. The strange 'St Judas' attempted to reconcile such opposites; its five linked sonnets concerned the events that led to the Crucifixion of Christ as felt in the conflicted mind of Judas Iscariot. It was difficult to understand; it was modern in that images were used instead of statements of themes. 'Derek Walcott is a poet of whom any community might well be proud. Let us hope then that this significant voice in West Indian literature may continue to be heard often in the many years to come.'[15]

Simmons was himself writing to introduce Walcott to the West Indies. Between late January and late February, versions of his '25 Poems by Derek Walcott . . . An Appreciation' were published in both St Lucian newspapers, in Trinidad, and twice in Jamaican publications. Simmons's comments are interesting because of his closeness to Walcott, who had selected the poems in the volume without his assistance. Simmons said that while Walcott's poetry can be difficult because of elusiveness, obscurity, or profundity, there was nothing superfluous. Walcott was a poet of images, words, ideas, which dance in the mind, jostling, coming and going, flickering on the fringe of understanding. Simmons argued that a poet must symbolize the disorder of the day. There was a fatalism showing the influence of Rilke through Sidney Keyes and Dylan Thomas. 'Both Sides of the Question' is Sidney Keyes revised topically as Walcott writes elegies for Hugh Etienne and Desmond Du Boulay, two St Lucians killed in their bombers over Germany. 'Saint Judas' is profound and obscure.

Among the reviewers, Revd E. C. Maclaren Mural, MB, PI, in the *Voice of St Lucia*, was both shocked and lifted by the poems. There were such contradictions as 'The logic of genitals is the rule by reason' in the same poem as 'man is light and lovely as a star'. He felt Walcott's previous poems 'fatalistic' and hoped that Derek may learn to 'discern the things that are not seen in the things that are seen'.[16]

25 Poems was rapidly being brought to the attention of those with an interest in West Indian culture and, at the urging of Frank Collymore, Walcott published a second edition, about 250 copies, in Bridgetown, Barbados. Collymore got the second edition ready for the printers. Walcott (3 March) was now hoping to make a small profit as many people wanted copies, including Alan Steward of the British Council, James Rodway, and A. J. Seymour in British Guyana. Steward wanted one hundred. Walcott had 'by' on the cover of the first printing, but, copying Faber, 'by' was omitted in the second edition. The Barbados edition of *25 Poems*, now thirty-nine rather than thirty-five pages, appeared in April. 'Of Time and the River' and 'Travelogue' had been revised since the first printing.

Walcott (12 May 1949) informed Collymore that he would come to Barbados in August. He was working on a second book, *Epitaph for the Young*, which he wanted to publish as soon as he could pay off the second printing of *25 Poems*. Harrison of the British Council said he would contact Selden Rodman, whose anthologies of poetry were among Walcott's early influences, and who became one of his friends and a constant reviewer. Harrison also sent a copy of *25 Poems* to John Lehmann of *Penguin New Writing*. Alan Steward was British Council Representative for Barbados and Windward Islands; John Harrison was Art Officer of the British Council. Walcott often came into contact with them through the extra-mural department and mutual friends. They both took a strong interest in Walcott's poetry, an interest he treated with some suspicion as he suspected he was being patronized because of his colour.

I have not located the savage review of *25 Poems* in the Port of Spain *Gazette* by the Catholic Archbishop, but Albert Gomes, the writer and politician, devoted his 'Behind the Curtain' column in the *Trinidad Guardian* to the second printing of *25 Poems*. The article titled 'All West Indians Should Read Book of Poems by St Lucian' said Walcott is the most talented West Indian poet, but Gomes was annoyed by the dense thicket of imagery and imitations of Auden and Rilke, Spender, Dylan Thomas, Eliot, and Whitman. Gomes did not like Eliot's poetry and thought him and Modernism a bad model for the young. He noticed that, despite the Modernist form, Walcott's content was often romantic, more the sick heart of Keats than the thick hide of Auden. Gomes foresaw that Walcott might 'give to the West Indies its greatest treasures of poetry', and concluded 'These poems should be read by every West Indian'. Wayne Baxter in the Trinidad

Evening News also claimed that *25 Poems* should be sold abroad to show others what West Indians are capable of.[17] Walcott was becoming a young star within the West Indies, famous within the small but active literary circles, often criticized for the same complexity of language and thought that was part of his unique attraction.

After the war some local radio stations occasionally broadcast readings by West Indian writers, but the major attraction was the BBC programme *Caribbean Voices*, which lasted 1945–58, a one-hour weekly radio literary magazine. Originally the idea of the Jamaican writer Una Marson, who worked for the BBC in London, the material was usually first assembled in Jamaica by Mr and Mrs Cedric Lindo, who sent it on to England. The BBC was receptive to employing West Indians on its staff and many writers worked for them on a regular or freelance basis, including V. S. Naipaul, and helped with the *Caribbean Voices* programme, as did many of the London literary establishment. Broadcasts of Walcott's poems not only increased his fame within the West Indies, but brought him to the attention of the London literary scene. The BBC *Caribbean Voices* programme was the first paying market for West Indian creative writing and Naipaul has suggested that *25 Poems* helped make the idea of a West Indian writer respectable.[18]

After receiving *25 Poems* from Simmons, Collymore (22 January 1949) forwarded some poems to Henry Swanzy in London along with a letter saying that here is a great poet who just turned 19. It is of interest that Collymore and some others instantly felt Walcott to be a great poet; throughout his career that would be the response of many writers. Swanzy immediately used the poems on the BBC *Caribbean Voices* and wrote to Walcott for a copy of the book. This is part of a sequence of those passing on Walcott's poetry with high praise, which runs from Simmons to Collymore to Swanzy to Roy Fuller to Alan Ross and William Plomer to Robert Giroux and Robert Lowell. Because of the interest by Swanzy and Fuller, some major British writers of the period, Stephen Spender and Christopher Fry, came to hear of Walcott.[19]

Simmons (8 March) wrote to the *West Indian Crusader* quoting a BBC *Caribbean Voices* announcement that on the 20 March programme it would broadcast a review of Walcott's *25 Poems* which it described as 'an important collection . . . strongly influenced by Dylan Thomas and the new schools of writing in English [*sic*] and America, but with an individual voice of remarkable poetic richness and density of image'. Simmons suggested readers should tune into the broadcast on Sunday, 20 March at 7.15 p.m.[20] Those who did heard nine Walcott poems or parts of poems read on *Caribbean Voices* by George Lamming, and introduced by Henry Swanzy. Walcott listened to the broadcast at home in a darkened drawing-room with his back turned towards surrounding friends and family, pretending to be nonchalant, yet lapping it up. Walcott's poems would continue to be broadcast on *Caribbean Voices* for almost a decade, until July 1958. At first the poems were taken from his publications; he submitted poems directly to London from 1951 to 1954 when he was studying in Jamaica. *Caribbean Voices* was the first paying market for his poetry.

Henry Swanzy (30 March 1949) wrote to the poet Roy Fuller saying that he had mentioned Walcott to Julian Symonds. Walcott was the most interesting poet so far from the Caribbean. The BBC had already broadcast a selection, but would Fuller care to discuss them with attention to details? Swanzy (8 April) wrote again, in reply to Fuller, that he knew little about Walcott except that he was 19 or 20 and a schoolmaster. Swanzy suggested a talk of fourteen minutes on 22 May. Noticeable in the letters of Swanzy and others within England is a touch of amusement about things colonial. Coming from those who were actively helpful to Walcott this may seem odd, and it seems to have led to, or touched on, some resentments on Walcott's part. As I follow the various letters between those outside the West Indies and Walcott, I am reminded of Montaigne's observation that it was uncertain whether he played with his cat or the cat played with him.

Fuller's talk (22 May) spoke of *25 Poems* as the most promising first book of poems he had seen for some time. He noted that the main influence was the early Auden of *Look, Stranger*, the early Auden of dry, terse, knotted, understated, epigrammatic verse in which there is ambiguity of level or subject. He described Walcott as using natural contemporary speech, drawing his images from contemporary situations, and easy, flippant, and satiric as well as serious and difficult. Auden's sonnet beginning 'Sir, no man's enemy, forgiving all' was the direct model of Walcott's first poem 'Inspire modesty means of nightly verses', which could refer to prayer or poetry. Walcott had learned from Auden significant ambiguity, fresh imagery and intelligence, and the omission of the definite and indefinite article to make his work very dense and stark. Walcott's 'Call for Breakers and Builders' had Spender's 'Oh young man, oh young comrades' in mind, but Auden was more significant to Walcott when he was referring to St Lucia as 'bright as advertisements'. Walcott's 'Carnival for Two Voices' called to mind MacNeice's use of the eclogue with two contrasting punning speakers in a colloquial voice. Fuller rather wrongly assumed that Dylan Thomas was a passing influence on Walcott who would stick to precision, wit, common sense, and universality—Fuller's own version of Auden.

Fuller said that the influences made possible the high level of *25 Poems* as Walcott, unlike other West Indian poets, knew he needed a tradition on which to build. Walcott's talent was the invention of impressive compressed phrases, images, and lines which appeared fresh, imaginative, and stayed in the memory. He made use of his island, he translated topography into poetry, he used and combined periphrasis. He thought in compressed, concrete vivid images as did the great poets of the past. Fuller correctly urged listeners to buy 25 *Poems* as it might become a collector's item.[21]

The quality of 25 *Poems* still seems exceptional for such a young poet. Six of the poems, including 'To a Painter in England' and 'Elegy' (the 1948 'In my Eighteenth Year') would be republished in *In a Green Night: Poems 1948–1960*. The highly selective *Collected Poems 1948–1984* would include 'Prelude', 'As John to Patmos', 'A City's Death by Fire', and 'The Harbour' (titled in 1948 'The Fisherman Rowing Homeward').

St Lucia previously had no published creative writing beyond the occasional poem in school magazines or the local press, but beginning in 1949 there were self-published volumes by Walcott, Hunter Francois, and Howick Elcock, followed by little else for some years beyond Walcott's publications and a volume of Father Jesse's verse. Francois, a few years older than Walcott, enjoyed reading, music, and the arts. When Walcott heard that Hunter Francois wrote poetry, he visited him, discovered shared interests—both admired the black pearl poem in Steinbeck's *Cannery Row*—and encouraged Francois to self-publish a volume. The *West Indian Crusader*, on Saturday, 8 October 1949, acknowledged receiving a copy of Francois's *First and Last Poems*, said that he was a barrister-at-law, and noted that the first poem was a Kiplingesque parody on unrequited love.

Walcott wrote a short introduction to the volume:

The work in this volume has a despairing Dowson-like note. The author almost buried them when I offered to put his poems out. I am glad to offer them here.

This is an important phase for the islands. When you speak of independence people think of public buildings and paved streets. I mean it is time to hear the voice of the West Indies. H. J. Francois does not use the public address system, he is not even modern, but a voice turned down to a compelling whisper.

I hope that he is heard. The despair, the mask of jocularity, the Cynara posturing are all part of us.

D.A.W. Castries April '49[22]

The cover (reproduced here in black and white) is in an interesting light blue-grey on which has been printed a blue Walcott drawing which combines the motif of a classical bust with a reduced Cubist version of it. The actual printing of the design appears to have been done by a heavy industrial press. Francois's 'Foreword' thanked H. D. Boxill for encouragement and said 'Without you, Derek, I should never have troubled to publish.'

Over the years Walcott and Francois would remain friends. Francois symbolized to Walcott part of the world in which he was raised and which gave birth to his poetry and St Omer's painting. Francois, a Methodist, had a love of Western classical music which he played on the phonograph. He played and still plays jazz piano. He was for years a drinking buddy of Dunstan St Omer. Luther

Francois remembers as a child often being awakened late at night when Hunter and Dunstan would return from night clubs and insist that Luther join them as a trio. Luther Francois, a jazz saxophonist, was first trained on violin and says that his father's main concern was his musical education.

Hunter would later become Minister of Education and argue that four years of Latin should be compulsory in the secondary schools of St Lucia. Seemingly quiet, shy, but with a twinkle in his eye, Hunter Francois was always doing the unexpected and being in the midst of controversy. His claims for the relevance of Latin to St Lucia were backed by long quotations from L. S. Senghor concerning how those who created Negritude had learned from studying Greek and Latin. His insistence that the various Church schools follow the same syllabus as the state schools led to a noisy controversy. Hunter would see that Dunstan St Omer was appointed to the Ministry of Culture, a position which gave him a secure income and allowed a creative approach to the arts, and he and St Omer were behind the appointment of Roderick Walcott as Director of Culture, which for a time brought him back from Canada. Hunter Francois eventually withdrew from politics, turned environmentalist, purchased a bay which he wanted to keep from being developed, and where he lived while raising cows which he milked. To interview him I had to learn his milk route and where he was likely to stop to play the piano. Walcott has mentioned Hunter Francois as a poet who was a government minister as an example of his St Lucian context, and indeed Hunter Francois is very much St Lucia, especially the St Lucian élite. Hunter Francois is said to have puzzled the Haitian military by lecturing them about the importance of poetry and Shakespeare.[23]

While Walcott would have been exceptional any place there was a welcoming context for him. A community of West Indian poets and critics had developed with a strong relationship to a regional nationalism, but they had no poet at home in the modern movement, no poet with the kind of complexity found in the work of Auden, Thomas, and Hopkins. Walcott had this, a sense of vocation, and a sensitivity towards social and racial conditions, while avoiding the limitations of protest verse. Concerned with his poetry, with his mulattoness, with St Lucia, he was part of the regional awakening and cultural decolonization without becoming lost in abstractions, glibness, one-theme politics, or incoherent rage. He was an intelligent artist first, a speaking subject with his own life and feelings, not a discourse, yet part of his time and place.

The *Caribbean Quarterly* began in 1949. It was at first only forty-eight pages an issue, published by the Extra-Mural Department, and edited by Philip Sherlock, Vice-Principal, and Andrew C. Pearse (ACP), the literary editor, who since late 1948 was Resident Extra-Mural Tutor in Trinidad. The *Caribbean Quarterly* was meant to create a bond between peoples of the region by enabling them to learn about and discuss their lands, history, and the world around them. The first issue became available in St Lucia during August and was on sale at the Resident Tutor's Office. The Saturday, 6 August *West Indian Crusader* carried an article saying one hundred copies were sent to St Lucia and readers were advised to subscribe in future.

The *Caribbean Quarterly* reflected what was thought culturally significant at the time. The first issue had reviews of Beryl McBurnie's Little Carib Dance Company, V. S. Reid's novel *New Day*, *Focus 1948* edited by Edna Manley, and *Kyk-Over-Al*, volume 2, no. 7. The Little Carib had been formally opened on November 1948 by Paul Robeson who was then in Trinidad. Reviewing *New Day*, Sherlock's attention was, on its politics, how, for example, Reid represents the folk, the past, and the historical parallels to the present. *Focus*, reviewed by A. J. Seymour, included writing by George Campbell—'one of the most important poets in the Caribbean' who had moved to New York—and Philip Sherlock. Pride of place in the issue was the republication of D. A. Walcott's 'The Yellow Cemetery', from *25 Poems*, with a short explication by A. C. Pearse.

The explication shows how some of Walcott's poetic characteristics and themes were already seen as offering an alternative to the political and racial affirmations of the period. The comments are still useful for understanding the methods of Walcott's poems and plays. Pearse mentions that for those unfamiliar with modern verse the poem may be difficult. The cemetery near a beach in St Lucia is the starting-point for reflections about life and death, which are conveyed by the reader's response to colours, suggestions, and associations, and not solely to the sense of the words. The images are used to carry meaning and there are symbols in the background; the image of the cock crowing at sunrise recurs three times, images of lighted candles recur throughout the poem. Other images suggest life being reborn from death; cradle and grave are linked as the bushes and candle images to the Crucifixion and Resurrection, associations strengthened by 'stone' and 'sea'. Walcott uses deliberate ambiguities, distorts grammar, and at times may be unintentionally obscure. The rhythm keeps changing according to mood, topic, and thought, with much use of internal rhymes, half-rhymes, assonance, and alliteration. Noting that there is a suggestion of a political solution to racial antagonism, Pearse asks why a young schoolmaster should be so in love with death and have such a sense of the futility of human struggle? Why this gospel of love when the approach to faith appears mournful? Is it a universal view of man or 'knowledge of his island-society's present condition and past history'? Although the 'message may be different from the patriotic affirmation of the Jamaican Vic Reid's *New Day*' the poem enriches the literature of the West Indies.

Having sold over 500 copies of *25 Poems*, which was reviewed in St Lucia, Trinidad, Barbados, Jamaica, and London, and already at the age of 19 having been described as the best of West Indian poets, with articles and talks devoted to his work, Walcott had achieved more international notice than he might have expected if he were a young American or British poet. He was, without knowing it, part of a larger movement, a change in the sensibility of our age in which those on the margins of the cultural establishment were to become a new establishment, a counter-tradition, part of, while challenging and outside of, the tradition.

During 1949 Walcott began publishing poems in *Bim*. Some of the poems express an anger at racial and social injustice. 'Letter to Margaret' speaks of 'Black laughter from those who cannot understand | The wrongs of the social ladder.' In August he visited Collymore in Barbados. One result was the uncollected 'Letter for Broodhagen', of interest because of Broodhagen, a now forgotten Caribbean artist, and its context:

> How I met him, his splayed hands talking,
> His squat energy carrying in a finger's luggage,
> Eyes, birds, lightning-striped tiger, or dove-stone girl walking,
> Sewing the sinews, knotting and threading their eyes
> In his tailor shop, stripping the quick, draping the dead,
>   mocking our age
> Of eaten linen.[24]

Karl Broodhagen was born (July 1909) in British Guyana of African, Dutch, French, and Portuguese ancestry. Around 1924 he moved to Barbados where, until about 1945, he primarily worked as a tailor, which he continued to do for years after. Although he claimed that his tailor's eye led him towards becoming a sculptor and painter, his family in British Guyana included a sculptor, a watercolourist, and a cousin who was well known for her ceramics and murals. His father was an amateur painter who dabbled in various arts and crafts including woodwork and weaving. During the 1940s Broodhagen began to gain attention as a painter and sculptor of heads which he did rapidly. Among his friends and early models were George Lamming, Grantley Adams, and Major Noot. The latter was an Englishman who, becoming headmaster of Combermere, asked Broodhagen to start an art department, the first in any Bajan secondary school.

Frank Collymore (1893–1980) also taught at Combermere School where among his pupils was George Lamming, whom he encouraged to write. By the time Walcott met him, Collymore was 56, a published poet, the author of short stories, a painter, thought of as a good actor, part of the local Green Room, and through *Bim* a leader in the emergence of West Indian literature. He was soon to be author of the still standard *Notes for a Glossary of Words and Phrases of Barbadian Dialect* (1955). Barbados and Collymore represented to Walcott everything desirable about England and Englishness: civilization in contrast to barbarian St Lucia. Barbados was Derek's 'fatherland', land of his white grandfather, a little England.

After returning home Walcott sent Collymore a playful thank you note filled with literary business (26 September), in which he moved quickly through a range of tones and manners from public schoolboy playfulness to what he described as his usual telegraphese in which he appeared to be bossing around his former sponsors who already seemed like sluggish elders. Within nine months of being introduced to Collymore by Simmons, Walcott was fully in the inner circles of the West Indian literary scene, had another book in print, was lining up a printing of his first long play, and was shepherding articles and reviews for Collymore and *Bim*.

Epitaph for the Young: XII Cantos, Walcott's second self-published volume of poems in 1949, was printed by the *Barbados Advocate*. It did not sell well, received less attention than *25 Poems*, and its thirty-eight pages have dropped from sight except for a few dedicated Walcott scholars interested in how it anticipates some of his later writings. Modelled on *Portrait of an Artist* and Pound's *Cantos*, the twelve cantos are a journey of experience from birth to manhood with each canto focusing on a theme. It is filled with autobiographical allusions and parodies:

> Alas poor Warwick,
> He was a gentleman, no doubt impressed
> By the attentive courtesy of worms.
> I hold his tenantless sockets to my skull,
> I am thy father's spirit, doomed to G Forms.

The structure, by canto, is (1) Birth, (2) Solitude, (3) Awakening and disillusion of love, (4) Ambition, (5) Wreck of Faith, (6) Drought and sterility, (7) Escape to sordid reality, (8) Contemplativeness of life and death, (9) Lust and sensuality, (10) Thirst for knowledge, (11) Love, cleansing, and purifying, (12) Assertion of faith. The resolution is love of Mary! Walcott was to use a similar method in *Omeros* where each book has its general theme.

The poems are autobiographical, yet satirical of the West Indies, filled with literary echoes and imitations of Dante, Joachim du Bellay, Anatole France, Baudelaire, Eliot, MacNeice, and Auden among others. Walcott soon felt that such poetry was too distant from his society, but that he had to get it out of him. One line was to be remembered and used as the title of George Lamming's classic coming of age novel,

> In the room the clock thunders on the mantel
> The brittle china shepherdess holds
> Her crook like a question sign, asks
> Why your complexion should have held you from me.
> You in the castle of your skin, I the swineherd.

Walcott was attracted towards white women who were unlikely to be his because marriage to a brown man was socially a step down. In a way he was in a similar position as a poet; what was he doing in black St Lucia? The nationalist, racially conscious, and Modernist were in productive conflict.

Keith Alleyne's review in *Bim* offered a useful analysis of the structure and of Walcott as a rebel who refused to write as a Negro poet:

> A classical Alas,
> For naked pickanninies, pygmies, pigs, and poverty,
> Veiling your inheritance, you kneel before
> The sessile invocation of the thrush, the sibilant yew-trees.

Many of Walcott's basic themes are in the poem. There is the Walcott embarrassed with borrowed poetic clothing, and already questioning definitions of culture as tradition in contrast to creativity:

> Ten zebra-clothed niggers in a palm cafe
> Beat on happy drums, their basic savagery.
> Black reckless waist of a dishwashing princess.
> 'Where is your culture?' Prejudice is white
> As the spittle from an estaminet.
> A tradition is not made, it evolves
> Through those who are not concerned with history.

Swanzy wrote to Walcott about *Epitaph*, suggesting it should have ended after the eighth part. It does become rather obvious:

> They fawned over the fact my mind was maimed,
> Dissected at each tea-party the surprising abortion
> Of my contradicting colour . . .
>
> I teach the word, to a class of several colours,
> That shall grow up to wear their father's flesh.
> Mixture of faces.

Walcott answered three years later; he remembered reading the letter at the cinema and wondering what he was doing in such a savage place among the natives. More Montaigne's cat?[25]

In *Public Opinion* A. L. Hendriks, a West Indian, reviewed *Epitaph for the Young*. While conceding that Walcott might make a 'permanent contribution to English Literature' and that his poetry may 'rank him high in the world of literature', Hendriks clearly disliked the volume for its 'obscurity', 'intellectual exercises', starkness, classical references, bits of foreign languages, and unusual grammatical constructions. Hendriks, a West Indian poet of an older aestheticism, saw the poem as bleakly Modernist and perhaps predictably praised the line 'Cry, O colour of perpetual dolour', but otherwise found the volume too clever and lacking merit. Hendriks did see the book as a youthful personal Odyssey of disillusionment, revolt, and despondency concerning religion, love, carnality, social class, colonialism, literature, and colour.[26] As the reviews show, by 1949 Walcott already had many of his themes. Besides writing of art, nature, race, culture, and religion, he felt alienated, superior, and had a sense both of being betrayed and likely to betray.

St Mary's at the time had a 'wall magazine' on which weekly writings were displayed from which a selection was published in the Annual. In his senior year Walcott was editor, but because of the fire there was no 1948 Annual. The combined *St Mary's College, St Lucia Annual Magazine 1948–1949*, consisting of seventy-three pages plus another twenty-two of advertisements and oddments, was one of a small number of regional secondary school publications including *The Harrisonian* and *The Collegian* from Barbados. It included a photograph of the college staff, apparently four foreign white priests and four secular local brown or black men including 'Mr. D. Walcott'. Another photograph showed Revd Brother Lawrence, Walcott, and the Macbeth Group—who performed scenes from *Macbeth*, one of three dramatic presentations at the College that year. Besides reminiscences and poems about the Castries fire, articles on the Trinidad Carnival, and 'The Wall Magazine', there was an article on 'Derek A. Walcott — Poet' by L. M. D. [Revd Brother Liam Dromey], followed by extracts from published reviews of Walcott by Fuller, Gomes, Collymore, Swanzy, and ACP, and an otherwise unpublished Walcott poem, 'By the Dying Water'. Walcott 'known to you for his recent publication of *25 Poems* which aroused such widespread and provocative interest' taught art.

The article noted that Walcott had become much discussed beyond the West Indies, mentioned his wide range of serious reading at an early age, his paintings, sketches, and the production of his play *Henri Christophe*. The writer spoke of his perplexed admiration for the poetry and mentioned that others had disapproved of what Walcott had written because of his obsession with failure, violence, death, and embittered memories. The critic claimed that Walcott lacked Christian Faith and Hope and that he used Christianity without conviction and reverence—objections which would still be made about Walcott in some St Lucian Catholic circles even after the Nobel Prize. The critic felt that while such turbulence is not unusual in a young artist and part of the transition from adolescence to maturity, it was expressed with unusual starkness in *Epitaph for the Young*. It was hoped that he would be a great poet and find himself in harmony with the Christian tradition.[27]

'By the Dying Water' seems purposefully obscure more in its subject and argument than the local details which aim at ingenuity. The title and first stanza imply an analogy between the end of spring and the speaker's own loss of faith:

> By the dying water, in the sun
> By the slim branches, and the spacious
> Grief of the whole season's end
> I stand remembering that one
> Who was my comfort before my griefs were gracious.

The subject could be loss of any object of love including Christ. The next three stanzas, rhymed and of various lengths, move back and forth between suggestions of the poet as a Hamlet who has destroyed his love, retains its relics, and makes poetry by twisting reality. 'Now my abortions must create the style, | I must chip honesty to bits, and groan by guile.' The diction of the poem hovers between the religious and secular—'Grief', 'Griefs', 'comfort', 'remembering', 'Gracious'—and in places could satisfy any follower of William Empson seeking ambiguities. There are echoes of George Herbert's 'Sacrifice', some 1920ish contrasts, 'static waltzes under stone', and the resistible 'quack of duck, and saxophone'.

The Convent of the Order of St Joseph of Cluny needed a large backdrop for its Christmas concert. It was 480 square feet in total, painted on both sides, and took all Walcott's spare time for six months to paint. Although he hated priests and the Church, he was physically attracted and felt love towards the nuns. In particular he attracted Sister Annunziata; he painted to impress her and refused to be paid. These years would be recalled in *Another Life* where Sister Annunziata 'sat by the white wall | of the convent balcony' listening to the piano 'as Anna played | in the rivering afternoon, | arpeggios of minnows | widening from her hand'. Walcott was attracted to the cloistered life as it would allow him peace to be a poet and control his lechery.[28]

5

$\sim\!\sim\!\sim\!\sim\!\sim\!\sim\!\sim\!\sim\!\sim\!\sim\!\sim\!\sim\!\sim\!\sim\!\sim\!\sim\!\sim\!\sim$

1950 The St Lucia Arts Guild and *Henri Christophe*

As a result of the 1948 fire, St Mary's College early in 1950 moved to its present site in Vigie. Garth St Omer, who sat his Higher School Certificate in December, joined Walcott as a junior master while Revd Brother Liam, who had told Walcott about the Irish literary renaissance, returned to Grenada. Walcott was teaching extra-mural courses as well as at St Mary's. His extra-mural art class in drawing and painting met on Tuesday each week at 5 p.m. at St Joseph's Convent. When the Resident Extra-Mural Tutor, B. Easter, left for Jamaica for a month in mid-February, his English classes were taken by Walcott, who taught poetry. In May the general course in English language and literature would be given by the Resident Tutor assisted by Walcott.

A major event of the year was the founding of the St Lucia Arts Guild by Derek Walcott and Maurice Mason. The Arts and Crafts Society, which Simmons had started, represented an older generation and was partly expatriate. It was in a British tradition of amateur handicrafts. The Arts Guild was younger, St Lucian, more creative, modern, and intellectual. It developed from the Junior Wesley Guild and those meetings and readings by Derek's friends on the Walcott veranda. It was backed by Simmons and other intellectual elders among the Protestants, lapsed Catholics, and those who returned from abroad. Alix Walcott became its 'mother'.

Seventeen young people met at St Mary's College on Thursday, 9 March 1950, to form the Arts Guild for encouraging the arts in St Lucia and the cultural uplift of the West Indies. Its officers were Derek Walcott (President), Naomi Theobalds (Vice-President), Leonard St Hill (Secretary-Treasurer), and Garth

St Omer (Assistant Secretary). Derek and Maurice Mason were elected leaders of the literary section, Dunstan St Omer was in charge of art, Leonard St Hill would lead drama, and Ruth Theobalds music. Also present were Pamela Walcott, Roderick Walcott, Kenneth Monplaisir, Primrose Bledman, and Howick Elcock. The official founding of the Guild was on the 23rd.

Although the Arts Guild still reunites for the performance of a play on a national occasion, its main period was 1950–68. Briefly under the leadership of Derek Walcott, and then of Roderick, it gave St Lucia a modern culture, promoted the work of Derek and Dunstan St Omer, then that of Roderick, tried to encourage other dramatists, produced plays, held national Arts Festivals, toured to other islands, and for two decades was the centre of the arts in St Lucia until Roderick moved to Canada after which it lost energy.[1]

Derek began writing plays when he was 16. Most are lost and only vaguely remembered by those involved. 'Flight and Sanctuary' is said to have involved an escape from and return to civilization. 'A Simple Cornada' was about revolutionaries. 'Another World for the Lost' concerned a bored young girl and suicide, and like others of his early plays (and some of the poems) was thought depressing. It was performed at Clarke's Theatre, a movie house where 'concerts' and other events were sometimes held. 'Cry for a Leader' appears to have been about nationalist politics.[2] As the boys and girls went to separate schools, Walcott's plays from the start were mostly written with male roles. By late 1949 he was already referring to a group of his friends who did readings of his plays as the Arts Guild or the Methodist Guild. He regarded the Arts Guild as evolving from earlier 'concerts', play readings, and other cultural events by the Methodists.

Perhaps more broadly it developed from the meeting between the St Lucian Methodist emphasis on the English language and its culture and a new regional nationalism and interest in folk culture. The modernizing tendencies of those who sought advancement and status as the clerks of the Empire combined with what was a global movement towards decolonization. The Arts Guild was the St Lucian equivalent of such movements elsewhere. It was a similar decolonizing élite, except that due to the island's smallness and its complex relationship to France and Catholicism their 'acts of resistance' and the creation of a new modern national culture were different from what they would be, say, in India or Africa. There was the upward progress of West Indians through the colonial administration, the challenge to the authority that the British had allowed to the Roman Catholic Church in educational and cultural matters, the rediscovery of the island's creole folk culture, the assertion of a modern European and St Lucian culture, and later the hopes offered by an independent West Indian Federation.

During these and the following years there was cultural nationalism in the air together with an awareness that the region was moving rapidly towards self-government and eventual independence. During the war St Lucia had been silently changing, with locals taking over positions of authority formerly reserved for the British. The Arts Guild was part of what has been termed a silent revolution during which the colonial order was replaced by a new generation with a different perspective. The Arts Guild did not reject European arts, it lectured about them and brought their performance to an island where this previously had been rare. Its radicalism was in being high brow, Modernist, and in recognizing local culture and encouraging creative artists. It received sympathy, even help, within the Catholic community from St Joseph's Convent, which took a more liberal attitude towards culture than the FMI Fathers led by Father Jesse. The Arts Guild held some of its first productions at Catholic venues with the notion of building bridges.

Primrose Bledman's 'Introducing Dunstan St Omer' in the *Voice of St Lucia* (10 May) was one of many articles the newspaper would carry by and about members of the Guild. Dunstan, who then worked at the La Clery Public Library, was painting murals, using local and classical subjects, at the Palm Beach Aquatic Club. He had returned to St Lucia from Curaçao in December 1949 and since then had painted a self-portrait and entered four paintings in the previous month's Industrial Exhibition in which he took three special first places. His *Rape of Castries* depicted the fire of Castries although he did not witness it. St Omer still speaks of this painting as his equivalent of Derek's 'A City's Death by Fire'.[3]

The next week the newspaper mentioned that there had been comment about the possible immorality of St Omer's themes. To dispel such ideas St Omer read a paper before the Arts Guild which the *Voice of St Lucia* was publishing. St Omer argued that it is difficult to find vulgarity in art as Art is broad and its boundaries uncertain. Art is a representation or product of the soul and as the soul is an image and likeness of God, who can set limits to God? The artist is the medium who captures nature and conveys it to others. Truth changes as do customs and opinions. Only the unmoved mover is unchangeable and can be trusted. The critic should look for virtues in art not for faults; reactions reflect the judge. Art is life, art is pure. People wrongly claimed that Renoir, Rodin, Cézanne, and Toulouse-Lautrec were vulgar, but the painters were concerned with suffering, beautiful forms, and patterns.[4]

Derek Walcott's 'Introduction to The Work of Dunstan St Omer' provided an analysis of his friend's paintings. The article mentioned that at the 25 July meeting of the Arts Guild there was an exhibition of four paintings by St Omer— *The Rape of Castries* showing in classical style the fire in Castries in June 1948, a seascape, a Cubist portrait of Walcott, and a Cubist landscape. Walcott claimed that St Omer was essentially pagan, naïve, and loved things for themselves. He was unacademic but prolific, powerful but not solid. St Omer's sense of line was personal. He learned to paint from comic books. He was volcanic, a disciple of Renoir, Delacroix, Rubens, Michelangelo. His seascape had little in the way of swaying palms, but had a lot of Harold Simmons in such colours as pure purple, green, yellows, and in the heavy technique, the use of the tree self-consciously to form a frame at the expense of the rest of the landscape. The use of bright colours tended to flatten the landscape, and was in keeping with claims that West Indian arts should be localized with lots of local atmosphere and colour. This could be a danger. 'We have been sickened to boredom with "Tropic" poetry that are little botanical litanies to the poinsettia and the poui.' This could turn St Omer into a bad landscape painter, a bad Van Gogh using lots of strong yellow. He was 'self-consciously modern but not modern'. The head of the poet was 'a marvel of rhythm', solid, yet split into angles. After describing what superficially sounds like a Cubist analyst of a face, Walcott says the experiments are in pure colour, a contrast of primary colour with no half-tones. 'One is tempted to nickname this prismism.' It appears a kind of primitivism laughing at Modernism, a volcano of colour, sometimes lacking dramatic harmony. But there are various cubes and other geometrical solids suggestive of Picasso and Cézanne. About the landscape, 'If Mr. Cézanne painted the first square apple, Mr. St Omer has painted the first square coco-nut tree.'[5]

While Walcott wanted to interest viewers in St Omer, he reveals what was to remain an essential difference between the poet and painter over the decades. Walcott is analytical, critical, concerned with detail, educated in art history and technique, while St Omer had a spontaneous natural talent with line and colour as a draughtsman and painter. St Omer's taste could be schoolboyish, an unsophisticated taking on or parodying of the characteristics of other artists, which resulted at times in an unsubtle vigour, even in maladroit portraiture, but he was unquestionably a painter and had rapidly arrived at his own style, a reductive, somewhat primitive, but often highly effective version of some aspects of Van Gogh, Cézanne, and Cubism.

From the time he was 16, Derek had been writing one-act plays; some were radio plays of which *Harry Dernier* was later published. Such plays were short, as most theatre in the West Indies then consisted of scenes from Shakespeare or one-act sketches performed at schools or as parts of 'concerts'. Walcott wrote a short play based on the Paolo and Francesca episode in Dante's *Inferno*, a natural theme for a young writer, especially one involved in relationships crossing religious and colour boundaries. Swanzy (19 May 1950) wrote to Fuller, sending him the script for 'Paolo and Francesca' and asking for an eight-minute talk. Nine days later *Caribbean Voices* broadcast 'Paolo and Francesca. Senza Alcun Sospetto' with Fuller's introductory talk. Fuller thought Walcott should have altered Dante's story more to make it more contemporary, rather than quaint. Walcott does make it more youthful and sensuous, he has shown the immaturity of the lovers without making them less tragic or lessening the physical attraction of the lovers for each other. Walcott is more interested in adolescent love than

Dante. Walcott as a young dramatist was exploring literary styles and here the model for the verse seems Jacobean, John Webster, or late Shakespeare. If the metaphysical manner remains modern, the use of 'thee' and 'thou' is archaic. Walcott is best when the poetry slows up and breathes. The play has some lovely passages, but the subject is not right for Walcott.[6]

Early in 1949 Roderick, who had been reading a book about the Haitian revolution, suggested to Derek that it might be the subject of a longer play in verse. The history of Haiti was in the air at the time. The second issue of *Caribbean Quarterly* included an article on Toussaint L'Ouverture by W. Adolphe Roberts. As Derek thought about the idea for *Henri Christophe*, he felt that there were parallels to St Lucia such as the poverty and the Church telling people to accept their life. In Haiti the tyranny of slavery was overthrown through revolution which brought about a new master, in St Lucia the new master was the Roman Catholic Church. Walcott worked on *Henri Christophe* for half a year and finished it during September 1949. His friends hoped to stage it, but as he could not duplicate it in St Lucia he asked Collymore for help. Two months later (11 November) he told Collymore that plans to stage the play at the Roman Catholic school had run into problems. The priest wanted to read the script to see whether the morals were Catholic. Did he want innocent tyrants, and virgin soldiers and whores? Walcott told Collymore that the play was more Napoleonic. The next month (7 December 1949) Walcott thanked Collymore for arranging for the printing of *Henri Christophe* in Barbados. The St Lucian production was put off as many in the cast left for Curaçao. Walcott had Leonard St Hill in mind for Christophe and suggested that Collymore also use him for a proposed production in Barbados. He had been making drawings for *Henri Christophe*. Marlowe was a model.

With models from Elizabethan and Jacobean drama, the result was very poetic language, a play and a main character drunk on words. Although the issues were to remain part of Walcott's vision, the high Elizabethan–Jacobean style is the romanticism of a young man discovering the riches of English verse drama at a time when the arts were becoming less rhetorical. *Henri Christophe*, like many of Walcott's early plays, offended the Church because its attitude towards God was angry and blasphemous. It spoke of a white God. The Roman Catholic Archbishop in Trinidad called Walcott a 'savage'.[7] Because of its subject-matter, the Haitian revolution and the establishment of the first independent black state in the Americas, *Henri Christophe* was relevant to the times and was soon being performed by the new West Indian drama groups in Jamaica, Trinidad, and London as well as in St Lucia. Its history epitomizes the story of the founding and creation of West Indian drama. Walcott paid for its first publication (in Barbados in 1950). It was not until mid-May 1950 that Walcott received advance copies. He asked (15 May) Collymore to send copies to

Mrs Cedric Lindo, Albert [Bertie] Gomes, Errol Hill, Noel Vaz, and Gloria Escoffrey (for *Public Opinion*). It was first performed by the St Lucia Arts Guild (1950), broadcast on *Calling the West Indies* (BBC, 1951), performed by West Indian students at the West Indian Student Centre, London (1952), then at University College of the West Indies, Jamaica (1954), and in Trinidad, (1954). Errol Hill, the older Trinidadian dramatist and director, was involved in many of these productions as he or his brother established groups to perform the new West Indian plays. *Henri Christophe* was the first play performed by Errol Hill's Federal Theatre in Jamaica; it was revived by Walcott's own Trinidad Theatre Workshop (1968).

During June Derek Walcott again contributed to the *Voice of St Lucia*, this time concerning 'The New Verse Drama'. His mind was obviously on his own plays. Modern drama had become realist, and people like to see themselves, but Walcott questioned the permanence of documentaries. It was more important to forge a new rhythm for modern metrics and speech. He claimed that we lack an Elizabethan sense of the heroic and dislike bombast and high rhetoric; our prose is not poetic. What can be done? We could revive Elizabethan ways by using history as Eliot and Christopher Fry had done, but Fry had gone further in brightening up the antique for 'our drab realistic stage'.[8]

Two weeks later (30 June) Walcott wrote to Collymore that he was disappointed with the lack of poetry in Eliot's *Cocktail Party*. He claimed that Mittelholzer's novel *A Morning at the Office* gives the best sound, taste, and feel of West Indian life, but the plot is too orderly, and objects are linked too programmatically to characters. There was a large stock of themes for young writers in the West Indies. He was now working on a two-act play, a comedy or a metaphysical tragi-comedy, concerning the devil, Carnival, and English dowagers. This was to become *The Charlatan*, a play he would work on for almost three decades without getting right.

Copies of *Henri Christophe* were becoming available and Maurice Mason (3 August) read a paper about the play to the Arts Guild. Mason said that *Henri Christophe* was the first book by Walcott he enjoyed from cover to cover, mainly because he was able to understand most of what the author was driving at. 'The language is fairly heavy but definitely not as soggy as in his *25 Poems* or his *Epitaph for the Young*.' He felt that *Henri Christophe* suffered from being too well written. The language was above such characters as Christophe who could not read or write. No illiterate would speak or think some of the lines attributed to him. While such loftiness was needed to bring out Christophe's ambition and force of personality, it was not needed for a messenger or professional murderer. The play was too wordy, and wordiness risks being boring on stage. The play could use some humour. There was too much of 'Walcott' in the play, too much of his likes and dislikes, his philosophy. It needed some domestic scenes, more scenes with women. There were many excellent similes, metaphors, and turns of phrase. It was good reading, but difficult to predict what it would be like on stage as it would be in early September.[9]

Before then, however, there was an exhibition at the temporary Education office of over thirty paintings by Dunstan St Omer and Derek Walcott, which was reviewed by Harold Simmons in the *Voice of St Lucia*. This was the first exhibition for both. St Omer dominated the show with two-thirds of the paintings, but many lacked finish and craft. He was, however, the artist, stimulating, earthy. Simmons thought Walcott sophisticated but not a painter. 'Words and imagery are Derek's forte, the brush with discipline will be Dunstan's citadel.' Both took an interest in each other's work, even painting from the same palette. Although Simmons says that a few works, such as *Rock of Ages* and *Ruin and Vision*, could have been painted by either, the title 'Rock of Ages' was part of St Omer's churchiness while 'Ruin and Vision' belonged to the spidery side of Walcott. St Omer's *Bread-fruit* was a stylized composition. His *The Rape of Castries* used a vulgar classicism for the fire when 'that hot gospeller had levelled all but the churched sky'. Walcott's *Tribute to Braque* created a sensation, a typical Braque still life embroidered with cobwebs.

The outstanding work at the show was No. 11, Abstract Portrait (*The Poet*). This is an abstract portrait of the outstanding poet in the British West Indies today, Derek Walcott, a clever and yet puzzling motif of juxtapositions of blues and reds, cubist in conception, yet without obvious cubist conventions . . . with squiggly lines relieving the bold angular parody of Walcott's Poetry.

The companion-piece to No. 11 was No. 3 'Prismatic Landscape' again by St Omer. 'Prismatic Landscape' was a synthesis of Cézanne but more economical in tone and form, and the colours pleasing in choice, laid flat.

The styles ranged from Surrealism to conventional portraiture, the latter being very poor. Neither was a good painter when imitating older styles, and it was suggested that they should concentrate on West Indian subjects and feelings.[10]

On Saturday, 2 September 1950, an advertisement appeared in the *West Indian Crusader* saying that the Arts Guild 'which has just sponsored an Art Exhibition of Dunstan St Omer's work, will present Derek Walcott's verse play *Henri Christophe* at St Joseph's Convent Saturday September 9 and Monday September 11 under the patronage of the Acting Administrator and Mrs Cools-Lartigue'. The notice was headed 'A Community is judged more by its cultural activities than by its social or political aspect'.

On Friday, 8 September, the *Voice of St Lucia* carried some puff concerning the next day's show. 'The story in verse of the events surrounding the rise and sudden fall of Haiti's Black Monarch Henri Christophe. . . . Bringing into play the intrigues of the all ambitious Blacks, Whites and Mulattos, the subtle racial dissension living at first side by side in quiet submission, but suddenly unleashed after the death of Toussaint L'Ouverture.'[11] This was the first production by the Arts Guild and, except for the plays of Errol Hill and Errol John staged by the Whitehall Players from 1948 onwards in Trinidad, might be thought of as the start of modern West Indian drama. In the same issue, same page, there is an article by Eric Williams about the significance of the eighteenth-century revolutions on the British West Indies.

The *West Indian Crusader*'s reviewer said that this was probably the first time the tragedy of King Christophe was dramatized in 'these parts'. 'There were times we could not agree with [Walcott's] interpretation. Christophe was not a master of intrigue; all he understood was war and work; all he wanted was a strong fortress and power for the good of his people.' The ending could have been improved by having the corpse borne way with others weeping for this 'great and good man who found so much to do in so short a time in an age of blood'. The play was poorly attended on Monday.[12] Walcott, however, had already started to master the promotion of his poems and plays.

Lucille Mair Mathurin in the *Voice of St Lucia* more correctly claimed that *Henri Christophe* was destined to be a landmark in West Indian drama. It was profound, mature, and had scenes of great subtlety; it made demands on the actors. Walcott called it a tragedy of a race and of personal bewilderment. The nuances of the verse and symbolism required thought. The Arts Guild was not yet up to such a challenge, they were too often amateurs awaiting cues, often unsure of their lines or delivered lines upstage where their faces could not be seen. The prompter was audible. There was too much senseless movement and pacing up and down the stage. The make-up was poor and incongruous. She thought Leonard St Hill had an impressive stage presence and a fine voice with a good range, but he failed to develop Christophe in the final acts where the ex-slave degenerates into an insane despot; the corruption of Christophe was at the heart of the play.[13] Over the years as he himself learned from professionals, Walcott would try to move West Indian theatre beyond such amateurism as senseless movement and incongruous make-up, but for the region such a play as *Henri Christope* was a radical new start.

Whatever Walcott, or other West Indians at the time, published was noticed throughout the region. W. E. Gocking in the *Trinidad Guardian* praised the richness of poetry in *Henri Christophe* and the tragic if fumbling grandeur of the main character. Gocking noted Walcott's taking liberties with history, mentioned a couple of minor errors (Christophe was born in St Christopher not Grenada and preferred to be called Henry, as in English, rather than the French Henri), and that the verse of the characters was insufficiently differentiated. He felt that Walcott apparently was more concerned with the quality of the poetry than with setting the characters in relief from each other.[14]

A review in *Kyk-Over-Al*, from British Guyana, praised the power of the poetry which reminded the critic of Cyril Tourneur. Writing in English about kings is bound to be filled with echoes; here they included Marlowe's Tamburlaine, Eliot's Beckett, Shakespeare's Caesar on the Lupercal, and the death of O'Neill's Emperor Jones.[15]

Henri Christophe gave the Caribbean a history comparable to European or North American history; such a usable past is part of any nationalist movement. It gave a complex, serious insight into West Indian history in which black racial pride and the desire for racial revenge was seen as dangerous and self-defeating. The message was universal; blacks can become tyrants and act as badly as whites, while some whites will work on the side of blacks. It also looked with sympathy on the mulatto, who, having mastered the ways of the French, was mistreated by the blacks.

The usual significance of the Haitian revolution for the West Indian colonies and the uniqueness of Walcott's approach can be seen from Eric Williams's 1951 article. According to Williams, the Haitian revolution and the Haitian Declaration of Independence made the slave trade politically untenable. Slavery was abolished in the British West Indies in 1833, in the Danish and French islands in 1848, in the United States and Dutch islands in 1863, and in Cuba and Brazil in 1880s, because after 1804 every slave holder had to fear the rise of a local Toussaint L'Ouverture and a second Haiti. A moral argument for slavery had been that it brought slaves into contact with a higher civilization and that life in the New World was an improvement over Africa. But the Haitian soldiers proved that Africans were brave and that character is independent of species. The Haitian revolution destroyed the plantation system as the workers seized the land, whereas where the slaves were emancipated by decree the plantation system survived with the slaves becoming share croppers or paid labourers.[16]

After meeting in November 1950, the Arts Guild went into recess until the following February when, Leonard St Hill said, they planned to open in April with two short plays by Derek Walcott—'Three Assassins' and 'Paolo and Francesca' —which would be performed with six speeches from Shakespeare. Marlowe's *Doctor Faustus* was scheduled for May.

Walcott had failed to gain the island scholarship to England in 1948 because of low marks in Mathematics. It was not offered in 1949, but after the fire aid was given to Castries including some possible scholarships to the new University College of the West Indies in Jamaica. In mid-May Walcott and L. G. Campbell were awarded scholarships under the Colonial Development and Welfare Scholarship Scheme. Campbell was to study for a diploma at the College of Tropical Agriculture in Trinidad. Derek Walcott was offered three years to study English, followed by a year for a Diploma in Education. Walcott hoped that the Diploma year would be in England, at Oxford. This was the first intake of Art students at UCWI and entrance required outstanding potential beyond high academic achievement. Years later Barbara Gloudon described her envy of those who were accepted: 'Back then, you had to do better than best. The University brought together the cream of the crop, the elite of Caribbean students. How I envied them.'[17]

Each likely student was interviewed by Philip Sherlock, who, looking beyond academic ability and other talents, was concerned with maturity and likely contribution to the university and, in future, to the regional community. Sherlock told me that he was impressed by having a poet and someone aware of French culture. At the time Walcott told Sherlock about *Henri Christophe*. Philip Sherlock, himself a poet, knew Simmons and Collymore and had already come across Walcott's poetry in *Bim*. He was interested that Walcott came from a French-speaking culture and that he was a painter as well as a poet. Walcott appeared outstanding. Sherlock arranged for him to have a scholarship and intended to remain in contact after he came to Mona. Although religion would not come into it, and he was thought to be agnostic, Sherlock came from a Methodist preaching family. Garnet Gordon, of St Lucia, was also one of the ten members on the provisional council of UCWI. If this were the 1990s it would have been argued that the Methodists were overrepresented.[18]

Walcott was of two minds about leaving. He loved St Lucia and had already decided that he was to be its artist, but as a Methodist there was little chance of advancement at St Mary's, which remained the only secondary school; and the truth was he was becoming bored and anxious to move on. He had been a junior master at St Mary's for two years. Walcott left on Monday, 25 September, for Barbados, where he would visit the Collymores, and then proceed to Jamaica where his classes at University College would start in November. Although he would always be nostalgic for the world of his childhood, St Lucia before the 1948 fire, his friendship with Dunstan and Simmons, most of his life from now on would be as an exile. He became the Odysseus of his imagination, his life a journey. His poetry and plays became the home he lost, and exile was to become one of his themes.[19]

Part II

Jamaica, Grenada, Greenwich Village First Exile

6

1950–1954 University College of the West Indies, *Poems, The Sea at Dauphin*

THE University College of the West Indies was started in 1948 because England could no longer produce enough doctors and teachers for its colonies as they moved towards self-government. To ensure standards, the degrees and syllabus were until 1962 those of the University of London and most staff had British university experience. The first faculty was Medicine, followed by Extra-Mural Studies which Philip Sherlock, who helped create University College, saw as providing some cultural glue, in the form of the performing arts, for the proposed Federation. First there were science students, meant to become medical doctors; as of 1950, a BA in the Liberal Arts was offered to about twenty students a year as preparation for a B.Ed., as a way of producing more teachers who until now could only study in the region for a teacher's diploma. Walcott was in this first intake.

During 1950–3 he was enrolled for a BA in English Literature, French, and Latin. He would have liked to study Spanish, but decided to stick to what for him would be easy subjects so he could concentrate on his writing. English and his other courses were no challenge, but he surprisingly enjoyed studying linguistics. Detailed analysis of the organization and sound of language contributed to his awareness of how poetry is put together and how its art might be discussed. Decades later he would show his poetry classes the many structures of grammar, syntax, and sound, as well as variations of rhythm, pitch, and register, within a few lines of a poem. His understanding of contrasts between kinds of English, of subtle half-rhymes, and of the movement of the voice in poetry or on the stage, were sharpened by the formal study of language.

Otherwise the university for him was a way to get away from St Lucia, and meet people from other islands. His hall of residence was initially the army barracks of Gibraltar Camp, then Taylor Hall when the 'new' halls were opened to students. Small, select, composed of the élite from the schools of the region, the class produced many of the leading actors, stage directors, and writers who would energize West Indian culture for decades. Walcott was somewhat more than a leader. There was no other student who had published several volumes of poems and plays and whose work was broadcast on the BBC. Philip Sherlock was an admirer; Walcott was even given a special room for himself in which to paint.

Soon after coming to Mona, Walcott founded a student paper, the *Barb*, and was its editor, columnist, and main artist. It was rapidly replaced by the less angry sounding *Pelican*, also his baby. He was a member of the Literary Society, the Scribblers' Group of creative writers, and the Arts Society.

The *Barb* lasted two issues, 26 November and 8 December 1950. The first issue is described on its cover as 'The Campus Fortnightly'. The magazine was typed and cyclostyled. Each issue had a drawing by Walcott as a cover. According to the first *Barb*, the University Players, of which Walcott was also President, was looking for one-act plays to perform, and had done a reading (for several years their usual form of performance) of Shaw's *St Joan*, which was attended by Noel Vaz, who was part of the Extra-Mural Department and who had studied drama at the Old Vic in England and been an assistant to Tyrone Guthrie. The December *Barb* has a humorous 'Sant-Ad Claus' on the cover, a Santa who distributes advertising for various local products, a self-mocking way of mentioning the inclusion of ads in the issue. There is also a remarkable page signed by 'The Editors' quoting in full the sonnet 'The Eternal Event' by the Catholic martyr Robert Southwell (1561–95). The Christmas editorial also mentioned St Jerome and quoted the passage by St Augustine that had been cited by T. S. Eliot in *The Waste Land*. The page has many small drawings by Walcott.

In December *Bim* published a scene from a play in progress; 'Robin and Andrea', a witty verse comedy about race, sex, lust, magic, and art, was to reappear over the years as *The Charlatan*, one of Walcott's often produced, revised, and unpublished plays.

Reports of the period mention Walcott's habitual blue jeans, his wit and repartee, his haughtiness. He was more likely to be found reading art books or painting than in his classes. He had an especially sharp and intimidating tongue where women were concerned, drank too much, was often depressed, and was thought a genius. Such depressions and a grim view of life lasted until about 1958 when he was commissioned to write a pageant for the West Indian Federation and discovered Trinidad, his second home.

Jamaica was a foreign country. The eastern or southern Caribbean colonies had been linked by their closeness to each other and in many cases by a shared history of an underlying non-English-speaking culture. They were mostly small, and life took place in the open or at beaches. Jamaica was long settled by the English, physically distant from St Lucia and Trinidad, large enough for people to forget the sea. It did not have the 'bohemian' latin ways of the south with their Spanish- and French-tinged cultures. It was historically a slave and plantation island in ways that St Lucia was not; it was physically and psychologically closer to Haiti, Cuba, and the American South.

Even the linguistic situation was different. Because of the late importation of large numbers of slaves, Jamaica has a dialect, or 'nation language', in which English is strongly influenced by African languages. The islands to the south were part of a French and Spanish linguistic belt, in which those languages had early incorporated African survivals to produce local French or Spanish patois which existed along with the recently imposed use of English. Walcott's pronunciation as a St Lucian is different from Standard British English, but St Lucia does not, like Jamaica, have a strong dialectical form of English.

University College was filled with West Indian intellectuals who wrote poetry, filling the anthologies of the period with political sentiments and coconut-tree verse. It supported the arts through the Extra-Mural Department, which published *Caribbean Quarterly*, promoted theatre workshops, and eventually published plays. It is difficult to imagine anyone more supportive than Philip Sherlock (director of the Extra-Mural Department and himself a poet), but Jamaica and University College offered Walcott little that he did not already have. He had excellent teaching at St Mary's College, where he had a general education that ranged from Latin poetry to learning about Joyce, Yeats, and the Abbey Theatre. On his own and with friends he had read modern poetry and studied modern art. He had taught at St Mary's College and given university extra-mural courses. Walcott's mind was made up about what to do with his life and about his interests before he came to UCWI.

Walcott was offended by the Britishness of UCWI and the attitudes of the British staff. The students had to attend lectures in red gowns, unsuitable for the heat, and were expected to attend a college table with the same rules as at Oxford or Cambridge. Walcott distrusted whites. Decades later he would recall an Englishman, Professor Croston, the head of the English Department, implying the scenery of Jamaica was inferior to that of England:

Walcott told the story of how, when he was a student at Mona, he was travelling through Bog Walk, scenic valley in Jamaica, along with Professor Sherlock, a Jamaican, and an English Professor [*sic*], when Sherlock commented; 'Beautiful, isn't it.'

To this the Englishman replied 'It is like a meaner sort of Wye Valley.'

'Which means' Walcott interpreted for his audience 'that the Jamaican landscape can break its ass trying, but it would never quite achieve the effort required.'

'This typifies the kind of experience we have been subjected to in every single nerve-end and aspect of our lives as colonials—a life of humiliation even in a remark like that.'[1]

The British built their new universities outside the cities to provide a place of retreat from urban hustle, bustle, and fashion. Compared to such older redbrick universities as Leeds, the new universities appeared bright new Edens. The UCWI was one of the first and was thought one of the most beautiful universities in the world; the location with its view of the mountains remains impressive. If for the Jamaicans the mountains were symbols of liberty and associated with the Maroons, escaped slaves, Rastafarians, and other forms of resistance to British colonialism and white rule, to Walcott the mountains were solemn, enclosing him in his loneliness far from the sea, beach, and coastal life with which he was familiar and which was the subject of much of his writing.

In St Lucia travel was difficult, but the roads mostly followed the coast and there were buses and small boats for transportation. Simmons and other friends had automobiles. Castries was a small but active world in which Walcott was at the centre socially and culturally. Castries was compact, the houses small, everything was within walking distance to the harbour. When St Mary's College moved from central Castries to Vigie, it was a bicycle ride. Jamaica is much larger, the roads go through villages between which the land often still appears uninhabited; in places there are uninhabitable cliffs and hills through which a path has been cut. Jamaica is as beautiful in its own way as St Lucia, but if you were a highly sensitive, lonely, heavy drinking, young West Indian writer and painter subject to depression and conscious of how the mountains blocked your perspective, cut off the sun's rays, and made the day seem shorter, you might well feel enclosed, caged, saddened, and want again the inclusive boundless freedom of the sea and the light associated with it. One of the Walcott paintings that have survived from this period is a landscape of Newcastle, Jamaica, in which swatches of colour flattened out towards abstractness.

Walcott despised UCWI, thought the curriculum predictable, and run by the English. He parodied 'Lycidas':

> 'The shaggy top of Mona high'
> To match the dry gullies and the shaggy hills
> That enclosed Mona High School[2]

Two decades later Walcott's 'Gib Hall Revisited' caught the mood of displacement, a displacement made worse by University College being so obviously British, so much, Walcott felt, an imitation of England, during a time when it was exciting to discover the Caribbean and its cultures, an excitement which in later years was tinged with a sense of loss:

> In those raft-planked bunkhouses christened Gibraltar
> by World War II D.P.s, as if they knew
> we'd drift like displaced persons too, but even further
> from Europe than the homesick, homeless Jew[3]

For many of the students an attraction of UCWI was that there were so few whites; here was a place where browns and blacks did not always have whites over them. Walcott, however, felt University College was a provincial perpetuation of a fading Empire that English ways still governed. The administration and staff seemed to him decent, dependable, second rate; they could have been doing the same jobs, teaching the same texts, in Singapore or Nigeria. The British were now part of an educational system being imitated in their provincial colonies, a system which would continue unchanged as local people replaced the British. There seemed no relationship between what they studied and life off campus. Walcott still feels guilty that he did not pursue Latin further. He should have studied more Virgil and Ovid. The problem was not discipline, but he felt disconnected from the system. His dissatisfactions as a student were far from unique, but for those who felt they belonged at Oxford, the new colonial university colleges seemed second rate. There was, however, a further alienation for many from the southern Caribbean. Jamaica appeared upper middle class, stuffy, snobbish, while the Jamaicans thought the southerners strange and bohemian. Few knew the Creole culture and language of Walcott's St Lucia. Friendships developed, but in general the Jamaicans and those from the southern Caribbean did not like each other.

Walcott, who remains conscious of death, thought of himself as a Chatterton, Keats, or Shelley who would die young and astonish the world by his talented youth and loss. His life became the Students' Union and the drinkers who hung around drinking beer—Danny Campbell, Allan Kirton, Val Rodgers, Don Bogle, Vernon Smith, Dunstan Champagnie, Bill Brooks, Ronnie Llanos, and Harry Major. Dunstan Champagnie was noted for his immaculate dress, unusual cocktails (which Walcott praised until he learned they included something 'unmentionable'), his broad taste in the arts, and his interest in Walcott's paintings of which he still has a few among a select but impressive collection of Caribbean art. Walcott worked on his poetry, painting, plays, and painted a mural with the help of 'Sleepy Smith', whom Walcott liked to hear recite Homer with a Bajan accent. Walcott only knew St Lucia although he had visited Grenada and Barbados a few times. The university brought various peoples together, their connection the future Federation. That was the excitement. Despite Walcott's reputation as aloof and sarcastic, he was, among his circle, thought fun-loving, a prankster, punning, but focused on what he was doing.

The leaders on campus were medical students and returning graduates, mostly Jamaican. They could go home, had local friends, and knew their way around the downtown nightclubs. The campus was a small enclosed world, the student body was smaller than many local schools. Eventually the Trinidadians began to set the tone on campus. They were a large group, had their own ways, their own version of English, participated in the arts, and had their own culture with the calypso and especially the steel band. The student union became their centre. Several of Walcott's close friends, Archie Hudson-Phillips and Ronnie Llanos, were Trinidadians.

Walcott's *Barb* died after its second issue and was resurrected on Sunday, 14 January 1951, as the *Pelican*, still 'The Campus Fortnightly' and still using a drawing by Walcott on the cover as well as having for its emblem a cartoonish head of a pelican with an arrow in its mouth (meant to represent the satiric *Barb*) and a mortarboard on its head. Amusing drawings of the pelican emblem appeared throughout the magazine. The editorial board listed Derek Walcott as Editor. The cover was by Walcott, cartoons by Bill Brooks. The idea originally behind the new journal was to have two journals, a Walcott satiric *Barb* and a larger, more general campus *Pelican*.

Walcott moved through various student clubs, occasionally showing up for a meeting without becoming involved. The Scribblers was for intending writers, Walcott was already a published writer. He was, however, interested in the Dramatic Society and its offshoot, the University Players. The campus was surprisingly alive with theatre. Most of the productions were readings, but some, especially a later *King Lear* with Slade Hopkinson, are still spoken of with awe. Hopkinson came to UCWI a year after Walcott, rapidly became one of his circle, a friend, even a rival. Hopkinson had won student drama prizes in Barbados, was bright, intellectual, a poet, director, and dramatist, and for decades one of the best actors in the West Indies. Walcott's involvement with the University Players during this period is a bit confusing as there were more announcements than productions. Volume 1, no. 4 of the *Pelican* announced in April that Walcott's production of *Richard II* had been cancelled and Walcott would instead direct *Oedipus Rex*. The play would not be actually produced until late 1954, directed by Slade Hopkinson.

An unusual letter to the editor appeared in the radical nationalist *Kyk-Over-Al* during 1951. 'Three Evenings with Six Poets' describes meetings with writers in Jamaica by a group of first-year students from British Guyana. The first night there were three Jamaicans, Una Marson, P. M. Sherlock, and W. A. Roberts, the latter of whom was thought to lack West Indian interests. The second meeting was with Walcott. The third evening consisted of Frank Collymore and H. A. Vaughan. The author of the letter claims that this was all new to them, having previously known nineteenth-century English poetry and a bit of T. S. Eliot.

The five older poets were treated with polite respect; it is obvious that Sherlock's 'Pocomania' was more to their taste than Roberts or the now old-fashioned protest poetry of Una Marson (better known in her youth as a poet of the new hedonism). Collymore was thought easy, likely to appeal to everyone, direct, and realistic. Vaughan was concerned with social issues and wrote better than most about race.

The hero was Walcott, 'the lone figure of a man standing on an intellectual promontory in the ocean of time. A solitary figure, gesticulating and expressing himself in a curiously fascinating manner which seemed foreign to most of us. And though he spoke English he made the language seem different and exciting and new to us . . . He may be the prophet . . . In fact, we feel it in our bones . . . 'Several lady members emphasized this conviction.' The Walcott the students met was angry about racial matters, unlike the Walcott who a few years later would proclaim his two heritages and see the British also as victims of foreign imperialism in the past. 'Derek Walcott does not conceal his feelings about the race problem in the West Indies . . . [he] knows nothing of poetic detachment from contemporary problems.' They admitted being so impressed by the poetry of *Henri Christophe* as to lose track of the story, but he met their desire for something different. 'His poetry is forever pregnant with delightfully original metaphors, dazzling similes, photographical phases that baffle with suggestion.' Besides Walcott's mixture of friendliness and distanced reserve, he fascinated the group with his 'manner of speech' which they did not understand but liked. He seemed too young to be so old, to carry such a weight, to be infected by European fatalism. Perhaps he is just going through a stage of Wastelandism which he will outgrow? But he is a genius.[4]

Walcott the genius attracted women despite, perhaps because of, his distance and caustic wit. Eros was often on his mind and the subject of his poetry. Many of the poems of the fifties remain unpublished and concern conflicts between love, lust, and the relationship of poetry to corruption. 'Sambo Agonistes', published in *Bim* during 1951, is a powerful, youthful, sardonic, Byronic poem in which life is a journey from innocence. There are such motifs as leaving mother, the confusion of love with sex, the relationship of lust to death. The language powerfully mixes puns, slang, a few West Indianisms, and learned literary allusion:

> I was lonely and young and on hills all the birds
> Did me a Danae with their showering turds,
> I was a sagaboy, augur with words.
> The stars were gold tacks that pinned the black drop
> Of the sky, I saw them as the humanist Wop.
> To whom Virgil was a kind purgatorial cop,
>   I jumped in the fire.

Following Nietzsche's death of God:

> I had gone through the towns with two jokes in my sockets,
> Carrying my heresy in empty pockets,
> And hysteria had showered me in its buckets,
> And as long as I lived I was soiled by the smoke
> Of my lust and my art when the inward tongue spoke,

> For a nigger poet is twice the world's joke,
> My soul had no buyer.

The thirteen seven-line stanzas, rhymed aaabbbc, are followed by a fifteen-line Envoy which reads like a seventeenth-century funeral epitaph addressed to the reader:

> I shone like you, my pride was star,
> But mark how myself in a dirty pan,
> Have often envisaged the Fall of Man,
> So Prince and Lady, and Kentucky Home
> And Dante and Virgil, and Wherever I Roam,
> This is my goodbye to my pain and art.
> I open my book and now you can
> Remove the withered rose of my heart.[5]

While Walcott was still an undergraduate, he was already beginning to have international recognition from those concerned with West Indian culture. *Henri Christophe*, produced by Errol Hill, was broadcast on the BBC *Caribbean Calling* in two instalments, on 4 and 11 February 1951. G. A. Holder in *Bim* thought the reading uneven and under-rehearsed. He mentioned the actors' seeming embarrassment during the first broadcast; they attempted to turn the verse into prose by clearing their throats and adding hesitations. The second broadcast was better with more decisive readings. Holder's review was itself dramatic. 'I was listening at a wayside loudspeaker when the rain began to drizzle and three or four people took shelter. Two men, barefooted, were talking when *Christophe* momentarily flared up; then his voice grew quieter,

> Anyway he died, broken, grey and quiet
> White-haired as the moon and stumbling just as lost
> Through peace-fleeced colonies of clouds, a foolish, mad old man.

The two men stopped talking and even when the rain had ceased, they remained listening to the end of the play. At that late stage they could not have followed the events; they were held by the poetry, striking in its vividness and beauty . . . I thought of the Elizabethans.'[6]

Swanzy interviewed Stephen Spender on *Caribbean Voices* in August 1951. Spender had recently heard George Lamming at the Institute of Contemporary Arts, and Lamming brought the work of other Caribbean writers to his attention. Spender spoke of an impression of a different world from his own. The interview is amusing as Spender was unprepared. He called the Bajan George Lamming a Jamaican and at one point discusses the influence of Valery on a poem by H. D. Carbery, which Swanzy then mentions was actually by John Figueroa. It is now easy to laugh at Spender's inability to get his colonies and colonial poets right, and to regard it as imperial condescension. Spender, however, was important and very busy then; for him to speak on *Caribbean Voices* was a triumph for Swanzy and the writers who were still mostly unknown. They might not have agreed with Spender's claim that there was a now international modern poetry to which each country contributed its own distinctive part, but Walcott, working during the summer for *Public Opinion* in Jamaica, was happy to know that Spender and Fuller would be reading his poems and showing them to W. H. Auden and T. S. Eliot. The second half of the broadcast consisted of R. B. Le Page reading and commenting upon Walcott's unpublished 'A Packet for Eros', a sequence of seven poems.[7] One of those discovering Walcott's poetry was V. S. Naipaul, who was an editor of *Caribbean Voices* and worked as a free-lancer at the BBC. In 1966 in Uganda he would introduce Paul Theroux to Walcott's poetry by quoting from 'As John to Patmos'. According to Theroux's *Sir Vidia's Shadow*, Walcott is one of the few living writers Naipaul respected, quoted, and treated as an equal.

In November 1951 Walcott's *Poems*, his third privately printed pamphlet of verse, was published in a volume of forty-six pages by the City Printery, Kingston. It consisted of thirty-two poems, three revised from *Bim* during 1949–51. 'Margaret Verlieu Dies' was later revised and published as 'A Country Club Romance'. These poems are not much known. They are mostly social satires with ethical concerns in the manner of Auden or visions of life as a process of dying in the manner of early Dylan Thomas. The volume begins with 'As for our tickling love' for Pamela Walcott, which says that we are our own hells, that pain is purgatorial, and leads the mind to seek something above itself. The concluding four poems are 'We Exiles' with its vision of birth and life as an exile from death, 'At the Break of Mist', in which a mother dies while giving birth to a child born dead ('A joy and a death'), 'The Sisters of Saint Joseph' (the convent near Castries), which questions the cost of faith,

> Behind the stained water of the lucent panes, they
> Bend their white monotony of prayers,
>
> Their lips turn pages of their mediation,
> Selling identity for coins of faith.

and 'The Eye is Never Broken', which concerns the universal desires of hope, love, and self-pity, the consequences of being born. Every heart

> . . . must exist alone,
> While under our venial wish
> It hears knock through the flesh
> The impatience of the bone.

Other *Poems* use Jamaica or the West Indies as a setting for a consideration of relationships between white and black and how to respond to a historical past of slavery. Two recurring symbols are a blonde tourist in sunglasses and a rich Jew in exile from Europe. In these poems Walcott explores some of the dominant themes of his later poems and essays, sometimes taking positions he would soon reject or which the concluding poems in the volume transcend. In 'The North Coast at Night':

> What History cannot instruct
> Is healing, and how not to hate
> The white hands' usufruct
> of slavery. 'To be great,'
> The gull screams, 'learn to absolve
> Us.' We must learn not to love
> Those whom an accident
> Of lust have bred in pink,
> The gull's impeccable tint

This is followed by 'The Sunny Caribbean', a poem of five stanzas each of which increases in length by one line from the original four lines to a concluding eight-line stanza. It argues that little can be done about the past, all is settled at death:

> And fate, spinning the roulette of islands, says,
> History can not pardon, they cannot feel.
> Who expect the dice to be always favourable, and praise
> Ubiquitous with niggers, nothing will teach
> The islands of flesh, the umbrella on the beach,
> But death, like a smiling croupier, fixing the wheel
> For the blonde in sunglasses and the expensive shoes
> And the fisherman crushing a season under his heel.

As a volume there is a rich deep poetic vision which marries social satire of types to reflections on history and a spiritual concern with the soul.

From these poems and such better-known lyrics as 'A Far Cry from Africa' and 'Ruins of a Great House', written a few years later, it appears that in his early Jamaican years Walcott's anger at racial discrimination, slavery, and imperialism was finding its place within a larger perspective of humanity fallen from birth, troubled by desire, and painfully prepared for an unknown future after death.

The *Public Opinion* reviewer mentioned that Walcott was earlier introduced to a meeting concerned with West Indian literature as 'a young man of startling talent, perhaps the most astonishing yet produced in these islands'. The reviewer found extraordinary that Walcott's influences were the modern poetry of W. H. Auden and Dylan Thomas, questioned how a young West Indian could allow himself to be identified with such nihilism and anarchy rather than have an optimistic approach towards life. As Walcott seemed likely to develop into a significant poet, local critics were going to have a rough time adjusting to such extravagance. Walcott's *Poems* showed someone learning his craft who took his talent for granted. They lacked aural interest and did not stick in the memory as they lacked concrete imagery although there was a wealth of metaphor. There was more thought than feeling.[8]

Walcott's writings were too extraordinary for some West Indians. In the *St Mary's College, Annual Magazine 1950–1951*, Barry Auguste also argued that while Walcott's poems were good they suffered from too much intellect and were devoid of music. He felt that as a preparation *Henri Christophe* demanded recognition for its expression, subtle feeling, honesty, wisdom, and West Indian symbolism. Walcott's earlier writing suffered from hypochondria. *Christophe* was 'devilish in the range of its language', Elizabethan, romantic, alive, vigorous, dramatic. In rather inflated language, Auguste claimed the play would live and not be outshone by later Walcott writings.[9]

The production of *Henri Christophe*, 25–7 January 1952, directed by Errol Hill, in the theatre of Hans Crescent House, Colonial Students Residence, London, was thought symbolic of the West Indies coming together politically and culturally, a foreshadowing of Federation. At 1 Hans Crescent, in the West End of London near Hyde Park, there was from 1950 a British Council residence for students from British Colonial territories. It accommodated 220 students and was used to introduce them to the English way of life. It was very British with High Table, a semi-formal first sitting during dinner, and no domestic duties beyond making one's own bed. Besides being a hostel it was used for lectures, exhibitions, concerts, and dances. It figures in many stories and novels about the period, especially by West Indians.

The production of *Henri Christophe* included many actors who would become leading West Indian writers, artists, teachers, and politicians. The production seemed an anticipation of cultural and political independence, a foretaste of the West Indian Federation. The cast included the novelist George Lamming (Barbados), the Trinidadian playwright and actor Errol John, the Trinidadian dramatist Frank Pilgrim, Maurice Mason, Roy Augier, and Kenneth Monplaisir (St Lucia). Ray Robinson, from Tobago, was to become one of the few Trinidadian politicians sympathetic to Walcott's Theatre Workshop. (Robinson's father was a Methodist minister, another Methodist!) The play was directed by Errol Hill (then studying at RADA), the stage-manager was Noel Vaz, and the assistant stage-manager was the Trinidad artist Carlisle Chang. Christophe was performed by Errol John, and Hill played Vasty the secretary to Christophe. The *Voice of St Lucia* claimed that Walcott was praised in the English press as having abilities above those of many dramatists in London's West End.[10]

Following the publication of *25 Poems* Christopher Fry brought Walcott to the attention of Longman, who invited him to submit a novel or some work in prose. There was a surprising lack of response by Walcott to all the attention he was getting from London. He did not reply to those who wrote to him. As usual he was conflicted, proud of being noticed by famous writers, angry at what he felt to be condescending attitudes towards him as a colonial and brown. Time was passing and Walcott hoped to move beyond self-publication. Earning a living as a writer meant living and publishing in London. Like other West Indian poets, he turned to writing a novel, which is what British publishers wanted; at UCWI he worked on a novel, one of several extended works in prose Walcott would write that failed to catch fire. After the London production of *Henri Christophe*, he unsuccessfuly tried to break into the British literary market.

Three years late he replied (12 February 1952) at length to Swanzy. After discussing the anti-white anger that was hidden in *25 Poems*, and how reading Auden helped him towards economy, he claimed to have changed from his earlier self: he now saw art as an enquiry, not the beating of drums. Walcott felt he was the romantic hero in *Epitaph*, striking non-tropical poses, although the experiences were real and he was sincere. It was a way of purging himself of Pound and Eliot and made him see even more clearly that he was not part of the world immediately around him. He had been writing a novel for the past three years to send to Longman. Walcott (6 July) sent Swanzy the novel. His letter speaks of a clerical or pedagogical career facing him unless he can publish.

Walcott also apologized to Roy Fuller (26 March) for not replying to a much earlier letter. Walcott ascribed his failure to either laziness or fear of having been overestimated. Then the letter suddenly takes life as he talks of what it is like to live in a small town on a small island and his ambitions of having readers abroad. Such ambitions could have only brought despair in St Lucia. Walcott's whole life was poetry, he had put aside everything else for it, but received little in return. He had submitted without acceptance to the *New Statesman*, the *Listener*, and the *Times Literary Supplement*. Walcott had little hopes of finding readers interested in the West Indies—even in the West Indies there were only a few. He had by now written so much that was unpublished he did not know what to do. He no longer felt that getting to England would help as British publishers would not be interested in a book of West Indian poetry. He was sending Swanzy a novel, three verse plays, and some poems, and some material to Fuller, who had offered to try to help him publish.

The novel, 'A Passage to Paradise', the title parodying *A Passage to India*, was rejected by Jonathan Cape as disgruntled, violent, adolescent, heavy handed, and offensive to everyone, especially the British administration. Swanzy read it and lost enthusiasm, but sent it to John Lehmann, who was in financial trouble and not interested, and to a West Indian writer whom Swanzy trusted and who thought there was insufficient action and, whether intended or not, the characters appeared to be voicing Walcott's opinions. The West Indian writer appears to have disliked Walcott's poetry as well. The novel viewed white colonials as degenerate, and treated an American Captain badly. The West Indian intelligentsia are seen as very anti-white. There was a foolish Carl Bemminger; Peter Cadmus, an over-sensitive young black who feels inferior around whites; Margaret Vertlieu, a semi-literate, married, needing men. Apparently the novel ended with the Castries fire, with Peter using the fire for observation. The Cape reader thought Walcott had a racial chip on his shoulder. In a letter to Swanzy (20 October 1952), Walcott said England had itself to blame if colonials felt that way, but he agreed that the novel was overwritten; it was in varied styles. Some of the characters and plot situations eventually found their way into *In a Fine Castle* and later *The Last Carnival.* It was a young man's novel about the end of the late colonial era with a decadent plantocracy, upper civil servants, a rogue preacher, adulteries, drunks, limited opportunities, colour awareness, and silent boundaries.

Walcott was in St Lucia from 11 July 1952 until he returned to Jamaica in October. The new Methodist school opened in April. Alix Walcott had been acting head of the primary school for the past five and a half years as no male headteacher could be found. This was in addition to being headteacher in the infant school, her thirty-fifth year at the school.[11] The Arts Guild Festival of the Arts started on Monday, 6 August, with an art exhibition at the new Methodist school. While most of the work was by Dunstan St Omer, others exhibited and some works by Warwick Walcott were included, thus demonstrating the lineage of St Lucian art, Warwick Walcott to Simmons to Dunstan and Derek. There was also an exhibition of a collection of Japanese prints. The relationship between the Arts Guild, the Walcotts, and the Methodists was clearly continuing as the Arts Guild held its Christmas party at the home of Alix Walcott. The President Lucius Mason moved a toast to the health of the members. They sang carols, and finished with 'Auld Lang Syne' and the National Anthem. Meanwhile Maurice Mason, who was now a law student in London, was heard reading carols on a radio broadcast from a Methodist church.

Slade Hopkinson joined UCWI as Walcott was starting his second year. Hopkinson was Secretary of the Dramatic Society and President during 1954–5. He acted in and directed many of Walcott's plays in Jamaica, and, along with Errol Hill and the Walcotts, was one of the main directors of the period. The Dramatic Society of UCWI produced nothing until 1952 when it did two one-act plays before a small undergraduate audience at the old Dramatic Theatre, Derek Walcott's *Harry Dernier*, with Walcott directing, and a British farce.

Originally intended as a radio play lasting twenty minutes, *Harry Dernier* was supposedly written when Walcott was 16 years old; it was published in Barbados as *Harry Dernier: A Play for Radio Production* during 1952 with a dedication to Leonard St Hill, accompanied by a quotation from Dorothy Sayers's translation of the entrance to the circle of treason in Dante's *Inferno.* The broadcast on the BBC with Errol Hill as Dernier was reviewed in *Bim* in December 1952. With the last man in the world as its subject, the play is about the love of self, of a woman, and of God. The world is sex, creation, sin, and death. The play asks, what is man? He argues with God, is not on speaking terms with him, but must trust him. No consolation is offered.

An experimental play which would have been at home on the BBC Third Programme during its high culture years, and which belongs to what one might call the Eliotic phase of late Modernism, *Harry Dernier* appears to express Walcott's own views about sex and love, living and sin. The dialogue is staccato, thoughts fade or are implied. It begins with Harry Dernier, a defrocked priest and scholar, speaking slowly after some apocalypse caused by an atomic explosion:

> Who am I? Who daren't explore
> The fringes of my hand? The horizon had become
> A boundary of bone. The wind's wicked today, huh . . .
> Talking to yourself again, Harry.
> Who's Harry though?

Along with some sound effects of wind, sea, and birds, there is a woman's voice, Lily the Lady (Lilith), a former singer, who wants to breed to renew life, and whom Harry loves but rejects as:

> Of the primordial sin. Now with you alive, the three loves come
> again,
> The desert blossoming like the rose. Isaiah.
> God, Sensual, and self love.
> We must be cautious, although God and man
> Are not on speaking terms. We must trust in him . . .

Harry believes 'Our sin is flesh', wants Lily to repent, refuses to repopulate the earth, and hears her voice no more as, the play ending, he discovers her skull:

> It's that skull. There's the skull, Duchess of Malfi still,
> That's Lily. She died, Dernier, she died too,
> Your filthy last . . . My mistress' skull . . .
> Silence again . . . a bird's voice, Dernier . . .

He is left burning and muttering.[12]

Three years had passed and Walcott tried to catch up with his courses at the last moment. He fainted at the Student Union from drink and overwork while trying to study for examinations in Milton, nineteenth-century French literature, and Virgil's *Georgics*. Alix had her heart set on his having a degree from Oxford and he expected to go to England after graduation. Early in 1953 Roderick Walcott told Collymore that Derek would study at Oxford or Cambridge for a year. At some point this became the Department of Education at Bristol University. Later (25 June) Walcott wrote to Swanzy from Jamaica sending a sequence of thirteen sonnets, 'Well of Being', and asked if it could be broadcast by the end of summer as in October he would start at Bristol and would need money. It was broadcast on 20 September on *Caribbean Voices*.

Walcott left Jamaica after his June exams and stopped off in Barbados on his way to St Lucia. Ellice Collymore says that Derek was at their home when they heard that a Bajan friend had got a third-class degree. Derek claimed that as the friend was a better student he would probably fail. Early in August 1953, the *Voice of St Lucia* welcomed his return, and the Extra-Mural Department wanted him to give some talks. The June Arts degree results were officially announced in October 1953. There were three firsts. Walcott was one of the thirteen who were awarded a second-class degree. There were five thirds and eleven passes.

In August the *Voice of St Lucia* announced that Derek Walcott, who had recently returned from UCWI, would direct his second full-length play in St Lucia the following month 'before he leaves for England to enter Bristol University'. (George Odlum was already at Bristol, with a first-class degree, and head of the Student Union.) *The Charlatan* is in three acts and is 'a metaphysical verse Comedy'. It was to be produced under the auspices of the Arts Guild. *The Golden Lions*, a Walcott play about the colourful West Indian politician Alexandre Bustamante, was supposed to be produced by the Arts Guild later in the year. Robert Penn Warren's *All the Kings Men* was an influence on the play. The article was wrong; the two plays were not produced and Walcott did not go to England.[13]

Although Walcott understood that he was originally awarded a fellowship to Oxford to do an Honours degree followed by a Diploma in Education at Bristol, St Lucia would not pay for him in England without knowing his examination results. John Figueroa claims that the French professor took the examinations to England to mark during the summer and was unreachable. The results were only available in September, by which time it was too late for any British university to accept Walcott for 1953–4, despite an intensive effort by Figueroa and others. Vernon Cooper has written another version according to which 'through the negligence or otherwise of certain Departments of the government of the day' the scholarship did not materialize. Sherlock remembers nothing about late French results. It is impossible now to separate the various strands of this story.[14]

Walcott was in Castries until October 1953 when he returned to Jamaica. Having failed a second time to get to England, Walcott enrolled in the Faculty of Education for a one-year D.Ed., the first offered at UCWI, but was resentful and attended few classes. As no one expected him to finish the academic year, St Lucia was advised to withdraw his scholarship and send him to England the next year, but instead the authorities were willing to pay for him to study in Jamaica for another year, which was thought continuing stupidity. Why could he not be sent to England for the good of everyone including the West Indies? Alix blamed Boxill, who, as Education Officer, had control over scholarships, and, as a Catholic convert, was getting back at the Methodists including his godson. Whether or not that is correct, Boxill steered St Lucians away from Oxford and Cambridge.

At the end of the 1952–3 academic year Errol Hill returned from London and joined the staff of the Extra-Mural Department as Drama Tutor. Although he had already directed several of Walcott's plays, Hill first met him in 1953. Walcott would come to his flat and listen to jazz records. They shared the view that there was an analogy between the birth of Irish renaissance drama and the situation in the West Indies. Over the years they would argue over many matters while remaining friends. Hill would be influential in publishing some of Walcott's early plays and in his commission to write a pageant for the 1958 West Indian Arts Festival.[15]

John Figueroa, the poet, after living in London from 1946 to 1953, also returned in 1953 and was Walcott's tutor during the Education diploma year. Figueroa knew Walcott's poetry since about 1949 and had met Walcott previously when he returned to Jamaica for a month. On first meeting Walcott, he immediately quoted his 'Nursing neurosis like a potted plant'. Although he thought there were great lines and poems, he did not immediately feel, like Collymore, that here was a great poet. There is a certain disciplined seriousness about his responses, a moral dislike of the unconventional as likely to cause excess and harm. Although Figueroa and Walcott seem very different, they shared being poets, believed in form, in the classics, the promotion of a West Indian literature, and the importance of good teaching. Both men are religious, although in different ways.

Derek attended Figueroa's lectures, went to teaching practice with him, and was interested in the ways Figueroa explored language in school classes. Walcott's own way of looking carefully at each word in any text comes from a time when literary critics, classical scholars, and those in the British educational system weighed and examined every word for its tonalities, ironies, paradoxes, history, rhetoric, and concreteness. Although Walcott had contempt for his classes, he took teaching seriously. He had been teaching since primary school and had his own ideas and methods. The poet Velma Pollard remembers that when she was in the sixth form at Jamaica College Walcott did a teaching practice with her class. His method consisted of a very detailed word-by-word explication of Coleridge's 'Lime Tree Bower my Prison', which was one of his favourite poems. Detailed explication was to remain part of his teaching technique, whether with students or actors.

One day Figs took a depressed Derek on a drive to Guava Ridge where they walked among some ruins. Walcott said nothing. About a year later he told Figs that he got a great poem out of that day, 'Ruins of a Great House'. One of Walcott's best-known poems, it first regards 'the disjecta membra of this Great

House' as 'The leprosy of Empire', mocks the aestheticism of Keats's Grecian Urn by recalling slavery,[16]

> 'Farewell, green fields,
> Farewell, ye happy groves!'
> Marble like Greece, like Faulkner's South in stone,
> Deciduous beauty prospered and is gone,
> But where the lawn breaks in a rash of trees
> A spade below dead leaves will ring the bone
> Of some dead animal or human thing
> Fallen from evil days, from evil times.

Anger at the past, at history, at religion and imperialism, 'the abuse | Of ignorance by Bible and by sword', and the continuing treatment of the African-Americans in Faulkner's South, is complicated by 'men like Hawkins, Walter Raleigh, Drake' being both 'Ancestral murderers and poets'. 'The world's green age then was a rotting lime', the New World like the Old is a product of man's fall. We are all guilty, all victims, all sinners, and art, the great house, and the poem, is a product. Thought and reflection lead to compassion and universalism rather than anger and polemics:

> Ablaze with rage I thought,
> Some slave is rotting in this manorial lake,
> But still the coal of my compassion fought
> That Albion too was once
> A colony like ours, 'part of the continent, piece of the main',
> Nook-shotten, rook o'erblown, deranged
> By foaming channels and the vain expense
> of bitter faction.
>   All in compassion ends
> So differently from what the heart arranged:
> 'As well as if a manor of thy friend's . . .'

A biblically based rumination on the 'ruins' of greatness, the literary echoes contribute to the sense of a mediation on both colonial and universal history. The outlines of Walcott's vision were already falling into place, the Dylan Thomas view of life as leading towards death had been radically enlarged to include history and empire as being sins carried to the New World in a way that replicates humanity's first fall. Nothing lasts, except perhaps literature and fame; to be born is to die; living is dying; only memory preserves, but memory is burdened by awareness that accomplishment is usually founded on evil.

'A Far Cry from Africa' was also written about this time, as a result of a student quarrel about Kenya. It is in part a poem about Walcott's supposed divided heritage, his black blood and white culture, in relationship to imperial policy in

Africa, but it is more significantly about universal guilt and the need for compassion rather than taking sides:

> Corpses are scatterd through a paradise.
> Only the worm, colonel of carrion, cries:
> 'Waste no compassion on these separate dead!'
> Statistics justify and scholars seize
> The salients of colonial policy.
> What is that to the white child hacked in bed?
> To savages, expendable as Jews.

Echoing and alluding to Auden, Walcott comments:

> Again brutish necessity wipes its hands
> Upon the napkin of a dirty cause, again
> A waste of our compassion, as with Spain
> The gorilla wrestles with the superman.[17]

Walcott was struggling with racial hurts and anger at slavery, colonialism, and black poverty, which he saw were becoming self-wounding obsessions. Better to accept that history consisted of people conquering and enslaving others, that in a fallen world all were potential victims and oppressors. Although the New World was really no better than the Old, it was better to try to start again without bitterness. Walcott's later writings develop this vision which he was shaping during his Jamaica years. It blends Christian notions of fall and compassion with those of New World exceptionalism and the restoration of Adamic innocence. What prevents it from becoming a cliché is that the tensions never settle, the hurts and anger continue to erupt.

Walcott also had other obsessions. He met Faye Moyston soon after he came to Jamaica in 1950. She was pretty, very upper-middle class, light brown, a graduate of a private school (to which she was chauffered), and was secretary to Philip Sherlock, now Vice-Principal, who encouraged her to assist Walcott by typing his manuscripts and preparing stencils for the two college publications that he edited. Soon Walcott began to court her by leaving poems in her typewriter at lunch time. Several people mention that she would tear up the poems and say something like 'silly boy', but Walcott is persistent with women, and she was aware of him as Sherlock's favourite. Affection grew. They would be seen together and by the end of his first year she was regarded as Walcott's girl friend. When Faye went to the University of Birmingham during 1951, Walcott regularly wrote to her, sent her poems; she told the men she met that she had a boy friend back home.

Although Faye was impressed by Walcott's reputation as a genius, she was not an intellectual, not deeply interested in the arts, did not like bohemian ways, was bothered by the loudness, heavy smoking, and drinking of Walcott's friends.

She was attractive, dressed well, liked to be admired, enjoyed dancing, took dancing classes for exercise, but was thought passive and withdrawn. She was in
Ivy Baxter's dance group, captained a netball team, and she and Derek often
played table tennis. About once a month he would take her to dinner. Walcott
was prudish, criticized her for showing her legs, and suspected her and his
friends of betrayal. She expected a future in which her husband supported her
while she raised a large family. Walcott, however, lacked many social graces,
never learned to dance or drive a car, was often moody, and was sarcastic about
others, especially women; he was once flattened by another student for making
remarks about his girl. Despite his rudeness towards women Walcott attracted
them, including the 'Kay' of 'Brise Marine'—'K with quick laughter, honey skin
and hair | and always money.'—a wealthy upper-class Jamaican. She was an
older student and had a crush on Derek during the first year when he knew Faye.

Over the years Walcott wrote several poems about his relationship with
Faye—including the strangely old-fashioned 'A Leave Taking' 'to F.M.' when he
was thinking of breaking up,

> O Love, remember me,
> For the light would have been thine, if I were a giver,
> The lights on the water,
> And the light of the hills of your country at evening
> And the cloudglow at evening, and the light in the bird's last crying
> Had I owned them or borrowed them, and I would give thee
> For a gift the globe revolving the stars,
> Orion, Andromeda, and the stately constellations,
> To keep the child's wonder in you,
> A gift for your innocence.[18]

Walcott told her that because of his poems she would be remembered, but the
Faye poems are uncollected and sometimes unpublished and unquotable, as they
were only broadcast on the BBC *Caribbean Voices*. Some are extremely convoluted and show Derek troubled about sex and his relationship to Faye, whom he
views as a temptress. The confusion is surprising as, based on his poems, Walcott
is thought to have had affairs during his time with Faye.

On Sunday, 20 September 1953, Faye would have heard being broadcast from
London 'The Well of Being' '(to F.M.)', a linked sequence of thirteen sonnets
Walcott had dedicated to her, which lasted more than fifteen minutes and
took more than half of the programme. The poems, never published, have a late
nineteenth-century poetic manner, and are concerned with how love has become
lust and brought chaos and guilt to what was once innocence; yet this wild
intensity is itself richer than what was lost. Like Samson, his passion has taken
him outside his faith and brought damnation. The vocabulary of sin, corruption,
agony, grace, destruction, need, indecision, is Victorian and Arnoldian, as Walcott

alludes to an emotive world of hell, violence, faction, pits, sins, dungeons, and errors, in which each person lives isolated and blinded in contrast to the distant pure stars. At the heart of the sequence is the claim that human need and love for a woman have made Walcott into God's enemy.

As in much of Walcott's poetry there is fear of death and annihilation. There is also a declaration of passion and its dangers seldom found in the later poetry. The Samson symbolism often occurs during this period. Walcott in his early twenties felt that he was being misled from his ambitions as a writer and his religion by the power of sex and the intense private world created by intimacy. That Faye was Roman Catholic contributed to his sense of going wrong. It needs, however, to be remembered that Walcott was always intense, driven, and had a need to be in love. He also liked Matthew Arnold's poetry and his reading influenced his expression and vision of reality; it is not easy untangling the inter-personal from the intertextual.

The second ceremony of the Presentation of Graduates took place on 11 March 1954. It was the first for Arts graduates. In the final examinations the previous June, twenty candidates had passed in Arts, fifteen in Science. There were also fifteen medical students, the first group who had entered in 1949, doing their exams.[19]

Henri Christophe, directed by Walcott, assisted by Mary Brathwaite, sister of the poet E. Kamau Brathwaite, was performed in the open air at the Jamaica Dramatic Theatre after the graduation ceremonies on 12–13 and 16 March. It was the first production of the year by the University Players, who had been want-ing a West Indian play. The cast included Rex Nettleford (who was to become famous as Jamaica's leading dancer and choreographer) as General Sylla and Slade Hopkinson as Dessalines. Walcott's friend Hopkinson was thought the best and most experienced of the actors in the group. Archie Hudson-Phillips was Vastey. This was Walcott's first production of the play since 1950 in St Lucia.

A few years later the *Pelican Annual* commented that the audience could not have failed to be impressed with the programme indicated—in the play writ-ten by Derek Walcott, produced and directed by Derek Walcott, with the set designed and made by Derek Walcott. The production became part of the mythology of this period of UCWI history because of a Walcott prank. A visit of the Queen to the graduation ceremony coincided with the plans for the production. After Walcott suggested that they needed the highly ornate official chair for his production some students then engaged in an elaborate plot to hijack the chair which, having obtained, they realized they could not publicly use. The return of the chair became a general campus student event, a sort of festival celebration, commemorated in a photograph that is still republished as an example of the good old days at UCWI. There were many dignitaries in the audience including the Haitian Consul, but the production was thought tedious, and Walcott a dramatist not a director.[20]

Lloyd Stanford was Henri Christophe. Stanford, a first-year student, first learned of Walcott when a friend gave him *25 Poems* to read. Stanford was excited by the idea that a fellow West Indian student wrote 'A City's Death by Fire' when he was 18 years old. He purchased *Epitaph for the Young*, which he still has, and auditioned for *Henri Christophe*. Walcott knew clearly what he wanted the actors to do, would pace off steps and count pauses, explain characters. Walcott was patient and curiously shy for someone who already had a reputation as a genius and was at the centre of a coterie. When he wanted Stanford to recite a soliloquy in a certain way, Walcott would not himself do it in public, but took Stanford to the Modern Language Department lab where Walcott recorded what he wanted and left before the recording could be played back. Stanford later took the part of Henri Christophe in *Drums and Colours*.

The Sea at Dauphin was first read at a December 1953 meeting of the Drama Society. In June the UCWI Dramatic Society announced it would produce short plays by Sean O'Casey and Errol Hill and Walcott's *Sea at Dauphin*.[21] *The Sea at Dauphin* was first published by the Extra-Mural Department UCWI, Trinidad, as Caribbean Plays no. 4. Set in an area of St Lucia that is still unreachable in bad weather, *The Sea at Dauphin* is influenced by Synge's *Riders to the Sea*, but, instead of stoicism and fatalism, Afa is angry and defiant, and curses God for the life he has given the peasants, the priests for telling them to accept and be thankful for such a life, and the whiteman. Afa makes poetic similes in which God and the awful environment are associated with the colour white. Such colour symbolism and associationalism was and remains a Walcott technique. There are, for example, the dangerous white waves that threaten the fishermen who must brave the rainy, windy sea or starve. Instead of a God of love, Walcott offers a God of life as a predatory food chain of conquerors and victims. In a speech which upset the St Lucian clergy, Afa turns and empties his fish pail on the sand:

That is God! A big fish eating small ones. And the sea, that thing there, not a priest white, pale like a shark belly we must fed until we dead, not no young Frenchman lock up in a church don't know coolie man dying because he will not beg! . . . This scapular not Dauphin own! Dauphin people build the church and pray and feed you, not their own people, and look at Dauphin! *Gadez lui!* Look at it! You see? Poverty, dirty woman, dirty children, where all the prayers? . . . Dirt and prayers is Dauphin life, in Dauphin, in Canaries. Micoud. Where they have priest is poverty![22]

When *Sea at Dauphin* was performed in St Lucia, Walcott was summoned by the Archbishop, which he ignored. Walcott had in mind the church in Gros Islet in which the statue of Mary was surrounded with gold, while the surrounding neighbourhood of the church consisted of the shacks of poor fishermen.

During his last year at UCWI Walcott gave informal classes in oil painting for the Art Society, and he sold some of his paintings at Sangster's bookstore. Slade

Hopkinson in March 1954 revived the *Pelican*, which lasted a few more issues as a cyclostyled publication; Walcott helped design it. A new Music Room in the corner of the Students' Union was officially opened on 22 May. Among its decorations was a painting by Walcott.

He sat his examinations with disdain. For some examination he supposedly replied to the question 'What is the difference between a ruler and a king' that a ruler is a foot long but a king will go to any length. He left UCWI with a recommendation as a teacher rather than a professional qualification.[23] There were some demonstrations by students in Walcott's favour, but he ignored the situation. There was a feeling that something should be done and Walcott was later offered a chance to write an essay, which he did not do. Later, in the early 1960s, he embarked on a dissertation that was never finished.

For someone who thought of himself as descended from teachers, who had immense respect for the older generation of West Indian schoolteachers, who taught at various times and ways (in schools, poetry or theatre workshops, and at universities), and would continue to think of himself as a teacher, Walcott was self-destructive about obtaining the usual qualifications for a teaching career, whether a Diploma in Education or a Ph.D. There was Walcott the writer with the artist's instinct to rebel, there was the Walcott who had already educated himself beyond his teachers, there were the examples of his father Warwick, who was mostly self-educated, his mother Alix, who had only qualified to teach infant school, his friend Harry Simmons, who was consulted by professors at Harvard and Oxford, there was the then current British notion that a BA was sufficient for a school or university teacher, but there was also an artist's instinct of self-preservation from being drawn into the deadening security of a steady job and the well-laid-out career of a colonial schoolteacher.

Walcott's friend Garth St Omer was soon to write several novels about St Lucia and UCWI in which the Walcotts, Dunstan St Omer, and others of their circle are models for characters. A career as a teacher or headmaster in one of the private schools on a small island was a trap to be avoided. In this Portrait of the Caribbean Artist, such security and middle-rank social position ends in frustration and narrowness. Castries is portrayed as a tight small world in which shades of skin colour are associated with how close people live to Columbus Square; women and men fear that sexual intercourse will result in pregnancies and the traps of children, marriage, family responsibilities, and frustrated dreams. It is necessary to get away before it is too late. Emigration from the West Indies is driven as much by the desire for adventure as financial betterment.

Walcott had similar feelings, but fate seemed to keep closing that escape route to England and his own acts of rebellion were keeping him in the West Indies. For the next few years Walcott would continue to think of England as where he must go to have a career as a writer and to see his plays properly produced by professional theatre companies. Though he often wrote to Collymore and others of England as a dream of paradise, he seemed to know that staying in the West Indies was essential for his writing. The idea of living in Europe left him feeling uncomfortable. Walcott had an eye for opportunities, an unflagging dedication to his career, but there has always been a stubbornness, an assumption that what will happen will happen and what is not fated will not happen. Instead of being a dissatisfied West Indian immigrant in London, patronized and discriminated against, he remained among a society, culture, and landscape that he knew and could be said to have created as he learned to portray in his art its various forms, whether the colours of the sky or the sounds of voices. He returned to St Lucia, once more thinking of living as a painter, having been, it is said, the only person to have failed a Diploma in Education at the University of the West Indies.

7

1954–1957 First Marriage, *Ti-Jean and His Brothers*, J. P. Harrison

THE *Voice of St Lucia* noted on 6 July that Miss Faye Moyston, a guest of Alix Walcott, had arrived from Barbados on a short holiday. Faye wanted to see if she would like the island to which Derek intended to return. While awaiting Derek, who arrived ten days later, she was introduced to the Arts Guild crowd by Roddy and Dunstan and enjoyed herself. Sherlock had warned her that Derek would not be a good husband, and Alix also told her that Derek was not the kind of man to marry as he was too involved with his work to give attention to a wife. Derek, however, wanted to have a family; family was important to him and would remain important. Although sceptical of the marriage, Alix wanted to regularize the relationship and pressed for a large public wedding. Faye was Roman Catholic, but the local priest surprisingly raised no objection to a church marriage.[1]

On 25 August 1954, Derek Walcott and Faye Althea Moyston, both 24, were married at the LaClery Chapel, Vide Bouteille, a church which Dunstan had decorated earlier with a mural. The bride was given away by Harold Simmons. She was attended by Mrs Lucille Mair Mathurin. The bestman was Roderick Walcott, who was then in the Lands & Survey Department. H. D. Boxill and Julian Theobalds were witnesses. Afterwards there was a reception at the house of Mr and Mrs E. F. Auguste at Micoud Street.[2]

Derek was irritable at the large reception and asked the Mathurins to drive him and Faye to a place outside of Gros Islet where he assembled some local musicians who played traditional music throughout the night, while Faye danced and Derek played bongos. Immediately afterwards, Thursday, they flew to Grenada where Derek had been appointed for four months as Assistant Master at Grenada

Boys' Secondary School, St George, to teach Latin and English, replacing A. N. Forde, another poet, who was on leave. He also taught some extra-mural classes. Faye remembers thinking they were living in a lovely house on the hill over-looking Market Square and she expected to be happy, but the first day Derek spent painting scenes of the harbour, and his time would be divided between his teaching, painting, and going to the library to study art books.[3]

Although he had a reputation as a good teacher and Faye was admired for her looks, dress sense, and having landed a job in the Governor's office, Derek was unhappy in Grenada. He did not want to teach. He wanted to live on St Lucia and paint. Grenada was called Spice Island and, according to a long unpublished article he later wrote, Walcott made up his mind to dislike the nutmeg, ginger, and allspice for which it was famous. St George, the capital, is a beautiful town built in hills around a harbour; he had decided it was Georgian colonial postcard pretty. The inland crop was cocoa grown on estates; he decided cocoa was a slave crop. Grenada was regarded as socially higher than St Lucia, more British, more orderly. St George had a red or high brown plantocracy and a larger black mer-chant class than St Lucia; inland there were black peasant co-operatives. Walcott disliked the social distinctions based on class and shade. Grenada was famous for its school, but he felt trapped, regimented, and bored; he had to wear a wool jacket and tie. He hated the headmaster.

Although he felt alone in the West Indies as there were no other poets of his stature, and no one seemed to have his dedication to a career as a writer, he had a central place among a dedicated group of people creating a modern regional theatre. In August Errol Hill produced *Sea at Dauphin* in Trinidad for the New Company and the Whitehall Players. Walcott prepared a special script for Hill filled with drawings and a personal note to the effect that despite differences of opinion, he appreciated Hill's encouragement and help and felt that they shared a cause, the creation of a West Indian theatre. The production was negatively reviewed by J. S.Barker, 'Not the Stuff for a West Indian Theatre' in the *Trinidad Guardian.*[4]

Three months later, on Saturday, 27 November, Hill's Whitehall Players and his brother Sydney Hill's New Company produced *Henri Christophe* in Trinidad for the first time. It opened at the USO Building for six performances. Two people who would soon be part of Walcott's Trinidadian years were Selby Wooding (Vice-President) and Claire Creteau (Secretary). Errol Jones was Henri Christophe. As the second production of a Derek Walcott play in Trinidad that year, it received much attention. Sydney Hill introduced the play and its historical background with five articles in the *Trinidad Guardian.* Eric Williams, already the leading politician, wrote a prologue for the production.

On 8 October Walcott sent Roy Fuller three unpublished poems, two of which are still among his best known. His brief comments to Fuller put them into perspective and offer an illustration of his way of organizing related short poems into a linked sequence. Walcott says that 'Africa, Patria Mia' (unpublished), 'A Far Cry', and 'Ruins' should be read as an emotional sequence in which 'Ruins' clears the bitterness and regret of the first poem. These poems had been written in Jamaica during the past year and reveal Walcott trying to come to terms with what he felt was his divided heritage as African and European. They move from Africa as a place of origins to an apparent conflict between his black skin and white language, which prevents him from choosing sides concerning the Mau Mau struggle in Kenya, a conflict which is resolved when he realizes that the imperial British were themselves in the past conquered slaves of the Romans. One tries to be angry and intellectually take sides, but real compassion for the world reveals the falsity of simple political views.

'Africa, Patria Mia' was not published, but apparently seeded a longer poem, 'Origins', which first appeared in the 1964 *Selected Poems*. 'A Far Cry from Africa' was first published during December 1956 under the broad title 'Poetry and War', preceded by a quotation from Dylan Thomas in *Public Opinion*.[5] It precedes 'Ruins of a Great House' in *In a Green Night* and *Collected Poems* so 'Ruins' is seen as the answer to the problems raised by the now famous lines:

> How can I face such slaughter and be cool?
> How can I turn from Africa and live?

Walcott hoped that if it were too late to use the poems Fuller might place them elsewhere or pass them on to Swanzy. If some lines were obscure that was the way they came to him and he feared editing would lose them. He knew that some lines were awkward, but he was trying to avoid smoothness and slickness. As there is no market for writing in the West Indies, Walcott had self-published and himself sold four booklets of his writings, but he could not afford to continue doing so. He had twenty poems written since 1951 that he would like to see in print, if only to get them out of the way. He could send Fuller his three verse plays as well.[6] Fuller sent the three poems to Geoffrey Moore in July 1956, to be considered for the *Penguin Book of American Poetry*. Walcott (5 November 1954) wrote to Swanzy saying the poems were coming to him and that he and Faye were saving money to come to England.

Henry Swanzy took his farewell from the *Caribbean Voices* broadcasts with 'The West Indian Predicament'(14 November 1954), a programme of unpublished, discontented poems illustrating some tensions in the region which he felt were the source of self-expression. The poets included Derek Walcott. Much of the discontent was with provinciality and the working class, but Walcott's 'Hatred by Moonlight' concerns the way his own awareness of racial prejudices had resulted in his hatred of whites and a desire to hurt white women. There was conflict between such anger and the actual tenderness he felt towards the women he loved, that which attracted his hatred became that which he loved. There is nothing by way of personal or communal revenge that can compare to the sweetness, order, and permanence of art. The best insult is to forgive enemies and dazzle them with writings. Art is a means to transcend social wounds.

The poem, with its allusions to his own self-hatred at being black, and the symbolism of the white moon, is late Yeatsian in its display of clipped self-revelations, its offering of an autobiographical story, and in working through its argument towards a triumphant reversal. It looks forward to the killing of the mulatto woman in *Malcauchon* and, more important, the beheading of the white apparition in *Dream on Monkey Mountain.* Like most poems of this period, it remains unpublished.[7] During November Walcott learned that 'Letter to Margaret', written in 1950, was translated into German and published in a West German anthology of black poetry from Africa and the Americas.

He returned with Faye to St Lucia (13 December) to help with the production of his *Sea at Dauphin,* which was to be presented at Wesley Hall, at the new Methodist infant school, on Friday, 17 December. The play had already been read twice, in late November and early in December, over the local experimental radio station. Suddenly everyone was in St Lucia. Errol Hill, UCWI Staff Tutor in Drama, had arrived expecting to take part in the production and a production of one his own plays. Mittelholzer, recently returned to the West Indies after working for the British Council in England, turned up for a week and visited with the Walcotts. The American anthropologist Dan Crowley, Harry Simmons's friend, had been in St Lucia since early November gathering folk materials after coming from Trinidad where he had been working with Andrew Pearse.

The Sea at Dauphin was regarded as part of the rediscovery of local folk culture and its renaissance. The *Voice of St Lucia* promised that the Arts Guild would stage a 'Conte' (a local folk dance) accompanied by a special drum during scenes of *Sea.* Two members of the Arts Guild would dance the Conte, which they had practised under the supervision of an experienced dancer, and a drummer had been instructed by a local master. Walcott learned early the need and ways to obtain advertising and promotion. A short run was announced, followed by claims that the play was being repeated because of demand. The Saturday and Sunday *Voice of St Lucia* carried articles saying 'Walcott Play Staging again on Monday' and 'Arts Guild Play Being Repeated Tomorrow Night'.[8]

An anonymous reviewer of the Friday performance mentioned that the play was local in authorship and language and described it as 'Life in the raw, realistically portrayed; life's puzzlement and frustrations, unfortunately unexplained and unresolved'. The reviewer commented upon the declamatory speeches and restricted action. Afa was as tempestuous as the seas and compassionate despite his denial of such weakness. The fishermen were neglected by God. The priest was made too ineffectual by the dramatist. A letter to the *Voice of St Lucia,*

Tuesday, two days later, commented in detail on the lighting (which suggests that the Walcotts early on had an unusual awareness of stage lighting to create atmosphere) and shows how the theme was understood. 'Its message of eternal verities—that work is hard, that the Sea is cruel, that Old Age is lonely and that Sympathy may harden into bitterness—but that Life carries on and though the Old Man dies the Boy is there to take the empty place in the fisherman's boat. A brave message'.[9]

This message was disagreeable to Father Jesse, who as Catholicus returned to his harassment of the Walcotts with a letter to the editor. He had not seen the play, but had read it twice since it was produced. Jesse claimed that some of the pidgin English is obscure and some Creole words are inaccurately phonetically represented. His main objection is to Afa's blasphemies. Jesse argued that all that is true of life is not fit for human eyes and ears, and reminded readers that St Lucia still legislated against the use of profane words. The official representative of Christianity in Pere Lavoisier is shown 'in pitiable fashion'. The play insinuates that white priests are the cause of poverty. Afa represents the spirit of soured, fatalistic, morbid disbelief.[10]

Walcott stayed on in St Lucia where he did some part-time teaching for a term at St Mary's and, according to Faye, became a beachcomber. He was glad to be back; he had not liked Jamaica, nor Grenada, did not want to go to England, and talked about remaining in St Lucia all his life. This, the life of the beachcomber, would remain a constant fantasy. Later, whenever he was faced by a crisis in his career or private life, Walcott would imagine himself as an aged, white-haired, weather-faced misanthrope living as a solitary, writing poetry, in a hut on the beach in St Lucia, or perhaps as a castaway on some little-known island.

Faye worried that there was no future for Derek in St Lucia; a permanent appointment for a Methodist at St Mary's was unlikely. Alix (on the verge of retiring) told Faye that they could live with her, and she would support them until Derek, whom she pampered, became famous and could live from his writing. Faye, now pregnant, thought this a poor idea and wrote to Sherlock, who found a desirable job for Derek at Jamaica College. Although Faye enjoyed Alix, she felt confined; Derek's work always took precedence, although he seemed resentful if she spent time with others. Derek had taken her to see Harry Simmons, proud of his mentor, but Faye had met Simmons in Jamaica a decade earlier when at the age of 15 she had begun work and he was following some course. Walcott did not seem to enjoy it when she and Simmons began talking about events in the past.

The Walcotts returned to Jamaica in May 1955. At Jamaica College, Kingston, Derek taught English, Latin, and French. They lived at 5 Wellington Drive which was close to both the College and UCWI.

Barbara Gloudon, now a well-known Jamaican journalist, actress, and businesswoman, remembers:

Derek Walcott held sway on campus and off. To be admitted to the inner circle of his Sunday night sessions in his flat at Wellington Avenue, you had to be quick with wit, knowledgeable in the arts and have a skin thicker than a crocodile's. Derek's tongue was razor sharp, and many a Sunday night we watched people retreat from the session . . . chopped up because of their lack of knowledge and faltering sense of humour . . . Slade Hopkinson, Ronnie Llanos and people like that, skilled in the dramatic arts, were the heroes of the day. Everyone abounded in creativity. Sunday mornings on campus was a ritual . . . it began with the opening of some art exhibition or other . . . people would come for morning drinks, stay for lunch, linger for tea and have to be swept out round midnight. Somehow, food always materialized and drink was endless . . . the talk incessant.

Gloudon mentions the wit of the St Lucian novelist Garth St Omer and the satiric Trinidadian picong of Archie Hudson-Phillips. This was the first time very bright, creative, educated young people from the islands were coming together, talking, learning about each other, listening to each other's music, forming friendships, marrying, having children. They also met at Carmen Manley's; on Sunday evenings a smaller group, including Garth St Omer, the St Lucian historian Roy Augier, and Shirley Gordon, an English academic, sometimes met at the house of John Hearne's mother.

They not only talked political Federation, but were beginning to experience it socially, culturally, romantically. Gloudon met her first Barbadian (until then regarded as amusing stereotypes), heard her first steel band recording (from Antigua!), Sparrow and 'Eastern Caribbean calypso' (in contrast to the Jamaican mento version), and was converted from Keats to West Indian literature by reading Mittelholzer's *Morning at the Office*.[11]

Faye gave birth to Peter in June. Dr Hoyte, Derek's friend, was the paediatrician in charge of the delivery. Peter's godfather was Roy Augier. They lived in a small two-bedroom flat, with one bedroom kept as a studio for Derek's painting. Derek was devoted to his work and not satisfied with his paintings; he destroyed a portrait of Faye when she was pregnant, as he found it difficult to capture her rounded features. Walcott often had trouble with portraits—he also destroyed one he painted of Roy Augier. The best paintings I have found of his Jamaican years are abstract landscapes and a Modernist abstract still life.

Faye learned about great painters as Derek would lie in bed with his arm around her reading. Walcott was fascinated, even obsessed, with their baby and would have Peter sleep with him; soon Peter would not sleep on his own. Derek did not seem to worry about supporting his family; he dedicated himself to his art. John Hearne was also at the College, and he and Derek would drink together late into the night along with Slade Hopkinson, Errol Hill, and Roy Augier. Derek and Hearne often visited Figueroa, who disapproved of the heavy drinking and what he considered the bohemian self-centredness of the two writers. Faye's friends considered their apartment underfurnished, 'bohemian', 'eccentric', in contrast to the large homes, well-groomed lawns, and well-bred stuffiness of the Jamaican upper-middle class.

Derek and Faye shared few interests. She was concerned with social status, liked to go for a drive on Sundays, but had to be the driver as he has never learned to drive a car. He did not dance. Faye was not much of a cook, but as Derek liked pineapple, she often served it to him. Soon the marriage began to fracture. Many people speak of Walcott's behaviour towards Faye, the verbal abuse, the telling her not to speak. Later poems, in which he mentions his love of his work, the landscape, St Lucia, the folk, and his children, will question whether he loves individuals, especially his wives.

An uncollected poem written during 1955 shows a troubled Walcott feeling very much a sinner whose ultimate justification before his Maker will be to have used his talent as a poet without the corruptions of his sexual life and ambitions. 'Words for Rent' is addressed to Peter, but becomes a confessional poem about fallen man, alluding tangentially to Derek's private life:

> For my son, asleep tonight,
> For all sons, fatal good
>
> Flesh, corruptible brood, sown
> In the cradles and laps
> Of this ark of our world, alight
> Through seasons of immortal stars
> Or orchards of yellow suns,
> For fathers, guessing the maps
> Of their time, whether wars,
> Women poverty or trust can
> Harm their breakable wills,
>
> . . . . .
>
> A brass sun for the twilight
> And another when mourning rise,
> I would keep cold, numberless man
> I lonely and wandering in bed
> From all the monsters of harm
> That drink at the wells of his heart
> Or cloven stalk through his head.

'Words for Rent' is characteristic of Walcott's uncollected poetry from the late 1940s into the 1950s. Even the title offers a complex pun on 'rent' with contrasting possible significances. The poem is over 170 lines in long stanzas of differing lengths; the long sentences often run over into the next stanza without a break and are often but irregularly rhymed. There is much internal rhyme, near rhyme, assonance, and alliteration. The consciously angular irregularity within a feeling of regularity, the biblical echoes, which quickly become ambiguous as they shift between kinds of meaning, the incantatory accumulation, are suggestive of Dylan Thomas, Henry Vaughan, Shakespeare, Herbert, and Quarles:

> That my heart has risen and waned
> for beauty bought at such a price,
> While ageing I hear tides race
> As I stand, unholy erect,
> In a cataract of good and bad love,
> A hub of this turning place,
> I would suffer more than enough
>
> Through dry or torrential season
> If my veins put out one leaf
> To cure mankind of its own reason.
> But all I possess is words . . .

Written soon after the birth of Peter, and addressed to him, the poem is about the father writing poetry, poetry which is in part about how the father pays for his sins by writing poems:

> But never to absolve my guilt
> My crude, ill-humoured deeds
> Will these words ever pay the rent
> Of my soul on earth on hire,
> For my heart break gift of my spent
> Ambition and desire . . .[12]

The summer of 1955 *Kyk-Over-Al* carried three untitled Walcott poems.[13] 'Though suns burn still, remembering pyres' consists of four stanzas, an extended sonnet in shape and movement, having a sonnet rhyme scheme, but with lines of varied metrical length. The conclusion seems to be that the dead are remembered by their efforts, especially by poetry:

> But from his rest, dead
> Tongues proclaim his height,
> Like stars on hill graves,
> His death the shadow of another light.

The style is Walcott Jacobean with its contrasts, paradoxes, Sir Thomas Browne formality, and Burtonian melancholy, but also Dylan Thomasesque in places: 'height' for instance, and its celebration of continuity after decay through some other kind of existence. The economy, discipline, tightness, and plainness in these poems are suggestive of, say, George Herbert. The poem, 'When I dreamed I found', in that curious twenty-one-line length Walcott will often use later, is a Herbertian allegory, although presumably about his own marriage:

> I know love is dead,
> Which lives by content,
> And an evil thing
> In imprisonment.

The third poem, 'He who fears the scattered seed', is explicit and explains some of the tensions that were in Walcott's relationship to Faye and which would influence later relationships:

> Fear is the harlot of desire,
> And her cunning virtue gives
> Heaven a countenance of fire,
> And a stranger to your wives.

Walcott's poems about such emotions strikingly contrast the intensity of desire, especially outside his marriage, with feelings of guilt, vice, and damnation. Fires lead to hell's fires, whether between people or after death. For a poet who supposedly no longer believed in religion, Walcott was, and remains, haunted by fears of punishment. There was something self-destructive in Walcott's openness to his feelings and imaginings. Rather than repressing conflict, he seems to want to dwell on the devil in man while using a judgemental vocabulary. Such Baudelairianism was, of course, a major strand of modern literature and especially appealing to someone young and troubled by desire, but it will reappear later when Walcott is older, more experienced, hardened, and more cynical, a man and poet of the world and worldly.

During June the old French town of Soufriere in St Lucia was destroyed by a fire and Walcott wrote an unusual article about it which appeared in the *Voice of St Lucia* and the *Daily Gleaner*. It was very structured, poetical, broody, moody, depressed, almost Jacobean, less about facts than loose ruminations around Soufriere as a topic as well as a place. Walcott begins by quoting Kingsley on 'the loveliest little bay . . . green wooded slopes . . . the rearward mountains . . . The whole glitters in blazing sunshine. But behind, black depths of cloud and grey sheets of rain shroud all the central highlands in mystery and sadness.' He then mentions the French origins of the name Soufriere for the smelly sulphurous volcanic springs that are used for bathing as an all-purpose cure. Instead of sulphur the area now smells 'of ashes, burnt leaves, parched paper and of the carcasses of the household animals that panic and are always stupid in a fire'. Walcott then takes up 'carcasses' to recall that seven years earlier Castries was also destroyed by fire. It is impossible to 'write the obituary of a town' one has loved. After mentioning the destruction of other cities ('by courage, like Coventry'), he recalls the appearance of parts of Soufriere, 'the colour of the sea around their piers'. The recurrence of so many disasters in the West Indies, like too many deaths in a family, results in a fatalism, a weariness. In scenes of such physical poverty how is it possible that the damage can be valued in pounds. The poverty is of spirit, 'a wheel stuck in continual poverty, whose hub is always the Church . . . the real democracy is disaster . . . all men are equal in such a paralysis.' Anticipating a theme of his later work, Walcott contrasts the actual disaster to the picturesqueness of poverty as seen from abroad. Soufriere was actually 'almost prosperous', although there were many small villages dependent on it. Soufriere is seen by Walcott as an image of St Lucia, 'the malheur or bad luck of this island' so often harmed by hurricanes, fires, and wars, continually struggling with poverty and needing to beg assistance from others.[14]

For a newspaper article this is very literary and poetic ('a hotel ironically called the Phoenix'). One expects seventeenth-century spelling. There are small echoes from Donne ('Their deaths diminish us') and Eliot ('if you came like Kingsley along the coast'). It is filled with comparisons, 'as pocked and scabrous as the moon', 'like too many deaths in a family', 'like any kind of prosperity it had too many relatives'. There is also Walcott the visual artist: 'the salmoncoloured nets forever drying, and the chrone green, lucid water . . .' Analogy, the pictorial, and elaborate syntax come together in 'it was one of those old world, charming towns, that deserved to die the death of a good, whitehaired generous Creole spinster, not so violently'.

The ways Walcott orders his prose here and some patterns of argument are similar to those later associated with V. S. Naipaul. There is the beginning with a citation from a Victorian travel writer, the building of paragraphs around phrases from the citation, and such world-weary paradoxes as the monotony of poverty and disaster. Even the humour can be similar, 'the flies in the innumerable little shops dozed in the air'. Unlike Naipaul, Walcott enriches rather than diminishes his subject. There is criticism, particularly of the Church, but also a great affection. 'It was really lovely . . . it was the loveliest town of that island', and Walcott fears that the memory of it will be lost when it is rebuilt 'in neo-Corbusier blocks'. Soufriere would suffer the fate of Castries after 1948.

During 1956 Faye moved out, taking Peter with her. She had wondered about Derek's relationship with several women in his circle, but felt insecure and angry when he was often seen with a teacher at UCWI. Derek was unwilling to accept how she felt about this and tried to act as if nothing had changed. His relationships with women would often follow a similar pattern. He would fall in love, intensely court the woman, but after having won her he would turn his attention towards his own work, assuming that the marriage or relationship would remain unaffected. There would be arguments, verbal abuse, and occasional physical abuse. There was the reluctance to give up the relationship, a bohemian attitude towards social conventions and legality, even a reluctance to make decisions. West Indian notions of family, a household, fidelity, and marriage can be baggy, but for Walcott there was also a Methodist streak of guilt and self-torture. He was a family man even if he found it difficult to remain romantically in love.

The Sea at Dauphin was becoming a West Indian theatre classic. John Wickham reviewed it in 'A Look at Ourselves' in *Bim* 6 and Slade Hopkinson revived the *Sea at Dauphin*, with Archie Hudson-Phillips in the lead role, for the University Players, as part of an evening of short West Indian plays. Walcott was present at each rehearsal, a *de facto* director quietly giving suggestions. The production was itself revived by Mary Brathwaite for the 1956 Adult Drama Festival, where it took first prize for best West Indian play. The chief minister Norman Manley and his wife attended and gave prizes. In *Public Opinion* Basil McFarlane appreciated the use of mime and observed that the play's potential for theatre was astonishing, but it was not the work of a seasoned playwright. Hounakin was an impossible character to portray, there were long expository speeches, and the heavily accented small-island speech, larded with French, did not help.[15]

During August there were rehearsals of *The Wine of the Country*, a one-act play by Walcott, who was director. The cast included Slade Hopkinson, Archie Hudson-Phillips, and Ronnie Llanos. They hoped to open in August at the Dramatic Theatre at UCWI. In *The Wine of the Country* a black Englishman, Carl Bemminger, is retiring from the administration of an isolated area of St Lucia, and hopes to marry the daughter of Margaret Vertlieu, owner of an estate, and take her to England. The daughter turns out to be like the mother, a degenerate Europe colonial, lustful, incapable of remaining faithful to any man, and, like her mother, happy to bed but unwilling to marry someone of darker skin. In the play everyone drinks too much, and the foolish Bemminger's antagonist is a young local black, Williams, who despises him as a colonial tool, an imitation white, whom he will replace. In *Wine of the Country*, there are references to characters and events that can be found in *The Sea of Dauphin*, as if Walcott saw the two plays as part of a larger vision or a contemporary history of St Lucia.[16]

Geoffrey Moore (26 July) returned Walcott's 'Near La Guaria' and 'Africa, Patria Mia' and some poems by Wilson Harris to Roy Fuller, who had asked Moore's help in placing them. Moore accepted 'Ruins of a Great House' for *New World Writing* and wrote to let Walcott know. During November 'Ruins of a Great House' was first published in *New World Writing*. The original version lacks the introductory epigraph from Sir Thomas Browne with its melancholic view of the futility of all endeavour, and its wide range of reference and strongly argued opinions.

Meanwhile Roderick Walcott was beginning to find his own voice as a cultural critic and dramatist. In the *Voice of St Lucia* he mocked the politicians and their proposed Federation. They could not even decide on a capital. The Federation was not a great revolution, but personal political bickering by politicians without statesmanship or vision of nation. What is being built is West Indian theatre. 'It is the only true medium, we believe, which is working in the tested spirit of West Indian miscegenation.' Errol Hill's efforts to establish West Indian drama are not unheeded. Yet there is not a proper theatre-house in the entire West Indies. Once a capital is decided we must begin with a local theatre group, and produce West Indian plays. We need a strong professional theatre comprising the best talent from all over the Caribbean and a theatre building for it. The company might include Errol Hill and Sydney Hill of Trinidad directing a play by Derek Walcott or Edgar Mittelholzer, with a cast consisting of Errol John, Errol Jones, and Ronnie Llanos of Trinidad, Slade Hopkinson of British Guyana, Marvis Arscott of Jamaica, Frank Collymore of Barbados, with sets by Colin Laird of Trinidad painted by Dunstan St Omer and Carlisle Chang of Trinidad, with a programme by George Campbell of Jamaica. There is a need for local films, a good publishing house, sponsorship of art exhibitions, and a national symphony orchestra. Who knows what new creations might evolve? Roderick's article might be thought a seed for Derek's later Trinidad Theatre Workshop.[17]

Roderick had started writing plays as the Arts Guild needed a writer, and Derek was in Jamaica, and Garth St Omer was teaching in Dominica. So that the plays could be performed on any of the islands, Roderick's plays were not set in any particular West Indian island, and dialect was not stressed. *The Harrowing of Benjy* concerns a Rastafari vagrant preacher and interest focuses on his character. *Shrove Tuesday March* is based on a steel band war. *The One Eye is King* shows how a city slicker fools villagers. Roderick was interested in local characters, was influenced by American films, would write about local customs, and would be concerned with spiritual redemption and forgiveness. The general compassion offered in Derek's poetry is clearly Christian charity (love of God through love of others) in Roderick's writings.

Harry Simmons reviewed the Arts Guild presentation (29–30 June) of the three one-act plays by Roderick Walcott. While showing present-day life on the islands, he wrote that each was too long, too verbose 'like a great deal of West Indian conversations'. While West Indians would enjoy the banter, rude jibes, crude melodrama, and seeing themselves on stage, each play lasted forty-five minutes. Benjy was a Rastafari. 'The author admits having been . . . influenced in creating Benjy by the character of Jonas in *The Golden Lions* by Derek Walcott. Other influences have been the real Benjy in a draft novel by Derek Walcott, plus a preacher called Corinthian McClarday in Robert Penn Warren's novel, *World Enough and Time.*'[18]

Although Derek Walcott had written occasional articles in the *Voice of Saint Lucia* and other newspapers and had worked during the summers as a student on *Public Opinion,* his career as a journalist began in 1957. He quit teaching and became a feature writer doing satirical sketches and book and art reviews.

Public Opinion was a Jamaican weekly with a long, distinguished tradition of mixing left-wing nationalism with coverage of the arts. Many poets, writers, and intellectuals had worked for it. The poet Basil McFarlane was general arts reviewer during 1955–6. Between 19 January and 10 August 1957, Walcott published one to three articles a week, almost all of which appeared in an arts section on pages 6 or 7. So far forty-four have been identified, an average of about one and a half a week. Most are signed Derek Walcott or D.W., a few are unsigned. A few articles concern such topics as the crisis in school teaching because of poor pay, the lack of government support for the arts, and the Federation. There are art, film, theatre, and book reviews, and nine satirical character sketches, along with a few satirical essays on such topics as Jamaica's attempt to create a Coat of Arms, School Festival plays, and an internal television to be used by medical doctors. One of the early essays concerns West Indian writing; four are about West Indian poets, including George Campbell.[19] Errol Hill had returned to Jamaica where he formed the Federal Theatre Company. Walcott reviewed the Federal Theatre Company's evening of one-act plays, including Roderick's *Benjy*.

Despite their separation Faye and Walcott remained on amicably hostile terms. Faye had been advised she could ask the Pope to annul her marriage on the grounds that Walcott had prevented her from following her faith—the person who told her was powerful enough to have his own marriage annulled on such grounds—but she said that Derek had never tried to interfere with her relation to Roman Catholicism. Derek, however, tried to make Faye attend a cultural event with him and her lawyer had the bruises photographed; they were used as evidence for divorce. The actual serving of the divorce papers had an element of farce suggestive of two still young people at savage play. Derek had been in St Lucia and returned to Jamaica before going on to Trinidad as part of his work on the pageant and asked if he could stay at Faye's apartment. Faye agreed and while she was driving him in her car, her lawyer served him with the papers (25 October 1957). Her heart sank and she felt sorry for what she had done, but Derek barely glanced at the papers, tore them up and threw them away, and left the country. He did not appear before the judge when the divorce was tried and refused for several years to accept that he had been divorced (June 1958). Derek told Faye that she could find other men, but theirs was the love that counted and he invited her to, and introduced her at, the 1958 West Indian Arts Festival as his wife.

Some of the complicated emotions that went into the final stages of his marriage to Faye, and which I think were repeated in the collapse of later marriages, can be found in two seemingly formal exercises in the Cavalier manner, Two Themes on an Old Lute, he published in *Bim* at this time. 'Go, Lovely Worm' begins

> Go, lovely worm,
> Bid her who uses now my heart for hers,
> Wearing bright flesh as she does veiled airs

and concludes

> Sing how I worshipped her and she loved everyone,
> How both our natures to thy cold bed come,
> Then, lovely worm,
> Consume her name here in destruction.

'A Lost Age' begins by praising seventeenth-century English writers,

> When two shipwrecked voyagers we must age
> On desert islands to drown in guilty seas,
> They may, perhaps, my turbulence assuage

Both poems are sardonic about the love of a woman. While Walcott is a master craftsman interested in the techniques and forms of art, the source of his writings is in his experience. When at his most classical he can be at his most personal.[20]

By now it was more than six years since Walcott had last published a volume of his poems. He had found little interest in them among foreign publishers and paying journals. He was also dissatisfied with his poetry of this period. After the initial acclaim a decade earlier, he appeared to be making little progress as a poet. By contrast his plays were central to a lively new theatre scene in the West Indies. On 16 March 1957, the Federal Theatre Company opened Walcott's *Ione,* 'a play with music', at the Ward Theatre, Kingston, Jamaica, directed by Ronald (Ronnie) Llanos. The cast included Lois Kelly-Barrow (Ione), Carmen Manley (Helene), Errol Hill (Victorin), and Archie Hudson-Phillips (Achille). During the year it was produced in Trinidad and published later in the year as Caribbean Plays No. 8 and was the second three-act play in the new series. Because of its length —fifty-four closely printed double columned pages—it was also listed as Long Play 1. The play was dedicated to the actor Archie Hudson-Phillips, Leith Tompson, and 'Harold Simmons, painter, who showed me more of my own island than I could find alone'. Errol Hill was thanked for 'technical advice with the script'.[21]

An extremely powerful play, set, like *Sea at Dauphin,* on the north-east coast of St Lucia, *Ione* takes place at Aux Lyons among the Neg Djine, descendants of Guineans who settled after emancipation. *Ione* is another of Walcott's works which involve mulattos, bastardy, and ownership of the land. Half-brothers lead two tribes who war over the land. The Alexandres are mixed blood, or bastards. Victorin is proud that he is a full-blooded Guinean, but Ione, his daughter is having a child by an American, and his other daughter, Helene, has a son with Achille, an outside warrior whom she was forced to marry to increase her father's land. Achille causes the smaller battles to become total war when he kills Diogene, son of Alexandre, who has bedded Helene. He also kills his own son, leaving Victorin heirless. The play blends the local and classical, the fight between two tribes resembles the Trojan War, a version of Virgil's epic. Theresine is the prophet foretelling doom, a local Cassandra or Tiresias. The Beggar acts as the chorus. Other classical conventions are the unities of time, place, and action. Helene, Achille, Theresine look forward to a similar but more developed use of classical characters for local life in *Omeros*. Behind the story are certain local concerns, such as the way black St Lucians in the past divided themselves into two different African groups, and the continuing disputes about land ownership, especially among mulattos and those with complicated family lineages. Walcott has said the play was based on events in St Lucia and it is difficult to avoid thinking that some of his family history led him to this subject.[22]

Ione had much publicity from February onwards, with at least four pieces in the *Daily Gleaner* before the Federal Theatre company's opening in mid-March, an article by Michael Manley (son of Norman Manley, the soon-to-be Prime Minister) in *Public Opinion*, followed by reviews in the *Daily Gleaner*, *Public Opinion*, and *West Indian Review*, and Walcott's letter to the *Daily Gleaner* in reply to Norman Rae's unfavourable review. The Trinidad production by the Company of Players was less controversial. *Ione* is powerful, but has not been revived since 1957 except for a 1996 production in Martinique. In 'Modern Theatre', his reply to Rae, and 'Christianity and Tragedy' in *Public Opinion*, Walcott claimed that no one knew what form West Indian theatre would take but that modern tragedy is always concerned with man's fight with his god.[23]

Walcott seemed to be marking time, but there was soon one of those major breakthroughs that are characteristic of Walcott's life. The Extra-Mural Department proposed that the celebrations for the opening of the West Indian Federation in Port of Spain during 1958 consist of a play about the previous four centuries of the region's history. The 'Unit' government agreed to the play and an Arts Festival. After looking at some scripts, the Department during June 1957 asked Walcott to write the pageant for the West Indian Arts Festival that was intended in 1958 to accompany the opening of the first West Indian Parliament, as the many British colonies in the region became a Federation and self-governing. The pageant was meant as the central event of the Festival and Errol Hill urged Faye not to divorce Derek at that time as it would interfere with his writing. The Arts Festival was to bring Walcott into a long relationship with the Rockefeller Foundation. John Harrison of the Rockefeller Foundation had been approached by Sherlock to help with developing theatre in the Extra-Mural Department and with the Festival, especially with the pageant.

John Parker Harrison joined the Rockefeller Foundation in 1956 as an Assistant, later Associate, Director for the Humanities, after having taught at several American universities. Beside his professional specialization in Latin America, he had a strong personal interest in theatre, which was in keeping with the Rockefeller Foundation's decades of supporting regional Little Theatre in the United States and theatre research in universities. With the movement of decolonization that had followed the Second World War and the subsequent Cold War, the Rockefeller Foundation became involved in helping the new universities that were being developed as the colonies prepared for independence. Sherlock thought that the performing arts were a means to create a common culture among the various groups in the West Indies. After approaching the Ontario Shakespeare Festival for help, Sherlock was directed to Harrison, who at first reluctantly involved the Rockefeller Foundation.

In June Harrison was in Trinidad as part of a trip through South America. He spoke about drama with Beryl McBurnie, whom he thought wild, and Noel Vaz, whom he trusted. Both McBurnie and Vaz said that talent left the region as there was no core around which to work. Walcott was the best playwright and literary talent and would leave for England to see his plays better performed. Vaz feared that the proposed dramatic pageant would be a mess and wanted Tyrone Guthrie to be brought in to help, but the script needed to be by a West Indian.

Walcott's concerns had been with how to use Caribbean subject-matter and speech in alien forms. He was soon attracted towards creating a West Indian acting style. In August there was the first Creative Arts Summer School (sponsored by the Extra-Mural Department along with the Adults Drama Festival Committee and the Jamaica Social Welfare Commission). There were two courses, in dance and drama, and some subsidiary courses in such areas as theatre management, West Indian theatre, and community recreation. The aim was to foster a better understanding of drama and dance, to train community leaders, and to improve practical knowledge for those involved in the community theatre. Errol Hill was director of drama studies. Reuben Silver, visiting tutor, was drama director at Karamu House, Cleveland. The director of dance was the Jamaican Ivy Baxter, but the star turned out to be Beryl McBurnie from Trinidad, who was visiting tutor, assisted by another Trinidadian, Jeff Henry. The Summer School introduced Walcott to the work of Beryl McBurnie, an energetic dynamic dancer who a decade earlier had returned to Trinidad from working professionally in the United States to build her Little Carib Theatre. Hardly more than a shed in her backyard, the LCT soon became a legend. McBurnie, who had worked with some of the best modern dancers in the United States, had researched folk dances throughout the region and brought them together in the first local modern folk dance company.

Roderick Walcott, who attended the Summer School, wrote about its significance over two issues of the *Voice of St Lucia*. It was the first time Caribbean dance and drama were linked at UCWI. Besides lectures on acting, speech, make-up, movement, and lighting, movement in ballet was taught by Ivy Baxter and Caribbean folk dancing by Beryl McBurnie. 'During the week the rehearsals of Beryl McBurnie were beginning to draw interest from both students and members of the public alike. Dynamic evening sessions in the West Indian Dance were developing into something more novel and vibrant in interpretation, clearly individualistic because of the intense personality of the tutor . . . it was for some a first glimpse of genius propelled by mastery of communication.' McBurnie fused the various dance traditions of the region while Hill's talk about West Indian theatre produced volatile discussion. All great cultural eras spring from some great school of thought or fashion, and the significance of the Arts Summer School was accentuated by national consciousness. Hill's lecture brought this into focus. It became apparent to those in search of a 'West Indian Style' in the theatre that the new West Indian artist must be a versatile performer, and that the art of the dance and the actor must merge and evolve into something novel and vibrant in expression. 'The unlimited resources that folklore provides was made clear' by McBurnie.[24]

As a result of seeing McBurnie's company, Derek Walcott would want to create an acting style which was West Indian in body movement and gestures, a style of acting close to dance.

In September, on a small Rockefeller Foundation grant, Walcott, Vaz, and Hill travelled to Stratford, Ontario, and New York to consult Tyrone Guthrie about the West Indian Arts Festival. Guthrie was unwilling to take responsibility, said it should be directed locally, and gave Walcott some advice such as using Hardy's *Dynasts* as a model. The group then discussed the situation with Harrison. Staying in a New York hotel, Walcott was scared of the big city and recalled his time in rural St Lucia when his aunt Sidone would tell him and Roderick folk tales. He rapidly wrote a play based on such tales, *Ti-Jean and His Brothers*, and sent it to Roddy, handwritten with illustrations for the scenery, costumes, and suggestions as to who should act the parts. Such rapid writing was unusual for Derek, who normally had to labour over his plays. Throughout his career, however, Derek's manuscripts and typescripts have been filled with drawings and paintings offering his vision of what he imagined on stage.

By mid-October planning for the Caribbean Festival of Arts was underway and Walcott had written a first draft of *Drums and Colours*. The various islands were to be represented by drama, dance, and painting; the Arts Guild was likely to prepare two plays, Derek's *The Sea at Dauphin* and Roderick's *Banjo Man*. The Central Organizing Committee for the West Indian Arts Festival suggested that a collection of verse be published for the Festival and that the next issue of *Caribbean Quarterly* be used for the purpose. Potential contributors from the Windward Islands were at first told to submit material to Derek Walcott in Castries before the end of November, but as he was too busy the resident Extra-Mural tutor took over.[25]

Walcott left Jamaica with Noel Vaz in December for Trinidad. His marriage had ended before he left, but he was reticent about his personal life and continued to speak of Faye as his wife. He went on to St Lucia for the production of his new play *Ti-Jean*. Bruce Procope, who was a member of the Central Committee of the West Indian Festival, arrived separately, and a St Lucia Arts Committee for the Festival was hurriedly formed including Harold Simmons (editor of the *Voice of St Lucia* from late 1957 until April 1959), Kenneth Monplaisir (President of the Arts Guild), the Resident UCWI Tutor, the Minister of Social Services, and a few others.

Roderick Walcott's 'Preview' of 'Ti-Jean and His Brothers' argued that all stories are part of a universal story that Adam's seed took around the world. The Ti-Jean legend is found throughout the French-speaking Caribbean and appears to have its origins in French folklore, although it is often said that the Caribbean version shows the influence of African trickster tales. Such folklore and culture should be preserved especially in these days of nationalism. The basic plot of Walcott's play is that the Devil, bored, wants to feel emotion and will reward whoever will make him lose his temper but will eat the losers. Gros Jean, the older brother (representing physical qualities) is given such impossible tasks as catching a goat that has magical abilities, catching seven fireflies, and counting all the leaves on the estate where he is a labourer. He soon tires, is caught smoking by the Devil-Planter (representing the white man), who nags him. Gros Jean loses his temper and is eaten. Mi Jean, the middle brother and a fisherman (representing philosophy), has more patience than Gros Jean at doing physical tasks. He refuses to speak with the Planter-Devil until tricked into a discussion of the difference between man and beasts. Mi-Jean claims to have a spark of divinity within him, but loses his temper when the Devil says man makes more noise than animals; the goat Mi-Jean is chasing is superior. By contrast Ti-Jean, the younger brother (representing common sense and rebellion) disobeys whatever the Devil says, and does whatever will get the Devil-Planter angry. Instead of tying up the goat he castrates and kills him. Instead of counting the leaves on the estates, he tell the workers to burn down all the estates. When the Devil loses his temper, Ti-Jean asks for nothing and the Devil is made to feel a fool, thus bringing about the return of Gros Jean and Mi Jean. Ti-Jean leaves home to make his way in the world. Although the play obviously refers to racial, economic, and class matters, its main message is spiritual. Slade Hopkinson said that its message is that one must earn the world—only by renunciation of the material world is it possible to be spiritually content.[26]

Harold Simmons reviewed the production critically. He felt that the last scene dragged along without purpose and lacked rehearsal. The production was started by Roderick but he did not finish it as he thought Derek would return in time to produce his own play; Derek, however, only returned ten days before the opening. As would at times happen with productions with which Derek Walcott was involved, the opening night was bad, a nightmare, but the production improved on the second. Some people prudishly objected to the curse words.[27]

The Rockefeller Foundation continued to have a role in Walcott's career and the emergence of a modern West Indian culture. This was a consequence of the promotion of Modernist high culture into the period of Cold War and decolonization. Towards the end of the Second World War the Rockefeller Foundation, in supporting high culture as part of the transition to peace, had brought together Southern conservative Agrarian new critics with New York ex-Marxist intellectuals to form a new consensus of those favourable towards Modernist literature, whether it be the poetry of Eliot, Pound, and Stevens, or the European Modernist novels of Kafka, Dostoevsky, and Proust. Freudian and Marxian analysis, angst, existentialism, and social democratic politics bedded with formalist analysis, explication of texts, and respect for traditions, even religion, as *Partisan Review* and *Kenyon Review* started sharing mutual interests and tastes, and their contributors applied to the Rockefeller Foundation for support. While the actual funding available was small, the effect was large, bridging two previously different groups of intellectuals and critics, and by 1954 the Modernist tradition had become the natural crown of the Humanities tradition of Western culture; the Bible, Homer, Virgil, Dante, and Donne led to T. S. Eliot and Kafka.

One curiosity of this union was the wedding of the Agrarians, regionalists who emphasized sensuous, local, lived experience, with the intellectualism, cosmopolitanism, belief in the unconscious, and *Zeitgeist* thinking of the New Yorkers. Nostalgia for some supposedly unfallen Roman Catholic Europe, for some mythic pre-historical primitivism, for some unity of being, which was part of a radical European right (and noticeable in the writings of Yeats, Lawrence, and Eliot) was now part of a cocktail with a central European Jewish anxiety concerning identity, instability, deracination, and the contradictions of freedom. Walcott, reading modern literature and critics in St Lucia and Jamaica, imbibed this vision as I did at Columbia University.[28]

By the mid-1950s Rockefeller concern with postwar culture was being influenced by the Cold War. Funding was denied those suspected to be Communists, while support was available for those attending conferences organized by the Congress for Cultural Freedom. Funds were made available to overseas projects at the new universities and other institutions, as former colonies prepared for national independence. The sums were small and grants were carefully evaluated for the usefulness of the proposed projects and the chances of their succeeding; most projects were turned down, and the officers showed a remarkable nose for what proved to be worthwhile in the way of scholarship or creativity. In the past Rockefeller Foundation aid had gone to medical schools abroad to wipe out tropical diseases or to English departments for scholarly projects, so that aiding the new universities of the rapidly dissolving British Empire was not a major departure, and was in keeping with former interests. Only the context had changed.

Such help was given to the new University College of the West Indies, the University College of Ibadan, and other new universities, with the emphasis on medical schools and similar professional areas where research was likely to be beneficial to the public. To a lesser extent there was help establishing theatre departments, or the study of local culture. Cultural decolonization speeded up as local scholars and artists were encouraged by the attention and small grants they received. Wole Soyinka and Derek Walcott were among the beneficiaries. Both were unusually intelligent, educated in the Western classics, well read in Modernist classics, poets with a concern for the structure of texts and the ambiguities of words, and fascinated by myth; they were social democrats with a strong instinctive dislike of repression and therefore of Stalinism. Both dramatists created a modern regional literature by themselves researching part of the folk tradition and by using recent scholarship by others concerning local traditions. They were associated with the new university colleges, Soyinka with the University College of Ibadan, Walcott with the University College of the West Indies. Both opposed the backward-looking nationalism, traditionalism, and black racism that were at various times the ideology of some African and Caribbean governments, and both found it possible to be universalists with deep roots in their local culture.

8

~~~~~~

1958 The West Indian Festival of the Arts, *Drums and Colours*

ON 8 February 1958 Walcott arrived in Port of Spain and stayed at first with Bruce Procope, a lawyer who was co-chair of the Festival Committee. He had an introduction to Irma (Billie) Pilgrim from John Hearne and soon moved to 6 Bengal Street, St James, a house co-rented by Veronica Jenkin and Pilgrim (later Goldstraw) where he stayed off and on for a few years. Jenkin, a British schoolteacher, was active in the arts. Pilgrim, who was educated in England, is from a well-known West Indian family that includes the dramatist Frank Pilgrim. The house was a gathering place for artists and intellectuals, and they always had a place available for Walcott for which he chipped in with a financial contribution whenever he could. Decades later Walcott would still smile recalling a Queen's Counsellor, Selby Wooding, who played quatro (a small four-string guitar) into the night. Laurence Goldstraw, a British naval officer with a strong interest in the arts, had heard of Derek Walcott and wanted to meet him, and was told by Billie, whom he was seeing, that Walcott was staying at her place. Walcott had found a lively, racially mixed group of those interested in the arts, a friendly river in which to swim.

Port of Spain had a reputation for the arts. Trinidadian dancers were famous abroad and leaders in 'black' modern dance at the time. Cruise ships stopped there for its fabled night life, floor shows, and for the shopping. Its private schools were excellent and many of their graduates went to England for further education. Colour and class made for differences, but they were not firm in Trinidad. It was for a long time a Spanish colony without settlers. When it was conquered by the British it became a refuge for those in the Caribbean fleeing the effects of the French Revolution and later the revolutions of Latin America. There had been many free blacks and mulattos, and the period of slavery was short. After emancipation it had imported workers from Madeira, China, and in large numbers from both north and south India. There were communities of Amerindians who had bred with Africans, there were black Americans who had fought for the British. The various nationalities, origins, shades, religions, and other social complexities, along with education, meant a place of rich differences rather than tightly held distinctions. In any case the distinctions of the past were breaking down. The American presence and base during the Second World War had brought money, opportunity, social mobility, and a casualness about class and race. It was a time, as the famous calypso had it, of working for the Yankee dollar; this could be done in many ways, as a driver, a builder, or on one's back.

During and after the war, Port of Spain attracted a group of educated progressives interested in politics and culture. After the austerities of England, the colonies offered a new world of opportunities including the experience of being part of a society in rapid change as it moved towards decolonization. Except in a few places, such as Kenya and Rhodesia, England was rapidly and willingly shedding its colonies, which it could no longer afford. India had become independent, Ghana became independent in 1957, and the West Indian Federation was to follow in 1958. As racial, religious, and other barriers were broken, as new educational opportunities were offered, and as the local arts became valued alongside European arts, those who shared in this experience inhabited a charmed circle.

Port of Spain was such an area. As the capital of the future federation, it attracted bright energetic young West Indians from Jamaica and the other islands, who saw it as a place of jobs, patronage, social, and cultural life. It attracted Walcott, who, having already moved from St Lucia, Grenada, and Jamaica, would now take root.

When Walcott arrived in Port of Spain, he was homeless, shell-shocked from a broken marriage, and wanted to avoid his past. He had planned to leave the region, but did not know how. Port of Spain offered him hospitality, friendship, a new start. Trinidad offered variety in its many races, cultures, religions, mixtures. When Procope took him by car around the island, he was struck by the Indian villages. Port of Spain was cosmopolitan and yet small, manageable, a collection of villages. There were some old families—white, black French, Spanish—but many families were immigrants from small islands, like Barbados, Grenada, St Vincent. There was a history of French culture, but more significant was the Spanish heritage. Older people often still spoke a Spanish-based Creole. Trinidad was near South America, small boats went back and forth to Venezuela. Architecturally the city was a treat. There were old wooden French buildings like in Castries before the 1948 fire. There were large mansions around Queen's Park. Port of Spain, like Castries, is a waterfront city surrounded by mountains.

Port of Spain was a centre of the new West Indian culture with the first theatre groups, Beryl McBurnie's Little Carib and other dancers, calypso, steel bands, and a wealthy community that could support the arts. As the temporary capital of the new West Indian Federation, it was the likely site for a national theatre. Besides Trinidad only Jamaica could afford professional artists. The other islands were too small and too impoverished. Walcott came to Trinidad with introductions to its upper bohemia, was treated well, fell in love with the city, then with Margaret Maillard, and would remarry. He would not, however, become a Trinidadian; he was St Lucian. As much as he admired calypso, steel band, and Carnival, he remained a small island Methodist and the hard-working son of a teacher. He could not join in the street jump-ups; his infidelities left him with a sense of guilt and damnation.

Trinidad was also known as the sink of Caribbean corruption, but it was energetic and proud of its many peoples and local culture. Eric Williams, the leader of the main political party, would later prove to be another corrupt tyrant, but for the present he was a black London University intellectual who had written excellent books about the relationship of slavery to capitalist imperialism and looked benignly on the arts. Williams was engaged in a struggle with the Hindu Indian community, who feared that independence would leave them at the mercy of a then black majority, but the circles in which Walcott moved were pro-Williams, pro-Federation, West Indian nationalists. Several of his actors were members of the government or top civil servants. Beryl McBurnie had been one of Williams's students during the days he was a schoolteacher.

The Arts Festival and the emphasis on theatre in the UCWI Extra-Mural Department had been designed to overcome the many religious, racial, ethnic, and regional differences in the West Indies. The creation of a secular cultural space in St Lucia, however, accentuated the difference between the Roman Catholic hierarchy and the Methodists. Noel Vaz, director of *Drums and Colours*, had arrived in early January to take stock of St Lucia's entry to the West Indies Arts Festival and to take Walcott to Trinidad, where casting and rehearsals would begin in February. Vaz met with the *ad hoc* St Lucia committee. Soon afterwards the Arts Guild decided to present *Sea at Dauphin* and Roderick Walcott's *The Banjo Man* as its contribution to the Festival. Rehearsals started in late February with the idea of mounting local productions on 10–12 April at the Roman Catholic Boys' School to raise funds for the trip to Trinidad. This soon led to a crisis that was discussed throughout the West Indies, and which was part of a continuing battle within St Lucia between the Anglophone modernizing minority led by the Methodists and the conservative Roman Catholic hierarchy, concerning education, culture, and the Church's role in society. In the 1990s, even after Derek Walcott was awarded the Nobel Prize in Literature, there were those in the Church hierarchy still complaining about the Walcotts and questioning whether Dunstan St Omer, who had devoted his life and art to the Church, might not have fallen into heresies and become a bad influence. Indeed as the Church itself modernized with local black priests—some of whom would become interested in liberation theology, black theology, and St Lucian cultural nationalism—attitudes towards the Walcotts and St Omer became the focus of heated skirmishes concerning control of the direction of the local Church.

The Banjo Man became Roderick's best-known play. The Banjo Man himself is a Dionysian figure, a wandering homeless artist and entertainer who tells jokes and stories, who sings and plays music for dancing. He is necessary for important social functions and is loved by the women who see in him the opposite of their husbands. He loves, leaves, often leaving a future child behind. The play itself is in part a recreation of the La Rose Festival, a St Lucian custom with a history of perhaps 200 years. Most St Lucians traditionally belonged to either the Rose or the Magrit, Marguerite, society, which dressed up, elected kings, queens, and other members of a court to preside over an annual festival and parade, part of which was devoted to satirizing or competing with the other society. A form of Carnival, with mixed European and African origins, the festivals were a subject of anthropological research during the mid-century by Simmons and Daniel Crowley. (Roderick Walcott's play includes a visiting American anthropologist who is recording the festival without being aware of what is happening in front of him.) Dunstan St Omer has made paintings of a contemporary saxophonist whom he describes as his Banjo Man, his version of the Dionysian artist living for wine, women, and song.[1]

After ten weeks of rehearsals, the Arts Guild, in mid-March, withdrew *The Sea at Dauphin* and *The Banjo Man* from the Festival after the Vicar-General ruled *The Banjo Man* immoral and forbade its production and Roman Catholic actors from performing in it. The parish priest of Castries refused the use of the Boys' School for fund-raising productions of *The Sea at Dauphin* and *The Banjo Man*. The Roman Catholic members of the Arts Guild followed their Church and refused to participate, causing the Arts Guild to cancel St Lucia's participation in the Arts Festival. Harold Simmons protested against the control the Church exerted over the actors and the control of the Church over St Lucia's culture. The situation caused much outcry in the region, where it was seen as an example of conservative outsiders opposing the flowering of West Indian arts and nationalism.

The decision of the Guild to withdraw was taken at a 6 March meeting of a committee comprising B. H. Easter (chair), H. D. Boxill, Kenneth Monplaisir, Roderick Walcott, Dunstan St Omer, Harold Simmons, and two others. Grace Augustin was on the committee but did not attend. The *Voice of St Lucia* reported that 'the majority of the committee did not endorse the play, and Mr. Harold Simmons resigned from the Committee in protest'. After Simmons withdrew from the committee Kenneth Monplaisir and Roderick Walcott refused to participate further.[2]

The same issue of the *Voice of St Lucia* carried a heated column by Simmons in which he called those who banned *The Banjo Man* dictators of the theatre. This was not the first time the arts and the expression of West Indian culture had been banned. In April 1944 the Roman Catholics on the Board of Censors banned the film *Green Pastures* as misrepresenting heaven. In 1945 when the steel band was beginning in Castries there was an outcry against it. The headmaster of St Mary's College threatened to expel students who played in steel bands. 'The West Indies will only have an art . . . when we are allowed the freedom to express freely our emotions as a result of experience of our way of life and our people. In the Caribbean especially, there can be no great art unless there is the freedom to weld the international traditions of culture with that of our local expressions or style.' Simmons described *The Banjo Man* as a slice of life about a loud-mouthed strolling minstrel-wastrel who drinks heavily and brags of his seductions without being made contrite. He claimed that there was now an inquisition against showing the everyday life of the island—that some would say that the play about the La Rose festival was banned by a priest who belonged to the rival Marguerite society.[3]

Charles Gachet, FMI, Bishop of Castries, on 15 March defended the judging of *The Banjo Man* by the standards of the Church's faith and morals. True Christian freedom is the power to choose what is good and right and to reject what is bad and wrong. No one ever said that everything that passes for art should be permitted. The Church is not against local culture and Pope Pius XII said that religion should not be identified with Western culture. But this play would give St Lucia a reputation for corrupt morals. 'Some have taken advantage of this incident to defend false notions of Freedom and Nationalism . . . We ask all good Catholics to stand firm in the defense of Christian Civilization.' This statement was read at the Masses in the Cathedral.[4] It is thought that Jesse was advising Gachet who would have instructed Father Vrignaud, who made the original decision about the play. This was a replay of the match about '1944' with more players and more at stake, but the issues and sides were mostly the same as before.

The following week, 22 March, Harold Simmons's regular Spotlight column was given over to two guest columns concerning the withdrawal of the Arts Guild from the West Indian Festival of the Arts. There was also an editorial note published along with the article claiming that both the correspondence and the opinions expressed by the columnists 'do NOT necessarily Express the views held by Editors of the VOICE'.[5]

B. H. Easter pointed out that there really was no committee. When Derek Walcott and Bruce Procope came from Trinidad in December, they called some people together who were asked what St Lucia would contribute to the Festival. Since there was no one representing the government, Easter as Extra-Mural Tutor became chair of the informal group. As the Arts Guild was heavily represented on the committee, the drama side was left to them. Easter did not read the play until March, by which time there was already a controversy. He felt it could not be presented as 'the whole effect of the Play was to glorify drunkenness, fornication, seduction and general lechery'. He was not surprised that the Roman Catholic authorities disapproved; it would have been banned by any censorship body. He was surprised that there was no official censorship of the stage in St Lucia as there was in England. He hoped this would not discourage Simmons and the Arts Guild from 'further activities within the limits imposed by the conscience of a Christian community'.[6]

Kenneth Monplaisir as President of the Arts Guild replied that during its eight years it had been non-denominational, non-political, and did not encourage class prejudice. At its inaugural meeting they had discussed the matter of art and morality and decided that if truth is expressed honestly then the question of immorality should not arise. At St Joseph's Convent they deleted Scene 4 of *Henri Christophe* as some Sisters claimed that some lines spoken by a character were heretical. After the Methodist Minister objected to showing J. S. Barker's *Bond of Matrimony* at the Methodist school because it contained gambling and concubinage, the Presentation Brothers allowed them to show it at the College. *The Sea at Dauphin* was attacked by Catholicus. Before *The Banjo Man* and *The Sea at Dauphin* were even read by the Arts Guild, Monplaisir had received correspondence objecting to the morals and complaining about blasphemy. The Guild had shown the scripts to Fr. Vrignaud and had discussed his objections. But it was known that Catholic Youth League members had been asked to withdraw and it was too late to recast the play. Many actors thought there was nothing wrong with the play, the producers had toned down or deleted some words and parts of the script, but Fr. Vrignaud still said there was no way the play could be changed to make it acceptable. He had also objected to parts of *The Sea at Dauphin* which he claimed were objectionable although the play had already been staged throughout the Caribbean and in London. The Arts Guild had tried to help CYO members put on shows. It was not anti-Roman Catholic, but the Arts Guild did not intend to stifle self-expression in its quest for West Indian culture. The common heritage of St Lucia is 'our slave background' which should be depicted in art and which people fear.[7]

The same day the *Voice* published a letter to the editor from Catholicus (Father Jesse) dated 16 March, in which *Banjo Man* is characterized by 'incidents, remarks, suggestions and allusions of drunkenness, fornication, seduction and lust'. There was a shocking piece of blasphemy in the story of God playing dice with the Devil for a drink of rum. The hero was a scurrilous old rake who seduced women and fathered bastards. *The Sea at Dauphin* irreverently used God's Holy Name several times, and even more objectionable than the story of forbidden fatalism was profanity bordering on blasphemy. Another letter, this one titled 'Vive La Rose', in the same issue signed by 'La Rose' complained that *The Banjo Man* portrayed 'our country people' unfavourably before the world and that 'a strong sex element and cuss words' were not art and culture. The Vicar-General was right. The dramatist could always write another play using a different subject.[8] Forty years later I would hear echoes of the dispute when John Figueroa, who is Roman Catholic, complained to me that John Hearne and Derek Walcott believed only in art to the exclusion of other matters.

As the life of the cultural organization was involved because of the publicity and the high-handed behaviour of the Roman Catholic clergy, Roderick felt it now necessary to discuss issues the Arts Guild had avoided during its eight years. Artists were aware they were privileged to be endowed by the

Creator's greatest gift to mankind, the gift of creation. With the greatest gift comes the greatest agonies, the sins of the super ego, of indolence, of despair in his dedication. It gnaws at his very existence, and he cannot hide his candle under a bushel or bury it in the ground like the man in the parable. . . . Consequently, the abuse of his God-given graces in such unethical practices as over-indulgence, plagiarism, and self-inspired messianic propaganda are some of the cardinal sins of which the artist must give an account to his Maker.

Roderick Walcott's Methodist assumptions are revealed in the allusion to the parable, although at times his vocabulary seems Roman Catholic. Roderick agreed that the possible sin of overindulgence was central to the present controversy and admitted that some artists had been guilty of such indiscipline. Works sacrificed to the altar of hedonism and usually forgotten included the *Decameron*, Shakespeare's 'Venus and Adonis', and some novels by Zola. The artist, however, must be honest to the creative urge and in seeking truth interpret life's complexities. Artists had often quarrelled with their patrons as Michelangelo quarrelled with Pope Julius II concerning the decoration of the Sistine Chapel.[9]

Having introduced the topic of art's relationship to the supposedly obscene and past wrong-headedness by those in authority, Roderick Walcott went on to ask who would have burnt the first draft of James Joyce's *Ulysses* or slashed Rubens *Rape of the Sabines*? To have harmed Rodin's *The Kiss* would have been criminal. People should not prevent or destroy works of art even if they are at first thought to be obscene; time will determine what has truly reflected life and used the artists' divinely given talent. The work of Diego Rivera, 'the Western Hemisphere's greatest painter', was not retouched to comply with the Church. 'This mirror up to nature, this life-capturing preoccupation we call art' must 'catch the essence of living'. All arts, whether the music of Palestrina or the dance of the Watusi, were the creator serving the Creator in dedication. There could be no immorality in Truth. 'Sin, or immorality, was created by Man.' Immoral topics were not in themselves obscene. Plays by Sophocles and Shakespeare treat of incest, parricide, despair; parts of the Bible have been called immoral. Fornication and bastardy would always remain moral issues in St Lucia because common-law marriage was the Creole way. The West Indies was ashamed of its ancestry and because of its pseudo-European middle-class affections decried preserving its cultural origins. Passages from *Banjo Man* were called obscene although the play has a moral theme if examined more closely. Roderick claimed to have used the realism of the American theatre to show a Creole country festival.

His assumptions were similar to those of Derek, although Derek's opposition was later more likely to be politicians and the politically inspired rather than Catholic priests, but both come to argue for the independence of art from its relationship to God; it is a divinely given gift which imitates God's Creation. True art necessarily must be mimicry of the Creator and the created.

The controversy continued with the Catholic leadership attacking the *Voice of St Lucia* (owned by the Methodist Gordons and edited by the Methodist Simmons) and those who criticized Father Jesse. The Church was using the controversy as a means of enforcing conformity among its followers. No one could have assumed that Father Jesse as Catholicus could go unanswered and uncriticized after publishing articles in the newspaper which claimed that art was immoral if it used bawdy language or depicted immoral behaviour, yet the Church was claiming that right. The controversy was not about a play but about the authority of the Roman Catholic priesthood in St Lucia at a time when it felt threatened by a vital Protestant secular culture, led by the Methodists, and by the West Indian Federation. Over the decades the British administrators and the Church had learned to live together, but could the St Lucian Church still be given such consideration in a West Indian Federation?

Philip Sherlock, Extra-Mural Studies, and UCWI had pushed the theatre as a means of bringing the various peoples and religions of the region together into a shared culture, but the new West Indian theatre had become a source of conflict between St Lucian Methodists and Roman Catholics. The bringing together of people into an arts group and the putting on stage before the public of a play which identified local traditional culture with a pagan vitalism, indeed which could be interpreted as symbolizing the pagan vitalism of the artist, threatened the authority of the priesthood. Like many other groups which feared assimilation, the Church wanted greater separation. The 5 April issue of the *Voice of St Lucia* carried on the front page, along with the report of the Bishop's complaint at the behaviour of the *Voice*, a large lithograph of Dunstan St Omer's *The Crown of Glory*, specially done for the Easter issue. 'Dunstan's religious temperament promises to make him our principal Religious Painter of the Federation. In this drawing he symbolizes the passion of Holy Week and the Triumph of Easter, with the sufferings of the West Indian People and Glory of Freedom in the attainment of Nationhood.'[10]

In Trinidad Derek was being lionized. The 'Who's Who in the Festival', prepared by the Central Committee of the West Indian Festival of Arts, compared Walcott to Lord Byron. He became famous overnight with the publication of *25 Poems*, which were praised by Roy Fuller, Louis MacNeice, and George Campbell. He was reported to be preparing a new volume of poetry. His *The Wine of the Country* and *Ione* were described as recent plays written before he left Jamaica as were *Crossroads* and *Ti-Jean* which were presented by the Montego Bay Players and the Arts Guild. As a painter Walcott was not thought to have found his style which was described as ranging from Cézanne to Braque.[11]

On 22 April Princess Margaret inaugurated the first Federal Parliament of the West Indies. The Federation, which lasted until 1962, was intended to bring the various peoples of the region together into a political and economic union with the size and status of such dominions as Canada or Australia. Culture, especially theatre, was supposed to be the cement. On 23 April, the evening following political Inauguration Day, the West Indian Festival of the Arts opened with Princess Margaret, the Governor-General, and the Prime Minister of the new West Indian Federation at a special performance in which all the territories of the Federation were supposed to participate.

Although he could not bring *Banjo Man*, Roderick Walcott reported on the Arts Festival in two articles in the *Voice of St Lucia*. For the opening night the dancer Geoffrey Holder returned to Trinidad from the United States. Ivy Baxter's group did semi-classical ballet to Jamaican poems. The Little Carib offered less pretentious dances, especially the effective McBurnie *Spirit* (which Derek was later to use in *Dream*), and Louise Bennett was amusing. St Vincent presented the Bamboo Entertainers, a four-piece string and flute country band. Roderick thought the drama section of the festival disappointing. Hill's *Ping Pong* should have been better. Douglas Archibald's *Anne-Marie*, which concerned the emergence of 'West Indian coloured society', had good direction and acting, but lacked an ending. The highlights were in the dance section. While Ivy Baxter's work was tame Broadway, it offered showmanship, zeal, and sensitivity. Her classical abstractions on folk themes suggested that her destination might not be national consciousness. The Little Carib mainly interpreted national dances with intense vibrant authority, but McBurnie's choreography lacked imagination and range. The popular Jamaican pantomime *Busha Bluebeard* had high quality dancing and songs, but crude humour.[12]

The main event of the Festival was Walcott's 'epic' or 'pageant play' *Drums and Colours*, which had five performances between 25 April and 1 May at the Royal Botanical Gardens in Port of Spain which seated 3,000. This was an immense project, with a cast of about eighty, in which some scenes were first rehearsed on the home island before being brought to Trinidad.

Although British Guyana had decided not the join the Federation, it sent various woods to be used for the stage and wings. This was an imitation of the

Stratford, Ontario, Shakespeare Festival stage, with a fixed permanent gallery at the back from which the stage projected outward, around which the audience sat on three sides, the first time such an 'Elizabethan' stage was used in the West Indies. It was a three-level, open-air apron stage, with many entrances. The 'wings' were a work of art consisting of eight beautiful woods. Such a stage, with no detailed scenery, put emphasis on the spoken word and action. Exits and entrances could be rapid. It was assumed that such a stage, as explained by Noel Vaz, who was the producer as well as now the Extra-Mural Drama Tutor in Trinidad, 'should create a style of acting too which is broad, three dimensional, and as dependent on physical vitality as is pure dance'. In his own contribution to the Festival souvenir publication, Walcott wrote that he was 'lucky to be the first West Indian writer to use a stage so suitable for our drama'. Many of the ideas Walcott would use for his own Theatre Workshop were already being offered, including some he would need to oppose, such as that the tropics were ideal for a Greek open-air theatre. Some Festival performances were ruined by rain.[13]

The Arts Festival had become, as its organizers feared, a larger event than the West Indies could handle on its own. The Trinidad government wanted but was unwilling to pay for it and was criticized for what it did spend. The Canada Council helped and the Rockefeller Foundation sent several assistants including John Robertson, who stayed for two months and planned the lighting design. Vaz was responsible for handling the hundred or so people involved each night.

Roderick reported that *Drums and Colours* was visually patterned so that the steps upon which the heroes ascended led to harsh lights and the end of each age. This was what the heroes shared. Each hero represented an epoch's tragedy. 'Columbus' humiliating return to Spain marks the Age of Discovery, and guilt . . . rests heavily on his snowy head.' In the final section there is a comic rebel, Pompey, a 'calypsoldier', an heroic parody like Falstaff in *Henry IV*. Roderick wrote that the play was long, no audience should be expected to attend more than three hours. It was an Herculean task, had brilliant writing and good acting, but it was untidy in its shape and the direction was not up to what was required. But nothing like it had ever been attempted before.

In the original Foreword to *Drums and Colours*, Vaz explained that Walcott's theme was War and Rebellion as illustrated by 'the lives of "four litigious men", Columbus, the discoverer, Raleigh, the conqueror, Toussaint, the rebel, and Gordon, one of the first martyrs of constitutional rights—betrayed, corrupted, misjudged or mitigated against'.

In the last section, from Emancipation to Federation . . . he makes his comment on nationhood in the poignant speech of Pompey, the shoemaker, as he dies in the arms of his comrades . . . Walcott seizes upon the disturbed moments of crisis in the lives of his four protagonists . . . the play reveals . . . the ideal of endeavour which prompted these pioneers and the irony of circumstances in which they suffered seeming defeat.[14]

It is often assumed that national political independence was viewed with unbridled optimism in the former colonies and that those who had their reservations were complicit with the colonizers rather than wise before their time about the ways of politicians and all rulers. *Drums and Colours* illustrates Walcott's sceptical humanism. History teaches that all races and nations are alike, that revenge is wrong, that empires and personal life end in failure and tragedy. Two years later Wole Soyinka, commissioned to write *The Dance of the Forest* to celebrate Nigeria's independence, would also look at history with disillusionment, warning of never-ending cycles of war, corruption, tribalism, and enslaving of other Africans. The best writers of the independence generation were sceptical, partly because they were products of Modernism and distrusted political rhetoric, but also because their experience of life and themselves had already warned them.

Walcott realized that the play would never again be mounted with such an expensive full-scale production and thought of it in terms of a series of one-act plays. He wrote it in a way that made it possible to take sections and play them as self-contained segments by using linking passages already provided in the text. Roderick was later to edit and adapt the play into a more cohesive structure for the Arts Guild. Besides the historical progression, the language evolves as it changes with each period, so that each has a different style of language and a different manner of acting.[15] The Haitian and French Revolutions are written about in a style close to the Alexandrine, while in the Gordon section Walcott uses some dialect. He had in mind Thomas Hardy's *Dynasts*, also a dramatic epic in various styles of verse and poetic prose. In Hardy's verse play, Napoleon creates a new order, whereas in Walcott's the Haitians become insane tyrants rather than true liberators.

Drums and Colours begins with a framing device that Walcott was to use in several of his plays, including *Batai, Dream on Monkey Mountain*, and *The Joker of Seville*, in which there is an introductory scene that leads into the story. Here there is a Carnival in which people decide to make a masquerade of historical events.

In the first episode about Columbus, Paco, a West Indian of mixed Spanish-Indian blood, is confused and told not to trust nations but persons. There is only one race, Man. What could have been an opening act of blaming the Spanish turns into a scene of reconciliation expressive of the Federation. Then the scene shifts to Spain from where Africans are being sent to the West Indies as slaves and a Jew asks whether he could go there and live in peace. We are reminded of the Inquisition and the burning of Jews and later of the notion of the Wandering Jew. We are reminded that the Africans 'sell each other after their battles'—in other words all are guilty. One of the slaves, the son of an African king, is Mano, the same name as one of the characters in the prologue. Then comes a scene in which some soldiers play dice in a way that recalls the Passion, while the

Africans lament in the hold of the ship. History is being repeated in the Passion of the black slaves and also in the Wandering Jew. The Africans come from different tribes and one even from a victorious tribe who was sold and shipped by mistake. The Africans begin to see that they share customs and the same God, while earlier the sailors had spoken of God, thus showing that mankind is the same. As a British ship is sighted, the slaves on the ship revolt, and the Jew tells one of them that he will try to protect him; they will be outcasts together in the new world, the implication being that everyone in the New World is an outcast or Wandering Jew.

The next episode is set in Elizabethan England. Paco, now an old beggar, is given money by Raleigh to tell him of El Dorado, which is a lie and a form of revenge on the Europeans for what they did to the Indians. A chorus comments on the destruction of the Spanish Armada and on Raleigh's being freed by James I on condition he find El Dorado. Raleigh also has a vision of freeing Latin America from Spain and forming a British empire in which natives and the English would marry and breed. Raleigh sees a parallel between himself and Columbus; both are visionary explorers, rebels against their mercenary monarchs. When Raleigh questions Berrio about El Dorado, the old Governor of Trinidad complains at the English attack: policy should not be governed by European politics, which might be translated as the islands must have their own history, federation, view of politics, and shared identity and interests. The governor represents the tradition of European settlers for whom the region is now their home rather than Europe. Raleigh defeating the Spanish and Raleigh's own death mark the end of an age, and show that people of various nations are really the same. El Dorado is a myth which ruins people who seek gold. Raleigh's son sings a ballad 'Gather ye money, while ye may' a parody of Robert Herrick's 'To the Virgins', 'Gather ye rosebuds'.

There is an interlude, and Pompey from the prologue returns to address the audience in colloquial prose. We are told an amusing story about a black Barbadian servant who is more upper-class British in manner and attitude than an English sailor whom he looks down upon as a drunken poor white. This joke on the black Barbadians who regarded themselves as British is followed by the death of Raleigh, then a chorus about history and forgiving and learning to love 'our brothers'.

The third part concerns Haiti, which had been French for less than 100 years and had a large class of free black plantation owners, before the slave revolt of 1791 led to a free-for-all civil war. Races and factions fought until Toussaint L'Ouverture gained the upper hand, put down the rebellion, made the peasants work, invited back the landlords, and in 1801 made himself Governor-General. At the end of 1801 Napoleon sent his brother-in-law, General Charles Leclerc, to regain French authority. Walcott begins at this point. Leclerc admired Toussaint, thought he was right to abolish slavery, and wanted to convince Napoleon that he was wrong about the man and the people. Leclerc is cynical about romantic notions of liberty; he has seen how the French Revolution ended, and believes in order, but he is an élitist who believes more in good individuals who rule well. In this playlet Anton is the half-European, half-African figure, the illegitimate son of the landowner Armand Calixte. His mother was a slave. He is divided, a Haitian, but he is fearful because two mulatto Haitians who had fought in New World wars for freedom were tortured and executed. By contrast Toussaint was a slave before becoming a victorious general. He is devoted to France but also to the abolition of slavery. Anton knows that black slaves hate mulattos like himself, who are free and appear part of white society. Anton calls Pauline Leclerc 'White and lovely as the moon', anticipating the image of whiteness as a moon or moon goddess found in Walcott's later plays. Anton refuses to help put down a slave uprising and, ironically, is killed by the slaves for having a white father. Toussaint finds him and lifts his dead body, and the scene creates an image of Christ carrying the cross. Toussaint becomes a redeemer who saves his people and dies. Dessalines and Christophe replace Toussaint. In 1804 Dessalines claims he is Emperor, and Christophe calls himself King in 1811. Dessalines wants to kill whites and burn everything in the region. The new age is 'the black man's turn to kill'. In the play Dessalines and Christophe appear to have conspired with Leclerc to trap Toussaint, who is sent to France and dies in 1803. Dessalines is assassinated by a mulatto like himself.

By including Haiti, Walcott was warning about the possible failures of West Indian freedom, while Gordon is used to represent the present era, from Emancipation to the Federation. Gordon significantly is a bastard mulatto, his father a white Jamaican planter. Gordon became a merchant and Baptist preacher as well as the leader of a small reform movement. Elected to the Assembly in 1863, he challenged Governor Edward Eyre, who accused him of helping create the Morant Bay black rebellion of 1865 and had him hanged. Gordon's death became an important issue in England with Thomas Carlyle, Lord Tennyson, Charles Kingsley, Dickens, and Ruskin supporting Eyre, while John Stuart Mill, Darwin, Huxley, and Spencer wrote against him.

This final episode is introduced by a scene involving a quarrel between a white plantation owner and his black slave housekeeper, Yette (who was in the prologue). She predicts the coming failure of the sugar market and the ruin of the planters. There is a meeting of slaves at a nonconformist Christian mission. Pompey, a revolutionary preacher, is missing. He is a force of nature; after being clubbed to death by the Sergeant, Pompey rises 'resurrected'. Gordon then reads a short unheroic speech he will give before the Jamaican Assembly concerning liberty. Next we are shown Pompey as a revolutionary. Calico, the ruined planter, is captured by Yette, who has become a rebel and part of the political vanguard. She recruits him and Pompey to a Maroon camp. To show that the West Indies has no real power, Walcott portrays the camp and its leaders comically. Mano is now General Mano, commander of the Maroons. A Chinese cook is now General Yu, who believes 'An army travels on its stomach'. There is also Ram, an East Indian so addicted to rum that he says life was better under Napoleon. The rebellion thus includes others, not only blacks. Ram tells Pompey 'history not a judge, not a prophet, not a priest and not a executioner . . . Don't grudge'. As often in Walcott's writings, women are a species of their own. Women are victims yet detached from the men they look on. Yette says 'man is a beast'. When Pompey kills Yette, Calico and Yu know and pray in 'the multitude of names for the eternal God', showing the many cultures that are part of the West Indies. This is a play with no hero, except Pompey, the parody calypsoldier, the common person. There are parallels to emancipation and independence (which in this context is the Federation). As everyone leaves, Pompey is resurrected and says 'Don't leave me behind, the most important man in this country'. The unknown person is the hero, the most important.

I do not need to mention the number of motifs in the play which recur in Walcott's work, some of which, while common to Caribbean history, might be thought to have autobiographical sources. While *Drums and Colours* was too ambitious as theatre, it was a major cultural event and widely reviewed. Two headlines provide a summary of criticism. '*Drums and Colours* seeks to trace evolution of West Indian Consciousness', '*Drums and Colours*—Guts at Least'. Veronica Jenkin in *Bim* was concerned with how Walcott was learning to handle and move beyond his influences.[16]

Walcott was the young star of the pageant, wooed by an international West Indian, especially Trinidadian, artistic and social élite. He was offered the chance to sit with Princess Margaret, which he modestly refused. He invited Faye and Peter and treated Faye as his wife. Many of Walcott's friends from St Lucia and Jamaica were in the play as well as new and future friends from Trinidad. The cast included Leonard St Hill, Lloyd Stanford, Ronnie Llanos, Errol Hill, Jeff Henry, Horace James, Peter Minshall, Sydney Hill, Eunice Bruno, Jean Miles, Peter Ireson, Robert Head, Freddie Kissoon, and Errol Jones. Margaret Maillard, who was to be his second wife, was one of the three people in charge of sound. Clare Creteau, with whom he stayed, was house manager. There was an enormous round of social events, such as the Trinidad Art Society's Bal des Beaux Arts, a costume party with a steel band until 3 a.m. Walcott was already well known in West Indies artistic circles through his publications, the productions of his plays, and the *Caribbean Voices* broadcasts. He was socially sought after, the young, handsome, terribly intellectual, incredibly creative, if at times moody, prince, the rightful heir who would attract followers.

Drums and Colours was commissioned by the University College of the West Indies, which first published it, slightly revised, in a special issue of the *Caribbean*

Quarterly (1961), and then republished it decades later in a special Walcott issue of the *Caribbean Quarterly* in 1992. When Walcott asked to be paid for the first publication, he was told that he had already been paid as part of his fee for writing the play.

It needs to be kept in mind that Derek Walcott's notion of a career as a West Indian dramatist did not seem so unlikely at the time. He was only unique in thinking he could be a professional while remaining in the Caribbean. Alongside the take-off of the West Indian novel, there was a West Indian drama movement in Britain comprising several groups. In May *Adella* by Barry Reckord was staged at the King's Theatre, Southsea, with a new title, *Flesh to a Tiger*; it then moved to Cardiff for a week, then to the Royal Court Theatre in London where it opened on 21 May with Cleo Laine in a production by Tony Richardson.

Although *Drums and Colours* had preoccupied Walcott from mid-1957 for a year, his career as a poet continued. An early version of 'Tales of the Island' in *Bim*, 26 (January–June 1958), shows him trying to get a factual autobiographical plainness, and a Hemingway flat dispassionateness, into sonnets:

> Chapter 10.   you can't go home again
> That second summer I returned. We arranged
> To stay somewhere in the villages, . . .
>   . . . but except
> For the first few hours it was suddenly different,
> As if either the country or myself had changed,

After the Festival Walcott remained in Trinidad where he produced and directed *Ti-Jean and His Brothers* at the Little Carib Theatre on 27–9 June and on 2 July in San Fernando. The cast included the well-known local actor Horace James as Mi-Jean, the popular playwright Freddie Kissoon as Ti-Jean; the Mother was acted by Errol Hill's sister Jean (Hill) Herbert on opening night and afterwards by Veronica Jenkin. Most important Errol Jones took on the triple role of Devil, Old Man of the Forest, and Planter, because Ronald Williams was tied up in government business. Those involved with the production were already part of the local artistic, cultural, professional, and even government élites. The architect Colin Laird played clarinet in the small orchestra and designed the set. After *Ti-Jean* Walcott returned to St Lucia for the remaining three weeks in July.

Walcott's interest in the Ti-Jean folk legend, along with his use of patois in *Sea at Dauphin* and *Ti-Jean*, was part of a creolization movement among the brown middle class. The valorization of Creole, the attempt to make it into a modern literary language, was a product of those associated with the Arts Guild. Harry Simmons's American friend and anthropologist Daniel Crowley produced an easy-to-use orthography in which to write Creole, based on English modifying Haitian (rather than Martiniquan) spelling. Each letter would represent one sound only, except for a few common conjuncts from English, 'th', 'ch', 'ng'. Consonants were pronounced approximately as in English. Simmons approved and published it in the *Voice of St Lucia*.[17]

Over the next year or so a few poems would be published in Creole as part of a campaign to bring the oral culture of the island to the same prominence as written English. During February 1958 the *Voice of St Lucia* published two 'Ballades Creole pour Harry Simmons par Derek Walcott' consisting of 'La Plainte Un Vieux Femme' and 'La Plainte Un Vieux N'Homme' followed by Walcott's note that the first poem is based in theme and structure on Villon's 'La Belle qui fut Heaulmière'. 'La Plainte Un Vieux Femme' concludes:

> Moi ja diné à sur grand table,
> Moi tais connaitre vin blanc, dentelle,
> Moi tais ni amoureux comme sable,
> Un belle ti fille passeé s'autres belles
> Et toute ca tait bein agréable.
> Mais quand s'autres deboût en miroir,
> Songez la paine dún blanc bougie,
> Gardez par un fenêtre our voir
> La vieux reine sale, sou, acoroupie
> Qui tait comme un chose en marbre,
> En marbre, vraiement, un marbre en noir.

Walcott claims that Villon's language has a similar power and immediacy to St Lucian Creole. Creole is not primitive and obscene; it is vigorous and imaginative. Walcott would make similar claims during 1995 and again cite Villon's poetry and language in contrast to the academic orthography that was coming into use and which makes St Lucian look on paper like a language from another planet. Walcott's two poems are close to French and the orthography is similar to Crowley's.[18]

The next month the *Voice of St Lucia* published a poem in Creole, 'Il Faut Paller', by Irvin Gray, praising Derek Walcott for showing how to write in the language and Simmons for having encouraged such an example:

> Mal tete mwen calmer Samedi passé
> Comme mwen lis un Poem Walcott
> Ses un problem qui bien solvé
> Pour é crit ballad en Crèole.
>
> .   .   .   .   .
>
> Monsieur Simmons dávoir l'honneur
> Pour un belle ti ballad comme ca
> Coulait de yeux un plume si chèr
> Et dédiqué pour lui seulement.
>
> Un belle lecon nour kai apprendre
> Merci Monsieur Walcott, merci . . .[19]

There were several related issues and we are now perhaps more familiar with the complexities and ironies than were intellectuals and folklorists in the past. The preservation of folk history and its language involves change, modernization, selection, and standardization. The 'raw' Creole of the country and the Frenchified, Anglified, Creole of Castries would be different in lexis, idiom, grammar, and pronunciation. Is the aim preservation or standardization for renewal? Is it to allow the poor and country people economic, social, and cultural equality with the Anglophone élite or is the purpose nationalist and racial 'respect' by the élite? Much of the nationalism that has accompanied decolonization was the work of a middle-class colonial élite seeking cultural respect and political power. Walcott writing in the *Voice* about the literary possibilities of Creole, and translating a French classic into Creole as an example, might be said to be part of the middle-class élite addressing the middle class. Before such cultural nationalism is dismissed, it needs to be said that when St Lucian Creole was eventually systematized in accordance with academic standards, the results were visually grotesque and thought unusable by many. Pedantry can be worse than the bourgeoisie. My impression is that in St Lucia the promotion at this time of Creole and its culture by English speakers, and especially by the Methodists, meant that it gave them, as late immigrants, a usable local history that they might be said otherwise to lack. As English replaced French Creole the latter became a form of 'pastoral' in which European sources were emphasized.

In the *Voice of St Lucia* the brilliant West Indian Marxist historian Gordon Lewis claimed that the recent growth of middle-class self-consciousness was reflected in the development of the West Indian novel (in which middle-class writers portrayed picaresque social types), in the new respectability of Carnival in Trinidad, and in the concern for the previously suppressed Creole cultural heritage. He believed that their professional bias was thought by some to qualify their claims to represent the nation. The UCWI had created a new subgroup of intelligentsia with various competing schools, notably those insisting on an English European heritage and those claiming that West Indian culture must come from the masses. 'The onslaught of the St Lucian Catholic hierarchy on the Walcott brother-playwrights and in Mr Walcott's press attack upon Mr Sherlock, the latter episode in particular, dramatically emphasizing the truth that with the common enemy of British colonialism passing from the scene, the national progressive movement will reproduce the inevitable tension between the trade-union wing and the intellectual wing, so richly documented in the British experience of the Labour Party, in the Beatrice Webb *Diaries*.' The ideological vehicle for the middle-class advance would be West Indian nationalism. To prevent the intranational strife that happened in Haiti between brown élite and black masses, he urged intellectuals to work with the labour unions to join social justice to political liberty. In the same issue of the *Voice* there was an advertisement for the Arts Guild production of three St Lucian one-act plays of the West Indian theatre.[20]

In July Sherlock lectured in St Lucia about Ghana. Sherlock still mentions his surprise that Walcott did not have the same reverence for Africa and the history of resistance to slavery that was common in Jamaica. This was a standard difference between those from the south Caribbean and the Jamaicans. The histories of the two areas were different, but there was also the specific social location of the St Lucian Walcotts and the Methodists in making a secular space for art and education outside Roman Catholic authority, in which the revival of the Creole culture, which English was displacing, had its role.

For two generations the Walcotts had a central role in the creation of a St Lucian and West Indian culture. While Derek was the new star in Trinidad, the St Lucia Arts Guild toured to Dominica, where it presented two plays at St Gerald's Hall, Roseau. Dominicans said they had not seen such good performances in the West Indies. The Guild performed *Talk of the Devil* by Allan Weekes, his first play. Roderick Walcott's *Flight of Sparrows* had already been produced twice in Jamaica and won an award. The play concerns juvenile delinquency and the conversion of a murderer. Such conversion and Christian forgiveness are often found in Roderick Walcott's plays. At the end of the year there was a farewell party for Mrs Alix Walcott, retiring headteacher of Castries infant school.[21]

During the Arts Festival Derek Walcott met John Robertson. Robertson had worked with Joseph Papp during the summer Shakespeare in the Park, was stage-manager at the Phoenix Theatre, and was generally trusted by Harrison as knowledgeable, practical, and committed to serious theatre. Robertson thought Walcott exceptionally talented. Returning to New York in July, he told Harrison that it was essential for West Indian dramatists to have a theatre that could produce their works well. He felt that Walcott was likely to leave for London, but Walcott would learn more from New York theatre, especially off-Broadway, than from a university drama department.[22]

Robertson remained in contact with Walcott and began thinking about possible courses should he be granted a Rockefeller fellowship to study theatre in New York. There was a New Dramatists group at the Phoenix which Walcott could observe as it mounted productions and maybe join. José Quintero would accept him for a twenty-week course in directing. Harold Clurman's acting classes might be beneficial. Walcott could learn scenic design from Lester Polokov, basic scenic design from Lee Watson, and survey styles from Robert Fletcher. He might be an observer at the Actors Studio. Philip Sherlock (now Vice-Principal of University College) would be in New York soon. Would Harrison like Robertson to discuss with Sherlock how Walcott could contribute to the future department of drama?[23] A few days later Robertson again contacted

Harrison to ask whether Walcott had at last asked for the proper forms to fill in. How long would it take for the application to be approved? Robertson needed to know whether to keep the places open for Walcott in the courses he had arranged.

The *Voice of St Lucia* reported on 4 October that Walcott had sent a telegram to his mother saying he had been awarded a Rockefeller fellowship and was leaving for New York the following week. The *Voice* noted that the recommendation for the award was made in Jamaica and was a recognition of Derek's talent in Jamaica. Then followed in italics: 'His equally talented twin-brother and playwright Roderick still holds a very minor post in the St Lucia Civil Service! (A prophet is not without honour, save in his own country! Ed.)' The editor at the time was Simmons.[24]

9

1958–1959 A Village Life, John Robertson, *Malcochon*

In October 1958 Walcott went to New York for nine months on a Rockefeller Fellowship to study drama. John Harrison had prepared an elaborate programme for him, but Walcott avoided most of it. He did get together with, indeed depended upon, John Robertson, the lighting designer the Rockefeller Foundation had sent to Trinidad for *Drums and Colours*. Robertson arranged for Walcott to attend directing classes under José Quintero and observe productions at the Phoenix Theatre, and helped him find others with whom he could share a loft. Robertson and Walcott got along well. Robertson would tell others with Walcott present a joke about Walcott's first visit to a Village laundromat when he was instructed to separate white from coloured clothing. Walcott probably made up the joke on himself.

After being told that his first choice of a hotel was full, Walcott was directed to the Hotel Colborne at 79 Washington Place just north of 4th Street, west of Washington Square and Fifth Avenue, a place for transients. He had a small green room, minimally furnished with a shared bathroom and with one window looking on to a brick wall. Greenwich Village was a radical change from Jamaica or St Lucia. The night he arrived there were strange animalistic noises, sobs, and groans in the next room. Strange sex? Torture? Murder? Drugs? Illness? The next day the deskman was uninterested in Walcott's account and unwilling to invest-igate and, Walcott imagined, possibly save the victim. America struck Walcott as loud and snarling, especially after being brought up to speak softly in the educated British manner.[1]

He had trouble adjusting to New York, its crowds, and size. As often when faced by a strange world he turned towards his memories and his art. During his first weeks in New York he drafted *Jourmard or A Comedy Till the Last Minute* based on eccentrics he remembered from St Lucia. He sent it to Roderick. Jourmard is educated, a poet, but has become a joker begging for money. At Easter he thinks up a prank on church-goers. He will be put in a coffin, have it nailed shut, and he will be resurrected the following day. A vagrant who hates him appears to go along with the gag, but at the conclusion of the play abandons him. Among his lost plays, such as 'So-So's Wake', Walcott had experimented with this curious form of a comedy suddenly ending with tragedy. *Jourmard* was played as part of evenings of one-act plays for a decade and then, unpublished, dropped from sight.[2]

Walcott wanted to study scenic design, acting, and stage direction, as he and the West Indies needed technical knowledge of theatre production, even, for example, how to make simple sets to use in schools. He wanted to study professional theatre, and the Rockefeller Foundation provided financial support during a time when he had none and none was likely. The fellowship was for twelve months and initially paid $250 a month. He first studied scenic design under Lester Polokov but soon saw that he lacked the background and stopped attending. West Indian theatre was unlike the large expensive shows with which Polokov was concerned. Walcott instead often went to theatres on and off Broadway, making sketches and studying on his own.

He studied directing with José Quintero on Monday nights, then would go to the Phoenix Theatre where Norris Houghton was forming a repertory company. Walcott was interested in the Actors Studio, but there were no West Indian actors in New York, and not many black actors. He saw his plays as being performed by black actors and there was nothing like that in New York in 1958. He was there a decade too early.

If there were he was unlikely to know. He lived essentially a Village life, a life of off-Broadway among struggling artists, mostly white, where the choice was between high culture and the Beats. Midtown meant visits to Broadway theatres and Rockefeller Foundation offices. Brooklyn was a distant land and Harlem scared him. He was an artist and artists lived in the Village if they could. He tore up the poetry he wrote, met some editors of Village publications, wrote two one-act plays, revised his other scripts in the light of what he was learning about staging, often went to the movies, and went with friends to local bars. A few of his play scripts were passed around to see if there was any interest, but he planned to return to the West Indies for a career as a dramatist.

John Robertson was stage-manager at the Phoenix Theatre and Stuart Vaughn a director. Walcott would watch productions take shape from early readings through rehearsals to the striking—taking down—of the sets. He saw in rehearsal at the Phoenix a revival of George Farquhar's Restoration comedy *The Beaux Stratagem* with the musical comedy star June Havoc, who had learned from vaudeville how to catch and keep the audience's attention and the importance of pace. While in New York he saw T. S. Eliot's *The Family Reunion,* which uses allegory to blend classical myth with modern realism. He attended opera. At the Circle in the Square he saw an open-stage arena production of Genet's *The Balcony,* and productions of Wilder's *Our Town,* Behan's *The Quare Fellow,* and Geraldine Page in Williams's *Summer and Smoke* directed by Quintero.[3]

By 1958 José Quintero had become perhaps the most influential director of serious plays in the United States. Quintero was born in Panama and after studying in California began directing at the Woodstock Summer Theatre in 1949. In 1950 he co-founded and became artistic director of the Circle in the Square. Between 1952 and 1956 he won each year at least one major award such as the Obie, Tony, Page One Award, Outer Circle Award, or Drama Desk Award. He had directed outstanding productions of Tennessee Williams's *The Glass Menagerie* (1949), *Summer and Smoke* (1952), Lorca's *Yerma* (1952), Jane Bowles's *In the Summer House* (1953), Behan's *The Hostage* (1954) and *The Quare Fellow* (1958), and Schnitzler's *La Ronde* (1955). The production of *Summer and Smoke* brought Geraldine Page to stardom. Walcott was seeing off-Broadway at the right time.

Quintero was becoming known as the foremost interpreter of Eugene O'Neill. O'Neill's widow had refused permission to perform his plays until Quintero obtained the right to direct *The Iceman Cometh* at the Circle in the Square in 1955. This was a tremendous success and ran for two years. Because of it Quintero was given permission to direct the American premiere of *Long Day's Journey Into Night* at the Helen Hayes in 1956. He also directed O'Neill's *A Moon for the Misbegotten* at the Festival of Two Worlds (1958) in Spoleto.

Walcott had already come into contact with professional directing and acting through Noel Vaz and Errol Hill at UCWI and through the staging of his pageant. Quintero's productions, however, were a model Walcott kept in mind. Working with the Method, Quintero made actors go beyond their inhibitions to their guts, yet his productions were stylized, hierarchical, slow, lacking movement, static, filled with silences, gestures, and tableaux. They were evocative, symbolic, focusing on personal emotions, and treating other characters as a choral response, but the productions lacked spatial action. Walcott's productions were to become similar in their blending of Method acting to slow pace, silences, tableaux, and gestures, but Walcott had other aims, including the distanced alienation of Brecht.

The Circle in the Square might also be seen as a formative influence on Walcott's notion of a little theatre; originally a bar it was a three-quarters arena stage with a backdrop, and the audience sat around the playing space at tables with the action at times flowing into the audience area. Later at the Little Carib Theatre and especially at the Basement Theatre (itself a former bar) Walcott worked in conditions closer to Quintero's Circle in the Square and the off-Broadway tradition than to the Little Theatre movement of the previous generation with its emphasis on conventional proscenium stages and staging.

Through Robertson Walcott met Jim and Mimi who invited him to share an apartment in the Village. Jim wrote bad poetry and was working on an off-off-Broadway play; Mimi, a stage and costume designer, earned money as a sales girl. There was another couple, Duane and his girl-friend Jerry. Duane, a mystic, shuttled between White Plains and the Village until he left Jerry and disappeared from the scene. The apartment was a fourth-floor walk-up loft at 148 Spring Street. Spring Street at the time was socially and physically real Bohemia. During the fifties the area south of the Village was mostly old industrial buildings, almost abandoned, which were often illegally turned into spacious but barely furnished artist studios. Because not approved by the city for living, the studios seldom had much or anything in the way of toilets, baths, kitchens, or individual rooms.[4]

Walcott lived in the loft for six months. The main feature was the large central room with its tall windows, the large work table, and a Tiffany-ish lamp:

> Through the wide, grey loft window,
> I watched that winter morning of my first snow
>
> .   .   .   .
>
> a snowfall of torn poems piling up,
> heaped by a rhyming spade[5]

There was a toilet but no bath, a kitchen, two bedrooms with partitions, and furniture that was found discarded on the streets. Walcott had a desk; a partition was added so he could have a bedroom.

He was overwhelmed by New York and its confusing subways, and tried to stay within areas he knew such as the Rockefeller Center in midtown, or in a Village comprising the Phoenix Theatre on 12th Street, the Circle in the Square Theatre, Sheridan Square, Cooper Union, and John Robertson's apartment on Hudson Street. The lower East Side frightened him.

This was the time of the Beats, Grove Press, *Evergreen Review*, Artaud, Brecht, the Theatre of the Absurd, loft theatres, Zen, reading poetry to jazz, Indian clothes, coffee houses, the Limelight Café, life on the road, and going to San Francisco. The Beats and *Evergreen Review* had mixed a new popular American self-expressive Whitmanism with the old and new European avant-garde. Walcott was interested in Brecht, Kurosawa, the Theatre of the Absurd, European avant-garde high culture, but felt threatened by the free-form American populist culture that was in the air. Others were going to the Limelight Café and listening to the Beats, but Walcott did not feel part of that. Broadway at that time was usually musicals and off-Broadway the place for serious plays, such as Tennessee Williams and the Europeans, Genet, Beckett, Betti, Ionesco, and Arrabal. There was a new generation of American dramatists such as Albee and Jack Gelber (*The Connection*, 1958) who interested Walcott more than the poets. There was no black theatre; he did not know black actors. He avoided his relatives in Harlem, a dangerous place. He planned to return home.

He was already a father and divorced. At first New York meant loneliness, having to take care of himself, continual sexual frustration, not knowing where to find a woman:

> Starved, on the prowl,
> I was a frightened cat in that grey city.
> homesick, my desire
> crawled across snow
> like smoke, for its lost fire.[6]

Casual interracial sex was new to him. Walcott enjoyed drinking in company and Greenwich Village bars offered a social life. He was not always wise, at times could be thought insulting, and there was at least one bar fight between his friends and racist toughs. He drank at all the right spots for an artist at the time. Le Roi Jones (soon Imamu Baraka) at the Cedar Tavern mocked Haiti as nothing, whereas Walcott, though far less dark, felt the Haitian revolution represented black dignity and self-respect. There were also the White Horse and the Minneta Tavern. He met Frank O'Hara, Robert Frank, some writers, editors, painters, and sometimes showed them his manuscripts, but basically he was a lonely outsider, studying theatre and finding his way around a sometimes violent Village.

He was, however, becoming close to Harrison who trusted Walcott's judgement. A project for books about, and an anthology of, Latin American writing had been floated; in January Harrison asked Walcott's opinion of Wycliffe Bennett, Coulthard, W. Adolphe Roberts, Claire McFarlane, and other Jamaican literary figures. Walcott mentioned their better qualities as well as their affectations, Jamaican perspective, and uncertain literary tastes.

In April the Herbert Berghof–Uta Hagen Drama Studio opened at a new home. The Trinidadian Geoffrey Holder danced, and Walcott complained to Harrison that there were no drums as he wanted to play. Harrison noted that Walcott had been approached by a literary agent wanting radio and television scripts for Sidney Poitier. After reading some issues of *Ebony*, Walcott decided that he was not the one to write for Poitier. During the course of the evening the conversation took a more serious turn when John Robertson and Tom Patterson joined Harrison and Walcott, and they discussed the future of the performing arts in the West Indies. Patterson, having created the Ontario Stratford Shakespeare Festival, was now President of a Canadian organization which wanted to challenge Sol Hurok's monopoly of international tours by leading theatre and dance companies. Patterson had brought the Little Carib dance group to Stratford and wanted to book them for a tour in 1960, then bring them to New York in 1961, but they needed better management and direction. Would the Rockefeller Foundation commission new ballets and send Robertson to help McBurnie set her house in order for international touring? Maybe University College or the Trinidad government could request Robertson and lend him to the Little Carib as manager? The Little Carib had possibilities and might make money locally by attracting tourists, but it was essential that it be developed into both a training school for the arts and a repertory group for dance, theatre, music, and other arts.

A week later Harrison, Robertson, and Walcott discussed Patterson's plans for the Little Carib. Robertson begged off; the Little Carib was primarily a dance, not a theatre, company, and he was an outsider in the West Indies who would wear out his welcome. Robertson would consider working for a theatre group, like the St Lucia Arts Guild, or if some talented actors could form a theatre group in Trinidad. (It is difficult not to suspect the hand of Walcott in this idea.) Harrison said there needed to be some legally registered group to which funds could be awarded; neither the present Little Carib or Arts Guild met this requirement. One of the sources of the Trinidad Theatre Workshop, which would occupy years of Walcott's life, was conversations like this during the Rockefeller fellowship.

Walcott was to return to these years in several poems, in an unpublished chapter of an unfinished autobiography (of which I have made use), and in 'Solo to the Hudson', an unproduced Gelberish play he wrote in the late 1970s which takes its details of the late 1950s in the Village from his experience of the period. Little of Walcott's poetry from this time has survived—rather episodes were recalled later. Walcott often mentioned the difficulties he had writing poetry in New York that winter. *In a Green Night* includes several 'fragments'.

'Greenwich Village, Winter' describes the difficulty of truthfully writing a life, 'Each word, | Black footprints in the frightening snow'. There were the timeless universal problems of writing poetry and the violence of New York, but there was also his awareness that in North America he was a 'black'. 'The Muse hath a stone breast in America. I rest dark hands thereon.'[7]

Christmas season in the Village formed the basis of 'God Rest Ye Merry Gentlemen' with its drunken narrator seeing in an all-night diner someone beaten to a pulp. Outside was danger and the confusions of good and evil, the reversals of colour stereotyping, the fears of northern white rather than black tropical evil: 'I longed for darkness, evil that was warm'. 'The night was white. There was nowhere to hide.'[8]

In 'A Village Life' in *The Castaway* Walcott addressed the now two-year-dead John Robertson:

> All that winter I haunted
> your house on Hudson Street, a tiring friend,
> demanding to be taken in, drunk, and fed.
> I thought winter would never end.

Being away from the West Indies, cold, divorced, at times broke, Walcott was toughened by New York:

> And since that winter I have learnt to gaze
> on life indifferently as through a pane of glass.

Not all was loneliness, foreignness, fear, and toughening. In 1971 Walcott published 'Reveries of Spring Street' which he revised for *Sea Grapes* (1976) as 'Spring Street in '58' (a poem appropriately dedicated to the 'New York school' poet-action painter Frank O'Hara, himself the embodiment of the 1950s Village and *Evergreen Review*):

> Dirt under the fingernails of the window-ledge,
> in the rococo ceiling, grime
> flowering like a street opera.
>
> .   .   .   .
>
> There was dirt on the peach tan
> of the girls of the gold Mid-West,
> ou sont ces vierges?
>
> .   .   .   .
>
> and one caught style from others like a cold,
> and I could look at Mimi washing her soiled feet
> as life imitating Lautrec.
>
> In Spring Street's dirty hermitage, where I
> crouched over poems, and drawings, I
> knew we'd all live as long as Hokusai.[9]

The Spring Street commune eventually unravelled. The others were jobless, living off his grant, and towards the end Walcott was almost penniless, awaiting his monthly Rockefeller money, sleeping between meals of cornflakes.

In March his stipend was increased to $300 a month and he moved out of the apartment. Returning to the Hotel Colborne he was depressed living alone in a small room facing a concrete wall. There he first began to write *Dream on Monkey Mountain.*[10] Like many of Walcott's plays it was to evolve for many years through many versions before being produced and eventually published. And like many of his major works it was to gain in texture and depth by being a product of different times and places. Its origins were in memories of St Lucia, Walcott's feelings of estrangement in New York, and his reading in contemporary literature and thought. The Fanon quotation at the start of *Dream* is from Sartre's preface to *Wretched of the Earth*, which was published by Grove Press. Fanon spoke to Walcott's own sense of a disassociated self; Walcott understood the stages from hallucinations to disassociation of the self to madness. He had been troubled since youth by his blackness, conflicted by Britishness in Jamaica, and now in New York he, like others before him, like, say, Naipaul in London, had reached the metropolitan promised land and found his own loneliness and smallness in an uncaring, seldom shining world.

The difficulties Walcott had in writing poetry might be explained by his inability to understand and distance the rich but confused experience of New York, where he felt himself to be an outsider with a foreign accent, a curiosity with black skin and British speech, yet neither an American black nor English. He worked on at least three plays which, while using new techniques and embodying some of the tensions of his Village life, are set in and dramatize St Lucia. It would take a few years before his feelings about New York settled and could be recollected in poetry.

He was also feeling the effects of the breakdown of his marriage and divorce. It is reductive to offer psychological interpretations of complex symbols that have been consciously and unconsciously evolving over decades through various drafts, but when Makak beheads the White Goddess in *Dream on Monkey Mountain* might not Walcott have been trying to kill off his attraction to Faye? The Apparition, the Moon Lady, White Goddess is his muse, his Venus, romantic love, the attractions of the Sleeping Beauty, innocence and virginity, all women. We now see her in racial or cultural terms or as some version of Robert Graves's White Goddess, the embodiment of poetry in a real-life muse. Walcott was aware of such significance and developed it in later versions of the play, but the actual origin of the Apparition, first known as the Moon Lady, is the white-faced spirit woman who appears to the potter in Kenji Mizoguchi's *Ugetsu* (1953). In Mizoguchi's film two contrasting women die needing love. Walcott was haunted by the film while staying at the hotel.[11]

Kenji Mizoguchi's *Ugetsu* (1953) is set in the sixteenth century and concerns two brothers and their women. Walcott saw a parallel between the misty rainy mountainous terrain of Japan and St Lucia, and took from the film the image of the pale-faced female spirit (*Ugetsu's* ghostly Lady Wakaka, the Apparition in *Dream on Monkey Mountain*), and the powerful image of beheading the woman (used in both *Malcochon* and *Dream*), which frees a man from his obsession (as Genjuro must kill Lady Wakasa to return to his wife). Mizoguchi's film is poetic in its moody, haunting lyricism, historical stylization, use of myths, mixing of the living and dead, slowness, and circular form (beginning and ending at the same place); the model is Noh drama. Just the film for Walcott at this point in his career, a film which can be seen as having many of the features that interested him in Japanese art and Brecht's theories as a possible way to create a West Indian theatre.

The ghost woman first appeared in the 'woman' in *Malcochon* who is accused by her husband of unfaithfulness and having given herself to 'the shabine', the 'red nigger that thinks he is a white man' for a bottle of bad rum.[12] She is 'that half-coolie bitch' with 'long hair and smooth skin'. When her husband questions her faithfulness she mocks him, 'She only shaking her hair and laughing in my face and saying "Kill me, yes, kill me."'[13] The attractions of the light-skinned, half-Indian 'coolie' woman in *Malcochon* are those of the Apparition in *Dream on Monkey Mountain*, where the naming of her as an Apparition shows Walcott's awareness of the fantasy of owning what is desired. Such motifs recur throughout Walcott's plays. In *Franklin* an Indian wife of a white man kills herself after having a child by a black lover; in the earliest version the Franklin character was a mulatto. In each retelling there is the basic obsession with, and death of, a light-skinned or brown woman who cannot be totally possessed and who is unfaithful.

Another Japanese film Walcott saw was Akira Kurosawa's *Rashomon* (1950). Set in a feudal Japan which appears to Western eyes alien in landscape and values, *Rashomon* tells a story from different perspectives in accordance with each person's sense of honour. The same device is used in *Malcochon* as is the symbolism of the rain to suggest a bleak evil world, and the seeking shelter from the storm as a way to bring together characters to tell their versions of a story which is then unexpectedly concluded in the present. Roderick Walcott, following Derek's lead, would use a similar technique in his play *Malfinis*.

One result of his time in New York was the lasting influence of Japanese arts, Brecht, and film on Walcott's work. He went to Village movie houses and was conscious of the power of films, especially Ingmar Bergman and Japanese cinema. He had studied Japanese costumes through Japanese woodcuts and liked the simplicity of Japanese theatre with its contrast between rich costumes and bare sets, which he thought were like the Caribbean with its Carnivals and other self-displays. The peasants, rain, poverty, mountains, and forests were analogous to St Lucia.

Walcott became certain that one model for West Indian drama should be Oriental theatre. It was stylized, so that one could have a West Indian acting style and need not worry about lacking the decorum of, and having different body movements from, the British. Oriental theatre was also minimalist in terms of scenery; the West Indian theatre would be unable to afford, and foolish to try to copy, the West's expensive detailed realism of presentation. The Japanese Noh plays showed him how to use a bare stage, which was needed because of the poverty of the West Indies, with just light. Too much energy in Western theatre went into simulation of reality, Walcott's theatre would be a folk theatre, without much in the way of props. A non-realistic theatre was also necessary for a theatre of action and a theatre of poetry; realistic settings meant people having conversations, rather than rapid changes in emotion or poetic speech. Walcott understood that his folk theatre was also part of an avant-garde of the time represented by such directors as Peter Brook and Jerzy Grotowski who were trying to get away from the limitations of realism and strengthening the theatre through story-telling, dance, and music.[14]

The first clear sign of this Japanese influence can be seen in the one-act play *Malcochon*. The alternative title is 'Six in the Rain'; Mizoguchi's *Ugetsu* is mostly based on the eighteenth-century Japanese 'Ugetsu Monogatari', which translates as 'Tales of Moonlight and Rain'. 'Malcochon' is St Lucian Creole for white rum. The six in the rain are an Old Man, his Nephew, a husband and wife, Chantal (the old man of the forest and charcoal burner), and Moumou a young deaf mute). The Old Man has slept with his brother's wife, the brother killed the woman and was hung—the brother is father of the Nephew. (Variations of Walcott's incest theme.) Each tells his version of the story. Throughout there is a pattern of imagery implying white power—white thunder, white rain, waves as white teeth. Chantal, who says he is drunk and will not judge, recalls the drunken judge in Brecht's *The Caucasian Chalk Circle*. The play warns against mistaking revenge for justice or justice for truth, a concern of both Derek and Roderick Walcott, as can be seen in the latter's play *Flight of Sparrows*. Neither priest nor Church is needed as an intermediary between Man and God. Man communicates with God through nature, a Walcott theme since '1944'.[15] *Malcochon* is dedicated to John Robertson.

Walcott started in the Village as a lonely black cat, but he was meeting people and showing them his work. For a time Grove Press considered publishing a volume of his poems. Don Allen of Grove Press wrote to him at 148 Spring Street. He had read the poems and plays Walcott had left with him and asked Walcott to type a copy of 'A Far Cry from Africa' for publication in *Evergreen Review*. When *Dream on Monkey Mountain* was complete Walcott should send it, along with a short play Allen had already sent on to Arabel Porter, and another short play or two, to Barney Rosset at Grove Press. Allen thought *Dream* was well written and had moving scenes, and would tell Rosset that they would make a good Grove Press book and possibly an *Evergreen Review* issue. Allen suggested that Jack Kerouac contact Walcott. Walcott's 'A Far Cry from Africa' was republished from *Public Opinion* in the Spring 1959 *Evergreen Review* alongside poems by Pasternak, cummings, Lowell, Corso, Ginsberg, Merrill, Ashbery, and Olson. Allen was at that time Walcott's contact with Rosset, who met but did not know him. Allen says he broke the contact when Walcott insulted a friend.

The Village in the 1950s sat uneasily atop an Italian neighbourhood then known for its occasional violence towards beards, blacks, and Others. As a student at Columbia University I had difficulty distinguishing between charming Italian restaurants and unwelcoming streets. Walcott had similar problems. 'Bleecker Street, Summer' mentions

a month of street accordions and sprinklers
laying the dust, . . .
It is music opening and closing, mia Italia, on Bleecker
ciao, Antonio, and the water-cries of children[16]

In 'Blues' he recalls being mugged on McDougal or Christopher Street during the summer at an Italian festival:

. . . I wasn't too far from
home . . .
I figured we were all
one, wop, nigger, jew

.   .   .   .   .   .

My face smashed in, my bloody mug
pouring, my olive-branch jacket saved
from cuts and tears,
I crawled four flights upstairs.

.   .   .   .   .   .

Still, it taught me something
about love. If it's so tough,
forget it.[17]

While in New York Walcott's West Indian career continued. The *Trinidad
Guardian* of 7 January 1959 published him for the first time; Walcott had sent
an article from New York about the possible demise of *Bim.* A month later, 8
February, the St Lucia Carnival Committee in conjunction with the St Lucia Arts
Guild produced *The Story of Ti-Jean,* based on the play by Derek Walcott. This
was really his brother's show as the script, choreography, and direction were by
Roderick. Little more than a week later, on 16, 18, and 20 February, Derek's own
Ti-Jean and His Brothers was performed at the Dramatic Theatre, UCWI, Jamaica,
sponsored by *Public Opinion* (which Slade Hopkinson edited), and directed
by Slade Hopkinson. The importance of the sponsorship can be seen from
Hopkinson's article, ' "Public Opinion" To Back Walcott Play', which trumpeted
the properly financed production of the play.[18] Hopkinson wrote that while
plays do not make money, they seldom lose it, but theatre groups lack money to
risk on productions. *Public Opinion* would try to set an example by backing
Ti-Jean. This would be the third production of *Ti-Jean,* the first in Jamaica. Earlier
productions were in St Lucia, directed by Roderick Walcott, and Trinidad,
directed by Derek. The cast included many of Walcott's friends: Ronnie Llanos
as the Devil/Planter; Franklin St Juste as Ti-Jean; Mary Brathwaite as the
Mother; and Slade Hopkinson as the Bolom.

Walcott had sent a handwritten copy of *Malcochon* to Roddy in St Lucia with
suggestions for casting, along with drawings for costumes, scenery, and staging.

Like many Walcott plays *Malcochon* has an earlier incarnation and is said to have developed from 'Cross Roads', no copy of which is known to exist. *Malcochon* was staged 12–13 March by the St Lucia Arts Guild at Castries Town Hall along with Roderick Walcott's *Shrove Tuesday March*. Roderick Walcott directed both plays. Proceeds were in aid of the forthcoming Arts Guild Tour to Trinidad. This was the first production of *Malcochon*; the cast included Dunstan St Omer as Charlemagne. Another bill of two one-act plays followed, 28–9 April, *Jourmard* by Derek Walcott and *The Trouble with Albino Joe* by Roderick Walcott. Directed by Roderick Walcott they were presented by the St Lucia Arts Guild at Castries Town Hall, with a cast that included Dunstan St Omer. The production design was by Dunstan St Omer who says that the part of Jourmard was written for himself by Derek.

On 12 June Walcott asked for his Rockefeller fellowship to be terminated on 20 June; he left New York three months before the conclusion of the fellowship. His brother Roddy was taking the St Lucia Arts Guild to Trinidad, where it would be performing six one-act plays by the two Walcotts during July; the Guild was the pioneer in performing on other islands. As often in Walcott's life there is no clear single reason for his decision to move on; there is always a complex of reasons. They included the mugging, the tour, the desire to start creating his own theatre, loneliness, the discomforts of living in a loft and a hotel room, the ambiguities of being a mulatto in a nation which was divided by colour.

Walcott wanted to form a theatre company. He had been learning methods of analysis, seeing the kind of discipline needed to create a coherent style. He wanted to use theatre techniques from around the world to create a new West Indian acting and stage style. He wanted something like the peasants in Japanese films, something like the simplicity of Brecht, along with West Indian folk traditions. He wanted to follow in his mother's path as a teacher. There was no place for his vision in New York. How could plays in West Indian dialect be done in New York? The only 'black' film was Lionel Rogosin's *Come Back Africa*. He wanted to write for a new theatre, as Yeats had in Ireland, not for New York. He did not even have the paper qualifications to teach in the United States.

New York and his divorce had toughened Walcott. There was no protective mother or wife, no servants, no one cared about his publications in the West Indies or the BBC *Caribbean Voices*. He was a man of 29 who had moved from country to country, who had lived a winter among artists, hustlers, and loners. There was the problem of the custody of his son. Derek and Faye wanted careers, both were on the move, both wanted Peter. 'Time's Surprise' notes how instead of crying tears for a broken heart he now finds below such 'pools of pity lies | The heart of adamant'. I assume the pun on 'lies' means that the hard heart deceives with tears.[19]

Walcott often returned in his writing to those nine months in the Village although they became mixed up with his short 1957 trip: 1958–9 became 1957–8, as in his unpublished play 'Solo to the Hudson', where four men after the war in Vietnam isolate themselves in a room to meditate and get away from contemporary America and instead recall what it was like in 1957–8, or was it, they wonder 1958–9, in their loft on Spring Street when they were young, new to New York, and innocent.

In the West Indies Walcott was already a prized big fish, in New York not even an anchovy. He knew, however, New York was where he had to make it. John Hearne had warned him of how easy it was to earn a literary reputation in the West Indies and settle into satisfaction without the competition of publishing abroad. Most West Indians went to England, but Alix's side of the family chose the States. From his childhood on, American culture had been part of his world. He read American comic strips, saw American films, read American literature. As someone raised in a British colony, whose paternal grandfather was a 'British' Bajan, he might think of himself as British, but New York, not London or Paris, was by 1959 the centre of the modern cultural world. He would soon be back, and he would continue to gravitate towards it; even in his sixties after his home-coming to St Lucia he would once again also become a New Yorker, a villager, a Greenwich Villager.

Part III

~~~~~~

Trinidad Second Marriage, Second Home, Professional Writer

10

1959–1962 Little Carib Theatre Workshop, Alan Ross, Jonathan Cape, *In a Green Night*

DURING August, Walcott was in Castries, where he told the *Voice of St Lucia* that Trinidad would offer him better chances and support to develop than St Lucia. He returned to Port of Spain where Beryl McBurnie agreed that he could start a weekly actors studio at her Little Carib Theatre. The Little Carib Theatre Workshop, later the Trinidad Theatre Workshop, was to remain Walcott's obsession for decades. He hoped to create an equivalent of Brecht's Berliner Ensemble, a playwright-director-led drama company of world class, which would evolve its own distinctive acting style based in part on the depth of character-ization of the Method and on the physical expressiveness of West Indian dance. He expected to take local amateur actors, even beginners, and turn them into complete professionals, capable of mime and dance, earning their livelihood from the stage. This company would stage his plays, along with those of other West Indian dramatists, and take them on tour abroad. In a part of the world where there was little amateur theatre, no professional theatre, and where an evening of one-act plays performed for a night or two was thought all there was an audience for, he wanted to earn his living as a dramatist-director. It was an absurdity Walcott still does not accept as flawed except by the politicians, local businesses, and others who refused to give him the support he needed. Political independence meant little, it was cultural independence he wanted—the West Indies, with himself as leader, to be on the map of world culture. The region would remain economically dependent on others, but those who judged the Caribbean by its poverty and history would be proved wrong.

West Indian theatre shared British concerns with diction, manner, and the exterior of characters, whereas in New York Marlon Brando, Eli Wallach, and Lee J Cobb were driving themselves to get to the truth of character. Walcott wanted a theatre which would have a similar obsessive self-exploration, but in a West Indian-sounding English.[1] He wanted actors who could do Ibsen and Shakespeare and modern avant-garde as well as West Indian plays. The same attention to craft that he gave to his poetry he expected from his actors. At the Little Carib dancers and actors could work together, with the actors learning to use their body while the dancers were learning to speak on stage. It was especially the movement and mime of the dancers that he wanted.

He had already come into contact with most of the Trinidad theatre world. He knew who had talent when he invited local actors to participate in a weekly theatre workshop; others had to audition. Several of the best actors, who became the core of his Workshop, were from San Fernando, the second largest city in Trinidad, and moved to Port of Spain to work with him. The Theatre Workshop was Walcott, and when he was not there it barely functioned. The early members already had local reputations, and, in a few cases, such as the dramatist Douglas Archibald, were known abroad. Walcott's leadership was not easily accepted and people drifted away. Not everyone wanted to be part of a high-brow Actors Studio. Attendance and paying dues were erratic. The Workshop was initially to develop acting and other skills which the members could bring to their own companies.

On 11 December 1959, before a small, invited, audience, including a representative of the Rockefeller Foundation, there was the first Little Carib Theatre Workshop production, six scenes from four plays—Errol John's *Moon on a Rainbow Shawl*, Tennessee Williams's *This Property is Condemned*, Shaw's *Saint Joan*, and Arthur Miller's *The Crucible*—and an adaptation of 'Basement Lullaby' from Sam Selvon's prose. Walcott directed four of the scenes. The actors included Errol Jones, who would be his principal actor and part of the inner core of the Workshop for the next forty years. Margaret Maillard was in charge of properties and front of the house. Walcott's programme note described this as a studio production. He did not want to perform in public until he had developed his own company from the workshop, and that would take years.

While laying the foundations for what he hoped would be a career as a West Indian dramatist, he supported himself through journalism and became a writer for the *Trinidad Guardian*. In November Walcott reviewed a local theatre production, there were two more reviews in December. After 24 January 1960, his articles on a variety of cultural and artistic topics appeared at least once a week, usually in the Sunday edition. The Thursday and Friday editions also carried some coverage of the arts to which he contributed. The fifty-five articles he published during 1960 were at first signed 'Derek Walcott Guardian Staff Writer' which was gradually replaced by the initials 'D.W.' and then a byline. Starting late 1963 he began a weekly 'Focus of the Arts' column and averaged two articles a week until July 1967.

He became, as he was earlier with *Public Opinion,* an all-purpose arts critic covering films, dance, local theatre, art exhibitions, and literature. He reviewed Carnival, calypso shows, pieced together bits of news, announcements, and comment into columns, and wrote long essays on West Indian theatre, literature, painting, and popular culture. His taste was excellent. He knew that the West Indian novel had blossomed and felt that some of the first novelists appeared to be running out of steam. He followed the novels of V. S. Naipaul with the attention that a major artist gives a rival. Walcott was interested in, although at times puzzled by, the Guyanese poet and novelist Wilson Harris, whose work viewed the Caribbean as a New World continually in a process of transformation. The vision had similarities to his own attack on the burden of history, but Harris's presentation, influenced by Latin American Magic Realism, appeared surreal.

The reviewing of art exhibitions appealed to Walcott's own interest in painting. The film reviews may seem so many words wasted on bad films, but Walcott was and remains in love with cinema. Films offered a chance to study acting, plotting, use of symbols, and sound, along with camera technique. Just as he wanted to be a painter, he still wanted to make films. The theatre reviews helped him understand the problems of local productions, find actors for his own Workshop, and set cultural standards by which his own work would be judged. Reviews of dance, calypsos, steel bands, and Carnival contributed towards his awareness of Trinidadian culture and how it might be integrated into his own theatre and poetry. This was important as he was a St Lucian in Trinidad, a very different society. Once he became a staff writer his role grew rapidly. He expressed his opinions clearly, argued with views he disliked, and covered an immense range of arts with impressive knowledge and concern. He was controversial, confrontational, and shaped local awareness and taste. His reviews of West Indian literature remain enlightening and should be collected into a book. The painting and dance criticism comprise a history of those arts in Trinidad during an important decade.

In his first two months on the staff of the *Guardian* Walcott published a parody of the libretto of *Yeomen of the Guard,* discussed the relationship of calypso to popular poetry, wrote a general essay on the Beat generation, an article on problems of make-up on the Trinidadian stage, reviewed the now famous calypso singer Mighty Sparrow, along with two books about Carnival, and reviewed a Haitian dance company that performed at Queen's Hall. His energy was amazing, especially as Walcott continued to write poetry, hold theatre workshops, travel between the islands, and have a full private life.

Walcott the art critic moved into an area where criticism was mostly reporting on local social activities; he brought to it a new seriousness. The venues Walcott covered now seem preposterous—schoolgirl art shows, exhibitions in backyards and restaurants—but that was where the art was shown. Walcott recognized the better, now internationally known painters—such as Peter Minshall and Jackie Hinkson. His reviews reflect his concern with the relationship between West Indian and Modern art. Commenting upon the Trinidad Art Society's November 1960 exhibition, Walcott argued that European culture continued to limit the imagination of the West Indian artist, whether painter or writer. Instead of taking inspiration and models from such regional sources as Mexican painting and pre-Columbian art, local middle-class artists wish to be compared with Picasso, Chagall, or John Osborne. There is a primness found in the still lifes, studies of flowers, lifeless nudes, and various -isms. For Walcott 'bad art is a reflection of social manners'. There is a parallel between such art and West Indian 'deference to and imitation of a foreign accent'. 'West Indian verse suffers from this as well. The inflection of the metre, which affects structure, or if you wish, form, is imported.' For all the artificiality of the local Africanisms that is better than Trinidad's polite, flabby, colonial Victorianism.² West Indian colours in art and literature must be brighter, stronger than those of Europe. Vigour, however, is not enough. There is also discipline. Walcott's creativity required unsettled tensions, exploring opposites, a Whitmanesque inclusiveness of unresolved conflicts to express what he felt was his situation and that of the West Indies, the New World mulatto.

Port of Spain had a vibrant new intellectual and artistic community as represented by *Opus: A Review*, edited by the Barbadian short-story writer John Wickham, who lived in Trinidad 1946–62. His co-editors included Walcott's friend Irma Pilgrim. As the Federation had brought many talented people to Trinidad, some civil servants decided to start an equivalent to *Bim*. Word was spread and a small group including Oliver Jackman, the architect Colin Laird, Pilgrim, and other friends of Walcott, met in Wickham's office at the Federal House. *Opus* lasted three issues, one of which was devoted to architecture.

The first issue of *Opus* included Veronica Jenkin's review of the first production at Queen's Hall (Shaw's *Caesar and Cleopatra*), Walcott's otherwise unpublished poem 'A Missal of Devotions From Her Faith', followed by an article on his Little Carib Theatre Workshop. The December issue included Walcott's poem 'Castiliane'.³ 'A Missal of Devotions From Her Faith' consists of fourteen stanzas each of two lines and describes a painting of the Virgin by Fra Angelico.

> Twin figure of opal.
> Virgen Madre, give us a sign;
>
> Bless this blue period
> From a forgotten calm.

The unsigned article on the Little Carib Theatre Workshop is probably by Walcott. Over the years he would often plant articles about the Workshop, which might be revised by others. 'Every speech or gesture must be interpreted not in the light of its surface content or its immediate effect but as a product of the psychological and physical forces that go to make up the humanity of the character at that moment'; 'not one word should be spoken or finger moved without a consciousness on the part of the actor of how the word or gesture fits in with his perception of the character'; 'the extent to which human (and therefore dramatic) character can be probed is unlimited'; the 'most convincing element of humanity is the fact that the more there is on the surface the more seems to remain underneath to be brought to light'. 'The training of amateur actors in this country . . . has been confined to the British Council type of course in movement, mime and voice' that sharpens the actors' tools but not the approach to the study of the part. There is no training for directors. In the Little Carib Theatre Workshop small groups are formed to study, produce, and perform short extracts from plays of all kinds; each performance is followed by a severe, frank discussion and criticism. Performances are arena style with little help in creating the illusion of reality. The development of technique must not be restricted to the conventions of the proscenium presentation. Walcott is chairman, he directs some rehearsals but offers no theories. From a few pages of a play it is possible to extract infinite significance. Each rehearsal raises further problems. There will eventually be a series of public performances of one-act plays, then perhaps a full-length play with the idea of improving local acting and audience standards.

Noel Vaz wrote (2 May 1960) from UCWI that he hoped *Drums and Colours* would be the next issue of *Caribbean Quarterly*.[4] Vaz wished Walcott were in Jamaica. Trinidad had more raw talent but lacked knowledge of theatre technique. The Trinidadian back-to-the-village view was only useful for backyard productions. A West Indian style is only possible from a theatre that in its own context looks, feels, and smells professional to people elsewhere. West Indians must stop justifying the slapdash as authentic. Local productions, especially where playwrights are also producers, lack organization. In his recent show with Ivy Baxter, the producer, musician, dancer, and writer co-operated and the best parts were improvised during rehearsals. This takes time but is how drama should be created. Walcott should convince McBurnie of this. Walcott should not begin by writing a literary play and fitting dances and music to it. He should start with some ideas for scenes, set, and a brief scenario and add lines as the artists develop the materials in workshop. Let the scene come alive before enclosing it in writing. In the theatre the poetic results from condensation, economy, silence; words should be used sparingly, at climaxes. Such a play will only have a slender text, twenty lines could result in an hour's great theatre; save poetry for printers. Improvise a situation endlessly in various styles as a way to create a rich and pure theatre.

Vaz was and remained an influence on Walcott, who often expressed similar ideas. Vaz knew it is necessary to workshop or rehearse continually to find what is worth while and to learn organization to present material properly. What is professional will differ according to the situation, but, as audiences throughout the world recognize and respond to the difference between sloppy and professional productions, one should work towards mastery. Vaz regarded theatre as a joint or communal creation by a group of artists working together under the guidance of a director rather than as a literary text garnished with other arts. There was and remains a tension in Walcott's way of looking at theatre between a literary approach and the improvisational, between the playwright-producer and the separation of responsibilities.

Port of Spain had its amateur theatre companies and such dramatists as Douglas and William Archibald, both successful in the United States, and earlier Errol John. It was for a time part of a circuit of tours by famous international artists. Walcott had claimed 'no new West Indian play of merit was produced in Trinidad during 1960', but there were local productions of Gilbert and Sullivan, Shakespeare, and Brendan Behan. The high point of the year had been a performance by José Limon and his dance company sponsored by the United States Information Services. During 1961 the Theatre Guild American Repertory Company on tour to Latin America stopped off with three plays, Thornton Wilder's *The Skin of Our Teeth*, Tennessee Williams's *The Glass Menagerie* with Helen Hayes, and *The Miracle Worker*. Alan Ross was one of many writers and editors who visited the West Indies during the 1960s. They often came with introductions to Walcott or he interviewed and wrote about them for the *Trinidad Guardian*. He no longer felt cut off from the outside literary world.[5]

Shortly after the New Year 1960, Walcott met the poet and editor Alan Ross. This was the dry season before Carnival and Ross was in Trinidad covering the Test Matches for the London *Observer*. Ross, a friend of Roy Fuller, was soon to replace John Lehmann as editor of *London Magazine*. For more than a decade Walcott was to publish regularly in *London Magazine*, which was his breakthrough into the London publishing and literary market, and Ross was his friend who helped open doors in England.

A *London Magazine* existed 1732–85 and 1820–9. It began its third incarnation in 1954 under the editorship of John Lehmann, editor of *New Writing* and *Penguin New Writing*. In 1959 Ross and Maurice Cranston took over the actual editing, assisted by the Australian Charles Osborne, until 1961 when Ross officially became editor and renumbered the publication as a New Series. Born in Calcutta (1922) Ross considers himself an Anglo-Indian. By the time he met Walcott he had published over a dozen books of poetry, prose (especially about travel and cricket), and various anthologies.

Ross's *Through the Caribbean: The M.C.C. Tour of the West Indies 1959–1960* (1960) is an example of the close links at the time between cricket reporting and the literary world. Writing about sports not only provided income and means to travel, but it also contributed to an international literary circle as London-based writers met their counterparts in the colonies, found mutual interests, became friends, and helped each other. In sports, as well as the arts, colour and class barriers were lowered and people judged by their abilities. In the recent past, writing about cricket had celebrated the English village, the village green, the olde Englande of those, such as 'Q' (J. C. Squires), who opposed Modernism in the arts. The war changed that. For many in the colonies, such as C. L. R. James, cricket was a way to be both British and nationalist by beating the British at their own game. Ross met and mentions such members of the West Indian literary scene as A. J. Seymour, Frank Collymore, John Figueroa, even Father Jesse (as an historian), along with C. L. R. James. Derek is called 'the most talented poet in the Caribbean' and Ross quotes from Walcott's 'A Map of the Antilles', which was printed in the *London Magazine* in August 1960, about the time Ross's book appeared.

Walcott took Ross to the Miramar where 'the girls used to do the limbo naked and then dance barefoot on the glass broken off the tops of beer bottles. They seemed never to cut themselves.'[6] The real night life of the city took place in the large dockside crowded dance-hall, the Miramar, with a multiracial crowd of pimps, prostitutes, toughs, a steel band, drummers, and calypsonians. There was a cabaret beginning with a limbo dancer, then various orgasmic Caribbean drum-led dances, followed by the bottle dance. Sacking was placed on the floor, empty beer bottles collected and their tops broken to produce jagged fragments tossed on the sacking, then a dancer would come on stage, work his way around the glass and leap upon it as the rhythm built, gyrating, trampling, crunching, before cartwheeling through it, standing on his hands, and then leave the stage. Mambo music would start while the crowd drifted away to other open-air clubs.

Walcott's poetry was starting to be published in magazines beyond the Caribbean. He submitted poems abroad that he had already published in the West Indies. In Canada the Winter 1960 *Tamarack Review* republished Walcott's reinterpretation of a well-known passage from Thomas Traherne's *Centuries of Meditations*, 'Orient and Immortal Wheat':

> Nature seemed monstrous to his thirteen years.
> Prone to malaria, sweating inherent sin,
> Absolved in Limacol and evening prayers,
> the prodigy, dusk rouging his peaked face,
> Studies the swallows stitch the opposing eaves
> In repetitions of the fall from grace.[7]

Tamarack Review had a good reputation and paid. Richard Weaver, the editor, wrote (22 March) that he liked Walcott's work. He planned to use four poems and *The Sea at Dauphin* in a West Indian issue which should appear in early April.

The initial three 'Tales of the Islands' were accepted (21 March) for *Between Worlds*, a new international literary magazine published by the Inter American University of Puerto Rico. Although contributors were not paid, the magazine of over 190 pages included part of a Spanish play by Ramon Sender, a poem by Herman Hesse, a chapter of a new book by Henry Miller, two stories by Robert Lowry, writing in French by Man Ray and a cover design by Man Ray, poetry by Robert Lowry, James Purdy, Edward Dorn, William Burroughs, Gregory Corso, Sir Herbert Read, and, from India, Srinivas Rayaprol. Poetry was published in English and other European languages and ranged from Dadaism to the Beats.

John Lehmann (16 June) accepted six poems for *London Magazine* and offered to submit others elsewhere. Although Lehmann was still editor, Alan Ross was making decisions and doing the work; Ross changed the letter to seven poems. *London Magazine* in August published 'A Map of the Antilles' along with 'Pays Natal', 'En Mi-Carême', and 'A Sea Chantey'. The October issue carried 'A Lesson for this Sunday', 'A Letter from Brooklyn', and 'Allegre'. This was Walcott's first appearance on the British literary scene beyond *Caribbean Voices*. Besides bringing him to wider notice, *London Magazine* paid, published well-known authors, and had an influential readership. Ross also had an unlimited appetite for Walcott poems and recognized that his new friend was a major writer. Charles Monteith, a director at Faber, had published John Hearne's *Voices Under the Window*, Wilson Harris's *Palace of the Peacock* (1960), and commissioned Andrew Salkey (then working freelance for the BBC) to select and edit *West Indian Stories* (1960). Monteith read *London Magazine*, enquired about Walcott, but heard that Ross and Fuller had already brought him to Cape's attention. Ross had sent a manuscript of the poems to Tom Maschler with the comment that Walcott is the best prospect he knew.

Besides *London Magazine*'s publication of Walcott's poetry, there was the first professional production of his plays in England. Lloyd Reckord was establishing the first black theatre company in London and began with two Walcott plays. He sent Walcott (7 July) a letter of agreement; for radio, television, film, or further stage productions Reckord wanted World Performance Rights. *Sea at Dauphin* and *Malcochon: Six in the Rain* had their English première by Reckord's New Day Theatre Company in association with the English Stage Society at the Court Theatre, Sunday, 10 July 1960, with Reckord directing. Reckord then hired the Tower Theatre in Canonbury, Islington, for two weeks, with performances on Tuesday, 12 July–Saturday, 16 July, and Monday, 18 July–Sunday, 24 July. Kenneth Young found the plays only partly successful. The 'central idea' of *Sea at Dauphin* 'seems to be that poverty can drive men to fish, even when the seas are high and dangerous'. Young found Chantal in *Six in the Rain* interesting, comic, and fearsome, but thought the play fussy with its play within a play and self-conscious poetry. Reviewers complained about the diction and difficulty understanding what was being said. K.J. in the *New Statesman* noted that Reckord was an inexperienced producer, and thought *The Sea at Dauphin* looked amateurish, a play for West Indian schoolmasters, but showed talent. *Six in the Rain*, however, was worth a trip to Canonbury, a 'genuinely indigenous' 'West Indian Noh play. Rewarding in spite of the production.'[8]

Reckord hoped to reopen at a fringe West End theatre early the following year, but wanted either another one-act play to replace *The Sea at Dauphin* or for *Malcochon: Six in the Rain* to be expanded into a full-length play. Reckord paid Walcott 10 per cent of the take at the Tower Theatre, £22. 12s. (about US $125), along with £5 for the Court Sunday performance. Reckord, who was a television actor, wanted to put New Day on a more permanent basis, and tried to get television people interested in Walcott's plays. Nothing came of it.

During July 1960 Derek and Margaret Ruth Maillard moved to a house at 156 Duke of Edinburgh Avenue in Petit Valley near a river, in bamboo groves, below a heavily forested mountain in Diego Martin Valley just outside Port of Spain. Margaret was active in artistic circles, a dancer in Beryl McBurnie's troupe, and a painter. She had studied for a degree in England and was part of the Port of Spain élite of those with foreign qualifications. A few months later the Walcotts moved to a new house at 165 Duke of Edinburgh Avenue, Petit Valley, with more space. This was to remain their home. Margaret was an attractive black French Creole, with Indian, African, and European blood, from a well-established family which disapproved of unconventional ways. Because of Margaret's concern with convention, she and Derek were self-conscious about living together. They were married at the Registry in Chaguaramas. The newspapers listed Margaret as a trained Almoner, daughter of Mr and Mrs G. Maillard of Woodbrook, Port of Spain. She gave up Catholicism for Derek.

Walcott was later to write in 'For Mildred' (an aunt, one of Warwick's sisters who died in Port of Spain):

> I settled on this city casually
> too, by a commission;
> it was, like yours, my last known
> refuge. I said, I would press on
> abandoning it, instead . . .

he married, had children, created a theatre company, and became a member of the community. His wife was not only the 'embodiment' of the city, Margaret was important to Derek's career. She was well connected locally and with the Trinidadians who had lived in England; she was attractive and wined and dined visitors, they loved her. She had her own job, provided the family with a steady income, and devoted herself to Derek's work. She did everything she could to help Derek's theatre group, to gather the local social élite in support of his plays, and to charm foreign editors, writers, and publishers. Everyone still asks 'how is Margaret?'[9]

During September the *New Statesman* published 'In a Green Night'. Although still dense and requiring attention, Walcott's poetry was emerging from the purposeful obscurity characteristic of late Modernist experimentalism. Filled with allusions to Andrew Marvell's 'Bermudas' and 'The Garden', along with echoes of Wallace Stevens, it tells the Walcottian fear of losing youthful passion, of time passing, of death:

> The orange tree, in various light,
> Proclaims that fable perfect now
> That the last season's summer height
> Bends from each overburdened bough.[10]

The next month Walcott sent Ross a copy of *The Charlatan*, a full-length comedy, and asked that it be passed on to the Court Theatre, or perhaps Joan Littlewood. Walcott described it as taking the wind out of many West Indian pretensions; the racial mixture and comedy is better than any long melodrama about racial problems. V. S. Naipaul had returned to Trinidad on a grant (which resulted in writing *The Middle Passage*) and amused the Walcotts with his stories of literary London.

The Greenwich Village contacts continued. Alfred Leslie, a friend of Robertson, had accepted *Ti-Jean* for *The Hasty Papers*, a one issue Little Mag. During June 1960, a film club was started in Port of Spain. Members included Bergman's actor Erik Strandmark. Among the films Walcott saw were Bergman's *Smiles Of a Summer Night* and two of Satyajit Ray's. Walcott asked Leslie how he could get *Pull My Daisy* for the film society as no one had answered their order. He wanted Leslie to telephone Robertson and Frank.

Andrew Salkey included an extract from *The Sea at Dauphin* in a BBC Christmas programme for broadcasting on Boxing Day. The copyright department wrote (23 December 1960) that Walcott would be paid one guinea less tax. The tax was 7*s*. 9*d*. in the pound which meant that Walcott would eventually be paid 12*s*. 10*d*. after 8*s*. 2*d*. was deducted from £1. 1*s*. As someone not regularly resident in the United Kingdom, Walcott could claim a refund and a voucher was enclosed. Walcott would need to obtain the proper claim forms from his local tax office after receiving from the BBC's bankers a mail transfer. By then he had already been sent at least four letters on the subject, not including the actual payment of 12*s*. 10*d*., say US $2.50. Walcott might not be able to live off such royalties, but he was certainly contributing to the upkeep of administrators at the BBC, their bank, and both the British and Trinidadian tax offices.

The copyright department of the BBC wrote once more, wrote on 24 February 1961, to inform Walcott that he would receive one guinea less tax for the broadcast of a minute and a half of his work. This time the poem 'As John to Patmos' would be read on *Calling the Caribbean* the next day and repeated on March 4. The accounts department would write making payment.

Walcott worked on his poetry and plays over the Christmas holidays. Shortly after the New Year he sent (4 January 1961) Ross a full manuscript of a book with new poems meant to replace an earlier manuscript, which had contained some prose poems. Walcott was going to St Lucia on holiday for two weeks starting on 14 January. Ross wrote on 18 February that he would become editor of *London Magazine* in April and wanted more poems. By 27 February the Walcotts had returned from their holiday in St Lucia, and Peter, Walcott's son by his first marriage, was now living with them.

After Faye, who had decided to move north for better employment, sent Peter temporarily to Alix in St Lucia, Derek took him to Trinidad, and what had been an amicable divorce turned bitter.

Walcott, although a loner, has a strong sense of family and responsibility for family. He emotionally needed a son, but he was also very private, even secretive. Faye only learned through others of his new marriage and what she felt to be the unfair removal of Peter to Trinidad; Derek had not told Alix of his divorce until some time afterwards, and Alix, who was ill at the time, wrote to Faye that everything had been a surprise, and she could not keep Peter from his father. Later Alix was to be asked to live with Derek and Margaret to look after Peter, but that did not last long.

The first issue of Ross's *London Magazine* New Series (April 1961) included Walcott's 'Cadaver' and 'Simply Passing Through', along with creative writing by Philip Larkin, George Barker, and Ted Hughes, and articles or criticism by John Fuller, Jon Whiting, George Macbeth, John Bayley, Christopher Hollis, and Harold Acton. The standard was high. There was at the time no other literary review with such broad interests, including music, painting, and drama, and of such quality.

After Ross sent Walcott a telegram saying Jonathan Cape was accepting his poems, Tom Maschler wrote (16 June) that Ross had given him the manuscript of *In A Green Night* and that William Plomer, who was Cape's poetry reader, enjoyed it. Maschler was sending a standard contract, but instead of half the advance being paid later he could pay all on signature. Maschler (then the wonder kid among British editors) still edited the Penguin New English Dramatists series and wanted to know more about Walcott's plays in case he might be of some help. Three weeks later Cape sent a form for UK tax relief which would allow payment to be made directly to Walcott without deductions. Cape (25 July) thanked Walcott for the completed tax exemption application, but noted that it had not been certified by a Trinidadian tax office; it was being returned. Over the years as Walcott published and worked in many countries, his correspondence and notebooks were to be filled with notations concerning taxes.

Walcott (19 June) congratulated Ross on the new look of *London Magazine*, the expansion of its range to include theatre and art criticism, and the spacious setting of poetry. He thanked him for helping place his manuscript with Cape, especially as Walcott had been depressed by the lack of prospects of having his poems published in a proper book. He returned to Maschler (23 June) the signed contract and 'Islands', which he wanted as the penultimate poem in the volume. Walcott was concerned about the order. From the poems he had recently sent Ross, 'Bronze' was to be at the end. 'Castiliane' should be next to 'A Careful Passion'. He removed a few poems, such as 'The Statesman' which had appeared in the 1951 *Poems*, and two prose poems, 'The Fall' and 'Paysage'. Besides being concerned with the shape and contents of the volume, he wanted to make further revisions before the type was set and thought that he might want to make some further changes in proof as poems look different in print, but he hoped not too many as he was anxious to have his poems published in a book, an event he had long awaited and for which he thanked Ross and Cape.

Walcott said that he was working on a second book of verse, which would include two long poems, both of which are in sections. The first, shorter one, was already finished, but too long for the present book of lyrics. He was still working on the second, which would be finished early in 1962. His best plays so far were *The Sea at Dauphin* and *Malcochon*, which had been performed in England and one full-length play, *Ti-Jean and His Brothers*, a folk fantasy. There was also *Dream on Monkey Mountain*, which he wanted to send to Maschler after he finished revisions. He would be proud if he appeared in the Penguin New English Dramatists as the series was in all the bookstores. Walcott would like to edit a large historical anthology of Caribbean writing, from Cuba to British Guyana, but, as he lacked the scholarship, he needed help with languages beyond English. He concluded by asking for the full advance of £50 now for his first book as the book would run into thirty-five editions and sell well on both sides of the Atlantic. Maybe as critic for the *Trinidad Guardian* he should review it himself?

During August Maschler wrote that he was determined to find Walcott an American publisher for what had become *In a Green Night: Poems 1948–60*. Did Walcott have any contacts? They were still awaiting the necessary form to pay the advance. Walcott replied that he had published in *Evergreen Review* and knew Barney Rosset.

The Extra-Mural Department at UCWI was ready to publish *Malcochon* and another play. Others wanted *Ti-Jean*, but Vaz knew Walcott was thinking of revising it. He needed to know (9 August) whether Grove Press would be publishing *Malcochon* or *Ti-Jean*. Vaz offered many ideas which Walcott accepted or later adapted; here his remarks look forward to the 1970 revised *Ti-Jean* with André Tanker's music. There would be an Arts Festival in August with a prize of £150 for the best musical and Vaz was wondering about turning *Ti-Jean* into something like an opera, perhaps using a Jamaican composer at Juillard. Vaz said that *Ti-Jean* should be severely cut, especially the long complex passages (which would be good for Walcott who must learn to extract). Each prose section might be set within a different musical idiom (speaking on key, intoned, half-sung) in which case each character should be in a different style. This would help discipline Walcott's writing; the last scene especially needed more form.

John P. Harrison (2 September 1960), now Associate Director of the Humanities at the Rockefeller Foundation, wanted to know whether the Little Carib and Port of Spain would be a proper focus for West Indian theatre and would the new UCWI Trinidad campus with Sherlock at its head have an influence on the situation of performing arts. Harrison (12 September) thought he should come to Port of Spain when the Theatre Workshop and the Little Carib were operating normally and not specifically at Carnival as Walcott had suggested. Harrison would try to meet Peter Minshall, whom Walcott recommended, and Procope, Sherlock, and McBurnie. Walcott's letters were encouraging about his workshop and Harrison on 14 April looked forward to meeting Erik Strandmark. On his way back from South America he would stop in Trinidad. He would accommodate his schedule for the Minister of Education and Sherlock, and hoped to spend at least Sunday with Walcott. He wanted to be acquainted with Walcott's work, the Little Carib Theatre, the performing arts at the UCWI-Trinidad, and the beach. He wrote again ten days later that he would be in Port of Spain 1–5 June, leaving early on the 6th.

While in Trinidad Harrison discussed how the Little Carib might be turned into a semi-professional theatre company with its own building. Colin Laird was expected to plan for a New Carib Theatre suitable for 268–480 seats, depending on arena or proscenium staging, for which the Rockefeller Foundation would provide a lighting and a stage machinery system. 'The emphasis in the New Carib is on experimental theatre and dance, on lighting and movement, with a minimum of stage scenery.' Once a site was found, a public appeal for $250,000 would be announced. A semi-professional dance and drama company was planned.[11] After returning to the United States Harrison wrote (14 June) to confirm the travel grant for Laird to study theatre architecture in the United States and Canada during July and August. George Izenour at Yale agreed to talk to Laird, show him various theatre plans, and discuss the problems concerning the new Little Carib.

During August 1961, Herbert Machiz, the American off-Broadway director, visited Port of Spain to examine theatres for the Rockefeller Foundation. Walcott quoted him in the *Trinidad Guardian* as saying 'The present Carib is inadequate for anything else but workshop and teaching', but that the New Carib design was 'ideal for a more intimate form of theatre'.[12] Machiz and Walcott got along well and Machiz suggested that Walcott should apply for an Ingram Merrill

Foundation grant for poets. Machiz's room-mate could help arrange it. He also wanted to help develop the Theatre Workshop. Walcott sent his application for the Ingram award to Harrison for forwarding, but Machiz needed, on 5 January, to remind Walcott to send copies of his work to the Ingram Merrill Foundation so they could be considered at the 9 February meeting.

After returning to New York Machiz wrote (28 September) that he had given Harrison a complete report of Walcott's accomplishments and problems in Trinidad and suggested that he put together a team of people for four to six weeks to give intensive training in all aspects of theatre. Walcott should write officially to Harrison on official stationery explaining in detail what Machiz did in Trinidad and what Walcott wanted him to do in future. Walcott's Workshop was on the brink of something which could be terrific.

Beryl McBurnie was a good dancer with a strong personality and powerful friends; she expected to get what she wanted. Harrison (5 October) wrote to Walcott that McBurnie had sent to Yale University someone who understood from McBurnie that Harrison would arrange a fellowship. Harrison had never seen or heard of this person previously! He would talk with him but what did Walcott think? Harrison would consider fellowships for advanced training if that person would really make a major difference in developing the Little Carib, but McBurnie could not just send anyone and expect the Foundation to offer financial support. Harrison had spent an evening with Machiz who was hoping to arrange a $3,000 grant to free Walcott from journalism for a year. He was sending Walcott a copy of Donald Allen's anthology of *New American Poetry*.

Financial support in the West Indies remained more difficult and it took energy even to get what was earned. As *Drums and Colours* was now published, Walcott (13 October) wrote to H. L. Wynter, Director of Extra-Mural Studies, UCWI, Jamaica, that he would like his promised advance, based on 15 per cent of the selling price. He also asked about the status of, and various matters concerning, *Malcochon*. They were going to print the first version but he had sent a second version. No one mentioned a fee. He could not remember what Hill paid him for *Sea at Dauphin* in the same series, but he was paid before the play was published and he would like his money now for *Malcochon*, with the *Drums and Colours* royalties.

Walcott had heard from Slade Hopkinson that their friend Ronnie Llanos intended to produce *The Charlatan* in November for the First Season of Plays by the Jamaica Drama League at the new Little Theatre in Kingston. He wrote (13 October) to Llanos granting permission, but wanted £5 a performance and suggested he be given a percentage. The letter was more concerned with details of staging, which Walcott clearly wanted to supervise at least through the mail. Walcott was happy to hear that Slade was coming to Trinidad.

Eugenie Galperina, Foreign Committee, Union of Soviet Writers, Moscow, sent (18 October) a small anthology of West Indian poetry translated into Russian. The poems were taken from anthologies and Galperina asked Walcott for more poems and some plays. The anthology, 'The Time of Flambeaux-Trees', mostly translated from French, consisted largely of 'Negro' and 'nationalistic' poems, along with Walcott's 'As John to Patmos' and 'Words for Rent' published as 'Two Hieroglyphs on the Passing of Empires'. The most represented writers were Jacques Roumain (four poems), R. Camille (five poems), René Depestre (nine poems), and Claude McKay (seven poems). There were also three poems each by E. M. Roach and H. A. Vaughan.

William Plomer was determined that Walcott's poetry should gain recognition. He was one of the judges, along with C. Day Lewis and Patrick Kavanagh, for the Guinness Poetry Award. Although the judges did not select Walcott's 'Sea Chantey' as one of the three awards, they wanted to give some recognition of its merit and offered an additional award for the poem. The award winners were to be kept secret until Tuesday, 31 October, at Goldsmiths' Hall, London.

Walcott now replied, on 15 September 1961, to an old William Plomer letter, which he claimed to have kept in a trouser pocket where it was washed by the family cook. He quoted some lines by Ezra Pound about the delight of having friends (or letters) 'come from far countries', called poetry a blessed occupation, mentioned knowing Plomer's writings and his gratitude to Roy Fuller and Alan Ross for helping him publish, his own lack of a circle of poets, and how much it meant that a book of his would now be printed by a good publisher.[13]

Ross returned from Italy where he had been trying to recover from a recent mental breakdown. He was pleased (26 October) about the Guinness Award which he was honoured to accept for Walcott and predicted that 'Walcott' would soon be known throughout the world. Ross, however, proved unable to be at the ceremony. The *Trinidad Guardian* of 27 November carried a full report about the Guinness Award for poetry. John Hearne received the award on Walcott's behalf for 'A Sea-Chantey', a poem which begins with Walcott spelling his Caribbean with the exoticism and beauty of Baudelaire's vowels; it is in part a dedication of himself to the music of West Indian words and sounds as well as sights:

> Anguilla, Adina,
> Antigua, Cannalles,
> Andreuille, all the l's
> Voyelles, of the liquid Antilles,
> The names tremble like needles
> Of anchored frigates,
> In ports of calm coral,[14]

Robert Graves (then Professor of Poetry at Oxford) and George Barker received the main £250 awards, the former for a sequence of twenty-one love poems, and the latter for his 'Roman Odes'. William Snodgrass was awarded £100 for 'Heart's Needle'. Walcott received a special award of £50 ($240) as did Rex Warner, the latter for a translation from Greek of 'The King of Asine' a poem by George Seferis. Over 3,000 poems were considered, all those published in the British Isles July 1960-June 1961. Only Warner then lived in England. Graves lived in Majorca, Barker in Italy, and Snodgrass is American. An anthology of poems from the competition would be published, in the spring of 1962, as *The Guinness Book of Poetry, Number Five*. These were the fifth and final awards presented by Arthur Guinness, Son & Company.

Ross (2 November 1961) was planning a poetry issue for February. He sent some questions to be used as a basis for 3–500 words of Walcott's views about poetry, requested a poem and a photograph by 1 December for the issue. Walcott (24 November) sent replies and the photograph. He mentioned floods which took some lives and covered his floors in mud and ruined some clothing. He had just had the proofs of his book.

Several years after Walcott had studied with Stuart Vaughn at the Phoenix (and had been told by John Robertson to send Betty Lord his short play manuscripts) Betty Lord of the play department wrote (6 July) asking to see the script of *The Charlatan*, which Harrison had told her about. She was hoping to do a new play or two next season. John Robertson had already written after a long period of spiritual blight and trouble, including breaking up with his woman. He was unhappy working at the Phoenix, but it paid his bills. Harrison kept telephoning, but Robertson felt alienated, tactless. Walcott should know that while several people wanted to produce *Malcochon*, Robertson felt it would neither result in money nor fame unless Walcott supervised it himself. He believed that Penelope Potter and Betty Lord were serious and meant well, but Walcott should refuse permission to perform the play unless they brought him in to supervise the production.

Alfred Leslie wrote (10 October) from New York complaining that Walcott never replied to his letters. This was urgent. Robert Nichols, poet and playwright, of Judson Poets Theatre thought *Malcochon* a masterpiece and wanted to produce the play, but first needed to contact Walcott. He had come to see Leslie personally. Should Leslie show Nichols the other two Walcott plays he had, *Sea at Dauphin* and *Jourmard*? Leslie had tried to reach Walcott through John Robertson, who was touring upstate New York with a Shakespearian play for the Phoenix, but Robertson had said Walcott never answered letters. Leslie's letter was breathlessly written and misspelled in an amazing mess of black, yiddish, even Latino English, without any regard to sentence structure.

Walcott gave Nichols tentative approval to produce *Malcochon* at the Judson and (13 October) told Leslie to show him the other two plays, but wanted to know what kind of cast, setting, and director Nichols would have. Robertson had been in the West Indies and could explain what Walcott was after, but Robertson had not answered his last letter. The Judson Poets Theatre could use *Hasty Papers* for the acting script. Walcott would send some ideas, including a tape for accents and music. Walcott wanted a copy of *Pull My Daisy* from Grove Press. He complained that Leslie's agent never replied to the local, Port of Spain, film club about showing *Pull My Daisy.*

bob nichols—no caps this time—thanked Walcott (14 November 1961) for his friendly letter. nichols was a playwright himself and interested in Noh theatre. He loved the control, brevity, form, and lyricism of *Malcochon*. The Judson was indeed the church Walcott remembered. In the past it had had an art gallery and magazine, on Washington Square South. He enclosed his theatre schedule for the year and wanted it returned as it was his only copy! The company still needed to make a final decision about doing *Malcochon* and who would direct it. There would be no money in it for Walcott, but their last play had been taken to the White Barn Theatre and eventually to Broadway. The Judson Poets Theatre is small, seating about seventy-five, three-quarters round, in the choir loft. The next month Robert Nichols, now with capitals and at a different Village address, again wrote to Walcott. *Malcochon* was now planned for late January and rehearsals would soon begin. He wanted his schedule returned.

Plans continued to use a new Little Carib Theatre for the teaching of performing arts by the University of the West Indies, by McBurnie's dance company, and by Walcott's theatre company. Bruce Procope had sent to Harrison a copy of the Articles of Association and Certificate of Incorporation of the Little Carib Theatre, along with a list of those needing advanced training. The list included actors, musicians, dancers, set designers, a bit of everything. Harrison (20 December 1961) asked Walcott about priorities and who would really develop. Procope mentioned that Walcott and McBurnie were planning a summer school in dance and drama for 1962. Herbert Machiz had already discussed a six-week seminar in theatre by professionals of which he would be in charge. Harrison wanted to know if the Little Carib was ready for such a large effort? He could send Machiz for ten days to discuss the seminar and what should become a national theatre. The Chairman of the Executive Committee should write requesting Machiz's visit. Harrison understood that Walcott and George Williams were making a list of lighting equipment. They should not depend on Rockefeller support unless there was a successful national appeal in Trinidad by the LCT in support of their new building. Three weeks later Harrison asked whether the Little Carib's Board of Director's was willing to go ahead with the seminar as planned by McBurnie and Walcott. He needed to know immediately; otherwise it would be too late and difficult to get support for the Little Carib on the scale that had been discussed. Harrison again (5 February) complained that he had no official request from the Little Carib about Machiz returning to discuss the seminar. Machiz was, however, awarded a two-week travel grant to help plan a summer season of dance and theatre at Little Carib. Harrison was going with Machiz to Yale to see a production of Errol Hill's *Man Better Man*. While there he would discuss with Izenour and others whether George Williams might be accepted for six months as a special student to study lighting.

The January *London Magazine* published 'Fregata Magnificens' (which would be revised as 'Man O' War Bird' for the 'Tropical Bestiary' sequence). This was a different poem from Walcott's 'Man O' War Bird' in the December 1953 *Bim*. The Man O'War Bird had a personal significance; its emblematic meaning later was described in 'A Latin Primer' in *The Arkansas Testament*. It was, he wrote, his 'phoenix'. Unable to find his own voice, imitating European models, he, one Saturday, near Vigie, watched a frigate bird:

> its emblem in the cirrus,
> named with the common sense
> of fisherman; sea scissors,
> *Fregata magnificens*
> *ciseau-la-mer*, the patois
> for its cloud-cutting course;
> and that native metaphor
> made by the strokes of oars,[15]

As Stephen Spender, recently in Trinidad, had said Ross was ill, Walcott (14 February) sent Charles Osborne 'Origins', the long poem that he had been working on for several years and wanted published entire in a single issue. Osborne rejected it (6 March) saying that he, Ross, and others felt it did not work.

Ronald Bryden returned in February to Trinidad to see his parents. He had read some of Walcott's work in *London Magazine*, and telephoned him to request poems for the *Spectator* of which he was literary editor. Walcott came to Bryden's parents' house for a drink and as a result wrote 'Verandah's End', about an elderly couple at the end of the Empire. They became friends and Margaret Walcott the godmother of Bryden's son. 'Origins' was too long for the *Spectator* so Walcott also sent Bryden a shorter poem, but he was irritated by Osborne's rejection and complained (28 March) that 'Origins' was his best poem.[16]

The Ingram Merrill Foundation (12 March) granted Walcott $3,000 in aid of his writing. Walcott would the next year, on 2 May 1963, be awarded a further $1,500 for six additional months. By contrast, Wycliffe Bennett (27 March) wrote from the Ministry of Welfare and Culture, Jamaica, concerning the £9 royalties still outstanding for the use of *The Charlatan* during the Season of Plays sponsored by the Jamaica Drama League of which Bennett was President. The League had no money and could not pay now. Walcott had written several letters on the subject and Bennett was annoyed. Walcott eventually received £5. Such were the problems of earning a living as a West Indian dramatist.

Maschler (28 November 1961) sent Walcott the jacket proof of *In a Green Night*. The blurb said that this was Walcott's first collection of poems to appear in England and indicated 'that he may be the outstanding poet in English of his generation. His work is of exceptional interest, not only for its sensibility and sensuousness, its technical skill, and its memorable themes, lines and images, but also because of its success in resolving the conflict, or antithesis between his Caribbean allegiances and evidently passionate love of the English language and literature.' Maschler was going to New York and hoped to find Walcott an American publisher. During March he sent Walcott an early copy of *In a Green Night*. The official publication date was 16 April 1962. The first impression was 2,000 copies in sheets, but initially only 500 were bound. It took until 1967 to sell the 2,000 after which there were reprints at the end of 1967 and during 1969.

Bryden (6 April) had been reading a review copy of *In a Green Night* and asked Walcott to send more poems for the *Spectator*. He said he had never thought in his time to read a world-class literature about West Indian society and landscape, and that the only British poets of Walcott's calibre were Gunn and Hughes. He urged Walcott to come to London and shine. He looked forward to seeing Derek and Margaret again if they came to London in September, and added that since returning a week ago from New York, he had been catching up with reading correspondence and literary life. There were contradictory reports about Ross's condition. Bryden thought 'Origins' great. Auden and Gunn would be writing for the *Spectator*. Walcott, through Ross, Fuller, and now Bryden, was being taken up by influential literary London although he was not part of it.

Cape mailed an early copy of *In a Green Night* to Robert Graves who (April 13) responded with 'Derek Walcott handles English with a closer understanding of its inner magic than most (if not any) of his English-born contemporaries'. Now Walcott had a greatly supportive quote from one of the giants of English poetry in the first half of the century, a giant who had been dismissive of Yeats, Eliot, and most other poets. He soon had Robert Lowell, the current monarch of American poetry, actively supporting him. Walcott had moved beyond being the best West Indian poet backed by Simmons, Collymore, and other regional critics.

The Graves quotation might be seen in a broader context—the context of what was becoming Commonwealth literature and what now is thought of as post-colonial literature. The novels of Patrick White, V. S. Naipaul, Chinua Achebe, and other writers from former colonies had been greeted with critical acclaim, but mostly for their exoticism, politics, or for reporting about abroad. They spoke of the colonies, decolonization, even national, racial, and cultural differences, but their significance was seen as largely in social, anthropological, and political reportage. Graves said something different and more important. This West Indian, this colonial, understands and uses English creatively better than most, perhaps all, of those born in England. This was the real handing over of the Empire, of the language and its heritage, of the future of English, to the former colonies, and the acceptance that English was no longer a British preserve. It was not a question of Americans being more numerous or the United States having more economic power, rather here was a coloured West Indian who 'handles English with a closer understanding of its inner magic than most (if not any) of his English-born contemporaries'. Warwick and Alix Walcott, the Castries Methodist schools and St Mary's College, Walker, Simmons, the bilingual culture of St Lucia, the range of Englishes and dialects used in the West Indies, had produced a mastery of, and sensitivity towards, English not likely to be found in England.

The great masters of English in our time—Walcott, Naipaul, Rushdie, Soyinka—have been writers from former colonies where the use of English is in conflict with other languages or where standard English is the dialect of the minority. In such places English must be learned and used with care like a precious jewel to be preserved, and such careful use is part of belonging to a social and educated élite, an élite that finds part of its cultural self-definition and claim to superiority in its possession of English literature. Education and careers are devoted to mastery of English language and literature, a mastery made more creative and sensitive by the pull of other influences and perspectives. These other influences are part of the richness brought to the language and literature. With Walcott's generation of writers English literature became truly international, no longer the preserve of a few 'white' nations.

In a Green Night was dedicated to Alix Walcott. In the acknowledgements Walcott wrote 'I should also like to thank Mr. Alan Ross for his encouragement and assistance'. The volume was the work of a mature poet. Walcott had put his experiments behind him, out of the sight of most critics. There were no prose poems, no imitation avant-garde obscurities, little of his racial and sexual rages. Themes included leaving home, loss of religious faith, the passing of the Empire and its ruins. Analogies are made between various homes, heaven, this world, and the Caribbean; man is an exile bitterly seeking home. 'In a Green Night' expresses Walcott's fear of losing youthful poetic intensity and vision, but promises that age and experience will not 'quail the comprehending heart'.

There were forty-two poems selected from over a decade, most had been revised since their first publication. The first six poems were republished or revised from *25 Poems* (1948). Many of the poems are sequences; 'Tales of the Islands' is a sequence of ten poems and 'Fragments and Epitaphs' consists of seven. Besides radically revising the style of the 'Tales' sequence since the prosy-1958 *Bim* version, Walcott replaced the original chapter 10 by a new version of chapter 11. Chapters 1 to 3 ('La rivière dorée', 'Qu'un sang impur', and 'La belle qui fut') were already in their third versions. *In a Green Night* was the first publication of 'Pocomania', 'Parang', 'Islands', 'Bronze', and most of the New York poems, such as 'Bleecker Street, Summer'.

The sonnet sequence 'Tales of the Islands', at the centre of the volume, shows that shifting between registers and varieties of English helps express the social and cultural range of the Caribbean. John Figueroa has often pointed to Sonnet VI which opens 'Poopa, da' was a fête! I mean it had | Free rum free whisky' as the real beginnings of the use of dialect in West Indian poetry. Others had tried, often unsuccessfully, to use dialect for realism; it usually sounded American or was used for comedy. In Walcott's sonnet a society came alive with its complex, ironic interaction of classes, cultures, and ways of speaking:

> They catch his wife with two tests up the beach
> While he drunk quoting Shelley with 'Each
> Generation has its angst, but we has none'[17]

Naipaul had urged that writers sending stories to the BBC *Caribbean Voices* should use dialect and he had used it for conversations in his own fiction. It would still take time before Walcott could use it for the authorial voice.[18]

The volume accepted a complicated West Indian and personal history with intelligence and craft while remaining lyrical. There was a real West Indian landscape. Besides examining his personal and the colonial situation, *In a Green Night* was rich in Walcott's allusions to, and imitations of, paintings and aspects of European art history. Walcott the painter and student of art history was present in titles, allusions, ideas for, and models of, poems, even in the way he visualized space, shifting angles of vision up and down, back and forward, using varied perspectives, colours, sketching land- and seascapes, still lifes, monuments, and portraits. 'The Polish Rider' is also the title of a painting by Rembrandt and the poem uses as its subject an engraving by an earlier painter, Albrecht Dürer. In 'Roots' the ruins of the fort at Vigie are likened to those in paintings by Nicolas Poussin and Giovanni Bellini. The hawk in 'Choc Bay' changes perspectives as it moves through the sky; there is a foreground, background, a seascape. The fourth stanza alludes to Botticelli's *Birth of Venus.* 'A City's Death by Fire' recalls Turner's romantic *The Burning of the Houses of Parliament.*[19]

Walcott, who subscribed to and would let no one touch the British weeklies and Sunday press until he had read the literary pages, found himself reviewed by Cyril Connolly in the *Sunday Times* along with books by Robert Graves, Robert Conquest, and *The Guinness Book of Poetry 1960–61.* Connolly, who had heard about Walcott from Ross, mentioned the two one-act plays performed at the Royal Court, called Walcott a fresh, original voice: 'a beautiful sport of heredity and environment' who takes risks. He praised the 'Tales of the Island' sonnet sequence and recommended that readers buy the book.[20]

The early reviewers noticed many of Walcott's continuing characteristics as a poet. F. N. Furbank in the *Listener* mentioned the melancholy, the 'fresh and stinging colours, luscious melody and intense awareness of place'. There is 'joyful apprehension of the immediate physical world' and a 'metaphysic of natural mutability and renewal' which Walcott uses 'to come to terms with the immutable historical wrongs of his people'. Furbank noted the use of vignettes of social debris, the masterly transitions from bitterness to reconciliation, Walcott's images of himself as shipwrecked, condemned to be a migrant, and of his heart as a coal ready to flame. The poetry 'hums with echoes of Villon, Dante, Catullus, and the metaphysicals'. The remarkable 'Ruins of a Great House', about a slave-owner's mansion, is 'strung on a frame-work of quotations from Browne, Donne, and Shakespeare'. History has made Walcott a citizen of the world. Walcott has a remarkable ear and deliciously handles metaphor.[21]

Hugo Williams, in the *London Magazine*, wrote that Walcott's poetry is rich, confident, never runs short of fresh pleasures. Williams said Walcott uses the page as a canvas; he praised Walcott's 'new colours', 'vocables', 'extravagance'. The iambics are light and versatile; the line endings, especially final lines, are well finished. While this is poetry of a high level, more selectivity would have been better; there is a bit too much of the self, at times muddy, self-pitying, 'superfluous epithets', over-ripe words, a tendency towards archness, and smugness. In the *Spectator* John Montague understood Walcott as a nationalistic romantic developing a language with local imagery. He questioned whether Walcott's struggle with conventions and his sensibility could be accommodated in English; it seemed crippled in comparison to exultant St-John Perse (who in 1960 was the first writer from the Caribbean to be awarded a Nobel Prize).[22]

When West Indian reviewers discussed Walcott's place in defining a regional tradition, they raised questions about the future of English literature. The poet and historian Edward Brathwaite, then an extra-mural tutor in St Lucia, carefully examined how Walcott's poetry since his first self-publications offered an evolving personality and relationship to the region. John Figueroa felt Walcott had 'drawn on all the strands of his heritage and used the opportunities which it affords so fruitfully' ranging from Horace to 'le loupgaron' and 'Parang'.[23]

C. L. R. James, who followed the new West Indian writing with attention, recognized something of more significance than most reviewers were aware. His review of *In a Green Night* touches on many of the main issues of West Indian literature, such as the consciousness of self-division, the need to build on the elemental while having a modern perspective, the sense of the region as a whole, the necessity for the artist to be true to art and self while somehow speaking from within a culture. Walcott's determination to live in the West Indies 'for a writer of poetry . . . is a heroic determination'. He claims poetry is the most difficult of the arts and Walcott is the first West Indian poet. He knows what he is doing and has his own vision and the technique for it. He sees the West Indies, especially the islands, the seas, the fishermen. He rejects the foreign and educated West Indian stereotypes, occasionally satirizing them. He is aware of the twentieth-century need to find a philosophical basis of experience, but he does not impose this on the people he describes. 'We have produced a poet, an authentic poetry-centered poet. Whatever else we do or do not do, that is something.' 'For centuries we used the language and literature of the English people. Now we are adding to it. Let no one underestimate what this means, to them, to us, and to other English-speaking peoples.' This was a declaration of independence, a recognition that the literatures and cultures of Europe would be changed by the former colonies as the latter learned to find their own voices and see themselves for what they are. Commenting on Walcott's 'A Map of The Antilles' (about Odysseus in the Circean seas), James observed: 'We are a new people who have first to learn what we are. Nowhere else have I ever been made so aware of the various islands of the West Indies as a West Indian entity.'[24]

By contrast the poet A. N. Forde, in *Bim*, argued that Walcott's concern was with the self, and that his being born in the West Indies was immaterial, despite claims to the contrary and the West Indian 'atmosphere'. It would be wrong to expect anything else as the only mentors available were the English tradition. Forde praised the way Walcott had developed from the Dylan Thomas-like language and sentiment of 'A City's Death by Fire' to the dramatic instinct and nuanced tone of 'A Careful Passion'. 'A Country Club Romance' has a Naipaulian satiric eye. Forde felt that Walcott was restless, uncomplacent, and obsessively aware of time, time wasted, and death.[25]

William Carr, an Englishman who had moved to the West Indies to teach at the university, used *In a Green Night* to criticize those who would reject Europe and seek their origins in Africa. To him Walcott's invocation of Marvell in the title suggested a desire for elusiveness, balance, poise, and clarity. 'Ruins of a Great House' offered many opportunities for outrage, but he felt Walcott saw that the Great House was not just a place of imperialism and slavery, it was also the culture that formed the poet. In this poem and in 'A Far Cry from Africa' Walcott spoke of hurts, crisis, self-recognition, and real feelings in contrast to falsified emotions. 'A Careful Passion' looked at an adulterous love affair with the eye of a novelist. Passion was not genial (Carr was to leave his English wife and family); Walcott noted its many complexities with stringency, compassion, and understanding. A year later Carr returned to 'The significance of Derek Walcott' for a broadcast produced by the Extra-Mural Department of UWI. Carr claimed that Walcott, in the by now already famous lines about Africa and love of the English tongue, was the only local writer to face up to the dilemma concerning the necessary European and English sources from which West Indian poetry would need to develop. The artist must recognize that the culture which produced the slave-trade also produced Shakespeare, and Donne, and Marvell. Only an understanding of that ambiguous relationship could cleanse something of the cruelty or change it into something to be lived with.[26]

By 1962 the West Indian novel was well established. Besides the earlier novels of Selvon, Hearne, and Lamming, Naipaul had published four books including his classic *A House for Mr Biswas*. Wilson Harris had published *The Palace of the Peacock*. Now Walcott had shown that poetry could capture the complexities of the society. Gordon Rohlehr later praised *In a Green Night* as 'a landmark in the history of West Indian poetry, liberating it at once from a simple mindless romanticism, weak historicism, over-rhetorical protest and sterile abstraction'. Walcott tried to come to terms with 'a tangled cultural heritage which offered both a vision of unbearable brutality, and the promise of rich variety'. While hearing an inner affirmation even in Walcott's usual melancholy, Rohlehr noted the sense of 'void' and fear of the drying up of the poetic impulse.[27]

Maschler (5 July) sent Walcott reviews of *In a Green Night*. Cape had so far sold 588 copies which he thought good for a first book of poetry. The copyright department of the BBC continued to find Walcott a source of activity. Philip Sherlock's talk, 'Outlook from the West Indies', broadcast on 4 August 1962, on the General Overseas Service with two repeats, had quoted six lines from 'As John to Patmos'. The BBC would pay Walcott a guinea, less tax, although legally it was entitled to seven overseas broadcasts for its original guinea. He would hear from the accounts department next. The *Listener* was planning to print Sherlock's speech and as reprinting fees come under a different Act from broadcast fees he would be paid a further guinea this time without withholding tax. This would need to be dealt with by a different section of the accounting department. Sherlock also included twelve lines from Walcott's 'A Country Club Romance', which was published in *In a Green Night* and discussions concerning payment were taking place with Cape!

One request unexpectedly influenced Walcott's work for over two decades. Ross on 9 August asked Walcott to write an article for a new series concerning the end of school-days and the start of professional life. This forced Walcott to think about a significant period of his life. The article took several years, and was followed by years of attempting to write a continuation, which evolved into Walcott's great long autobiographical poem *Another Life*, which was followed by an even longer attempt at writing a prose autobiography. Several of Walcott's most important essays in turn derive from material in the unpublished unfinished chapters.

II

~~~~~~

1962–1964 Robert Lowell, Farrar, Straus and Giroux, Gerald Freund, *Selected Poems*

THE West Indian Federation lasted 1958–62. Guyana never joined, Jamaica wanted to go its own way, and Trinidad feared being swamped by the needs of the smaller islands, especially Grenada, who in turn feared dominance by Trinidad. The many ethnic and religious groups distrusted each other and were uncertain whether the regional Federation was bad or independent small nations worse. Whereas the Federation put power into the hands of a university-trained, often brown, bureaucracy, the politicians could keep power in their own hands by exploiting nationalism and racial tensions. Trinidad ended the Federation on 31 August 1962. With the end of the Federation some of the islands could not afford independence or preferred being colonies of England. It was another five years, in March 1967, before St Lucia became an Associated State, controlling its own internal affairs, but with England responsible for defence and foreign affairs. It took a further twelve years, until February 1979, before St Lucia became an independent state within the Commonwealth. Walcott continued to have a British passport, and decried small island nationalism as economically unsound, racially divisive, unable to support the region's artists, or encourage the development of a modern culture.

Erik Strandmark, a friend of Walcott since 1960, was famous in Sweden as an actor, teacher, and director in the Royal Dramatic Theatre. He wrote and directed *Beautiful Susannah and The Elders* and had major roles in over thirty films including Ingmar Bergman's *The Seventh Seal*. On a visit to Trinidad he had married a local woman and made Port of Spain his home, only returning to

Sweden to work. He was active in the film society (importing films that would otherwise have been difficult to obtain); he helped with an exhibition of African art, and directed a production of *Twelfth Night* that Walcott reviewed. When Strandmark suggested that he write a play for television to be shown to Bergman, Walcott wrote the first version of what was to be *In a Fine Castle*, originally a story of a French Creole family living in an elaborate mansion, inspired by Stollmeyer's 'castle', on the rim of Grand Savannah park. The Stollmeyers, local plantocracy, were part of the Port of Spain society in which the Walcotts circulated. The family was well known and included several well-known sportsmen and Hugh Stollmeyer, a painter.

Strandmark died on Saturday, 5 January 1963, when his private airplane crashed in sight of his friends at Trinidad's Piarco Airport. Two weeks after Strandmark's death, 19 January, a benefit for his family was held at the Little Carib Theatre. Walcott, George Lamming, Samuel Selvon, Slade Hopkinson, and Errol Hill read. Paintings were hung by Carlisle Chang, Sybil Atteck, and others. After Erik's death, Margaret and Derek were pillars of support for his wife Ena Strandmark, spending time with her, and making her drive a car again. Strandmark had captured the Nordic imagination, leaving security and fame for life in the tropics. His death left his wife and two children without support and a fund was established in Sweden so that they could live there. Walcott wrote, and dedicated to Ena, the Rilkean-titled 'O Trees of Life, What are your Signs of Winter?', first published in *Selected Poems*:

> . . . I imagine her
> This winter at a window,
> Shawled, in an empty room
> With two forgetting children,
> In the blue globe I brought
> Her when he died . . .'

When I visited Stockholm during 1994 people at the Royal Theatre still spoke highly of Strandmark, and Ena recalled a Port of Spain where Derek and Margaret Walcott were the young charmed prince and princess of an artistic circle. 'It was a time of wine and roses.' All those with cultural interests came to their parties, and invited them to their parties; this was a social and cultural élite.

Walcott first met Robert Lowell and Elizabeth Hardwick when they stopped in Trinidad during June 1962 on their way to Brazil under the auspices of the Congress for Cultural Freedom. Lowell had heard of Walcott through Bob Giroux, who learned of his poetry through Maschler. Walcott knew that they were coming for a poetry reading and lecture and met them at the airport. As a reporter he wrote an article for the *Sunday Guardian*, 'Poet From the Land of Bean and The Cod'. He later claimed to be so flustered he called Hardwick 'Edna

St Vincent Millay', to which she replied 'I'm not that old yet'. Like many amusing stories about himself that Walcott tells, it may be exaggerated. The Lowells planned to stay only a few days, but they so much enjoyed the company of Derek and Margaret, including a few days at a cabin on a cliff overlooking the Atlantic, that they stayed for ten. That was the beginning of a long friendship. At the cabin after the others had gone to bed, Lowell by gaslight read some of his poems from *Imitations* and asked Walcott what he thought of the Hugo and Rilke translations. Walcott felt honoured, and at various times would recall the meeting.

His own development as a writer was influenced by Lowell, who brought his life directly into his poetry, and by the Lowell of *Imitations* who 'had made the body of literature his body, all styles his style, every varying voice his own. The *Imitations* were not appropriations, but simply a rereading of literature in his own ... accent.' The friendship and influence were possible because Walcott and Lowell shared a love of literature, an erudition, the ability to quote and parody poets, a love of language and learning. The poetry of both echoes with centuries of poetry in many European languages—with poetry as a language of forms, phrases, sounds, metres, words, separate from specific cultures and languages. They both were New World aristocrats masquerading as democrats.[2]

The Walcotts often borrowed or rented the beach camp at Toco owned by the father of a friend of Margaret, Grace Phelps, and would go there at Christmas. One of Walcott's friends showed me a photograph from this trip with the pole of a beach umbrella bisecting the animated face of a Lowell sitting in a beach chair while prominently in the foreground is Walcott's back with his swimming trunks slightly below half-mast. An historical document lacking decorum.

Eight months later, after Cape sent Farrar, Straus a copy of *In a Green Night*, Robert Giroux asked Lowell for a report. He wrote (9 March 1963) that Walcott is the best 'negro' poet in English and very promising, he might well become much better. He has colourful descriptions of scenes and subjects, he has a Hart Cranean feeling for rhetoric, and the passion that makes a poem a poem. Lowell had used 'Bronze' the past summer in his 'anthology' at readings. Walcott shows that a negro and Trinidadian can be in the same league as good American and British poets, and that his race and place might even be an advantage. The poems are in places stiff, filled with echoes, but they are powerful. Lowell hoped Giroux would publish them. Giroux responded (22 May 1963) to Cape that he was interested; Walcott lines remain in his memory. Robert Lowell understood that Walcott was working on a second volume and Giroux thought a combined *Selected Poems* would have more success in the United States. Cape knew nothing about a second volume. Would Giroux consider publishing *In a Green Night* from sheets that Cape would supply? Giroux still preferred a selected volume. Cape hoped (17 June) Walcott had a second volume ready; it would help sell a volume of *Selected Poems* to Farrar, Straus for the United States.

The Walcotts were planning to be in New York during September as Derek had some money left from his fellowship, wanted to catch up with theatre, and hoped to speak with Straus or Giroux. This would be Margaret's first time in New York. She wrote (12 July) to the Lowells about the coming trip and amusingly listed an improbable group of people to meet, including Barry Goldwater, Sonny Liston, and David Belasco. During August Margaret wrote again to the Lowells saying that Derek had made someone read a poem from *Imitations* five times at a drunken luncheon. Cape informed Giroux that Walcott and his wife would be in New York from 14 September.

The Walcotts stayed for three weeks in a room with kitchenette for $50 a week at the Chelsea Hotel on 23rd Street. They went to films by Antonioni and Fellini, plays by Pinter and Genet, museums, and listened to jazz. As usual Derek made use of everything. He wrote 'Derek Walcott Looks at off-Broadway Theatre' for the *Trinidad Guardian*; the Trinidad Theatre Workshop would later perform plays by Pinter and Genet. Walcott had planned to stay at a midtown hotel, but with Lowell's help the trip was lengthened and partly financed by $300 from the Farfield Foundation. The Farfield Foundation for over a decade would fund the arts, especially in former colonies. It eventually was revealed as a channel through which CIA moneys could be used for those thought likely to support the West during the Cold War, especially those involved with or helped by the Congress for Cultural Freedom, which the Lowells were. It is too easy for those who ignore Soviet funding of intellectuals and artists during this period to assume that the CIA invented Modern African Literature. Most of the writers and editors were innocent about the ultimate source of American aid.[3]

The Lowells held a cocktail party for their friends among the New York literary intelligentsia to meet Walcott. By way of thanks he sent (28 October) what was intended as an amusing letter consisting of a cod interview by Malcolm X of Elizabeth Hardwick and Lowell's Spanish cook Teresa, which Walcott claimed was published in *Paris Review*, and which was being sold as anti-American propaganda in Clifford Sealy's Port of Spain bookshop. (Sealy was a Trinidadian writer, editor of the slim *Voices*, and book dealer.) The letter is in many voices, filled with multilingual puns and allusions. Partly in mock-Spanish and filled with attempted in-jokes about New York artistic and intellectual life, it recalls the cocktail party attended by William Meredith, Frederick Seidel, Susan Sontag, Robert Silvers, Jack Thompson, Howard Moss, and Henry Rago.

When Lowell recommended publication of Walcott to Robert Giroux, he brought him into what was to become a close-knit group of writers, especially poets, and New York intellectuals. Walcott soon became a surprising adjunct of 'The Family', a group of New York Jewish intellectuals. Through Lowell, Hardwick, Giroux, and Roger Straus, Walcott was invited to international conferences of intellectuals, invited to contribute to *Partisan Review*, later became one of those who wrote for the *New York Review of Books* (of which Hardwick was a founder); while remaining a West Indian writer he was becoming part of the New York literary world.

Walcott was coming to know those at the centre of American literary life. Farrar, Straus was to become the major American poetry publisher, the American equivalent to Faber, and connected to *Partisan Review*. Many of those mentioned in Walcott's letter to Lowell would have some role in Walcott's career. Moss as poetry editor of the *New Yorker*, the best paying and most widely read publication that published poetry, later became Walcott's main magazine market. Sontag was, along with Lowell, Hardwick, and Straus, part of the *Partisan Review* group. The door was not only opening to the New York literary establishment, it was also opened towards Boston. Lowell was part of the literary establishment of both cities. Walcott was eventually to be appointed to what was thought of as Lowell's former position as a professor of poetry at Boston University. I am making it sound like a laying on of hands to the future heir of the firm; it was not that easy or obvious. And putting it in such a fashion is to ignore Walcott's West Indian life, which was his main life, and his British sponsorship which was, through Ross, Plomer, Cape, and Bryden, extraneous to New York. Still, Walcott understood that the future was with the United States, that as a West Indian he was American, and that his intellectual home was among the cosmopolitan Modernist culture of the New York intelligentsia rather than the British tradition.

Farrar, Straus was a newish company which Roger Straus purchased from Farrar with family money. Related to the Guggenheims and Macys, always dressed in the best handmade clothing, Roger Straus was at first treated as a rich foolish upstart Jew by the then largely WASP New York publishing scene, but Farrar, Straus and Giroux has turned out to be the only major publisher established after the Second World War that has survived into the twenty-first century. Straus surprised his rivals by locating and keeping the publishing company in unfashionable, low-rent Union Square and by building a solid reputation. He became part of the New York cultural world, being a trustee or a senior officer of *Partisan Review*, the Guggenheim Foundation, the New York Institute of Humanities, and PEN. He was interested in European fiction and ideas at a time when they were coming into fashion in the United States. A bright extrovert, Straus enjoyed being around writers, enjoyed travel, enjoyed international business. He had charisma; other publishers complained that their writers changed house after meeting him. He recognized talented people, trusted them, knew how to use and promote them, concentrated on high culture, knew what would sell, was willing to invest, and would wait for future profits. He was to publish more writers awarded the Nobel Prize in Literature than any other publisher in the world. His authors would include Elizabeth Bishop, T. S. Eliot, William Golding, Herman Hesse, Neruda, Isaac Singer, Nadine Gordimer, and Philip Roth.

If his list was and remains especially known for its poets, it was due to Robert Giroux. Giroux had studied at Columbia College with Mark Van Doren and edited the *Columbia Review* in which he published John Berryman and Thomas Merton. Poetry was difficult and expensive to set in print, and revisions in proofs were costly, but Giroux wanted poetry to be given attention and look good. In 1955 Giroux moved from Harcourt Brace to be editor-in-chief at Farrar, Straus. Seventeen well-known authors followed him including John Berryman, Randall Jarrell, Jack Kerouac, Robert Lowell, Bernard Malamud, Thomas Merton, and Flannery O'Connor. In 1964 he became a full partner of Farrar, Straus and Giroux. Giroux was not only a working editor, he created a tradition of acting as an agent, submitting poems to journals, handling requests for readings, and building the careers of his writers. Farrar, Straus and Giroux treated its writers as part of a family in which temperament was expected, outbursts permitted, attention was required, and loans given. Reading memos between Giroux and others at Farrar, Straus later when Walcott's career began to take off, one can feel a sense of excitement disproportionate to likely financial returns. Many of the writers became friends, attended each other's readings and parties, and published in each other's magazines.

Derek and Margaret charmed Giroux, who wrote to Cape (1 October) as soon as he received the manuscript of *Selected Poems*—which at this time consisted of twenty-three poems from *In a Green Night* and eighteen new poems. He offered an advance of $400 for United States rights. Walcott had suggested his placing poems in American publications and Giroux would do this, without commission in little magazines, for 10 per cent in commercial magazines. Walcott wanted the advance, but Giroux explained it must go through Cape, which would take 10 per cent. *Selected Poems* was scheduled for publication during May 1964.

Walcott always revised his writings on their way towards publication. He soon wanted to change selections in the book, especially material in Part II. The second part should start with the new long poem 'Origins'. Walcott had worked on it for two years and revised it again after returning to Port of Spain. 'Origins' (for Veronica Jenkin) was influenced by Césaire in its concerns and long lines; its lyricism and diction is like St-John Perse. It is another of Walcott's Odyssey poems, the odyssey of evolution, the odyssey to the New World, especially from Africa. Walcott wanted Lowell to look at 'Origins'. Giroux sent 'Origins' to Lowell, saying Walcott did not want to use it unless he agreed. 'Mania of the Dogstar', revised and retitled 'Dogstar', showed the influence of Lowell in dropping initial capital letters at the start of lines, which changed the effect from isolated lines of verse to prose-like continuity. It mentions three friends dead in a year. 'Choir of Statues', dropped as unclear, was an especially nihilistic, pessimistic poem in which, instead of the older Christian notion of eternal rings of light, there is stillness around inactivity while immortality is petrification. All life creates its extinction.

On 28 October 1963 Walcott wrote a long letter to Ross to whom he had not written for some time. New York was costly for them, London was out of the question, and they had to go into debt, but it was worth it; otherwise Walcott feared becoming rusty. He had met Frederick Seidel, who was under Lowell's influence, and who had published *Final Solutions.* Walcott thought the poems powerfully phrased, and that the book had a dramatic spine. Ross had written a negative report on a proposed anthology by Wycliffe Bennett of West Indian literature and Walcott agreed. Walcott wanted to edit an issue of *London Magazine* with good writers: Naipaul, Hearne, Lamming, Harris, Selvon. Margaret was having a baby. Farrar Straus would put out a selection of Walcott's poems in the spring, which Walcott saw as an extension of Ross's help in publishing with Cape.

In mid-November Walcott suggested to Giroux dividing *Selected Poems* into three parts with 'Origins' as Part II. He had letters from universities in Texas and Yale about possible readings in 1964. John Harrison, now at the Institute of Latin American Studies, University of Texas, Austin, wrote (30 September) that when Walcott was in the United States he could give a lecture or reading at Texas and stay with the Harrisons. Harrison would try to arrange readings at Texas, Yale, and a third university which, combined, should more than cover costs.

Walcott published his first 'Focus on the Arts' column in the *Trinidad Guardian* on Saturday, 7 December 1963. Starting on 11 December this became a regular Wednesday column on page 5 of the *Trinidad Guardian* and consisted of news and opinions on a variety of topics. During the next two years Walcott would usually write a 'Focus on the Arts' column for the Wednesday *Trinidad Guardian,* an arts review for the *Sunday Guardian,* and an essay or feature piece for its Sunday Magazine. There might also be a short piece on other days. Walcott published about one hundred articles during 1964, about sixty in 1965, about eighty in 1966.

His 'Focus On The Arts' column for 1 January 1964 was mostly a review of Alan Ross's recent book *The West Indies At Lords.* Besides remarking on some local painters, Walcott mentions that Denis Williams's *Other Leopards* is 'the most interesting novel of the year for me'. Williams, an excellent Guyanese painter and African art historian, had indeed written one of the classics of West Indian literature. Walcott's short review is a marvel of insight, summation, compression, and style. The novel 'traced the breakdown and gradual anthropological throw-back of a West Indian intellectual baffled by Africa and his Western heritage. Mr. Williams' style is impressionist, his sense of humour profound, and he has excellently located the germ of our cultural schizophrenia.'[4]

The Sunday articles are more unified, think pieces. Four days after writing about Ross and Williams, he was lamenting the lack of a spiritual purpose since the Federation collapsed; although the region is culturally one, the artist has no nation. Within the region the Catholic–Creole nations, like Martinique and St Lucia, have more in common than St Lucia has with Barbados or Antigua. Trinidad should be the most culturally creative because of its wealth and multiracial composition, but it lacks a cultural policy. Perhaps a revolution, such as in Cuba and Haiti, or at least revolutionary social tension, is needed to create national self-expression in which the artist and citizen could be united? Walcott objected to attempts to bring back to the West Indies artists living in England. They feel secure in English culture; they have the outlook of an older generation, that is why they live there. Patronage instead is needed for new local artists through an arts council, scholarships, a theatre, a building where talents could be trained and performing arts produced. As usual Walcott defines regional needs in terms of his own. He will argue consistently that there is a culture to which he and other local artists belong, a multiracial, multilingual culture which includes Césaire from Martinique and St-John Perse from Guadeloupe. Stop imagining that Naipaul and those who made it in London are going to return, that is another colonial heritage to want back those who have fought their way to success abroad. Put your money into those who work as artists in the West Indies regardless of national origins or race. Their need is for scholarships to study abroad and places in which to perform. This requires money, and a policy about how to spend the money.[5]

The 'Focus On Arts' columns allowed Walcott to enjoy himself as a public figure, although behind the amusement was the usual message that good art results from technique and hard work. Local artistic activities were mostly repetitious and predictable. Most of the six pieces in the new National Art Exhibition are, 'as paintings, pathetically incompetent, but as acts of patriotism, invaluable . . . They are mostly primitives, which is a euphemism in these parts for people who can't paint.' Walcott then makes an analogy between bad primitive painting and bad poetry. 'Like some of the poets they assert that they don't need to know anything about art to paint. Grammar is a hangover from the colonial mentality. Drawing is for Europeans. The banners are self-expression.' *Voices*, a new literary magazine in Port of Spain, shows just such faults. There are the therapeutic writers who 'work themselves up to an orgiastic frenzy', those who are 'incomprehensible', and a few offering an 'anarchic image of revolt. Only the poetry is revolting.' The magazine however looks good and should be supported. While Walcott amusingly observed that 'his opinions deplete the ranks of his friends', there was obviously a readership that enjoyed Walcott's views, wit, and superiority. These columns that Walcott was grinding out several times a week for six years are a golden spot in modern journalism.[6]

In the late summer of 1962, Harrison left the Rockefeller Foundation to be Director of the Institute of Latin American Studies at the University of Texas, Austin. He was replaced by Gerald Freund, who was to have a role in several important events in Walcott's career. Besides his decade at the Rockefeller Foundation, Freund was from 1980 to 1983 Vice-President at the John D. and Catherine T. MacArthur Foundation, where he started the Prize Fellows Program, the so-called Genius Awards. Later he was director, president, or consultant to several organizations concerned with philanthropy, including the Whiting Writers' Awards. In August 1962, Freund and Harrison flew to Trinidad where they were met after midnight by Derek, Margaret, and Peter and driven to the new Hilton where they talked until morning. Walcott drank too much and frequently criticized members of the Little Carib board; he had resigned himself to establishing a theatre without the university. This was Freund's first meeting with Walcott, who showed him scrapbooks for intended productions of Beckett and Brecht. Freund thought him temperamental, irascible, erratic, someone whose life was made stable by his wife, but the Rockefeller Foundation would need to trust his judgement concerning artistic matters at the Little Carib as, Freund thought, Beryl McBurnie was mystical, unreliable, and artistically not outstanding. Freund was impressed by Slade Hopkinson, who was teaching Latin in a school, and by the painter Peter Minshall. Plans for turning the Little Carib into a regional theatre and for co-operation with the university soon foundered. No money was collected for the building, the government failed to supply any land, and consequently the Rockefeller Foundation did not supply lights and generally lost interest except in Walcott's theatre workshop. The university, now independent from London, but without a West Indian Federation to support it, was coming under political and financial pressure from the demands of local politicians.

   The first public production of the Little Carib Theatre Workshop consisted of two one-act plays. Walcott directed Slade Hopkinson in Samuel Beckett's *Krapp's Last Tape* and Hopkinson directed the West Indian Dennis Scott's *The Caged* at the Little Carib Theatre, 11–13 May 1962, both Absurdist plays. McBurnie is said to have shown her disapproval by loudly flushing the theatre's toilet during Hopkinson's excellent Krapp. Walcott's notebooks include a attractive drawing of a set design and poster for *Caged*; these drawings in his notebooks are, I feel, much more successful works of art than his later full-scale painting. They are looser, freer, with an excellent sense of colour and mood, probably derived from the need to consider lighting and costumes. Walcott was then working on two full-length plays, including a revision of *The Charlatan*, which was soon produced by the San Fernando Drama Guild. Directed by Dennis Scott, it won first prize in a competition held to celebrate the opening of Naparima Bowl at San Fernando, one of the few places outside of Port of Spain to perform plays in Trinidad. Walcott received TT $120 royalties. Walcott and Slade Hopkinson then directed *The Charlatan* at the Little Carib (7–10 December) as a Theatre Workshop production, which included Arnold Rampersad (later famous as a scholar of Black American literature) and Jean Miles (the future subject of Walcott's poem 'The

Silent Woman'). The lyrics were by Walcott and the setting was based on a design by Peter Minshall. This was the first real production of a play that had existed in various forms since at least 1950 and which Walcott was to continue to revise until 1977.[7] There is a mimeograph version from the 1950s printed by the UCWI, from 1962 the University of the West Indies Extra-Mural Department.

It was over a year before the Theatre Workshop made another public appearance, this time trying to find a niche between New Year and Carnival with two one-act plays. *The Lesson* by Ionesco and Walcott's *Malcochon*, both directed by Walcott, were produced 22–4 January 1964 at the Little Carib Theatre. The Workshop was becoming a company and now included such future regulars as Eunice Alleyne, Slade Hopkinson, Claude Reid, Errol Jones, and Stanley Marshall. Lighting was by George Williams, already a former Rockefeller Foundation Fellow. The *Trinidad Guardian* review praised the show. The two plays were repeated at the university and later at the Naparima Bowl, where in August Walcott's comedy *Jourmard* was produced by the San Fernando Guild and later entered in the West Indian one-act play section of the 1965 Arts Festival.

Now thought of as Naipaul's opposite, Walcott was often in agreement with his analysis of the problems of the West Indies, but whereas Naipaul saw the region as the victim of its history which resulted in a crude culture, racial strife, and the lack of political and moral stability, Walcott replied that the cultural creativity of the region would come from its lack of a historical tradition. Naipaul had left Trinidad for Oxford around the time Walcott went to the University College of the West Indies. After 1960 he occasionally returned to see his family in Trinidad. Sometimes he would see Walcott. Walcott in turn read and reviewed Naipaul's books as they appeared.

Why did Walcott settle in Trinidad? A 1986 *New York Times Magazine* article appears, as do many of Walcott's works, to be partly a reply to Naipaul. He has in mind the opening of Naipaul's *Mimic Men*, with its allusion to St Augustine's *City of God* with its contrast between the imperial and heavenly city. Walcott claims that Port of Spain offers the 'possibility of the ideal city' with the world's peoples and cultures 'intermingling'. It is exotic, a bazaar, but the people speak one language. The skyline is picturesque, a mixture of architectural styles and periods, the streets recall the nations of the world—Bengal, Lucknow. It is not the orderly imperial city, but a place of Carnival, of contrasting tastes. Walcott reverses what Naipaul criticized in *The Middle Passage*. Where Naipaul saw a noisy, shallow, half-formed society of too many races and cultures which lacked reverence, taste, and ideals and preferred the con man, Walcott offers a spicy stew, a callaloo. Trinidadian mimicry is the thousands of costumes at Carnival. Port of Spain lacks a decent museum, but its historical places are associated with great steel bands and calypsos. 'The calypsos are not merely popular rhyme. They have a force as personal, as responsible as François Villon's.' The calypsos are personal, expressions of the artists. Port of Spain has the necessary vulgarity of a city, of Rome. 'Towns become cities through . . . their satire.' Walcott speaks of the trees, flowers, hills of Port of Spain. It devotes itself to the artist connected with Carnival, the designers, and musicians. To live for Carnival is an aesthetic.[8]

Walcott began writing about Naipaul in a November 1961 *Sunday Guardian* with an article about and review of *A House for Mr Biswas,* 'A Great New Novel of the West Indies: The Man who was Born Unlucky'. This was followed the next year by 'History and Picong in *The Middle Passage*'. Each book was reviewed and there were general articles and, when Naipaul visited Trinidad, interviews. 'The Achievement of V. S. Naipaul' in the *Sunday Guardian* of 12 April 1964 followed on from Naipaul's recent Hawthornden prize in England for *Mr Stone and Knights Companion,* the third major prize he had won. Naipaul at 32 already had published six books and a seventh was announced for later in the year. Walcott knew Naipaul was his rival, a rival already far ahead of him in accomplishment and success, but who had followed a different path, and with a somewhat different temperament, which, Walcott felt, would eventually limit his achievement, and allow Walcott to be first.

Walcott's article is careful in its praise and reservations. Naipaul had already written what is 'probably the finest novel by a West Indian', *A House for Mr Biswas,* his 'nostalgic and affectionate portrait of family life'. It is thinly disguised autobiography and is like the great Russian novels in its sense of generational change. The portrait of failure, rootlessness, and disinheritance which result in 'material greed and spiritual emptiness' is symbolic of all the races of the region. It has a compassionate sense of the absurd, not the philosophical absurd, but determination mixed with self-delusion and grandeur. The humble are endowed with dignity.

Walcott was speaking about himself, seeing in Naipaul's writing a West Indies he knew, but he also distanced himself from Naipaul, the Naipaul who had left to have a career in London, the Naipaul who lived among the exiles who would never return except on visits, the Naipaul who was becoming a London literary personality and who wrote about Trinidad from memory, a Trinidad that had by then changed, and to which, one senses, Walcott was laying claim. Naipaul has re-created life, but he lacked innovation. His novels were based on traditional models, his prose was a model of reticence, he distrusted exuberance. Walcott seems to have seen Naipaul as his opposite, yet recognized that Naipaul was the one West Indian writer who would continue to develop.[9]

In September there was Naipaul's *An Area of Darkness* to review. Walcott claimed that the West Indian sensibility could only define itself after retracing the middle passage of the slaves from Africa or of the indentured labour from India (a view he would later use in *Dream on Monkey Mountain* and *Omeros*), but the nostalgia for origins only led to disappointed exile in London. *An Area of*

Darkness revealed Naipaul as a dispossessed colonial. Instead of the distanced, supercilious, mocking traveller of *The Middle Passage*, Naipaul in India was afraid to enter and be lost among the Indian crowd with its degradation, fantasy, and fatalism. Unlike the carefully constructed prim sentences of the earlier books, here the writing was looser, the sentences longer, as Naipaul examined himself and his relationship to India. The book was a self-portrait, seldom calm. As a colonial Naipaul had worked hard to go to London thinking it was the centre of his world; it was not. By returning to India, Naipaul lost what it had meant for him. He was now a displaced person in London with no place to which to return.[10]

While Walcott tried to be objective, there was another problem beyond differences of personality and ideas. Walcott disliked the clear, unmetaphoric, understated, distilled prose Naipaul had mastered. Walcott was a poet in love with metaphor, a Modernist, someone who brought his larger-than-life personality into his writing, someone who approached theatre by writing powerful scenes rather than through a well-structured story. Reviewing *The Gift* Walcott was delighted by Nabokov's puns, parodies, ambiguities, voices, puzzles, and indifference to plot and realism—life was too simple and repetitive.[11] This was the kind of prose he admired. Long before he met Joseph Brodsky, Walcott was already at heart a Russian writer. Maybe it was that Jewish ancestor he sometimes imagined?

In mid-February 1964, Giroux wrote that Walcott's corrected proofs of *Selected Poems* had arrived and that all his changes were improvements, but the proofs had taken too long to reach Walcott and a way must be found around this problem in future. Maybe Trinidad customs would appreciate packages marked 'Poems, damn you'? Publication date was now set for 18 May.

Giroux (7 May 1964) sent Walcott advance comments, from Louis Untermeyer, Marianne Moore, and May Sarton. There is also a quotation on file from Babette Deutsch to the effect that Walcott was a strong and original poet. Untermeyer (23 April) said it was a long time since he had read such an original and exciting new book of poetry. Marianne Moore (n.d.) claimed, however, to feel ill from some of Walcott's language and descriptions. Walcott (29 May) thanked Giroux for a well-produced book. Giroux (2 July 1964) congratulated him on the recent birth of his daughter Elizabeth and told him of William Jay Smith's forthcoming review of *Selected Poems*, 'Inner Magic' in *Harper's*. Walcott had met Smith in Barbados during 1962. Smith's wife, the poet Barbara Howes, edited one of the first anthologies of Caribbean writing.

Selected Poems brought together 'the best poems' from *In a Green Night* and new poems written since 1960. The cover included Robert Graves's increasingly famous remark about Walcott's understanding of the inner magic of English. There was also a quotation from *The Sphere* about the wry sadness of a Caribbean

Eliot. *Selected Poems* appeared on Farrar Straus's list along with John Berryman's *Homage to Mistress Bradstreet* and *77 Dream Songs,* T. S. Eliot's *The Elder Statesman* and *On Poetry and Poets,* Lowell's *Life Studies* and *Imitations,* and books by Hardwick, Mary McCarthy, Jacques Barzun, and Edmund Wilson. He was in good company.

Selected Poems includes twenty-three of the forty-two poems from *In a Green Night,* the previously unpublished 'Origins', and fifteen of the twenty-seven poems that would appear in the British edition of *Castaway.* Several poems had been revised since *In a Green Night,* including (once more) 'A Far Cry from Africa', 'Return to D'Ennery', 'Brise Marine', and (also once more) 'Conqueror'. Of the new poems in the volume, five were published in *London Magazine* during 1962–3, three in *Bim* during 1963, and one each in *Encounter, Spectator,* and the *Beloit Poetry Journal* between December 1962 and September 1963. Each of these eleven poems was revised for publication in *Selected Poems.* Whereas *In a Green Night* represented the best work of a decade and a half, Walcott was now publishing his poems almost as soon as written, and in the months between magazine and book publication the poems were revised. While it would be a mistake to assume that each poem in every book can be dated by its place in what is also a consciously structured work of art, the poems tend towards a chrono-logical order.

'Origins', a seven-part sequence, modelled upon the long lyrical Modernist epic-like sequences of Eliot, Césaire, and St-John Perse, was printed as Part II of *Selected Poems,* after 'Bronze', which concluded the *In a Green Night* selection, and before 'Castaway' the first poem of Part III. Walcott regarded 'Origins' as being between his early St Lucian poems and those he wrote in Jamaica. Thirty years later he would include it in his *Collected Poems,* where it follows the early 'The Harbour', the third poem he saved, which had appeared in the 1948 *25 Poems* as 'The Fisherman Rowing Homeward' and before 'A Far Cry from Africa' and 'Ruins of a Great House', 'Origins' taking the place of the unpublished 'Africa, Patria Mia' in the sequence Walcott sent Plomer. For a major Walcott poem 'Origins' has received surprisingly little attention, perhaps because it is more like a French than an English poem. It is, however, central to the vision found in Walcott's poems.

In 'Origins' phrases and passages from other writers are silently incorporated or set off in quotation marks and used for their resonances—puzzlement as to the sources being a way to focus attention on the complex associations of the words, while the learned or lucky reader's ability to recognize them bring an additional pleasure. There are several recurring implied narratives of the 'I', a Ulyssesian Odyssey of birth, evolution, the European discovery of the Americas, the middle passage from Africa to the New World. The obliqueness is in Walcott's early manner, the manner of the BBC *Caribbean Voices* poems, but without such torturous complexity of syntax and argument. There is more economy and selectiveness as the themes emerge, Pound-like, as a series of images, references, and quotations, in some multi-argument, to form an emblem of the many 'Origins' of Walcott, the West Indian, and the New World. In section I:

> Nameless I came among olives of algae,
> Foetus of plankton, I remember nothing.
>
> Clouds, log of Colon,
> I learnt your annals of ocean,

he knows the Odyssey story but nothing of the Amerindians who greeted Columbus, and he quotes a passage from a school book about primitive minds watching the skies for magic. There is a gap in his history. Section II combines images from Africa, the Old Testament, and Egypt. It attempts to recall the Jews in Egypt, speaks of being an animist lost between African and Greek gods, of having undertaken a 'Guinean odyssey' from the Mediterranean to the Caribbean:

> These islands have drifted from anchorage
> Like gommiers loosened from Guinea,
> Far from the childhood of rivers.

Section III of 'Origins' printed in italic script is an extremely lyrical evocation through images of a supposed peasant childhood in villages, among '*children | like black rocks of petrified beginnings in whose potbellied | drought the hookworm boils*', and a contrasting Persean white colonial dream world of church and care which here becomes a mulatto's fear of Africanness and blackness: '*the odour of fresh bread and mother's skin, that knew its own skin | slowly (amber, then excrement, then bronze)*'. Throughout the poem recurring images of water, rivers, sea, bind the various themes into a personal, racial, and dream-like voyage. In section IV images of a now no longer remembered exodus combine with memories of childhood as part of a process to define the self. Although the old gods of Africa have died, he attempts to stitch together two worlds 'Like the whirr of my mother's machine in a Sabbath bedroom'. The speaker, clearly Walcott here, is sea-wrecked and 'Seeks, like the polyp, to take root in itself'. The short section V imitates the Psalms as those who come to the New World attempt to name it, sing a new song, and make religious emblems of fall and redemption in this new Eden, 'Christening the pomegranate', 'bitter Cytherean apple', 'Shaping new labials to the curl of the wave' in praise of an indifferent blue-eyed God.

Section VI, in italics, is an ironic psalm-like call to forget Caribbean origins in Africa and India. The middle passage has produced amnesia, a second self, but as a consequence the mind is dry, without the sweetness of faith. Walcott is obviously thinking of himself here. Section VII returns to the theme of life as an Odysseyan voyage and return. In rapid and contrasting images it praises those who recall origins, especially of Africa, bring rebirth, work on sugar plantations, build cities, and bring hope of a Caribbean racial rainbow:

> 'We praise those whose back on hillsides buckles on the wind
> To sow the grain of Guinea in the mouths of the dead,
>
> .   .   .   .
>
> Whose sweat, touching earth, multiples in crystals of sugar
> Those who conceive the birth of white cities in a raindrop
> And the annihilation of races in the prism of the dew.'[12]

'Origins' is a rich poem, rich in imagery and theme, not reducible to a single message, but interpretable. It has been ignored by those wanting more obvious messages. It concerns the loss of faith in the gods of Africa as a result of the middle passage, the learning of European myths and the seeing of the world through blue eyes while trying to discover what he really is, the need to make an imaginative voyage of recovery to Africa as part of the process of healing spiritual wounds, and the need to overcome or stop wallowing in black self-hate and see that the Caribbean will be multiracial bronze, a place of white cities as well as impoverished peasants, a place where Old Testament stories of the Jews become applicable to blacks, where life is similar to that of the ancient Greeks, where language must be relearned, the world renamed. It offers a vision which Walcott will develop and expand over the decades, but which remains mostly unchanged.

William Plomer had recommended that Walcott be invited to contribute to a volume of fifteen new poems that the Arts Council of Great Britain was commissioning to celebrate the Shakespeare Quatercentenary. By the rules the poems had to be fourteen to fifty lines and take as a starting-point some quotation from Shakespeare. Although half the poems had to come from outside England, the other poets were mostly from the British establishment—Edmund Blunden, Charles Causley, Roy Fuller, Thom Gunn, Thomas Kinsella, Laurie Lee, Hugh MacDiarmid, Dom Moraes (the Indian poet who was then living in England), Peter Porter (an Australian who lives in England), Stephen Spender, Vernon Watkins, David Wright, along with the Americans Randall Jarrell and W. D. Snodgrass.

Walcott's 'Goats and Monkeys' uses the opening scene of *Othello* as the setting and is prefaced by 'even now, an old black ram is tupping your white ewe'. The poem treats of how the perception of racial difference heightens lust, and divides the world, but the poem is also indirectly about racial hate, self-hate, original sin, power, disillusionment, even the relation of the colonial to the imperial and of black to white culture. In Walcott's interpretation of the play what drives Othello to madness 'was not his racial, panther-black revenge' but 'horror of the moon's change, | of the corruption of an absolute':

And so he barbarously arraigns the moon
for all she has beheld since time began
for his own night-long lechery, ambition,
while barren innocence whimpers for pardon.[13]

Othello is the bull, the cuckold, the eternal male, driven by desire, by imaginings, by idealization, by fears, by anger, absurd yet deadly, the dark side of the self, that which has been projected upon blackness: 'this mythical, horned beast who's no more | monstrous for being black'.

Eric White of the Arts Council wrote (3 April 1964) that if Walcott has preserved the worksheets he could be paid an additional £10 by the National Manuscript Collection of Contemporary Poets, which was being set up by the British Museum and the Arts Council. Payment for the poem itself, £30, would follow. Walcott replied with some worksheets of 'Goats and Monkeys' and some notebook pages of a recently finished unpublished poem, 'At Lampfall', which showed his methods of composition. The Festival of Poetry was part of the Stratford Shakespeare Festival that summer and the fifteen poems were printed for a special souvenir programme. Some of the poems were included at the opening recital at the Guildhall, Stratford-upon-Avon, Sunday, 5 July.

When Eric Dalton of Evans Brothers asked for permission to use 'Winter' and 'Greenwich Village' in volume I of John Figueroa's *Caribbean Voices*, a two-volume poetry anthology intended for schools in the Caribbean, Walcott replied (14 September) that he did not want any of his poems from the BBC *Caribbean Voices* included without his permission. He has over the years avoided republishing such early work. Maschler had sent some Walcott poems to Chad Walsh for an anthology of modern poetry. The anthology progressed slowly towards publication and Walsh wrote in July saying he hoped his anthology would be published in the summer or autumn of 1964. Walcott sent him some new poems. Waddell Austin on 11 May 1964 had asked permission to reprint 'Tarpon' from the September 1963 *Encounter* in *Best Poems of 1963*. Eighty poems published in the United States and England were to be included and eligible for one of the three prizes in the sixteenth annual Borestone Mountain Poetry Awards. Walcott would win awards in 1964 and 1977. Permission was also asked on 17 June to include Walcott's 'The Royal Palms' in a forthcoming anthology of negro verse, edited by Anselm Hollo, in the Pocket Poets Series.

On a Farfield Foundation grant, Walcott attended an International Congress of Poets in Berlin, 22–7 September 1964, where he talked with J. P. Clark, Wole Soyinka, and Césaire as well as meeting Auden and Borges. He saw the Berlin Wall, a production of Brecht's *Coriolanus*, Duro Ladipo's Yoruba opera *Oba Kosa*, and Olivier's *Othello*. The following month, October 1964, he discussed the Congress in the *Sunday Guardian* over two Sundays.

While he was away Walcott's columns continued to appear. Shortly before the Congress L. S. Senghor had been on an official visit to Trinidad; the government had not arranged for him to meet any writers. Instead of an interview Walcott wrote 'Necessity of Negritude' for the *Guardian*. He discussed the movement as part of a division between those who argued for the arts as universal and those who saw them as having such essential racial characteristics as 'soul'. He suggested that negritude was part of the experiment in racial self-analysis, the opposite of integration, and that most poets found it impossible in English to create poetry which was identifiably black without unnaturally distorting language and technique. While Senghor writes from a living mythology, Césaire from nostalgia and protest, both write within French culture, and in the French language, which is flexible to ideas, abstractions, and philosophy. Senghor and Césaire, like Perse, use surrealism and other concepts that have not worked well in English, which provide them with what appears a freer, more natural expression, than older poetic forms, but which require much discipline. While negritude offers an assertion of pride to the descendants of slaves, it can only be part of the cultural heritage in the New World.[14]

While in England he saw his publishers, charmed Tom Maschler, and, during the first week of October, read poems for *Many Islands, Many Voices* a BBC special about the Caribbean. He interviewed Ian Hunter, Director-General of the Commonwealth Festival planned for 1965, who commissioned him to write a poem. Walcott would discuss in the *Trinidad Guardian* some anthologies of West Indian literature scheduled for publication during 1965 in connection with the Festival.[15]

On his way back from Europe Walcott stopped off in the United States for readings. The most important was on 15 October at the Solomon R. Guggenheim Museum. Walcott was the first on the 1964–5 calendar of Ten Poetry Readings presented by the Academy of American Poets; other readings would include Randall Jarrell, C. Day Lewis, William Meredith, A. R. Ammons, Wendell Berry, Louis Simpson, Gary Snyder, Stanley Kunitz, and Jorge Guillen. Walcott told Hirsch that before the reading he had a wild electric razor haircut which left him angry and embarrassed and thinking of wearing a hat.

Robert Lowell's introduction of Walcott at the Guggenheim meant approval by the most influential American poet. Lowell said that Walcott was his friend, he quoted Graves about Walcott's understanding of the inner magic of English and added that Graves seldom gave such bouquets to other poets. (Lowell himself seldom gave such bouquets to American poets.) Lowell continued by saying that Walcott is unlike but as good a poet as any in the United States or England of his generation. His powerful vehemence and resonance recall Hart Crane. Lowell appears to have thought Walcott was born in Trinidad and remarks on the possible advantages of living in a world populated by 'Negroes' and Indians with a British culture, and a history of Spanish conquests, galleons, and Robinson Crusoe. The Trinidadian poet is more like a South American or French poet than an American. Lowell reminded the audience that not long ago William Faulkner was thought provincial and limited by his Mississippi subject-matter in contrast to Thomas Mann or Gide; now it may be Trinidad's turn to be at the centre. Lowell praised the descriptions of Trinidad in Walcott's early verse and mentions that a few years ago Walcott began a new more abstract manner, perhaps like René Char or Léger. The new poems were an advance in their haunting mixture of almost surreal imagery with particularity of locale. Walcott's way of looking intensely at the local scene while sensing some ultimate absolute eternal blankness, Lowell suggested, was similar to, but different from, the void of Valéry and Mallarmé.[16]

Walcott amusingly played up to the audience's awareness of his being a new face on the scene. He said that it was like Yeats introducing Edgar Guest, that he was tempted to read Lowell's 'For the Union Dead' instead of his own poems, and that while he always wanted to come to a New York poetry reading, it was as a listener. He then introduced and read 'A Far Cry From Africa', 'Ruins of a Great House', and parts of 'Tales of the Islands' and 'Parang'. There was some applause, which Walcott later claimed that he assumed meant that he was to have finished, so he walked off stage.

'A Far Cry from Africa', he said, was written ten years earlier after a student quarrel about events in Kenya. Walcott felt that the Mau Mau were politically right, although he questioned their methods, but he could also understand the British soldiers. Cruelty was necessary for both, but he could not accept such cruelty. Rather than tolerance the poem expresses his feelings of conflict, pain, and distance. 'Ruins of a Great House' also treats of racial and cultural schizophrenia, the conflict of language and racial origins. References and allusions to English poetry are built into the structure. Working outside the context of a tradition he needed the security of the British poetic tradition. Colonial poets had to master a tradition before they could break with it. Walcott said that with political independence race was no longer an issue, and probably had not been in his time. 'Some Tales of the Islands' are sketches modelled on chapters of Hemingway's *In Our Time*. The portraits have their origins in imagination, rumour, and experience. Walcott had tried to compress the form of the Hemingway short story into loose sonnets and write dispassionately.[17]

Ralph Lennox reported on the reading for the *Trinidad Guardian*; Walcott was modest, pleasant, and in control of his voice and lines. He claimed that the spirit of negritude was alien to West Indians, and acknowledged the influence of Perse and Césaire. Walcott, during a telephone conversation with Lennox, said that Ralph Ellison told him that he was not a negro and Walcott said that that was right, he does not feel like one, but did not want to be quoted.[18]

On 20 October 1964 Walcott recorded twelve of his poems, along with comments, in the Recording Library of the Library of Congress, Washington, for the Archive of Recorded Poetry and Literature. Giroux sent ten copies of *Selected Poems* to the poet William Meredith for Walcott's reading at Connecticut College, New London. Walcott visited Yale University and Boston by train. He met with members of the Yale Drama School and among other matters asked why the graduates of John Gassner's course were mostly Broadway lighting or costume designers rather than playwrights.[19]

The trip is recalled in 'Lines in New England' (first published in the 1965 Cape edition of *Castaway*), where he quotes Whittier's 'Snowbound' about the American Civil War, and thinks about the history of battles with redcoats and redmen, British and Indian:

> . . . Outside,
> an Indian summer whose trees radiate
> like veins, a salt-blue pond,
> where I imagine a crazed, single deer-
> skinned quarry drinking, the last
> Mohican, Redcoat, redman, their thirst-
> ing, autumn battle-ground,
> its savage lacerations healed
> by salt white spire and green field.[20]

Walcott sees the United States as a related but different heritage, where the past is not really 'healed' as long as there is 'separate but equal love'.

'Lines in New England' is marvellous Walcott of this period with its self-questioning, 'Why am I so far north | who dread . . .', and the many ways in which Walcott's own sense of form has, under Lowell's example, loosened to give an illusion of free verse. Those long sentences appear to move casually through lines seemingly of arbitrary length until you stop, look more closely, and, starting with the end rhymes, begin to see the many patterns, even such literary echoes as from Marvell's 'Definition of Love', a poem Walcott will often imitate, and even Marvell's 'To His Coy Mistress' in 'their power clamps the jaw | tight with abhorrence and with love'. Walcott establishes a basic beat of three stress and six syllables early, a pattern regularized in lines 4 and 5:

> Geese creaking south, a raucous
> chain unlocking winter's cavernous
> barn, cross me
> going the other way.
> Why am I so far north,

The formality is broken up by having modifiers at the end of lines and the nouns at the start of the next lines (raucous | chain . . . cavernous | barn).

Walcott had learned much from Lowell. It is not just that Lowell did similar scenes; Lowell and Walcott share that technique (which Eliot made famous) of making poems from phrases and images in the poems of others. The dropping of the capital letters at the beginning of lines to get a more prose-like feel to the stanza, so that each line does not stand out as verse, is a technique which Walcott learned from Lowell.

Many of the same stylistic and autobiographical freedoms can be found in 'November Sun' (also first printed in the British *Castaway*) but written in Trinidad and added to the sequence found in the *Selected Poems*:

> Look, they'll be pierced with knowledge
> as with light! One boy, nine years in age
> who vaults and tumbles, squirrelling
> in his perpetual spring,
> that ten-month, cautious totterer
> my daughter.
> I rarely let them in.[21]

The references are to Peter and Elizabeth, his first daughter, born in January.

Because British and American editions of Walcott's first volumes of poetry are different it can be difficult to see his development clearly. A British reader, for example, would not have had access to 'Origins' before the 1986 *Collected Poems*. That poems from *In a Green Night* follow parts of 'The Castaway' sequence in the American *Selected Poems* means that readers need to consult the British edition to see the full power of the sequence and have a clear view of Walcott's devlelopment as a poet. Until a Complete Walcott is published, the study of his poetry will depend on the arbitrariness of the edition the reader has available.

Whereas *In a Green Night* shares in the concern with cultural identity noticeable in Walcott's work of the fifties and in the writing of other West Indians at the time, *The Castaway*, like much West Indian writing of the sixties, attempts to define the Self. The title poem (probably 1962, maybe early 1963) came about when Walcott chose to spend a weekend by himself at a beachhouse in Trinidad and wrote 'The Castaway'. He 'had an image of the West Indian artist as someone who was in a shipwrecked position . . . the beaches around here are generally very empty—just you, the sea, and the vegetation around you, and you're very much by yourself.' There are variations on the Crusoe theme, including the idea that 'every race that has come to the Caribbean has been brought here under situations of servitude or rejection, and that is the metaphor of the shipwreck'. You look around and must make your own tools 'whether that tool is a pen or a hammer, you are building in a situation that's Adamic'. There are such ironies as the assumption that Friday is being civilized when it is the people who come here who need to be 'recultured' and learn that races must live together. There is also the 'erasure of the idea of history'. In the Caribbean the surf is always wiping the sand clean, the huge clouds change rapidly. 'There is a continual sense of motion in the Caribbean—caused by the sea and feeling that one is almost travelling through water and not stationary.' There is a different, larger, clockless, personal notion of time.[22]

The Baltimore *Evening Sun* found *Selected Poems* 'one of the most impressive collections to come from a young writer in a long time. It is somber and beautiful poetry' which explores 'extremely complex and abstract ideas by means of full, easy, brilliantly evocative physical images'. Robert Mazzocco, in the *New York Review of Books*, thought Walcott exotic, unlike other contemporary poets, lush, preoccupied with the self, Hart Crane-ish, a showman, yet brooding, offering a world of scenic delights, often implying racial matters, at times a bore, but with such gifts as musical textures, the eye of a painter, ambitious craftsmanship, and a lively moral and an imaginative response. The *New York Times*'s Christmas book review section listed *Selected Poems* among the best books of the year and printed 'Missing the Sea', along with poems by Lowell, John Berryman, Theodore Roethke, and L. S. Senghor.[23]

Maschler had enjoyed Walcott's recent visit, but asked (1 December) if he had actually posted the manuscript of the new volume. He praised Walcott's letters, nerve, charm, and talent; he also knew Walcott was aware how easily he could get away with things and Maschler did not mind. Would Walcott do Cape an anthology? Talk of Walcott putting together a West Indian anthology would continue over the years without anything coming of it.

12

~~~~~~

1965–1966 *The Castaway,*
The Trinidad Theatre Workshop

MEANWHILE there was a dust-up with Errol Hill. After criticizing Hill's Dimanche Gras show for the past two Carnivals, Walcott had written his own, *Batai*, which he asked Hill to direct. Hill said no, but sent Walcott for review a copy of *3 Plays From the Yale School of Drama* (edited by John Gassner), which included *Man Better Man*. Hill's play had gone through many transformations: originally a prose revenge drama, it was now a calypso verse play filled with songs. In his 'Focus on the Arts' column, Walcott claimed Hill had debased his play by changing it from dialect into an inconsistent mess of dictions ranging from American slang to Elizabethan. How could any actor say 'since I was a po po, knee-high to a grasshopper'? Hill had ruined a powerful naturalistic play written in prose by forcing it into unnatural four-beat rhyming calypso lines. Walcott was annoyed that both Errol John and Errol Hill, two pioneers of West Indian drama, had modified the West Indianness of their plays for American tastes. The Broadway production of Errol John's *Moon on a Rainbow Shawl* even had an upbeat American ending.[1]

Hill's sarcastic reply (3 February) praised Walcott as 'having appeared more than once in the printed edition of Caribbean Plays, published by the Extra-Mural Department under my editorship', 'the leading (or is it second leading?) Negro poet published in America' (Walcott had recently been awarded second prize in poetry at the First World Festival of Negro Arts in Senegal; first prize for poetry went to the American Robert Hayden), 'the undisputed leader of an active theatre workshop . . . [that] it is hoped, will be felt some day on the local theatrical scene', and 'above all . . . arbiter of standards and tastes in the artistic world of Trinidad, being the only published critic on literature, drama, dance, cinema, painting, sculpture and calypso'. As the Trinidadian argot of *Man Better Man* was difficult to follow in Jamaica, Hill had even before he went to Yale started revising the play into a musical with dance; the calypso verse smoothed transitions. Why did Walcott impute base motives? Hill challenged Walcott's ear for local speech; the passages sounded Trinidadian to him. 'This from an outsider who has been living with us a mere five years! What arrogance!'[2]

This argument has often been misunderstood. Walcott claimed that naturalism is limited, it loses its power and truth when made into something else, something more elevated. Prose can not be turned into poetry by changing the form. The resulting inconsistencies are shown in the play's language, verse rhythms, and style. Walcott continued to feel it a humiliation for educated West Indians to attempt to sound British or American; provided one speaks clearly it is the task of others to understand. That is as true about theatre as poetry. Hill, in Walcott's view, had earlier sacrificed the dignity of West Indian speech for British diction. Few West Indian actors could feel at ease using such a diction. Now Hill was as unnaturally imposing a local verse and musical form on the play in the hope of reaching an American audience. Each writer must work towards expressing an inner voice, which is likely to be the speech of an educated West Indian with the many shifts in registers, dictions, and tones that are characteristic of the Caribbean. Hill's diction had become unnatural, literally unspeakable.

Batai was itself an experiment with the possibilities of local forms. Rehearsals started on 14 February and continued until the performance on the 28th. The show was narrated by Slade Hopkinson and many of the actors were from the Workshop; Margaret was business manager. Derek was paid $1,000 for the script and as director. Produced by the Carnival Development Committee at the Savannah under the patronage of the Governor-General and his wife, *Batai* was a disaster. Everything went wrong from the band arriving late to the new sound system failing, with the result that the actors were unintelligible to most of the audience. Heavy winds and complex learned symbolism suitable for a Jacobean masque did not help.

The Dimanche Gras show was originally a revue, consisting mostly of comedy sketches and dances leading up to the finale of the calypso contest and parade. It is performed on a large stage before an immense audience seated on opposite sides, basically a parallel stage on which two audiences need to be addressed. Hill had the previous two years scripted and directed the productions while trying to integrate the various elements, including a Calypso King contest between the two halves of the show and the competition for King and Queen of the Bands, into what he hoped would become a national form of theatre. Now Walcott tried to add a sociology and history of Carnival around these events, attempted too much, and lost most of his audience within thirty minutes. The classical allusions and analogies did not help. Douxdoux is like Dido, Queen of Carthage, Port of Spain is like Athens, and Bat is blind like Homer and Milton.

The unpublished *Batai* might be compared to a Stuart Masque written for one performance, a frame for a visual and musical symbolic ceremonial entertainment rather than a drama with plot, action, and character psychology. Just as the Court Masque led up to the celebration of the monarchy and its social order through a concluding dance, so *Batai* concludes with the crowning of the King and Queen and runner-up contestants of the annual Trinidad Carnival, the Calypso King and the Roadmarch. A Carnival is not just a celebration of disorder and social release, it is also a celebration of the various competitive arts such as the masquerades, costumes, and music that make up the Carnival and which have their hierarchy of kings, queens, and runners-up. *Batai* offers a history and justification of the order that it celebrates—what the narrator describes as a season of wit and rhyme in bloodless battles. Much of it reads like Music Hall repartée and banter.

Batai is also like an early Jonsonian comedy in that the audience is introduced to character types—here conventional Carnival masquerades. 'A Pierrot' is the drama master who arranges the characters and scenes. The characters perform pantomime movements illustrative of their role while the choir sings appropriate songs. For Bat it is the Executor's Theme 'Sans Humanité', which recurs in the pageant as a motif. Carnival is a Celebration of the Life Force, of the will to conquer, and a protest against the Death facing each individual. A traditional Trinidadian song, which Walcott regards as representative of the brutality, instinct for survival, and need to assert oneself that is part of the Caribbean psyche, 'Sans Humanité' will later be used as one of the motifs of *The Joker of Seville*, which is also a celebration of the Life Force and will to conquer as a protest against Death. In 'Origins' and *Batai* Walcott is asserting a Shavian or Nietzschean personal philosophy that is as much part of his vision and life as the sensitivity, guilt, and pessimism common to his poetry.

Hill described *Batai* as 'an unmitigated calamity', not a failure but 'a selfish abuse of the Trinidad Carnival theatre to satisfy the ego of the producer'. 'Walcott was attempting an historical survey of Carnival, based on an article by Andrew Pearse in the Carnival issue of *Caribbean Quarterly*.' Instead of trusting in 'the indestructible masquerade spirit of the Trinidadians, which perhaps he does not truly apprehend', there was a 'tedious narration', 'silence and stillness on the yawning expanse of stage'. Hill claimed that Walcott was so in love with his own artistry that instead of the expected display of movement and colour he supplied a serious play filled with alien classical allusions to illustrate his ideas about the nature and development of Carnival, and that this proved terrible theatre on a large stage before ten thousand people expecting to enjoy themselves.[3]

Walcott normally wrote several articles each year discussing Carnival, usually one about the tents and one about the Dimanche Gras pageant. This year he discussed the Original Young Brigade Tent (6 January) and the Mighty Terror, a new calypsonian dressed as a matador (17 January). His seeing, being part of, and writing about Carnival contributed to the imaginative world of his writing. He would later adopt the mask and some of the diction of a calypsonian, along with alluding to the history and form of the music, in his great satire, 'The Spoiler's Return':[4]

> so back me up, Old Brigade of Satire,
> back me up, Martial, Juvenal, and Pope
> (to hang theirself I giving plenty rope),
> Join Spoiler' chorus, sing the song with me

The brilliant Trotskyite writer C. L. R. James had returned to Trinidad to cover the Test series for the *Guardian*. James had a few years earlier been part of Eric Williams's government, proved himself absolutely ruthless, and was suspected of forming his own faction to replace Williams, who forced him into exile. James then revealed the corruption, tyranny, and hatred of Indians in Williams's party. Williams naturally assumed that James's return had more to do with politics, probably the 1966 election, than cricket, and interned him under house arrest at his sister's, as a subversive. Williams also declared a limited state of emergency. (This led to James attempting to form an unlikely alliance with Rudranath Capildeo's largely Indian Democratic Labour Party. Capildeo is related to V. S. Naipaul and the situation sounds as if it could have been taken from Naipaul's *The Mimic Men*.) Walcott was discussing the situation with a friend when he saw Williams in a big car with a police escort. Walcott walked over and shouted 'Release C. L. R. James!' Williams's fear of James was part of a regional attack on free speech by those in power, which would intensify during the late 1960s and early 1970s as the Independence leaders were challenged.[5]

In March V. S. Naipaul also returned to Trinidad, his first visit since *Middle Passage*. When Walcott interviewed him for the *Trinidad Guardian*, Naipaul was as usual amusingly outrageous, as usual in a state of nervous exhaustion, continually saying the opposite of the expected and desired. It was Carnival time and he disliked Carnival. He sounded an imperialist, declaring that being in a colonial society meant being on the margins of something larger and that created aspirations. People formerly tried to speak better than they had since Independence. The world is being proletarianized; apartheid South Africa is 'the absolute triumph of a European proletarian culture'. Travelling is repetitive, the same events seem to recur. He had nothing to say about India, but having accepted money from a publisher, he had to write *An Area of Darkness*, or refund the money. He would write a word such as 'ruins' on a page and just stare at it for a day. Naipaul felt that people never abandon allegiance to a community or the idea of their community. In Trinidad where people were insecure they destructively acted and reacted upon each other.

During the interview Walcott appears to be pressing his views on Naipaul. When Walcott mentioned that Lamming had written of a connection between artists, even cricketers, and society, Naipaul replied 'I am not a cricketer', which was misleading. Naipaul still practised cricket bowling for exercise. Walcott pressed on by saying that such a connection is inevitable. Naipaul returned: 'To the writer it is incidental.' Walcott thought multiracialism resulted in a Trinidadian sense of laughter found in Selvon and Naipaul. Naipaul: 'I really don't know.' Walcott claimed that the people in *Miguel Street* were portrayed with much tenderness and compassion. Naipaul: 'I wouldn't like to have them to breakfast.' Naipaul claimed he never laughed at his characters, that would be 'bad manners'.[6]

During March Walcott spoke about 'West Indian Poetry, a "Search for Voices"' for an Extra-Mural Seminar, at UWI, Mona, part of a series concerning 'The State of the Arts in Jamaica'. He read 'Origins' and said that he was trying to get a similar quality in English to Francophone Caribbean poetry. He claimed that poetry is a high art which the ordinary person is not likely to understand. You could not grab the first working man and say 'have you heard this one?'[7]

This was his first trip to Jamaica in six or seven years; much had happened including the breakup of the Federation, the fostering of nationalism on each of its former components, Walcott's divorce, his second marriage, and the making of his home in Trinidad. Walcott might speak of being at home throughout the Caribbean, but he was seldom at ease in Jamaica, although he had many friends there. It was British, black, socially more stratified than St Lucia or Trinidad. Nationalism was intertwined with its slave past and a history of resistance. In the first of his *Trinidad Guardian* articles on the trip, he began by contrasting the landscapes:

The West Indian landscape now resembles its novels. To leave behind the sunny, huddled alleys of St James, the savannahs with thatch huts and bamboo flagpoles for the dry, soaring ranges of Jamaica is to move from the pages of Naipaul and Selvon to those of Hearne. The distinction is more than physical. Both islands have become nations. Each has had to evolve, because of geographical distance, a 'separate identity'.

For Walcott the only links remaining between the new small island nations were the writers and the West Indian Test team.[8]

Walcott's week in Jamaica resulted in three articles, articles which like many he wrote moved from their immediate subject to broad issues concerning the arts and culture in the West Indies. Rex Nettleford and his National Dance Theatre Company of Jamaica was now three years old. Nettleford, who had been at UCWI with Walcott was also a major artist, intent on a career as a dancer, choreographer, and director within Jamaica. He had been able to take a different path in his ambitions as an artist from Walcott. He did well in his examinations and was a Rhodes scholar at Oxford. For two years, 1957–9, he choreographed for the Oxford University Dramatic Society and the Oxford Opera Group. He put on revues at the Edinburgh Fringe and for the Lyric Hammersmith in London. He studied African dance in Nigeria and Ghana, and gave dance courses at American universities and to professionals. He had been an extra-mural tutor at the university and was now Director of Studies at the Trade Union Education Institute along with being artistic director of the National Dance Company of Jamaica.

Walcott had not seen Nettleford's Jamaica National Dance Company perform, but it was what he wanted. Within three years it had a repertoire of nineteen Jamaican works, some folk based, some modern, and offered a 'season' lasting a month, which was sold out in advance. It received a small subsidy from the government and had already travelled to the Stratford Festival in Canada and the Nassau Caribbean Dance Festival. There was a company of sixteen developed from dance workshops held in Kingston or drawn from other, already existing, local companies and schools, such as the Ivy Baxter School.

During April Walcott discussed C. L. R. James's lecture on Wilson Harris; the next month Walcott reviewed Harris's *Tradition and the West Indian Novel.* Whereas James saw Harris as a philosopher in the high European tradition, Walcott sees a poet drunk on words and the imagination, like Rimbaud, someone mad enough to transfer such a vision directly to prose, a less disciplined Borges. Walcott claims that Harris, Lamming, and other West Indian writers share this love of language that wrestles with syntax and rhetoric rather than story and character; this distinguishes them from Proust, Faulkner, or Joyce whose distortions of naturalism result from extreme compression. Harris's perceptions and metaphors at times appear accidental, but have a greater power than those of any other West Indian intellectual. Although Harris objects to the old-fashioned realism of other West Indian novelists, he draws from the common European myth kettle. Trying to create his own myths, he bloats his characters. Walcott was obviously puzzled by Harris. Here was someone with tremendous linguistic and poetic powers, published by Faber, although seemingly undisciplined, uncompromising, and obscure. Harris was making art from the very excesses Walcott was trying to control, clarify, and compress.[9] Other West Indian writers Walcott wrote about during 1965 included Michael Anthony, Mittelholzer, Austin Clarke, Sam Selvon, and the poets A. L. Hendriks and E. M. Roach. He reviewed *Bim* 41 and *From the Caribbean,* an anthology of short stories edited by Salkey.

A hurried, handwritten letter (27 May) to Alan Ross said that Walcott was sending 'Leaving School' at Margaret's urging to meet the deadline. (Walcott had had lots of time; Ross first mentioned the article in 1962.) Because of insufficient postage the proofs of his poems 'Veranda', 'Laventille', 'A Village

Life', and 'Coral' meant for the June issue of *London Magazine* came too late to return for that deadline.

'Laventille', dedicated to Naipaul, was inspired by a visit to a shrine where Walcott was a child's godfather. There is a description of Laventille, then of Walcott climbing the hill, the christening itself, and reflections afterwards as Walcott descends towards Port of Spain. Laventille, part of a mountain range around the city, is filled with an overwhelmingly black population in violent slums. Criminals live openly and during times of political instability the inhabitants descend on Port of Spain to loot the shops. It is often used as a symbol of Trinidad in its literature. Walcott calls it 'the height of poverty' for blacks and his poem is about imprisonment in body, poverty, colour, the island, and the New World. He alludes to calypsos about illegal immigrant Grenadians living close together in Laventille; they breed like 'felonies'. The poem is crammed with such puns. Steel band began here, especially the Desperadoes. Life on the hill is harsh, even the rain is harsh. Socially you climb by going down from Laventille to the city. The birth of the child leads to Walcott's renewed awareness of the plight of poor blacks, thus there is a birth and rebirth. The poem criticizes browns for being alienated from and not helping poor blacks; the poor blacks suffer in ways browns do not. There is no meaning in such suffering; there is no appropriate religion for those of African descent in the Americas, as all are victims of cultural amnesia resulting from the Middle Passage. Nothing was reborn. This is a poem of heavy alliteration, harsh sounds, and unexpected and unrhymed couplets.[10]

During the summer Walcott taught at the UWI Summer School, which was attended by five members of the St Lucia Arts Guild including Dunstan St Omer and Roderick Walcott; and he became involved with a frustrating experience as a result of his desire to break into film making.

Early in the year he had reviewed Fellini's $8\frac{1}{2}$, Richard Lester's Beatle film *A Hard Day's Night*, John Frankenheimer's *The Train*, John Ford's *Cheyenne Autumn*, and Bryan Forbes's terror film, *Seance On a Wet Afternoon*. The French New Wave and experimental art films were in fashion, but not in Port of Spain, where their dialogue was drowned out by boos; objects had been hurled at the screen. Walcott himself objected to the hermeticism of Godard. He disliked abstraction and what he thought experiment for its own sake. A film buff, he was learning their techniques, noting the difference between what made successful film art and what was pretentious. It was a natural direction for a dramatist with a strong visual sense who was also a painter. How was he to break into that still foreign world when he was struggling to keep a theatre workshop going, and there was no West Indian film?

Lionel Rogosin, director of *On the Bowery* (1955), *Come Back Africa* (1959), and other well-known protest films of the period, approached Walcott about revising Naipaul's 'A Flag on the Island' for a film. Rogosin had spent part of 1965 in

Jamaica trying to get a feel for the West Indies, as he had in mind a musical about a working-class hero in the slums. He read the new West Indian writers, felt *Miguel Street* and *A House for Mr Biswas* had the sympathetic treatment he desired; so he asked Naipaul to write a story to be used for a film. Rogosin visited Trinidad with Naipaul and brought Naipaul to New York, but the satire and irony of 'A Flag on the Island' was not what he wanted and Naipaul was unwilling to change it. After Naipaul angrily withdrew, Rogosin turned to Walcott. Walcott had started by writing lyrics for the music and then began to exchange ideas for the film with Rogosin; he visited New York for discussions, worked hard on the script, but was reluctant to change Naipaul's story in a radical way. Rogosin then took the script to London, but could not get financing. Naipaul eventually published 'A Flag on an Island' in a book with that title together with some other short stories.

Rogosin recognized two great West Indian writers, but was unable to see that they rejected the stereotypes of protest art. Decades later he still assumed that Naipaul had changed in his view of the West Indies after *A House for Mr Biswas*, not seeing that part of the bitterness of the first four books was as much a protest at Trinidad as against colonialism. The London promoters who claimed there was no market for a film about West Indian music and refused to finance Rogosin's project were wildly wrong. They missed the beginning of the worldwide interest in reggae. A film similar to what Rogosin had in mind was made by others and was a success, the classic *The Harder They Fall* with Jimmy Cliff. Rogosin apparently had not recognized the importance of the Rastas when in Jamaica. Trevor Rhone had not then opened the Barn Theatre, yet it was Rhone writing about Jamaica who might have been perfect for what Rogosin wanted, whereas Naipaul, Walcott, and probably Trinidad were inappropriate. Unfortunately Walcott had invested much time and many hopes in the project and its collapse left him, as was becoming customary, in financial difficulties.[11]

'Commonwealth literature' originated during the mid-sixties at a time when the new national literatures were trying to establish themselves and finding commonalities; this was the start of international interest in Caribbean, African, and other new literatures. Walcott, along with Naipaul, Wilson Harris, Achebe, Soyinka, R. K. Narayan, and Patrick White, was one of the stars of this new constellation. Later many writers would agree with Naipaul, already a star of the London literary world, that Commonwealth literature was a way of putting others outside the canon as second-rate, like a regional literature, but at the time Walcott, trying to earn a living as a writer in Trinidad, saw the advantages of promoting the new literatures. Many Commonwealth, British, and European critics still like the notion of Commonwealth literature as it indicates that part of the history and culture of many former British colonies is shared and still links nations in many areas of the world. Commonwealth literature tends to be affirmative, proclaiming the importance of writers and literarary traditions, whereas the more recent post-colonialism is an American takeover of the movement towards cultural decolonization and is concerned with the guilt of Western imperialism, guilt towards the treatment of minorities in the West, and a hands-off attitude towards Others. Commonwealth literature assumes I am interested in literature and that I have a right to criticize injustice, whether by whites or blacks. Post-colonialism assumes my interest is politics and that if I criticize black tyrannies rather than white then I am betraying the movement.

Hill's *Man Better Man* represented Trinidad at the Commonwealth Arts Festival in England during September and received good reviews. There was a Commonwealth Poetry Conference in Cardiff, 20–4 September, attended by George Lamming and Louise Bennett, but not by Walcott or Roach who declined invitations in protest against the Commonwealth Immigration Bill, a new, unfavourable policy towards immigrants by the British government. Roach's poem 'Calypso Caribbean', written for the Festival, was performed at the Royal Court Theatre, 27 September, and included in the Festival's souvenir programme. Walcott had not finished his poem. Walcott, who had a British passport and could have migrated to England, was always conscious of the racial situation there, how it had affected other writers, and how it was then changing for the worse. A year later he would review Douglas Hinds's *Journey To an Illusion* (Heinemann, 1966), an angry report about black life in England. Walcott thought this by now an old story which would only get worse, and was better treated by satire and irony than rage.[12]

He wrote several articles about the Commonwealth Festival, discussing the decline of England, the new immigration policy, Trinidad's representation at the Arts Festival, and Commonwealth literature. 'Commonwealth Literature' in the *Sunday Guardian*, 17 October, surveyed such recent events and publications as the 16 September *TLS*, the *London Magazine* Commonwealth issue, the new *Journal of Commonwealth Literature*, Heinemann's *Commonwealth Literature* (edited by John Press), comprising papers presented at the 1964 Leeds conference which initiated Commonwealth Literature studies in England.[13]

He did not mention his part in the big September 'Commonwealth 1965' issue of *London Magazine*, which included his 'Leaving School', his poem 'Dogstar', and his one-page introduction to 'Some West Indian Poets', followed by his selection of works by George Campbell, Basil McFarlane, A. L. Hendriks, Dennis Scott, E. M. Roach, E. McG. Keane, Ian Macdonald, Martin Carter, and E. L. Brathwaite. It was not totally a Walcott issue; it also included Hal Porter's 'Melbourne in the Thirties', poetry from Australia and New Zealand by Judith Wright, James Baxter, Peter Bland, Louis Johnson, and Fleur Adcock, paintings by Russell Drysdale, and an article about Patrick White's plays. From the proportion of the issue which was Walcott's he, however, could have been a nation on his own.

Walcott claimed that West Indian literature in verse began with Claude McKay's ballads, and that many of the novelists, such as Harris and George Lamming, were originally poets, but that with the lack of publishing houses in the region, the writers became exiles, writing novels for the London market. There was little encouragement for poetry in the islands, beyond such popular forms as calypso and folk songs. The challenge was to find a specific personal tone and create forms without becoming distant. How were they to retain the rich expression of dialect without losing the syntactical power of English? The strongest poetry realized this conflict. Essentially this is another statement of Walcott's distinction between, and hope to use in a dramatic way, the forms of high culture and the raw materials of local life.[14]

In February Walcott had lost the use of the Little Carib Theatre when McBurnie, increasingly living off her theatre, forced cancellation of a private performance of the Theatre Workshop; she locked them out for not making payments towards her mortgage. The attempt to turn the Little Carib Theatre into a regional Arts Centre had come to nought. The government had offered no site, no money had been raised for a building, no association had been formed with the university; as a result the Rockefeller Foundation terminated its support. Freund wrote in his diary that these were talented individuals who would always be at strife with each other.[15] As the Theatre Workshop was an *ad hoc* group, it would be impossible for the Rockefeller Foundation to help. Walcott was avoiding the Rockefeller Foundation, but Freund hoped they would remain in contact.

Without a regular place to meet the Theatre Workshop was barely alive until mid-October when the disused bar in the basement of Hotel Bretton Hall was 'discovered' and reconversions started to turn the space into what became the Basement Theatre, to be used for rehearsals and performances by the, now, Trinidad Theatre Workshop. The architect John Gillespie, Errol Jones, Margaret and Derek, Selby Wooding, and Fred Thomas formed a committee which raised $800 for the Basement Theatre. A small theatre of sixty to ninety seats was created in which the audience was crowded on three sides of the stage on the same level as the actors. The room was painted black to improve the concentration of the actors and audience, and there was no space for scenery beyond a painted backdrop. Lighting equipment was primitive and required continual invention. There was no dressing room or room to store props.

There was another pleasant surprise in October when the 23 October issue of the *New Yorker* carried a 'Letter from Port of Spain' that said Walcott was the best poet in the region, quoted from 'Tales of the Islands', and mentioned that Walcott had followed Yeats's policy in adopting a persona, the Castaway.[16] Giroux then contacted Howard Moss at the *New Yorker* and wrote to ask Walcott (27 October) whether he wanted Farrar, Straus and Giroux to act as his agent in submitting poems to journals. It would be to the advantage of Farrar, Straus and

Giroux to have his poems better known before their appearance in books. Giroux claimed that poets often write excellent prose, as for example Elizabeth Bishop's story 'In the Village' in *Questions of Travel*, which he was sending. Had Walcott written anything in prose about his life or the region? He also sent Lowell's book of plays, *The Old Glory*.

Walcott (1 November) informed Giroux that he was already writing an auto-biography and had about seventy pages. He had not seen the *New Yorker* article, asked for a copy, sent love to the Lowells and Straus. Walcott mentioned that the poems he was sending, except for 'Almond Trees' and 'Crusoe's Journal', had already been published in *London Magazine* and would be in the Cape edition of *The Castaway*. He thanked Giroux for the books, Bishop was new to him, a revelation. Giroux (8 November) sent Howard Moss 'Crusoe's Journal', calling it extraordinary. Although Moss liked the poem, others at the *New Yorker* voted against it. Walcott still had not broken into the *New Yorker* poetry market.

The attempted autobiography had developed from 'Leaving School'; from 29 April 1965 for two years Walcott worked towards a long continuation in prose. Between September and November he worked almost daily on the first notebook, he then started a second. He began again in 1969. The passages, usually of a paragraph or a few pages, were remembered episodes, epiphanies, or essayistic. The model Walcott had in mind was Boris Pasternak's *Safe Conduct*. His approach was similarly selective, elliptical, at times self-consciously superior or ironic in tone, poetic, with each small section meant to stand on its own. Little attempt was made at chronology or narrative continuity. These passages, carefully written and often transcribed from drafts, fill two notebooks and eventually were the raw material of his book-length poem *Another Life* (1973). Some lines, even paragraphs, of prose were taken directly from the notebooks and without much change beyond lineation became marvellous poetry. Once Walcott moves beyond journalism his prose often becomes poetic—mood, impressionism, epiphanies, and posturing—the opposite of Naipaul's directness and transparency.

Walcott mostly avoids family history, avoids the mucky details, the excess, that are at the heart of a prose view of life, which allows the linkage of cause and effect. Instead the reader would have been offered a carefully censored and controlled portrait of the speaker as he wishes to appear. The confessional is not confessional, the story is only by implication a story. While the example of Hemingway might explain such erasures, Walcott had come to regard Hemingway, and the other Americans he read in his teens, as a 'romantic natur-alist'. He wanted more irony, more satire like James Joyce's *Portrait of the Artist as a Young Man*. He wrote of himself as a quadroon, which he puns on as quarter moon. He was already writing about approaching middle age and dead friends, regarded others as parasites, and was aware of tendencies towards paranoia. He saw himself a self-reliant Protestant, unlike Dunstan St Omer, who as a Roman Catholic felt pride, damnation, and despair. The two notebooks are now at the University of West Indies Mona Campus. The first book has seventy-three pages of writing by hand or typescript pasted in. The second book continues on to page 125.

Walcott wrote to Ross apologetically about his prose in the 'Leaving School' essay (11 November); he called it his first published prose, thus dismissing years of journalism. He was trying to translate a Césaire play, but the level of French was difficult. He was interested in Ross's last book in which he writes of how a breakdown is followed by strength, elation, and creativity from anguish. He hoped Ross would publish a Commonwealth anthology and suggested an issue on Commonwealth theatre including Soyinka, J. P. Clark, and Patrick White. The next burst of energy would be in Commonwealth theatre. Walcott claimed, as he would often do in the future, that a real poet's theatre is emerging, but it is not known because not published (later he would say because there are few places to perform it). Contributors to the issue might include Charles Osborne for Australia, Soyinka and Ulli Beier for Nigeria, himself, and someone from Jamaica.

During November Walcott visited Guyana, enjoying the pleasant, colonial, bland appearance of Georgetown in contrast to its recent violence, and remarking on the army helicopters, jeeps, and armed soldiers. In London at the time there were meetings concerning independence and shortly after Walcott left, Cheddi Jagan called a strike which plunged the nation into strife. Walcott, however, was there as a judge for the Fourth National Drama Festival, not for politics. He was envious that since 1960 Georgetown had a Playhouse (owned and operated by the Theatre Guild of British Guyana) at a good location, with lighting and chairs. There were eight weeks of rehearsals between productions. 'Amateur groups in other territories suffer a deep psychological dispiritedness because they have no sense of property, of a place to work which belongs to them, and what tires them most is the physical problem of adapting halls and centres to playhouses, renting chairs, storing scenery, and finding rehearsal rooms. To visit the playhouse is to realise how rootless such groups are.' The Guild was also racially mixed, unlike most West Indian theatre groups.[17]

The Castaway and Other Poems was published in England by Cape on 21 October 1965. It was slightly shorter than *In a Green Night*, sixty-four pages. The first impression was 1,500 copies, a thousand of which sold by the end of the year; the other 500 took two more years, followed by a reprint of 500 which took three years to sell out. It consisted of twenty-seven poems or sequences. Besides the fifteen from *Selected Poems*, all revised, six poems had been first published in *London Magazine* between December 1963 and June 1965 and since revised. There was a revised 'Goats and Monkeys', and five poems not previously published, apparently written during the past two years. The title 'Laventille'was misprinted as 'Laventville'. A second misprint was 'Whither' for the poet Whittier quoted at the start of 'Lines in New England'. Four of the revised poems had new titles. 'Rivers' was now 'The Voyage up River', 'Beach House' was now 'Lampfall', 'Postcard' had become 'Codicil', while 'Verandah' was now spelled 'Veranda'.

The power of *The Castaway* is the wide range of associations Walcott brings to symbols. *The Castaway* uses Crusoe and Prospero as personae; its themes include race in such poems as 'Goats and Monkey', and class in 'Laventille'. He is a castaway in the world, the New World, in the community, language, and literature, cut off from Europe, from Africa. Not only are blacks castaway from Africa, but whites from Europe. Just as Naipaul fears Indians will disappear in the West Indies, so Walcott recognizes that his own whiteness will be lost. The fear is racial as well as cultural. There is also the philosophical sense of the subjective self and the imagination (as in a Wallace Stevens poem) being distinct from the world; the imagination is alone, exiled. The situations of the mulatto, the artist, the religious are analogous, all are castaways. Walcott is a castaway in having lost his faith, in being a Methodist among Catholics, in having lost Eden. He is a castaway from home, family, and friends, whether in St Lucia, England, or Greenwich Village. The world is dangerous, violent, driven by blind desire, and procreation is disguised as love. It is a world of purposeless change, in which everything leads to annihilation. We are castaway in a meaningless universe. Each person is a wanderer, seafarer, an exile, an Odysseus travelling towards death and annihilation.

Walcott gave a lecture on 27 October at the university about 'The Figure of Crusoe; on the Theme of Isolation in West Indian Writing'. It remained in his notebook unpublished until 1993. In it he compares himself to a lonely man on a beach making a bonfire from dead bushes and twigs. The poet does something similar with memories, thoughts, used parts of his life, and from the ritual creates the pure light of Dante's Paradiso, the reality beyond Plato's shadows on the cave. Such calmness is unlike the visions of madmen and saints. It is serene, orderly, the result of contemplation. The poet's world becomes remote, yet all persons and objects are equally holy. Walcott's Crusoe is, like Proteus, a shape-changer: Adam, Columbus, God, a missionary, Defoe, Protestant, craftsman, existentialist, beachcomber, derelict from an old novel, Prospero, someone who can name, shape, and baptize a still virgin part of the new world.[18]

The use of Robinson Crusoe as an image of the castaway is part of Walcott's continuing use of the European literary tradition to provide analogous symbols for his own condition and the Caribbean. It is also related to his use of Odysseus in *Epitaph for the Young* and other poems. Odysseus leaves home, is a quester, a wanderer, but eventually returns home, although changed. Walcott's sense of analogy, of the various applications of Crusoe's situation, gives an unusual richness of metaphor, significance, and tone to these poems, the central attitude being of alienation, distance, of building a new civilization among those unlike himself. The attitude is of someone superior among those he wishes to be part of, and whom he tries to regard as equal, but who will remain distant and different. The gulf between himself and others cannot be bridged except in poetry. Variations of such images and themes are found in such future works as *The Gulf*, *Pantomime*, *The Fortunate Traveller*, and, of course, *Omeros* and *The Odyssey*.[19]

In 'The Castaway',

> The starved eye devours the seascape for the morsel
> Of a sail

Over three decades later Walcott, the returning Odysseus, in *The Bounty* uses a similar image to denote his restlessness, the personal insufficiency of restive meditation and homecoming to a small island:

> The sea should have settled him, but its noise is no help.
> I am talking about a man whose doors invite a sail
> to cross a kitchen-sill at sunrise, . . .[20]

The metaphors have become enriched over the years, the vision perhaps more complex, as in the later poem the existential and personal castaway is among a God-given bounty of life. A kind of faith has returned.

The Castaway is similar to other Walcott volumes of poetry in its linked vocabulary and images creating complexity of associations. The racial white and black, the youthful edenic green, and other colours take on multiple meanings, sometimes religious and moral, often the result of exact observation. In 'The Castaway':

> The salt green vine with yellow trumpet-flower;
>
> . . . .
>
> . . . the dog's faeces
> Crust, whitens like coral.
>
> . . . .
>
> The ripe brain rotting like a yellow nut
>
> . . . . . .
>
> That green wine bottle's gospel . . .
> Clenched seawood nailed and white as a man's hand.

'The Swamp' begins 'Gnawing the highway's edges, its black mouth'; other colour and road images are 'White mottling its root', 'Its black mood', 'Backward to darkness, go black'. 'The Swamp' concludes 'Like chaos, like the road | Ahead.' The next poem, 'Dogstar' begins 'The dogstar's rabid. Our Street'.

Walcott had been anticipated by Saint-John Perse's 'Images à Crusoé' in *Éloges*. He considered Perse part of his heritage, accepting that the white colonial is part of the culture of the region. Both poets share a sense of exile and distanced irony, a mixture of concise accurate description and high lyricism often obliquely expressed, the paradoxical, almost narcissistic, focus on the poet's personal world, and the creation through poeticizing of a Caribbean world. Here is the opening of 'Écrit sur la Porte' from *Éloges*:

> Mon orgueil est que ma fille soit très-belle quand elle
>   commande aux femmes noires,
> ma joie, qu'elle découvre un bras très-blanc parmi ses poules noires;
> et qu'elle n'ait point honte de ma joue rude sous le poil, quand je
>   rentre boueux.

> My pride is that my daughter should be very beautiful when she
>   gives orders to the black women,
> my joy, that she should have a very white arm among her black hens;
> and that she should not be ashamed of my rough, hairy cheek when
>   I come home covered with mud.

This could be used as an example of the ways patriarchy, white racial prejudice, and class domination were built upon plantations and the exploitation of blacks, but the power of such verse is because it does economically, rapidly, and with its own self-aware ironies notate the characteristics of a society. There is dignity in an ideal of a way of life, and there are the details to make it flesh:

> En souriant elle m'acquitte de ma face ruisselante; et porte à son visage
>   mes mains grasses d'avoir
> éprouvé l'amande de kako, la graine de café.
> Et puis elle m'apporte un mouchoir de tête bruissant; et ma robe de laine;
>   de l'eau pure pour rincer mes dents de silencieux.

> Smiling she forgives me my dripping face; and lifts to her face my hands,
>   oily
> from testing the cacao seed and the coffee bean.
> And then she brings me a rustling bandanna; and my woollen robe;
>   pure water to rinse my mouth of few words.

In 'Pour Fêter Une Enfance' Perse celebrates his mother, her maids, the trees, the gardens, the sea, the boats, the volcanoes, coffee, coco plum, mangoes, even the flies. They represent a lost paradise, the childhood he can never recover. While in 'Vendredi' from 'Images à Crusoé' Perse offers Friday's resentment in being colonized:

> Vendredi! que la feuille était verte, et ton ombre nouvelle, les mains si
>   longues vers la terre, quand, près de l'homme taciturne . . .
> Maintenant l'on t'a fait cadeau d'une défroque rouge. Tu bois l'huile des
>   lampes et voles au garde-manger.

> Friday! how green was the leaf, and your shadow how new, your hands so
>   long towards the earth when, beside the taciturn man . . .
> Now they have given you a cast-off red coat. You drink the oil from the lamps
>   and steal from the larder.[21]

While Robinson Crusoe is one of Walcott's masks for the writer, the mulatto, and other situations involving the outsider, alienated, and shipwrecked (Naipaul's image for those races that empires brought to colonies for plantations and then abandoned), a continuing presence is the biblical garden, Eden, especially as alluded to in Andrew Marvell's 'The Garden'. Walcott in St Lucia contemplating the sand, sea, and palms is like Marvell's speaker. Behind the opening poem, 'The Castaway', there are the Garden's vines, palm, the contrast between action and contemplation, the multiplying thoughts, the greenery, the Godlike annihilation of art and self—but, here, for Walcott, religion is a 'wrecked ship' in contrast to those sailing to Marvell's 'Bermudas'. Instead of Gospel greenery, there is dryness, loss of faith, sand. The imitation Jacobean, Senecan echoes of Eliot's 'Gerontion' contribute to a symbolism as dependent upon literature as nature:

> Pleasures of an old man:
> Morning: contemplative evacuation, considering
> The dried leaf, nature's plan.

The artist's mind itself has become God, the making of analogies the divine act of creation—a creation here, however, dependent upon analogies to an already existing nature world and a known, if no longer accepted, gospel. In 'The Flock': 'I | awoke this sunrise to a violence | of images migrating from the mind.' As suggested by the diction, Walcott sees 'The style, tension of motion and the dark, | inflexible direction of the world | as it revolves upon its centuries | . . . year after year with images of flight'. He hopes that 'Till its annihilation may the mind | reflect his fixity'. At the end Walcott confesses:

> I labour at my art.
> My father, God, is dead.
>
> Past thirty now I know
> To love the self is dread
> Of being swallowed by the blue
> Of heaven overhead
> Or rougher blue below.
> Some lesion of the brain
> From art or alcohol
> Flashes this fear by day:
> As startling as his shadow
> Grows to the castaway.
>
> Upon this rock the bearded hermit built
> His Eden:
>
> .   .   .   .   .   .
>
>   . . . all the joys
> But one
> Which sent him howling for a human voice.[22]

While British reviewers saw that Walcott had an unusual command of the nuances, textures, and harmonies of English, there were some reservations, a feeling that the poetry was at times vague and portentous. Alvarez in the *Observer* observed that the poems concerned loneliness, especially the loneliness of a poet. Walcott was angry, uneasy, guilty, alive, melodramatic, the best poet from the West Indies. Maurice Wiggin in the *Sunday Times* wrote of the pyrotechnical vocabulary, the many images, the intelligence, the density, the glow, the discipline. Walcott combined, according to Richard Kell in the *Guardian*, 'a strong rational structure with great imaginative intensity'. Graham Martin, in the *Listener*, thought Walcott at his best used a 'richly tentacular language in a descriptive-metaphoric mode'. Destructive Nature provided only momentary pleasures and led to death, the only defence being art. The anonymous reviewer in the *TLS* thought the poems serious, dramatic, angular, filled with observation and content, as well as being melancholic and sensuous. Walcott was maturing rapidly, this was a better book than his first, but it was in places a bit portentous and the focus on isolation was uncompelling. There were too many dull aphorisms.[23]

Ross claimed that while Walcott shared in the pervasive West Indian melancholy of heat, rain, and longing (typical of colonial writing where life is elsewhere), Lowell's influence could now be seen in a 'more laconic, open manner, a greater definition'. Some earlier poems were almost impenetrably dense, 'the paths of meaning trailing off or twisting confusedly . . . dependent clauses piling up and the sense collapsing under their weight . . . an attachment to the comma rather than the full stop'. Such syntax emphasized the overblown at the expense of clarity. The landscape came through more vividly than the poet. Such flaws were less true of the new volume. 'He has exchanged exclamation for the flat statement, the verb has taken over from the adjective.' There was 'a rewarding approximation between the physical shape and texture of his poems and their subject matter'. Walcott was more concerned with history than himself, and masked his 'natural warmth', but no West Indian poet had previously catalogued and reinvented the region so miraculously.[24]

Gordon Rohlehr was later to note images of fire throughout, suggestive of withering rather than purification; time's fires would wither mind and life, but ripen experience into art. There was a sense of void, distance, and alienation already noticeable in *In a Green Night*; life was empty. There was a gulf (the title of Walcott's next book) between the author's persona and those he observed. He stared at others, at society. Walcott was seeking a cold indifference like the later Yeats, but an indifference that would include commitment, something between dry loneliness and helpless rage.[25]

In January, Therese Mills of the *Trinidad Guardian* asked five local intellectuals for 'The 5 best books of 1965'. Walcott listed six titles, Nirad Chaudhuri's *The Continent of Circe*, Robert Lowell's *For the Union Dead*, Elizabeth Bishop's

Questions of Travel, and Christopher Isherwood's *Exhumations*. He also included W. H. Auden's *About the House* and Philip Larkin's *The Whitsun Weddings*, 'books which I re-read and enjoy at least once a fortnight'. C. L. R. James recommended *King Lear* and *Moby Dick* along with books by E. P. Thompson, Gilberto Freyre, and Dubois.

A major event of 1966 was the opening of the Basement Theatre, which led to the rapid development of the former Little Carib Theatre Workshop into the Trinidad Theatre Workshop and its first season. Rent was $3,000 a year. The theatre was too small to make a profit, but as this was the first semi-professional little theatre in Port of Spain, no one knew what to expect. For the first time lead actors might be paid, perhaps $5 or $10. This was in its own small way the start of professional theatre in the West Indies—what Walcott hoped to build into the foundations of a career as a West Indian playwright-director-producer. Despite its many limitations, the little Basement Theatre was a home, a place to rehearse, to perform, even a place for the actors to meet and practise with each other, to talk over their parts and socialize. There were now usually two workshops a week, followed by hard social drinking. When not used for rehearsals and workshops, the theatre was used for poetry readings, try-outs by other drama companies, an art exhibition, a miniature all-purpose arts centre, something Port of Spain did not and still does not have.

Since the failed attempt to turn the Little Carib into such a centre, Walcott's plan to earn a living from the theatre in the West Indies appeared even more unlikely. His idea of the theatre workshop and his belief that the region could have its equivalent of an Irish Renaissance depended on transforming local arts from amateurism to professionalism. This required an arts centre, a theatre, training local artists to international standards, training by outsiders, scholarships to study abroad, sponsorship, and a paying audience. Throughout the year and in subsequent years Walcott wrote in the *Trinidad Guardian* about the problems and needs of West Indian artists, especially performing artists. This was part of a decades-long, magnificent, but ultimately futile wish to make Port of Spain into an international centre for the region's art. To Walcott it seemed obvious that if the government would not do the job on its own, it could support the Trinidad Theatre Workshop and enable it to become a national company. There was money, work, and talent for only one company. Peter Minshall, Trinidad's most promising scene designer, had gained his diploma from the Central School of Arts in London, but where could he find work outside of Carnival when he returned to Trinidad?[26]

The first of the Theatre Workshop productions in the Basement Theatre at Bretton Hall Hotel was a double bill, 7–12 January, of Walcott's *Sea at Dauphin* and Edward Albee's *Zoo Story*. Walcott directed both. The casts included three of the four core members in the company, Claude Reid, Albert Laveau, and Errol Jones. Stanley Marshall, one of the other foundation members, worked backstage.

The idea was that no one would be a star and tasks would be shared, even roles exchanged during productions, an ideal sometimes practised. The Theatre Workshop's production, 14–27 April, of Eric Roach's *Belle Fanto*, was a new if rather old-fashioned play about a Trinidadian village. Directed by Walcott, this was for a time the longest run for any play in Trinidad. Reviewers noted that J. B. Priestley, in Trinidad to give some lectures, came with the local British Council representative, and commented on the acting, especially that of Errol Jones. Despite its claustrophobic size the Basement Theatre was within months being described as a national shrine and used to support the call for a national theatre. Earl Lovelace wrote that while theatre could promote cultural and racial integration, there was a danger that the Workshop actors and other creative artists would go abroad if society and the government could not provide professional conditions.[27]

As the Workshop began to expand and accept new members, Walcott's method of interviewing some applicants became controversial. Walcott always was thought a sharp judge of character, someone who observed others and knew how to lead and use them. He often 'tested' people when he first met them by creating a potentially humiliating situation and watching how they handled it. A young woman who came to the Basement Theatre and asked how to join was told to take a broom and pretend she was sweeping the room. Later a white actress would be asked to stand on one leg and recite a nursery rhyme; she recited 'Baa, Baa, Black Sheep' over and over.

During January 1966 Walcott stopped being a regular staff member with weekly assignments for the *Trinidad Guardian*. His relationship to the newspaper for the next year or so was as a member of staff on a monthly retainer of $100 and payment per article at freelance rates. The details are unclear, but Walcott may have exaggerated a disagreement with an editor so that he could find more time for the theatre and his own work. He wrote to the Rockefeller and Farfield Foundations asking for temporary help for six months or a year so he could stay on in Trinidad. This led to long discussions within the Rockefeller Foundation as Freund tried to convince others that support of Walcott could be justified within existing policies. At the end of the month (31 January) Walcott explained to Giroux that he had been told that his arts reviews were too obscure. Walcott claimed that the *Trinidad Guardian* wished to get rid of him, but was concerned that the union would create problems. He was sending ninety pages of the 'project'—the story of his life—and wanted an advance if possible. He had money problems and needed about $200. He sent his love to the Lowells and Straus. Giroux wrote back on 9 February that he kept trying the *New Yorker*, as they paid the best rates, but without success. Although he thought 'Leaving School' well written it lacked 'story'; he would, however, try to make an advance on the autobiography.

Frank Platt, Executive Director of the Farfield Foundation, telephoned Freund (17 February) to say he could make a $1,500 grant to keep Walcott going, and hoped the Rockefeller Foundation would find a way to make an exception to its rules so it could make a larger grant. Lowell wrote to Freund on 21 May a supporting letter in which he described Walcott as brilliant, his standards of the highest. Although his perspective and materials were Caribbean, which is where he belonged, he was making a contribution to American letters. He deserved and needed support.

Roderick telephoned Derek to tell him that Harry Simmons had committed suicide on Saturday, 7 May. Simmons had stopped being a leading intellectual and artist, an influence on the bright young. He had given up jobs, chased young women, lost his wife, and, despondent and isolated, had drunk himself to death; it took several days for his death to be discovered. Walcott's 'Tribute to a Master' was published in the *Trinidad Guardian*. Walcott described him as 'one of the finest water-colourists the West Indies has produced . . . a federalist before the politicians . . . [he helped] to create a community of writers and painters among whom Sybil Atteck and the late Edgar Mittelholzer'.

He preferred humble subjects, the chronicle of the country life that he knew well; fishermen at work, peasants, country dances, the firelight of kitchens, portraits of simple people, and he made us see that these were subjects that were worthy of our young and confused gifts.

Since January Walcott had seemed unable to decide whether his autobiography should be in prose or verse. Simmons's death decided the issue; the prose continuation of 'Leaving School' started its journey to becoming the long poem *Another Life*.[28]

After *The Castaway* gained the 1966 Royal Society of Literature Heinemann Award for poetry (£200) Walcott was made a Fellow of the Society, joining Naipaul along with Graham Greene, Lawrence Durrell, Noel Coward, and Agatha Christie. Maschler agreed on 21 June to collect the award. He was glad to learn that Walcott was working on a new book of poems, what would become *Another Life*, that might be available as early as October.

The Extra-Mural Department published *Malcochon* in Caribbean Plays, but Walcott wanted a commercial publisher for his plays, with international distribution, advances, decent royalties, and reviews, just as he now had for his poems. Maschler was willing to consider publishing the plays, although they were unlikely to be profitable, and asked to be sent the published and unpublished scripts. He was concerned about how many copies had already been printed by the Extra-Mural Department and whether they had been republished. The scripts were then with Louis James, who had moved from the University of the West Indies to the University of Canterbury, Kent; he had requested them for the

Oxford University Press Three Crown series which mostly published Third World writing in paperback.

Maschler renewed discussion of an Anthology of West Indian literature. He wanted first refusal; if he could not use it he would send it to Collins under plain cover as Walcott's agent. Walcott was concerned that he could not find enough good material. He was not satisfied with the selection in *London Magazine*, and felt he needed such prose writers as Naipaul, Harris, and Lamming. Maschler wanted to know whether Walcott had cleared copyrights? The West Indian poetry anthology and the idea of a volume of Walcott's plays dragged on, although Maschler was favourable in principle to both.

The reasons why Walcott was having problems putting together a good anthology can be gathered from his comments about anthologies edited by others. He praised Barbara Howes's *From the Green Antilles* for discovering early works, including 'neglected' writers, and for excellent excerpts from works in progress. While Walcott's 'Missing the Sea' was the first work in Howes's book, it is true that it is still a good selection in four languages, ranging from Naipaul, Selvon, and Hearne to St-John Perse and Césaire, Nicolas Guillén and Alejo Carpentier. Walcott thought G. R. Coulthard's *Caribbean Literature, an Anthology* suffered from predictable selections, sentimentality, and bad verse. Coulthard replied by objecting that publishers, including Walcott's own, charged too much.[29]

The famous play agent Margaret Ramsay (24 August 1966) told Maschler that Walcott's talent was literary rather than dramatic; being in blank verse *Franklin* might seem pretentious. The real trouble, however, was that no one was likely to want it as it would take too much study to produce, unless John Barton could be interested. The opening of the play was excellent and Ramsay had thought of trying to find a composer, perhaps Britten or Richard Bennett, to turn it into an opera. Ramsay was not certain that Walcott should be a playwright, but he was going to succeed as a writer, and she wanted to read future scripts by him.[30]

During August Walcott taught and directed at the UWI summer school where he found some new actors for his workshop, which was preparing for its first repertory season in the Basement Theatre. The 'season' lasted for a month, twenty-six nights (excluding Mondays), a major step towards regular semi-professional theatre after decades of West Indian amateur groups performing one-act plays on one weekend. There was, 6–15 October, Jean Genet's *The Blacks*; 20–2 October, the second run of Roach's *Belle Fanto*; 26 October–5 November, Wole Soyinka's *The Road*. The plays were meant to be part of the company's regular repertory, but only *Belle Fanto* was performed again, as *The Blacks* was felt to be shocking and *The Road* difficult. The casts included Errol Jones, Stanley Marshall, Albert Laveau, and Claude Reid. Among the other regulars was Hamilton Parris, an excellent actor who had performed in a local light opera society. Walcott directed the three plays. Admission was $2.

While the Trinidad Theatre Workshop first season included a range of plays from Roach's old-fashioned naturalism to the avant-garde violence of Genet and the avant-garde ritualism of Soyinka, each of the three plays is about 'race', about being 'black', whether it be the social conditions of the poor in Trinidad or the Yoruba myth and rituals of Soyinka (which in *The Road* are contrasted to Christianity).

Early in 1965 Walcott had written about LeRoi Jones in 'The Theatre of Abuse' and about 'T. S. Eliot—Master of an Age'. Walcott had been thinking about the problems that would be part of his own work. It was necessary to rise above the simplistic protest art of the United States to a wild poetry of abuse as found in Genet's *The Blacks*. This required masks, changing roles, and revelations of self-hatred by the social underdogs. *Murder in the Cathedral* showed the difficulties of communicating interiorized changes of mind and being.[31]

Walcott normally introduced his productions with newspaper articles on the play or notable aspects of the production. He claimed Genet's *The Blacks* was the great play about blacks, as its rage against God and bourgeois values is a rage against the white God. When this God dies, black stops being the colour of sin. For blacks to perform the play increases its theatricality and is part of a tradition of black carnivalesque parody. Walcott's own anger at a 'white' world found in *Malcochon* and *Sea at Dauphin* assumed brotherhood with Genet and other rebels; the white God was the existing order of injustice and limitation.[32]

As *The Road* has seldom been performed except when Soyinka himself directed it, Walcott's production has more than a historical interest. A dozen years later Walcott wrote an unpublished 'Essay on Soyinka's *The Road*'. Walcott was not at ease with the obscurity of Soyinka's poetry and plays; of the new African writers he seems only to have known the work of some Nigerians and preferred the poetry of Christopher Okigbo and J. P. Clark. This would explain why the Theatre Workshop often rehearsed Clark's *Song of a Goat*. Walcott, however, realized that Soyinka's *The Road* is a great play and the Professor one of the great characters of modern theatre. Walcott felt that Soyinka's ritualistic drama is difficult to perform honestly without faking what makes it unique to the dramatist's vision and to his culture. It has passages in Yoruba. Walcott's actors could not speak Yoruba and using phonetic transcription was thought dishonest. The same problems occurred with the African drumming and chanting, which risked becoming exotic Africana if faked according to Trinidadian notions. The main problem was that Soyinka assumes that the actors become possessed by gods and re-enact Ogun's dangerous journey through chaos from the world of the spiritual to the human. At the climax of the play there is possession after a ritual mask is put on and a death, a killing, as the actor becomes drunken Ogun blindly slaughtering those around him. This is the vision of the Road the Professor has sought and now finds in death. Walcott believed that a Trinidadian actor could not participate in the experience the way one of Soyinka's actors could. Walcott felt that the Trinidad Theatre Workshop production could at best treat only the surface of this great play.

Walcott sent Giroux (10 October) his recently finished *Franklin*, wanting to know whether the Lowells thought the play needed a stronger ending. Giroux replied on 11 November writing that he felt Franklin and Major Willoughby rather flat characters. Was this because they were relics of a doomed and vanishing past?

Walcott (16 November) told Ross that for the past two years he had been working on a long poem that began in 'Leaving School'. He was deliberately writing factual, prosaic verse as he wanted the poem to read like a work of fiction without leaving space for pausing, reflection, or admiration. It would be difficult to excerpt. He hoped to have a full version by the New Year when they returned to the beach house. Walcott again mentioned that he would like a *London Magazine* issue on Commonwealth theatre, its problems and influences. He had just finished directing and designing three plays for the first repertory season of his Theatre Workshop and would like to write a book about the struggle. The letter concludes with humour which in those days would be described as masculine.

Among Walcott's articles during 1966 is 'Patterns of Existence' in which he argued 'the anguish of every art is that it is continually groping to escape from itself. Van Gogh would have plastered thick sunlight onto his Provence canvasses instead of pure paint, if he could. Language, especially in the form of poetry, gropes for an algebraic precision, in which letters have the unchanging rigidity of numbers.' What appears to be an argument for abstract formalism as a result of the inability of the arts to mimic reality curiously turns into its opposite, a proclamation of a tightly packed minimalist naturalism as the highest art, the true poetry. This idea would become increasingly significant to Walcott, as he attempted to move from an elaborate metaphoric style to the seemingly nonmetaphoric. Walcott would a decade later return to such ideas and argue that the most poetic drama is in the understated realism of a Chekhov. He admitted not having finished reading *Dr Zhivago* but praised Pasternak's autobiography *Safe Conduct* as a minor masterpiece. The prose of *Dr Zhivago* was too poetic, better savoured in fragments that could become dull if taken in excess, whereas Pasternak's poetry had the compression of a novel; the poetry was like Hardy's in including everything, in naming a world, in its humanness.[33]

Selden Rodman, well-known editor, anthologist, and critic, had been studying art in Haiti, came to Trinidad (19 December) and soon became friends with Walcott. Derek told him that all the criticisms Naipaul made of Trinidad were true but irrelevant: Walcott could not leave Trinidad, this was where he belonged. After Rodman gave him a copy of *South America of the Poets*, Walcott began reading Borges and Neruda with more care.

13

~~~~~~

1967–1968 Rockefeller Grant, First Tours

BETWEEN 15 January and 11 February 1967 Walcott wrote five articles on Carnival and related matters such as calypso technique and Carnival costumes. These were among his last pieces in the *Trinidad Guardian* as a member of the staff. After much discussion the Rockefeller Foundation agreed to grant Walcott $10,000, paid in quarterly instalments of $833.33 over three years, March 1967–70, to enable him to devote himself to artistic activities. Having secured another source of steady income, he resigned from being a regular arts critic, citing conflict of interest in reviewing drama as his reason.

He soon told the Rockefeller Foundation that to keep his pension he had agreed to continue to contribute articles to the *Trinidad Guardian*. These were articles on West Indian literature, including two concerning Edward Brathwaite's *Rights of Passage*. Walcott had known Brathwaite's sister in Jamaica, had seen Brathwaite's work in manuscript, and was interested in it, especially in the use of different voices. He adapted some of it for his Theatre Workshop. Later, as critics tried to polarize West Indian poetry between an Anglo-Walcott and a Black-Brathwaite, a view Brathwaite seemed to encourage, Walcott was to make fun of some of the latter's bravura displays, but Brathwaite was one of the few West Indian poets in whose work Walcott was interested. Naipaul was the subject of one article and shared another with Wilson Harris. The publication of *The Mimic Men* resulted in another article, also broadcast locally, in which Walcott claimed that while *A House for Mr Biswas* was great, and *The Middle Passage* was outrageous, *The Mimic Men* chronicled a decline towards the 'madness and anonymity that all Naipaul's books record'. Naipaul appeared embittered, pessimistic, and untrusting of racial integration and West Indian economic development; even West Indian gaiety depressed him. While this is the start of a shift in his evaluation, Walcott apparently saw himself, his usually repressed hidden side, in Naipaul, 'the impatience, the schizophrenic scorn, the paranoid self-detestation'.[1]

'Another Kind of Sentimentality' in the *Sunday Guardian Magazine* (12 February 1967) discussed Walcott's own angry feelings while young. As a young colonial he had thought of whites with envy and bitterness; he had seen and still saw history as the exploitation of blacks for profit by whites. He had tried to exorcize this, but he could still justify his passion. For him all West Indian theatre had race as its subject in the sense that the characters must be 'defined by their attitudes to such a history'. Walcott had been puzzled when a young black poet and dramatist disagreed with him and said that there were other important topics. People liked to pretend that class had replaced race and that Trinidad was a multiracial Utopia, but this was not so. People only hid their feelings in politeness.[2]

The scenario surrounding Walcott being fired by the *Trinidad Guardian* is puzzling. Apparently a number of articles were expected as the editor wrote early in 1968 (10 January) complaining that Walcott had submitted nothing for three months. As the *Trinidad Guardian* still counted on him for reviews, weekly articles for the Sunday edition, and for the editorial page, the editor wanted to know whether he should make alternative arrangements. Decades later, after the Nobel Prize, the *Trinidad Guardian* was to deny it fired Walcott. It seems likely that a dispute was magnified as Walcott needed more time for his theatre company and wanted to be released from reviewing other drama companies and having the regular obligations of a member of staff. He still hoped to earn money from journalism.

The Trinidad Theatre Workshop had a hit (14–19 April) with Errol John's play *Moon on a Rainbow Shawl* at Queen's Hall. This was the first time the Workshop had used a three-dimensional set, worked on a stage with a proscenium arch, and booked the large Queen's Hall. By local standards they were no longer a small arts theatre. The total audience was in thousands rather than hundreds. The production was originally planned for four nights, and could have continued longer if the hall had not already been booked.

Besides work on his next book of poetry the main events of 1967 were the tours by the Trinidad Theatre Workshop. These were necessary for Walcott to keep his actors performing and toughen them; they offered a potential profit, and would bring his plays to wider attention in the region. Walcott still thought in terms of the West Indies rather than Trinidad and hoped his theatre company could eventually tour internationally and perform at Edinburgh and other festivals. Indeed to become a professional company they would need to become a regional touring company; he would be their artistic director, usually direct their plays, and they would produce and perform his plays. This was another grand idea that became too expensive and difficult, but provided some of the best theatre the West Indian has seen. The first tour was to Barbados, and became a model for the hard work and intensive schedule that became normal when the Workshop travelled abroad. The Workshop prepared for the tour by performing Walcott's *Jourmard* and Albee's *Zoo Story* at the university on 21 June. Walcott and others arrived on 29 June in Barbados and began creating a theatre where there was none previously. This meant putting up lighting and sound, doing the electrical wiring, finding seats, and much else. As the Workshop had no real lighting equipment, much of it was improvised along with what could be carried by passengers on airplanes. Curiously, because of Walcott's interest in art and because of the artistry of John Andrews, a former dancer who was learning about lighting, the Workshop became known for its lighting, and decades later when it performed in Boston its lighting design for *Dream on Monkey Mountain* struck professionals as among the most subtle and complex they had ever seen.

Others in the company arrived the next day, rehearsed, and that night performed *Zoo Story* and *Jourmard* at St Winifred's School, followed by two performances of *Belle Fanto*, at 4 and 8 p.m. on 1 July and a matinée on 2 July. They then returned to Trinidad where Walcott continued working on the film script of 'A Flag on the Island'. On 14–16 July, *Zoo Story* and *Jourmard* were performed at the Basement Theatre before overflow audiences, and on 23 July and 28 July *Belle Fanto* was taken to Tobago and San Fernando. There were other performances around Trinidad before the workshop left for Canada and Guyana.

Canada, as part of the Empire, now the British Commonwealth, had a long-standing relationship with the West Indies and was often the destination to which West Indians emigrated. It did not have the colour bar of the American South, and there was an interest in cultural exchanges. There were West Indian communities in large cities. Fred Hope, a former Walcott actor who had helped raise funds for the Basement Theatre, was Co-ordinating Secretary of the Caribbean Centennial Committee in Toronto to which he invited (16 May) the Workshop. He said that the Committee would cover expenses in Canada for not more than twelve people who should try to arrive a few days in advance to relax, rehearse, and make stage alterations for two or three plays. He also asked Walcott to take responsibility for what Carlisle Chang and others would send to the Centennial.

The Canada trip soon became part of an epic journey with many events, including a Toronto wedding between two members of the Workshop and several recordings for radio. The trip itself was long and tiring, as they flew island to island, changing airplanes and going through customs with lighting equipment carried on their laps; there was an immense backdrop for *Dream on Monkey Mountain*, which was to première in Canada, although only the first half had been rehearsed. There was none of the relaxation Hope had hoped for. Besides rehearsing *Dream* during the day it was necessary to find a different theatre from the shell on Centre Island which proved noisy and windy, and let in more than it kept out of the Caribana Festival, an event more devoted to dance, music, song, and drunken crowds than theatre. Beginning 5 August there were several days of performances of *Belle Fanto, Jourmard,* and *Zoo Story* before the Workshop gave up; *Dream on Monkey Mountain* premièred at the Central Library Theatre on 12 August for one night, and *Zoo Story* and *Jourmard* were performed the next night.

They left Toronto on 15 August, overnighted in Trinidad, and opened at the Theatre Guild Playhouse, Kingston, Guyana, 17–19 August, with *Zoo Story* and *Jourmard,* and continued, 21–3 August, with *Belle Fanto* and, 24–6 August, with *Dream on Monkey Mountain.* The shows were at first poorly attended as no one knew what to expect from the company. After they left critics said that it was by far the best West Indian acting they had seen and that the Theatre Guild should itself encourage more West Indian plays. The Workshop lost in Guyana the profits made in Barbados. While in Guyana Walcott recorded two radio programmes, a discussion of theatre in the Caribbean with Slade Hopkinson, and a poetry reading with Martin Carter.

Nine months later *London Magazine* published the six-part sequence 'Guyana' which Walcott revised for *The Gulf.* The first part, now also titled 'Guyana', was originally 'The Survey'.[3] Walcott was working on the poems which later went into *The Gulf.* After Che Guevara was killed, 9 October, on orders of the High Command of the Bolivian Army, photographs were made and internationally published. The photographs of the revolutionary hero of the Left seemed, according to some, comparable to Mantegna's *Dead Christ* and Rembrandt's *Anatomy Lesson.* Walcott's 'Che' makes a similar comparison, perhaps more accurately noting the dramatic dark–white contrasts in a photograph that was both highly realistic and strangely iconic, like a Baroque statue or portrait of Christ —'In this dark-grained news-photograph, whose glare | is rigidly composed as Caravaggio's'. A year later, 6 June 1968, he wrote 'Elegy', very much a 1968 poem:

> Our hammock swung between Americas
> we miss you, Liberty. Che's
> bullet-riddled body falls,
> and those who cried the Republic must first die
> to be reborn are dead,
> the freeborn citizen's ballot in the head.[4]

'Che' immediately precedes 'Negatives' in *The Gulf,* the two poems meant as a pair. After viewing television news clips about the Nigerian–Biafra civil war, and the killing of Ibos, Walcott addresses the now dead poet Christopher Okigbo, admitting his Africa was an actor in *Dream on Monkey Mountain* screaming 'The tribes! | The tribes!'. Now for a moment he sees Ibo 'bug-eyed | prisoners of some drumhead tribunal'. The pun on dumb | drum catches some of the distance from Africa which Walcott recognizes along with his anger that Africans should act like whites towards Africans. The poem appears simple, but its various ironies are complex:

> The soldiers' helmeted shadows
> could have been white . . .
>
> entering . . . the tribes, the tribes, their shame—
> that central city, Christ, what is its name?

Walcott sees the trial scene in *Dream* and the citation of many absurd charges by its radical black African tribunal as foretelling the tribal conflicts of Africa. As a black he is humiliated by Africans killing Africans, yet he and those watching television are distant from the war, know little of Africa, and will soon forget it.[5]

Dream was on Walcott's mind. He sent Ronald Bryden (30 November 1967) a copy for comment and told Maschler that if Cape published a volume of his plays Bryden might write the introduction. Walcott said he was enjoying doing the film script of Naipaul's 'A Flag for the Island' for Lionel Rogosin.

As the Workshop developed into a theatre company, Walcott wanted another director and other professionals to help him. Freund was thinking how to help André Gregory, who was leaving the Los Angeles Inner City Cultural Center. Gregory, now also famous for his films, already had a reputation as one of the best young American theatre directors, who had led the Theatre of the Living Arts in Philadelphia. He had worked with Herbert Blau and studied at the Brecht Theatre in Berlin, as well as doing productions off-Broadway and in Los Angeles. Freund thought that Gregory might be the American director that Walcott needed. He suggested a travel grant so Gregory could visit Trinidad for a week to explore a longer visit. Walcott spoke with Gregory on the telephone and asked if he could come to Trinidad in late January to meet and see the Workshop and plan for a later visit.

Already famous as a drummer and singer initiated into the Trinidadian Shango cult, Andrew Beddeau, who had worked for McBurnie, joined the Workshop in December. His drumming and chanting added to the power of *Dream on Monkey Mountain* which, with the company enlarged to thirty, was performed at Queen's Hall, 26–30 January 1968. This was its first staging in Trinidad. Ross was in Trinidad and attended a rehearsal unknown to Walcott. Returning to England Ross received a rather jumpy and jumbled letter (22 February) in which Walcott mentioned he had been in bad shape with too much work, drink, frenzy, fear, and exhaustion. There had been a drunken quarrel about the movie script, which

Walcott hoped would blow over, he was trying to finish it. Ross had sent a telegram asking for poems and accused Walcott of worrying his poems out of existence. Walcott sent some, but requested prepayment as he needed money. He had 'lent' Ross sections of *Another Life*, which he wanted back to show his publishers. He was working hard, with help, on a translation of Césaire's *Cahier* with notes from a Caribbean perspective. He thought Césaire a loud but tremendous poet.

The next week (29 February 1968) Walcott wrote to Maschler that he hoped soon to have ready a book of short poems and *Another Life*, the verse-autobiography which had started in prose. Like many of Walcott's works *The Gulf and Other Poems* had a different title until shortly before it was completed. As late as 22 November 1968, Maschler thought he was contracting 'The Homecoming', the title of the centrally placed poem in the volume, 'Homecoming: Anse La Raye', with its themes of being distanced and exiled from the ordinary St Lucians of the fishing village as a result of education, ambition, and travel. The poem is addressed to the novelist Garth St Omer:

> Whatever else we learned
> at school, like solemn Afro-Greeks eager for grades,
> of Helen and the shades
> of borrowed ancestors,
> there are no rites
> for those who have returned,
>
> .   .   .   .   .   .
>
> for once, like them,
> you wanted no career
> but this sheer light, this clear,
> infinite, boring, paradisal sea,
> but hoped it would mean something to declare
> today, I am your poet, yours,
> all this you knew,
> but never guessed you'd come
> to know there are homecomings without home.[6]

When in New York the previous December Walcott had discussed his manuscripts with Giroux, who had been thinking of combining 'The Homecoming' with those *Castaway* poems not in *Selected Poems*. Walcott felt that because of the work involved and its length he wanted more than the usual £50 advance from Cape for *Another Life*.

It was necessary to postpone the Festival for the opening of the Creative Arts Centre at Mona as furnishings and theatre equipment from England were held up. Still hoping to open the Centre with a Festival in June, John Hearne now decided to have a Derek Walcott Week and asked him (23 January) to come on

Saturday, 16 March, before the students left for vacations. As there would be no examinations that would be a good time for readings and talks. The Walcotts' second daughter, Anna, was born on 7 March 1968, a week before Derek went to Jamaica, where there were displays of photographs of Walcott and the Trinidad Theatre Workshop, manuscripts, theatre notebooks, and paintings. There were readings from Walcott's poetry by Walcott, John Figueroa, and Dennis Scott, and a lecture by Walcott on the 'Origins and Operations of the Basement Theatre, Trinidad'.

Mervyn Morris's lecture, 'Walcott and the Audience for Poetry', discusses some of the contexts in which Walcott was creating. Citing Walcott's 'Castiliane' ('Girl, you were wise, whoever lived by verse? | The future is in cheap enamel wares'), Morris claims that there is no community of serious poetry readers in the West Indies, what taste there is remains limited to the Romantics. Twentieth-century Modernist poetry and such influences as the Elizabethans and Jacobeans are neglected in the schools. West Indian intellectuals are obsessed with politics and race; by contrast Walcott's poetry is 'exploratory'.

Morris then explicates passages from 'Ruins of a Great House' to show how the allusions to Donne's *Devotions* enrich and complicate the poem, which can be read in various ways, including ironically. An emendation of punctuation in 'Ablaze with rage, I thought | Some slave is rotting in this manorial lake' makes it, in the American *Selected Poems*, 'Ablaze with rage I thought,'—a much more complicated statement, including possible criticism of unthinking anti-colonialism. In *The Castaway*'s 'A Village Life' the possible puns on Uncle Tom Cat as well as 'Spade' make a seemingly simple poem difficult because it conveys a complexity of emotions. Comparing the 'Margaret Verlieu Dies' in *Poems* with its later 'A Country Club Romance' version in *In a Green Night*, Morris notes that while the lines have extra beats the language and rhythm are tighter. This is mostly new critical emphasis on economy, ambiguity, art as complexity and shows a context of Walcott's work and reception far different from the politics and folk nationalism assumed to dominate West Indian criticism. That Morris is himself an excellent poet adds to the interest of the lecture which except for details could have so far been delivered in the United States or England.

The lecture suddenly takes on a different weight as Morris compares the 1958 version of 'Tales of the Islands' as published in *Bim 26* with *In a Green Night*. Whereas before Walcott had aimed at a Hemingwayesque flatness, a dispassionate prose-like observation, now the poems are rewritten to be rhythmically tight, conversational, make use of many tones and dialects of voice and class, which sharpens their ironies, and makes them more West Indian in cadences and complex cultural situations. Chapter VI was already famous among those who followed West Indian poetry. Originally it began:

> Garcon—that was a fete—I mean they had
> Free Whiskey and they had some fellows beating
> Steel from one of the bands in Trinidad

Now it read:

> Poopa, da' was a fête! I mean it had
> Free rum free whisky and some fellars beating
> Pan from one of them band in Trinidad

While the excitement comes from the language, there is a complex social situation, a hedonistic society, the alienated writer, a black Oxbridge graduate, and the implied question whether the vacuity seen by the speaker is different from his own. The poem is also ambiguous about the voodoo sacrificial ritual mentioned by the educated speaker, as it is at once horrifying and yet more emotionally profound, primitive. Morris claims that the supposed conflict between middle-class West Indian speech and folk speech may be less sharp than suggested by Walcott's *London Magazine* 'Some West Indian Poets'. Walcott himself often unobtrusively interweaves West Indian English into his poems. Such natural West Indianness speaks as directly or indirectly to society as attempts to write dialect poetry, which is really just another form of art-speech. Walcott's main direction has been towards greater complexity of significance within a simpler surface. 'Tales of the Islands' required an inventive criticism which blended concern with artistic standards and local cultural assertion with recognition of innovation such as Walcott's use of the West Indian voice with its mastery of many registers, and suggestions that both the folk and educated may be without real cultural roots.[7]

That week the Literary Committee of the Barbados Arts Council (19 March) informed Walcott that *Franklin* was unanimously adjudged the best three-act play in the Play-writing Competition. The judges included Frank Collymore and Edward Baugh. Walcott was sent $200.

During May Walcott was working with Harold Major on a translation of Aimé Césaire's 'Journals of a Return to my Own Land'. (Major's name was later crossed out on the typescript.) There were the usual revisions with prepositions being added in place of others, and the poetic word being wrong. At times the translators were puzzled as Césaire's great poem is surrealist with many images more suitable for a Dali painting than Négritude. The ten draft pages of the translation that survive are not promising, but Walcott integrated some tropes into his own vision, including the notion that one could use nouns in an elemental way to communicate great, simple but magical notions as did primitive man. This would remain a Walcottian ambition as late as his Nobel Prize acceptance speech. Walcott would modify Césaire's praise of those who invented nothing (in contrast to Europe) to a New World amnesia towards the past which results in a new start. Walcott hoped Ross would publish the translation with an essay and drawings of the photographs of the beaches on Martinique.

For the Trinidad and Tobago Festival of 1968 the Trinidad Theatre Workshop performed *Henri Christophe* at Queen's Hall (26–8 April) and two weeks later at Naparima Bowl (11 May) in San Fernando. The first night was attended by Gregory who had come to Trinidad a few weeks earlier. In July the Trinidad Theatre Workshop was forced to leave the Basement Theatre at Bretton Hall Hotel after a problem with the owner; it remained homeless for two decades, rehearsing at such places as the Zoo and a high school.

Walcott had sent *Another Life* to Giroux and Maschler early in May and asked Maschler to place sections in British journals that pay, as he expected Giroux to do in the United States. Plomer, however, was disappointed with the poem. He was worried about Walcott's reaction to a rejection and talked to Ross who had seen it earlier; Plomer learned that Ross and Margaret Walcott also felt it was not yet right for publication. It was decided that Plomer would explain what was wrong while Maschler would offer to publish if Walcott insisted, but, as he understood Walcott needed the money, Cape would prefer to contract the book for some future date and pay an advance now. On 11 July Walcott asked for the return of the manuscript as Plomer had agreed with Ross that the long poem needed more work.

Walcott thanked Ross (12 July) for the recent issue with 'Guyana'. He sent five poems including 'O. S. Moses . . . the Man and the Myth'. Walcott again appeared distracted, he would later call it almost hysterical, and was uncertain whether he had already sent Ross these poems. One of the topics that recurs in these letters is of Walcott continuing to revise poems that he had already submitted, some of which were already set up in proof. He now had another book of poems almost ready which he had been working on for months; he was sending some to Ross as he was broke and needed money. He had been paid on acceptance for 'Guyana' and Walcott now wanted advance payment for the new poems. He told Ross that he had been working steadily on his poetry, the translation, a film script, and at the theatre as they prepared for their Jamaican tour. He was going to Washington to read at the Library of Congress in October and maybe at the University of Texas. He had not yet received a promised TT $900 bonus from Rogosin for the film script. Money was a problem. Walcott telephoned Giroux who wrote to Maschler (19 July) asking if there were some way to speed up paying Walcott. Perhaps Farrar, Straus could pay him directly instead of going through Cape? Maschler objected that Cape only took 10 per cent and wanted to handle the rights. This appears to have left Walcott smouldering. He needed money and Farrar, Straus would pay for its own editions, whereas Cape wanted uniform editions which it would control.

In August Walcott taught a three-week drama course at the University of the West Indies summer school at which, as there were far more women than men, he directed a production of Aristophanes' *Lysistrata*. This was the Third Annual Summer School in St Augustine.

Roy Basler, Director of the Library of Congress Reference Department, had invited Walcott (26 March) to inaugurate with Robert Hayden a new poetry programme. The date of the reading was scheduled for 21 October. The master of ceremonies would be William Jay Smith, who was planning the programmes before assuming his duties as the Library's Consultant in Poetry. Each poet would read about twenty minutes so that there would be time for introductions and discussion. Smith had a copy of the Cape edition of *In a Green Night* and wrongly assumed that the Farrar, Straus *Selected Poems* was the same. If the poems were not from that edition, Smith needed copies as educational television required planning; he would like Walcott to spend 22 October reading some further poems. There was a need to decide which poems were the most visual for television and for scripts to be prepared around the poems. Perhaps they could work in a short play or a scene?[8]

Walcott replied at length (17 September) to Smith saying that he had just returned from a busy four days travelling between the islands to arrange a tour by his theatre company. He planned to fly from Barbados on Sunday, 20 October, to New York, then come to Washington the next morning. He would stay on for whatever Smith wanted including further readings; he hoped to earn money so he would still have free time after his Rockefeller Foundation fellowship ended. He wished to go to the theatre in New York and spend time with Lowell and other friends. Walcott had a number of visual suggestions; he mentioned that 'The Gulf' concerns inner conflict, ghettos, and fires and covers an area from Texas to the West Indies; 'Two Elegies' could be illustrated by a photograph of Che Guevara and of Biafra where Okigbo died. 'Blues' concerns a mugging one night in the Village. He had recently written a 'folk fantasy', *Dream on Monkey Mountain*, and was translating *Cahier D'Un Retour Au Pays Natal*. He would send about ten glossy stills soon, but what fee would the Library pay the photographer?[9]

The Trinidad Theatre Workshop toured (10–26 October) with *Dream on Monkey Mountain* and Roach's *Belle Fanto* to Antigua, St Lucia, Barbados, St Vincent, and Grenada. The five-island tour required incredible energy. A few members would arrive in advance to build and wire the stage. As soon as the actors arrived they would rehearse, nap on stage, and perform. Often because of demand there would be several shows a day. Many in the audience had never seen a play before, certainly not a West Indian one.

Dream on Monkey Mountain had an especial relevance for St Lucia as it was based on Walcott's memories of its society and the people he had known in his youth. *Dream* reflects the language problem in St Lucia where Creole is in common use in contrast to the English of the government and courts. Makak was based on 'Makak D'Augier', Augier's Monkey, a rough fellow who worked for an Augier, got drunk every weekend, and would be put in jail after hitting people and breaking up bars. His employer would then bail him out. Makak is a protest character in a line of succession from Afa and Chantal; Walcott intended him to show the stages of a progression from protest though revolt, madness, and destruction to purification. Makak also has sources in previous dramatic literature; he brings to mind Ibsen's Peer Gynt and Brand, O'Neill's Emperor Jones. Walcott, as in other early plays, uses a peasant to explore his own feelings, ideas, and contradictions. The play is partly about the dangers of imposing the psychological hurts of the brown middle-class intellectual on the West Indies. Makak is tempted into being a hero and tyrant by others. For Walcott the real heroes are isolated individuals, poor folk, artists, those without communal power.[10] Lestrade represents the high brown colonial who learns the ways of whites, remains excluded, and turns into a revolutionary. In this play of many puns, symbols, allusions, and literary echoes, the characters have (as in Ben Jonson's comedies) symbolic names. Makak is Creole for monkey and thus ape. Makak and Lestrade want to return to Africa, but Africa offers the Original Sin of tribe against tribe. Lestrade in Africa echoes Milton's portrayal of the fallen Satan in hell. Moustique's bad foot is meant as a sign of a devil.

Walcott left the company in Barbados for his poetry reading at the Library of Congress where he and Hayden shared a seventy-five-minute poetry reading and discussion at the Coolidge Auditorium, Library of Congress, which was recorded for the Archive of Recorded Poetry and Literature. This was offered as a Two Negro Poets evening, with mention of Hayden having been awarded the main prize in 1966 at the First World Festival of Negro Arts in Senegal and Walcott also having been given an award by the Festival for his poetry. The programme was broadcast in Washington and made available to the National Educational Radio network.

A result of the trip to Washington was 'Postcards 1. Washington', one of Walcott's few direct comments on contemporary American politics. Outrage about the war in Vietnam is expressed in the contrast between President Johnson's face on television, the nearby White House, a Washington aflame with autumnal leafage, and television images of 'Buddhist's robes, | charred'.[11]

A year later the *Chicago Tribune Magazine* was to publish the first version of 'Cold Spring Harbour', a place on Long Island, in which Walcott recalled himself as a child reading books about a world of snow and wanting to be part of it. He would ask himself why now, after his early dreams were destroyed, he was fearfully plunging into such a white world:

> That was a child's sorrow, this is
> Children's play through which you cannot go,
> dumbstruck at an open door,
> stunned, fearing the strange violation
> (because you are missing your children)
> of perfect snow.[12]

Significantly 'Cold Spring Harbour' is followed in *The Gulf* by 'In the Kitchen' which recalls an innocence before he stewed (an Elizabethan pun) 'in the imagination's drab adulteries'.

By American standards Cape's advances were small, and after a discussion with Giroux in which he was told to be tough Walcott felt he might earn more by himself selling his American rights to Giroux as the Cape and Farrar, Straus volumes were different books. This bothered Maschler who would have liked to increase his print runs and add to his profits by selling copies or sheets to the United States, but who also was concerned about the possible harm to Walcott's career if there was no standard edition and confusion about who held the rights for republication of poems in anthologies or other editions. The situation was getting messy and later proved to be so. Giroux lunched with Maschler who agreed to release American rights to Walcott and to wait to contract *Another Life* until after Walcott's revisions. Giroux said that there were enough new poems to add to half of *Castaway* to make a full book already.

Walcott's letters during December and for a few months after seem in a different mood, anxious, pressing, like someone tense trying to break through a barrier. Walcott asked Cape either to publish a volume of his plays or *Dream* by itself. He wrote to Giroux (17 December) that he was thinking of a volume that might include *Dream, Sea, Malcochon, Henri Christophe*, and 'What the Twilight'. He knew Farrar, Straus and Giroux did not usually publish plays, but they had published Lowell's. He was also hoping that *Another Life* could be published during the spring of 1970 when he would be 40 years old. *The Gulf* was promised to Cape. A similar letter (also 17 December) to Maschler mentioned that with the tenth anniversary of the Trinidad Theatre Workshop approaching, in August, he wanted 'What the Twilight Says' published along with, at least, *Dream*. He was hoping the Workshop might have a long retrospective season and was thinking of changing its name to the Trinidad Repertory Theatre. The need to record and celebrate his role in, and vision of, West Indian drama was important to him. He also seemed obsessed with anniversaries. He sent Maschler (20 December) the manuscript of *The Gulf* and told him that he had sent Giroux a copy along with the selections from *The Castaway* that were not in *Selected Poems*. He wanted advances on this and other future books as he needed the money.

He apologized (17 December) for taking so long to thank Ross for the advance he sent when Walcott had financial difficulties because of lack of payment from

Rogosin. He also thanked Ross for his comments on poems he felt did not work, which Walcott had since revised or scrapped. He had finished a new book with more flexible and relaxed rhythms. Ted Hughes and Patrick Garland had arranged for him to be invited to Poetry International 69, but only a third of his passage would be paid. Could the Arts Council or Cape help with costs?

Over Christmas and the New Year the Walcotts were at Toco, Rampanalgas, where Derek made more drawings for a mid-nineteenth-century version of *The Beggar's Opera* and notes for a possible production of J. P. Clark's *Song of a Goat*. Earlier in the year he had made sketches for a possible revival of *The Blacks* with the setting, masks, and costumes mostly in black and white. As usual he examined his finances and found that he had spent more than he earned for the year.

Although Walcott was a central figure in the generation that formed West Indian literature—he was the one who stayed home, he was the one who created theatre groups, he wrote about the arts in local newspapers, he was actively involved in the literary scene of Trinidad and St Lucia—his role was oddly neglected by the first intellectuals and critics who concentrated on novelists and those with clear social views. Ivan Van Sertima's *Caribbean Writers: Critical Essays* (1968) has fourteen essays, none of which are about Walcott. It could be said in Van Sertima's defence that he was concerned mostly with the writers of the 1950s and that his book ends in 1963; since then he felt there was little to add. By 1963 almost all the authors Van Sertima discusses were in exile in London and the poets among them were writing novels for the British market.

14

1969–1970 *The Gulf, Dream* at Waterford and Los Angeles, Gordon Davidson

RETURNING from the seaside (5 January) Walcott wrote about Soyinka for the *Sunday Guardian*, and reviewed Zeffirelli's film *Romeo and Juliet* for *Art and Man*, a new magazine published in Trinidad. After mentioning Soyinka's imprisonment for his political activities, Walcott grandly proclaimed 'the very choice of poetry is the choice of a prison'. For such reviews he was paid thirty or forty Trinidad dollars. He was also working on and publicizing the Trinidad Theatre Workshop's dramatization of six stories by Samuel Selvon.

His emotions were erratic as from day to day he got on or off the wagon. He was depressive and seeking a fight with Maschler. Walcott claimed to Giroux (20 January 1969) that Cape was hampering his development as a professional dramatist. If Cape would not publish his plays then Oxford or Longman would. Such seeking hurts and picking fights occurred when obligation, loyalty, or love conflicted with feelings that it was time for his career to move on. This usually coincided with financial problems and what appeared to be better opportunities. This time there was an anticlimax. Maschler (22 January) offered £100 advance for *The Gulf*, twice what Cape gave other poets. After Cape and Farrar, Straus and Giroux exchanged contracts for *The Gulf* (18 February), Giroux wrote that he wanted to include half of *The Castaway* with *The Gulf*. The British and American editions again would be different.

Maschler (7 March) decided to publish a volume of Walcott's 'television plays'; if Farrar, Straus and Giroux did not wish to join in the printing he wanted

American rights. He had been sent *Franklin, Henri Christophe, Dream on Monkey Mountain, Malcochon, Ti-Jean,* and *The Sea at Dauphin,* but he remained uncertain what to include. As a book of plays that had not been produced in Britain would be difficult to sell he offered an advance of only £100. He sent a contract and notified Louis James and Bob Giroux. If Walcott definitely wanted to come to the July Poetry Festival Maschler would try, but could not promise, to get him a grant for the airfare.

A holiday in Barbados in late January or in February had become part of Walcott's annual schedule. There is an unfinished self-interview in his note-books dated February 1969 in which Walcott discussed his views about Barbados. While he disliked the self-abasement and selling of the country that accompanied tourism, he admitted Barbados felt more lively than most of the region. He and his family had recently had a good time there and his friends were now in positions of power and without the old prejudices that Bim was a shire of England. How could Bajans have taken pride in the history of England, in being English? Yet Walcott knows why, he is part Bajan, Walcott is a Bajan name. When he was 18 or 19 he was attracted to Barbados because of his Bajan teachers and because of Frank Collymore. Whereas St Lucia was wild and exuberant, Barbados appeared civilized, settled, ordered, literate. Most West Indians felt and still feel they are English, but before Independence Barbados openly accepted its debt to British civilization in such forms as black knights, cricket, public schools, and Latin and Greek classics. Walcott admitted his debt to his Barbadian teachers. English history, customs, and literature were exciting to someone from a rigidly Catholic, French-Creole island. The decorum of being English made C. L. R. James, George Lamming, Austin Clarke, and Edward Brathwaite. It was something they could use or rebel against. By comparison writers now lack education. Barbados is itself changing and becoming international or American. Barbados continued to be part of Walcott's world as part of his family was there. During 1969 his *Henri Christophe* would be acted there, he would teach a summer course, and at the end of the year visit Alix, who had moved to Barbados.

Walcott was in Guyana from 8 March for two weeks assisting in the production of his *Franklin* by Guyana's Dramatic Society in an open-air old barn, as the Theatre Guild's stage was being repaired. In contrast to the homeless Trinidad Theatre Workshop the playhouse in Georgetown was well equipped and seldom used. The actors were University of Guyana students, including Ken Corsbie; the Director was Michael Gilkes, then a university lecturer and dramatist. Walcott was to receive $450 from the university for royalties on the production and $15 which Bill Carr added as honorarium for a tutorial in the English Department. Gilkes (2 June) hoped Walcott had by now received the $30 for *Sea at Dauphin* which Radio Guyana used in 1968. Corsbie and Gilkes would soon leave Guyana, as it turned into a black nationalist dictatorship, and contribute to the creation of the next wave of Caribbean theatre centred in Barbados, often using Walcott's plays.

The first American production of *Malcochon* had been at the Judson Church, directed by Larry Kornfeld with music by Al Carmines. The second production of *Malcochon* in New York began on 25 March at St Mark's Playhouse in the Village, around the corner from St Mark's Place. The Playhouse, seating about 140, is in the same building as the larger St Mark's Theatre. There were thirty-two performances directed by Edmund Cambridge for the Negro Ensemble Company as part of an Evening of One Acts. Reviews were not good and Walcott did not like what he read of the production, but he earned royalties of $820. This was the start of Walcott's relations with the Negro Ensemble Company, which would become the best-known black drama group in the United States and would produce his *Dream on Monkey Mountain* and other of his plays. John Melser reviewed the production for the *Trinidad Guardian* during the third week of the run. Although it was a wet day the house was nearly full with a mostly black audience that enjoyed every joke about racial matters. Melser said that Walcott has a dramatist's visual imagination and sense of situation, but his plays are over lush. *Malcochon* is concerned with how people are bound together and yet separated by passions and crimes.[1]

During mid-June the Workshop, directed by Walcott, performed a double bill of plays about middle-class adultery, Harold Pinter's *The Lover* and *Stepchild, Stepchild* by Oliver Jackman, Walcott's long-time Barbadian friend. The production was controversial because it featured two white women who had recently joined the Workshop, Helen Camps and Judy Stone, along with two white male actors and Slade Hopkinson, who had moved from Guyana to Trinidad. Walcott was criticized as favouring his white actors and being concerned with middle-class issues. Jackman's play about an interracial marriage was little more than a sketch.

Walcott wanted the Workshop to have more professional training, but it was proving difficult for the Rockefeller Foundation to aid a Trinidadian theatre company. George White, Director of the O'Neill Foundation, was touring the Caribbean from 23 March to 5 April for the Rockefeller Foundation; he visited Walcott and saw a private performance of *Dream* and part of *Blacks*. After White returned to the United States he said that he wanted to bring the Trinidad Theatre Workshop to Connecticut.

Walcott, Freund, and André Gregory agreed that the O'Neill's summer Play-wrights' Conference would be a good way for the Trinidad Theatre Workshop to gain professional training while showing its own wares to Americans. Lloyd Richards, already famous as a black actor, teacher, and director, would be in charge and Gregory wanted to go to Waterford to help if the Workshop was coming. As, however, White could not afford to bring them to the Eugene O'Neill Memorial Theatre in Waterford, Connecticut, and the Rockefeller Foundation could not help within its policies, the Workshop seemed stranded until Dale Wasserman, author of *Man of La Mancha*, agreed to pay for their travelling expenses. Fourteen members left for the United States on 6 July.

Walcott continued on to London from the United States for Poetry International '69. Beyond the £50 towards his travel expenses and the £40 from the Poetry Book Society as Walcott's fee for reading, he received £5 a day; Maschler also contributed £50 and Ross helped. Walcott was expected to attend all four performances 10–13 July at Queen Elizabeth's Hall, and to read from his own poems on 10 and 13 July, for twenty minutes each time. He read ten of his poems on the BBC; Argo later used five in a recording entitled *Poetry International '69* for which he received about £50.

He returned to Connecticut where, after weeks of participating in workshops, readings, and forums and receiving professional training, the Trinidad Theatre Workshop performed *Dream on Monkey Mountain* 1–9 August and left for Trinidad the next day. As the cast consisted of amateurs with regular jobs an opportunity was lost to perform at La Mama in New York.

The play was a great success with those who were at Waterford, including Elizabeth Hardwick, who covered theatre for the *Partisan Review*. Samuel Hirsch, the *Herald Tribune*'s drama editor, described the Workshop as 'a remarkably supple and resonant group of talents, men and women able to speak like classical actors and move like dancers'. It is an 'ensemble of extraordinary power'. The critic for the *Day*, New London, praised the beautiful, strange poetry, and thought the production fascinating and the company 'amazingly good'. *Variety* judged *Dream* powerful, but too long and rambling for Broadway. Walcott was lionized and there were many vague offers for *Dream* by producers along with well-intended advice about how to avoid the corruptions of Broadway.[2]

The O'Neill production of *Dream* was the beginning of Walcott's breakthrough into American theatre and major changes in his life. Increasingly more time would be spent in the United States for meetings, revisions, rehearsals, productions; the grander possibilities of American wealth and fame would challenge and eventually push to the side Walcott's 1959 dream of creating a national Caribbean theatre company with its own style. Long periods alone in hotels would result in additional strain on his marriage, finances, and temper. The immediate consequence of Waterford was that White recommended *Dream* to NBC and Gordon Davidson offered a 1970 production at the Mark Taper Forum in Los Angeles.

It was at the National Playwright Conference at Waterford that Gordon Davidson of the Contemporary Theatre Group and Michael Schultz of the Negro Ensemble Company first saw *Dream on Monkey Mountain*. By September it was planned that the first commercial production would be produced by Davidson, with Michael Schultz directing, at the Mark Taper Forum, Los Angeles.

After the United States Walcott and Slade Hopkinson were invited by the Extra-Mural Tutor, Barbados, to conduct a Drama Workshop, 23 August–3 September, at Combermere School. Each was paid $500, which included their expenses and transportation. They were expected to cover Theatre Organization, Production, Stage Management, and Acting Techniques. There were morning sessions 9 a.m.–12:30 p.m. and evening sessions 5–8 p.m., excluding Saturday, 30 August, and the evening of Sunday, 31 August. At the end of the seminar there was a one-act play.

While in Barbados Walcott worked on the foreword to *Dream on Monkey Mountain and Other Plays*, which became 'What the Twilight Says'. He claimed that his plays are written for countries that still think of theatre as a luxury of metropolitan countries. His plays have their origins in poverty, humiliation, and uncertainty and they are meant for the poor. Their assertion of pride seems simple, but for his generation of West Indian writers the problem was the struggle against colonialism with its past of slavery and spiritual indenture. Writers were naming what was around them, disciplining dialect into the popular and personal. After independence the identity problems of ridiculously small nations became self-inflicted, like the dramas of youth, as they worshipped folk or tribal forms and tried to get rid of the imported. The ambitions of the dramatists are curtailed by those wanting folklore as official entertainment. The artist is worse off than before. Maybe he has brought this situation on himself in wanting a metropolitan replica, a theatre isolated from the calypsonians, folk dancers, and Carnival. When young he tried to learn how to create monumental characters from the greatest playwrights. It is amazing that after so many years of apprenticeship of modelling on others the result should be original.

Walcott claimed to have lived by the creed of the Abbey Theatre and Yeats's 'to write for my own race, and the reality'. He had no concern for the modern theatre; one had to describe in the text itself such effects as a forest or changes in light and place. Poverty itself recreated the unities of classical theatre. Settings had to be simple. But what was he to do after *Sea at Dauphin*? Naturalism meant artifice, a lessening of language. He had always written plays as poetry, but he was undergoing a problem of identity, similar to the political problems of the islands. He searched for a theatre with the precision, vigour, and refined mimeticism of St Lucian dance and found it in Oriental theatre, in Noh and Kabuki. Yeats had reinvented them for a literary audience, Walcott wanted vulgarity. He wrote plays, rewrote them, and kept returning to the same dead end of naturalism. Dialect was no longer enjoyable on its own, farce and backyard tragedy were too easy, and the drawing-room theatre of expatriate groups seemed remote. During his year in New York he decided to avoid Western theatre and looked carefully at the drawings of Hokusai and Hiroshige, listened carefully to Calypso, sought Japanese films. He began working again using fable, superstition, and legend; he wanted a theatre that was visually strong, mimetic narrative, closer to ballet than folk opera, where plot could be learned from gesture or the body. He wanted a technique in which the actor would be singer, dancer, narrator. *Malcochon* and *Ti-Jean* developed from this. *Dream* developed from *Malcochon*, because the Trinidad Theatre Workshop was then part of McBurnie's folk-dance company. Dance can create archetypes without the complex psychology of individual characters. He started limiting himself to an archetypal central figure, one from Hokusai's art and his childhood's fears and admiration, a mad old woodcutter who danced his pain.

He wanted a bare stage, a clean storyline, the inclusion of all forms of theatre as one. He felt all West Indian theatre should be like this. He hoped in future to write some naturalist plays, but this book of plays was meant to be taken whole, read as a history of his search. The plays were written without expectation of being published outside the West Indies. They are not exotic, nor is West Indian society. Walcott claims dialect is dying, and sees the theatre as beginning in popular culture and needing classical form.

He wrote to William Plomer (15 August) thanking him for his continuing interest in his poetry. Plomer had supported him for the Society of Authors' Cholmondeley Award, announced in May, of £650 for 'The Gulf'. Plomer was correct about *Another Life*, which Walcott had been revising. Money from the award made rushing into print less urgent. The Poetry Festival gave him a chance to meet many poets who had encouraged him, including Roy Fuller and Alan Ross. Walcott was thinking of accepting an offer as visiting Commonwealth writer at Leeds University, which he unflatteringly metaphorized as Greenland in contrast to the University of Sussex-Italy.

He wrote to Ross apologizing that he had only stopped briefly at his office. He was continuing to translate Césaire, and suggested a *London Magazine* edition of six West Indian poets to be edited by himself. It would include George Campbell, Martin Carter, E. M. Roach, Wayne Brown, and Basil McFarlane. As in other letters of this period Walcott mentions stress between himself and Margaret, his drinking, obscene speech, and frayed nerves. He blames heavy drinking for his conduct, yet is fascinated by how it lets loose a madman within himself that he both fears and yet feels he has the strength to use, although it takes its toll on others.

The immediate expression of how drunkenness might lead to exploring the conflicts of the soul and bring enlightenment is *Dream* itself, with Makak representing some of Walcott's own continuing insecurities concerning colour, lack of relation to Africa, and unwillingness to adjust to the brown bourgeoisie; Makak is an outsider, a really isolated person, haunted by the 'white muse' (whiteness,

European culture, and poetry as in Robert Graves's myth of the White Goddess as Muse). While the notion that the artist must descend into the depths and
experience some form of insanity is part of the romantic tradition that Walcott early
inherited from his study of Van Gogh and others, the closer influence on him
would be Lowell, Plath, and the confessional poets of the late 1950s and 1960s.

Surviving in the West Indies, finding the time and resources to create an international career, took self-control and an acute sense of opportunities if Walcott's
immense talent was to be realized. Keeping the Workshop going was itself an
impossible task, only possible by someone who was highly practical, knew how
to obtain advertisements, reviews, rehearsal halls, keep a company together,
as well as write, direct, and produce plays. But he needed the elemental, the
Dionysian as well as the Apollonian. Drink, unfaithfulness, obscenity, violence,
were ways for a time to tap the uncontrolled chaos of emotion, to turn his conflicts and repressions into art, as well as offering momentary relief from stress.
I have a sense that Walcott's life was at various times marked by crises which
were partly self-induced and from which he would emerge stronger. It is necessary to enter the abyss of chaos and nothingness before being reborn.

During October Walcott was offered a playwriting fellowship of $3,500, plus
living and working quarters at Waterford, by the Eugene O'Neill Foundation–
Wesleyan University Program; he declined by indefinitely postponing the offer.
He also received a $3,500 fellowship grant from the Audrey Wood Foundation
to continue his theatre work in Trinidad. Wood was Tennessee Williams's agent.
There was a surprising link between Williams and Walcott. Walcott kept planning to produce Williams's plays and Williams had even at one time promised
to go to Trinidad to help. Williams's plays were, of course, the height of serious
theatre a decade earlier during Walcott's days in the Village, but there was
another connection as can be seen from Walcott's own *In a Fine Castle* or from
some of the plays of Douglas Archibald: the West Indies had its own romantic,
artistic, decadent white plantation society in the recent past. Some of Walcott's
early plays, early poems, and the lost novel, allude to a not so romantic decadent
colonial St Lucia. According to *Variety* (22 October) the Trinidad Theatre Wokshop
planned to produce *Camino Real* in December and Williams might go to rehearsals
if his health allowed.

George White had brought Walcott and *Dream* to the attention of NBC which
agreed to show a film about the play and company as part of a new television
series about experimental drama. In connection with the filming of *Dream on
Monkey Mountain* in Trinidad, Walcott was given $10,000 by NBC to help the
Trinidad Theatre Workshop and $3,000 for himself. This would enable him to
stay in Trinidad during 1970 instead of taking up the visiting professorship at
Leeds. At the end of the month Hugh Robertson, an editor of *Midnight Cowboy*,
arrived to film for NBC a one-hour television version of *Dream on Monkey*

Mountain with the original cast. Rehearsals were 3–10 November with the actual shooting lasting until 4 December.

Filming in Trinidad presented many problems, but the worst was Robertson's decision to do a shortened version of the play rather than a documentary about Walcott and his theatre company. Walcott wanted a celebration of his efforts and his actors, Robertson instead cut down a three-hour play to fifty minutes. There was the problem of hiring local technicians, most of whom had never worked for television. It rained eleven days of the nineteen-day schedule, and they went five days over schedule. The company had to be moved by trucks across rain-soaked poor roads. One day a twenty-five foot snake was found on the set and there were invasions of scorpions. For three days some workers were paid not to use a power saw near the site of the filming. It was necessary to rent cattle. Sixty-five locals in Cumana had to be hired for the market scene.

During May Walcott had been sent proofs of *The Gulf* with instructions to return them by the end of the month. There were so many heavy revisions that in June Maschler asked to see the printer's bill, with Walcott's share separated, before it was paid. The seventy-one-page *The Gulf and Other Poems* was published in England by Cape on 23 October 1969 in 2,000 copies, 500 more than *The Castaway*. Cape also republished *In a Green Night* and *The Castaway*. *The Gulf* consisted of thirty-four poems (of which 'Metamorphoses' was a sequence of three, 'Postcards' comprised two, and 'Guyana' six.) About two-thirds of the poems were being published for the first time, many of the others had appeared in *London Magazine*.

Giroux (18 November) told Maschler that Walcott had not sent the text of all the plays for a volume and that Walcott wanted separate contracts with Farrar, Straus and Giroux and Cape (rather than letting Cape handle the American rights). Giroux said that this was not his own idea, but it might be necessary. There is indeed a tense, disturbed tone to some of Walcott's notes of this period. Some unpublished poems appear to be about love affairs, temptations, and ending an affair that had been off and on for several years. He missed his children when he was not at home, and ambition, constant travel, too much work, drink, financial worries, guilt, paranoia, fantasies were having their effect. The white moon had become his personal image for what was leading him astray. The Rockefeller grant would soon be over.

His main literary and theatre market was shifting from England to the United States. Maschler (3 December) agreed that Farrar, Straus and Giroux should publish *Dream on Monkey Mountain*. Giroux wrote to Walcott that he wanted to include the 'Twilight' essay as an Introduction. He only had *Malcochon* as it appeared in *The Hasty Papers*. He needed any corrections and he needed scripts for *Sea* and *Ti-Jean*. When Walcott (6 December) sent Giroux the proofs for the American edition of *The Gulf,* only one poem had been heavily revised. Walcott was exhausted from a month of torture over the filming of *Dream*. He was to get a $500 advance on delivery of *Dream on Monkey Mountain and Other Plays*, more than twice what Cape advanced.

During December Joe Papp considered producing *Dream on Monkey Mountain*. The first reader of the script thought it exciting and the recreation of an entire society, but difficult to stage and probably not right for the Public Theatre; it should be recommended to the Negro Ensemble Company. Papp thought *Dream* a beautiful folk play which might be done later in their Experimental Theatre.

Roy Fuller reviewed *The Gulf and Other Poems* in *London Magazine*, where he said the theme was a journey from, and return to, provincialism, a return sharpened by awareness of life elsewhere as in the racial violence found in 'The Gulf'. He said the volume in places suffered from fuss, clottedness, and 'syntactical clumsiness', with accumulations of subordinate clauses. Walcott's imaginative and descriptive powers are remarkable, and his fresh combinations of words are exciting, but his poems have not reached his full potential.[3]

In the *Express* Clyde Hosein said that many people would find incomprehensible the sweeping, audacious, involved language of Walcott's new poems. The poems are comments on his private life and complaints at the burdens of living. He is sensitive, intelligent, harassed by conscience and duty, seldom happy with the world, melancholic by temperament.[4]

Gordon Rohlehr's long review in the *Trinidad Guardian* noted that at the launching of *The Gulf* in Port of Spain, Walcott said that constant contemplation of disaster teaches faith in family, friends, and love as the way out of absurdity. Rohlehr, however, thought the poems show that the 'void' is within the poet's mind and heart, and projects itself on all he sees. The land is empty or blighted, the sea far away, the moon unattainable. If the void is within the poet all the love seems like despair. Rohlehr then moves from the personal to the political. The Great Falls of Guyana offer no revelation, unlike in Wilson Harris's *Palace of the Peacock*. Georgetown seems a wasteland. There is nothing about a decade of racial civil war, killings, imbecile governments, and foreign involvement in Guyana. Walcott claims domestic truths as absolute and seeks a plain style, a dry bleached, hard style that works best in 'Blues', 'Elegy', and 'Negatives', where, faced by irreconcilable harshness, the attitude is forget it. While nationalists have questioned whether there is any use of pessimism or introspection in the West Indies, society is anxiety ridden. People felt betrayed by intellectuals and politicians. Rohlehr offers as examples Walcott's 'Codicil' and 'Gib Hall Revisited'. Walcott wants to preserve himself from the crippling narrowness of the group, of provinciality; he wants to preserve an identity detached from opportunistic nationalism and the mindless hedonism of Carnival.[5]

During 1969 Walcott became friends with Basil Paquet, one of the returning American veterans who fuelled the anti-war movement. Paquet wrote anti-war poetry, ran the small 1st Casualty Press, published two anthologies about the war, and worked with Joseph Papp towards a show publicizing the Movement. He married the Trinidadian Sandra Pouchet, who was writing a dissertation on Caribbean literature at the University of Connecticut where they helped arrange a reading by Walcott. Lowell was actively involved in the peace movement and Basil felt Walcott was on their side; indeed it was impossible to read or lecture at American campuses without being against the war. Walcott was increasingly involved in readings, lectures, and directing and productions of his plays along a New York–Connecticut–Boston axis, as well as in Los Angeles.

After spending Christmas and New Year 1970 working at the beach house, Walcott visited Barbados where his mother was now living with Pamela and her husband Leonard St Hill. While there he gave a twenty-minute lecture on West Indian Theatre and its economic possibilities to the United States Men's Luncheon Association of Barbados. Decades later he would still be giving such lectures to foreign businessmen.

Peter Donkin arrived in Port of Spain on 31 January and began taping a fifty-minute *Ti-Jean and His Brothers* with Workshop actors for the Canadian Broadcasting Company. He also recorded an interview concerning *Ti-Jean* and another broadcast consisting of Walcott reading poems and excerpts from his plays. The CBC recordings were profitable. On top of what Walcott and the actors were paid at the time of recording, a one-hour broadcast of the play was to earn Walcott $1,000; copies were distributed to five radio stations in the Caribbean which might pay to use them.

Walcott had been erratically on the wagon for two months. He kept track of his drinking in his diary; on 11 February he had two Camparis and a glass of wine. Drink resulted in hallucinations and hangovers. The next day Walcott's diary erupted with annoyance at his mother's continual praise of his father's abstinence. He wrote that Warwick was a prim bigot, constipated at the sight of drink, a perfect amateur. It was a miracle he ever married! Walcott then wittily covers himself; he lies, he loved Warwick although he never saw him. Such conflicts over his mother's image of his father appear at other times in Walcott's writings. The material from the diary kept finding its way into *Another Life* where he asks: 'how many would prefer to this poem | to see you drunken in a gutter'?:

> We drank for all our fathers,
> for freedom, as for mine,
> how Mama'd praise that angular abstinence,
> as if that prim-pursed mouth instantly clicked
> at the thought of a quick one,
> 'Your father never drank,'
> self-righteous sphincter![6]

Robertson's version of *Dream on Monkey Mountain* was the first show of that season's NBC *Experiment in Television* series, on Sunday, 15 February. While it reached an audience in the millions the reviews were bad. The *Washington Post* found the play confusing; there was no clean seam where reality and fantasy met. *Variety* described the show as rambling with competent acting but incompetent writing and a lightweight story. The characters argued endlessly and were unintelligible. The direction by Robertson was pedestrian. The reviews upset Walcott, who blamed Robertson. In the future, he decided, he must make his own films; he worked up his confidence by telling himself he had a natural visual sense and years of experience directing his plays. He was especially bothered by references to the actors as non-professional, which he interpreted as unprofessional. To make his films Walcott thought he still needed Robertson to whom he soon (24 February) suggested setting up a company that might get government assistance for films of *In a Fine Castle*, *Franklin*, and a calypso documentary featuring Sparrow.[7]

While Cape still avoided publishing the plays as there was no major production planned in England, in the United States *Dream* had been performed at the O'Neill, on NBC, and was about to open in Los Angeles. There was a clause in the production contract for *Dream* at Waterford saying that acting copies could be published by the O'Neill. When George White intended to exercise this option, Giroux objected. Giroux had recently introduced Walcott to Bridget Aschenberg of the International Famous Agency, who for two decades would be his drama agent and find herself in situations where Walcott's desire to have his plays in print or performed conflicted with her sense of what a professional dramatist should earn. George White now told Aschenberg that Grove would be publishing an anthology of O'Neill plays including *Dream*. Giroux (19 February) asked whether Walcott had signed anything with Grove or White as this would abort the Farrar, Straus edition. On 23 February Margaret returned to John Lahr at Grove a cheque for $214. 25. The next week Walcott sent to Giroux and Cape the finished play manuscript and a draft of 'What the Twilight Says'. He supplied two of his drawings for the end pages.

Walcott soon came off his wagon. His three-year Rockefeller grant ended, which meant that from now on, apart from Margaret's salary, he was dependent on his earnings as a writer. On 5 March there was a Black Power march in Port of Spain, the beginning of a long period of marches and near revolution that made Walcott angry, fearful, and depressed. During the early 1970s the West Indies were plagued with imitation Black Power and Cuban revolutionary movements. After Stokely Carmichael had been banned from Trinidad, there were demonstrations during the 1970 Carnival. They expanded into street marches, violence, and fire bombs. What was first seen as justifiable protest by the young and poor became racial. Mulattos and other light-skinned people who tried to join the demonstrations were insulted and threatened: Indians refused to participate. Intellectuals and university teachers who joined the demonstrations were rejected as leaders; this was a revolt, not a discourse. Areas of Port of Spain were set on fire and looted, sections of the army supported the revolutionaries, and the government began to crumble. In late April there was a curfew and state of emergency. The Coast Guard and police remained loyal, however, and during May re-established order with the indirect but visible backing of the Venezuelan air force and the American navy patrolling near the coast. The story, mixed with events from a more shadowy uprising in 1973, can be found in V. S. Naipaul's *Guerrillas*.

Walcott's dream of a revolution in West Indian culture led by himself and his theatre company appeared to crumble. For several years he had unsuccessfully sought a visiting professional director and further professional training for his actors. A way had been found to channel Rockefeller funds through the O'Neill Foundation to send Jay Ranelli who, because of his American schedule, could only go to Trinidad in April for four or five weeks. The actors found his rehearsals interesting as he allowed them more freedom of interpretation than did Walcott. This abruptly ended; with the curfew and state of emergency Walcott had to cancel a week's run, 10–17 May, at Queen's Hall of the new, longer *Ti-Jean* with André Tanker's music, directed by Walcott, and Genet's *The Balcony*, directed by Ranelli. Ranelli returned to the United States (24 April). $4,000 wasted!

Years later in the drafts of his unpublished autobiography Walcott would try to express his conflicting feelings about the 1970 revolt. At Woodford Square he listened to the orators screaming for power over their microphones and proclaiming that only pure black would be allowed to survive. He felt threatened and worried about his children's future in Trinidad. His first priority was the safety of his house, to which he returned by taxi. The driver warned him that the placard bearers, who were holding up traffic, were dangerous. Hearing shouts of 'black is beautiful' Walcott thought about the implications; did it mean that he and his children were ugly? He felt guilty for himself having written of the beauty of blackness while being socially advantaged. Later, on a Sunday morning, he and his family were returning from the beach to Port of Spain when at the waterfront they suddenly faced a crowd of shirtless young black men happily shouting that the army was with them. Walcott thought the revolution had come if the crowd could so easily parade when public assemblies had been banned. He got out of the car and joined the marching as he wanted to be part of the crowd, to feel part of its collective happiness. Some of the army had indeed joined the revolution, locking up their commander. Walcott kept making a comparison of Red Square with Woodford Square, kept thinking of how Claude McKay and other West Indians had joined in with revolutionary movements, but this seemed less like a revolution than a riot which had become an organized march.

A revolt, however, was taking place within the Theatre Workshop where Slade Hopkinson led an attack on Walcott at the 3 May General Meeting. Hopkinson, who was ill with kidney problems, had become carried away by the political climate, and angry that his plays were not produced; he accused Walcott of everything from financial mismanagement to dictatorial leadership. At UCWI Hopkinson had appeared Walcott's equal, an intellectual, a poet, a dramatist, director, a great actor, a professional journalist, and editor. He was still a good actor and a marvellous teacher who inspired his students, but his star had stopped rising. His Rockefeller fellowship to Yale had ended without a doctorate, his plays had no following, his rehearsals were shambles, his anthology of writing for the Caribbean schools tended towards progressive clichés. He joined the marches, chanted slogans. Less than a decade later Hopkinson was to admit he had been in the wrong, but at the May meeting Walcott, drunk and wild, resigned from the Trinidad Theatre Workshop, refused any longer to speak with Hopkinson, and indeed threatened to take legal action if his handling of finances were again questioned. Walcott never forgave Hopkinson. Walcott had a knack for bringing people together, binding them into a community around himself through work, shared activities, fame, dreams. Those who belonged felt fortunate, but Walcott could be nasty towards those he distrusted or felt did not contribute enough. There were whispering campaigns and other indications that someone was to be got at. The Trinidad Theatre Workshop was supposedly a democracy, there were meetings and consultations, governed by carrots and whips; disagreements, however, were regarded as rebellions.

Walcott's messianic imaginings had not left him. He felt that people expected leadership from him, but he felt betrayed, and was aware that he had expected betrayal. 'Twilight' had spoken of betrayal; he felt a Moses, a Christ, and a paranoid. There was always a Judas. Talk of censorship was in the air and this was even more frightening to him than the anarchy of the streets. Now there were going to be lies about loving the poor. He should be a lighthouse to others, instead he was being irrational, drinking, self-hating. He desired to return to the discipline of work and the love that should go with it.

Luckily he had been developing a different life in the United States where (22 April) the Center Theatre Group of Los Angeles paid him $1,000 as an advance for first-class professional stage performing rights for *Dream on Monkey Mountain*. Gordon Davidson, the CTG Artistic Director, had at the O'Neill promised to use Trinidadian actors and to present the play as a Trinidad Theatre Workshop production, but this was impossible; no Foundation was willing to pay to bring the actors; more insurmountable was Equity's objection. There were also artistic problems. On the basis of the Waterford and television productions Davidson felt that Makak and Moustique needed other actors, although Slade Hopkinson might play Lestrade! He did bring Beddeau to Los Angeles as it was easier with a musician than an actor. *Dream* was to open at the Mark Taper on 27 August.

Walcott was disappointed that the Trinidad Theatre Workshop would not be performing in Los Angeles; he still thought of the company as part of himself, and of himself as being capable of making West Indian theatre, including his actors, part of world culture. In a long letter (13 May) Walcott recalled for Davidson the history of *Dream on Monkey Mountain*. When offered a production in the United States without his actors he felt like saying, Get thee behind me, Satan. Another voice said, Ahead of you is your life, your art will profit. He knew he had blinded himself to his actors' faults, but the play was created by them. Many of Walcott's drawings and scripts of the early 1970s were to show a devil or snake tempting him. This was the start of a slow fall and planned departure from his West Indian Eden which was to go through many phases before he actually left, never completely shutting the gate against his return.

His drinking remained a serious problem. His diary for 2 May mentions six scotches and two beers. He was troubled by his sexual fantasies and worried about madness. He continued working on the film script of *In a Fine Castle*, which after the attempted Black Power revolution changed from a character study of the decadent white Creole plantocracy to their relationship to current black Trinidadian politics. He needed money. He started planning for a smaller version of the Theatre Workshop, Aquarius Productions, Group III, with $500 capital. He would be director and the actors could invest as partners. He would use a small group of loyalists, perhaps a dozen, with whom he would make films, tour to Tobago, Grenada, Barbados, and St Lucia. His diary several times mentions that degeneration results from hating the abstract 'they' and others. Later, during September, the Trinidad Theatre Workshop met and voted to bring Walcott back as Artistic Director on his terms.

Whit weekend, 15–17 May, Walcott wrote a 'Letter from Trinidad' (unpublished, intended for *London Magazine*) at a beach-house he had rented away from Port of Spain with its 9 p.m. curfew. The 'Letter' was another attempt to sort out his emotions about the political events in relation to class and colour. He saw the middle classes and light-skinned soaked in guilt; nothing had changed politically. The Black Power revolution was unbelievable, the Caribbean had a history of violence, repression, and torture, which was being glorified by the revolutionaries. In a comment that might be applied to himself, he claimed that the more white a mulatto was the more likely he would be troubled by being black and conscious of racial humiliation, unlike the poor blacks who were resigned to their race but wanted economic improvement and were likely to join any movement offering hope. This had brought the region a history of tyrants who began by being 'tribal' heroes of the masses. The masses put up with dictators because they were used to obedience, but eventually they destroyed them. The modern

Dessalines and Christophe were Duvalier, Machado, Trujillo. The leaders were called Papa, Uncle, never Brother. The essay spoke well of Castro as combining brotherhood and Papa-ism in the form of Comrade, while opposing the horrors of capitalism and racism.[8] Walcott's own confusions are shown in a punning note he made in which Red-Afro-Saxon Protestants are termed RASPs. The next day (18 May) he was even further wrapped in doubts and feelings of betrayal, recalling Lowell's hurting remark that he used people. He then went off to Barbados for a week of heavy drinking.

After returning home on 28 May he pointed out to the new management committee that legally he and Errol Jones owned the Theatre Workshop as they, along with Stanley Marshall, were the founders and the signatories of the bank account. He claimed that the Trinidad Theatre Workshop died on 3 May and he proposed it be resurrected as Group IV Theatre over which he would have absolute authority. He intended to go ahead with the tour of Ti-Jean under his own name and by 7 June he had the play in rehearsal.

The new Ti-Jean and His Brothers with music by André Tanker was performed as a Trinidad Theatre Workshop production 25–7 and 29–30 June. Although the audience loved the new version, the reviews were mixed as critics were uncomfortable with a musical form which was more than a fable with music and much less an opera. For the audience to return home before curfew the show started at 6 p.m. and ran for ninety minutes. The Trinidad Theatre Workshop then took the production of Ti-Jean on a seventeen-day tour to Grenada, St Lucia, and Barbados.

While playing in St Lucia some actors from the Workshop stayed at Walcott's old house on Chausee Road. Many allusions in the 'Twilight' introduction published with Dream on Monkey Mountain only become intelligible in terms of the recent past of the Workshop and Walcott's tours with the company to St Lucia. Parts of the essay are set in St Lucia during the tour, although as often with Walcott's poetic prose the movements back in time make the specific scene and periods difficult to distinguish. A visit (12 July) to the Sulphur Springs at Soufriere along with memories of his early love for Andreuille, appear to have resulted in Another Life's 'this circle of hell' section (Part Four, Chapter 19), with its condemnation of:

> Those who peel, from their own leprous flesh, their names,
> who chafe and nurture the scars of rusted chains,
> like primates favouring scabs, those who charge tickets
> for another free ride on the middle-passage,
> those who explain to the peasant why he is African,
>
> .   .   .   .
>
> they measure the skulls of with callipers
> and pronounce their measure
> of toms, of traitors, of traditionals and AfroSaxons.

They measure them carefully
as others once measured the teeth
of men and horse, they measure and divide.[9]

While in Barbados *Ti-Jean and His Brothers* was taped on video. Walcott returned to Trinidad on 20 July for a day before he and Margaret left for the Mark Taper rehearsals.

Dream on Monkey Mountain at the Mark Taper Forum ran 27 August–11 October. Michael Schultz directed a cast including Roscoe Lee Browne (Makak), Ron O'Neal (Lestrade), and Antonio Fargas (Moustique). During rehearsals Walcott gave a long note to Michael Schultz explaining details of the play's symbolism. The note is interesting as an indication of Walcott's way of seeing his play. As the West Indian search for roots is blocked by amnesia, there are various signs of this blankness as when Makak says he is lost. The crossroads is the sign of the cross and symbolic both of indecision and of healing. Moustique is the Judas in the play, he does not know where to go and spins to choose a direction that brings death. Moustique is a materialist, degraded by the profit motive; he moves instinctually to the market. His spin should be a moment of arrest, as in Japanese theatre, when the audience wants to comment. Lestrade deliberately forgets his race, then becomes a frantic convert. He is baffled by law, by its changes, by it not being the same as morality. He is angry with his people and wants them disciplined. All of the actors should be aware of blank signposts that paralyse (the signposts I think are one of the influences of Soyinka's *The Road* on *Dream*). Souris mocks but believes in the possibility of vision. Awareness of being lost is a moment of illumination; Souris who rediscovers the bounty of Eden should have the pathos of a child, an innocent (like Ti-Jean). The forest is a circle of enchantment, a clearing whitened by the moon, an eden surrounded by horror, madness, hallucination. Here Lestrade goes mad, re-enacts the death of his race so it can find itself again like Adam or like Crusoe in wonder of a new world. The actor should think of a forest in the morning, still, grass growing, dew. Not surprisingly Walcott felt such implications were lost in the acting.

The play was an immense success, the reviews among the best I have ever seen. Dan Sullivan in the *Los Angeles Times* was one of the many reviewers who said it was not to be missed. With superb control, poetry, and theatrical power *Dream* reveals the black unconscious and creates a manhood-restoring myth. The language is wed to the heartbeat. Roscoe Lee Browne is immense. It is a dazzling, gorgeous production of stage poetry. What LeRoi Jones has tried to do in the theatre, Walcott has done. Beddeau's drumming keeps it together.[10]

Polly Warfield called *Dream* 'a play and a half, or maybe three'. A work of 'genius'. It is 'almost . . . a theatrical masterpiece', an original, yet 'compounded of a thousand fragments, evocations, influences', while being 'deeply black'. The production is 'visually beautiful'. Ron O'Neal is brilliant, unforgettable. 'One longs to see the play again.' The scene where Makak beheads his white apparition was greeted with 'spontaneous applause'. Tom Tugend claimed Walcott was a genius and there was almost too much good theatre for one night. The play offers white and black power, classical poetry, calypso, satire, protest, fantasy and reality, greatness and degradation. Makak is unforgettable, a Christ-Don Quixote, 'who explores the black experience, which would be white, if it could, one moment and kill the whites the next, with self-brutal self-honesty'. Hazel La Marre said the 'most amazing feat of the entire spectacular is the magnificent artistry of Roscoe Lee Browne. What he does with his voice alone is startling. He thunders like a god, growls like an animal, whines in his grief and cajoles'. 'The whole show is wonderful.'[11]

The reviewers were excited by the way the poetry was blended with music, drumming, and dance. Jim Guthrie described the play as a 'visual poem' and said it was 'a joyously lyric celebration of West Indian Culture'. Jeanne Pieper claimed that the only problem with *Dream* is that it says too much at once on too many different levels. 'Yet you never really feel overwhelmed. You just wish you could see the play again soon.' Pieper was fascinated by the discussion afterwards between some members of the cast and the audience. Kimmis Hendrick mentioned the electric response of the black audience to the play. 'The non-black knows there's more to this than meets the white-trained eye.' 'Roscoe Lee Browne . . . holds the audience breathless by his total absorption.' Richard Vale said that 'in poetic richness, blended with folk vigor and color, it towers above the entire plane of contemporary theatre'.[12]

Dream was nominated for four awards by the Los Angeles Drama Critics and was a financial as well as critical success; Walcott received over $7,000 in royalties. It was, however, difficult to find a New York producer willing to take it on. Schultz (8 October) fruitlessly tried to talk Joseph Papp into staging *Dream on Monkey Mountain* in Central Park during 1971.

After New York Walcott went to the University of the West Indies, Jamaica, for a term. At the end of October he premièred *In a Fine Castle* as a play (not film) at the Creative Arts Centre. Walcott directed; Richard Montgomery, who had a brilliant reputation in England before drifting to Jamaica was designer and his soon-to-be wife Sally Thompson did costumes. This was the beginning of a long association between Walcott and the Montgomerys. Walcott would think of this version of *In a Fine Castle* as a work in progress from the late 1940s. The play would not be published until 1985 when, much revised, it became *The Last Carnival*. In 1992, even more radically revised, it would be acted in Birmingham (England) and Stockholm.

After living out of a suitcase for about five months, Walcott returned home early in November. He had been asked to plan, find the local contributions, and edit for André Deutsch a book about Trinidad to be introduced by a big name personality. While Walcott was in the United States Diana Athill, director at André Deutsch, wrote (9 September) that it had been decided to do the 'X Introduces Trinidad and Tobago' book rapidly. She felt that Walcott was becoming too heavily involved in other commitments and would be glad to be relieved of editorial duties. Instead he was asked to write 'On Choosing Trinidad'. Besides being paid $250 for the essay he would be paid for his work in planning the book and finding contributors.

Whenever a new year approached Walcott's diaries were increasingly filled with things that needed to be done and deadlines that were passing. For 20 November there were eleven urgent tasks to do, such as preparing a brochure for the first ten years of the Trinidad Theatre Workshop, finishing his lecture for the January Commonwealth Literature Conference in Jamaica, finishing 'On Choosing Port of Spain', finishing a lecture on West Indian drama which he was to give on 3 December at the university (and for which he was to be paid $50). He also needed to hire a secretary typist.

Such tension had its consequences. Walcott's diary for Monday, 23 November, noted that he had been drunk all weekend, and slept through his party for John Hearne. The low point was later in December; while drunk Walcott was violent to Margaret, then slept for two days. His diary was filled with remorse, self-pity, awareness that he was repeating faults from his first marriage, and self-lacerating admissions that he loved no one except himself. As usual he then returned to the discipline of work, on *Another Life*.

Some days were filled with urgent telegrams. Walcott had to make a decision about a visiting professorship in California for the coming year. When Walcott learned that Gordon Davidson (22 December) had optioned *In a Fine Castle* for the Mark Taper Forum for the following year he was elated and one of his first thoughts was that he might be able to get Albert Laveau a leading part in the production. He remained bitter about the Workshop and Black Power. He drafted 'A Patriot to Patriots' (it was published in Guyana during 1972) for a projected book of unpleasant Brechtian 'Poems of Theatre and Politics'. The book was never finished. At the end of the month he was at Toco writing, this time for the conference, about the betrayal of the West Indies by those seeking to return to their supposed origins.

Selden Rodman's highly favourable review of the American edition of *The Gulf: Poems* in the *New York Times Book Review* (11 October) was titled 'Caribbean Poet of Elizabethan Richness'. Rodman said that *The Gulf* is about alienation whether in Texas or at Carnival, and that Walcott, a formalist, is one of the best poets at present. Aschenberg sent Papp a copy of the Rodman review. Giroux (4 December) sent Walcott an advance copy of Chad Walsh's *Book World* review of *The Gulf*. Giroux said that few poets have had such glowing comments; he had already read the review to their sales people. Chad Walsh claimed that as Walcott refuses to simplify the many lives in his skin, the appearance of a unified soul in his poetry is an aesthetic and moral achievement. With *The Gulf* he is a major poet. 'Few American poets have caught as much of the confused national scene as Walcott in the title poem.' 'Walcott is already one of the half-dozen most important poets now writing in English. He may prove to be *the* best.' From a well-respected poet that was praise.[13]

The Gulf appeared the same year as Edward Brathwaite's *Islands*, the final volume of his three-part trilogy, which began a decade of comparisons between the two poets and what their work represented. Whereas Walcott in *The Gulf* increasingly felt alienated from the Caribbean, Brathwaite assumed that West Indians are of African descent and regarded Africa as the West Indian's spiritual home, although the West Indies has become his physical home. Whereas Walcott writes of self, family, friends, as an individual, Brathwaite was seen as the voice of the community, speaking with the many 'we' voices of black people on both sides of the Atlantic. He wrote in dialect, 'American negro', Creole, and made a 'straight transcription of an Akan drum salutation'. Walmsley wrote of 'Walcott's enslavement to the iambic pentameter'. While Walmsley's preference was for the more 'popular' poetry of Brathwaite as expressing the hopes of the young, she concludes by saying that the two poets should be celebrated, a conclusion somewhat undermined by her suggestion that Brathwaite has somehow made poetic life easier for Walcott, allowing him to be himself rather than feeling he need speak for the region.[14]

Dream on Monkey Mountain and Other Plays was published in mid-December and made available what Walcott regarded as the core achievement of some twenty years of work in the theatre. A few early plays had been available in West Indian editions, but even these were out of print, had been revised, and were difficult to obtain. *Dream on Monkey Mountain and Other Plays*, like *In a Green Night*, was a selection of earlier work, and powerful because the earlier experiments and failures were not in sight. *The Sea at Dauphin*, *Malcochon*, and *Ti-Jean and His Brothers* formed a seemingly straightforward record of a developing cultural nationalism, exploration of problems of colour, and increased mastery of theatrical technique, leading directly to *Dream*. Now that there was a body of his work as a dramatist, Walcott would need to be seen as a playwright as well as a poet. Besides making a core of plays available, the volume included 'What the Twilight Says', an impassioned obliquely presented discussion of the Trinidad Theatre Workshop and Walcott's aims. Between the weaker, explicit, 1969 unpublished Foreword and this classic, there was the revolt of the Trinidad Theatre Workshop, alluded to in the essay, and a reason for its passion, allusions to betrayal, and conflicting emotions.

At the end of the year Walcott made a list of major accomplishments during 1970. Most of his earnings were royalties from plays, especially in North America. The Mark Taper *Dream* had paid over $7,000, the CBC *Ti-Jean* $1,000, but the twenty local performances of *Ti-Jean* had only paid TT $500 in royalties. Poetry paid little. The exchange rates at the time were £1 = United States $2.40 = TT $4.85.

The opening speaker for the ACLALS conference in Jamaica 2–9 January 1971, was Edward Kamau Brathwaite addressing 'The Function of the Writer'. V. S. Naipaul, on the panel, was humiliated by hostile local black militants in the audience. The next day there were panels concerning 'Literature and the Folk' and 'African Literature and the Oral Tradition'. Walcott was to speak on 'The Poet in the West Indies', but, I have often been told, warned by friends that Brathwaite's supporters had arranged a reception similar to Naipaul's, he wisely excused himself at the last minute. Behind the withdrawal there was another story. Walcott had been rewriting *In a Fine Castle* at Rampanalgas, and returning home after eight days on the wagon he again slid heavily off. He was trying to do too much, and the political climate was getting to him. He had prepared some notes criticizing those who betrayed the West Indies by imagining returns to origins instead of creating the New World. All races in the West Indies arrived wounded and it would take time to heal. The speech was tentatively titled 'The Stricken Conscience'. Walcott wrote further drafts of 'Farewell to the Actors', in which clerks and housewives betray him, while in 'Another Farewell to the Actors' the finest are his friends and he, a Prospero, recognizes their ten years of servitude.

Part IV

Trinidad Black Power, Preparing for Exile, Musicals

15

1971 *Dream on Monkey Mountain* in New York, *New Yorker*

ASCHENBERG telegrammed Walcott (21 January 1971) that the Negro Ensemble Company wanted *Dream*, based on the Los Angeles production, for New York. Schultz would direct and Roscoe Lee Browne would come to New York; Ron O'Neal, Tony Fargas, and Afolabni Ajayi would repeat their parts. Although the theatre was small the prestige would be good. Gerald Krone, the business manager for Negro Ensemble Company, said they were keeping their slogan, 'themes of black struggle'; it never made sense, but was needed to receive foundation support. All the leading actors would work for the minimum Negro Ensemble Company salary of $130 weekly. Walcott should come to New York in March as three weeks of rehearsals would begin on 16 February. The Negro Ensemble Company would pay for Walcott's round trip fare, but not a per diem. He could stay with Schultz or Hugh Robertson (who was awaiting a revised script of *In a Fine Castle* before taking a film option).

Dream on Monkey Mountain was presented by the Negro Ensemble Company, at St Mark's Playhouse, 9 March–18 April, for forty-eight performances. Other plays in New York at the time were *Oh! Calcutta!* and Arthur Miller's adaptation of Ibsen's *An Enemy of the People*. *Dream* progressed from a shaky start to a hit. Only four seats were sold for the first night of previews, twenty-eight for the second night, and fifty the third. Opening night sales were eighty-eight seats, thirty-five the next night, and eighty-five the third night. On Friday, 19 March, sales went up and from then on the theatre was sold out, including the two shows on both Saturday and Sunday. Walcott left on 19 March in the morning for Trinidad after the third night of *Dream*.

Clive Barnes's review in the *New York Times* seems made up of quotations for future advertisements: 'a beautiful bewildering play by a poet', Walcott 'writes with a mind clarified with the clouds of literature', 'the language is a variation of white, the thought is interestingly black', 'rich in comic incident'. Of Lestrade, 'the pistol knows no color'. Barnes regarded the play as a poetic allegory, but appeared uncomfortable with what it was saying; he had been near an intense argument that did not interest him. 'Walcott is counselling . . . a 20th-century black identity rather than an attempt to impose a reversal to a pre-slave black identity. But much of the play's interest is in its spectacle and poetry.' Edith Oliver, a *New Yorker* staff writer who was interested in off-Broadway and black theatre, wrote 'This production is the richest and strongest that the N. E. C. has ever given us, and in the service of a masterpiece. *The Dream on Monkey Mountain* is a poem in dramatic form or a drama in poetry, and poetry is rare in the modern theatre. Every line of it plays; there are no verbal decorations.' She valued 'the absolute trust that Mr. Walcott engenders in his audience, convincing us that there is a sound psychological basis for every action and emotion'.[1]

John Lahr's rave review in the *Village Voice* praised the play and Walcott more than the production. Lahr regarded the shifting dream world, 'a mayhem of images', as that of Carnival, of masking and testing identities. The review was Lahr at his most brilliant, writing as if each paragraph was meant to offer at least a line for quotation: 'language and sound emerge with glistening freshness', 'psychic triumphs over colonial castrations', 'the extraordinary vigor and surprise in Walcott's language', 'full of fresh air and raw wounds', 'a sensory assault which makes us aware of our cultural blocks', 'Walcott's theatre is a search for the authentic voice in his culture', 'it takes the popular modes of a people—its tales, its music, its dances—and fuses them into a new prophecy', 'the play's original-ity . . . makes it exciting'. Lahr implied that Walcott was the great dramatist of the age whom others would need to follow. 'If our theatre is to be liberated from imitation and our language from mimicry, it will need creators equal to his tenacity, intellectual passion, and humour.' Lahr's review brilliantly restated the core theme of *Dream on Monkey Mountain*; Makak's drunkenness was a revolt which in rewriting white history tried to rewrite black history, but Death challenged all identities. Freedom came from embracing rather than escaping identity.[2]

The Negro Ensemble Company production led to a temporary estrangement between Rodman and Walcott. Rodman, a white critic who had spent decades studying and promoting black and Latin American culture, was disturbed by the production. Rodman was interested in the regeneration theme in Walcott's plays and *Dream*, like much of Walcott's theatre, is a play about regeneration; after Makak kills the white muse he is purged, he awakes from his dream, and he returns home accepting who he is and the beauty of where he lives. Life is a bounty rather than hell. *Dream* reflects the conflicts about not being white and about living on St Lucia that Walcott felt in his teens when he wrote *Epitaph for the Young,* but what troubled him in his late teens and early twenties had now become valued. A humiliating personal conflict had been faced, felt, and thought through, and in the process of purgation found to be a source of strength, the sources of humiliation were seen to be bounties. Rodman, however, thought that the Negro Ensemble Company production emphasized anti-white politics especially as New York advertisements showed a clenched Black Power fist.

Rodman's discomfort is significant. Reviewers had commented upon the way *Dream* had stirred blacks in the audience. Walcott's works are made from contradictions, from saying too much at once, from radical shifts, from contesting voices, and multiple perspectives. The same Walcott who was threatened by Black Power slogans felt them as intensely as he rejected them. *Dream* assimilated a decade of revolutionary slogans and violence into what was a mediation upon being born 'black' in a 'white' world and offered a release of the resulting humiliations. In *Dream* purgation is by way of imagined violence, symbolic action. The Negro Ensemble Company brought out the potential violence, the anger at whites behind Walcott's claims to forget history and start anew. This was a difference between theatre and poetry. The former realizes itself in events, deeds, violence, the latter in thought and the imagination. Walcott's poetry is meditative, autobiographical, distanced, but the power of his plays results from externalizing the introspective into action. Theatre is usually best as action, extremes, show; the Negro Ensemble Company knew what it was doing, it purged black wounds by an emphasis on violence towards whites. Walcott made a point of seeing Rodman in California later and renewing their friendship.

Rodman was a friend of Frank MacShane, head of the Writing Division, who invited Walcott to an international conference at Columbia University 12–14 April which was being co-sponsored by the School of Arts and the Institute of Latin American Studies. Those invited included Jorge Luis Borges and Mario Vargas Llosa; there was a show of Cuban paintings and Brazilian films. MacShane asked Walcott to prepare a talk which might be printed, discussing the relationship between art and society to the environment of Latin America. Walcott's lecture (13 April) received much praise and would be published and republished as 'The Muse of History'. The lecture argues that given a history of slavery, humiliation, victims, and the guilty, the correct, brave, choice is to see the New World as without a history, as a new start. There is a continuity of theme between the revised *Ti-Jean and His Brothers, Dream on Monkey Mountain, Another Life,* and many of the essays, in that it is first necessary to enter the self to recognize desires, and then to see the uselessness of racial revenge, before lifting the burden by accepting the self, its own history and where it lives, and turning the struggle and acceptance into art. Walcott's own family history has become representative of 'the race', 'the new world', and humanity. While Walcott will offer many variations of such themes, it is a story of paradise lost and regained. 'The Muse of History' is striking in finding a racial epic in the African–American spiritual, each song being fragments or recapitulations of a larger epic of an historical physical dispossession which finds redemption through spiritual belief. The essay powerfully concludes with a recapitulation of Walcott's life and acceptance of being an American:

I accept this archipelago of the Americas. I say to the ancestor who sold me, and to the ancestor who caught me I have no father, I want no such father, although I can understand you, black ghost, white ghost, when you both whisper 'history', for if I attempt to forgive you both I am falling into your idea of history which justifies and explains and expiates . . . I, like the more honest of my race, give a strange thanks . . . that exiled from your own Edens you have placed me in the wonder of another, and that was my inheritance and your gift.

The first publication of 'The Muse of History' was in Orde Coombs *Is Massa Day Dead?* (1974). In the same book Edward Kamau Brathwaite asserted that Walcott was a humanist 'concerned with converting his heritage into a classical tradition, into a classical statement'. Brathwaite assumed that Walcott would find himself increasingly alienated from 'the folk movement . . . below'. In a 1988 interview Walcott was to claim that poets do not look at history as a sequence of events. 'Poetry has no temporality, it does not work in that kind of sequential time. It not only forgives' (recalling Auden's poem about Yeats), 'it absorbs a lot of things.' The experience of slavery could be treated in many ways. It was not the same in the Caribbean as in the United States, life in Central America was not like in Harlem.[3]

An event took place at Columbia University concerning Borges that Walcott wrote up later and tried to publish as a magazine article. It is an excellent, complicated, descriptive piece about the radicalism of the 1970s. A radical in dirty casual clothes suddenly went up to the conference table and explosively ranted that Borges was reactionary, dead, useless, wrote fantasies while Latin America and the Third World were suffering. The situation was made more poignant by Borges being blind, and by his age, his vulnerability, and his stylish fastidiousness. Walcott described him as immobile, quiet, trying to be ignored. Walcott the painter watched Borges's face carefully, noting the changes from humility to patrician, from concern with the ideas of others to patronizing. Interrupted, Borges was impassive, more lizard-like, even more stylish in his seeming lack of fear. Walcott, who often dismisses political ideas as lacking the violence of real politics, claimed that the scene was bad rhetoric in which the radical's ideas counted for less than his too-literal style. What could the radical do? A graceful formal style would betray the notion of revolution. At the time Walcott was angry that someone would try to humiliate Borges, try to pour filth on a great writer. A year after the conference Walcott claimed that all the sociological thinking about the problems of Latin America was reflected in the radical's anger and sense of futility. His rage paid respect to Borges and Borges understood the futility, a futility which neither Borges nor the radical could do anything about.

The Columbia conference was the beginning of Walcott's friendship with Daniel Halpern. With Paul Bowles, Halpern edited the literary journal *Antaeus* from Tangiers, where he was teaching in 1969. He read the British edition of *The Gulf* and kept writing to Walcott asking for poetry for his magazine. During 1970–2 he was a Fellow at Columbia University and in January wrote to Walcott once more asking for a poem. They went together to hear Borges; Walcott remained busy, he was much in demand, needed payment for his work, and seldom replied to letters. Halpern had still had no poem from Walcott when he wrote (21 September) asking for something for issue 5. He had material by Jane Bowles, Anthony Hecht, Donald Davie, Charles Simic, and an interview with Auden, but needed Walcott.

There was soon a small circle of poets in New York with whom Walcott was close and who remained friends over the years. It included Mark Strand who between 1969 and 1973 was teaching at Columbia, Yale, Brooklyn College, and Princeton. Strand had an apartment in the Village where they often met. By the late 1970s the group would include Joseph Brodsky and Susan Sontag. They often had dinner together, enjoyed displays of amusing, even amazing, erudition about poetry and the arts, attended each other's readings and lectures, read together. Walcott was lively and outgoing in those days, whereas in recent years he has become more distant and withdrawn.

After the Columbia University conference Walcott went to Jamaica for the first tour there by the Trinidad Theatre Workshop. Earlier (21 January) he had made a list of thirty things to do in preparation for a tour to Jamaica of *Dream* and *Ti-Jean*: these included typing the cast list, calculating fares, estimating salaries, compiling a property list, compiling a costume list, selecting quotes for publicity, ordering twenty-five copies of *Dream* at discount rate, designing pro-grammes and posters and getting estimates, seeking ads for the Jamaican tour, getting contact prints for *Ti-Jean*, preparing biographies of actors, telephoning Queen's Hall for bookings the weekend before the tour, and writing various letters. This was typical of Walcott's responsibilities in keeping his theatre com-pany going. He was Management, Publicity, Agent, Producer, Dramatist, Acting Coach, Director, Artistic Director, Designer, Ringmaster, and his own assistant. Margaret helped with many tasks, and a part-time secretary was hired who had a full-time job elsewhere.

The Trinidad Theatre Workshop, with a cast of eighteen, performed *Ti-Jean and His Brothers* (16–25 April) and *Dream on Monkey Mountain* (26 April–1 May) at the Creative Arts Centre, UWI. Some critics have claimed that this was the best production by the Trinidad Theatre Workshop in Jamaica and perhaps the finest West Indian theatre they have seen. The final performance of *Dream* was attended by the leaders of the two major Jamaican political parties, Edward Seaga and Michael Manley. The tour was made possible by the financial backing of Pan-Jamaica Investments, a group of businessmen with whom Ralph Thompson, himself a poet and painter, was influential. Beside what Walcott earned as director of the plays, he was paid a royalty of TT $25 per performance, TT $200 for the eight performances of *Dream*; TT $225 for the nine *Ti-Jean* performances.

On 22 April Giroux sent to Maschler Denis Donoghue's favourable review of *The Gulf*, 'Waiting for the End', in the *New York Review of Books* and asked when Cape would publish the *Dream* volume. Aschenberg told Giroux that Walcott had finished rewriting *In a Fine Castle*, which had film possibilities. Farrar, Straus and Giroux planned to publish it during the spring of 1972.

During May the Dartmouth Players produced the American première of *Ti-Jean and His Brothers*, directed by Errol Hill. Hill had planned to return to the University of the West Indies after a stint at the University of Ibadan, Nigeria, but there was no suitable position and he moved to the United States. He took up an appointment at Dartmouth in 1968 and after a few years felt it time to do a Caribbean play. *Ti-Jean* was one of his favourites. The contrast between Walcott and Hill, and the argument between them about the uses of Carnival as a model for West Indian drama, have been exaggerated by critics hoping to line up artists into opposing camps. West Indian disagreements are family arguments voiced strongly at the time, later forgotten except by interested bystanders. Over the years Walcott and Hill would remain friends while quarrelling over the direction local theatre should take. Hill has now premièred Walcott plays in Trinidad, Jamaica, England, and the United States.

On Monday, 24 May, Aschenberg and Robert Giroux went to the Village Gate (a famous jazz club) for the Obie award ceremony. On arriving they were told that Walcott was flying in from Trinidad to accept his award personally. This was unlikely, but until the last moment they were uncertain. It was very hot, with 700 people crammed in. Elaine May presented the awards and the three judges were Harold Clurman, John Lahr, and Edith Oliver. *Dream on Monkey Mountain* was awarded the best foreign play off-Broadway. Elaine May announced that Aschenberg would accept the award for Walcott. Aschenberg mailed Walcott the Obie award, but he did not receive it. Three weeks later it still appeared that the award was lost in the post and Aschenberg would need ask the *Village Voice* to issue another. It was awaiting Walcott at the post office, which had failed to notify him.

Samuel French wanted the North American stock and amateur rights to *Dream*, but Aschenberg had put them off until after the Obie award so they might raise their offer, which was originally $1,000 and had gone to $1,500.

French would publish an acting edition and pay Walcott 10 per cent on copies sold. Aschenberg suggested accepting the offer as it would make the play better known to acting groups. Giroux was not happy with Samuel French publishing a cheap edition of *Dream* as this would cut into sales of the Farrar, Straus and Giroux edition of the four plays which could be published as a Noonday Press edition. Walcott's contract with Farrar, Straus and Giroux did not allow him to authorize the Samuel French edition, but Giroux reluctantly agreed. Aschenberg asked Walcott to make certain all his contracts went through her as IFA contracts provided for such acting editions. Giroux wrote (21 October) that while he would like to continue with Farrar, Straus and Giroux handling contracts for poems, plays, and other books, Aschenberg should take care of theatre and production rights.

At the time of the Columbia conference Howard Moss (13 April) wrote to Walcott in Trinidad asking him to submit poems to the *New Yorker*. Moss said that while in Antigua during 1970 he had read a volume of Walcott's poetry and now welcomed contributions. It is difficult not to assume that the attention Walcott had received in connection with *Dream* helped, especially after Edith Oliver's review. This was the beginning of Walcott's relationship with the *New Yorker* which became more significant than *London Magazine* as his career progressed. The *New Yorker* paid best and established reputations. Walcott's undated reply from Trinidad to Moss's letter was short, almost cool. He thanked him, sent some poems, and mentioned that he had been working on a long poem for the past five years. Although Moss (8 June) accepted 'The Muse of History at Rampanalgas', the length was a problem as the *New Yorker* had a backlog of long poems and other poems that needed to be used before book publication. Moss needed an idea of book publication date and some months' leeway. There were other problems. The poem needed editing to clarify meaning, and it was filled with unfamiliar references. Was Rampanalgas a river, a house, a town? Moss could not find it in an atlas. Later when Moss (2 February 1972) sent off an author's proof of 'The Muse of History at Rampanalgas' he tried to 'correct' Walcott's French, but saw that something was wrong if corrected. The checking department tried to locate the names of the slaves mentioned and, failing to do so, tried the Trinidad Consulate without success! Moss thought the poem marvellous, but who are the people? Walcott replied (28 February 1972) that Rampanalgas is a small isolated fishing village on Trinidad's north-east coast where Walcott and his family stay at Resthaven Cottage. (It is also the scene of 'Almond Trees' in *Castaway* and 'Hawk' in *The Gulf*.) Walcott did not know the origin of the name Rampanalgas, but the names of slaves are irrelevant as the point is their anonymity. He purposely used ungrammatical Creole French, but would accept it being corrected. He admitted that his punctuation often was a problem and left the corrections to Moss.

It is too easy to regard Moss's letters with amusement; he had recognized a marvellous poem, a central poem in Walcott's work, and accepted it for an American publication whose readers would have little idea of what Walcott was writing about. They were unlikely to have much sympathy with being asked to accept such allusions as Rampanalgas. Now we are used to literature with unexplained references to India, the Caribbean, Australia, or Africa. Post-colonialism, globalization, and internationalization have made readers accept words and terms that a few decades ago would have required a footnote or the embedding within the text of an explanation. Walcott was in the vanguard of writers from the former colonies expecting readers to take his work on his own terms. Some of Moss's other comments point to difficulties that are so common to Walcott's writing that they are part of his style. There are words with uncertain reference which look forward and backward, there is a lack of verbs, the syntax may be erratic, punctuation is erratic in terms of clarifying meaning. Walcott had inherited a Modernism which embodied experimentation, ambiguity, and difficulty, but times were changing and Dylan Thomas was perhaps the last major poet in that mode, a mode that required much faith in finding significance within the ambiguous. Walcott's poetry would benefit from the kind of close reading and editing that Moss and Strachan would give it, requiring it to have the accuracy of good prose. Walcott was himself moving towards clarity; Moss asked questions that Walcott needed to be asked.

Walcott replied (1 September 1971) from Tobago to thank Moss for his suggestions. He accepted that his punctuation was casual and his grammar at times indifferent, which he explained as trying to catch the movements of West Indian speech. Most of the suggestions involved minor corrections of weight of punctuation and making the reference clear. Walcott told Moss that he had been working towards a draft of his essay, 'The Muse of History'. Moss thought 'The Muse of History at Rampanalgas' so extraordinary he sent a copy to Giroux. A month later Moss sent a check of over $1,000 to Walcott as half-payment and asked to see other pieces.[4] Moss rejected some other poems, but asked Walcott to send more.

Of the rejected poems 'For Mildred' would later be published as part of 'On Choosing Port of Spain'. 'Desert Song' shows Walcott's continuing feelings of betrayal by supposed friends and by inferior poets. A year later A. J. Seymour's *New Writing in the Caribbean* would publish Walcott's 'A Patriot to Patriots', which begins 'Respect my silence. A head used to betrayals | is scared to show its tongue.' Again there are references to betrayal, especially by poets, and to disillusionment:

> 'Respect my quiet. I have seen revolution turn
> into a barbarous, betrayed riot,
>
> . . . . . .
>
> believe in my bitterness, believe this venom.
> I no longer listen to such wrongs.'

Walcott's rejection of the burden of a history of slavery and black humiliation was part of a context in which those claiming to represent such a burden had produced local tyrants and were destroying his theatre company and calling him inauthentic.

The failed Black Power revolution of 1970 led to those in power taking on the rhetoric of class and racial guilt. Not only was Walcott under fire for being insufficiently black, but the physically blacker and ideologically more negritude Rex Nettleford and his Jamaican Dance Company, which was visiting Trinidad, were also not black enough. Walcott's article in the *Express* (20 August) mocked those who, now safe from revolution, had turned its fury into fashion and slogans. Walcott accused Trinidad of importing revolutions, revolutionary language, and white bourgeois guilt. 'Beat me, insult me . . . I'm guilty, I ignored you, but I see the light, black brother.' 'It is degrading to make a defence of a company of this quality, but the accusations have been aired, and that, unfortunately, is the odour of our time. In the colonial consciousness definitions of soul have become as intricate as mediaeval heresies.' Nettleford's revolution was in defying abstraction.[5]

Between *The Gulf* (1969) and *Sea Grapes* (1976), Walcott's only book of verse was *Another Life.* It was a major book, but it mostly recounted life in St Lucia. The Black Power revolt of 1970, the fights and betrayals, the accusations, and how the government had used the situation to pass laws to silence opposition, had their effect on Walcott. The poems written during 1971–2 show his bitterness, even fear. In June he published in *Tapia* a 'Poem' later retitled 'Preparing for Exile':

> Why do I imagine the death of Mandelstam
> among the yellowing coconuts,
> why does my gift already look over its shoulder . . .

'Preparing for Exile' would be followed in *Sea Grapes* by 'Party Night at the Hilton', a poem occasioned by Grenada's leader visiting Trinidad, where, imagining himself 'in that air-conditioned | roomful of venal, vengeful party hacks', Walcott thinks 'Fear those laws | which ex-slaves praise with passion'.[6] Some of Walcott's friends attended the party, but he stayed away in disgust. The political poems of *Sea Grapes* begin in the early 1970s, although it would take another five years before they appeared as part of a volume of Walcott's poems.

The Talk of the Town section of the *New Yorker,* 26 June, included an interview, 'Man of the Theatre'. Walcott was described as having hazel eyes, longish hair ('sideburns but no Afro'), and a casual muted elegance. Walcott said that *Dream* was about the West Indian search for identity and what colonialism does to the spirit. The first half of the play is white, but when Lestrade becomes an ape, the play becomes black, and the same sins are repeated, the cycle of violence begins again. At the end Makak is like a drifting tree that puts down roots in the New World. Makak must face reality, he must sell to the public at market on

Saturdays to make a living. Walcott said he could never be a Trinidadian, he was too much a Methodist to be irresponsible. He was working on *In a Fine Castle*, a play that concerns the contrast between Carnival, which people take seriously, and revolution, which is treated as fun.[7]

The Negro Ensemble Company was invited to perform two plays in Munich for a week in August during the 1972 Olympics. They wanted to take *Dream* and tried to reassemble the original company, which was possible as Roscoe Lee Browne said he would like to tour Europe. The Negro Ensemble Company paid $1,000 for two options on *Dream*, for touring in the United States and for overseas touring. They wanted to break in the production in the United States before taking it to Munich where the Kammerspiele has 700 seats. There were more problems about bringing *Ti-Jean* to the United States with the Trinidad Theatre Workshop as the Negro Ensemble Company had its budget slashed. Steve Lathan told Aschenberg he was trying to get National Educational Television or some other network to sponsor the filming of *Ti-Jean* in Trinidad with the Trinidad Theatre Workshop.

By now Walcott was dreaming of having two theatre companies, one touring and playing in North America, the other in Trinidad. It was a great, unlikely, idea. The Workshop had grown to thirty actors and could train more if there were more opportunities to act. Walcott felt that Laveau and others were of international standard. Walcott himself was becoming a hot theatre property, meeting influential investors, producers, actors, and directors; America was seeking black culture, importing foreign theatre and dance groups, why not the Trinidad Theatre Workshop with Walcott directing his plays? It now sounds impractical—African-American actors would object through Equity to the competition, Caribbean speech and stories are obscure to white and black Americans, the Trinidad Theatre Workshop was insufficiently polished—but who knows what might have been if some investor had taken the challenge? Walcott had friends in the West Indies who might have helped if the Americans and Canadians had been seriously interested.

As Michael Schultz was to direct *In a Fine Castle* at the Mark Taper, Walcott was shuttling between Trinidad and Los Angeles when he was interviewed several times during May and June by Umberto Bonsignori for a 1972 University of California Ph.D. dissertation that has many interesting and sometimes incorrect facts.[8] Rehearsals of *In a Fine Castle* were to began on 23 July, but Davidson decided to reschedule it for the 1972 season. Frank von Zerneck sent Aschenberg (21 June) $1,000 as a further non-returnable advance. Aschenberg (16 July) wrote to Joseph Papp at the New York Shakespeare Festival asking him whether he would be interested in having the Trinidad Theatre Workshop for a two-week engagement to perform *Ti-Jean and His Brothers*. She mentioned Walcott's success with *Dream on Monkey Mountain*, said that Michael Schultz knew about *Ti-Jean*, and mentioned that *In a Fine Castle* would be opening at the Mark Taper the following April.

Walcott's Trinidadian loyalties conflicted with the American market in which, even after his Obie, he still only had a toe or two. Big money and fame in the United States required big stars and an amount of commercialization very different from the high art which Walcott had brought to West Indian literature. Walcott wanted Albert Laveau in the Los Angeles Mark Taper *In a Fine Castle,* he wanted a film made of it with Trinidad Theatre Workshop actors, he wanted the Trinidad Theatre Workshop to tour in the United States with *Ti-Jean,* and he wanted Aschenberg to represent the Trinidad Theatre Workshop. She had to tell him that the moving picture industry was unlikely to make any deal concerning *In a Fine Castle* unless it received very good reviews and much publicity at the Mark Taper. Hugh Robertson's interest was not real money. The only black star then big enough for Hollywood was Richard Roundtree, who played Shaft the black detective, and he was already signed to do eleven films. He was a client of the International Famous Agency and if he liked *In a Fine Castle* Aschenberg could make a deal. He was interested in being in the Mark Taper production, but Schultz said he was not a good stage actor and would not use him. There was nothing Aschenberg could do at present about getting Laveau into Equity, as he had no offer from an American producer. Gordon Davidson and Schultz considered Laveau an amateur. Davidson was busy working with Leonard Bernstein concerning the opening of the new JFK Center in Washington. He and Schultz wanted to shoot some documentary footage at Carnival to use in *Castle* and as promotion for a film. Turning to other matters, Aschenberg had an offer from the Back Alley Theatre, a good black amateur group in Washington, who wanted to do sixteen performances of *Dream.* If Walcott approved they could go through Samuel French concerning fees. She had asked Ellen Stewart, Joe Papp, and George White about a *Ti-Jean* tour. She was reluctant to be an agent for the Trinidad Theatre Workshop. Walcott was invited to Lake Forest College as a poet in residence for a short period during 1971–2. She had told Lake Forest College that he could come in February for two weeks prior to going to Los Angeles for rehearsals.

Pan-Jamaican Investment Trust broke even on the Trinidad Theatre Workshop tour. Ralph Thompson (19 July) regarded breaking even as semi-commercial, unlike charity, and likely to lead to further underwriting. He had come back from a week in New York, where he had talked with Michael Shultz and George White about producing *Ti-Jean* off or on Broadway. He felt that there needed to be a formula reflecting the relationship of creative talents from developing nations and developed countries such as the backers in the developed nation putting up 70 per cent and entrepreneurs from developing nations committing 30 per cent. Estimates of costs ranged from $200,000 to $500,000. Thompson's plan never got off the ground. Instead Lloyd Richards invited Walcott to direct a student production of *Ti-Jean* at New York University which led to a production by Joseph Papp.

Stephen Bostic, Executive Director, Virgin Islands Council on the Arts, visited Port of Spain the week of 16 August. The Trinidad Theatre Workshop staged a reading and after Bostic returned to the Virgin Islands he reported to the Council, which accepted the idea of a Walcott residency. This was the start of what became a long relationship between Walcott and the American Virgin Islands. He would at various times tour with the Trinidad Theatre Workshop, hold workshops, help develop local theatre groups, and be a visiting professor at the College, later University, of the Virgin Islands.

Selden Rodman wrote to Margaret and Derek (16 August) enclosing a list of final contents of the anthology which, at Walcott's suggestion, he had changed from '100 British Poems' to *100 British Poets*. The original list started with Beowulf, folk ballads, and Chaucer and worked its way through the centuries until it reached Ted Hughes's 'Pike', Walcott's 'The Polish Rider', and John Lennon's 'Eleanor Rigby'. Walcott suggested such further inclusions as 'Piers Plowman', Marvell, and Hopkins and this led to enlarging the project. Dutton had asked Rodman for a volume of Conversations with Authors and he agreed to do so if he could limit himself to ten writers. He wanted five Americans—Hemingway, Ginsberg, Frost, Kunitz, Mailer—and Borges, Neto, García Marquéz, Neruda, and Walcott, with Paz as an alternative.

While producing serious stage plays in Trinidad could not form the basis of a career, it seemed possible to tap into radio and television which needed local material. Several Workshop actors were performing as individuals, even doing television advertisements. For a few years Walcott and the Trinidad Theatre Workshop were to try to find a backer or some formula where they could be paid for adapting, directing, and acting in West Indian plays which could, they hoped, then be rebroadcast for a further fee and perhaps sold to other West Indian radio stations and even Canada. Walcott signed on 30 July for *Theatre Ten*, a radio series, commissioned by 610 Radio, with Texaco as sponsor. The first programme was Roderick Walcott's *The Harrowing of Benjy*. Derek adapted his own *Henri Christophe* into two forty-five-minute segments which he directed. Other programmes included Walcott's *Sea at Dauphin* and Brathwaite's African play *Odale's Choice*. By local standards these paid decently. Walcott earned TT $800 for *Henri Christophe* and TT $240 for *Sea at Dauphin*.

Lloyd Richards, of the Theatre Program, New York University, School of the Arts, confirmed by letter (5 October) that Walcott was to direct a production of *Ti-Jean* with students from the New York University acting programme. Rehearsals would be from 29 November until 18 December, and restart after the Christmas break on 3 January, 1972, with the production opening on 13 January for five performances. The students would do voice and body warm-ups 9–10 a.m. and then be available Monday to Friday for rehearsals 10 a.m.–1 p.m. and 2–6 p.m. as well as the weekend before the opening. While performances by students were not reviewed by newspaper critics and not open to the public, many people interested in the theatre would be invited. Walcott would be paid his air fare plus $2,000 for royalties and directing fees. It might be possible to bring Tanker along for a couple of weeks; there would be $1,000 in total for Tanker's air fare and fee. Richards urged him to come early in November to learn about the school, meet and cast students, and discuss technical needs. This would be beneficial to the students and Walcott. It might contribute towards interest in the Trinidad Theatre Workshop and perhaps a future production. If Walcott came to New York during early November it would be possible to discuss plans for next summer, when Walcott wanted to do *Ti-Jean* and other plays with the Trinidad Theatre Workshop at the O'Neill.

On 5 October the Trinidadian architect, John Gillespie (with Walcott's co-signature) wrote to John Compton, the Prime Minister of St Lucia (with a copy to the Minister of Education) enclosing a report prepared in September concerning a Creative and Performing Arts Centre requested by the government and in part based on discussions between Gillespie and Walcott. This was a better and grander version of a proposal which had been developing since McBurnie's Little Carib and which continues to circulate today in Walcott's proposed Arts Centre on Rat Island. Trinidad, St Lucia, and several other eastern Caribbean islands lacked a suitable place for theatre, dance, and other performing arts. Gillespie and Walcott proposed two theatres, an amphitheatre for large folk festivals, and a little theatre seating 300. The amphitheatre could be used for visiting orchestras and ballet companies, the little theatre for local drama groups, chamber music, film societies, and poetry readings. The proposal concerns mainly the little theatre. As usual nothing was done about it. Twenty-five years later those staging cultural events in St Lucia would need to choose building a football stadium, erecting a tent, or using two new tiny open-air stages behind expensive restaurants distant from city centres.

Meanwhile the Trinidad Theatre Workshop produced *Ti-Jean and His Brothers* in Port of Spain at the Town Hall, 13 October, and 23–4 October at Queen's Hall. *In a Fine Castle,* designed and directed by Walcott, was produced by the Trinidad Theatre Workshop 28–30 October at Queen's Hall. An excerpt was published as 'Conscience of a Revolutionary' in the *Express* (24 October). There was a second run, 28–9 November and 2 December, at the Town Hall. During November Trinidad passed an amended Sedition Bill banning the publicizing and discussion of political matters if they contributed to stirring up tensions between the various ethnic groups. *In a Fine Castle* and much of Walcott's writing might be thought to treat of such topics. Whereas Trinidad's Constitution had guaranteed freedom of thought and expression, the new Sedition Bill made it possible to punish with five years' imprisonment and a $10,000 fine 'seditious' statements and publications. The promotion of 'feelings of ill-will and hostility between different classes or races' was already defined as a form of sedition under the Sedition Ordinance. Walcott took such repression of expression seriously. For a writer the essential freedom is of expression. It is self-identity as a person and artist as well as a career. *Dream* and *In a Fine Castle* were concerned with the destructive effects of black self-hate, slave history, and racial guilt and revenge, but from *Henri Christophe* onwards he thought that racial divisions threatened the region with tyrants, whether black nationalists, Stalinist imitators, or fascist promoters of a national 'folk' culture. At the same time as the *New Yorker* was celebrating Walcott, he was interviewed by Therese Mills in the *Sunday Guardian*. 'Right now there is an aura of fear of free expression.' 'There is no climate of free opinion now in this country and this is where the theatre can confront the cultural policy of the State.'⁹

Walcott left Trinidad for a two-week poetry tour of universities in the United States to be followed by work on the New York University *Ti-Jean*. On Tuesday, 2 November, he was in New York and failed to telephone Howard Moss, who wrote to Giroux asking whether he could meet Walcott the following week. Walcott's tour was the first offering of the Connecticut Poetry Circuit and foreshadowed his later intensive reading tours in the United States and Europe. A career as a poet meant promoting your poetry. From now on a large part of his life would be spent on such reading tours. This was a tour to earn money, about $1,000 in total, and to make his poetry better known. He was to be paid a $100 honorarium for each reading, and as he did not, and still does not, drive, each college was supposed to drive him to his next engagement. Otherwise Walcott was asked to use public transport, make his own travel arrangements, arrange his own accommodations when there were no readings, and advise whether he would want his evening meal before or after his reading. He was told he should travel from New York to Hartford by Trailways or Greyhound for his Wednesday reading at Manchester Community College, where he stayed overnight. The next day, Thursday, there were two readings. He had to arrive at Central Connecticut State College in New Britain for a 3.30 p.m. reading and afterwards was driven to Trinity College, Hartford, for an 8 p.m. reading. He was sent a map explaining how to get from Manchester Community College to Central Connecticut State College, New Britain. Walcott was told to have a driver let him off at the Administration Building; he should then walk to the library, climb to the third floor, go to an office, introduce himself to the departmental secretary, and make himself at home!

After overnighting at Hartford he was expected at 4 p.m. on Friday at Miss Porter's School in Farmington for an 8 p.m. reading. Saturday, 6 November, was free, but William Meredith of the English Department at Connecticut College, New London, needed him on Sunday for a 4 p.m. reading. Monday was also free. John Malcolm Brinnin had earlier asked Walcott to read from his poems at Boston University for a fee of $300. Walcott would read on Tuesday at Yale University, New Haven, stay overnight, read on 10 November at the University of Hartford, and on Thursday he was expected at Wesleyan University for an 8 p.m. reading followed by a reception. He breakfasted the next morning with students, and was taken to the Middletown bus terminal to return, 12 November, to New York. Dan Masterson, poet in residence at Rockland Community College, had written a rave review of *The Gulf,* and invited Walcott to the College for three days for which he earned $1,250. Walcott stayed at the Chelsea Hotel 18–20 November and 28 November–11 December, while working on *Ti-Jean* for New York University.

The spring 1972 issue of *Haggis/Baggis* of Miss Porter's School has a drawing of Walcott by Joan Devine, class of 1972, with information that he came to Farmington 'on November 5, 1971, late in the rain. Rushed into reading, he relaxed with cigarettes between poems . . . Calmed he swung into a scene from *Ti-Jean and His Brothers,* a play he wrote for The Trinidad Theatre Workshop, and he read all the parts and the play came alive.'[10]

Walcott's finances were becoming dependent on American earnings. His earnings in American dollars for 1971 included $1,000 for the Connecticut poetry tour, $1,000 from the *New Yorker,* $1,250 from Rockland Community College, $1,500 from Samuel French for rights to *Dream on Monkey Mountain,* $1,000 from the Center Theatre Group, about $2,500 in total for the New York *Dream on Monkey Mountain,* and several smaller sums for royalties on his books, totalling a little under $10,000. Out of total earnings for the year calculated in TT dollars of about $21,500 only $2,000 were earned in the West Indies, of which a third were UK royalties from Cape. There was no paying West Indian literary market; West Indian theatre, which provided him with a society in which he could be involved, offered small rewards.

While in Tobago over the holidays Walcott wrote 'The Runner at Sauteurs (for Selden Rodman)'. It would first be published as Chapter 11, iv, in *Another Life.* The poem concerns the mass suicide of Indians in Grenada, who jumped off a cliff rather than allow themselves to be captured by the British. Over the years the fate of the Amerindians would become a Walcott concern. He was made an Officer, Order of the British Empire (St Lucia List) by the Queen in the New Year Honours List.

16

1972 *Ti-Jean* in New York, Joseph Papp, Pat Strachan

AFTER he returned to New York and the Chelsea Hotel (4 January 1972), *Ti-Jean* was performed 13–14 and 17–18 January by students at New York University. Lloyd Richards invited Papp to the show, and sent an official play report and letter concerning *Ti-Jean* to the New York Shakespeare Festival, in which he described the writing as poetic, childlike, beautiful without being pompous or picturesque. As a result Papp decided to do *Ti-Jean* with the New York Shakespeare Festival in Central Park during the summer. The audience would be about 2,000 a night and the stage immense. Papp, however, thought the New York University production static and conservative; he suggested that Walcott co-direct *Ti-Jean* in association with a young American director, preferably black, which Walcott refused.

Since admission would be free and there were no ticket sales, Papp and Aschenberg agreed to a flat royalty for seven and a half weeks ($3,750), along with round-trip transportation plus $25 per diem for Walcott, who would also get $1,000 as director and $250 to redirect for the Mobile Unit. Tanker would get $500 plus transportation and a per diem of $25. Aschenberg felt that the Papp production would improve the value of Walcott's plays as Papp was then the most important and influential American producer (after David Merrick). Until then Papp had only produced classics in the Park and paid no royalties. On Broadway the New York Shakespeare Festival had two big Tony winning hits in 1972, the Best Musical and the Best Play.

Walcott thought this an opportunity to bring the Trinidad Theatre Workshop to New York. He wanted Papp to see Laveau in *Ti-Jean* and also to consider if the entire company could do a play at the Public Theatre for a short run. Papp trusted Walcott and decided, sight unseen, to ask Actors' Equity to hire Hamilton Parris and Laveau. Papp (14 February) argued that while he wanted to develop black American actors, the two West Indians were essential for the flavour of *Ti-Jean*, a folk musical unlike what is usually meant as a musical. During the previous June a ten-minute segment of *Ti-Jean* had been filmed for eventual use on *Black Journal*; it was shown on WNET | 13 (29 February) where Walcott introduced it and discussed *Dream*.

After Walcott returned from New York to Trinidad, Schultz telephoned Aschenberg about film rights for *In a Fine Castle*. They agreed on $1,500 for the first draft by 1 April. Another $8,500 was to be spread over 1972. Walcott was supposed to be paid $10,000 on the first day of principal photography and $10,000 out of the first monies after the release of the film, along with 5 per cent of 100 per cent of profits, 10 per cent of producers' share of profits. Schultz was to be producer, Walcott associate producer. The total budget of $350,000, Aschenberg wrote (21 January), was much lower than usual and only acceptable as a labour of love. As the usual minimum for film rights would be $50,000 and $25,000 for screen writing, this was giving it away, but even given away nothing came of it.

Patricia Harting, recently hired as an assistant to Giroux, would soon become Pat Strachan and Walcott's editor from *Another Life* to *Collected Poems*. When his books were set first in England, by Cape, the type would be reset in the United States, and the punctuation changed; Walcott always made further revisions. Strachan continued Giroux's job of carefully reading manuscripts, submitting poems to well-paying or influential journals, handling correspondence concerning proofs, revisions, lectures, Walcott's whereabouts, and other matters, such as sending him (7 March) Rodman's review in the *New York Times* of the *Dream on Monkey Mountain* volume of plays.

Walcott and Tanker stayed at the Chelsea from Monday, 27 March, during the week of auditions for *Ti-Jean*. Walcott brought sketches for the costumes, and had already sent Papp descriptions of what he wanted for the characters. The descriptions included physical builds, skin colours, and voices. For the Frog Walcott wanted a male with a rich baritone voice, Hamilton Parris. Gros-Jean should be black, powerful, heavy, a countryman, and yet light on his feet, and have a bass or deep baritone voice. Mi-Jean should be lighter skinned, and have a fine voice between baritone and tenor, be nimble footed, younger than Gros-Jean, and have the intellectual ambition to go with his colour. Ti-Jean was crucial, the part required a 12 to 15-year-old boy with a good soprano voice, a defiant but winning smile, someone not too professional. The Mother should be a strong voiced Mammy. Maybe someone who knew Creole culture through Haiti? The Devil needed to combine an impeccable British accent (as planter) with a West

Indian accent (as Papa Bois) and have a powerful voice capable of classical verse monologues while being physically lithe, obviously Albert Laveau. There are other descriptions, such as the need for The Bolom to be small, child-sized, and acrobatic. Walcott had types in mind, visualized his characters, and race, class, voice, and diction were part of the picture. This is Walcott the painter as much as Walcott the dramatist. It would be difficult for others to cast actors for the roles the way he saw them and had cast them in St Lucia and Trinidad.

Besides the productions of *Ti-Jean* and *In a Fine Castle*, Walcott in New York was involved with a possible film, 'Vangelo Nero' (the Black Christ), for Dino de Laurentiis. He wrote from the Chelsea to Produzioni De Laurentiis in Rome that he would by the end of April send an outline, and after they had read it and there was agreement about the concept he would start to write the script, which would take him three to four months. He wanted $30,000 United States for the script, 20 per cent on signature, 60 per cent while writing, and the final 20 per cent on acceptance of the script. The production company would also need to reimburse him for any travel and foreign expenses, such as travel to Rome or Africa.

He was writer in residence at Lake Forest College from 4 April for ten days, returning to New York on Thursday, 13 April, and continuing on to Los Angeles 14 April–7 May, during which time he received a $25 per diem. Aschenberg meantime sent money to Margaret Walcott (17 April) as the telephone had been cut off at Walcott's residence in Trinidad! Papp's people were trying to telephone Margaret all day and night to get for Immigration the addresses and telephone numbers of the two actors coming from Trinidad.

The Centre Theatre Group of Los Angeles, with Edward Parone as the Resident Director, presented *In a Fine Castle* at the Mark Taper Forum as a New Theatre For Now production for six performances, 3–6 May. The NTFN productions, sponsored by a Rockefeller Foundation grant, were meant as experiments, with minimal staging, steps towards completing a work, not full-scale productions. For this version, unlike Jamaica, there were no projections of stills and films. Carnival was suggested by a soundtrack of steel bands. Set at the end of Carnival, the eve of Ash Wednesday, the play concerns the division between old and new in a social upheaval. It asks what is imported, what is imitation about art, politics, people, and revolutions.

The production was thought poor, but reviewers were divided about Walcott and the play. Dan Sullivan in the *Los Angeles Times* (10 May) found the characters thin and Brown a prig in love with his own alienation. The whites were stock figures of decadence, the language too poetic. Ron Pennington in the *Hollywood Reporter* (8 May) noted the delicate, beautiful poetry that looked back sadly on an inevitable but necessary historical change. He compared it to the sardonic romanticism of Tennessee Williams, but said that the actors lacked depth. The flat delivery seemed a mistaken choice by the director which did not do justice to the writing. The Los Angeles *Herald-Examiner* reviewer (13 May) found the production drifting without much understanding by the director or actors. The *San Gabriel Valley Tribune* reviewer (9 May) was uncertain whether bad acting ruined the play or whether it was a bad play. It had a good story idea. The dialogue was beautiful but too flowery to be real. The first half was of interest, but after the intermission it became a 'flood of speeches', and the ending was unsatisfactory (a complaint made of many Walcott plays).

The play requires an eastern Caribbean attitude, and indeed Walcott had in mind someone like Albert Laveau, someone laid back, concerned with art, unpolitical, sarcastic. Walcott told Bonsignori that Brown needed a Trinidadian actor, especially Laveau. The part required West Indian humour, sarcasm, lack of decision. The need was for someone who would care about a Watteau painting more than social justice. Even the Jamaican production lacked 'that kind of flipness'.

For a play which was never published as such (*The Last Carnival* is a later version) *In a Fine Castle* occupies a large place in Walcott's career. Drafts, versions, and productions and further versions keep showing up from the early 1960s onward. Many novels use a house as a symbol for a nation or culture. Here, instead of a house as a symbol for a land and its culture, there is the castle, which is also symbolic of colour. What is the white culture of the old families of Trinidad, what have they inherited from Europe, how have they changed, what is the West Indies inheriting from them? The castle and the Watteau painting that is shown throughout are like the moon or the white muse, the desired Other, that which is partly denied Walcott by being part black. It is, however, also part of the history, culture, and people of the region. It is a necessary part of Walcott's art, something he must understand. The original idea for the play was the mulatto inheritance of European culture, and of whiteness, from a decaying plantocracy. The fascination with this not-yet past has its parallels in Walcott's own training as an artist and his theory of art as modelling; begin by learning the classics and then use your own subject-matter in the forms you study. Walcott would also have had in mind the old French families in St Lucia and the ways in which his talents as a writer had brought him into contact with members of the white plantocracy. In Trinidad he had become friends with the Stollmeyers, large estate owners whose 'castle' was one of the fine old houses lining Queens Park. One the current Stollmeyers was a painter.

There is an undated pre-1970 television scenario, 'Un Voyage A Cythère', an early version of *In a Fine Castle*. It is really a twenty-seven-page short story about a young 'negro' reporter and art critic who interviews members of an old, now thoroughly decadent, French family about its art and past; he becomes involved with one of the women, Françoise, who in later versions of the play is Clodia. This is very much a pre-1970 version with no Carnival and no revolution. The negro reporter keeps saying there is no history worth being concerned with.

Anger at the past becomes repetition. The French family has had black lovers in the past and is part-black though white. In these early versions of the play it is easier to see the same personal obsessions about whiteness and white culture that went into *Dream on Monkey Mountain* and some of the early poems and the lost novel. There are also Walcottian obsessions about madness, suicide, the artist's alienation from society, and origins.

The *In A Fine Castle* story began to change as the failed Black Power revolution of 1970 and the attacks on Walcott as Anglo-black meant that his own ideal of a West Indian culture cross-pollinated by its various cultures and peoples was challenged by the kind of 'black' racism he had tried to avoid most of his life. Once more it was the politicians and politicized intellectuals who were thinking in terms of ethnic identity and race whereas Walcott felt that the various peoples living together in such small islands were in the process of forming a common society. Walcott identifies with Brown in the play, sharing feelings of exhaustion, of being tired of hating. We might now see Walcott's views as hybridity, creolization, or another fashionable term of post-colonial theory, but the recognition of Brownness as distinct from Black, as the future of the West Indies, and as part of the New World, was long a Walcott notion and followed from being raised culturally white while being mulatto.

The exhaustion theme recurs in Walcott work; its articulation is in part modelled on an existentialist motif, but it is also an insight based on Walcott's own knowledge that hate is tiring; it requires more and more fuel, extremism, anger. Racial hate unlike social justice cannot bring about reconciliation and must be self-defeating. It is especially impossible for West Indians to cleanse themselves of being part-white, of being culturally part-European. To treat language as servitude is to limit one's art; to say syntax is white and thus limit syntax to be black does not liberate, but is a self-made idiocy.[1]

The stage of *In a Fine Castle* is dominated by a copy of Antoine Watteau's *The Embarkation for Cythera*. In Baudelaire's famous 'Un Voyage à Cythère' the Ionian island Cythera is a dream place of love and beauty where Venus has her temple. Cythera stands in the same relation to European desire as does the Moon goddess or Apparition in *Dream*. It is the unobtainable ideal. The main characters include Oswald, the uncle of Clodia and of Antoine, whose father, François, is dead. François represents the European cultural inheritance of the islands, whereas Oswald sees the castle as only real estate. An alien to his skin, Brown prefers the great paintings of the West to political action. Brown's distrust of revolutionaries and those who love the poor is like Walcott's dislike of priests who love the poor. François's suicide represents the artist cut off from his country; he wants France the way West Indians want other countries. In one version Brown knew Antoine at school, where the boys tortured Antoine as a sissy interested in the arts. Clodia suffers like Makak—confusion, disassociation of self, madness. Clodia and Brown are two sides of Walcott. Brown, unlike Makak, cannot be freed by killing the image of whiteness as it is part of himself.[2]

The copy of the painting of Antoine Watteau's *The Embarkation for Cythera* is a symbol of people being together on the island and unable to leave. The painting shows that people share a common humanity; they all want their Cythera, their return to an imagined paradise. Walcott told Bonsignori that there is a connection between François the father and failed artist and Walcott's memory of his own father, Warwick, who would copy European paintings in watercolour. At one time Derek thought Warwick was a false Negro. Warwick was an imitator, not a real artist, like François, but that does not mean that respect for art or training in European art was wrong. Clodia is a girl in rebellion, disassociated, rich, dislocated, in pain, restless, feeling empty. You could find her in the films of Antonioni, Fellini, or Bergman.[3]

The first two drafts of the play did not have the black radical Shelley, only Brown coming into the castle as a photographer attracted to Clodia. Walcott felt that the play needed to come out of the castle to reality, it needed various points of view, including the hysteria of radical politics. In the version Bonsignori read, there is a meeting of the revolutionaries which results in the proclamation of a black tyrant who will lead the cause. This was Walcott's continuing vision of how racial rebellion leads to the Haiti of Henri Christophe, a theme taken up in his political poems. Sydney Prince, the leader of the black radical group, has a white wife. In later drafts Shelley, functioning as messenger, announces at the end that Elizabeth Prince has committed suicide off stage—the first martyr to the movement is white. Brown then leaves and there is a projection of Brown walking down an empty street and meeting some Carnival gang who are turning into revolutionaries, while a Creole family is sprawled on a lawn. Sydney marches past him. Earlier there was a scene in which Clodia, like Macbeth, sees the blood of guilt on her hands which others do not see. As late as 1992 Walcott would still be writing radically different versions of this play which obviously means so much to him, drawing on many experiences of his life, but which never settles into a final form.

Walcott flew from Los Angeles to New York on 8 May for a week, then returned to Trinidad where he started the script for 'Vangelo Nero' while workshopping *The Charlatan*, which he also hoped to sell to the United States. On 24 May he was invested at Government House, St Lucia, with his OBE. Between 12–29 May he made various notes on the life of a contemporary black Jesus. His Pan-African, Pan-Black vision belongs to New World diaspora sentimentality. On 18 May he wrote a 'proem' explaining that this life of Christ, who may be Jesus, is meant for and set in all of Africa, Ethiopia to South Africa, and will unite the tribes of Africa. Walcott continues with parallels to the Christian Christ; his will be a revolutionary martyr with a spiritual vision. Where the Jews suffered under the Romans, the Africans suffer under imperialism. In our age the whites are Romans, the Jews are black. Black martyrs include Haile Selassie and Patrice Lumumba. They are Christ-like, not Christ. So Vangelo Nero will be Christ-like but political. There is a basic experience of baptism (or calling), mission (service, revolution), sedition, arrest, trial, betrayal, torture, and public execution found in the lives of Lumumba, Malcolm X, Selassie. There is no more earthly paradise, it is corrupted (as in Africa). Christ figures are betrayed by their own people (Gandhi, Pease, Connolly, Che), but the New World African remains a hope.

Walcott's recurring obsessions can be seen in his notes and analogies. It is perhaps significant that Judas is first seen as a treasurer-revolutionary who signs a $30,000 contract with Caiphas, which Walcott describes as the 'deal'. Walcott sometimes associated the events visually with Trinidad and Tobago, even listing Trinidad Theatre Workshop actors for the characters, as if he might get them the roles. The biblical characters were divided into whites and blacks, Romans and Jews. Herod, Herodias, and Salome were to be black. The white Centurion would be Nigel Scott, Pontius Pilate would be Laurence Goldstraw, Joseph was to be Errol Jones.

Walcott had not been to Africa and the script is an Africa based on movies. Light is described in terms of Italian paintings or perhaps the Caribbean. There is a cave near a river in which an old man reads a book, and there are primitive drawings of the life of Christ. Some of the script is very poetic, like scenes for a pageant in verse, but the emotions are interiorized. It is difficult to imagine 'Vangelo Nero' as a film. By 30 May Walcott had written about forty pages of what often feels like poetic prose with rhymes. Dino de Laurentiis sent a telegram (10 June) saying that he thought the atmosphere and insight into a contemporary African Christ worth pursuing, but the scenes and outline lacked a clear story. Would Walcott come to Rome at their expense to discuss how to proceed? Walcott, however, went to New York for Ti-Jean. Was a great opportunity missed? Or would perhaps Walcott have ended up on Capri, a script writer of European art films?

He flew from Port of Spain to New York on 18 June for rehearsals of Ti-Jean, which started four days later. Margaret and the children came with him for a time and they had an apartment. The New York Shakespeare Festival that summer began at the Delacort Theatre, Central Park, with Hamlet, 20 June–16 July; then there were fifteen performances of Ti-Jean and His Brothers, 20 July–6 August, with book and lyrics by Walcott, directed by Walcott. Walcott had twice rewritten Ti-Jean since 1959 and the music by André Tanker was now part of it. He insisted that the contract say the music for Ti-Jean should always be Tanker's and that no other music be used in other productions. There were two Trinidad Theatre Workshop actors in the production. Hamilton Parris performed the role of the Frog; Albert Laveau took the triple role of Devil, Papa Bois, and Planter.

On the strength of his performance Papp invited Albert Laveau to stay on in New York. The season concluded with *Much Ado About Nothing*, 10 August–3 September. Gail Merrifield Papp remembers her husband's excitement about the power and beauty of Walcott's play and the risk in producing *Ti-Jean* in Central Park. Could it fill the stage and seats? It is difficult now to understand the risk or the uniqueness of the event, but it was the only contemporary play done there.[4]

The reviews were mixed. The critics praised the acting of Parris and Laveau, but generally did not like the play nor Walcott's writing, which they found shapeless, wordy, static, literary, and self-consciously symbolic. He was also said to be inciting an anti-white revolution. Walcott's directing was found indulgent. Some critics, however, praised the production as magical, warm, whimsical, eloquent, and a visual treat. For those who liked the play Walcott was sensitive and ironic with words. Whether the critics were favourable or not, they seemed uncertain what to say; the play was not translating into American.

Clive Barnes said Walcott 'is a poet who deals in symbols, sometimes very convoluted symbols . . . it seems possible that Mr. Walcott has set this play not in his native Trinidad but on Haiti . . . as pieces of theatre [Walcott's plays] are hard to take'. Douglas Watt in the *Daily News* thought the play 'annoyingly pedantic and pretentious'. William Raidy called it 'fresh and exhilarating', 'simply magic'. The *Christian Science Monitor* found the first act static and wordy, but the play generally 'a musical and visual treat'. All the reviews praised Albert Laveau.[5]

Walcott's early plays were meant for a little theatre. Although *Ti-Jean* has become a classic of West Indian drama and is constantly being revived, there were problems in producing it before a large urban American audience resistant to its folk setting and themes, confused by its mixture of West Indian speech and high poetry, and unlikely to make the various political and cultural connections to a late colonial world of a plantocracy, of class, and of 'shades', the differences between political and spiritual freedom.

Walcott now had an Obie and was a favourite dramatist of the most influential producer in Los Angeles; he was also in the process of becoming one of Papp's favourites. There were several people in the Joseph Papp circle with whom Walcott would work in future. The composer Galt MacDermot was involved with many Papp ventures, including the original production of *Hair* at the Anspacher Theatre during the 1967–8 season before the musical was sold to Mike Butler who financially backed the hit Broadway production. MacDermot was also the composer for the 1970–1 season's *Two Gentlemen of Verona*, which Mel Shapiro helped adapt into a musical and directed. This was an immense success and transferred from the Mobile Theatre to Broadway at the St James Theatre and was then taken to London. Walcott's connections in the American theatre world were expanding, and this would influence his vision of the future.

The Mobile Theatre toured the Boroughs with *Ti-Jean*, 9–27 August. Four performances were scheduled in Queens, four in Brooklyn, two in Staten Island, four in the Bronx, three in Manhattan. The Mobile Theatre was a group of eight vehicles that carried everything from a fold-out thrust stage, lighting, sound, a generator, dressing-rooms, and bleachers to chairs for 1,600 people. It took plays to communities outside Manhattan that would otherwise never attend theatre. The audience varied and could be dangerous. Mobile Theatre performances had been cancelled after bottles and rocks were thrown at the actors on stage.

The Mobile Theatre was also running into some non-theatrical criticism. Although Papp was openly a member of the Communist Party who pioneered many racial breakthroughs in the New York cultural scene, a group based on Long Island City complained (24 August) that he had not scheduled any performances in the poverty-stricken Long Island City-Astoria area of Queens, which had many blacks and Puerto Ricans. A week earlier another group had also written to Papp with the same complaint and had asked that one of the two performances in Bayside be transferred to the western side of Queens. The Association Progresiva Hispana de Queens, Inc. accused Papp of deliberately avoiding the Queensbridge area of Long Island City with its poorer Puerto Ricans and blacks. By contrast the Staten Island Council on the Arts complained that the arts were being advertised at the expense of the environment; *Ti-Jean* posters on telephone poles and trees were being blown on to roads and lawns.

Meantime, from 31 July to 6 August, the Negro Ensemble Company production of *Dream on Monkey Mountain* was at the Munich Olympics as part of the Cultural Olympics. It received extensive newspaper coverage in Germany. Although the German press kept contrasting the invitation to Hitler's refusal to award an Olympic medal to Jessie Owens, this was the Olympics where Israeli athletes were taken hostage and then killed by Palestinian terrorists.

Walcott was in the United States reading from his poetry and working on plays from 1 October for over a month. After a reading at the New School (2 October) arranged by Daniel Halpern, he began the season's programme of the International Poetry Forum, Carnegie Library, Pittsburgh, with a reading on 4 October for which he was paid $500 (of which $50 went to the International Famous Agency) and $300 expenses. Walcott had to send a handwritten and signed copy of one of his poems, which was to be photocopied and given to the audience at the reading. The next night Walcott read in a hall of more than a thousand seats at Hunter College, the first of a series of readings sponsored by the Center for Inter-American Relations. Invitations were sent to about a hundred people including Richard Howard, Tom Wolf, Adrienne Rich, Lillian Hellman, John Simon, Vera Stravinski, Robert Craft, Hilton Kramer, Philip Rahv, and Elizabeth Hardwick—the New York intelligentsia. A reception followed the reading.

He read along with Nikki Giovanni at New York University on 10 October as part of a series called 'Couplets: Double Poetry Reading'. Some of the students had seen *Ti-Jean* during the summer and requested him. He was paid $300 for the half-hour reading and a half-hour question and answer session. The reading took place in 'The Top of the Park' at Loeb Student Center, with the space set up as a cabaret with small tables for 120 people around a podium. Two days later, 12 October, he read at the University of Pennsylvania where Daniel Hoffman thanked him for being so generous with his time. Hoffman spoke with the managing director of the Walnut Street Theatre about possibly having the Trinidad Theatre Workshop. From 16 to 23 October Walcott was Frederick L. Gwynn Memorial Poet. This was a 150th anniversary event sponsored by the Trinity College Poetry Center, Hartford. Walcott was expected to have informal sessions with students, visit classes, read from his own poetry on Tuesday evening, 17 October, read the poetry of his contemporaries on Wednesday, and on Friday read from his plays.

Walcott kept going back and forth between New York, Connecticut, Boston, and Trinidad. He spent some time with Robert Lowell, who was in the United States in connection with being divorced by Elizabeth Hardwick and to arrange teaching at Harvard the following year. Lowell brought Walcott to the attention of Boston University, which asked about purchasing his manuscripts and letters for its special collections of manuscripts and letters, but nothing came of it.

In Trinidad the Workshop was involved in another attempt to earn from performing serious drama on radio. Starting late July Radio 610 broadcast Trinidad Workshop productions on Sundays on *Theatre Fifteen*. The series included *Jourmard* and *Henri Christophe*, both directed by Walcott. Later the Workshop planned for twenty plays on Radio 610 for the next season. Derek did not attend the 25 August–15 September Carifesta in Guyana where the St Lucia Arts Guild presented Roderick's *Banjo Man*, fourteen years after it had been banned by the Catholic Church in St Lucia and withdrawn from the West Indian Arts Festival.

On 8–9 December the Trinidad Theatre Workshop joined with the Repertory Dance Theatre to present a mixture of short plays and modern dance. The founder of the Repertory Dance Company, Arthur Johnson, was the successor of Beryl McBurnie in that he moved Trinidadian modern dance from modernized folk dance to modern dance itself. Walcott early became a Johnson supporter, reviewed his performances, and invited him to work with the Trinidad Theatre Workshop. Besides supporting a parallel art to his own theatre and poetry, Walcott wanted to heal the fracture that occurred when he and McBurnie went their own ways. Walcott was quietly, in the long-range way he worked, planning for there to be a Trinidad Theatre Workshop and a Trinidad Theatre Workshop Dance Company. On 12 December Walcott's *Malcochon* was filmed for Trinidad and Tobago Television.

In recent years Trinidad had become rich, the envy of the West Indies, through its oil. It had also become increasingly corrupt as oil contracts, even gasoline stations, were a source of percentages, pay-offs, and patronage. Few dared speak out. Besides laws effectively censoring the press, the governing party destroyed those who opposed it. On 14 December both the *Trinidad Guardian* and the *Express* published Walcott's 'The Silent Woman', a protest at the way Jean Miles had been hounded to death. Under the heading there were four lines from the Russian poet Anna Akhmatova:

> No, not under the vault of another sky,
> not under the shelter of other wings,
> I was with my people then,
> there where my people were doomed to be.

And Walcott's poem:

> Now the,
> the wheelers and winners with their shrugs and smiles,
> like all the other tyrants who have lived
> can settle with relief now
> to their appointments, luncheons and commissions
> that the final silence has arrived
> until another one, some woman
> or a man brave enough to have the heart of a woman,
> some accounts clerk, some public servant is broken
> again by the cost in agony
> of public service. Better to be broken, Miss Miles,
> better, than like the rest, to leave the truth unspoken.
> So come gentlemen, if you not busy, come Creon,
> come Stalin, take the black jackets off, and help Antigone
> lift up this woman.

There was another heading 'To Her Honour and Example' signed by thirty-three names, many of whom were associated with Walcott, the Trinidad Theatre Workshop, and the arts. It began with Margaret Walcott, then Helen Camps, Judy Boldon, Verna Joseph, Stephanie Laveau, and included Wilma Hoyte, Pearl Springer, Therese Mills, Therese Holder, Judy Hinkson, Jeanette Laird. Walcott's poem was later included in *Sea Grapes* (1976).[6]

Miles, a white woman from the local élite, was a friend of Margaret Walcott and part of her circle. Miles had supported Williams's political party and married black. Her lover was in Williams's cabinet and part of its corruption. When she denounced it, she was rejected by her lover and could not get a job to support herself or her children. She sought help from politicians who she thought were friends; they made false promises, slept with her, then bragged to others. Humiliating her because of her colour and class went along with punishing a renegade. Miles became depressed, took to drink, suffered from illness and a mental collapse. Eventually she was found dead in circumstances which led to rumours that the politicians had killed her with drugs. She came to represent the ways the Williams regime had changed from a decolonizing movement to a corrupt tyranny from which even its supporters, who included many of the Walcott circle, were not protected. To have spoken up in support of Miles at this point was an act of bravery as Williams and his followers were vicious and used thugs as well as the power of the government against opponents, most of whom it had driven from Trinidad. Years later Miles would be viewed as a national hero, someone to be commemorated, but at the time it took courage to stand up for her.

There was at this time another unexpected connection between Walcott and politics. When Walcott was in New York late October–early November 1972 the composer Gary William Friedman, who often worked with Gordon Davidson, left some tapes for 'Heavenly Peace' at the Chelsea. 'Heavenly Peace' was an idea for a play based on the Daniel Berrigan trial. This developed from Walcott's friendship with Gordon Davidson and those involved in the protests against the American involvement in Vietnam, and ended several years later in frustration and wasted energies.

Friedman suggested meeting in New York in early December. Instead Walcott (14 December) sent from Trinidad a first working draft of 'Heavenly Peace', a musical play based on Daniel Berrigan's poems. The script was prepared for Gordon Davidson, the director Gil Moses, and Friedman who were hoping to open it at the Mark Taper. Moses was a successful black director who in the 1970s had hits on Broadway before moving on to Hollywood and films. In the accompanying letter Walcott says the title is the best he has come up with, although the rock-operatic 'Feel my Fire', which he rejected, is actually from Southwell's poem 'The Burning Babe'. Friedman (19 December) was happy with the first draft of 'Heavenly Peace': it was good theatre. He liked many of Walcott's ideas, but he thought the speeches and scenes too long; there was not enough forward momentum and action. He was uncertain which poems were Berrigan's and which Walcott's; he was sceptical of using older, non-Berrigan poetry, such as by Southwell.

Although there was no promise the show would be contracted, Friedman wanted to move ahead rapidly. Walcott was leaving for the beach on the north coast on 23 December for two weeks during which time he could work on the script. He proposed coming to New York in mid-January for ten days for further discussions; he needed to be back in Trinidad in mid-February for Peter Donkin and the Trinidad Theatre Workshop. Walcott hoped to use the Trinidad Theatre Workshop to make a demonstration tape. He had in mind a small cast in which parts were doubled and tripled. While visiting at Rampanalgas, Basil Paquet saw some of Walcott's drawings for 'Heavenly Peace' and was told that the play was being dedicated to him.

One reason for writing a theatre script based on Berrigan's poems was Walcott's notion of the poet as martyr, the poet who suffers for his society while carrying the torch of freedom and truth. Walcott had thought of priests in St Lucia as reactionary, censors, evil; Berrigan was a poet-priest representing a return to a time of innocence when Christians challenged those in power and suffered for their beliefs. Daniel Berrigan, a Jesuit priest, had received the Lamont Poetry award from the Academy of American Poets and was nominated for a National Book award for his first book, *Time without Number*. He marched in Selma, Alabama, with Martin Luther King, Jr., and was a co-founder of Clergy and Laity Concerned about Vietnam. He was one of nine people who, in May 1968, took hundreds of files from a local draft board in Catonsville, Maryland, and set fire to them in a parking lot. Although the property damage was small, the symbolism was large and the Catonsville nine were charged with a federal crime. Berrigan became a star of the 'Movement'. He helped his more activist brother Philip in the pouring of blood on some draft files in Baltimore and travelled to Hanoi as part of the release of three American pilots. He believed in non-violent resistance in the tradition of Thoreau and Gandhi: it was necessary to break the law to live by the spirit of Christianity. As he had taught and counselled at Cornell University, the students at first treated him as a hero before, under the influence of the Weathermen, the Movement turned violent and revolutionary.

After the original trial, the Berrigans were freed while awaiting their appeal. They went 'underground' to further publicize their views; Daniel wrote several books, including his own dramatization of *The Trial of the Catonsville Nine* (1970), intended as 'factual theatre'. He was aware of the Living Theatre and other off-Broadway alternative theatres; he wanted avant-garde drama to become political. While Berrigan was hiding, *The Trial of the Catonsville Nine* opened in May 1970 in Los Angeles, directed by Gordon Davidson. Davidson had asked Berrigan to prepare a taped message for the opening night audience, which included FBI agents hoping that the author would appear in person.[7] The play then moved on to New York. On 12 August 1970 Daniel Berrigan was captured in Rhode Island by FBI agents pretending to be bird watchers. He was sent to Danbury prison on 14 December 1970. *The Trial of the Catonsville Nine* received in 1971 both the Los Angeles Drama Critics Award and a New York Obie award (the same year that Walcott's *Dream* won an Obie as the best foreign play). In February 1972 Daniel Berrigan was released on parole. In 1973 he published his *Selected and New Poems*, his *Prison Poems*, and during October upset many of his followers by making a speech before the Association of Arab University

Graduates in Washington, DC, during which Berrigan denied the right of Israel to exist.

Another major theatre project, which would also occupy Walcott for years, developed from Walcott's friendship with Ronald Bryden, who had moved from being a literary editor for British weeklies to becoming literary adviser to the Royal Shakespeare Company. The Royal Shakespeare Company had been thinking about Tirso de Molina's late Renaissance classic, *El Burlador de Sevilla*, the original of the Don Juan theme, and had asked Bryden to commission a translation that might be workshopped. Bryden wondered which English poet had a rich Shakespearian style and recommended his friend Derek Walcott who had earlier sent him *In a Fine Castle*. Bryden had told Walcott that the RSC could not do *In a Fine Castle*, as black actors went to New York. The decision whether to go ahead with the translation was likely to depend on Trevor Nunn, who was then directing *Titus Andronicus*. Bryden had not yet negotiated commissions, but guessed that Walcott would get between £500 and £1,500. Advances were made against royalties and one tried to get as much advance as possible as royalties on 50–100 repertory performances were small. Could Walcott find a way of getting his way paid to London when next in New York as there was much to discuss in terms of the script? Bryden would take care of Walcott from the moment of arrival and see that he was somehow repaid at the contract stage.

At the end of the year Walcott was hoping that *In a Fine Castle* would open on Broadway, that *Ti-Jean* would move on to the Public Theatre, and also that Farrar, Straus and Giroux would publish *Another Life* and *In a Fine Castle*. Bryden had sent Walcott's work to Peter Brook, who thought Walcott should join him and his group touring Africa beginning with Christmas in (very Muslim) Kano, Nigeria, followed by ten days at the University of Ife, then moving on to Dahomey, Togo, and Mali, and returning to Europe in early March. Perhaps the trip would provide material for something about Africa? Walcott did not accept. In retrospect an opportunity was lost. Imagine if Walcott had become part of that international avant-garde theatre scene to which Brook in Paris was central. Speaking Creole Walcott was already part of Francophonie. This, rather than New York, might have been the market for Walcott's ambitions in the theatre, but it would have meant working in permanent exile, working in French with the French administrative bureaucracy, writing in French. His poetry would have withered. New York rather than Paris or Rome would be his promised land.

17

~~~~~~

1973 *Another Life*

ON Walcott's forty-third birthday (23 January) the University of the West Indies, Mona, announced that he would be the first graduate of UCWI to be awarded an Honorary Doctorate of Letters. He received the Doctorate from Sir Hugh Wooding, Pro Chancellor, at the Graduation Ceremony on 3 February. During 1946 Walcott, as part of the choir, had sung before Hugh Wooding when the Methodist Synod met in St Lucia. The Methodists were no longer evangelicals and school teachers, they were leading members of modern West Indian society, but Walcott carried part of his religious upbringing with him and it found its way into his work. During February 1973 *The American Way*, the American Airlines magazine, carried Selden Rodman's long interview with Walcott recounting their friendship, and discussed black–white relationships using *Dream on Monkey Mountain*. The conversation then turned to the difference between the politics of colour and the way poets of all colours were engaged in creating the Americas by describing them. Walcott affirmed his belief in a God and claimed that his belief has never wavered.[1]

Shortly afterwards Daniel Berrigan wrote to Walcott that there were brilliant, exciting, moving moments in 'Heavenly Peace', along with speeches he did not like. Berrigan read the Rodman interview and hoped Davidson would send him *Dream on Monkey Mountain*. Berrigan and Philip were trying to get to Hanoi. The message was on a card which included a fragment of a poem by Denise Levertov and a painting by Vo-Dinh; proceeds from the card would go to the Fellowship of Reconciliation. Gil Moses's comments (9 February) on the second draft of 'Heavenly Peace' were the usual criticism about Walcott's scripts. Some scenes were difficult to follow with too many jumps, there was a lack of distinction between the imagined and reality. Why bring in the Arawaks, best to stick to

Vietnamese. What was the point of the Southwell trial? It seems obvious that the interest of Moses and Friedman in the play was political, Walcott's involvement had other sources. He wanted to be part of the American theatre world, but the topic also attracted him because the play was religious and part of a history of poets with strong moral beliefs opposing those in power. Moses worried that, between the poetry of Walcott and Berrigan, the play was abstract, intellectual. It needed to be more down to earth, closer to the horror and ugliness of the war. Moses wanted to change minds; Walcott seemed less convinced that this was possible. Two months later Gil Moses, who no longer got along with Friedman, withdrew from the project.

Lowell had been in New York several times that winter and had spoken during early January at an Ezra Pound memorial at the American Academy of Arts and Letters. After returning to England he wrote (19 February 1973) apologizing for seeing so little of Walcott the previous October in New York. He had read *Another Life* at one sitting and thought it tremendous. It was like a Proustian novel of recollection in which the past, especially youth, is caught and then lost. The best parts were the many descriptions of St Lucia, the recollections, and the autobiography when the central character understood and faced up to life. Some passages were a bit empty and he questioned the diatribes, which he called Poundish. The book reminded him that it had been a decade since he first met Walcott and he felt nostalgic. He imagined Walcott in Port of Spain with Margaret, warm, perhaps in the rain. Lowell looked out the window at grey sheep. He had sent off page proofs for three autobiographical books he had been working on since 1967. Although his technique and temperament differed there were similarities to *Another Life*. What had kept him and Walcott friends was that they both wrote about their life and all lives were really similar.

Rather than being warm on a beach with Margaret, Walcott was in Ohio with James Wright towards the end of February as part of a whirlwind tour of reading at Kenyon, Ohio State, Denison, Ohio Wesleyan, and other colleges and universities of the Poetry Circle of Ohio. The circuit consisted of a dozen colleges and universities, along with some associated institutions. Each paid $125 and expenses for a reading and it was possible to do two readings a day, or about ten a week. Walcott tried to arrange such tours to coincide with the publication of one of his volumes of poetry; *Another Life* was scheduled to be published in late March.

The tour stuck in Walcott's mind and is often alluded to among his private writings when thinking of his increased knowledge of the United States. There was snow everywhere, it turned dark early, life seemed very domestic and hidden, he was cold; he lived in motels and listened to other poets talk about the fear of being 40, middle-aged, and perhaps never making it and being forgotten. The poets talked of the suicides of American poets. It is the subject of Walcott's 'Ohio, Winter (for James Wright)':

> frost glazes the eyelid
> of the windscreen, and every barn or
> farm-light goes lonelier, lonelier.[2]

    While in Ohio Walcott discussed with the West Indian novelist and antho-
logist Ronald Dathorne plans by Heinemann Educational Books to publish
Walcott's *Selected Poems* in the Caribbean Writers series. Besides wanting to make
certain that the book was limited to the educational market, Walcott (16 January)
was anxious about the selection and critical commentary. Walcott met Dathorne's
class and Dathorne agreed that Walcott could help select the poems and would
be shown the introduction and notes in manuscript. The project was to drag on
for years; Walcott, dissatisfied with Dathorne's work, would eventually demand
that another editor take over.

    Walcott then returned to Trinidad where, during March, the Canadian
Broadcasting Company recorded a two-hour version of *In a Fine Castle* for
radio, produced by Peter Donkin; the next month (14–21 April) the Trinidad
Theatre Workshop performed *Franklin, a Tale from the Islands*, directed by Walcott.
Franklin is another one of those Walcott plays which has been produced in
different versions over the decades without finding a satisfactory final form. The
central theme is that people earn their right to 'belong' to a land and culture,
it is not a right bestowed by colour, history, or race. The play was to be taken
on tour to Jamaica and Walcott was hoping that the tour could be extended
to the United States where, once there, Lloyd Richards would arrange for the
Workshop to perform at Waterford.

    John Harrison had moved from the University of Texas to be Co-ordinator of
the American Assembly at the University of Miami, and he invited Walcott there
to lecture. His lecture (27 April) on 'The Caribbean: Culture or Mimicry', for
which Walcott was paid $200, has become one of the principal sources for dis-
cussion of his ideas. It is in part a reply to Naipaul's claim that nothing was ever
created in the West Indies, and to Naipaul's portrayal of the newly independent
nations as social volcanoes capped by ineffectual imitation Europeans. Walcott
claims that it is better not to have a past than be constantly aware of a history of
racial injustice. Walcott wants the social and political to be regarded as a clean
slate without guilt and victims; he views the arts as crafts which first should
be learnt before progressing to self-critical awareness. The new will at first be
unrecognizable because it will be unlike anything that existed previously. It is
necessary to begin with mimicry, the consciousness of mimicry being the start
of the new.[3]

    In New York, at the Chelsea, Walcott met a deadline (30 April) to write about
Chinua Achebe's *Christmas in Biafra and Other Poems* and Keorapetse Kgositsile's
anthology *The Word is Here; Poetry from Modern Africa* for the *New York Times Book*

Review. Walcott criticized the myth of Africa created by imperialism and by black nostalgia, saying that it was disproved by nationalism and the Nigerian civil war. The African writer was a modern individual, not part of a unified tribe or of one Africa. Walcott praised Achebe's prose as clear and serene and weighty, but felt that the verse lacked poetry. He said that it was bad poetic prose, or tough-guy realism, in chopped-up syntax aiming for tension. It lacked tones and variety, the line breaks were wilful, the nouns abstract, there was a lack of sustained or compressed metaphors. There were too many details, too many clichés. The review was not used.

Walcott had now been working on the Berrigan play for about seven months. He was excited by having several important projects going, indeed he felt elated, but so many different people were involved in these productions—producers, composers, choreographers—that his drafts seemed increasingly unfinished. Hands and Bryden wanted him to come to London, but Walcott was avoiding a tiring trip in the middle of so much else, including production details for the forthcoming Workshop tour of Jamaica. The tour in July involved two plays, large sets, complicated timing, and Walcott did not have time to fly to London.

He wrote (8 May) from Jamaica to Bryden of his fear that discussing the details might make him dry up; instead of his having a fixed idea, characters and scenes appeared in his head and remained in a state of chaos. The kind of co-operation needed in theatre threatened his way of working. First he had to get the chaotic but creative material into drafts, only afterwards could he revise and shape. Walcott was offering a view of artistic creation similar to T. S. Eliot's comments about writing poetry; there were two separate phases, an uncontrolled outburst of images, and a rational selecting, editing, and shaping. That Walcott worked in such a way shows why his plays so often have powerful scenes while lacking tight plots, whereas, because his approach to painting is analytical, it lacks the fire of chaos and is too tightly controlled. There was another reason for Walcott to avoid London. He was creating something different from the translation the RSC originally had in mind. The letter continued the next day (9 May) with Walcott asking exactly what the Royal Shakespeare Company wanted, an updated crib, a refreshed Tirso, a restored Old Master, or an irreverent homage such as Picasso's version of Manet's *Déjeuner* (which Walcott at the time thought of as a model for modern art that might also be useful to a Caribbean writer). While staying close to the original structure Walcott was moving towards his own Don Juan, an existentialist who challenges the silence of God. Walcott's Juan is not a hedonist, but someone who having known complete freedom finds it melancholy, sad, like an overdose of pornography.

Walcott flew from Trinidad to New York, where he got in some work on 'Heavenly Peace', on his way to a two-week conference at the Institute of African and Caribbean Writing in English at the University of Missouri, Kansas City (9–23 June). The United States had little interest in Commonwealth literature, but was discovering part of it as black writing. Directed by Robert Farnsworth and the poet David Ray, this was one of the first major American conferences concerning the new English literature. As visiting faculty Walcott was paid an honorarium of $250 along with expenses; in return the Institute asked for the right to videotape his participation and to publish his lecture in *New Letters*, a literary journal that Ray edited.[4]

The conference studied the writings of Achebe and Harris, along with, for three days each, Paule Marshall, Walcott, George Lamming, Kofi Awoonor, and Ezekiel Mphalele. The writers gave lectures, readings, and took part in the discussions of other writers. Chinua Achebe and Wilson Harris shared the first night; Walcott spoke on the second. Walcott's lecture, 'Views on Dialect and Tradition', was reported in the *Kansas City Times*: 'Revolution Rhetoric Clouds Writer's Search for Truth'. Walcott challenged many of the accepted ideas at the Institute which sounded like a Third Worldist, anti-war-in-Vietnam lobby. Walcott said that while each writer must find his own voice and truth, the 'third world' writer was being confused by demands to use revolutionary rhetoric and up-to-date dialect. Writers were caught between fear of losing 'the tribal truth' and wanting universal recognition. Revolutionary writers too often choose to write poetry thinking that it is easy and the rules can be broken; they hope to avoid reason and syntax. Walcott claimed that all writers from colonial and black backgrounds are revolutionary, the act of writing for them is revolutionary. Physical protests pass, but the revolution continues in the supposedly conservative writers who have patience.[5]

Many of the young academics interested in Third World literatures were there and their work appeared in *New Letters*. Noteworthy was Michel Fabre's ' "Adam's Task of Giving Things Their Name": The Poetry of Derek Walcott'. Fabre, from the Sorbonne, was the first professor to teach African-American literature in France. He began his state doctorate at a time when a French dissertation had to be written about a dead author and only one person at a time was allowed to work on the author. A decade or two would pass before another dissertation on the topic would be permitted. It used to be said that approved dissertation topics were passed on from father to son as part of the family inheritance. Fabre had spent a year in the United States, wanted to specialize in American literature, and on his way to see his supervisor read in the newspaper that Richard Wright, who then lived in Paris, had died. Fabre became an international authority on Wright. He was now moving into African-Anglophone literature and would introduce the study of Commonwealth literatures into French universities. This was the first time he had come across Walcott's poetry; his discussion of the ways folk, autobiographical, historical, contemporary, and international elements blend in the poetry and the poet's persona remains one of the best general essays about Walcott and points to such basic characteristics as how the autobiographical becomes the voice of a time, place, and region.[6]

Many of the lectures and writings by African and Caribbean writers were published in the special October 1973 issue of *New Letters*, which included four Walcott poems—'Semper Eaden', 'For Pablo Neruda', 'Rider', and the five-part 'O. S. Moses, the Man and the Myth'. The Audenesque, uncollected 'O. S. Moses, the Man and the Myth' reveals the conflicts between Walcott's hopes of fame and the effect of family responsibilities on his work. As in many of his drawings and writings at this time (an early draft of part of the poem is dated 29 June 1971) there is a serpent and an analogy between plunging into writing and having sex. The pen has become the serpent in the garden leading him to endlessly feed 'two hungry mouths'. After the fall, 'there was nothing left to do but work'.

> ... he knew he must go on
> belching forth journals, poems, critical pieces,
> theatrical designs, film-scripts, mixed media,
> a collapsed thesis,
> in terror of those oval, hungry mouths
> beside his bed.
> Fear shook his house.
> His wife and children cried.
> He whored to recollect his innocence,
> remorseful, but neat-wristed.

The Nobel Prize had already become a long-awaited Walcott desire; here it appears in 'his melancholy Russian phase':

> Ah, the Nobel!
> Just rest it on the mantel Ivan Ivanovitch,
> and sip the old nostalgovitch with me![7]

He then returned to Trinidad. As preparation for its second Jamaican tour, the Trinidad Theatre Workshop performed Walcott's *The Charlatan* at Town Hall, Port of Spain, 29 June–3 July. It was directed by Walcott and extensively revised with new songs; the music was done locally. For the July tour with *Franklin* (11–15 July) and *The Charlatan* (16–21 July) financial backing came from Thompson's Pan-Jamaica Investments. Prime Minister Michael Manley attended the opening night at the Little Theatre. Sets for the Jamaica production were by Richard Montgomery.

1973 was the year of the National Union of Freedom Fighters in Trinidad and the New Jewell Movement in Grenada. The NUFF consisted mostly of students and lecturers at the university, who had murdered some people and were now being hunted and killed by the police. The newspapers were forbidden to publicize the radicals or their fate. There has been little directly written on this period, although some 1973 events are incorporated into V. S. Naipaul's *Guerrillas* and Walcott's later play *The Last Carnival*.

'We Are Still Being Betrayed' in the July *Caribbean Contact* is a long interview in which Walcott claimed that politicians and intellectuals were betraying the Caribbean by using race to gain and hold power. The potential social revolution started by the poor in 1970 had become a Black Panther imitation blacker-than-thou movement with tyrannical possibilities. The West Indies was lucky in being powerless and not guilty of a history of evil. The interview shows that Walcott's vision, perhaps a vision he had always held, had deepened and its articulation become more religious. It had also moved beyond regional issues. He said that the twentieth century was a time of original sin as seen in Auschwitz and Vietnam. Naipaul's pessimism should be directed at mankind not the Caribbean. The West Indies was not corrupted to the same degree as those who had power. West Indians could still make moral judgements without the excuses of expediency and history. Vietnam and Biafra could be seen from the West Indies as clear moral issues, whereas most Americans were tormented by and yet unable to do anything about Vietnam. The conflict in his poem 'A Far Cry from Africa' was about good and evil, not about race. It was about innocent victims on both sides.[8]

In an unpublished manuscript concerning the New Jewell Movement in Grenada, Walcott regarded the main problem of the West Indies as ownership of land; the Caribbean islands remained plantation economies with the land and control of the economy in the hands of a few, usually foreigners or those who lived abroad. None of the parties, ideologies, or governments had tackled the problems of land reform. Instead they saw themselves in nationalist, internationalist, or racial struggles with imperialism, capitalism, or whites. They were not concerned with real peasants, those who worked the land, whose poverty was likely to make them thrifty and conservative; they saw them with romantic notions learned from ideologies. He viewed the revolutionaries of the '70s as Castro wannabees, who rejected the compromises and corruptions of an older generation of postwar nationalist politicians (Gary, Williams, Papa Doc), but, lacking any real economic programme, saw themselves in the romantic imagery of guerrillas, radical freedom fighters, leading Third World peasants. University based, they ignored the labour unions.

Walcott (25 July) wrote at length from Trinidad to Lowell. He was concerned about some reviews of Lowell's recent books and tried to cheer him up. According to Walcott, Lowell upset critics by his treatment of the American past; to Walcott history is a heap of dead facts, ideas, and trivia. Lowell by contrast brings together the whole of past and present, the trivial and the great in his vision and language. He moves between Jonathan Edwards and the present Watergate scandal while remaining large hearted and anguished. Lowell makes all experience immediate. He has chosen not to write in the older forms and harmonies and has opened himself to the clash of contradictions, made himself vulnerable. His greatness is that he does not defend himself, but shows the world his flaws, his pains, and does not pretend to epiphanies or take such postures as simplicity, serenity, or fury. His *Notebooks* can be puzzling, annoying, even dull, but they have power, movement, turbulence. Walcott says that he was often disappointed in the past by great lyric poets who wrote too sweetly and did not reveal what their times really smelled like. That made Walcott give more attention to prose. Then he discovered the modern world in Rimbaud, Pound, Eliot, and Auden. Lowell introduced him to Hardy's poetry with its real experience of life.

Walcott had hesitated over Lowell's revelation of his private pains, but came to see that the courage of such naked revelation purifies. Better to show what you are and feel than biographers embalming you. Lowell's life is filled with loss through the madness and suicide of friends. British poets know they have a small place in a tradition and can become grand old men in minor anthologies. In America it is different, a battle with fate. Walcott concludes that Lowell is too great to settle for some private peace, but he and Margaret love him and those he has loved and blesses him.

The letter expresses Walcott's continuing concern that history be regarded as dead facts and ideas in contrast to the immediacy of life, and that a superior poet is like an oyster creating a pearl by accreting and encrusting past and present. Posturing and personae are rejected, a poet is a martyr who suffers. The concluding, helpless blessing has parallels to Walcott's own poetry. The British reviews of *The Dolphin* were good and Walcott's letter found Lowell (7 August) in a better mood. He was pleased to be told he was too relentless to settle for private joy. After we die it will all come out, a larger part than art can digest. Autobiography is fiction, selective, an invention from what is lived. Life was not agonizing, it was a joy to write. Lowell would be at Harvard next winter.

Over the years Walcott had no suitable place to publish his poetry in Trinidad. *Bim* was Bajan, *Savacou* was Jamaican and associated with West Indians in London. The Trinidadian *Voices* was a tiny magazine even by little magazine standards. The situation changed with *Tapia* and its successor the *Trinidad and Tobago Review*. Progressive political magazines, they also gave serious attention to the arts and carried long review articles by local critics and writers. The first Walcott poem in *Tapia* was 'Commune', December 1972. Six poems that would appear in *Sea Grapes* were first published in *Tapia*. 'Non Serviam' is one of several that use listening to the rain as a means of expressing ideas. The poem is a single unbroken, somewhat Miltonic sentence of eighteen lines, with one semi-colon, and two commas, on the theme of rejecting racial hatred. The title has its ironies recalling the Devil's fall and Stephen Dedalus:

'but no, not even my race
can keep me from what I must write
or the rain from falling.'[9]

While the poetry might claim that Walcott's art was a force of nature, part
of the creation itself, letters continued to go back and forth about the early version of *The Joker of Seville*; who was the busiest, and who would travel where and
when to meet whom. Bryden thought Walcott was turning Juan from someone
without any moral sense to someone who, at the end of the play, was troubled by
a conscience. Walcott (10 September) wanted Terry Hands to come to Trinidad;
he should come in early November by which time Walcott would be into a second draft and the actors would have done a reading and could be left in Hands's
hands. What in London might seen artificial was natural in Trinidad with such
public theatrical forms as the calypso, stick-fighting, and picong, and where
there was communal participation. The ring was a metaphor of the play, an
arena for stick-fighting, cock fights, the bull ring, and for dancing; it included
the audience. Walcott was seeing his play in relation to his part of the world, not
London. Bryden (11 September) wanted to send Hands to Carnival, but Hands
was starting rehearsals of Peter Barnes's *The Bewitched* in mid-February. Bryden
wondered if he could somehow replace Hands with Peter Brook. *Joker* sounded
like the marriage of primitive and classic that Brook wanted, but Brook might
run off with the production and make it his version. Bryden (8 October) later
showed *Joker* to Brook who was thinking of working for the Royal Shakespeare
Company in 1974. Bryden felt that while *Joker* offered little to the leading RSC
actors, Brook's involvement might make further Arts Council grants more likely.

Walcott (24 September) thanked Tom Maschler for the Cape edition of
Another Life, but noted that the epigraph for Book 2 was cut off at the bottom.
As the RSC was thinking of doing *Joker* during the summer or autumn of 1974
could Cape publish it then? Walcott wrote that he was coming to London and
had some plays, especially a film script for *In a Fine Castle*, which he wanted read
especially by television people. He needed to earn money. Maschler, however,
did not want to publish *Joker* before the actual production as it was bound to be
changed.

Davidson (7 August) thought Walcott was still not getting to the heart of
'Heavenly Peace'. On the other hand he had enjoyed *The Charlatan* and although
he could not yet make an offer was interested in it for the 1974 season. Should
Michael Schultz direct it? In what proved an all-too-true question, he asked
whether it would be understood in the United States? On 7 October members
of the Trinidad Theatre Workshop made a demonstration tape of the Seven
Deadly Sins section of 'Heavenly Peace'. Walcott was leaving for New York
where he stayed at the Chelsea writing. As he had now been in New York

several times, once on a per diem from the Mark Taper, without contacting Davidson, sometimes without contacting Friedman, Aschenberg asked him to delay his trip to London. This resulted in a heated flap. Walcott claimed he was working on 'Heavenly Peace' as a Christian, was interested in the holiness of the Berrigan script, not its topicality or possible commercial success. He was an artist and would not be hurried even if on Mark Taper expenses. Davidson (1 November) tried to calm him. Having not heard from Walcott for months he had written in the hope of reopening lines of communication. He had faith in Walcott and his talent, but would like to hear from him once in a while and see him. While the episode throws light on Walcott's interest in the play, he often proved touchy when under pressure and would go ballistic when his motives were questioned.

He left for London on 28 October, returned to New York a week later. In London he saw Bryden, but not Trevor Nunn, at the Aldwych, and Tom Maschler and Alan Ross. He also talked to Jenny Sheridan of the International Famous Agency, London, who was handling his contracts in England. Walcott told her about his many play, film, and television scripts. She thought *Franklin* sounded promising and asked (10 December) for the stage and film versions. Maybe Truffaut would be interested?

The 'Heavenly Peace' project soon began unravelling. After Berrigan's anti-Israel October speech probable investors and some others began dropping out. Walcott seemed unwilling to accept the situation. There are several pages added to the 1973 manuscript of 'Heavenly Peace' which consist of a speech Berrigan made in 1972 to the Jewish community at Cornell about their aid in his release from Danbury prison; this concludes with a joint prayer in which some of the words are translated into Hebrew (added by Friedman). This was possibly added in the hope of bridging the gap that had opened between Berrigan and many Jews.

After returning to Trinidad Walcott (13 November) wrote to Frank MacShane that he had enjoyed teaching five classes at Columbia the previous year. They had also paid well. Although Walcott could understand the anger of black writers, as a West Indian he found their attitude self-defeatingly tragic and the sessions could be lacerating. He wrote that he would do a few more classes in future if they were scheduled close together; otherwise the cost of living in hotels in New York made occasional teaching prohibitive. He sent McShane the Borges piece.

During 14–19 November, Walcott and seven members of the Trinidad Theatre Workshop toured St Croix with a production of Scenes from *Dream on Monkey Mountain* and *The Charlatan* and *Franklin*. The programme included Walcott reading from 'What the Twilight Says' and a 'Preface' to *The Charlatan*, along with songs and scenes from the plays. There was a performance during West Indian Weekend at the College of the Virgin Islands, St Thomas campus. On

21 November, Walcott wrote the second part of a poem about infidelity on the beach in the Virgins, his calm afterwards, the impossibility of remaining faithful when away. The poem concludes by saying, Do not think, take a moment at a time. As so often Walcott takes refuge in art from conflict, the poem will outlast those it is about. The poem seems related to a slightly earlier (26 July 1973) poem about loss of trust. If Walcott could not remain faithful, he could not leave alone his feelings of sin.

Ruth Moore, Vice-President of the Courtyard Players, Frederiksted, St Croix, had tried unsuccessfully to contact Walcott in St Thomas. She wrote on 5 December to say that the Courtyard Players wanted to perform *Ti-Jean* under his direction. Was he interested and what would it cost? The Courtyard Players was a training group that ran workshop sessions during the year. They had recently begun a series of workshops with lecturers from New York University's School of the Arts. Interest in West Indian literature was high, and she and Stephen Bostic, Executive Director of the Virgin Islands Council of the Arts, had previously met Walcott in St Lucia. This was to be the start of a decade-long relationship between Walcott and the Courtyard Players.

With *Another Life* out of the way, Walcott had in May begun writing a prose continuation, a book he intended to call 'American, without America'. For the next decade he was to draft chapters, and make chapter lists. On Sunday, 25 November 1973, Walcott began assembling an incomplete draft of his still unpublished 'Isla Incognita' chapter which shows some of the problems he faced in writing the kind of non-chronological autobiography he wanted.

Written at his favourite beach near Cumana Village the first three pages use the landscape and sea to argue for the need to rediscover the island and the region. All knowledge has been inaccurate and without reference to the eternal nature of the scene. Faced with utter simplicity and desolation, how can revolutionaries complain? As often Walcott is self-consciously the Modernist writer, mocking the readers' desire for variety and movement, and alludes to Pasternak as an excuse to change to a snow-scene. There follows a typed page, previously written at a writers' conference in Ohio where Walcott and other poets talk about early middle age and the suicides of Crane, Berryman, Plath, and other American poets. Alvarez's book had argued that the isolation of modern poetry led American poets towards suicide and Walcott contrasts such a tradition, in which the poet will either become famous or remain unknown, with the traditionless Caribbean where poets are Calypsonians playing in public. Walcott mentions trying to enjoy the bleakness of Ohio as new to him and he contrasts the isolation of the poet with theatre, a community activity.

Pages 5–9 are handwritten and dated Monday, 26 September. Here, as in the November pages, the long cadenced sentences seem familiar in their rhythms until one admits that they bring to mind the narrator of Naipaul's *Mimic Men*, and indeed it soon becomes clear that Walcott is arguing with Naipaul and through him with Froude. Walcott's claim is that any comparison using a foreign point of reference is likely to diminish the local, the local becoming a poor version of a foreign original. History itself, with its demand for order and events, works against valuing and seeing the local correctly. To have a botanist name a specimen makes it part of official history and occults its local name, associations, and use. Walcott sees himself and his 'race' as only now learning to grow from the local soil without concern for European refinements, to make art from an actual apprehension of nature rather than accepting old names. The draft is followed by elaborate notes about how it could be developed and a poem mocking New York intellectuals for anguishing over the 'Triste Tropiques'.

With the American production of 'Heavenly Peace' likely to collapse, Walcott wanted to do the play with the Workshop which in December taped some further sections, but which decided it was too alien for them. On 13 December Walcott wrote to Friedman that they should go ahead without Davidson. The play could be done at a small theatre for a limited run. It was becoming one about pardon not guilt, raising the questions: Can we forgive? Can we forgive humanity and individuals and ourselves? Walcott knew we cannot resolve such questions, but felt art must go there; this was a great spiritual undertaking. While this is Walcott as the unrecognized heir of Southwell and Herbert, the great religious poets, I am uncomfortable with such large gestures. Themes of sin and pardon, fallen man and grace, often appear in his work, and, as in 'Heavenly Peace', are associated with Auschwitz, but they can sound a bit easy. What precisely is being questioned? Running together slavery, imperialism, the attempted extermination of the Jews, the war in Vietnam, and personal sins, loses their specificity, their difference, the reality of what has been done. Walcott at times is too 'protestant' for me, too much concerned with a vague personal sense of guilt, and too ready to grant a pardon which does not require renunciation and restitution.

Walcott and Friedman were in constant communication about 'Heavenly Peace', sending each other rewrites and tapes of the music. Friedman was thinking of including a statement that he disassociated himself from Berrigan's post-Vietnam views. The coalition of the anti-war movement was breaking up. Moses was out, Davidson unlikely to take the play, Friedman was disassociating himself from Berrigan. Davidson (4 January 1974) sent $250 each to Friedman and Walcott as a concluding payment in place of an option. He advised letting things cool before taking the play elsewhere. Aschenberg and Friedman sent 'Heavenly Peace' to Papp, who, after Friedman and three singers had performed the music for him, decided against it. With the New York theatre scene heavily Jewish and pro-Israel, Walcott was heavily investing his time and talent in a non-West Indian theatre project that was unlikely to succeed.

Harper's, not *Vogue*, bought the Borges incident, but it was never published. Giroux (18 December) sent the $300 directly to Walcott instead of crediting it to royalties. Walcott (28 December) told Giroux that the Mark Taper Forum had taken *The Charlatan*. He was giving Hugh Robertson drawings to take to New York for a possible animated film of *Ti-Jean*. Might they be used for a children's book? The Los Angeles office of IFA rejected *In a Fine Castle* as an interesting project that needed much work to make into a screen play.

Walcott was represented in a number of mainstream anthologies during 1973–4, including Philip Larkin's *Oxford Book of Modern Verse* (1973), which Walcott later said was 'One of the most flattering experiences' he had had. Larkin had avoided such fashions as Commonwealth poetry and chose good craftsmen and neglected minor poets.[10]

The main event of 1973 was the publication early in the year of *Another Life*. *Another Life* took seven years, and evolved from a prose continuation of the 1965 'Leaving School' essay involving a year of writing prose about Walcott's family, early life, friends, and first love. These early drafts can be found in two notebooks in the University of West Indies, Mona, library, and are at times brilliant poetic epiphanies, at other times pretentious ramblings, sometimes self-conscious pastiches—interesting facts and episodes, but lacking continuity. Scenes without plot. Then, during 1966, after Harry Simmons died, the prose started to turn into poetry. The resulting manuscript was rejected by Cape, and reached its present form in 1970–1 when the last two of the four parts were heavily influenced by the political situation and Walcott's personal life and mental state at the time. Some of its greatness lies in the complexity resulting from the various times it was written. The remembrance of the past is presented and commented upon by a now well-experienced author at mid-life, actively involved with the world, yet highly changeable, sceptical, disgusted, thankful, and filled with praise, anger, and blessings.

The title *Another Life* recalls Auden's *Another Time*, another book of poetry about growing up and what follows. *Another Life* is not just about the past, it is about the present, especially a Walcott twice married, unfaithful, who drinks too much, leads a theatre company, trusts no one or nothing beyond his ability with words, is in love with painting and the visual world, has found most politicians and intellectuals to be scum, and can constantly speak of the world as without purpose, a 'nothing', while praising and blessing it and those he knows as holy with the same awe and holiness as he praised nature in the poem he wrote at 14. As Father Jesse saw then, Walcott uses the vocabulary of Christianity, especially of Catholicism, for a personal and curious pantheism: curious because it is infused with Methodist guilt and has a New Worldish, almost Emersonian, vision of transcendence in the real, especially in activity, doing, experience, so that life is nothing except what you make of it. Yet there is a God, and all is holy, not just because you see it as such (in the American way), but because of your fear and trembling, anxiety.

A hodge podge? Hybridity? I have come to see it as Walcott's personal vision, a vision which, like much about Walcott, has remained consistent yet has grown, has taken in more and greater contradictions, is difficult to pin down to a linear rationality, and yet has become as rich and full, as much a world-view, a religion with an accompanying philosophy, as that of Wordsworth, T. S. Eliot, Robert Graves, Wallace Stevens, D. H. Lawrence, or other writers of the past two centuries. In his case it is not so much post-Christian as a personal adaptation of the Methodist and Catholic worlds of his youth to the scepticism of Modernism, existentialism, and other movements of our time.

There is the fullness of a nineteenth-century Russian novel about the poem, the large characters, the seeming digressiveness, the willingness to let something be itself as well as symbolic, the continuing presence of the narrator. Walcott's St Lucia could be, and at times is envisaged as, Tolstoy's Russia or Pasternak's. There are the occasional comparisons, Andreuille is Anna, but as later in *Omeros* Walcott's aim is not to equate, which in his view would diminish the Caribbean by saying it is lesser and therefore needs elevation by being compared with Europe. The aim is to treat the experience on its own as marvellous, sublime. If it mimics the literature of Europe it is because he as an artist needs such forms to craft the experience; the new begins in imitation, modelling, mimicry, and while never losing the sins or traces of the past, is new, unique, different. To keep speaking of it in terms of the past is to devalue, to be someone obsessed with roots, origins, and history.

And it is here, in the area of history, the topic raised towards the end of the book, in the sections written during the 1970s, that Walcott speaks as a New World writer, someone taking his place alongside Whitman, Neruda, Wilson Harris, someone answering Brathwaite and the negritudists. He denies history, it is like the sea, the waves, ever changing, dangerous yet nothing, which has brought various peoples to the New World, during which process they have undergone a sea-change, died, and been reborn, without memories. The new history starts here and now, not with ancestral lines traced back over centuries. The poem celebrates his youth, his teens, but also that of a specific time of St Lucian history; history begins here.

If one feels vaguely that T. S. Eliot's *Four Quartets* is as much behind *Another Life* as Wordsworth's *The Prelude*, the nineteenth-century Russian novel, and Pasternak's poetry and memoirs, it is because Eliot's seeing of his American past in British history, especially at Burnt Norton, is being challenged just as much as is Naipaul's claim that a lack of a history of achievement cripples the West Indies. In saying NO, that is not history, such history is bunk, I am history, Walcott is indeed a New World poet, someone perhaps even more needed now for a post-Vietnam, guilt-ridden, politically correct America than its more innocent prophets of the past. The issues of the present, the relations between the races, where to start, what to make of history, was being discussed, argued, and thought and felt through by such Caribbean writers as Naipaul, Harris, and Walcott before post-colonial was ever heard of.

William Plomer informed Cape that *Another Life* was one the most important poems written in his lifetime, and the 'grandest' poem to emerge from the West Indies. The poem is not just about the colonial and Caribbean, but also about the division between a religious view of humanity and the instinctive natural man. Plomer also saw the poem as concerning the need to assert a personal consciousness, to create personal mythologies, to respond to the local landscape.

Another Life was soon recognized as a masterpiece. Although commentary and some good criticism had been published about Walcott's poetry from the 1950s onward, he had mainly attracted the praise of other poets in reviews. The publication of *Another Life* was the impulse for a more sustained, more deeply researched, analysis of what Walcott was doing as a poet. As his critical writings are not systematic or well known, the poetry itself has usually been the necessary introduction to what he is doing. The autobiographical revelations, the offering of a context, the use of literary models, and the method of *Another Life*, influenced criticism which until then had often taken as its main perspective *The Castaway*. Edward Baugh's eighty-five-page *Derek Walcott: Memory as Vision: Another Life* (1978) was the first monograph published on Walcott, and provided, along with a sensitive reading of the long poem, details of his life and St Lucia.

Wordsworth's *The Prelude* is the only other significant verse autobiography in English, but Walcott's poem is more novelistic, more like Joyce's *Portrait of the Artist* or Pasternak's *Safe Conduct* in its impressionistic shifting narrative, epiphanies, and selectivity. Beginning with a memory of Vigie Peninsula, set in amber like an old painting (or a fossil) the poem recalls Walcott's youth, his education, the island's social history, the end of the colonial period, the influences upon him, the destruction of a world he knew with the 1948 Castries fire, his first love, the discovery of painting, his friendships with Harold Simmons and Dunstan St Omer, and recreates the joy of feeling that they were the first to see and paint St Lucia as it is. While, since his teens, Walcott had seen a comparison between Joyce's colonial Ireland and his Catholic St Lucia, Pasternak's poetry, *Safe Conduct*, and *Doctor Zhivago* were other influences. There were the self-conscious dissolves to seemingly unrelated scenes, the way a symbol could be used for different experiences, and such analogies as Walcott's first love to Pasternak's Lara.

Another Life is a symphony of styles, influences, imitations, echoes, colours, recurring themes, reharmonizations. As often in Walcott's writing of the 1960s and 1970s one wonders whether this might be in part influenced by, and a reply to, Naipaul. As in *Miguel Street*, Walcott's poem has a similar double narrative focus as child and as adult, scenes of local life especially as a schoolboy and shortly after graduating school—until now the model for both could be *Portrait of an Artist*—before leaving the island by airplane. Naipaul is both the model and anti-model. Instead of Hat, the father replacement is Simmons. One might contrast the difference between B. Wordsworth, the Pyrotechnicalist, and other Miguel Street fake or non-artists and the commitment to art in *Another Life*. Naipaul had written *A House for Mr Biswas*, the great West Indian novel, a semi-fictional account of his father and also about his youth and schooldays and the difficulties of being a writer in Trinidad. Walcott had replied with a novel in verse about his youth and the joys of learning to be a painter and poet in St Lucia.

Although at first the British reviewers, apart from the poet Elizabeth Jennings, were a bit hesitant in the face of a long narrative poem, *Another Life* was internationally recognized as an important new masterpiece. Kildare Dobbs in the *Toronto Star* said it is of such 'gravity and beauty that it establishes its author as one of the most considerable poets of our generation', the bright star of West Indian writers. *Another Life* is a poetic autobiography, a meditation on the emergence of the artist who has no adequate way to express himself except through metaphor. Like Adam he names all nature. The black boy longs to become white like his grandfather until he comes across lines of poetry that consecrate his blackness. His imagination resounds with the sounds and rhythms of the liturgy, evangelists, abolitionists. He offers us an alphabet of local heroes, he evokes places, sights, sounds, smells. He describes the island in a brownish yellow tinge, the sepia tint of memory.[11]

In the *Times Educational Supplement* Ned Thomas said that *Another Life* is characterized by the passing of time. The poem is vivid with personal consciousness, particular moments, shades of light, and life rather than rhetoric. Walcott has moved on from the isolated lyric to an ability to enhance life, to give it significance, bless it, rather than treat the Caribbean as a story of victimization. He has put St Lucia on the map of literary consciousness the way great novelists of the past gave a reality and immortality to Paris and Moscow, or Dublin. Thomas asked who will do the same for Birmingham and Cardiff?[12]

Much of Walcott's poetry and theatre might be regarded as a substitute for his life as a painter, an imitation of painting in other art forms. Within a decade scholars such as Edward Baugh were writing of 'Painters and Painting in Another Life'. *Another Life* could be seen as an autobiography within an artistic frame, an attempt to unify painting and writing.[13] There was a dissenting voice, worth mentioning for its objections. Alice Walker did not like *Another Life* because it was not a black American poem. 'There is a lot . . . that I do not like and much that I do not understand.' It was too long, too foreign, and too British in style. 'Very little that is recognizably Black West Indian survives.' Too much was said by way of 'names from Greek myths'. Walker found the poem difficult, obscure, and was willing to leave it to Oxford dons. She thought this a colonial poem without the sense of racial difference found even in academic black American poets.[14]

That was not the view of V. S. Naipaul, V. S. Pritchett, and Claire Tomalin, the literary editor of the *New Statesman*, the jury in 1974 for the *New Statesman* Jock Campbell award of £1,000, which went to Walcott for *Another Life*. The award was given every third year and only writers born in Africa or the Caribbean were eligible. The first three winners were Chinua Achebe (1965), Wole Soyinka (1968), and V. S. Naipaul (1971). Bryden had been invited to be a judge for the award, but turned it down because he knew Walcott too well. He did tell Tomalin that Walcott was the best West Indian poet. Tomalin claimed that Walcott's central concern was being a cultural orphan, amnesiac of traditions lost. *Another Life* was the first long narrative from the West Indies, one of the best long poems in English in decades, and sought reconciliation rather than anger. The poem was mostly autobiography of what was then colonial life, was vigorous and varied, there were passages of great beauty, and many literary echoes. Few English children would now be as well read as was the young Walcott.[15]

The year *Another Life* was published Dunstan St Omer was painting many of his now recognized masterpieces in St Lucia, including the mural on the wall behind the church altar at Roseau and the *Prometheus* at the Department of Continuing Education at the Sir Arthur Lewis Community College. Both works reveal how St Omer's transformation of Cubism into his own prismatism had deepened as he moved from abstract patterns towards a monumental figuratism and a consciously black Christian symbolism. His *Prometheus* who will bring wisdom and education is black and inspired by a holy dove. In his own way he made the long journey from imitation of European classics through Modernist art to a contemporary art about and peopled by St Lucians. The differences between Walcott's high-brown Methodism and St Omer's black St Lucian Catholicism remained.

His painting at Roseau, 1,500 square feet, behind the altar at the Church of the Holy Family, was unveiled and blessed at a special mass on Easter Sunday. The mural is one of the great works of Caribbean art. Transforming the general model of Renaissance religious painting into a central statement of contemporary black liberation theology, St Omer filled his mural with scenes from St Lucian life. For the first time local Catholics could come to church and see people like themselves in the religious art and symbolism. The Madonna is black, the face based on an African mask, the child has a face like a South African springbok, as St Omer believed that the most beautiful form in Africa. Instead of white Renaissance angels blowing trumpets there is a local fisherman blowing a counch shell and a local woman chantwell (the lead singer in festivals). The rays from the Christ child are black not white, the trees are banana plants. The mannerist derived group of figures on the left of the mural are clearly black peasants or labourers doing a local dance. One of the figures on the right of the mural is derived from the face of an American athlete, and two local white patrons are included on the right where noble patrons might be in the paintings of the past.

Although the theology is different, this is similar to Walcott's art in that a European form has been imitated and transformed to include St Lucian subject-matter and colour. Over the years St Omer would become controversial. For him Christianity would be useless without a black Christ. He wanted a religion of resurrection not the crucifixion. He would be asked to do murals and decorations for other Catholic churches in St Lucia and even Martinique; he would be asked to 'renew' the decoration of Castries Cathedral before the visit of the Pope, painting a remarkable series of rondells of black religious scenes. His evolving series of paintings of black Madonnas would be discussed as central documents of black Caribbean liberation theory, but some churchgoers would object that such local subject-matter felt irreligious, some older white priests would complain that St Omer's followers were changing Christianity, and St Omer himself would be questioned by Vatican-appointed theologians about the doctrine of his work.

As Derek Walcott became increasingly spoken of with pride in St Lucia, some important members of the Catholic hierarchy would question whether it was appropriate. The battles of Walcott's youth in St Lucia had not ended; they had become intertwined with the assertion of a black theology and had moved behind the scenes as black priests defended St Omer and the Walcotts. Without realizing it Walcott had in *Another Life* written a testament of what was the beginnings of a radical change in St Lucian culture that extended even into the Roman Catholic Church.

18

1974 *The Joker of Seville,* Galt MacDermot

WALCOTT remained in need of money; he had family responsibilities, insurance to pay, the cost of travel abroad, investments in performances of his plays, even expenses for heavily revising his works in proof. He borrowed money from Farrar, Straus and Giroux and from January 1972 to November 1973 had had a debit of $1,225; as of the end of March 1974 Walcott's account with Farrar, Straus and Giroux was still in the red. Largish sums passed through his hands for some plays, but he never struck it big and they were the exception. More common were such payments as $3 for 1974 from Caedmon Records for Walcott's poems on *West Indian Poetry and Poets of the West Indies.* Colonial Life Insurance wrote (7 October) about arrears of $2,350.73 on a mortgage loan of $16,000. Walcott wanted *The Charlatan* contracted as soon as possible so he could obtain a bank advance. Could Aschenberg (9 January 1974) send an official statement confirming that he would be getting an advance from the Mark Taper of $450? Davidson should soon send the ticket and the fee for taping the songs.

When John Figueroa mentioned coming to Trinidad for Carnival, Walcott (17 January 1974) told him to see *Joker* in rehearsal. He had revised a poem, 'To Return to the Trees', which he was going to dedicate to 'Figs' as a lover of Latin. 'To Return to the Trees' would eventually form part of a sequence concluding *Sea Grapes* where Walcott is alone in St Lucia and turns to the natural world as offering wisdom superior to that found in the classics. He had earlier in *The Gulf* dedicated to 'Figs' the powerful, Miltonic 'Nearing Forty'.

Ruth Moore had sent a Trinidad–New York open return ticket for Walcott to come to the Courtyard Players Theatre School on 21 January. He replied that he would be bringing costume designs, music, a revised text of *Ti-Jean*, and that he planned to meet the actors, start casting, and select the orchestra for the March rehearsals. On 26 January Walcott flew from St Croix to New York and returned on 7 February to Trinidad, where he spoke with Wilbert Holder about using his leave to go to St Croix for *Ti-Jean* and to Margaret about going away again for a month and then to Los Angeles for a further five weeks. Walcott wanted a contract from the Courtyard Players and proposed half or $250 on the first day of rehearsals and the rest on the opening night or in the middle of the show. He suggested the same for Holder. They could stay together to share expenses.

The Drama Department, New York University, asked him to submit another play for possible staging; he sent (8 February) 'Heavenly Peace', which by now had been rejected by the American Place Theatre, the Chelsea Theatre, and Papp. Walcott admitted that the subject might be dated and suggested that he work on the play at New York University during rehearsals, but pointed out that someone else would need to direct it as he was going to St Croix in March. He had been working on *Joker* with the Trinidad Theatre Workshop, holding rehearsals and designing costumes. He promised Bryden a final draft mid-May. Walcott left (4 March) with Wilbert Holder for St Croix, where a few weeks later the *St Croix Avis* reported on his directing, 31 March to 5 April, of a local cast for the production of *Ti-Jean*. 'Watching Walcott hone his people to professional sharpness is to see a man who simply will not accept anything but perfection, and the ladies and gentlemen of the company are working their hearts out for him.'[1]

Afterwards Walcott (9 April) went to Miami to see Harrison and then to New York to see Galt MacDermot who lived on Staten Island. Rehearsals for the Mark Taper production of *The Charlatan* were starting. The Mark Taper expected to hire André Tanker to compose the music and wanted him in Los Angeles for the rehearsals and previews (16 April–23 May), but Tanker declined. Walcott urgently needed a musical director and asked Galt MacDermot, who had worked with Papp's hit Broadway musical *Two Gentlemen from Verona* and had written music for the fabulously successful *Hair*. This led to MacDermot writing new music for *The Charlatan* and a long association with Walcott as a collaborator in many musicals. Walcott and MacDermot were both Commonwealth outsiders who got along well. MacDermot had Canadian, South African, and Caribbean connections. In school in Canada he had had a steel band, he had studied music in Africa, and he was related to Tom Redcam, one of the founders of Jamaican literature.

MacDermot led a jazz band, wrote music for films, and his classical music was frequently performed. He was one of those taking the Broadway musical in new directions, and while his music from *Hair* was top of the pops he wanted the musical, and the cinema, to become a new form for developing towards oratorio. He was a serious composer who retained roots in the 'vulgar' that Walcott thought necessary to his own art, and he had the contacts with big money producers that Walcott needed in the United States.

Walcott flew into Los Angeles on Monday, 15 April; the next day was the first rehearsal of *The Charlatan*, directed by Mel Shapiro, which began previews on 11 May, opened on 23 May, and ran for six weeks until 7 July. A central part of the story concerns an ageing white magician who wants to marry off his black daughter (the princess of myth) before he dies. He decides to sprinkle a love potion on a dying artist, but it is sprinkled around town and a Carnival becomes a real saturnalia. The wizard kills and then revives his ex-wife, a socialite. Lou Gossett took the role of The Mighty Cobo. Walcott thought the play miscast and badly misdirected, a likely disaster. He withdrew emotionally, told Margaret to stay home, and did not go to the opening; before the reviews appeared he flew to New York and returned to Trinidad. Farrar, Straus and Giroux planned to publish *The Charlatan* in late 1974; instead *The Charlatan* was never published commercially. There were some terrible reviews, although Henry Goodman in the *Wall Street Journal* thought it lively with good moments. According to Goodman the play used the myth of the conquest of Death by Love. The actors were charming, but the calypso enunciation was hard to understand and Goodman felt excluded. There was too much focus on myth, the play needed to be more explicit, a bit less like aimless revelry and Carnival confusion.[2]

Aschenberg (30 May) wrote a long, heartfelt letter to Walcott. Davidson had told her that Walcott listened to the show a couple of times then would not come to the theatre and did not sit out front for any previews. He had pleaded with Walcott, left messages at his hotel, but Walcott would not return calls. Davidson acknowledged that half the audiences walked out of the first three previews, but claimed it got better; by opening night the audience was enjoying itself and no one left early. If, Aschenberg asked, Walcott thought the production so poor why did he not discuss the problems with Davidson, Shapiro, and MacDermot? Walcott should have telephoned her or the Los Angeles office. He should have attended the opening as IFA Los Angeles people were there to meet him.

She tried to find Walcott at the Chelsea Hotel as she wanted to hear his side of the story. Davidson was bitter and desperate, said the play needed more clarity and shaping. He needed permission from Walcott for him and Shapiro to work on the script or bring in another writer. People told her MacDermot's songs and the physical side of the production were very good. Davidson still felt that the play would have a future outside and after Los Angeles, but nothing could be done if Walcott would not communicate. Aschenberg was distressed as Davidson has been Walcott's friend and sponsor.

Bryden (17 May) was trying to keep alive Walcott's interest in the Royal Shakespeare Company and the company's interest in the *Joker*. Time was passing and he needed material from Walcott to keep interest on the boil. Terry

Hands, who had been thinking about leaving the Royal Shakespeare Company and trying to make a career in Paris, had been away and returned inscrutable. He wanted a complete revision and a script session with Walcott. The play was unlikely to go into production during 1974. They needed a musical score. If Walcott could get the revision to them before July that would allow Hands a month before leaving on holiday and six months for music to be composed. Gordon Davidson had written to Trevor Nunn saying that *The Charlatan* was brilliant and had suggested the Royal Shakespeare Company read the script.

Meanwhile, the Courtyard Players' tour of *Ti-Jean* was a wild success. Ruth Moore (23 May) wrote that there had been twelve performances, seven in Frederiksted, two in Christiansted, one on Tortola, and two on St Thomas. Royalties were being paid to Samuel French. The local PBS station wanted to know what Walcott would charge for a one-time use of *Ti-Jean*; Chase Manhattan Bank might pay, but Moore hoped that Walcott could get National Educational Television to sponsor Walcott on his own for a large-budget full two-hour show. The letter was full of admiration and respect.

Walcott, in Trinidad, wrote to Bryden on 31 May that Tanker was unwilling to do the music for *Joker*, but that Galt MacDermot would and was willing to come to Trinidad. (Friedman had earlier refused.) On the strength of the St Croix *Ti-Jean* the Trinidad Theatre Workshop had been invited to the White Barn Theatre Festival in Connecticut. The invitation had come through Ralph Alswang, Artistic Director of the White Barn avant-garde theatre festival, Westport, Connecticut, who, on a visit to St Croix, had heard enthusiastic reports of *Ti-Jean and His Brothers*. Would the Royal Shakespeare Company allow the Trinidad Theatre Workshop to do five performances of *The Joker* at the White Barn Theatre Festival during the summer? It would not be a commercial production and it would not be reviewed. Hands and Nunn agreed to the performances if it involved MacDermot whom Bryden (12 June) wanted for the Royal Shakespeare Company. Bryden had earlier tried to get MacDermot, and had suggested something indirectly to Fugard, but Walcott and MacDermot would be better. But where was the rewrite? Should Hands come to the White Barn? Hands needed to be nailed down to dates as he was being offered big money to do musicals in the West End, and productions at the Comédie Française and the Vienna Burgtheater, which paid more than his Royal Shakespeare Company salary. 1975 was filling in. The Royal Shakespeare Company had a hit with Tom Stoppard's *Travesties*; this was on top of *Sherlock Holmes*, which was being taken to the United States by Merrick, and there was the Peter Barnes's *The Bewitched*, which was a critical success. Bryden urged Walcott to come on board soon by sending in the revised script before all the dates were taken.

Walcott wrote to MacDermot (20 June) that MacDermot's lawyer should work out details about *Joker* with the Royal Shakespeare Company. Walcott was hoping to stage *Joker* in Port of Spain 1–6 August. Could MacDermot get some songs ready in three weeks? When could he come to Trinidad? Walcott would like the musicians mobile to take part in the action. He wanted to use stickfight chants and would send some. Walcott sent eighteen pages of song lyrics. Some were then backed by 'traditional music'. The songs included 'Sans humanite', 'Little red bird', 'Whatever happen to big-foot Bertha', the stickfight 'Better watch yourself, old man', 'Let resurrection come', 'There is a sower in the sky', Raphael's 'Now whether Juan gone down to hell', and Juan's farewell. These are lovely lyrics; it is a shame they are not better known. Walcott is an excellent songwriter and there is a need for a volume of his songs, accompanied by melodies, from his many published and unpublished plays. It is another side of his work that still needs to be discovered.

As Walcott could not get *The Joker of Seville* ready in time, *Ti-Jean* and *Dream on Monkey Mountain* were taken to the White Barn. Walcott (15 July) wrote to the White Barn that neither play requires many properties. *Ti-Jean* needs a log, strong enough to support an actor, hexagonal with ends flat, covered with jute and painted to look like bark, about four feet long and eighteen inches wide. Staging would be in the round. It might be nice to have a floor cloth painted dark green with a leaf pattern. An old bicycle would be useful. Two amplifiers and microphones were needed for the music. Seats could be on the sides of the stage. *Dream* requires only two L-shaped, free-standing sections about six feet high to represent jail cells and a hut. It might be useful to have six soft drink crates and two three-legged stools. Walcott hoped to have about six wooden African spears made in Connecticut. He wanted the theatre available the morning after they arrived to rehearse straight through until *Ti-Jean*.

The Little Carib Theatre still lacked seating and decent lighting. Walcott (29 July) wrote to the Carnival Development Committee, Port of Spain, to borrow 350 chairs to stage *Dream* 1–6 August, to raise funds for the White Barn Theatre tour. Similar letters were sent on 22 and 30 September 1975 asking for the loan of bleachers for the reopening of *The Joker* at the Little Carib on 15 October for thirteen nights, and on 1 July 1975 for 350 chairs for the Trinidad Theatre Workshop Little Carib production of *The Seagull*. The Trinidad Theatre Workshop not only lacked a theatre, there was no appropriate little theatre with seats! *Dream on Monkey Mountain* at the Little Carib Theatre (1–6 August) was a fifteenth anniversary Trinidad Theatre Workshop production designed and directed by Walcott. On Sunday, 11 August, there was a run-through of *Ti-Jean* before an invited audience at 10 a.m., and this was followed by the Trinidad Workshop tour to the White Barn Festival in Connecticut.

Ti-Jean and His Brothers opened on 14 August. *Dream on Monkey Mountain* started on 21 August for a week. Straus, his friends, and some of the Farrar, Straus and Giroux staff travelled to White Barn to see *Dream*, but there was such a crowd afterwards around the Walcotts that Straus and his wife left. Walcott had been turned down for a 1974 Guggenheim fellowship, but Straus (28 August) sent the Guggenheim Foundation's forms to Walcott and suggested he try again.

Meanwhile, on 15 August, Vicki Little, of Hart House, University of Toronto, wrote to invite Walcott to read at a Poetry Festival to be held the week of 27 October. Besides sessions at which three poets would read there would be discussion groups. Could Walcott come for two or more days, read at one session and participate in one seminar? His expenses would be covered plus a modest fee. She sent the invitation to Farrar, Straus and Giroux along with a sample of what Monday, 28 October, might look like. It included Margaret Atwood, James Merrill, and Robert Lowell, and sounded very ambitious and crowded. Walcott did not reply until 9 September when he accepted by saying that nothing less than $200 was acceptable, but maybe even that was negotiable.

Frank MacShane (27 July) wrote from London where he was on sabbatical. He needed to fill a course at Columbia and hoped to broaden the students' ideas by using Walcott, Chinua Achebe, and Ezekiel Mphalele, and wanted Walcott to teach for a month or so in the autumn. Walcott would get paid $150 a class, but MacShane would try to get him other work. There had been a long postal strike in Trinidad and Walcott on 9 September received the letter inviting him to teach that semester. He could not leave until mid-October; $150 per class was not enough to pay for a hotel or apartment, so all his classes would need be within two or three weeks. He hoped he was not too late, perhaps other readings could be arranged?

'Heavenly Peace' had found no resting place; no New York commercial theatre was interested, but Gary William Friedman hoped it could be produced non-commercially by URGENT (Universal Relevance Group-Enterprise in a National Theatre), an off-off-Broadway group that had been in existence for a year and a half. Their productions ran for twelve workshop performances before about eighty people a show and no one was paid, but the plays were reviewed by first-string critics. Aschenberg thought this could be a showcase which if favourably reviewed might be moved elsewhere. Berrigan would go along with what Friedman wanted and Friedman wanted this as the situation otherwise was hopeless.

Walcott missed Aschenberg at the White Barn, and wrote (26 September) to tell her that MacDermot's score for *Joker* was excellent. He would be teaching at Columbia University around 21 October for two and a half weeks. Would this coincide with the production of 'Heavenly Peace'? Walcott had almost given up on the play. He would like to revise parts, but would not without a confirmed production. He asked to be told soon as it could affect his rehearsals for *Joker*. Even if no one got paid could URGENT afford subsistence as otherwise he could not spend much time in New York?

Walcott had received the tape of songs for *Joker* and wrote to MacDermot (26 September) that the music healed all the pain of Los Angeles. *The Joker* was moving away from what the Royal Shakespeare Company intended; that could not be helped, it must take its own direction. It was expensive to do *Joker*, but he would do the best he could to get a good cast and to make the play part of the Trinidad Theatre Workshop repertory along with *Dream* and *Ti-Jean*. There had been plans for MacDermot to come in mid-October. Walcott warned him that there would be little to see of the play, as there would be no rehearsals while he was away and as amateurs they only rehearsed at night. There could, however, be some early publicity for the show and studio recordings of the songs for *Joker* and *Charlatan*. He wanted to have the play put on by early December. MacDermot could help him think about the staging which would save time at rehearsal.

Howard Rosenstone of the William Morris Agency wrote (2 October) to Bridget Aschenberg to say that MacDermot was working on the understanding that he would have one-third ownership in 'the property' and that there would be an even fifty–fifty split in regards to all publishing. Aschenberg (21 November) wanted to know if this had Walcott's approval. The Royal Shakespeare Company rights expired a year from delivery of the first draft, which meant as of 31 December 1974. As the *Joker* was now a full musical as the result of Galt MacDermot's involvement, the contract with the Royal Shakespeare Company needed renegotiation.

The link continued to develop between Walcott and the Courtyard Players. Walcott along with some Workshop members were hired to give a theatre clinic, which they intended to use as the basis for a local production of *Dream on Monkey Mountain*. The tutors would invest their fees and some accommodation expenses in the production. Walcott wrote to Ruth Moore that he, Stanley Marshall, Astor Johnson, and Noble Douglas would arrive in St Croix on Sunday, 29 September. That afternoon they would have auditions for *Dream on Monkey Mountain*, especially the dancers. They would also need two singers. They would advertise two nights and reserve for a third. The first week they would like invitations to stay with people, but after that they could move in together. Margaret would like to come for three to four days. Could he accept Moore's invitation for the family to stay with them? They could use the flat downstairs and shop and cook for themselves. He needed to earn money on *Dream*. Could something be done to avoid the terrible problems with customs and immigration? They should arrange for *Joker* to be performed in St Croix on the way to Jamaica during 1975.

Walcott (16 September) wrote again to Ruth Moore. He had to go to Barbados now for a few days, instead of, as planned, on the way to St Croix. He was thinking of doing *Lysistrata* as there were so many women at the clinic. *Lysistrata* could be developed through improvisations, was fun, and could become part of the Court repertory. After Walcott reached St Croix on 29 September other tutors and actors arrived over the next two weeks. Under a grant from the Virgin Islands Council on the Arts, for nineteen days they conducted a theatre clinic for the Courtyard Players before the 12–14 October production of *Dream*.[3]

Walcott read at the Public Library, Port of Spain, on 17 October 'supported by dramatisations of his plays'. MacDermot came to Port of Spain and on 8 November participated in 'Songs from *Ti-Jean and his Brothers, The Charlatan*, and *The Joker of Seville*, along with the drummer Andrew Beddeau. This was a Trinidad Theatre Workshop production at the Public Library, as part of the Adult Education Programme.

Although Terry Hands (13 December) had seen MacDermot in New York and thought they were on the same wavelength, Bryden (26 November) wrote a long letter to Walcott in which one can see the Royal Shakespeare Company production of *The Joker* becoming less likely. Hands's flight would arrive in Port of Spain at 7.45 p.m. on Friday, 6 December. He hoped to see *Joker* on Saturday night, talk to Walcott and MacDermot on Sunday and during the day on Monday, then return to London on Monday night. Hands had been stuck with directing all four of Shakespeare's Henry plays and was in the middle of casting the entire Stratford season for the coming year. This caused problems scheduling *Joker*. Without Hands it might not be produced. Other problems included a financial crisis at the Royal Shakespeare Company in the midst of a national financial crisis with little chance of increased subsidies. Hands wanted to do *Joker* after the four Henry plays which meant aiming at Christmas 1975 or spring 1976 for the opening. It had taken Bryden a couple of weeks to get money for Hands to fly to Trinidad and for the fare for MacDermot to fly from New York to England. Even at that the Royal Shakespeare Company would only pay half the money, the rest came from an interested producer.

The Joker of Seville opened on 28 November and ran to 8 December at the Little Carib Theatre. Walcott directed and the music was supervised by Galt MacDermot. This was another fifteenth anniversary production of the Workshop. At 10.45 a.m. on Sunday, 8 December, there was a 'Parang Performance' with breakfast of 'sharkbake' (shark in baked rolls) and beer, introductory songs, bleacher seating, and audience involvement. Hands was impressed, this was real theatre with the kind of community participation that everyone wanted. That was the trouble. It was no longer a Brechtian study in class for London audiences. The Royal Shakespeare Company did not have black actors, an audience interested in the relationship of the Old to the New World, fresh green coconuts to drink, or 'sharkbake' to sell for breakfast. It was unlikely there would be sufficient London audience to sustain such a West Indian musical. *The Joker of Seville* would be revived by the Trinidad Theatre Workshop during 1975, have the longest run of any play in Trinidad at that time, and be Walcott's first popular success in Port of Spain, but it had stopped being a Royal Shakespeare Company project, although it would still take some time before that was clear. Nor was it clear when, during the first run, Walcott started courting Norline Metivier, one of the dancers, that it would eventually end his second marriage and contribute to a major change in his life.

Joker tries to bridge the gap between high and popular culture. Walcott regarded the American musical with its use of dance, music, and lyrics as a form of total theatre and a way to reach larger audiences, while offering a play that was highly stylized, anti-naturalistic, like Oriental theatre, like Brecht. From an artist's standpoint the musical is an interesting form to master, a way to avoid the static quality of serious, especially poetic, theatre. To get away from long poetic speeches, tell story through action, dance, and song, Walcott felt that words must be supported by gestures. What is lost by the ear can be picked up by the eye through body movement, mime, and dance.

T. S. Eliot had tried to transform the well-made, West End, upper-class social comedy into serious verse drama. Eliot's later plays had philosophical, religious, and mythic content, as well as the psychological and social. Walcott was trying a similar transformation of the Broadway musical into a vehicle for serious drama while West Indianizing it. Tirso de Molina's early seventeenth-century play was changed by Walcott into something very different, having the opposite meaning. The basic concepts of honour and vengeance in the Spanish play refer to family honour, one's name, sexual honour, and a blood code of revenge. *Joker*, like *Ti-Jean*, concerns problems of free will, choice, good, and evil. Walcott's Don Juan can be seen as being like Shakespeare's Richard III, an amusing villain who beats all the self-pitying goodies, but he is also a rebel, an Existentialist, a liberator, another version of Walcott.

Walcott had been learning from MacDermot about the musical as a form; he should explain less and let the songs carry more of the significance. The first production ended with 'Sans Humanité', a traditional Trinidadian song. That is the aggressive, unsentimental, realistic side of life. In the second run Walcott concluded the play with 'Little Red Bird', which shows how rebellion should lead to inner freedom. Each song is different; they range from calypsos to the operatic. The marvellous 'O Brave Fat lady' is a fourteen-line sonnet in iambics. The play shows Walcott's awareness of Freudian, Marxist, and other interpretations of the Don Juan legend, but such motifs add possible complexities rather than being an interpretation. *Joker* often seems self-referential. Rafael, like Walcott, had led a theatre group for fifteen years, and there is a play within the play. *Joker* is about acting, theatre, disguise, role playing. Unlike previous Walcott plays there are not many long speeches, and the speeches are different in manner according to character and situation.

Apart from costumes *Joker* does not require much in the way of scenery, props, or equipment. The set itself is minimalist, a theatre of poverty, and the text contains much visual description. It can be difficult to know what is happening in the plot without paying attention to what we are told we are seeing. There is much mime, use of freezes, spectacle, song and dance, and costumes. The mode is non-naturalistic, Walcott's own version of a Brechtian epic theatre. For the first production Walcott designed period costumes, but during 1975 Richard Montgomery redesigned the set and costumes. There are many images of clothing, capes, disguise, and impersonation, because society is itself wrapped in falsehood. Don Juan introduces the Carnivalesque, he brings the liberation of disorder, by taking on roles and playing at being part of the hierarchy. If others cheat by playing roles, why not Don Juan?

In *Joker* notions of honour and revenge easily are seen as analogous to the former slave's relationship to the whites. Is life to be driven by hatred and revenge for former crimes? Walcott does not even need to make the analogy, it is felt because part of an ongoing discourse in which Walcott has himself had his share. Many episodes, themes, and images in the play take on such a metaphoric or analogical characteristic. The theme of sexual freedom is universal or existential, but in the West Indies at the time was seen in terms of a challenge to tyrannical governments in the region. Some governments were pro-Cuban, some pro-American, some were black nationalist, others were not, but many were tyrannical, jailed and killed their opponents, and prevented free speech. In such a context *Joker* was interpreted as a cry for individual liberty, for personal freedom, against the repressive state.

This is a play in which events happen rapidly. Don Juan is given no time for reflection; he challenges God, property, restrictions, traditions, but is given no inner life, no metaphysical crisis, no examination of conscience. This is non-bourgeois art, Brechtian in its objectivity, externality, lack of interest in psychology. It has a purposely unfinished, disorganized, Carnivalesque feel. Its unity is not obvious as Walcott finds popular and folk theatre elements in the Don Juan legend. There are many symbols and adaptations of symbols as European materials become Caribbean. The sword fight becomes a Trinidadian stick fight; a shipwreck stands for the Middle Passage; the seduction of Tisbea shows the Old World possessing and corrupting the New World; Don Juan is the arch rebel, human libido and desire challenging limits and God, but he might be seen as the West Indian male, macho, dangerous, cunning, enjoying the playing of roles, unattached to society, irresponsible, and ironic. The play consists of ironies, jokes, paradoxes, comedy, farce. Freedom itself is illogical as there is always an absurd distance between desires and limitations. Don Juan's tricks bring out the worst of those he tricks; the comedy is West Indian reductive humour, mocking, verbal, extravagant, in which elaborate metaphors are used to mock, bring down, rather than praise. The play both celebrates and mocks death. Death is always present, but treated casually. People die for silly ideas, fight battles they cannot win. Don Juan, like a tired prankster or old whoremaster, is bored with life which is repetition without purpose, yet the play shows people reborn through experience, art, and legend.

The Tisbea New World section is in prose because prose is rational, Old World rationality being brought to the New World; Tisbea and Aminta fall, or are seduced, because their heads are filled with Old World ideas and ambitions. The New World and the peasant are no different from the people at court.

Walcott was not interested in European moralized concern with the Don Juan legend. What interests him is the West Indian exuberance in performance, the vulgarity, the popular theatrical elements. His Don Juan is less concerned with lust than how to get around a problem, how to get what is denied him. He desires what is forbidden.

The text has many images of sex, nature, hunting, bull fighting, spider and web. Life is driven, instinctual, intellectually absurd. The basic pattern is Paradise, garden of Eden, serpent, snake, fall. Some themes are Don Juan's rebellion against his class, Don Juan as phallus, Don Juan as driven by a never satisfied need for love, Don Juan as rebel against God, Don Juan as the only truly religious person who is angered by the silence of God and wants attention if only through damnation. There is a fall from innocence into knowledge (and freedom—the fortunate fall), corruption of the New World by the Old, corruption by pride, ambition, ownership. Don Juan is seeking, what he does not know. Sex is as close to a Holy Grail as he gets, and he becomes bored with it. You challenge death by living fully, freely, yet life is absurd, pointless.

For some viewers or readers there is the problem that freedom is portrayed in terms of a male seducing a woman, but many women see Isabella as a feminist given the choice between feeling violated or free. She is the one in the play who most fully develops, and gains control of her life. Like much of Walcott's work *Joker* is politically liberal; individual freedom is what counts. Repression is bad. It is clear from West Indian reviews on several of the islands that the *Joker* was seen as the voice of the people against oppression.[4]

Time is passing, a full life is a challenge to death, but Don Juan is too proud to go beyond rebellion and surrender himself to become creative. To love he would need humility, love of others. Once more a Walcott work seems to have its vision and themes in his awareness of his own personality. There is an under-lying sadness that there is no God or that God is distant and unknowable. Better to be damned than free in a meaningless world.

Don Juan has contempt for the peasants who create an imitation ruling high culture. Walcott wants free disorder, not just a reversal of power relations. Don Juan liberates others from the social order by his violation of it, but he destroys those who do not use their freedom. He himself, however, is destroyed by an inability to love, to care for, and to give to others. His freedom is negative, rebellion, rather than creative. While asserting an existentialist freedom he does not know what to do with it and finds life empty.

19

1975–1976 *O Babylon!, Sea Grapes,* Resignation

THE success of *Joker* pushed aside other projects, including an early version of the play *The Isle is Full of Noises* which Walcott wrote and planned to produce during 1975. *Joker* was revived in Port of Spain (13–23 March), taken to San Fernando (2 April), performed in St Lucia (7–13 April), reopened in Port of Spain (15–27 April), and taken to Jamaica (22 November–6 December). Negotiations continued with the Royal Shakespeare Company. There was a fruitless trip to London that further unsettled Walcott about the Royal Shakespeare Company's intentions. He kept revising the play, which became leaner although MacDermot added new songs. Walcott's original period costumes for *Joker* were replaced by Richard Montgomery's complex minimalist costumes that maximized textures and historical associations and showed that cultural traffic was not one way. The voyages of discovery were influencing European fashions. How the Elizabethan ruff was itself influenced by the New World, especially by botanical specimens, is suggested by a collar of banana leaves, the plumed helmet by a pineapple.

Walcott (29 January) failed to keep his appointment with John Compton, Premier of St Lucia, as he was tied up in Port of Spain, making arrangements for the LP album of *The Joker of Seville*. Two weeks later Compton welcomed the idea of bringing *Joker* and the Trinidad Theatre Workshop to St Lucia and Walcott was thinking of using the play as a basis of creating a St Lucian National Theatre on the Morne overlooking Castries. He asked Compton to speak at the opening about the need for a theatre in St Lucia. He told Compton that for *Joker* they would need a raised open stage, bleachers around it, at least four poles for lighting, some way to separate the audience from the musicians. There would need to be a local committee. It is difficult to imagine another dramatist discussing such details with the head of a government, but Walcott knew many of the leading West Indian politicians who were now heads of government. His relationship, although often strained, was probably closer to them than Shakespeare's had been with Queen Elizabeth or James I. While Walcott's tours often had such requirements if the production was to get off the ground where there was no theatre or management, his tours of St Lucia were always charged with emotional homecoming. He hoped that St Lucia would build a national theatre to which he could return, another unrealized dream.

Two weeks later (14–15 February) there was a multimedia event at the Little Carib Theatre with songs from *Joker*, dancing, Shango drumming, singing by Beddeau, and projections and poems by LeRoy Clarke, an excellent Trinidadian artist. There was also a party at the Little Carib for the release of the LP of music from *The Joker of Seville* on 8 March. This was the first LP record to be made of a Trinidad musical play; cassettes of it can still be purchased.

Hands told Bryden (21 February) that he still wanted to do *Joker*, but he could not do it Trinidad style with coconuts for sale at the door and children hanging over the fence. The idea now was for *Joker* to open at the Aldwych Theatre in October with rehearsals beginning mid-September. As Hands had to work with his designer on *Joker* during intervals at Stratford, it would be best if Walcott came to England for May. Bryden asked if Walcott could come to England both in May and October? As the Royal Shakespeare Company would not pay for two round trips, could Walcott come in May and stay on until the opening? The Royal Shakespeare Company would support him in May while working on the script with Hands. He could stay with the Brydens except for some weeks in the summer and could stay in London when Hands was in Stratford. Could he get spending money from Cape, the Trinidad government, or a Guggenheim fellowship? Perhaps with a Guggenheim or British Council grant he could bring Margaret and the family? Bryden wanted badly to have Walcott come to England and wanted to save a production that increasingly seemed unlikely to fly. Walcott could not spare the time and *Joker* took on a life of its own with the addition of MacDermot as composer, the Trinidad Theatre Workshop production, and Walcott's increased contact with American theatre producers. Walcott was never someone who would live for six months on spare sofas and in extra rooms to get a play into production. He had too many irons in the fire, a family to support. Bryden, working with a subsidized theatre company, had little idea how difficult it would be to get those grants or a publisher to support Walcott for months in England.

On 2 April there was a performance of *The Joker of Seville* at Naparima Bowl, San Fernando, and on 3 April Walcott flew to St Lucia. Two days later the Trinidad Theatre Workshop arrived and on Sunday, 6 April, began rehearsals. *The Joker of Seville* was performed 7–12 April not on the Morne but in Castries at Geest's Old

Banana Shed, with an extra performance on 13 April at Vieux Fort. The tour, like other performances of *Joker*, played to sell-out crowds and received great reviews, but with a cast of thirty the Workshop was not earning a profit on its biggest hit.

Royal Shakespeare Company rehearsals were now to begin on 8 September with an opening at the Aldwych planned for 20 October 1975. The Royal Shakespeare Company agreed to bring Walcott and MacDermot to England for two weeks in May. A West End manager was helping to capitalize the show in the hope of taking it to the West End. In late May Walcott was in London to work on *Joker*; he stayed with the Brydens, went for drives in the countryside, to the theatre in Stratford-upon-Avon and London, saw Maschler at Cape, and told him about his new manuscript of poems, *Sea Grapes*. The reader of *The Joker of Seville* for Cape thought it full of life, a treat, and great fun, recommended it, but wondered whether it would sell. Trevor Nunn, however, did not make time to see Walcott. Terry Hands was so knocked out by his work on the Henry epic that the discussions were not as useful as they might have been. Only Bryden appeared to care.

In contrast to the problems with the Royal Shakespeare Company several of Walcott's plays were being produced by amateur and small companies. *Malcochon* had been performed at the Commonwealth Institute, with permission from the Extra-Mural Department, University of the West Indies. There were productions of *Dream on Monkey Mountain* in New Orleans, Detroit, and Nashville during 1974 and an amateur production of *Ti-Jean* in Barbados during 1975.

MacDermot had found a film director possibly interested in *The Charlatan*. During March Walcott had listened to the tape of the Los Angeles production and made notes about how to develop it into a film script. He thought the Carnival setting would provide many good visuals and hoped the Workshop actors could be used in the film. He would go ahead with a step-by-step treatment of *The Charlatan*. This proved another dead end. There is a 1975 typescript of a musical film version of *Ti-Jean* with songs by Tanker and a possible cast list. There is also an animated film screenplay of ninety pages with music by Tanker. Two decades later Walcott would still be trying to make a film of *Ti-Jean*.

Edward Baugh had asked Walcott about the genesis of *Another Life*; during June Walcott wrote explaining that *Another Life* began when Ross asked him to write 'Leaving School' which grew and grew and suddenly became a poem. Was the University of the West Indies, Jamaica, interested in buying the *Another Life* manuscript and materials? Walcott wrote that he would like a letter saying the manuscript was sold and that the university would pay for it so he could get an overdraft from his bank manager. After some negotiations Baugh (16 June) replied that Walcott should send the librarian a bill for JA $5,000 itemizing the material included, but especially the valuable two handwritten exercise books, corrected proof copies, and the typed ledger notebook. The material should be brought to Jamaica rather than mailed.

The material was collated by John Figueroa (who was interviewing Walcott for a possible book on his poetry) and Walcott's secretary. Sandra Pouchet Paquet brought it to Jamaica on 8 July. There were two handwritten note-books, the first numbered 1–75, the second numbered 76–125; eleven unnumbered pages, and page proofs, manuscript, galley, fourteen pages of typescript, correc-tions, but no ledger with drafts containing a complete typescript of the poem with emendations made in 1970. Baugh (11 July) asked what had happened? Walcott should submit a bill for $4,000 and say he would send the ledger and a further bill later, otherwise the money would not come soon. Walcott said he would look for the missing ledger. As a writer trying to make a decent living he needed the money rapidly and not after a long delay; he submitted a reduced bill. He was paid TT $9,600 on 13 August, the equivalent of JA $4,000.

The Workshop was active 10–19 July with a surprising production of Chekhov's *The Seagull*. In an unpublished poem Walcott sees the play as being about him-self with Norline as the Seagull! The production was controversial because the majority of the cast were white members of the Workshop while the play was a European naturalistic classic, the kind of theatre the Workshop was assumed to be against. Walcott defended the production by claiming that Chekhov was one of the world's greatest dramatists, who understood the unpredictability of human nature, its longings, the comedy and poetry of not knowing oneself. The production was also part of a shift that soon became noticeable in Walcott's theatre towards more realistic plays, in prose, with an interest in the psychology of characters, and the use of smaller casts.

David Jones, Artistic Director of the Royal Shakespeare Company, Aldwych, cabled (1 August) MacDermott that the company no longer had sufficient gov-ernment subsidies to produce *Joker* until the next financial year; he proposed April 1976 as an opening date. Trevor Nunn also telegraphed that rehearsals had been postponed. It had now been four years since Walcott was approached about writing a translation of Tirso's play. Aschenberg replied that Walcott and MacDermot would not wait until April and wanted the rights returned. MacDermot talked to Papp and Aschenberg contacted others who might be interested. MacDermot hoped to mend bridges between Davidson and Walcott, but, as Walcott had hung up the phone on Davidson a year earlier, he felt the first move should be by Walcott. As it was going to be difficult to do a musical with a cast of thirty, their best hope was for someone subsidized like Papp.

Walcott tried to put the best face possible on the situation. He told Ralph Thompson (8 August) that he had withdrawn *Joker* because of American pos-sibilities. Thompson should put money into the show as it was a money maker. He now wanted Pan-Jamaican to invite the thirty-member cast to Jamaica for two weeks November–December. Thompson had earlier said yes, but Walcott needed to plan for the year. He asked Ruth Moore (8 August) would she like to have *Joker* on its way to Jamaica, in November? Passages would be paid by the Jamaican sponsors.

The play legally belonged to the Royal Shakespeare Company. Before there could be an American production Walcott needed a settlement from the Royal Shakespeare Company. He felt Bryden had falsely raised his hopes; in a long letter (15 August, possibly begun earlier) he said *Joker* was Bryden's creation; if not for Bryden he would have withdrawn earlier as all he had earned from it for a couple of years was under $2,000. The Royal Shakespeare Company should either say when the play was to be done, or make a settlement. Walcott could not keep dates open in the hope of a Royal Shakespeare Company production. He had written the play because of Bryden and Bryden's faith in him, but Walcott doubted that the Royal Shakespeare Company could do the play because of its style, cast, and the music. As Bryden left the Royal Shakespeare Company at the end of the year for a position at the University of Toronto, the friendship became frayed and was never to be the same again.

MacDermot told Walcott that Papp had listened to the music for *Joker* and might have a reading in September. Walcott wrote to Papp (19 August) complaining that the Royal Shakespeare Company would never produce *Joker*. Would Papp take over from the Royal Shakespeare Company? Would he buy the option and produce it? Walcott rather outrageously claimed that with MacDermot's music it had become a New World black show for the Don Juans in Spanish Harlem. Gil Moses could be the director. Could Papp bring Walcott to New York for the reading? The reading did not take place until 1977. Walcott also wrote to Brigid Aschenberg on 19 August that with a cast of thirty *Joker* appeared expensive, but that six or seven were musicians, and if Papp did it in the round in one of his theatres he would need no decor. Walcott sent the script for *Joker* to Davidson. He also asked Aschenberg whether Carol Dawes and the National Festival Theatre of Jamaica had obtained permission from Samuel French to do *Dream* at the Ward Theatre 16–31 August.

Walcott (19 August) replied to 'Dear Figs', who was then a professor in Puerto Rico, giving him permission forever to use whatever he needed from Walcott's work for his own writing about Walcott. *The Seagull* lost money, but Walcott felt they did it well. He had learned much about play-writing from directing it and the cast had learned much. Figueroa had been trying to arrange Puerto Rico as part of the forthcoming Trinidad Theatre Workshop tour. Pan-Jamaica agreed to pay the Trinidad Theatre Workshop's expenses to and from Jamaica for a three-week tour of *Joker* with thirty people including musicians. The problem was where to produce the play as there was much violence in Kingston; the Ward Theatre had no parking facilities and was unsafe. Walcott wondered about Pan-Jamaica underwriting two nights each in Puerto Rico (at a suggested fee of $2,000 a night), in St Croix, and in Barbados before Jamaica. He decided to write suggesting this to Thompson; he was trying to avoid the expense of overseas calls. Walcott asked Ruth Moore (19 August) about St Croix. The Trinidad Theatre Workshop would pay for everything, accommodation and the theatre. They could come for two days and give two performances. Thompson said they could keep what they earned.

MacDermot or his lawyers did not trust the Royal Shakespeare Company; what had begun in friendship and trust had become a legal wrangle. The Royal Shakespeare Company planned a season at the Brooklyn Academy (BAM) in May–June and thought about opening with *Joker* as an American co-production, but this meant a further delay. Two months after David Brierley sent a final version of a revised draft contract MacDermot's lawyers wanted more changes.

There were other squabbles. The difficulties of presenting a play in Port of Spain and the special problems at the Little Carib continued over the decades. Walcott wrote (1 September) crossly to the Little Carib complaining about a letter he had received in reply to a bill the Trinidad Theatre Workshop had presented. He had been told over the telephone that the cost of the Trinidad Theatre Workshop fixing up the Little Carib would be reimbursed or deducted from the rent. The Trinidad Theatre Workshop had made improvements which would help the theatre and pay for themselves. The Trinidad Theatre Workshop was trying to make a theatre that could be used. They were its largest user. Walcott was willing to discuss the bill, but felt insulted by the tone, with its implications that the bill was inflated. The Workshop had improved the theatre, they did not rent things and take them out. Walcott mentioned that the Little Carib lacked seating, it was roach-infested, had no security, the roof leaked, it had never been cleaned under the stage, the floor boards splintered, mirrors for the actors were needed, the lighting was useless and powerless, the building needed painting inside and out.

By the early 1970s the works of Walcott and V. S. Naipaul were becoming known to those following the new Commonwealth Literature; Twayne the publishers contracted books about them as part of a series of introductions to World Authors. Robert Hamner, an American who was commissioned to write the Walcott volume, first met Walcott during September 1975. Appointed a Fulbright Professor to Guyana, Hamner stopped off in Trinidad, looked up Walcott in the telephone directory, and was soon attending rehearsals of *The Joker of Seville* at the Little Carib Theatre. Hamner's *Derek Walcott* (1980) was the first survey of his life and work; for a decade it remained the basic source of information. Hamner was to publish various articles, an interview, bibliographical updates, and a collection of republished articles; along with Baugh and Goldstraw he put in place the foundations for scholarship and criticism of Walcott.

Ralph Thompson, as Group Managing Director, Pan-Jamaican Investment Trust, set out terms on 31 September for the tour. Economy fares and hotel accommodation (double occupancy) and three meals a day for thirty persons would be paid. Thompson would be responsible for the publicity. He was concerned about punctuality and laid out a schedule for transportation to and from the Guest House. Thompson enclosed a feasibility study based on 70 per cent occupancy of which 20 per cent were at student prices, bringing in a revenue of $14,000 Jamaican dollars. Transportation, hotel, and other costs would be $17,000 leaving a deficit of $3,000. The salaries of the director and actors for the period would be $2,000. For the tour to keep within the estimated cost, Thompson asked BWIA for ten complimentary return seats. After *Joker*'s run in Port of Spain, 15–27 October, the Trinidad Theatre Workshop, 22 November– 6 December, gave seventeen performances at the Creative Arts Centre at the University of the West Indies, Jamaica. It was a great success.

Joker has an important place in Walcott's theatre beyond the great quality of the play itself. Until then many of his plays were folk plays based on scripts he had started in St Lucia and Jamaica and had usually taken a decade of revision to find a form. The commission by the Royal Shakespeare Company to translate a European classic meant a new start, a new kind of subject and story, even a new form. Walcott transposed the story to bring in the New World, made it a study in freedom, and he made full use of the possibilities of the American musical as a form of serious theatre, an experiment already underway in revisions of *The Charlatan* with MacDermot.

After *Another Life* Walcott wanted to write short, compressed poems. Four poems, 'The Little Nations', 'Martial Law', 'Interior', and 'Natural History', had been accepted for publication in *Cooperation Canada* by the Canadian International Development Agency (20 March 1974) which paid £50 each. The four poems appeared in the March–April 1975 issue, three were never republished.[1] The claim of 'The Little Nations' is the irony that the new dictatorships ruling black nations are the result of the grass-roots parties and elections, not of foreigners and neocolonialists:

> no, the men in suits,
> in the Members' Stand
>
> have written the songs,
> and the bleeding choirs are conducted
> by police batons,
>
> beat the dead horse
> the Good Friday effigy
> of the honkey again to death,
>
> the straw man you kill
> will not cry mercy,
> nor the man on the guarded hill
>
> with the new flag
> the ridiculous currency,
> the not-so-secret police

This is Walcott as an Auden heir using regular rhythms, compressed metaphors, and re-enlivened clichés to write pointed ethical observations about society and politics. Such poems with their local Caribbean allusions and arguments seldom reached book publication. 'Interior' rejects politics, ideologies, and stereotypes; it is a poem preparing for exile. The retreat into the forest of the self is an exploration of the sources of pain, poetry, self-knowledge:

> with only a few classics for company,
> I am taking all I can carry,
> the bad poems, screen magazines, Dante,
> a good bonfire needs trash
> the soul soars high from detritus,
> all I need and more that I do not,
>
> I am carrying the memory of all the women I've known,
> who I lay with, and how many times,
> I have a carton packed tight with prejudices,
> the amount of them was amazing,
>
> and, anyway, I shall be going probably
> for a very short while, forever,
> it's startling how suddenly you can come upon
> the breathless, abounding Pacific,
> just so you can feel small.

Walcott was working towards what became *Sea Grapes*. The volume's original title was 'The Harvest', the title of a poem of which Walcott wrote two versions during May. He informed Giroux (7 August) that he was making major revisions to the poems and no longer liked the title. He hoped to send the typescript in a few weeks. Financial problems regarding *Joker* resulted in Walcott needing money; he was awaiting contracts for 'The Harvest' and *Joker* from Farrar, Straus and Giroux and asked Giroux to send an advance (minus Cape's 10 per cent) as soon as possible, even before a contract had been negotiated with Cape.

Walcott (14 August) sent Moss the great five-part 'Sainte Lucie' sequence, another example of Walcott working in larger forms than magazines were likely to print, and mentioned he would have a new book with Cape during 1976. A month later (19 September) Moss rejected the sequence, although he especially liked 'For the Altarpiece of the Roseau Valley Church' the concluding poem (itself a three-part sequence!) about Dunstan St Omer's mural behind the altar.

During mid-August Walcott wrote to Maschler that he now did not like at least a third of 'The Harvest'. As usual when readying a volume he had written new poems, made major revisions, and rejected some poems. Maschler complained that the proofs were due at the printer's in a few weeks; he needed the revisions immediately or at least he should be told when he could expect them.

It was good, however, to know that Walcott would be in London, he hoped to see him more than in the past.

Walcott (3 September) wrote a draft of 'Storm Light', an unpublished poem in the short-lined, three-line stanzas that he was experimenting with towards the end of *Sea Grapes*. The basic idea of the poem is the change in light from before a storm until afterwards, and watching for light during the storm, a symbol of resurrection. There is a suggestion that God is the source of bad experiences, testing man as he did Job.

Poems were coming rapidly now, and Walcott wanted to finish the book. He sent Giroux what was supposedly the final version of what had become *Sea Grapes* with a copy to Maschler. Cape (22 September) missed their schedule, but Maschler said he would aim for early spring. Giroux (26 September) preferred *Sea Grapes* to 'Harvest' for a title, and said that the revised poems are strong, this is Walcott's best collection to date. Giroux offered Cape a $500 advance. He hoped Maschler and Walcott would agree as there are no riches in publishing poetry.

Arthur Vogelsang, co-editor of *American Poetry Review*, accepted (9 October) 'Sour Grapes' and 'For the Altarpiece of the Roseau Valley Church, Saint Lucia'. Vogelsang thought the third section of 'For the Altarpiece' remarkable, but wondered about the second section which seemed more historical and developmental without the visionary quality of most of the poem. They would accept it as it was, but did it need more work?

'Sour Grapes' was within a short time published in four different versions— in the *American Poetry Review* in January 1976, in *London Magazine* in February 1976, and in the British and American editions of *Sea Grapes* where it is retitled 'Sea Grapes'. The poem is a reflection of Walcott's own situation at the time, his affair with Norline (his Nausicaa), his feelings of guilt, and has behind it *Joker*. It makes use of the analogy between the Caribbean and the Odyssey expressed in many of Walcott's writings, especially his later works. The speaker as in many Walcott poems sees the sail of a ship, imagines it as heading for home, and that it might be Odysseus:

> home-bound on the Aegean;
> that father and husband's
>
> Longing, under gnarled sour grapes, is
> like the adulterer hearing Nausicaa's name
> in every gull's outcry.

This became the opening poem of the volume with its universal conflict between 'obsession and responsibility', the role of the classics in consolation, and the return to a kind of harmony with the natural world in St Lucia.[2]

Belinda Foster-Meilliar at Cape acknowledged (23 October) receipt of two additional poems for what was now *Sea Grapes*, but she queried the situation concerning the copyright of poems republished from the *New Yorker* which usually insists on a full copyright acknowledgement. Could Walcott supply written permission?

Leonore Bishop, Walcott's secretary in Trinidad, sent Robert Giroux and Cape on 4 November a revised version of 'The Chelsea' in the hope that it would reach them before the proofs were set. The *New Yorker* had accepted 'Midsummer England' and 'Bright Field'. Bishop asked Cape to telephone Howard Moss to work out the copyright problems as they were confusing Walcott. Cape (10 November) wrote to the *New Yorker* for permission to publish 'To Return to the Trees', 'Sunday Lemons', 'Midsummer', and 'The Bright Fields' in *Sea Grapes*.

Moss (14 November) replied to Cape that although 'To Return to the Trees' had been published during 1974 the other three poems were awaiting publication. When did Cape intend to publish *Sea Grapes* as the *New Yorker* needed at least six months' notice? The *New Yorker* had bought first publication rights and that included England. If *Sea Grapes* was published before the *New Yorker* could use the poems, Walcott would need to return his fees. The same day Moss wrote a more friendly note to Walcott saying that he was irritated by the vagueness of Cape and wished Walcott had informed him of the situation instead of his publishers. How could the *New Yorker* avoid publishing Walcott's poems after the publication date if Cape did not send him the publication date? He hoped Walcott would send him some new poems soon. Four days later Moss wrote to Walcott to say that as the *New Yorker* would not use already published material he wanted to be warned if submissions were likely to be included in a book and if so when the book would appear. He also wrote to Cape admitting that he had already published 'Sunday Lemons', and apologized for the tone of his previous letter, saying he had had a bad day. He would try to publish the other two poems before *Sea Grapes* appeared. The Cape editor in charge of American permissions pretended (8 December 1975) to sympathize with having bothered him at the end of a bad day. Publication date was 11 March and unless otherwise notified Cape would acknowledge only the two poems.

Moss (1 December) sent proofs of 'Midsummer England' to Walcott and the next day proofs of 'The Bright Field'. He wanted them returned in time for the 12 January 1976 issue. He asked whether, in stanza two, line three, of 'The Bright Field' Walcott wanted that second hyphen? The passage is:

> Their sun that would not set was going down
> on their flushed faces, brickwork like a kiln,
> on pillar-box-bright buses between trees,
> with the compassion of calendar art;

This is a knotty poem which builds on a series of comparisons, metaphors, and other analogies. Some themes concern similarities between England and the

West Indies, between the colonials and the colonized, the futility of political history and the uselessness of anger about the past. The above lines continue with an extremely elaborate analogy between the crowds in the London underground and the harvesting of such plantation crops as sugar cane or wheat. 'Pillar-box-bright buses' has a potential complexity of response that 'pillar-box bright buses' lacks. The use of hyphenated compounds had been a feature of Walcott's early *25 Poems*; in his poetry hyphens and compound words still create manifold associations.

Walcott was in Ohio for two weeks during January 1976, with James Wright; it was heavily snowing. On his way back through New York he had bad news. He and MacDermot had hoped that Michael Butler, producer of the Broadway version of *Hair*, would take *The Joker of Seville* for Broadway, but Butler did not want to become involved with the Royal Shakespeare Company over rights. He was more interested in a reggae musical that Walcott and MacDermot were working on. The idea was to get the production off the ground in Trinidad and then bring it with the Workshop Actors to Broadway. The bad news was a disagreement concerning rights for *O Babylon!*, which Walcott saw as a play he was writing, would own as author, and which Butler would finance for profit from the production. Butler saw it as a 'property', a package including music and text that he would control and exploit.

The differences were spelled out by Butler in a long letter (12 January) in response to a telephone conversation with Walcott and MacDermot. A few weeks later (3 February) Butler sent copies to others. As a result of his experience with *Hair*, where the property had not been fully exploited, he felt all world rights including publishing should be with one producing company providing direction to associates, partners, touring companies, and others. Butler did not want to become involved with restrictive rights in which he could only do what was already agreed by lawyers; he wanted to integrate the exploitation of the whole package including the words and music. So far there was, according to Butler's film associates, a treatment without a complete score. There was not enough to promise investors that it would evolve into a film, play, concert, and television production. He wanted to get all areas prepared at the same time and then the project could be controlled from the centre using the best venue. Should it first be presented as a play or concert? If a play there might be problems getting Actors Equity to agree to West Indians. It was so expensive to produce a musical play that it might be better to start with a motion picture. He had financed a workshop in Trinidad, but it was now too late for a spring production of the play. If Walcott did not trust him enough to show him the latest version, how could they work together?

Walcott wrote to Robert Giroux (26 January) apologizing for not having kept an appointment on his way through New York, but he was shocked to learn of what he described as the cancellation of the Broadway production of *O Babylon!*. He had expected money at the end of January for a final draft; to cut expenses he had returned home. He was also annoyed that Cape was publishing *Sea Grapes* on 26 January. He would have liked it delayed until the American edition. He disliked the physical appearance of the Cape edition. The next day Pat Strachan sent the Cape proofs of *Sea Grapes* and a copy to mark up for Farrar, Straus and Giroux. She hoped to have galleys by mid-March. The British and United States editions would again differ.

Poems from what would be *Sea Grapes* were published in the *London Magazine* and the *New Yorker* during February and March. 'Midsummer, England', which was published in the *New Yorker*, was to win a 1976 Borestone poetry award. Moss was at this time still rejecting as many Walcott poems as he accepted. Pat Strachan (21 April) sent bound galleys of *Sea Grapes* to Mark Strand, Stanley Kunitz, William Strafford, James Wright, and Michael Harper. Giroux sent them to William Meredith and Robert Penn Warren. Michael Harper, Professor of English and Director of Writing Programs at Brown University, replied with a paragraph that could be used on the cover, saying that Walcott used images as a means of bringing forth an inner life. He spoke of a moral vision and transformation as redemption. Mark Strand wrote to Pat Strachan (10 May) that he had received the uncorrected proofs just before leaving for Italy and had taken them with him. There were some superb poems, among Walcott's best. Pat Strachan (30 April) sent Walcott copies of the recent *American Poetry Review* with 'Sour Grapes' and 'For the Altarpiece'. The *American Poetry Review* wanted to publish 'Sea Canes' and 'The Bridge' in June.

The same day as a production of *Dream on Monkey Mountain* opened in Hartford, Connecticut, 19 March, the Trinidad Theatre Workshop production of *O Babylon!* started a two-week run at the Little Carib Theatre. *O Babylon!* is set in 1966 Jamaica during the excitement of the coming visit of Haile Selassie, and contrasts the dreamy illusions of a group of Rastafarians with the ruthlessness of some local Mafia who want to develop Rasta land into a tourist hotel. The story is seen through the eyes of one of the participants, who years later is a successful entertainer. Trinidad reviewers thought it too MacDermottish, a Broadway musical or operetta, not realistic enough about Rasta life.

Walcott returned to New York in mid-May and continued on to California for poetry readings. As usual there were complicated plans about how and what extra readings might be fitted in, transportation, when he would be paid, what would be his expenses, especially for hotels during the trip. Just as the Trinidad Theatre Workshop's finances seemed to bleed away into rentals and other costs arising from being homeless, so Walcott's non-stop work created non-stop expenses, especially for transportation and accommodation. Hotel bills had to be paid and drivers arranged. The sums Walcott earned were small. Walcott's diary notes indicate that he expected to earn between $1,000 and $1,400 on the trip. Plans included a reading on Monday, 24 May, for $150; readings on 26 May at California Poly ($300) and at the University of Southern California ($500); on Thursday, 27 May, at Northridge ($300); on 31 May he would be in Santa Barbara. Walcott needed to be back in time for the June rehearsals of *O Babylon!*

During early June Robert Hamner interviewed Walcott and attended rehearsals at the Holiday Inn of a revised *O Babylon!* with new songs. MacDermot had sent tapes and most of the rehearsal went into choreography. Ten days later *O Babylon!*, with more songs by MacDermot, who played piano, was performed at Naparima Bowl, San Fernando, 14–15 June. After reopening at the Little Carib, the Trinidad Theatre Workshop was abruptly sent by the Trinidad government to Carifesta '76, Jamaica, where *O Babylon!* was performed 24–6 July at the Little Theatre, Kingston. Jamaican reviewers did not expect it to be a realistic study of Rasta life and thought it the hit of the large festival which included national dance companies from Cuba and Mexico. The final performance was attended by about seventy Rastas who showed their appreciation by beating on drums.

After years of surviving as best they could, often dependent upon Walcott's improvisations and will, the Trinidad Theatre Workshop was becoming organized. During April there had been two general meetings of a new board of the Trinidad Theatre Workshop and an election of officers. A schedule for the first full continuing season from July to December had been planned and season tickets sold. The season was to include *O Babylon!*, *Belle Fanto*, a benefit to launch the Theatre Workshop Dance and Drama School (of which Carol La Chapelle and Noble Douglas would be directors) with Roscoe Lee Browne, 'Revival', Genet's *The Maids*, and, at the end of the year, revivals of *Joker* and *Ti-Jean*. It was assumed that besides Walcott being paid as artistic director, director of plays, and for royalties on his plays, La Chapelle and Douglas would have salaries and Albert Laveau and Tony Hall would direct some plays. Jones, Marshall, and other actors would be paid. In August the Trinidad Theatre Workshop was registered with Walcott, Laveau, and Nigel Scott as partners. It was now officially a company from which Walcott and others could profit, but they would not be responsible for major losses. At the end of the month there was the third meeting of the board. The Workshop presented E. M. Roach's *Belle Fanto* at the Little Carib Theatre 2–11 September. This was directed by Albert Laveau, and was one of the few shows Walcott had not directed; Walcott's contribution was the set design and the painted backdrop.

Since the fracture between McBurnie and the Theatre Workshop in 1965 Walcott had hoped that the Workshop would itself become the home for a dance company. He had given his support to Astor Johnson, who stylistically was the successor to McBurnie in the development of modern dance in Trinidad. Johnson was for a time a member of the Workshop before establishing his own company. Then, with *The Joker of Seville*, many of the best young dancers joined the Workshop under the leadership of Carol La Chapelle and Noble Douglas, two dancers and choreographers who had recently returned to Trinidad after working and studying in the United States and Britain. La Chapelle had studied ballet, had the long thin body and limbs expected in European ballet, and she fused ballet with modern and West Indian dance. Douglas was built more solidly, moved more from her pelvis, and was more Afro-Caribbean in her dance. Her style seemed warm and emotional, whereas La Chapelle could be more vertical and abstract. Between them they brought variety to the further modernization of local dance beyond McBurnie's use of folk tradition. La Chapelle and Douglas forged ahead with a programme and a dance school under the umbrella of the Trinidad Theatre Workshop. Walcott was sympathetic to the dancers. The women were young, attractive, energetic. Many had studied and worked abroad, often with Martha Graham. Trinidadians were in American and French dance companies and his dancers thought in terms of international techniques and careers. They worked like professionals, had their own dance workshops as well as attending theatre workshops, and when not in rehearsals were at workshops four or five nights a week.

As Walcott's thoughts increasingly turned towards an American career he spent more time among the dancers. He still hoped to bring his Trinidad Theatre Workshop to the United States and turn his actors into stars on Broadway. If he could move the Trinidad Theatre Workshop productions of *Ti-Jean*, *The Charlatan*, *Joker*, and *O Babylon!* to New York his plays would be staged there as he wanted them; he and his actors would become famous, and he would prove the truth of his vision of a great world-class West Indian culture led by him, his plays, and his theatre company. The vision of being a Moses leading his people to a promised land was still there, along with the desire and need for money.

Whereas the female dancers understood such dreams, his main male actors were older; they had jobs with pensions that they did not want to lose, some had families to support, and the tours were already a strain on their lives and required using up vacation time. They were unlikely to leave Trinidad for an uncertain promised land in the United States. Albert Laveau had already tried, given up an excellent job to act in the United States, survived for a few years as a professional, worked with some stars, taught classes in New York, found that he missed his family, was limited to 'black' roles and black theatre companies, and decided to return to Trinidad, knowing that he was good, but that he lacked the necessary stomach, luck, and drive to be a star. He no longer had his promising career as an executive and he lost his appetite for acting.

From 28 October into November the Trinidad Theatre Workshop Dance Company presented *Revival*, an evening of various dances, at the Little Carib Theatre. Walcott was listed as artistic director and as one of the set designers.

Norline Metivier was one of the dancers. The show moved late in November to the Naparima Bowl.

In mid-November Walcott resigned from the Workshop, suddenly abandoning seventeen years of building a theatre company according to a plan he had formed during his time in the Village in 1958. He and MacDermot had been revising *The Charlatan* for the United States and Walcott wanted the Workshop to produce it instead of *Joker* during the Trinidad Carnival. The Workshop had already sold season tickets that included *The Maids, Ti-Jean,* and *Joker,* but Walcott went ahead with calling rehearsals for *The Charlatan* and had a rebellion on his hands as actors and musicians failed to show up, arguments flared, and insults were exchanged. Walcott took back the script and resigned. The Workshop was forbidden to perform his plays.

There was another reason. Margaret still devoted much of her time to helping with productions, but the marriage had been rocky since the late 1960s. With Derek often away, lonely, tempted, and under tremendous pressure, it became rockier. Then came the mid-life crisis. During the first production of *The Joker of Seville* Walcott fell in love with Norline Metivier, one of his dancers, who was young, very attractive, and fun to be around; he courted and besieged her and wanted her to go to New York with him. As the affair became visible the members of the Workshop took sides.

The Charlatan and Norline need not have led to Walcott's resignation nor the break-up of his marriage. They were manifestations of his own conflicts. Ever since the success of *Dream* at Waterford, Walcott knew that opening his plays in the United States meant abandoning his illusions of having them performed by his own company under his direction. He was earning little in Trinidad, saw a brilliant future abroad which required his being there, but did not know how, or want, to make the break, so became moody and picked fights. It was time to leave, but the Workshop was his family, Port of Spain was his social world, and he did not want to leave home. He wanted home to follow him to the United States, but it would not. In drafts of 'American, without America' he would later speak of having lost faith in his vision of a West Indian theatre; his home felt spiritually insecure, he was obsessed by his love of a younger woman, America now seemed a refuge rather than a market, and he felt a coward repeating what he had been doing.

There was also the political situation. Ever since the 1970 Black Power demonstrations, Walcott had been uncomfortable as critics accused him of not writing 'black' enough, as local governments became more tyrannical, and as the future of his children in the region seemed less secure. For several generations education, especially education abroad, determined social status. Walcott expected to provide such an education abroad for his children, but he was having trouble, despite all his work and Margaret having a good job, keeping up his mortgage payments and telephone bills.

A week before his resignation (7 November) Walcott filled in forms for a John Simon Guggenheim Memorial Foundation Fellowship to revise two volumes of his plays, to prepare his Collected Poems, and to continue working on his plays and poems in Trinidad, with some time in the United States. His references were Elizabeth Hardwick, Roger Straus, Mark Strand, and William Moody of the Rockefeller Brothers Fund.

A week after his resignation Walcott wrote to Terry Hands (23 November). Perhaps Hands could do *Joker* privately rather than with the Royal Shakespeare Company? He also wrote (23 November) to Daniel Halpern asking him to look further into Walcott teaching at Columbia or Princeton for a year, as he could not make a living in Trinidad. He thanked Halpern for previously arranging for him to teach some classes in New York and said that his plans for Broadway were on and off. He sent regards to Mark Strand. Two days later (25 November) Walcott wrote to Strachan. He was broke, having problems with creditors. Walcott again had hopes of opening *O Babylon!* on Broadway; the production had passed on to Harry Rigby who had not yet signed contracts. There was a new song version of *The Charlatan*, and he hoped to have a volume of *O Babylon!* and *Joker* ready in four or five months. He explained that he had broken with the Workshop due to indiscipline and that he wanted to rebuild his own company. He missed New York. He asked Strachan to tell the YMHA that he was stuck in Port of Spain at present, but that he hoped to be in New York early in 1977. Whatever the YMHA offered he needed more money. Walcott had often struggled in the past, but the focus now would be on money to survive if he really was going to leave Trinidad for New York. Even having a roof over his head could become a problem.

Over the holidays Walcott rehearsed *The Charlatan* and worked on a new play, *Remembrance*, for St Croix. On 31 December there was a read-through in the morning and a read-through in the afternoon. He went to Tobago 2–7 January, and for the next two weeks was involved in readings of *Remembrance* and preparing scripts. Productions were planned for St Croix, Trinidad, and, Walcott hoped, New York. As usual his notes were often about money. For *Remembrance* in Trinidad he would be paid $2,300 for everything including rehearsals, publicity, and set design; he would get $1,150 now and $1,150 on opening night to send to Margaret.

And as usual Walcott had a number of projects for plays from which little would come or would only come much later. There is a manuscript of his comedy *Beef, No Chicken* dated Trinidad 1976. It was not produced until 1981. He also wrote 'The Snow Queen, A Television Play' during 1976, which he rehearsed with Trinidad Tobago Television during 1977 when extracts and photographs were published.[3]

The new two-act version of *The Charlatan* was performed 13–23 January 1977 at the Little Carib Theatre without Errol Jones, Stanley Marshall, Claude Reid, or Albert Laveau, the core members of the Workshop. It was shorter and, using MacDermot's 1974 music, closer to a musical comedy. Norline Metivier took the role of Heloise Upshot. For the revised *The Charlatan*, now subtitled 'The Little Carnival' and described as a calypso comedy, Walcott wrote a six-page (single-spaced) unpublished article or preface on calypso as theatre, with notes on the calypso as a drama, together with two calypsos from *The Charlatan*. He claimed that the form had changed; there were no more contests between stars like Melody versus Sparrow, no more invective or picong, no more 'Sans Humanité' insults from the crowd at the loser. Now performers coddled the audience instead of insulting them. As prices went up, shows became elaborate and improvisation was lost. Real calypso as drama was Sparrow's 'Ten to One is Murder'. Walcott explicated the song and its allusions, which were based on a real event. Once you accepted the premiss that the odds against Sparrow were wrong, then the jury, here the audience, might decide to free him. Walcott noted the feminine endings of rhymes, the use of space for the speaker to imitate the events, and the violence, but admitted that most calypso was not up to this standard.

Sea Grapes had been published in London in April 1976, and in the United States in July. The Cape volume was a paperback, the American edition was in hardcover. Both editions have forty-six poems, of which 'Natural History' has four sections and 'Saint Lucie' five. The American edition has some later revisions. Eight poems had appeared in the *London Magazine*, four in the *New Yorker*, nine in other American publications, and six in *Tapia*. In *Sea Grapes* the many short poems reflect the places in which Walcott had travelled and worked in recent years, ranging from Ohio to London. Although all Walcott's volumes of poetry reflect his interest in art and painting, *Sea Grapes* is especially concerned with perspective, as the poems move from foreground to background to middle ground, or Walcott on an airplane looks down. There are conscious exercises in painterly genres such as 'Sunday Lemons', a still life. The five Sainte Lucie poems in the middle of the book include 'For the Altarpiece of Roseau Valley Church, St Lucia' about Dunstan's painting. There is a general movement within the volume from the Virgin Islands to a cluster of poems set in Trinidad written against the politicians and petty tyrants of the region, leading to 'The Silent Woman', the French Creole 'Sainte Lucie' at the centre of the volume, and then poems of other places, Colorado, New York, England, California, followed by a return to the Caribbean and the natural world. 'The Harvest' has behind it the Harvest Festival of the Methodists of Walcott's youth, a time of fruits, gifts, and thankfulness. For any poet there is also Keats's great 'To Autumn' with its sense of the sweet rich fruitfulness of experience and decay. Curiously Walcott modulates into one of his Herbertian allegories of life as a moral and spiritual journey, but one that is bitter and ambiguous:

>   . . . the usual ways
> of those who swore to serve truth with one hand,
> and one behind their back for cash or praise,
>
> .   .   .   .
> . . . I surrendered dreaming how I'd stand
> in the rewarding autumn of my life,
> just ankle deep in money, thick as leaves
>
> .   .   .   .
> What I soon learnt was that they had changed the script,
> left out the golden fall and turned to winter,
> to some grey monochrome, much like this metre[4]

The movement of the volume is from alienation from, and anger with, regional black politics and politicians to reaffirming his roots in the black Creole culture of St Lucia, travel abroad, and a return to the natural world. The sense of conclusion is clear in such titles as 'At Last', 'Winding Up', and 'To Return to the Trees'. Like most of Walcott's volumes it is made up of poems composed during the few years before the submission of the manuscript, indeed of poems written since the first version of the manuscript.

    If the notion of earning a living as a dramatist in the West Indies was a fantasy along with the notion that the Trinidad Theatre Workshop would somehow become a national and regional professional theatre company, a launching pad towards international stardom for its performers, a new dream was replacing it, to be rich and famous, or at least a successful and well-off dramatist in the United States. Walcott was now increasingly meeting the rich and famous who seemed interested in using his talent and ideas.

Part V

Tobago, St Croix, St Thomas, New York Starting Again

20

~~~~~~~~~~~~~~~~~~~~~~~~~~~~~~~~~~~~

1977–1978 *Remembrance, Pantomime, Joseph Brodsky*

WALCOTT was broke and felt cheated; he felt he had given up too much of his career for the Workshop and Trinidad. He used to feel a self-sacrificing martyr, now he felt a fool. Instead of a great national theatre, there were eighteen wasted years that could have been used to build his reputation and career abroad. The actors had regular jobs, security for themselves and their families, annual increments in their wages and pensions. Walcott felt he had nothing, only sourness. A problem with being a poet was loneliness. He did not usually form close friendships. He had wanted the communion of theatre, had needed to feel he was part of the Workshop; instead he was humiliated how dependent he had become on others. How often had he waited for the actors, tried to telephone them to see why they were late. He had convinced himself he could make Port of Spain a cultural centre, but the government was not interested in the Workshop nor in him as a national poet. Early in his career, when wounded by the collapse of his first marriage, he was welcomed to Trinidad, accepted, but there was no interest in what he wanted. Trinidad was different from Walcott. It believed in the hedonist 'fête'. One-third of the national income resulted from Carnival. For two or three months you danced, the rest of the year you prepared for Carnival. He did not like to join in crowds, wild dancing, surrender, abandonment.

Beginning again meant leaving his wife, his children, his house, perhaps Norline, who would not answer his telephone calls. Walcott did not want to leave his world. Having become the writer who stayed home, he lacked the courage to go. As often with Walcott there was no clear break with the past, none of the living for yourself in the present that has become the morality of our time. He was depressed, angry, self-pitying, conflicted. He would, childishly, think that he would return rich and as a patriot build that national theatre with professional actors. To go abroad meant exile. In the past he thought he could be satisfied with nature, with landscape; now he needed a woman, the latest incarnation of his muse.

He, however, also felt the need of the artist to empty himself to create. He believed that the artist cannot be at peace, be satisfied; the artist's life, as shown by the suicides of Edgar Mittelholzer, Harold Simmons, Eric Roach, Hemingway, and Plath, is self-destructive. To have peace is to be dishonest. Walcott blamed himself for having allowed situations to develop where he could say others had made him leave Trinidad; the honest writer would leave without making a scene. He was aware that this inner battle would never be the subject of his writing. The writer needs solitude, truth drives him on by inflicting pain. Walcott was aware of his dependency on the self-destructive, on chaos, but he also needed his muse: he wished it still were his wife, the one person who really knew him.

The crisis was finding expression in his unpublished autobiography (upon which I have drawn). He wrote (23 January 1977) that his life had been a fantasy. He had assumed by the time he was 50 he would be at least comfortably well off, instead he was badly in debt. His plans always begin with high hopes and conclude sadly. While the sun provided him with the climate to which other writers hoped to retire, he felt displaced and kept debating with himself about emigrating to the United States. Breaking up his ordinary life would be like leaving the Caribbean forever. He could not be alone, a hermit, a Crusoe living by himself. He wrote that like most American writers about nature he was talkative and knew little about it. He wrote about the sea but had never swum far out into it. Yet he felt the need for the sea, a fear he would dry out as a writer without it.

Even if Walcott wanted to leave for New York, how and where would he live? The next five years were transitional as Walcott worked his way into the American scene, often living in hotels in Tobago, in the Chelsea Hotel in New York, with friends in St Croix. He ate cheeseburgers, read magazines, was often alone writing. Margaret continued to handle his mail, but his life became a four-sided contest between his art, hustling his room and board, playing for the high stakes of success in New York and Hollywood, and paying for his family and Norline.

When the selection committee for the Guggenheim fellowship asked for some of his work, he replied (14 February) that he now had about a hundred pages of the first draft of a book of autobiography and essays, 'American, without America', which he planned to finish by September. He would bring some pages when he came to New York in March. Pat Strachan, who had pushed him to apply, sent (15 February) the committee four volumes of poetry, the *Dream on Monkey Mountain* volume of plays, a couple of essays, and mentioned that a second volume of plays was planned for later in the year, and that an autobiography had been contracted.

The same day Walcott wrote (14 February) teasing Daniel Halpern, whose letters were now headed by both Antaeus Press and Ecco Press, for being big time. After joking about soon reading at the YMHA and starting his own YMNA, and publishing in *Antaeus* with such small fry as Lowell, Gunn, and Auden, Walcott came to the point. He would be in New York in early March and would like to teach at Columbia. On Thursday, 3 March, Dan Masterson introduced Walcott at the Poetry Center, YM-YWHA, 92nd Street. Later in the month Walcott was interviewed by Sharon Ciccarelli in New Haven; this continued an interview started in January in Trinidad.[1]

In April Michael Schultz (now at Universal City Studios) wrote suggesting they work on 'The Black Emperor', a play about the Haitian revolution based on Percy Waxman's *The Black Napoleon (The Story of Toussaint Louverture)*, published in 1931. Schultz had not heard from Walcott for a while but he was excited by Waxman's book, and thought Walcott could use Toussaint's history to present many of his own views. As a studio was interested in developing the story, Schultz wanted to know if he and Walcott could agree on the treatment. Walcott noted (26 June) that he had several pages that he would mail to Schultz in a few weeks. He expected to complete the outline and send it and a covering letter, possible cast lists, and other information to Schultz and Aschenberg. He wanted an advance of $2,500 for script development, a further $2,500 for the first draft, and an eventual $25,000. He would work on the script throughout the summer. It became 'The Haitian Earth', an unproduced television mini-series, for Crystalite Productions, Hollywood, for which a general outline and nine segments and various scenes for the play were sketched. The story can be seen as having several interests for Walcott, including the tragic position of the mulattos who were humiliated by the white French and slaughtered by Toussaint. Then there was the universality of tyranny, civil war, and betrayal, whether in France or Haiti, whether white or black. Although a continuation of topics in *Henri Christophe* and *Drums and Colours*, this is a separate work which in 1984 became a major national theatre production, *Haytian Earth*, in St Lucia.

Walcott still needed the West Indies to première and develop his plays. For almost a decade Walcott continued to be actively involved in West Indian theatre. He would continue to mount or find others to mount productions in Trinidad. St Croix and St Thomas offered American money, West Indians, and a new theatre company needing help. Soon Barbados would offer the opportunity of well-staged productions with good actors and good directors. *Remembrance* was commissioned and first performed by the Courtyard Players, Dorsch Center St Croix, 22 April–1 May, at Frederiksted, with Walcott directing. Wilbert Holder came from Trinidad. This was the third Walcott play in St Croix; previously there had been *Dream* and *Ti-Jean*. It was the start of a new phase of his theatre; it was realistic, used a small cast, and was concerned with changing social and cultural conditions over the generations. It sympathetically recalls the colonial West Indians who mastered English culture, especially language and poetry, but lacked the courage to take equality through intermarriage. It portrays the generational conflict between such late colonials and the young radicals who, Americanized, are fearless, even dismissive, of such equality. The play has a complicated structure moving back and forth in time, and could be said to be both a commemoration of the past and an acceptance of the present. Although it could be interpreted as Walcott coming to terms with Black Power, it might also be seen as about his own conflicts with the memory of Warwick and the issue of whiteness, even with the possibility of living in white America.

Set in the old settled Belmont area of Port of Spain, *Remembrance* mostly consists of scenes from the life of Albert Perez Jordan, a retired schoolteacher in his mid-sixties who has also written some short stories. The play opens on Remembrance Day, 'seven years after the February revolution' in which he lost a son, a radical leader who will be commemorated by everyone except Jordan. Jordan, who was Acting Principal of Belmont Intermediate, is fond of quoting Thomas Gray's 'Elegy'. 'My mother, who was also a teacher, used to recite this same passage to me when I was your age.'[2] Walcott's own remembrance is accurate. The *West Indian Crusader* reported, on Saturday, 24 January 1948, that at a meeting of the Castries Town Board Mr H. Collymore moved that four scholarships for secondary education be created for the poor to attend St Mary's College and St Joseph's Convent. Collymore, who I am told was a black Anglican, said 'In the ranks of the poorer classes there is many a lawyer, doctor, philosopher, engineer, etc., whose natural talent is allowed to stagnate because of inadequate educational facilities. The Poet Gray has summed it all up in his beautiful lines from the 'Elegy written in a Churchyard'.

> Full many a gem of purest ray serene,
> The deep unfathomed caves of ocean bear,
> Full many a flower is born to blush unseen,
> And waste its sweetness on the desert air.'[3]

This could be a scene from *Remembrance*, but times have changed and outside the window Jordan's former students, radicalized, are chanting, 'Gray is ofay, black is beautiful . . . Jordan is a honky-donkey white nigger man!' As in many of Walcott's works the images refer to the work itself as well as to the story it tells. The play is an elegy for Jordan and what he represents, just as the grandfather clock which dominates the set recalls the past and indicates the present with which Jordan must come to terms. This is Walcott recalling his mother and an older generation of West Indian teachers and writers, even C. L. R. James, and is his own way of coming to terms with the black militancy of recent years. Generational difference is shown by Jordan's attraction and failure of nerve towards a white British woman in contrast to his son's easy, dismissive, relationship to a white American hippie girl friend.

Until now Walcott's theatre had been concerned with peasants, the folk, the heroic, and the mythic. While *Joker* and *O Babylon!* had freed him to treat new subjects, he had approached the musical as art theatre, verse drama, subsidized theatre with large casts. Such plays as *Remembrance, Pantomime,* and *Beef, No Chicken* would be concerned with the middle classes, recent or contemporary life, social change. They would be prose plays, require small casts, be low cost to produce, with more emphasis on psychology, although the characters would still be representative.

The American Virgin Islands, St Croix and St Thomas, during this transitional period of his life became important to Walcott. The Courtyard Players and other groups gave him a paying drama company with which to hold workshops and perform his plays. The College of the Virgin Islands would hire him as a Visiting Professor, even a Distinguished Visiting Professor, without expecting much in the way of regular teaching. He was treated with respect, had friends, even learned how to tap into American grants. There was not much competition, and it was preparation for moving on to the mainland. Walcott regarded St Croix as a part of the West Indies colonized by the United States. Its beaches and harbours were for white Americans seeking the sun, but black West Indians saw it as a stepping-stone, a place to wait a few years before moving northward. It was a place to practise being American before earning a green card and permanent residence. Then one could return to the West Indies dressed in American clothes and show off as a conqueror while being bored by the lack of activity and lack of modernity. Walcott was himself following a pattern he had known from his youth, a story already told in 'The Glory Trumpeter' about the inner defeat of the apparently successful exile. He was also aware that St Croix was, like Barbados and other tourist areas, becoming a kind of sex shop where light-skinned northerners came seeking sensual and erotic pleasure. Until recently many clubs had been white only, and many businesses exploitive, sending their profits to the mainland. It was also a place where many of the poems in his next volume were written, a place for writing chapters of that unfinished autobiography, 'American, without America', which was meant to recount his own migration to the United States.

The Star-Apple Kingdom, like Walcott's other volumes of poetry, began unexpectedly, came rapidly, and at times seems accidental, the result of chance meetings and events, although it is unified by Walcott's concern with West Indian politics, illusions about the region, his personal situation, and the role of a poet. His exasperation with the revolutionary and black militancy of recent years, the increasing suppression of human rights in the region, his financial crisis, and the break-up of his second marriage and love for Norline, combined in some poems, partly found expression in others, but once more he was an Odysseus, now departing from Trinidad in the opening poem 'Schooner Flight', northward through the Caribbean to the Jamaica of the concluding 'Star Apple Kingdom'. A complete version of 'The Schooner *Flight*', illustrated by Walcott, appeared in the May issue of the *Trinidad & Tobago Review*. The long poem 'Star Apple Kingdom' began on Rainbow Beach, St Croix. Walcott wrote some lines but did not know what the poem was going to be about. It was 'accelerated' by reading García Marquéz's novel *The Autumn of the Patriarch*. The Kingdom is Jamaica; 'He' is his friend Michael Manley, the young ruler in contrast to the aged despot in Marquéz's book. The ending, cracking an egg, opens a world, anything can happen.[4]

'American, without America', a story about his attraction to the United States where he would be a West Indian writer, should have been the logical next publication along with *The Star-Apple Kingdom*. 'American, without America', his unpublished autobiography modelled on Boris Pasternak's *My Sister—Life* and *Safe Conduct*, was a preoccupation throughout the 1970s and into the 1980s. It was a continuation of *Another Life*, although one version started even before Walcott's birth with the migration of West Indians north to the United States and Canada and the continuing awareness of this diaspora by Walcott and his family during his youth. The book would then recount various periods of his life, such as 1958–9 in Greenwich Village, and, after telling of the break-up of his second marriage, would conclude, in the earlier versions, with him on the edge of a decision about himself leaving for the United States. Fragments exist in such forms as a typed essay about Hemingway's Caribbean, handwritten memories written in early January 1977, and comments on the 1970 Black Power marches. His 1973 'Notes' for a proposal are three pages. This project existed in several forms; at one point it was to republish 'Leaving School' and 'On Choosing Port of Spain'.

The Hemingway section, written in Christiansted in St Croix, was first published as an essay in 1990. It explains Walcott's interest in Hemingway and in the painter Winslow Homer and suggests ways in which his work is related to theirs. *To Have and Have Not*, *The Old Man and the Sea*, and *Islands In The Stream* are Caribbean novels which take place mostly in Florida, Cuba, and the Bahamas, and in which the Gulf Stream is central. Thomas Hudson of *The Old Man and the Sea* evokes Winslow Homer in the Bahamas and paints similar subjects—storms, fishing natives—and in the same style, a realism formed by close observation of the natural world. Walcott claims that in Hemingway's prose the paragraphs are like the watercolours of Winslow Homer, especially in their transparency. There is a similar choice of topics, extreme sensitivity to light, the weather, colours, and the changes in seasonal winds. It is possible to criticize the melodramatic side of

Homer and Hemingway, the Victorian clichés, the great white hunter attitudes, but Hemingway and Homer are precise about nature. Truth is in the brush of the wash, the right words.

Walcott reads Hemingway's fiction biographically, even perhaps as an analogy to Walcott's own life. Thomas Hudson's concern with himself follows after Robert Jordan in *For Whom the Bell Tolls* having given himself to the poor of Spain. Hudson is Hemingway spiritually exhausted, a more truthful, realistic person who paints a private paradise rather than naturalist portraits of poverty. *Islands in the Stream* results from loneliness, failed marriages, ennui, fear, and cynicism; it is penitential. Hemingway wants to preserve nature. American literature and painting seek a detailed knowledge of nature, a return to primal joys, fears, and awe. Instead of social conscience we see a more truthful selfishness, remorse, humility, failure. So far Hemingway sounds like Walcott.

Walcott then turns on Hemingway with insights that anticipate both the recent questioning of the Western canon and reject what might be called the Empire Writes Back school of post-colonial criticism. With the emergence of new national and ethnic literatures, the supposed classics will be challenged unless really universal, really masterpieces. Hemingway's heroes are too much like a soldier of fortune in older romances or even a tourist on a rented boat enjoying 'Nature'. The new literatures must be more than corrections of the old. It would be as or more provincial to have a rewritten canon by blacks and browns, no longer exotic natives, staring back. What is needed is a greater compassion that crosses divides and hierarchies, a humility towards the craft of art, a humility towards nature, descriptions of the world through art which make you see your world better. This is Walcott criticizing the Hemingway he admired in his youth; it is also Walcott's response to recent claims that the Western literary canon is imperialist, culturally exclusive, and that all post-colonial literature is essentially Caliban answering back, cursing Prospero in Prospero's language.[5]

He was in New York, without Norline, 15 May–3 July. Strachan sent (4 May) a copy of *The Joker of Seville* to Robert Brustein, Dean of the Yale School of Drama. Henry Louis ('Skip') Gates, Jr., was teaching at Yale and for a time Walcott found himself ornamenting a movement by some African American intellectuals and artists away from the radicalism, black essentialism, and idealization of the culture of black ghettos. This was useful to both Walcott and the Americans. They appeared to have a major writer on their side; Walcott would for a few years be associated with Yale University which interested him because of its School of Drama. A decade earlier Freund and the Rockefeller Foundation had thought it the best place to study Drama; it was a good place to get started if he were to teach in the United States. Gates told Strachan that Brustein wanted to see Walcott. This was to lead to Walcott teaching play-writing at Yale the coming autumn semester for $4,000 on a grant from the Columbia Broadcasting System.

Walcott on 8 June was awarded a Guggenheim fellowship of $18,000 for twelve months starting in July, which would be paid quarterly. He replied (22 June) from the Chelsea Hotel that the fellowship would avoid the financial stress he had been under for the past two years, but must he give up the Yale appointment? As he had a family to maintain in Trinidad he would like both. Straus had already informed the committee of the CBS grant and Walcott was allowed to keep both. In estimating his costs for the year, Walcott assumed he would earn $10,000 beyond the Guggenheim grant, and included a possible trip to Haiti for the purpose of study. In September Walcott requested an advance of $1,200 on his October $4,500. He mentioned his separation from his wife, which he hoped was temporary, and his taking his daughters on a trip to New York in August when he returned on theatre business. Although the rent was only $125 weekly he was already $1,000 in debt to the Chelsea, which would extend no further credit. He had also been in Tobago writing. During these transitional years he often stayed at a hotel in Tobago when he was not in the Virgin Islands, the United States, or Trinidad.

Three days after Walcott read (17 June) at an MLA/NEH Summer Seminar in Afro-American Studies at Yale University, Robert Stepto, Assistant Professor of English and Afro-American Studies, wrote thanking him for his reading. The Winter 1977 volume of *The Massachusetts Review*, published early in January, would include six pages from 'The Schooner *Flight*' along with works by Chinua Achebe, Ralph Ellison, Robert Hayden, Ernest Gaines, Michael Harper, and six 'Odysseus Collages' by Romare Bearden. The issue mostly contained new material but reprinted Ellison on Romare Bearden. Stepto retyped 'The Schooner Flight' with Walcott's revisions for book publication in *Chant of the Saints*, which included five sections. The conclusion here is more optimistic than the version in *The Star-Apple Kingdom* as the various stages and revisions of the poem reflect his troubled relationship with Norline who was reluctant to leave Trinidad.

Chant of the Saints also included part of 'The Star-Apple Kingdom' and the Ciccarelli interview, which reads as if transcribed into academic prose. It also reveals some of Walcott's discomfort in talking to black Americans about race, which could mean Africa in his blood or the West Indies. He uses the term as Joyce did to mean Irish, in a nineteenth-century usage which could and can even mean the people and culture of a region. If it is absurd to speak of Americans as a race that is Walcott's point; the New World, whether white or black, whether in Brazil or Canada, shares newness, and has no single continuous history with Europe. Walcott often speaks of 'tribe', a metaphor for community, and his claim here, as in the 'Muse of History', is that such a tribal sense belongs to an oral culture and the continuities of the past, unlike the Americas where it is at best fragmented, as in the Negro spirituals. His tribe is the West Indian peasantry, but they are not only divided by many languages and education, but also by the lack of a common history beyond being castaways in the New World and having to start again.[6]

Henry Louis Gates, Jr., wanted Afro-American studies to be a serious academic discipline for which it was necessary to make available the materials to discuss, analyse, and teach black social and cultural history. Early the following year Walcott (10 January) was invited to join, as an adviser, the Board of Directors of a Complete Works Series of Afro-American authors intended to reprint a variety of Afro-American writers ranging from poets to historians and social scientists. Gates would be General Editor with an editorial board including Romare Bearden, Sterling Brown, Charles Davis, and Wole Soyinka. Although Walcott would often lend his name to major projects and journals of African-American literature, this was no more his cultural history than it was Soyinka's. Walcott was part of an international black cultural assertion that followed from decolonization; in the United States he was thought a black writer, but he was not part of black America, he did not share its national history or experience; indeed it threatened his own identity as a red, shabine, West Indian, someone who had left Trinidad in part because he was not black enough. The West Indies he was writing about was black, but it was also brown, red, white, yellow, and bronze.

Walcott hoped to begin rehearsals of *O Babylon!* on 31 May and to open in October at the Theatre Lab of the Kennedy Center for Performing Arts before, he hoped, moving it to Broadway. In New York during June Walcott heavily revised it, but somehow the play never was to get off the ground in the United States. There were even problems about publishing it. Cape and Farrar, Straus and Giroux were joint owners of the eventual volume, as Cape had rights to *Joker* and Farrar, Straus and Giroux to *O Babylon!*. Tom Maschler wrote (16 June) to Roger Straus that Cape's plans for a *Joker/Babylon* volume depended on productions in Britain. Walcott, back in Port of Spain, wrote to Maschler on 27 June insisting that his two plays be published in England during 1978 as one volume. If Cape was unwilling he would return the advance, ask to be released from the contract, and seek another UK publisher. This had the desired effect. Maschler wrote (5 July) to Straus that Cape would go ahead with the two plays.

Walcott asked Papp whether there would be a reading of *Remembrance*. Gail Papp thought they had a good cast available, but they needed a report on the script. The report called the play effective and subtle, noted its dream-like quality, wit, and humour, but seemed uncertain what was reality and what fantasy. Rather than just a play about colour and colonialism it was also about being in love without a lover, being without a country, about dreaming of beauty in life long after one has supposedly adjusted to reality. Walcott returned to New York for the reading (7 July) directed by Charles Turner. Roscoe Lee Browne was interested in the role of Jordan.

Walcott was at the Chelsea when a friend telephoned that Robert Lowell died (12 September 1977) in a taxi after returning to New York from England. The body was delivered to Hardwick's apartment. Roger Straus, Mark Strand, Susan Sontag, and Walcott travelled to Boston for the funeral (16 September) after which they went to Elizabeth Bishop's where Walcott met Joseph Brodsky; they soon became close friends.

He taught at the Yale Drama School during the autumn semester, commuting from New York where he and Norline (whom he had convinced to give up her job in Trinidad) lived at the Chelsea Hotel where he was making sketches for *O Babylon!*. Strachan (September 23) had just read another draft of 'The Schooner Flight' when Brodsky, now writing in English, came by the Farrar, Straus and Giroux offices with his elegy on Lowell and credited Walcott with a change in the text. The *New York Review of Books* wanted Walcott's address for a Lowell memorial service.

Walcott loved New York with its autumn weather, the falling leaves, the changing colours, the stylish women, even the advertisements and posters. He felt middle aged, autumnal, decaying, yet (as in Keats's well-known poem) decay was fermentation and life. He felt exhilarated. Aware that life was passing he also felt that life and his work were becoming more varied, richer; part of the growth was an awareness of being hopelessly in love, trapped with responsibilities, and filled with doubts. Living in New York while caring for his family in Trinidad was expensive. He asked the Guggenheim Foundation for another advance, this time of $2,200, to be paid into his New York account.

He went to Jamaica (18 November) for five days in connection with one of his plays; after returning he called (28 November) the New York Shakespeare Festival about *Remembrance* as Roscoe Lee Browne agreed to a March workshop. Papp wanted reports on Walcott's other work. A few days later Papp complained that he had twice asked for a report on *O Babylon!*. Gail Papp remembered reading two plays. The scripts had been given to a reader who was good at doing rapid reports. The report for *O Babylon!* was found—a standard rejection slip. The reader thought the plot predictable and that there was little of interest beyond the pro-Rasta position. Unless the music is exceptional it is a sermon. Gail asked her husband if he wanted another reading. The script was sent to Peregrine Whittlesey (Gerald Freund's wife) who backed off making any comment: she did not have the tape and she recommended it be sent to a third reader! *O Babylon!* was not going much further with the New York Shakespeare Festival.

After the semester at Yale Walcott was interviewed by Edward Hirsch at the Chelsea (28 November). Walcott lamented the fragmentation of Caribbean literature into national literatures. There is a West Indian cricket team, there is a West Indian literature in English, he fears Europe, fears being alienated, deracinated.

'Every West Indian has been severed from a continent, whether he is Indian, Chinese, Portuguese, or black.' 'The only possible realization in the West Indies is art. There is no possibility of the country becoming unified and having its own strengths except in its art. Because there is no economic power, there is no political power, Art is lasting.' Being brought up in an English colony he was contemporary with anyone using the language, but it had taken him a long time to find his own voice, to feel it natural and not a dialect.[7]

Walcott was lonely; busy with an international career, with friends in many countries, he remained an island, a jet-setting rather than floating island. Late in the year he wrote a draft of a poem 'Winter coming, Away from my Daughters'. He made a list of what he had accomplished during the year and of work ahead. He planned to stay at Crown Point Hotel near the airport in Tobago, now his usual base when not in New York or Port of Spain, for seventeen days, 5–23 December, where he would rewrite part of *Remembrance*, which Farrar, Straus and Giroux expected by April, and work on 'American, without America'. Then there were two new plays to draft, *North Rampart Street* or *Marie Laveau* and a revised *The Isle Is Full of Noises*. Once more he listed his finances, probable debts, engagements, and deadlines. Earnings included some readings, advances on finished manuscripts, Guggenheim funds, and teaching at Yale. There were taxes, the cost of hotels and transportation, money needed for his daughters and, especially, his son Peter and Norline. He would probably travel to Miami, 14–23 January, and then on 23–31 January to Jamaica, Oklahoma, and to New York in February.

At Crown Point he drew up possible cast lists for Caribbean and New York productions of *Marie Laveau*. 'Marie' interested him because of her background. Born in New Orleans in 1792, a free mulatto, she claimed that the La Veaux (*sic*) were descended from the noblest blood of France. On a page of his notebooks he quotes Sidney's 'Leave me, O love, which reacheth but to dust . . .', followed by a remark about self-pity, followed by a new poem 'Koenig of the River', dated Christmas Eve 1977, about a Conradian explorer at the end of Empire who has lost any sense of mission or purpose and who will soon vanish from the pages of history.

Walcott remained in Tobago over Christmas. He was emotional, feeling that he was part of a war between men and women. He knew he had treated his women badly and was worried about his children whom he was afraid of losing. He was afraid of exile. He was thinking of returning to Trinidad, but he was also thinking of big musical hits on Broadway, film rights, earning perhaps a half-million dollars a year. The actuality was less bright. Even with the Guggenheim he had borrowed over $1,500 from Farrar, Straus and Giroux during 1977. He paid back $500, his advance, and $480 from royalties.

On New Year's Day, 1978, Walcott wrote to Strachan from Tobago enclosing 'Koenig of the River'. He would have liked it for Halpern, but the *New Yorker* paid much more; he hoped to have another for *Antaeus*. Moss wrote (14 February) directly to Walcott saying he was delighted with it. Walcott (18 January) asked Strachan to send 'Sabbaths' to the *American Poetry Review*, which wanted a poem to go along with an essay about him in the March number, and to try 'Egypt, Tobago (For N.M.)' at the *New Yorker* or the *New York Review of Books*. He was 'sweating blood' awaiting his Guggenheim money. He had to go to New York for two days before Oklahoma and return to New York, the amount of time depending on Papp. Could he get readings from Dan Masterson at Rockland College or Frank MacShane at Columbia? 'The Star-Apple Kingdom' was sent first to Moss (31 May 1977) who felt that the poem (3 June) while beautiful required too much knowledge of Caribbean history and politics. Strachan asked (25 January) if she could give second choice on the poems to the *American Poetry Review*, which wanted more than one to go with an article. Could she send them 'The Schooner' as well?

During January Walcott was in Trinidad for the opening of a paperback book exhibition by the United States Information Service. He criticized the government for its failure to respect civil liberties and the press for not standing up to repression. 'This place is not a preserve of liberties . . . our journalists and commentators are regularly fired or investigated, . . . our writers are expected to think in a certain way . . . books are banned . . . every day we are losing more freedoms under the pretext of discipline and development.' The press in Trinidad carried no mention of Walcott's statement.[8]

In late January he was making more sketches for *Marie Laveau*. He had been paid $1,000 and expected two further payments of $2,500 plus a month's subsistence for the play, which was to open in St Thomas as a try-out for a possible Lincoln Center or Broadway production. During February he finished a still unpublished essay on Wole Soyinka's *The Road*, nine typed single-spaced pages, which he would send to Stepto for a book that Gates was planning. Like many of Walcott's essays it appears to have been put together by adding to earlier material, including production notes to his 1966 *The Road*, some notes concerning that production written for 'What the Twilight Says', and paragraphs written during 1971 or 72. Except for 'The Telephone Conversation' Walcott was not enamoured of Soyinka's poetry. He preferred the bright mosaics of Christopher Okigbo, and the non-mystic side of J. P. Clark.

The Soyinka essay was a major statement of his notions of theatre. Walcott claimed that *The Road* is written in the kind of prose that is poetry, like the prose of Genet, Brecht, and Beckett, which is poetry without aiming at poetic prose. Such prose is based on common experience, the vulgar, the humorous, unlike the solemn theatre poetry of T. S. Eliot. Great characters in drama suffer from sexual jealousy, flatulence, penny pinching; they stumble, bellow, calculate. They are fools, pitiful, but as they become wise their death transfigures. Once a writer sees such a person the other lesser characters are branches, opposites, other urges, not ideas. Soyinka's Professor is a great character, one of the few great ones of the modern theatre. Like Mother Courage the Professor is both ordinary and emblematic of a race or culture. Great drama is built around such figures as Hamlet, Oedipus, Othello, Macbeth, Falstaff, and Philoctetes, masks for the tribe or race. Without ritual and religion there is a thin naturalism. Great plays have absurd plot lines that a naturalist writer would not consider. Walcott's own aims and defence as a dramatist can be seen in his claim that great plays do not hold together as logical narratives. He did not like Soyinka's other plays, which he thought at times magnificent but obscure, tangled, even dull.

The essay then digresses into Method Acting which Walcott now regarded as an American technical achievement based on the precise observation of character, working in terms of phrases, incomplete utterances (just what he had brought to the Workshop almost two decades ago). Such a style is potentially poetic, but it lacks greatness as it closely follows what the writer intended. It is a method for directors and actors, artisans who distrust ambition and appearing foolish. American theatre has become unpoetic, the poets lack theatre technique. There are no characters in the American theatre with the tragic grandeur of Ahab. Ahab is America. The great tales are told and retold to unify society, religion, and culture. In the West Indies and Africa poetry is usual, rhyme contributes to order, and the poet belongs to theatre as he shares a common culture with the audience. In former colonies there is the excitement of conflicts between language, cultures, religions, which the poet must make into a coherence.[9]

He travelled from Trinidad through New York and arrived on 22 February in Norman, Oklahoma, where he was to be a juror for the $40,000 Neustadt International Prize for Literature sponsored by *World Literature Today* and the University of Oklahoma. Each juror has to nominate a candidate and Walcott nominated Naipaul about whom he was expected to speak, and compare with, other nominees for about fifteen to thirty minutes. Besides Brodsky and Walcott the jury that year included R. K. Narayan and William Jay Smith, along with writers from Finland, Denmark, Brazil, Germany, Hungary, and Austria. Narayan, who for medical reasons could not fly to the United States, sent a message nominating Graham Greene. The jurors met for the whole day on 23 February and for the following morning; Brodsky championed Czeslaw Milosz, who was given the prize. There was a banquet on the 25th, and the jurors left the next day.

Walcott was thought distant except when he was with Brodsky with whom he appeared good friends, staying up late at night, telling stories, reciting poems. At Norman, Walcott started the Horatian 'Forest of Europe', dedicated to Brodsky, about exile, friendship, and writing poetry during a time of evil. It was the first major work in which Walcott took up the theme of the fate of American Indians. History consists of evils, and of poets exiled for telling the truth:

'The rustling of ruble notes by the lemon Neva.'
Under your exile's tongue, crisp under heel,
the gutturals crackle like decaying leaves,
the phrase from Mandelstam circles with light
in a brown room, in barren Oklahoma.

There is a Gulag Archipelago
under this ice, where the salt, mineral spring
of the long Trail of Tears runnels these plains
as hard and open as a herdsman's face
sun-cracked and stubbled with unshaven snow.

    .   .   .   .   .   .

and every February, every 'last autumn,'
you write far from the threshing harvesters
folding wheat like a girl plaiting her hair,
far from Russia's canals quivering with sunstroke,
a man living with English in one room.

    .   .   .   .   .   .

but now that fever is a fire whose glow
warms our hands, Joseph, as we grunt like primates
exchanging gutturals in this winter cave
of a brown cottage, while in the drifts outside
mastodons force their systems through the snow.[10]

In late February Walcott, on his way back to Trinidad, returned to New York, where Brodsky had a flat at the Chelsea Hotel.

Walcott's close friendships have been with other artists, often with outsiders creating a place for themselves. Such friendships have also been with those erudite yet actively engaged in the arts. There was his father's circle of friends, Dunstan and Harry Simmons, Hunter Francois, Slade Hopkinson, Mark Strand, Halpern, and now, and most important, Brodsky. Brodsky was so totally dedicated to poetry, language, and culture that his fame as someone who stood up to Soviet Communist persecution meant little to him; what counted in Brodsky's own eyes was his loyalty to his art. His refusal to betray his art for political compromise had led to exile. His family was unable to leave Russia. Walcott felt he too was an exile, even a political exile, and he had also left a family and life behind. Walcott had not been directly forced out, but he felt that the lack of support for his Workshop, his inability to support himself as a writer in Trinidad, were due to his being mulatto, and his unwillingness to accept Williams and those like him. 'The Schooner *Flight*' was about this.

Brodsky and Walcott shared many of the same tastes in English poetry, and both were essentially loners who would write of their own world while teaching in American universities. Both were poets in love with words and sounds. Listen to tapes of Brodsky reading his poetry in Russian and you know you are listening to a real poet even if you cannot understand a word of it. Poets throughout the world read like that, sound like that. Walcott does not read in a similar projective way, his voice is more reserved, at times introverted, but his poetry has a complex organization of sound and rhythm, its own strong cadences, its own elaborate harmonies. It is as possible to enjoy a Walcott poem in English without understanding it, as with a Brodsky poem in Russian. Both poets may speak of many things in their literary criticism, but once Walcott met Brodsky he also began writing criticism which, once the noise is filtered out, is really about sound, cadence, tone, pitch, harmonies, metrics, caesuras, not ideas.

They enjoyed each other's company: the quoting, citing, alluding to, and parodying of poetry; they both were committed to literary culture during a time when the arts were being sidetracked into politics and social work. Brodsky was the embodiment of the St Petersburg grand tradition of Russian European high culture, Walcott was a product of Caribbean self-creation from its location as the confluence of so many peoples and cultures and empires of the world. They also shared an obscene sense of humour.[11]

Walcott met Brodsky during a time when his own poetry, as can be seen from *The Star-Apple Kingdom*, was changing and becoming more complex, sophisticated, cosmopolitan, richer than previously. From *The Gulf* to *Sea Grapes*, even in *Another Life*, Walcott had been working towards a plainer style, trying to get the power of prose into his poetry. For a poet with an instinct towards metaphor, who saw poetry as essentially metaphor, prose balanced his tendencies towards obscurity and complexity. Brodsky's familiarity with the classics of Europe, the classics of English poetry (which he had often read in the same anthologies as Walcott had in St Lucia), and his being part of the ongoing tradition of modern Russian poetry meant that in his company Walcott was part of something familiar yet much larger and grander. Both were exceptionally talented outsiders from opposite extremes of Western culture, with local cultures of their own behind them, who were now at the centre of the new Western empire. Both would see themselves as the new Barbarians who had conquered the new Rome by having excelled the inhabitants in mastery of their literary craft. Brodsky had arrived first, had the larger reputation and would open many doors, including those to the Nobel Prize.

Walcott has often mentioned how Brodsky has helped him, especially in the international world of literary prizes. Brodsky sang his praises in places previously uninterested in Caribbean writing. Walcott began imitating Brodsky's mannerisms, his habits, and his way with audiences at poetry readings and conferences. Within a few years he was more distant, harder to approach, forbidding, a man of the world, a 'gentleman'. Often Brodsky's mannerisms translate differently according to Walcott's personality; Brodsky's European reserve increased Walcott's appearance of disdain.

He was hoping to finish *The Star-Apple Kingdom* manuscript in early May. In Trinidad during March he finished another version of 'The Schooner Flight' and a draft of what he thought of as his Oklahoma Brodsky poem. He had also been thinking about Romare Bearden since he had received his copy of the *Massachusetts Review*. During 1995 Walcott recalled his first meeting with Bearden. Bearden had wanted to meet Walcott and a doorman at the Chelsea let Bearden and a friend, another painter, into Walcott's apartment. Walcott said Bearden was a genius with cut-outs, with scissors, who had not had the attention he deserved because he was black. Bearden was a storyteller who made narratives based on his own experience, and had an astonishing sense of colour. He got it right when he cut. The artist lived on St Maarten, painted St Maarten, and owed much to Matisse. The images and colours in his Odyssey collages are Caribbean. Walcott claimed that one of the most spectacular works of illustration is Bearden's Odyssey collages, which may have influenced his own *Omeros*. He shared with Walcott the Caribbean experience of the sea, of travel between islands, of parallels to the *Odyssey*, not to the classical white blanched-out epic, but to the epic as peasants travelling between islands on a small boat with sailors and pigs.[12]

Bearden had a place on Canal Street and Walcott wanted him to do a cover for his book. When Nanette, Bearden's wife, brought Strachan a colour transparency of 'The Sea Nymph' Strachan (13 April) thought the colours fabulous, but the cost of production and the increased price could be immense. She was going to see what might be done using four-colour separations, skimping on paper and binding material quality, and preparing the design in house. She joked that Farrar, Straus and Giroux could cut costs by running Walcott's poems together without stanza or title breaks, South American stream-of-consciousness style. The 'Sea Nymph' was used for the dust jacket of *Star-Apple Kingdom*, one of the few jackets without a photograph of Walcott or one of his paintings.

While at Crown Point, Tobago, Walcott had written *Pantomime*, an amusing comedy, one of his best and most performed plays. The hotel was then being managed by the retired English actor Arthur Bentley, who had come to Trinidad to manage hotels. Walcott has often claimed to have been impressed by the free and witty exchange between Bentley and his staff. Although Bentley was manager, he was an outsider, a foreigner, who to Walcott represented many of the English he had observed on the islands. Whereas the West Indian started with little, but felt secure, and hustled for opportunities, the British seemed soft, defeated, nursing old wounds. The play was muse-given, the voices were there in the hotel, and seemed to dictate the play, one of the few times since *Ti-Jean and His Brothers* that Walcott wrote a play without planning and long labour. Like many of Walcott's writings *Pantomime* has some sources in his own life—he performed in British-style pantomimes as a child—and is despite its naturalism a house of mirrors. It begins with the hotel owner, a former English actor, recalling a music-hall routine and the central action of the play is a conflict about his attempt to get a black employee, Jackson, to perform in a hotel production of a Robinson Crusoe pantomime and Jackson's refusal, which turns into a debate about European and Caribbean culture and behaviour. *Pantomime* was performed in the hotel, and was then produced by Helen Camps, a former Trinidad Theatre Workshop actress who got along well with Walcott, and who wanted something from him for her new All Theatre Productions. It ran 12–22 April at the Little Carib, directed by Albert Laveau, with Wilbert Holder as Jackson.

As a child Walcott knew the Crusoe story, had seen illustrations of it; he used Crusoe as a persona for the alienated individual and artist in his *Castaway* poems. He had wittily reviewed a bad Trinidadian Christmas pantomime of 'Robinson Crusoe', which had strayed so far away from the original form for him to describe it as 'a new art form invented in Trinidad, a theatrical lime. This doesn't only mean that it is a kind of lemon.'[13] Tobago, with its lovely beaches, is misleadingly advertised as where Columbus landed. *Pantomime* was his own, radical revisioning of the story.

Pantomime revises the Crusoe story as Trewe the English castaway turns out to be far weaker than his Friday, Jackson. If Trewe at first appears emblematic of British imperialism, or neocolonialism, white economic power, and domination, he is really someone who has failed in his career and personal life in England, a loser, a softie; he has come to Tobago because with his limited emotional and other resources the role of a hotel manager in the West Indies appears easier than life in England. Jackson, the black employee, is the one who is stronger, tougher, dominating, threatening. The seeming roles of master and slave are reversed in the emotional relationship and indeed in Trewe's dependence upon Jackson. The two men are continually adapting, modifying, and adjusting roles, they are players, actors, both in the literal sense and in relation to each other. The relationship is complicated because although there is the ease of give and take there is still the economic and racial difference, as seen in the contrast between Trewe's private bathroom and Jackson's use of the staff toilet. Trewe must understand that his emotional wounds, his feeling of exile and loss, can only be healed by a more realistic recognition of his dependency on Jackson, not just a superficial willingness to play Friday himself, but a deeper transformation. This would be the real revolution. Jackson already has, so to speak, political power, has long had legal and cultural equality, but for Trewe to go beyond such symbols of decolonization to acceptance of what has become a fact, that his own life depends on Jackson and the blacks, would mean living together in ways that might at present be uncomfortable to both Trewe and Jackson.

Walcott would make many interpretive statements about *Pantomime*, mostly suggesting the play was an amusing exercise in theatre genres or a kind of psychological boxing match in which two guys playfully, and sometimes not so playfully, throw punches at each other, until one manages to get beyond the defences and help the other towards healing some long-term problems. This is a shift from seeing the Crusoe–Friday relationship as mostly one of alienation, of just being a Castaway. In a 1988 interview Walcott explained the range of possibilities in Crusoe and Friday.[14]

'Crusoe in relation to Friday is emblematic of Christianising cannibals and converting people from savagery . . . The more involved aspect of it is: How does Crusoe feel? What does he become, isolated from his country and his language? Who is this man who only has himself to perpetuate?' Walcott then turns to a rather different question, 'What does Friday do for him?'

Walcott claimed that Friday's 'subservience is not surrender, it is sharing'. Third World writers are not concerned with dependency, what empire does to a colony, but rather what a colony does for the empire.

This is a remarkable twist in the discussion of empires and colonies, in which the supposed slave instead of complaining says I have helped create my supposed master and will save him from himself. It might also be understood as Walcott indicating that English poetry and culture cannot remain the same, indeed they have already been changing.

There was also a more personal source of *Pantomime*. In the many comments Walcott was to make over the years about *Pantomime* there recur the notion of two men coming closer together through quarrels and the notion of a cure. Around 1975 Walcott and Wilbert Holder went through a cure together at Alcoholics Anonymous and this is a subtext of the play, which uses the drama of the Holder–Walcott relationship during that period. Part of the rich complexity of the play and the reason why it often erupts into threatened violence and near collapse results from the wit and social message layered on this more personal drama.

Holder was an extremely powerful, sarcastic actor who later performed Jackson in productions in Florida and Minneapolis, and would overwhelm those on stage who did not stand up to him. A problem with this play is that most of the white actors who performed the role of Trewe, the Englishman, were mild and did not have the 'front' of Bentley. It is not a part for a guilt-stricken white liberal, but for a hardened performer, someone who enjoys the give and take of trading verbal punches. It is through this that the play within the play is created and Trewe begins to be cured. The play was an attempt by Walcott to move beyond the purposeful use of contradictions common to his writing and work towards resolution. Walcott's writing at this time shows an interest in psychology as he had himself consulted a friend about some of his worries and recurring emotions.

Strachan (16 May) sent Moss 'Forest of Europe' and 'In the Virgins'. These were among the three final poems for *The Star-Apple Kingdom* volume. Walcott would be in New York 14–20 June. Moss (6 June) accepted 'Forest of Europe', queried stanzas six and seven, where 'like' appeared four times, as well as in other stanzas. It might be intentional, but was not Walcott's usual practice, and Moss thought some excising might be considered. In the book version 'like' appears three times in stanzas six and seven. The conscious foregrounding of comparisons begins in the first line of the poem 'The last leaves fell like notes from a piano' and continues through the first eleven stanzas of the poem as Walcott helps the reader through an otherwise extremely complicated sequence of analogies that find their resolution in the clear but concentrated metaphoric language of the final five stanzas. I have always regarded this poem as influenced by Russian Modernist poetics, as well as a tradition of accretions of symbolism that can be seen in Lovelace's Grasse-hopper poem, to which Walcott's is related. Walcott has mentioned that Brodsky showed him that intelligence could be in poetry; Walcott felt he had formerly avoided it in his verse. There were ideas, argumentative structures, but now the poetry became more full of intellectual observation about the present and life. A level of comment was added between West Indian politics and the universal; this can be seen in the new volume in the 'Forest of Europe'. The discussion of Mandelstam moves from poetry's own politics of truth to the claim that the truest poetry is both a communion across centuries and an original language of primitive sound and inspired metaphor.

During a poetry reading at the Little Carib Theatre (24 May) Walcott said that 'The Star-Apple Kingdom' showed the dilemma of Caribbean politicians who must choose between democracy and socialism. Socialism could only be imposed by tyranny and force. The poem is about Jamaica and the choices faced by Michael Manley. It is about Walcott's own colonial inheritance and the humiliations colonials suffered from the English. He was also influenced by García Marquéz's compression of Caribbean experience into narrative metaphors in *The Autumn of the Patriarch*. Recalling the humiliation of hearing Professor Croston speak condescendingly of the beauty of the Jamaican landscape, Walcott's poem begins ironically with Jamaican cattle trying to appear like the British cattle pictured in a wall plaque inside a sugar baron's great house. There is also a portrait of the planter's family. Outside there is the scream of anguish that cannot be heard from the black servants. The young ruler contemplates what must be done to heal such screams, but there is the danger of revolutions becoming military juntas as so often in Latin America.[15]

The events of 1970 and 1973 remained on Walcott's mind along with the increasing militancy of regional politics. *In a Fine Castle* was evolving into what became *The Last Carnival*. Walcott wrote (6 June) a four-page film outline of *The Last Carnival*. Although it shares with the play scripts a love story between a black journalist and a rich white French Creole woman during the 1970 Trinidad Black Power riots, here several of the revolutionaries are killed by government forces, and the revolutionaries plan to slip a real tank and guerrillas armed with machine-guns, grenades, and mortars into the Carnival procession. The coup is prevented without the public learning how close they had been to a bloody civil war. Black Power, however, has divided the black man and white woman; he joins the marchers outside and she, feeling no longer accepted, leaves the country.

Walcott was in Port of Spain when a copy-edited *Star-Apple Kingdom* was sent to him with Strachan's questions (25 July). In each case she provided a substitute, but wanted his approval. There were minor queries such as capitalization, start of stanzas, punctuation. Strachan carefully edited Walcott, even questioning his vocabulary and suggesting phrases, but except in emergencies her suggestions were sent to him for approval. She was being troubled by the Yale and Columbia administrators. Halpern, who had started teaching at Columbia University in 1976, became Chair of the School of Arts in 1978. He hired Brodsky and Walcott to teach classes. Yale complained that Walcott wanted to teach at Columbia as well. Strachan replied that it was only for two hours a week. She promised Gates she would try to get Walcott to live in New Haven as he was required to be there three days a week.

Walcott (3 August) sent Yale a long delayed written acceptance that he would be Visiting Lecturer in Afro-American Studies for the first semester 1978–9. He was looking forward to working again with Robert Brustein in the Drama Department. He had some questions and problems. Where could he stay overnight in New Haven between classes and at what price? He would like an advance of $750 by 20 August to settle his domestic bills for a long absence and to help with travelling and hotels in New York during September.

Earlier (18 April) Strachan had sent Walcott the May/June *American Poetry Review* with Valerie Trueblood's piece about him.[16] The issue had a photograph of Walcott on the cover and several poems from what would be *The Star-Apple Kingdom*, including the title poem. Trueblood's largely descriptive survey of Walcott's poetry is full of insights. While *Another Life* is an evocation of paradise, his Eden always has a snake. *Sea Grapes* concerns home, wandering, responsibilities, obsessions, islands, the consolations of art, seeking and refusing peace. 'Lost Federation' and 'Negatives' are angry. His poems reveal an irritability with the world along with a calming vision in which a mind is persuaded from anger to resignation to delight. Walcott usually undercuts himself, he is a poet of finish and control, so controlled he does not need understatement. There are changes of tone and mood within poems. He can be passive, innocent, petulant, wistful, melancholic, comic, have second thoughts. There are few people in the poetry, there is loneliness, elegy, loss, but there can be awe and feelings of grace. When birds appear everything pauses; they are seldom used as metaphors. The descriptive language is sometimes from the past; talking of influences on Walcott is like talking about baking powder when you taste a cake.

Papp's New York Shakespeare Festival had a report (13 June) on the first New York production of Walcott's *The Sea at Dauphin* by the Urban Arts Corps (a member of the Black Theatre Alliance), directed by Leon Morenzie who had been in the 1972 *Ti-Jean*. The reviewer found that the West Indian dialect distanced him and the play did not touch him, although it seemed powerful and raised interesting questions. There was a reading of *Pantomime* on 29 June at the Ladies' Fort Theatre. The NYSF reviewer thought it a bit long and lacking in motivation, but intelligent and challenging with stunning monologues. A good director could get out some of the bugs. Walcott wrote to Papp (9 August) asking his plans for *Remembrance* and *Pantomime*. Meanwhile Trinidad and Tobago Television, 4–18 August, shot a version of *Pantomime* in Tobago, which was broadcast at the end of the month.

Walcott returned from Tobago on 22 August, worked some more on *O Babylon!*, and left for New York and the Chelsea on 3 September. This was to be his base until he rented an apartment at 404 Dodge Street, with Norline. He commuted by train between teaching at Yale on Tuesday and Wednesday (usually holding his three classes on one day) and Columbia where he taught 11 a.m.–1 p.m., regularly on Thursday. There were often play rehearsals in New York and some poetry readings at other universities. On Thursday, 21 September, he read at Wesleyan University, for which he was paid $300, but had to remain overnight. For the entire semester he earned over $10,000 from the two universities, but Norline often felt left out and bored.

At Columbia Walcott gave a course on 'The English Pentameter Tradition'. The first day he assigned 'a strong dose of classical pentameter poetry'. He had the class memorize the poetry of, and recite in class, Frost, Edward Thomas, and Larkin (whom they studied in depth). Walcott would himself recite from memory in each class. 'His voice had an island lilt to it that lent a special music to lines by Chaucer and Milton, Wordsworth and Hardy, Auden and Gunn. He knew the canon of great pentameter verse inside and out.' Walcott told his class the more severe the discipline the more the liberty obtained. He would quote Yeats's 'Out of the quarrels with others we make rhetoric. Out of the quarrel with ourselves we make poetry.' Walcott appeared to have a mission to make his students love the classics, and knew that they had to get the song of traditional verse in their ears before they themselves could sing. Outside class Walcott helped students revise their poems and joked about getting 10 per cent off their career.[17]

At Yale he was Visiting Fellow in Play-writing in the School of Drama. The visiting faculty at the time included Lee Bruer, Martha Clarke, John Guare, Arthur Kopit, Jan Knott, and George White. Robert Brustein was Dean of the School of Drama and Director of the Yale Repertory Theatre. Walcott taught along with Kopit and John Madden in Drama 17, Playwrights' Practicum, which involved the student in the practical side of a playwright's work in progress. He also taught Drama 27, Playwriting II, which he shared with Jean-Claude vanItalie. He was also in the Afro-American Studies Program.

Back in the Village after two decades Walcott began recalling his nine months there in the late fifties. During September he sent Edith Oliver 'Reveries of Spring Street', part of 'American, without America', about his months in the Village during 1958–9. Three weeks later he received a reply saying that the chapter lacked focus; it required too much revision for the *New Yorker* to encourage him to rewrite it.

He was also writing a play recalling his earlier Village days, *Solo to the Hudson*, which Walcott hoped to see produced in Port of Spain during August 1979. The play, dedicated to Galt MacDermot, has a prologue based on Paul Goodman's poem 'The Lordly Hudson'. It is set in a New York City loft on Spring Street in the Village in the seventies—the script refers to Nixon as the new president which is changed to ex-president—where three jazz musicians, veterans of Vietnam, try to cleanse themselves of guilt through Indian meditation. The play contrasts the Village of 1957–8 (when Walcott was living there) with the 1970s when the three have become disillusioned with their lives and society. They came to the Village with hope, now in early middle age their hopes have vanished. Even the Indian guru turns out to be a fake, a Trinidadian East Indian who worked for Americans at the army base (and who appears in 'The Rig'). After a week of trying to live without sex and junk food the three turn violently on their guru, as symbolic of the Americans' relationship to the Third World. The second act consists mostly of memories, including that of Castro marching into Havana (Walcott was in New York at the time), and ends with the group seeing that it is too late to drop out; they go separate ways.

The use of a small group of jazz musicians in a loft playing jazz and some other features of the play recall Jack Gelber's off-Broadway classic *The Connection*. Here the Connection is the West Indian guru rather than a black drug dealer. Walcott's play uses a characteristic of the avant-garde theatre of the 1950s and 1960s with its sudden shifts in levels of behaviour; here the realistic comedy of three impatient men complaining about their withdrawal from ordinary life suddenly turns into memories of killing in Vietnam and the beginning of what seems a ritualized murder of the guru, who survives by presenting a bill for his services. At the play's end there is the sentimental vision of others coming from the provinces to New York seeking action, most of whom will soon return home, but some will stay because of their love of the city. What film was that?

Solo to the Hudson is uneven, often trite, in places powerful, while lacking cohesion or a clear action. There is much intensity and theatricality, but too often you have heard or seen this before in other plays and in movies. Walcott had a few years earlier written a poem recalling 'Spring Street '58'. *Solo to the Hudson*, like many Walcott plays, has some autobiographical basis while being an expression of how America had changed from the fun of hippiedom to post-Vietnam disillusionment. Twenty years later, when Walcott returned to the Village in 1998 at the time of *The Capeman*, he reread the script of the unproduced *Solo to the Hudson* and pronounced it good.

He left, on 29 September, for St Thomas where at the instigation of Ruth Moore he was invited to speak at the Governor's Conference on Library Services. Carrol Fleming from California was living on a yacht, writing poetry, and earning money by contributing freelance articles to local magazines. Over the next few days she and Walcott went to the beach together, where he worked on the galley proofs of *The Star-Apple Kingdom* and she taped a long brilliant interview, parts of which were used in local newspapers, but the largest part of which was not published until years later in *The Caribbean Writer*.[18] It is an excellent exposition of Walcott's ideas.

Walcott told Fleming that painting gave him other ways to regard form and subjects than the platitudes of politics and literary criticism. The opposition between what others considered the universal and local, the centre and circumference, was in painting more a creative tension. Walcott explained that much of the Caribbean remained 'primal', Edenic; there were still totally deserted beaches; mountainous areas you could see that had had no inhabitants, probably not even Arawaks or Caribs, no explorers, not even woodcutters. The landscape, sea, and sky appeared vast. For a representational painter the intensity of the light, the blue of the bays, was fantastic. To represent it and not treat it as inferior to or a version of Italy or England was a new beginning. Much of Caribbean history took place on water—the voyagers, the sea battles—or on the fringes of the islands—the forts—and such history was rapidly lost; sea cultures were erased and renewed. In such a culture the poet was a Crusoe, an isolated explorer, but not in the sense of a European imperialist finding paradise. We owned this paradise. It was our possession. But writers of his generation also felt that they had behind them an 'English Tradition' of language and customs. Discovering and exploring identity could be bitter, as with Naipaul, or an elation. Walcott warned against feelings of inferiority, resentment, and superiority. Writers were engaged in a continuing process of learning and must know everything. It was wrong to say a Caribbean writer should not write a poem about 'snow', and it was wrong that a poem about a breadfruit should be treated as comical; breadfruits were as beautiful as cantaloupes.

I have often wondered about Walcott's instructions to actors to use their own pronunciation, as I knew that even within the West Indies the accents of other islands may make a play seem difficult. For him this is a matter of the power of the artist. To falsify the language you use will lead to a falsification of the work. A British reader should look up words the poet uses rather than expect Walcott to use familiar words. English is a world language, but tones get lost. National

Englishes are tones and the writer must be true to the sound of his voice, which will be the 'sound of his own race', not requiring any artificiality. Walcott is using 'race' as had James Joyce in *A Portrait of the Artist* to mean a blurring of ethnic and national cultures rather than 'colour' or 'blood'. Walcott believed that arguments over language were political or sociological; he, as a writer, had his own tone, his own voice. He was interested in the area in-between standard and West Indian English, such as how to avoid the speaker being too literary in 'The Schooner *Flight*'. He gave as an example of the uses of dialect 'and a wind start to interfere with the trees' with its suggestiveness and topical sensuality. If he had instead written 'the wind started to interfere with the trees' the meaning and effect of the sound would be different.

If Walcott wanted West Indian voices to have their own authority he also wanted readers to catch other cultural references and echoes when they were familiar with them. In 'Schooner Flight' he was writing a mini-*Odyssey* with an Odysseus travelling up the islands. There is also the *Pilgrim's Progress*-like journey taken by a ploughman through England in *Piers Plowman*. Using *Piers Plowman* means that English is no longer the property of Englishmen. The way Latin words exist but with local Caribbean meanings shows how things survive and are transformed; this is especially true of the Caribbean where, because of the smallness of the islands, languages become intensely varied. As expressions change so do their significance.

When Walcott returned to the mainland his October schedule was a lecture at Yale on Monday and classes at 10, 1.30, and 4 p.m. Tuesday. Gordon Davidson arrived on 13 October and Walcott hoped to show him a new draft of *Marie Laveau*. A week later he was putting his new plays into a sequence: *Remembrance, Pantomime, The Isle is Full of Noises, Solo to the Hudson, Marie Laveau*.

Early in November Walcott flew to Trinidad for *Encore*, two nights by the La Chapelle-Douglas Dance Company, to which Norline belonged, which had evolved from the Trinidad Theatre Workshop Dance Company. The Company might be seen as part of Walcott's long involvement with dance in Trinidad, starting with Beryl McBurnie through Astor Johnson to La Chapelle and Douglas. He then read at the University of South Florida and returned to Yale. On the 9th there was a short reading for the Academy of American Poets and on the 10th he was photographed in connection with an interview for the BBC.

In 1978 the BBC recorded a sequence of programmes about the Caribbean which was broadcast in late January 1979. David Pryce-Jones interviewed Walcott, Rex Nettleford of the Jamaica National Dance Theatre Company, and Elaine Perkins, who created *Dulciminia*, the latter a Radio Jamaica serial built around hustlers, prostitutes, and gangsters. At the time of the interview, mid-November, Walcott was in New York, living in Greenwich Village, teaching at both Columbia and Yale. He was enjoying New York after the turmoils of the

1. Derek Walcott writing poetry, St Lucia, *c*.1946–48.

FIRST AND LAST POEMS

HUNTER J. FRANCOIS

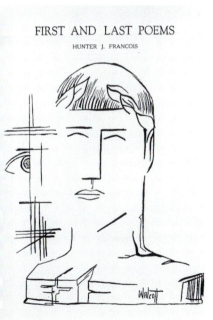

2. Derek Walcott, Junior Master, St Mary's College, St Lucia, 1949.

3. Derek Walcott's cover for *First and Last Poems* by Hunter Francois, 1950.

4. Derek Walcott being amusing, St Lucia, early 1950s.

5. Derek Walcott with Faye Walcott and new son Peter, Jamaica, 1955.

6. First Marriage, St Lucia 1954. Fay and Derek Walcott. Roderick Walcott behind Derek.

7. First Marriage, St Lucia 1954. Front row: Harold Simmons, Nigel Walcott, Alix Walcott. Second row: Fay and Derek Walcott. Third Row: Roderick Walcott behind Derek.

8. George Odlum, Howick Elcock, and Eric Brandford in Derek Walcott's *The Sea at Daupin* St Lucia Arts Guild, broadcast on WIBS, experimimental radio station 1954.

9. Derek Walcott's *Drums and Colours*, 1958, Trinidad. The West Indian Festival of the Arts for the inauguration of the West Indian Federation.

10. Derek Walcott's *Drums and Colours*, 1958, Trinidad. The West Indian Festival of the Arts for the inauguration of the West Indian Federation. Desmond Rostant as Anton Calixte, William Webb as a Slave.

11. Errol Jones and Horace James in Derek Walcott's *The Sea at Dauphin*, The New Company and The Whitehall Players, directed by Errol Hill, Trinidad, 1954.

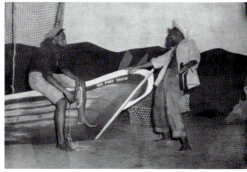

12. Derek Walcott in the early 1960s.

13. Derek Walcott, George White, and a critic at the National Playwrights Conference, Eugene O'Neill Theatre Center, Waterford, Conneticut, July, 1969.

14. Derek Walcott directing the Trinidad Theatre Workshop in *Dream on Monkey Mountain* at the National Playwrights Conference, Eugene O'Neill Theatre Center, Waterford, Conneticut, July, 1969.

16. Derek Walcott painting the portrait of Peter Ireson, Trinidad, 1969.

15. Derek Walcott's portrait of Peter Ireson, Trinidad, 1969.

17. Derek Walcott working in his studio in Trinidad, 1969.

18. Derek Walcott holding his daughter, Anna, Port of Spain, Trinidad, 1969.

19. Derek Walcott drumming, Albert Laveau to his left, in Central Park, July 1972, between rehearsals for New York Shakespeare Festival's production of *Ti-Jean and His Brothers*.

20. André Tanker, Ellsworth Primus, Hamilton Parris, and Adele Bynoe in Derek Walcott's *Ti-Jean and His Brothers*, Trinidad Theatre Workshop rehearsal, Trinidad, probably 1970.

21. Derek Walcott at home in Trinidad, 1974.

22. Derek Walcott, 1974.

23. Front (left to right): Norline Metivier, Nigel Scott, Helen Camps. Back: Carol LaChapelle, Stephanie King. Trinidad Theatre Workshop's production of Derek Walcott's *The Joker of Seville*, Trinidad, 1974. Period Costumes by Walcott.

29. Derek Walcott's poster for *O Babylon!* Trinidad, 1976.

30. Hamilton Parris as Raphael, Trinidad Theatre Workshop Production of *The Joker of Seville*, Jamaica, 1975, Richard Montgomery's costumes.

31. Carol LaChapelle as Ana and Norline Metivier as Aminta, Trinidad Theatre Production of *The Joker of Seville*, Jamaica, 1975, Richard Montgomery's costumes.

32. Derek Walcott's ink drawing of Priscilla for possible American production of *O Babylon!*, 1978.

33. Derek Walcott's watercolour notebook sketch for *Marie Laveau*, 1978.

35. Derek Walcott's ink drawing of Bambolla Marc for *Marie Laveau* with Maurice Brasch as Mark. 1978.

4. Derek Walcott's ink drawing of Bambolla Marc for *Marie Laveau* with Maurice Brasch as Mark. 1978.

6. Derek Walcott's ink drawing *emembrance*, Directed by Walcott for he Courtyard Players, St Croix, 1977.

37. Derek Walcott's watercolour notebook sketch for Papa Sam for his play *Marie Laveau* 1978.

38. A section of Dunstan St Omer's mural behind the Altar at the Roseau Church, St Lucia, 1973.

39. Dunstan St Omer with Derek Walcott at Waves beach restaurant, St Lucia, early 1990s.

40. Poster by Derek Walcott for his production of *Marie Laveau*, Trinidad, 1980.

41. Derek Walcott and Joseph Brodsky in front of Trailways bus at Hartwick Colege, New York, 2 October, 1980.

42. Rehearsal for *The Rig*, television film script and direction by Derek Walcott, for Bunyan, Trinidad, 1982.

43. Rehearsal for *The Rig*, television film script and direction by Derek Walcott, for Bunyan, Trinidad, 1982

44. Fran McDormand in front of Peter Walcott's canvas backdrop for the world premiere of *The Last Carnival*, Warwick Productions, Trinidad, July 1982.

45. Derek Walcott discussing *The Last Carnival* with the cast, July 1982. To the right of Derek Walcott are Fran McDormand and Cotter Smith.

58. Marie Richardson and Johan Lindell in *Sista Karnevaleu* (*The Last Carnival*) Kungliga Dramatiska, Stockholm, September, 1992.

59. Marie Richardson and Rolf Skoglund in *Sista Karnevaleu* (*The Last Carnival*) Kungliga Dramatiska, Stockholm, September, 1992.

60. Tine Matulessy, Marie Richardson (foreground), Olof Willgen, Rolf Skoglund and Annika Hansson (background) in *Sista Karnevaleu* (*The Last Carnival*) Kungliga Dramatiska, Stockholm, September, 1992.

61. Thorsten Flinck and Irene Lindh *Sista Karnevaleu* (*The Last Carnival*) Kungliga Dramatiska, Stockholm, September, 1992.

62. Derek Walcott addressing Trinidad Theatre Workshop actors during rehearsal of *Nobel Celebration*, Boston, 1993.

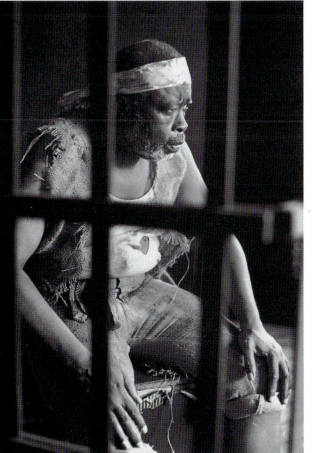

63. Errol Jones as Makak in Derek Walcott's *Dream on Monkey Mountain*, Trinidad, 1993.

64. David Dabydeen and Derek Walcott, Honorary Degree Ceremony, University of Warwick, 1998.

Trinidad Theatre Workshop. 'Why should one go down to an empty building, find the chairs, get a carpenter, sit on the steps waiting for actors who don't turn up? My generation has gone through a pioneering phase but it's still all to be done. There's no support. The Caribbean is a wearing-out place.' Jones saw Walcott at 48 poised for achievement with 'The Star-Apple Kingdom' already causing a stir in its cautionary advice to his friend Michael Manley, the Prime Minister of Jamaica, against following Castro. After Joseph Brodsky stopped over, Walcott said 'God is genuinely dead in some countries' and Pryce-Jones observed that they were an 'unlikely pair, except that both believe in the power of art to heal and redeem'. Walcott remarked that his strongest desire was to be a painter, but temperamentally he was not right for it. 'Now if there's one thing I'd like to do it's to paint.'[19]

During November Walcott read at Trinity College (15), was in Toronto (17–18), returned to New York for (20) Brodsky's reading at the YMHA, and read (29) at the University of Hartford. He read and lectured (5–6 December) at Brown University for Michael Harper; his last class was 14 December, just in time to return to Port of Spain for Helen Camps's 14–16 December second, different, production of *Pantomime* at the Little Carib Theatre. He was in Tobago 18–24 December, then returned to Trinidad, and returned to Tobago with his daughters 27–9 December. After readings and blocking of *Remembrance* in Port of Spain (30–1 December) he returned to Tobago for a week in January.

21

1979 *The Star-Apple Kingdom,*
Seamus Heaney

WALCOTT, Norline with him, returned from Trinidad to Tobago where he wrote
to Strachan (16 January) contrasting the mild peaceful landscape, for him a paradise and a sanitarium, with his domestic problems. He needed money for his
mortgage and taxes. Strachan should ask for at least $300 per reading, other-
wise, because of the travel, they were not worth his doing. He was going on 5
February to St Croix as a Visiting Distinguished Professor at the College of the
Virgin Islands and to rehearse *Pantomime*. He would teach at Rutgers University
from late March for two months. He had finished *The Isle is Full of Noises* and was
continuing to work on *Marie Laveau* and his autobiography. Norline would be
coming with him to New York where he hoped at Easter to bring his daughters
Anna and Lizzie.

Arnold Highfield of the College of the Virgin Islands met Walcott and Norline
at the airport for Ruth Moore. They stayed with him for two months. Highfield
was trained in French Creole culture, linguistics, and had studied anthropology
with a professor who was a student of Herskovits. He wrote poetry and followed
modern poetry. Although white and from the north, Highfield is married to a
West Indian. He and Walcott found interests in common, got along, and Highfield enjoyed Walcott's company. Each day Walcott would read Highfield's copy
of the *New York Times*, and they would talk about what they read.

Highfield thought Walcott delightful, witty, always aware of language,
making puns and allusions. Walcott was a pleasure to be around, an excellent con-
versationalist; he seemed to live in language and said that if he had any ability
with plots he would have been a novelist. He was more open with Highfield than

with most people. Highfield had recently visited Haiti and Walcott wanted to know about it. He also had a local television show and Walcott spoke about their making a film together. Highfield felt Walcott was like a child expecting always to get his own way, using a combination of great charm and bullying impatience. He would rapidly go from charming and amusing to having a go the local actors rehearsing *Pantomime*. He was in charge whether he was being amusing or short tempered. He expected Norline or Highfield to chauffeur him. When Highfield would accuse him of trying to use him by playing on his emotions or telling him some story, Walcott would laugh and admit it, even take Highfield into what he thought of as an amusing confidential joke, his ability to get what he wanted. Highfield appears to be one of the few to whom Walcott would talk proudly of his ability to get what he wanted.

On the topic of how society treats artists or matters of money, Walcott could lose his charm. He felt that the world owed artists; he gave a talk at the university the next semester in which he said people 'used' artists—artists should never work without payment. Walcott often found it difficult to listen to people who had no interest for him. He did this to one of Highfield's friends, but when he learned they shared a love of cinema and that the friend has an encyclopaedic knowledge of films, Walcott spoke incessantly with him.[1]

Norline kept up pressure for Walcott to marry her, but otherwise catered for him. She practised dance exercises and talked about choreography for future projects. Highfield felt that she had picked up Walcott's habit of speaking down to actors and dancers, something that was out of character as she really thought of herself as a dancer. Although Walcott said that he had learned his love of reading from his mother, Highfield felt that Walcott seemed to think women unintelligent. Walcott seemed able to shift to almost any point of view he wanted. Highfield showed Walcott some poems and was pleased when Walcott picked out three or four as being powerful and told him to continue writing. Since then he has started publishing his poems in magazines, giving readings, and seeing himself as a poet.

Walcott used the days for rehearsals of *Pantomime* or stayed in his room working and reading, but he and Highfield often talked at night. Walcott was then working on the script of *Marie Laveau* and some poetry. He would ask Highfield about social and cultural aspects of New Orleans as, except for voodoo, it was mostly foreign to him. He talked of wanting to have a hit on Broadway, and cited details of the number of productions, audience attendance, investment, and profits of Sondheim's musical *Sweeney Todd*. He regarded St Croix as transitional between Trinidad (Port of Spain for someone from the eastern Caribbean was the cultural metropolis where as an outsider from the smaller islands he had to make it) and the United States (where he felt alien but wanted to make it professionally and financially). *Marie Laveau* was intended for Broadway. Highfield felt that Walcott was one of the very few Caribbean writers who transcended matters of race and politics or who could see them from a distance. Brodsky came to St Croix to visit Walcott and they did a reading before perhaps forty people. Around Brodsky Walcott changed and gave him all his attention, distancing others. The famous Russian dancer Baryshnikov was then also in the Caribbean and telephoned Brodsky. Baryshnikov, who defected from Russia in 1974, was part of the Brodsky circle and someone Walcott was proud to have among his acquaintances.

Highfield was impressed by Walcott's range of interests and talents, but felt that Walcott may have been using him and that Walcott was upsetting some of the people in the community. He was impressed by Walcott's claim that writing is a reality in itself and creates its own reality and that a new West Indian person could be made by the word, the logos, in which there would be a new Adam, undivided, without reference to Europe or Africa.

In March *Pantomime* was produced at Dorsch Center, Frederiksted, by Southern Cross Productions, a new theatre company, and taken to St Thomas. There was a signing of *The Star-Apple Kingdom* at Jeltrup's Bookstore on St Patrick's Day.

When Walcott was elected to the Academy of American Poets, he wrote from Frederiksted to Pat (6 February) amusingly asking to borrow Bill Strachan's necktie and cape for the 23 May ceremony. And could she ask Isaac Singer, a Farrar, Straus and Giroux author who had been awarded the Nobel Prize for Literature in 1978, to share a bagel with him afterwards at Plato's Retreat, a something-for-everyone sexual club which at the time had become a must-see. (Beyond Singer's well-known interest in women nothing should be inferred from Walcott's remark beyond amusement.) Walcott would be in St Croix until early March and he wanted copies of *The Star-Apple Kingdom* to be sent to St Croix and to Margaret in Trinidad. He wondered whether Brodsky's flat might be free from early March for a month when he would be in New York for casting *Remembrance*.

He made a schedule and listed probable earnings until May; it mostly concerned *Remembrance* which was going to be workshopped at the Public Theatre. He assumed that Papp would pay $1,000 for the option. There was another $1,000 to be earned by designing the setting. A month of performances would earn possibly $3,000. If the play could be moved to Broadway for even three months he would earn $12,000. There was Helen Camps's probable production in Trinidad from which he would earn $100 a night of which $30 had to be paid to the Courtyard Players, who had commissioned the work. He would need to pay $150 to have the scripts duplicated. The BBC was to pay him United States $476 after the broadcast of the play. He might sell a long poem to *Kenyon Review*; he could teach twice weekly at Rutgers during April and May, earning $1,000 each month. He hoped to have $210 weekly as a per diem from Papp, or $840 for a month. This meant he could probably send home $4,600 at the end of May. And he hoped to be paid $1,000 by the BBC during the summer. As usual his financial calculations were optimistic and his financial needs led to problems.

Aschenberg had written to him (30 January) after speaking with Papp. The usual fee for workshop productions was $600, so far for *Remembrance* Walcott had had $900, a round-trip airfare, and a $50 loan from Papp. They had already paid him $350 for *Pantomime*. Papp was willing to pay a round-trip air fare, but nothing more. Walcott had been paid more than anyone. Rehearsals would begin on 26 March with the first of twelve performances on 24 April. Roscoe Lee Browne expected to be in it, and Papp hoped it would be good enough that it could be made into a full off-Broadway show. As the New York Shakespeare Festival was not paying a per diem there was no need for Walcott to come to New York. Perhaps while he was teaching at Rutgers they could let him have faculty housing, which would solve his problems about New York. He replied by saying she was fired. He complained to Strachan that Aschenberg's letters made him feel like a beggar. If necessary he would rather give her her percentage and go his own way. He explained that the blow-up concerned Walcott's coming to New York for *Remembrance*. He wanted her to ask Papp for a per diem and he wanted to move upmarket to the Algonquin from the Chelsea. Aschenberg had implied he was hustling Papp. Did she expect him to pay for a month in New York hotels from his own pocket?

He sent Papp (7 February) from St Croix a revised tightened *Remembrance*, and said he hated giving up the play as it was personal, his father and mother were in it, but his agent was treating it as a commodity. Then Walcott less directly approached the matter of a per diem. New York was too expensive for him to live there for a month, he had debts to pay and would need to borrow more. He must know if and when he was needed for auditions because between casting and rehearsals he could live in Tobago which would cost less. There is also an undated letter to Papp from Walcott in St Croix including a copy of the letter from Aschenberg that had upset Walcott. Walcott obviously felt humiliated; there is a mixture of anger, threat, and flattery. Walcott said that if he did not get a per diem then Papp could not have *Remembrance* or *Pantomime*. If he was going to lose money by American productions of his plays then he would need to remain a West Indian dramatist. The threat worked, he was offered $200 per week for six weeks plus return air transportation.

Walcott went to New York in early March. He was to be paid $5,000 in five payments, without fringe benefits, for teaching at Douglas College, Rutgers University, 5 March–30 May. This coincided with the New York Shakespeare Festival *Remembrance* and various readings in connection with the publication of *The Star-Apple Kingdom*. Strachan had scheduled 23–4 March for the Howard

County Poetry and Literature Society, Columbia, Maryland. He had to be there Thursday afternoon. On Friday morning he was to teach negritude poets, Césaire, Damas, and Senghor, read on Friday evening, and then on Saturday fly to Washington-Baltimore airport. For this he would earn $300 plus transportation. On Monday (26 March) he was to read at Hampshire College, Amherst, in the evening. Henry Lyman of WNCR wanted to tape a reading and interview him before or after for a special one-hour programme. He would earn $500, plus transportation. He should be there in time for an afternoon interview and leave early on Tuesday. The next week, Tuesday, 3 April, he was to read at Westbury College, SUNY, Westbury, Long Island, for $500 plus transportation. Two weeks later, Tuesday, 17 April, the gig was on the upper East Side of Manhattan. Walcott was to give a private reading of 'The Star-Apple Kingdom' for William (Terry) Kistler of Kistler Investment Co. who was also treasurer of Poets and Writers. There would be a buffet and dancing. Walcott would earn $300 and his cab fare.

Rehearsals for *Remembrance* began early in April for three weeks, and were followed by eighteen performances 24 April–13 May at the Other Stage, a small theatre with eighty-eight seats. The total attendance was under 1,400, and no one paid; it was treated as a workshop. It was directed by Charles Turner, who had directed *Dream* for the Hartford Stage Company and had worked for the Mark Taper. The cast included Roscoe Lee Browne and Earle Hyman. Edith Oliver in the *New Yorker* said it was a loosely constructed play, but none the worse for it, which slowed and darkened as it progressed. Its pleasures were in its details and lines. The writing was of a quality seldom heard in the theatre.[2] Other reviews were lukewarm whereas *The Star-Apple Kingdom* was receiving excellent comments.

On 30 April Walcott gave his first reading at Hartwick College in Oneonta, New York. He was to read at Hartwick almost every year, even after the Nobel Prize. Robert Bensen had begun teaching at Hartwick during the autumn of 1978. His job included bringing poets to the campus. He had met Walcott in St Croix, had read *Another Life*, and, deciding that Walcott should be the first poet on campus, he contacted Pat Strachan. Walcott was offered $300 and transportation, either two hours in a small airplane or a four-hour bus trip from Manhattan. Walcott flew with Catskill Airlines. The first reading was at the college's old coffee house, with poor lighting and noise from traffic, but Bensen and Walcott became friends and said they would try again in better conditions. Bensen, although trained as a Miltonist, began teaching a course in Caribbean literature and started taking his class in January to St Lucia and Trinidad where Walcott would read.[3]

The Star-Apple Kingdom was reviewed by the major newspapers and journals. When the 1979 *American Poetry Review* awards for the poetry published in its pages during 1978 were announced in the November/December issue, Walcott would be awarded $1,000 for 'The Star-Apple Kingdom' and other poems (vol. 7, no. 3). Walcott was not a popular poet, but he was selling about 2,000 copies a volume in the United States, which was good as most American poetry books only sold 1,000. The dedications in *The Star-Apple Kingdom* showed something of Walcott's increasingly complicated and international life in which the personal, the literary, and matters related to career were becoming the main stories. The book was dedicated 'For Margaret'. Besides the poems dedicated to Norline and Brodsky, 'In the Virgins' was dedicated to Bill and Pat Strachan, and 'The Saddhu of Couva' was for the Trinidadian literary critic Kenneth Ramchand. 'R.T.S.L' was an elegy to the dead Lowell. A short, compact powerful book of fifty-eight pages, it offered a world-weary Odysseus who in 'The Schooner Flight' had 'raptures', saw God bleeding, described the Captain as Christ-like, and talked about religion, language, poetry, his women, corruption, conflicting desires, and politics. Walcott had created a voice, a tone, a character who was both a persona and yet the embodiment of the complexities of the Caribbean.

> a rusty head sailor with sea-green eyes
> that they nickname Shabine, the patois for
> any red nigger, and I Shabine, saw
> when these slums of empire was paradise.
> I'm just a red nigger who love the sea,
> I had a sound colonial education,
> I have Dutch, nigger, and English in me,
> and either I'm nobody, or I'm a nation,
>
> But Maria Conception was all my thought
> watching the sea heaving up and down
> as the port side of dories, schooners, and yachts
> was painted afresh by the strokes of the sun
> signing her name with every reflection.[4]

Shabine. This was Walcott writing about his life by making up his Caliban, almost inventing a new word, Shabine, from a term which existed in French, in Haiti, and in Trinidad with other ranges of meanings. After 'The Schooner *Flight*' every educated West Indian would use 'Shabine' for a 'red' male as if they always had. A meaning had been invented, something named, which corresponded to a new West Indian recognition of the many cultures of which the region consists and that not all shades of black were 'black'.

It had paid off—those years of packing many kinds of significance into a poem, years of creating larger-than-life characters in the theatre, or writing in poems about himself as if he were a generation or a people, the slow working towards the incorporation of forms of Caribbean English into British and American English, the increasingly unselfconscious use of literary echoes, the public arguments about Caribbean politics. Increasingly the structure of Walcott's volumes of poetry was becoming apparent. The organization of individual poems and sequences was often similar to the arrangement of poems throughout the volume. Sometimes this appeared conscious, other times it seemed to be the way his mind worked. Here the northward movement from Trinidad to Jamaica (and towards the United States) in 'The Schooner Flight' was also that of the arrangement of poems leading to 'The Star-Apple Kingdom'. And there were other larger implied patterns such as implicit analogies to events during Odysseus' travels.

I remember reading *The Star-Apple Kingdom* and feeling that this was the best book of poetry that had come my way in years. It attracted international attention. Benjamin DeMott claimed 'The Star-Apple Kingdom' 'marks . . . the return, after an absence, of a moving public speech to poetry in English. And that places it with the headiest and rarest kinds of poetic experience—fruitful to people who practice the art and to all the rest of us, too.' Martin Harrison in the Sydney *Morning Herald* said *The Star-Apple Kingdom* was the 'book I've enjoyed most this year . . . no one I know writing presently in English blends so much originality and innovation . . . with themes so seriously dedicated to his neighbours' everyday concern'. The poet Vicki Feaver in the *TLS*, reviewing the 1980 British Cape edition, said 'Walcott has mixed patois and literary language before, but never to such poetic effect'. She commented upon the way Walcott West Indianized everything (Egypt, Russia) and the ways 'The Star-Apple Kingdom' returned to 'Ruins of a Great House'; both began with the colonial world as a vanished pastoral, and 'the poet's rancour is replaced by understanding and compassion'. '*The Star-Apple Kingdom* is the real thing: poetry that makes the hair rise.'[5]

It also brought Seamus Heaney and Walcott together. Heaney first met Walcott after writing an admiring review of *The Star-Apple Kingdom* in *Parnassus*, in the issue of Fall–Winter 1979. Walcott had previously read a bitchy review of Heaney's poetry and had scribbled an obscenity on it and sent it to Heaney though Farrar, Straus and Giroux, their mutual publisher. Heaney was in New York for a short trip and obtained Walcott's telephone number from Farrar, Straus and Giroux; they had a drink together, and Heaney enjoyed bantering with Walcott. Heaney had followed Walcott's work since the early 1960s as his themes were of interest to someone who grew up in Ireland. Heaney as a Catholic in Northern Ireland felt a kinship with Walcott being from a minority in St Lucia. They both shared a complicated relationship to English colonialism and the English language. They were both nationalists who disliked the narrowness of nationalism, felt the need to affirm their own use of 'English' in contrast to that of England. For both Joyce was the master who earlier had understood the problems that colonialism, nationalism, and matters of religion, language, and 'race', posed for the writer. They shared the love of Joyce, the feeling of having been youthful imitations of Stephen Dedalus, rebels for art against the Church and Philistines. They would both teach in the United States which, with its free-enterprise imperialism, imported the best there was while exporting its own culture and ideology. Heaney and Walcott also shared the notion of poetry being a meta-language, a language found in nature itself. Although Heaney may have influenced Walcott in this, the basic idea can be found in Robert Graves's *White Goddess* where it is traced back to the Celtic bards and a supposed language of the trees. After Heaney began teaching at Harvard they would meet from time to time. Both knew poetry by heart and would quote it, enjoying the sound. They were often joined by Brodsky. Heaney, Walcott, and Brodsky would feel a rush of energy, be lifted with language, jokes, puns, irony, *double entendres*, quotations, challenging each other, mocking other poets. For Heaney it was like when he was a young poet starting out in Belfast. At times Les Murray, whom Heaney knew from other contexts, came into the picture, although the four have only been together once, when Walcott and Brodsky were reading in Dublin.[6]

The power of the publishing circle of which Walcott had become part can be seen from the six Farrar, Straus and Giroux authors being honoured by the American Academy and Institute of Arts and Letters on 23 May 1979. Isaac Bashevis Singer was inducted as a member; Walcott was made an honorary member of the Academy and Institute; his friends Brodsky and Sontag were made members; the drama critic Richard Gilman received an award for criticism; and Joseph Caldwell was given a fellowship in creative writing.

Another honour came Walcott's way when the Director of the Welsh Arts Council (9 March) informed him that the Literature Committee had awarded him the International Writer's Prize. Worth $1,000, the award is intended as recognition of international achievement in literature and had previously been given to Eugène Ionesco (1974), Frederich Dürrenmatt (1976), and Astrid Lindgren (1978). Walcott was invited to spend a fortnight in Wales, preferably October or November 1980, as a guest of the Council, which would organize readings and seminars and sponsor a short book in Welsh and English introducing his work. Walcott replied from New York on 5 May by telegram confirming 14–28 October 1980 for his 'visit to Cardiff'.

Walcott returned to Trinidad on 24 May. On the 30th the American Embassy and Trinidad Theatre Workshop gave a reception to honour George White and members of the Caribbean–United States Theater Workshop Committee at Hotel Normandie, which was followed by a three-day conference, to plan theatre workshops for the Caribbean. The Committee included Walcott, Errol Jones, Helen Camps, Richard Montgomery, and Noel Vaz. Walcott directed *Remembrance*, 5–7 July, with Holder, for the Dinner Theatre at Hotel Normandie. The production company was run by Helen Camps, an Irish woman who had married a St Lucian, for a time had starred in the Trinidad Theatre

Workshop, and after Walcott left had started directing and producing plays in various settings including a tent. The Dinner Theatre was an idea of Arthur Bentley, the source of Trewe in *Pantomime*, who had moved from Crown Point to work for the Normandie. While profits were small by American standards, the actors understood what Walcott wanted.

During 1979 Stage One Theatre Productions, a non-profit company, was established in Barbados primarily to perform Caribbean plays. Stage One rapidly became one of the better drama companies in the region and between 1979–85 offered many excellent productions of Walcott's plays. Whereas the Trinidad Theatre Workshop had always been strapped for money, Barbados had money to put into culture. Stage One in 1979 produced *Ti-Jean* and *Pantomime*, *Remembrance* in 1980, and in 1984 would première *A Branch of the Blue Nile* with a black-tie opening. In 1985 there was *Beef, No Chicken*. Stage One Productions would tour the region in the same way as the Trinidad Theatre Workshop had done previously and, like the Trinidad Theatre Workshop, run into trouble when it tried to perform in the United States. Walcott's plays were becoming West Indian classics, regularly performed by companies throughout the region and taught in schools.

Walcott's theatre career, however, had been languishing in England. There was the 1960 production of two one-act plays and the disaster with the Royal Shakespeare Company about *The Joker of Seville*. Walcott's career as a dramatist was in the West Indies and the United States. In the late 1970s Black England started to make its cultural presence felt with its own theatres, directors, and famous actors. Television, government grants, a black middle class, a new generation of university graduates, and co-operation between the various immigrant communities meant that there was a market for plays about racial relations, West Indian generational conflicts, and the effects of modernization on 'home'. Suddenly, there was interest in Walcott's plays, especially the recent ones. The BBC broadcast *Pantomime* on 25 January 1979, with Norman Beaton as Jackson. *Remembrance* was broadcast in July on BBC Radio 4. The Keskidee Arts Centre planned a season of Caribbean plays with Walcott's works at the core. *Malcochon* was performed 22 February–1 April.

Walcott had planned to be in London for a month from mid-July for a Black Theatre Co-Operative production of *O Babylon!* for which he had written a shorter version, but he cancelled the trip with MacDermot as some youths wanted to use the Centre for something else and the actors were quarrelling with the producers. If he went it seemed unlikely he would be reimbursed for his ticket. Instead, he wrote to Strachan (6 and 21 July) that he was in Port of Spain to see Margaret and the children. Living at the Hotel Normandie was expensive as he had no kitchen, but there was a pool for his children and it was a good place to work. Poems were coming rapidly, short lyrics, unlike the long personae poems of *The Star-Apple Kingdom*. He especially liked 'Cantina Music'. (This was a poem in which Walcott developed an earlier theme about the fantasies of Caribbean life, here especially among the drinkers, movie-goers, and young radicals of Port of Spain:

> Bandidos of no republic,
> Sonora, Veracruz,
> your teeth flashed like daggers,
> your snarl was torn leather,
> you strode into the street
> at the hour of the firefly
> and, boots astride for the showdown,
> prepared to die
> if someone could name the cause,
> to play your last scene as
> you slowly waltzed into dirt
> to a joropo from the tin cantinas.[7])

He told Strachan that he resisted repeating himself and the 'significance' of his last book. He was letting the poems come as he could never tell when they would stop. He respected poetry too much to force it and did not know when he would start writing again. He was writing poetry directly on to the typewriter, which he had avoided until now. The real work was on the drafts when the original poem was erased out of existence. He already had about forty pages, enough for half of his next book (*The Fortunate Traveller*), which he was sending to her to see which ones she could place. He thought that around 50 writing came rapidly as poets had to confront old age and find a final style. He might seem to be writing too much, too rapidly, but death was coming when he would write no more. Money was a problem; he borrowed TT $6,000 from the bank, which he planned to pay back from his Virgin Islands salary.

Walcott then gave a report on his work. 1. *Pantomime* needed a better ending, but it and *Remembrance* had been produced and would make a book of plays. He would like a contract soon, perhaps $1,000? He would be 50 in January! He would like *Pantomime* and *Remembrance* published for his fiftieth birthday. 2. He had finished a complete draft of *Marie Laveau*. 3. *The Isle is Full of Noises* was going slowly and was difficult but would make a companion in politics to 4. *Solo to the Hudson*, which he was hoping to do in mid-August with Albert Laveau. Walcott was thinking about a volume of two plays every year, but knew that would be too much. 5. It seemed that published screen and television plays were becoming 'literature'. For over five years he had been working on a television script about the Haitian revolution with drawings and illustrations. It would make a big book of 350 pages and he would want one of his paintings on the jacket. 6. His new poems could be published in the autumn of 1980. 7. 'American, without America' should be ready during 1981 and could be published in the spring of 1982, 8. followed by his Collected Poems, in the autumn of 1982. If he needed money could he ask Farrar, Straus and Giroux for a thousand dollar advance on the book of plays and $750 for the new book of poetry?

Walcott wanted to get Peter into a school of architecture in New York such as Cooper Union or Pratt; he would like prospectuses. Peter should get away from Trinidad and as Derek was often in New York that would be best, but money would be a problem. Maybe he should lease an apartment the year round that Peter could also use as Derek was already spending $4–5,000 at the Chelsea on rent and expenses? He hoped to come to New York, probably 4–13 August, on his way to St Thomas where he expected to direct *Marie Laveau* while teaching. He should be in the Virgin Islands when term started in mid-August.

He wrote to Halpern (21 July) in Italy. He had written to Yale asking about a job for the autumn of 1980 and was now asking Halpern about Columbia. If not a course he could do a single poet as part of a course. He was in love with New York and was trying to get his son into architecture school there. The cost of educating his children and living in New York was too much to contemplate.

During the summer Jo Thomas interviewed Walcott at the Normandie, which, although thought classy in Port of Spain, she described as 'one of those hotels . . . bare bulbs and damp rooms . . . narrow and empty bar' but with a swimming pool. 'His office was two chairs outside the room that is his home while he is getting his second divorce.' The previous day local newspapers had announced that Walcott was getting the Welsh Arts Council Prize, but Walcott was not asked by the government to be part of the next Caribbean Arts Festival in Cuba. Walcott started work at 5 a.m., mixed tap water with instant coffee, and had a cigarette before the hotel restaurant opened at 7.30. By 10.30 he was a bundle of nerves. Walcott told Thomas that a poet was obsessed, obsessed by conscience, aware of his own inadequacy and the inadequacy of art. There was the will to create order, but once order was created in the poem it was finished and one began again. He complained that his reputation as a Caribbean poet was founded on money from elsewhere. Trinidad was indifferent to arts; there was no national art gallery, no theatre, only one library.[8]

From mid-August until the middle of December Walcott was writer-in-residence at the College of the Virgin Islands, St Thomas, where he gave a senior Humanities seminar on his *Joker of Seville* and worked on *Marie Laveau*. While at the College Walcott suggested to the Guggenheim Foundation (21 September) that application forms be sent to Earl Lovelace whom he recommended. On 16 November *Marie Laveau* opened for eight performances. Dennis Parker, College of the Virgin Islands drama professor, was producer, and MacDermot came and played piano for one performance. Walcott was unhappy with some of the cast and changed two of the female leads. He also made paintings of each of the characters, which are now the property of the University of the Virgin Islands. The local television station WTJX commissioned a television version for which he wrote a revised script.

Walcott gave several drama workshops on St Thomas from about 1978 on as he had made friends with John Morrow who was in charge of the local Arts Council. He liked St Thomas and claimed that if you listened on one of the main streets you heard all the voices and accents of the Caribbean. Although *Marie Laveau* was criticized as Broadwayish the audiences loved it. The only other place it was performed was Trinidad where the script was different, as Walcott had problems with last-minute cast changes and kept rewriting. Years later Parker asked Walcott why he had not published or put on further productions of the play, but Walcott said it needed more work. There is a video tape recording of the St Thomas production which I watched at Banyan Studios in Trinidad. I thought the play and music of more interest than I expected, but found the production stiff.[9]

During July and August Strachan started sending to the *New Yorker* such new poems as 'Jean Rhys', 'Piano Practice', and a revised version of 'Old New England', which would eventually appear in *The Fortunate Traveller*. Moss accepted (11 September) 'Jean Rhys', 'Old New England' (revised version), and 'Upstate' (which Walcott had written on his way back to New York from Hartwick College). He thought the poems wonderful, would publish 'Jean Rhys' as soon as possible but wanted to add her birth and death dates after the name, making it an elegy. Should there be another verb before 'Nuremberg's needles' in 'Jean Rhys' as the syntax was puzzling? Walcott did not want the Rhys dates published with the poem. Payment for these poems went directly to Walcott as the volume had not yet been contracted. The second stanza of 'Rhys' still was a problem and Strachan made some tentative suggestions. (It seemed from the manuscript as if Strachan in an emergency did some revising and I was curious about this, but she said that Walcott never allowed anything to be published that he had not checked himself.) On 10 October Strachan sent Moss 'The Man Who Loved Islands' and 'The Call'. Five days later she sent him a once more revised 'Jean Rhys' with the comment that while ambiguous the second stanza was pleasing. The punctuation was Strachan's and could be amended as Moss saw fit. (This conflicts with what Strachan told me. I felt she had forgotten. She looked back on her time of working with Walcott as extremely pleasant and might have blanked out small problems.)

Strachan had become Walcott's editor, booker of lectures and readings, organizer, secretary, correspondent. At times she appears the only stability in his life, the only one with an overview of where he should be and what he was writing. She often was planning his readings and stints as writer in residence a year in advance; reading tours coincided with the publication of books or the productions of plays. Walcott's rushing from place to place caused problems. Strachan wrote to Moss towards the end of November that she had sent the proofs of 'Upstate' and 'Old New England', but perhaps Moss should telephone Walcott in December. (These would become the first two poems in *The Fortunate Traveller*.) Moss did try to telephone on 12 December, but the next day he sent Strachan some minor changes in 'Jean Rhys' as he did not know Walcott's whereabouts and asked to have the proofs corrected and signed. Walcott had left the Virgin Islands for Trinidad the previous week. Moss again (19 December) wrote Strachan about 'Upstate', which included a reference to 'hoopoes' which do not exist in the United States. The line eventually became 'were the starlings as heartbroken as nightingales'. Communications between the *New Yorker* and Walcott or Strachan were at times unceasing. Brodsky also wrote, needing Walcott's translation of 'Letters from the Ming Dynasty' as soon as possible for his book which was going into production. In December the revised translation was sent to Moss.

The New York Institute for the Humanities invited Walcott (13 November 1979) to be one of a select group meeting on 1–2 February 1980 to discuss the relationship of literature and censorship. The Institute would pay for transportation to New York and a hotel for one night, but no fees or honoraria. The invitation was co-signed by Richard Sennett, Aryeh Neier, and Joseph Brodsky. Thirty-nine writers were invited to discuss the Aesthetics of Dissident Literature including Chinua Achebe, John Ashbery, Heinrich Boll, Julio Cortazar, Athol Fugard, Elizabeth Hardwick, Milan Kundera, Arthur Miller, V. S. Naipaul, Victor Navasky, Philip Roth, Robert Silvers, Joseph Skvorecky, Susan Sontag, Wole Soyinka, Tom Stoppard, Mario Vargas-Llosa, and Robert Penn Warren. It was politically a mixed bag of international, famous intellectuals, heavily weighted with *Partisan Review* and *New York Review of Books* writers. Many of the issues discussed had been, and would remain, concerns of Walcott's poetry and plays from at least 1970 onward. Indeed the meeting might be used as a commentary on Walcott's poems in which he sees writers as frequently exiled opponents of tyranny.

This was an unusually serious conference which began by questioning the relationship of expression and repression, even the complicity between enemies as a progression takes place between the censor, provocation, the needing to be provoked, and the creation of new forms of circumvention. If all societies are formed on repression, then all writers are accomplices, except when challenging their culture. Brodsky led a meeting about the benefits and pitfalls of censorship. This ranged from the cliché that 'suffering is good for the soul' to how censorship created a large body of serious readers and how writers created tones, styles, forms, and conventions to evade censorship. How did writing profit from its relationship to repression? A second panel, chaired by Richard Sennett, concerned cultural censorship. Censorship was part of society, in its taboos, aversions, and silences; it influenced writers through self-censorship, repression, and lack of confidence. Did deracination and a refusal to belong to a society limit one's being? Aryeh Neier chaired the meeting about the politics of censorship which explored the aims of censors. What would loosen or tighten their power? Why in defending some political *status quo* are censors drawn towards sexual and artistic repression while seldom objecting to the representation of violence? The general assumptions could be seen as those held by Brodsky and shared by Walcott. To protest acknowledged the importance of politics, yet art for art became a further trap. A non-political art was needed which by its nature could be understood as commenting upon politics in the way that Brodsky's ignoring of the Russian state was a criticism of its repressions, violence, and murders.

A few weeks later (30 November 1979) Sennett and Brodsky offered Walcott a fellowship at the New York Institute for the Humanities for 1980–1. There would be no teaching, no students. He would have his own office, $10,000 for the fall semester, possibly $7,500 in the spring (this money still had to be raised), and a free apartment in the autumn (which was promised to Kundera or Naipaul in the spring). He could teach elsewhere but had to be based in New York. The letter ended on a personal note saying 'do us the honour of joining your friends and other interesting people'. The apartment was a small brownstone mews cottage owned by New York University in the Village.

The New York Institute for the Humanities had been founded by Richard Sennett, Professor of Sociology at New York University, and John Sawhill, President of New York University, for artists, writers, intellectuals, and professors. Each year it elected thirty-five to forty Fellows. On Fridays the Fellows met for a sandwich lunch and one person would talk about his or her work. There was usually a small weekly seminar and various public lectures and large conferences. Once Brodsky, Walcott, and Heaney shared a reading. Fellows during 1978–83 included drama critic Richard Gilman (1978), Brodsky (1979), Sontag (1979), the Cuban poet Herberto Padilla (1980), David Rieff (1980), Walcott (1980), and John Guare (1982). In 1982–3 Walcott was made Associate Fellow. Many of the Fellows during this time were part of the Farrar, Straus and Giroux 'family'—Padilla, David Kalstone, Sennett. The Board of Trustees included Elizabeth Hardwick, in 1979 Roger Straus, and in 1981 Robert Silvers (editor of the *New York Review of Books*). Roger Straus was among the donors.

The Institute for the Humanities was partly financed by George Soros and had an especial interest in Eastern Europe. A small number of scholarships were available to foreign intellectuals. There were perhaps sixty members at a time; it was accused of forming a New York literary salon. The Institute might appear as a later continuation of the Congress for Cultural Freedom, *Partisan Review*, the democratic left, but while Sontag and Brodsky were among its leadership, the Institute included a variety of views, even those who might be thought pro-Soviet. Normally it provided little to its members except the use of an office. A few people used it for social purposes, but for most it was a place to meet other intellectuals and to hear or contribute to what was being said.[10] Walcott did not socialize much, but attended its lectures. On 14 October 1982 he listened to Nadine Gordimer lecture about South Africa and mentally compared the attention she received with that of an exiled black South African whose talk hardly any one in Chicago had attended.

The New York Shakespeare Festival reader (3 December) submitted reports on the scripts of *Solo to the Hudson*, *The Isle is Full of Noises*, and *Pantomime*. *The Isle is Full of Noises* was described as Walcott's version of a West Indian Greek tragedy and the plot summarized as being the story of a young black journalist who tries to save his island from his uncle 'Papa', a dictator. It was thought badly overwritten and needing trimming and shape, but with powerful language. It should be given a reading if only so Walcott could hear what it sounded like. Some later report described the play as a bore. *Solo to the Hudson* then existed only in fragments, mostly the first act and bits of Act II, and was thought amusing in places with beautiful language, but lacking dramatic conflict and development. Even the incomplete version seemed too long. It was recommended that the New York Shakespeare Festival ask to see the script later when it was further developed. *Pantomime* was described as a television play of about an hour in the manner of television heightened realism. The reviewer said that it was really a stage play, stronger on language than visual effects and should remain a stage play. It was too long and undeveloped, but interesting and should be workshopped. Of the three plays only *Pantomime* was performable, but it needed revision.

Pantomime was already being staged elsewhere. The British stage première of *Pantomime* was at the Keskidee Centre in Islington during December 1979. Irving Wardle in *The Times* seemed only to know of Walcott's published volume *Dream on Monkey Mountain*, and was surprised how different *Pantomime* was; he thanked the Keskidee for an 'introduction to this fine writer'. Walcott in Trinidad was happy with the reviews.[11]

Having decided in his teens that he lacked the natural abilities for a professional painter, Walcott had usually given his drawings and paintings as gifts to friends, or sometimes in payment for loans. Then Clara Rosa de Lima opened the Art Creators gallery in Port of Spain with Stella Beaubrun. De Lima, from a well-off South American–Trinidadian family of Spanish origin, soon became one of Walcott's major sponsors in Trinidad. Stella, originally from Grenada, was married to Michael Beaubrun, of the St Lucia Beaubruns. Within a year Clara would announce in a quietly excited voice that Derek had left with her for sale some paintings from *Marie Laveau*. This was the start of Walcott selling paintings and for many years, until the Nobel Prize, his prices would remain low, no more than those of other eastern Caribbean artists. There are quite a few *Marie Laveau* sketches around as Walcott was working on the play for over two years. There is an *élan* and freedom to the drawings and watercolours of this period as if Walcott was enjoying his subject, which included historical scenes with Norline in costume. Extracts from *Marie Laveau* were published in the Christmas 1979 issue of the *Trinidad and Tobago Review*.

Walcott had earlier noted that he was hoping to earn $6,000 by 15 December; he would need that for Christmas with the expense of living at the Normandie, the mortgage on the house, and going to Tobago. While in Port of Spain during January Walcott was interviewed (5 January) at length by Victor Questel about his plays and the Trinidad Theatre Workshop.[12]

As usual Walcott's life was becoming a topic of his poetry. At 'The Hotel Normandie Pool',

> Around the cool pool in the metal light
> of New Year's morning I choose one of nine
> iron-cast umbrellas set in iron tables
> for work and coffee . . .
>
> while a battalion of drunk married men
> reswore their vows. For this my fiftieth year,
> I muttered to the ribbon-medalled water,
> 'Change me, my sign, to someone I can bear.'
>
> .   .   .   .
>
> at fifty I have learnt that beyond words
> is the disfiguring exile of divorce.[13]

At 50 he was still a homeless, wandering Odysseus with no security, often financially broke, working hard in a seemingly fruitless attempt to earn a comfortable living, travelling with his love while having a wife and family to support, a family which included three children whom he loved, and a wife whom he felt he had wronged. He had also become a famous West Indian writer, part of the New York literary scene, a close friend of some of the major writers of the time, a major Commonwealth (or as Americans were starting to put it, 'post-colonial') writer, one of the international jet-setting writers who have become a characteristic of contemporary culture, as its promotion and market become globalized and the new national literatures become part of the world cultural market. A former provincial on the margins of imperial cultures, he was one of those who brought the new national literatures to world standards and attention. Most writers leave the provinces to make it in the metropolis. Colonial writers had to make it in the imperial capital; those who stayed at home were minor writers, regional writers. Port of Spain, for someone from Castries, was his first metropolis to conquer, but its possibilities had proved illusory. It too was one of the provinces. He needed the United States and especially New York. In his late forties he had started over, needing to make it in the new imperial cultural centre while knowing that his inner life would remain in the West Indies where, even there, he was homeless.

22

〜〜〜〜〜〜〜〜〜〜〜〜〜〜〜〜〜〜〜〜〜〜

1980–1981 New York, MacArthur Award

FOR Walcott's fiftieth birthday (23 January) there were celebrations in the Caribbean and England. He read four times in the West Indies within a week, including reading along with Joseph Brodsky and Mark Strand in Port of Spain, Tobago, and at the Black Rock Culture Centre, Barbados. From 14 February until late March, *Remembrance* was produced at the Keskidee in London, directed by the Jamaican Yvonne Brewster, with a West Indian cast including Anton Phillips; in February there was also a production of *Dream on Monkey Mountain* in Barbados by the University Players in which women were cast as Makak and Moustique. *Caribbean Quarterly* published a special issue devoted to Brathwaite and Walcott.[1]

Early in February Walcott was in New York and read (4 February) at the YMHA Poetry Center. He was introduced by Brodsky and spoke about working with Brodsky on 'Letters from the Ming Dynasty', which had appeared in the *New Yorker* the previous week, and later in Brodsky's *A Part of Speech*. It is a little-known collaboration and an example of Brodsky drawing upon a wide variety of literary conventions to write about art while alluding to politics at a distance:

> Soon it will be thirteen years since the nightingale
> fluttered out of its cage and vanished. And, at nightfall,
> the Emperor washes down his medicine with the blood
> of another tailor, then, propped on silk pillows, turns on a
> jeweled bird
> that lulls him with its level, identical song.

Walcott's reading was part of the Poetry Center's 1979–80 season which included Geoffrey Hill, Bernard Malamud, Richard Wilbur, I. S. Singer, Robert Penn Warren, and Elizabeth Hardwick. Walcott read 'The Schooner *Flight*', and his new poems 'Old New England', 'The Man Who Loved Islands', 'Easter', 'Jean Rhys', and 'Piano Practice'. He was paid $150.²

The next day (5 February) he gave the Katherine Garrison Chapin Memorial Lecture at the Guggenheim Museum for the Academy of American Poets. He was introduced by Mark Strand, who mentioned that Walcott had changed his passport from British to St Lucian. Walcott read 'The Insulted Landscape', dedicated to Susan Sontag, an unpublished verse essay based in part on 'The Star-Apple Kingdom'.³ He was paid $300. The audience came expecting an academic lecture on West Indian writing, instead they heard a somewhat obscure, swirling, highly metaphoric discussion of language in former colonies. 'The Insulted Landscape' attacks comparisons as humiliating West Indians and the West Indies. Whether imperialists see other lands as Edens or jungles, they impose their own concepts on them. The native becomes a mimic, an inferior of the imperial original, and the New World is turned into a Third World and the landscape is insulted. The imperial order cannot create poetry, poetry is born from chaos. Nor can dialect, as it is a mirror reversal of the imperial and sustains a sense of inferiority.

The Guggenheim was followed by a reading (6 February) at Syracuse University for $500, a reading in Rochester (7 February), and Bucks Community College (8 February), Pennsylvania, for $500. He was expected to go by train to Trenton where he would be met and taken to the Community College. He offered a poetry workshop at the University of Iowa (11–12 February) and was writer in residence at Hollins College 13 February–21 March. He had not made up with Bryden after the Royal Shakespeare Company fiasco and he missed the production of *The Joker of Seville* at the University of Toronto, directed by Paula Sperdakos, 6–16 February, which ran for eight performances. It had an amateur cast and as MacDermot sent only the melodies the score was done locally. Bryden used a long script that he had from his days at the RSC.

William Smith had arranged Walcott's visiting appointment at Hollins College, for which he was to receive $2,000 plus travelling expenses to and from Trinidad. The College offered housing and paid for meals at the College. Walcott was expected to visit writing classes and be available to the community during his stay, as well as participating in the Literary Festival by giving a reading and serving on the poetry panel. A pregnant Norline was with him. The March *London Magazine* published 'Sabbaths, St Lucia', 'The Saddhu of Couva', and 'Koenig of the River', as Cape was a year behind Farrar, Straus and Giroux with *The Star-Apple Kingdom*. Although Ross wanted Walcott's writings, the English literary scene had become an afterthought. Walcott's main market was the United States.

On 25 March Moss accepted 'North and South', the concluding poem of the first section of *The Fortunate Traveller*:

> Under the blue sky of winter in Virginia
> the brick chimneys flute white smoke through the skeletal lindens,
> as a spaniel churns up a pyre of blood-rusted leaves;
> there is no memorial here to their Treblinka—
> as a can delivers from the oven loaves
> as warm as flesh, its brakes jaggedly screech
> like the square wheel of a swastika. The mania
> of history veils even the cleanest air,
> the sickly-sweet taste of ash, of something burning.
>
> And when one encounters the slow coil of an accent,
> reflexes step aside as if for a snake,
> with the paranoid anxiety of the victim.
> The ghosts of white-robed horsemen float through the trees,
> the galloping hysterical abhorrence of my race—
> like any child of the Diaspora, I remember this
> even as the flakes whiten Sheridan's shoulders,
> and I remember once looking at my aunt's face,
> the wintry blue eyes, the rusty hair, and thinking
>
> maybe we are part Jewish . . .[4]

The long lines, sentences, verse paragraphs, and stanzas express an imagination that moves across continents, places, times, finding similarities: a perfect example of poetry as metaphor, yet also an example of how Walcott's writing was becoming richer in themes and vision perhaps in part because of his associations with the European, Jewish, New York intellectuals. A poem in part about the history of imperialism and hatreds and how we learn to live with them, it has behind it a deepening sense of man as fallen, a consciousness no doubt influenced by his readings and friendships, but perhaps by his own conflicts and conduct. Yet, and it is always 'but' when discussing Walcott, much of what is in this poem can be found in the obscure clotted verse of his teens and early twenties. It had taken Walcott decades to be able to express it, and this required years of practice as well as experience. Walcott had always understood poetry as metaphor; he was learning how to make metaphors so clear that another and still another metaphor could be built on them, and yet the poem moves forward as if it had plot and linear argument while in fact darting, circling, weaving, spiralling, taking on further possible meanings as it evolves.

During the editing of 'North and South' Moss (5 June) wrote to Strachan about some problems that needed more attention than usual. 'Fragments of paper swirl round the bronze general | of Sheridan Square' is slightly inaccurate; the statue of Sheridan in the Village is in Christopher Park, not Sheridan Square, but this could not be changed without a radical revision. About another problem Moss wisely suggested extending the parenthesis which followed to improve the clarity of the comparison: '(as an obeah priestess sprinkles flour on the doorstep | to ward off evil, so Carthage was sown with salt)'. There were other minor queries; the syntactical movement was at times difficult to follow. Moss hoped to see Strachan in East Hampton.

After finishing at Virginia, Walcott delivered the keynote address at a Comparative Literature conference at Brown University (23 March). The lecture included revisions from 'The Insulted Landscape'. Michael Harper also organized a reading at Brown for the English Department. He was at Sweetbriar College three days later.

A professorship in New York would have been ideal, but Walcott remained a foreigner travelling on a foreign passport; government permission was needed even for a visiting stint at Hollins. He lacked a Ph.D. or even an MFA, which universities often accept as a 'terminal' degree in Creative Writing. A small unconventional liberal arts college might make an exception, but Walcott was too serious about education, poetry, his work, and himself, for such a setting. During mid-March there was one of those situations that have at times occurred when he came into conflict with the ways of American universities. Walcott was to be interviewed for an appointment at Sarah Lawrence College and because of problems with his taxi he missed lunch with the writers teaching on campus. Instead of being interviewed by the faculty, he was met by students, who planned themselves to interview him, and who asked him to join them for a late lunch. A tense Walcott found some of their questions an affront and left. Exactly what happened is unclear as Walcott seldom discusses disagreeable incidents. Roger Straus, however, was angry and immediately telephoned and wrote to the President of Sarah Lawrence College. The exchange of letters between Straus and DeCarlo lasted into May with Straus wanting an apology to Walcott, while DeCarlo took an increasingly progressive educational position accusing Walcott of having been raised in the British system where professors are never questioned. The matter ended with Straus crowing that Walcott was now being interviewed by Harvard and DeCarlo wishing, in a tone which could be understood as insulting, Walcott the best at Harvard where he might find a circle to his liking. A trivial incident involving competing egos and even cultures, it illustrates Walcott's temper when he perceives an insult, and Roger Straus's eagerness to do battle for his authors. It would also prove an ironic foreshadowing of later incidents. At Sarah Lawrence, where Walcott's poems are often taught, the incident has become mythic, passed on as what might have been.

While Papp remained enthusiastic about Walcott's plays, there was among his associates a feeling that he was soft with Walcott, who was attempting too much at once. An undated memo around this time notes that Walcott had been paid

$500 for the option on *Pantomime* (and would be paid a further $500), $1,500 for an eighteen-month option, $500 for *Solo to the Hudson,* $1,000 for *Marie Laveau* as a work in progress, making $3,500. MacDermot was also paid $500 for his work on *Marie Laveau.* In March Walcott wanted to know if the New York Shakespeare Festival would renew options on the three plays; it was decided that there were few funds for the purpose and later in the month Walcott was told no. During May there was still another disappointing reader's report of *O Babylon!,* which was thought unworthy of consideration by the New York Shakespeare Festival without major revision as the characters and story were unclear and too difficult to be concerned about.

Walcott left New York at the end of March, stayed at the Normandie on his return to Trinidad, and then he and Norline moved to the colonial Queen's Park Hotel in Port of Spain for part of April. Walcott liked the hotel for its older ways and has made paintings of the horses on the Savannah across from it. He was back in New York for a Spring Semester poetry reading at Hartwick in mid-April, followed by four days participation, 21–5 April, in conferences and readings by the Academy of American Poets, honouring the United States visit of Les Murray, Vincent Buckley, and David Malouf from Australia. This was part of the AAP's new interest in Literature in English. He was paid about $1,000 as honoraria, per diem, and, hotel expenses, and was reimbursed travel.

Walcott was having trouble placing portions of 'American, without America'. The *New Yorker* turned down his memories of the village in 1958. Stepto was planning an anthology of Caribbean writing for which Walcott submitted the Hemingway's Caribbean essay, and expected to be paid $150, but the anthology did not materialize.

He returned to New York from Trinidad on 18 May for readings with Brodsky and Hecht at the New York University Poetry Center, co-sponsored by *Kenyon Review.* There were several events at the Academy and Institute including a lunch and ceremony, and a University/Kenyon party on the 21st when Roger Straus also held a party at his house in honour of Grace Paley, Larry Woiwoode, and Tom Wolfe. On 5 May Eve Gittelson, Associate Director of Publicity at Farrar, Straus and Giroux, wrote to Shad Northshield, Executive Producer of CBS-Television's *Sunday Morning* to tell him that both Derek Walcott and Joseph Brodsky should be at the party, and he might like to meet them as possibilities for the programme. Northshield had already shown interest. Gittelson sent him *The Star-Apple Kingdom,* told him that on 20 June *Remembrance & Pantomime* would be published, as would Brodsky's *A Part of Speech* on 16 June. She also enclosed articles about the two authors and a book jacket to show what Brodsky looked like.

On the return flight to Trinidad (22 May) Walcott wrote a sexual fantasy about some past summer of ambition, loneliness, sex, sin, vice, violence, and race in Manhattan, especially along 8th Avenue. Walcott saw himself and midtown

Manhattan in Baudelairean terms, with the streets filled with hookers, porno stores, rapid junk-food restaurants, and delirium-haunted violent men. Like many of these paragraphs—long, one-page epiphanies—the story ends ironically, in this case with a Moor clothed in purple (purple the colour of sexual passion) approaching a hooker with a blade in his pocket, a contemporary New York version of the Othello story. This and other passages written during May and June in 'American, without Americans' are filled with sexual longings, guilt, and feelings that he had screwed up his marriage. He even suggested (2 June) that his autobiography was a way to exclude Margaret and put her behind him. He wanted to become totally selfish.

Marie Laveau was revived 29 May–8 June at the Little Carib, directed by Walcott, produced by Walcott and Clara Rosa de Lima, with choreography by Norline Metivier. Derek designed the set, Peter Walcott was credited with set construction and decoration. The executive producer was Stella Beaubrun. Many in the cast were Americans from the Virgin Islands production. There was a clash of accents, Trinidadians who tried to sound like Americans made the situation worse. While Trinidadian critics were impressed by Walcott writing clear lyrics so that MacDermot's music could shine, they felt there was not much plot and that the play was weak, even trivial, in comparison to his other musicals. It may have been meant to be Broadway bound, but Port of Spain was in the opposite direction. Actually the play has more potential interest than most reviews noted. It comments on the search for whiteness among the high browns, assumes specific African survivals in New World voodoo, and, as can be seen from Walcott's drawings, it could be a visual treat. Of the many unpublished, really unfinished, Walcott plays, it is the one I would like to see developed and given a professional production.

Walcott remained in Trinidad for part of the summer. When *Remembrance & Pantomime* was published (20 June) sixty-five review copies were sent for publicity, far less than Walcott's books of poetry. During July he read at the D. H. Lawrence Festival Conference held by the College of Santa Fe, New Mexico; his fee was $1,000. He was at the Halcyon Beach Club, St Lucia, the last week of July. In August he and Sontag were in Port of Spain for a reading and in Tobago at Crown Point.

Early in September when proofs of 'North and South' and 'The Season of Phantasmal Peace' (the concluding poem of *The Fortunate Traveller*) had to be returned to the *New Yorker* for publication in October and December, Walcott was living at 19 W 12th Street. Peter was enrolled at the New School for classes in Painting, Drawing, and Drafting. The daughters remained in Port of Spain with Margaret.

Derek was working on a script for 'Wind, Sand and Stars: a musical based on *The Little Prince* by Antoine de Exupéry', another musical play intended for

Broadway that went no place. The production was to be directed by Mel Shapiro, the book by Hugh Wheeler, the composer John Barry, with lyrics by Derek Walcott. There was a question about Walcott's role in the production which seemed to repeat the mess with *A Flag on the Island* or even 'Heavenly Peace', although this time Walcott was paid as he worked. He had started in May on the lyrics for the songs, then by August was working on the script, but without an actual contract for it. By the end of August Walcott had written a possible outline for Act I. He was hoping to write four pages a day to produce a draft and worried about keeping his head clear of poems (!) so he could get on with the adaptation. By mid-September he had a first draft and as usual he made many drawings.

The completed first draft (dated 12 September 1980) was fifty-two pages, a two-act musical partly in verse with script and lyrics by Walcott. Walcott's typed notes show uncertainty about the assignment and likely results. He might receive $1,000 or $750 compensation for the draft, as at the end of September Hugh Wheeler had changed his mind about Walcott doing the book. If so he should receive $3,500 immediate advance on the songs he had done since May or maybe he would get $5,000 and that would be the end of his involvement, with the credits to the lyrics to be negotiated. He might get $1,750 advance as sharing the writing of the lyrics and $750 general compensation for working on an outline and the script. At the end of October he received a second payment, $1,500, and the balance then due was $1,000.

During the autumn of 1980 Walcott and Brodsky shared a Poetry course at New York University. Susan Sontag often attended and is said to have been very present. Walcott's diaries of this period are continually filled with financial notations of what he might earn, advances, actual earnings, when he would be paid, and how much he needed next. There are such notes as $150 cash for the weekend, outstanding $325, two more weeks before money, then next week $250. Many sums are small, apparently he thought of sending 'Map of the New World', 'Only In A World', and 'Beach Head' to *Antaeus* for $50, and then later decided to send them to *Kenyon Review*. Walcott included among his larger earnings and commitments the cost of a round trip to Trinidad at Christmas. What shows through the various diaries and notes besides Walcott's continual financial anxieties and the variety of work he was doing almost simultaneously is his concern for his family and a small group of friends. There are various reminders about presents.

As usual his schedule was super-hectic. A weekend in Washington (19–21 September) was followed by Brodsky's party in New York on Monday, teaching at Columbia on Tuesday morning, a flight that night to London for the Poetry Olympics until Sunday when he returned to New York, with classes again on Monday.

Michael Horovitz, of *New Departures*, had invited Walcott to be part of a major poetry reading and conference in London lasting several days. He flew into London on 23 September and was met by Margaret Drabble, with whom he stayed as a house guest. The Poetry Olympics were launched at Poets' Corner in Westminster Abbey, on Friday, 26 September, with Walcott, Gregory Corso, Anne Stevenson, Dennis Lee (Canada), Edward Limonov (Russia), Stephen Spender, Linton Kwesi Johnson, and John Cooper Clarke, perhaps a sign of how rapidly the British cultural establishment was accepting the increased importance of West Indian writers to an ethnically changing England.

After returning to the United States, Walcott read along with Brodsky (1 October) at Hartwick College, Oneonta, NY. They arrived on a Trailways bus where for five hours young toughs had filled the bus with ghetto-blaster music and the driver would or could do nothing. Brodsky was recovering from heart surgery, and was too upset to eat that night, but wanted ice-cream and beer, which were then not available together in any single place in Oneonta. Brodsky, who is normally reserved, began showing pictures of his family in Russia and talking about them to Bensen and his wife Mary Lynn. Bensen has photos of Brodsky and Walcott at Trailways on 2 October. A similar journey is recalled in 'American Muse' in which the poet is a 'Trailways fantasist'. Each writer was paid $350.

During the 1940s and 1950s Walcott could not get to England. Even during the 1970s the Royal Shakespeare Company found it difficult to bring him to work on *Joker*. Times had changed, transportation was less expensive, and Walcott was becoming an international figure. Now he was flying to London for the second time within a month. For the Welsh Arts Council International Writers' prize, Walcott flew from New York on 12 October, was met at Heathrow airport and taken to Cardiff where, 14 October, he read at the Sherman Theatre in Cardiff, 16 October at the Arts Centre Wrexham, 17 October at University College, Bangor, 20 October at Aberystwyth, and 23 October at the Dylan Thomas Theatre, Swansea.

As part of the Welsh Arts Council International Writers' prize-giving, John Figueroa gave a lecture, 'Protest in Walcott', in Cardiff (14 October) and there was a conference (17–19 October) about Walcott with lectures by M. J. C. Echeruo (then Professor of English at the University of Ibadan, Nigeria), Arthur Pollard (Professor of English at the University of Hull), and Christopher Heywood (University of Sheffield). Other speakers included John Ramsaran (of University College, Swansea), John Figueroa (now with the Open University), Kenneth Ramchand (University of the West Indies, Trinidad), and Ned Thomas (University College Wales, Aberystwyth). Walcott read from 'The Spoiler's Return' which he said could be seen as written in either heroic couplets or calypso metre.

'The Spoiler's Return' is one of the great poems of this period of great poems, easily shifting from calypsonian to classical satire, finding a place for Walcott in both traditions, and showing that poets, especially satirists, are the same in all cultures, and likely to be exiled. The persona is of the Mighty Spoiler, a famous calypsonian, now dead. The poem is filled with allusions to, and quotes from, various calypso singers and satirists, as well as politicians in Trinidad, such as Eric Williams (who remained in power from 1956 until his death in March 1981):

> Behind dark glasses is just hollow skull,
> and black still poor, though black is beautiful.
> So, crown and mitre me Bedbug the First—
> the gift of mockery with which I'm cursed
> is just a insect biting Fame behind,
> a vermin swimming in a glass of wine,
> that, dipped out with a finger, bound to bite
> its saving host, ungrateful parasite,
> whose sting, between the cleft arse and its seat,
> reminds Authority man is just meat,
> a moralist as mordant as the louse
> that the good husband brings from the whorehouse . . .⁵

This is Walcott the heir of Ovid, Juvenal, Boileau, Rochester, and Johnson, one of the great satirists of our time, although as his subject is often the Caribbean this side of his work is often ignored. Desire, guilt, disillusionment, conscience, being close to power, feeling spurned, and awareness of death are a good combination for any satirist; having a popular tradition, just the sort of tradition those in power assert as local culture, with which to blend the classical is unbeatable.

Ned Thomas, the Welsh nationalist, editor, novelist, and university lecturer was the main promoter of Walcott receiving the award. For Thomas there was a parallel between the situation of Wales and the West Indies. The small book he wrote, in English and Welsh, *Derek Walcott: Poet of the Islands* (*Derek Walcott: Bardd yr Ynysoedd*) was both an introduction to the poetry and discussed problems of cultural decolonization.⁶ 'Wales [For Ned Thomas]' was to be the first poem in the concluding North section of *The Fortunate Traveller*. Walcott regarded Wales as, like St Lucia, an impoverished colony with its own culture and language alongside the British, and he saw a parallel between its congregations and his own Methodism.

An interview with Fiona McKenzie during the Welsh Arts Festival brought out many of the conflicts that Walcott had managed to use creatively and his somewhat changing perception of himself. One reason Walcott felt he had been chosen for the award was that he wrote in what the Welsh considered a 'borrowed' language and therefore was regarded favourably by Welsh nationalists opposing English linguistic and cultural imperialism. While Walcott could sympathize with the Welsh, his own position was more complex, subtle, and evolving. English was a given in the West Indies, the question was the role of local varieties which some politicians and intellectuals had tried to make a basis of an inward-looking separatist nationalism or racism. For Walcott the shape of the discussion was wrong and had been twisted from the artist's and people's creation of language to political conformity. Walcott now no longer was willing to consider himself a Commonwealth writer, as that implied that the centre of culture was London and other literatures remained tributaries. Rather he felt himself an international writer, someone who wrote about himself but who expected universal understanding. A real nationalist would argue that the English should return to using Anglo-Saxon. 'Colonisation by Romans, Scandinavians and Normans has led to English being one of the most varied rich languages in the world. Walcott is continuing that process of enrichment with his "tropical glory of images." ' Walcott spoke of the richness and variety of English which by including in its range Anglo-Saxon, Latin, and Rastafarian offered choices in expressing the 'intensity of reality'.[7]

Pantomime was produced at the Sherman Theatre, Cardiff, directed by Yvonne Brewster, 23–5 October and received highly favourable reviews. Before playing Cardiff it toured for a week, 15–22 October, through Bristol, Bangor, Mold, Aberystwyth, and Swansea. While Walcott was in England *Pantomime* (10–18 October) was also produced by Helen Camps in Port of Spain. Soon afterwards Alwin Bully directed it for the People's Action Theatre in Dominica. It was becoming a popular play. Walcott was in Chicago several times during November and December in connection with a future production of *Pantomime* at the Goodman Theatre which he hoped to direct. He remained in New York and gave readings in the area including, 1 December, at the 92nd Street Y Poetry Center where, when Brodsky cancelled, Walcott read on his own.

Moss wrote to Walcott (25 November) that 'The Hotel Normandie Pool' was 'extraordinary', Walcott's poems were the best! A few weeks later Moss wrote to Strachan (16 December) saying that Walcott's final version of 'The Hotel Normandie Pool' was his favourite poem of the past decade or even longer. Strachan replied that 'The Hotel Normandie Pool' was a different and stronger version of what she had seen a month ago.

Walcott was one of the very few Commonwealth poets included in D. J. Enright's *Oxford Book of Contemporary Verse 1945–1980*. Walcott was still not known in Europe; this would still take some years, but Straus was trying to drum up interest. When Straus discussed a German translation with Suhrkamp Verlag of Frankfurt, Strachan noted that *Another Life* and *The Star-Apple Kingdom* were Walcott's best books of poetry, and that *Remembrance* and *Pantomime* were easily producible unlike the musicals. Adelphi was considering an Italian translation of some of Walcott's work and had assigned a translator. Straus, looking ahead, checked translation rights for Farrar, Straus and Giroux's agent in Milan. Contract rights to *Dream on Monkey Mountain* and *The Gulf* were unclear; they might belong to either Cape or Walcott, Walcott held rights to *O Babylon!* and *Another Life*, Cape held rights to *Sea Grapes* and *Selected Poems*, Farrar, Straus and Giroux held rights to *The Fortunate Traveller, The Joker of Seville, The Star-Apple Kingdom, Remembrance, Pantomime*, and several unpublished works.

Walcott returned to Trinidad after his classes had finished. He stayed once more at the Normandie Hotel and this year was interviewed on video tape (7 January 1981) by Ken Ramchand about his poetry. Walcott spoke often about religion in his life and poetry. While in Port of Spain Walcott continued to experiment with video at the Banyan studios.[8]

He taught at New York University and Columbia University again as he had the previous semester, earning about $870 a month at Columbia, $1,400 at New York University. His class at Columbia was on Monday, 11–1 p.m. He taught early in the week so as to have the rest of the week free for writing, readings, and travel. At the end of January Walcott with twelve suitcases and Norline moved from the apartment on 12th Street to an apartment earlier rented by Brodsky at 44 Morton Street, NY 10014, where he stayed until early March. He was still working on 'The Little Prince' for which he received $1,500 during February as a per diem for the month. During March he was to receive another $750 for half the month.

On 25 February there was 'An Evening with Derek Walcott and Galt MacDermot' featuring the première New York performance of the concert version of *O, Babylon!* This was a 'Concert in The Sanctuary' at Saint Peter's Church (where *Elephant Man* had premièred) on Lexington Avenue in Manhattan; Saint Peter's Jazz Ministry was presenting 'A Benefit for the Common' (an arts and theatre group at the church). The programme was in three parts. Walcott read from his works, then MacDermot's New Pulse Band, formed in 1979, played. After the intermission there were sixteen numbers from *O Babylon!*, several of which were performed by singers who had been in one of the productions of *Hair*. A recording of *O Babylon!* was available on Kilmarnock Records.

MacDermot invited the Papps to attend and they sent a reviewer who thought the music often disappointingly old-fashioned, sentimental elevator music. Walcott's lyrics improved the situation, but were thought to lack discipline and were like long recitatives. It was too much like *Hair* with reggae music, which itself seemed limited and always at the same tempo. Audience interest faded. The subject itself was uninteresting. *O Babylon!* was not for New York.

Around this time Walcott met Lawrence Pitkethly of the Center for Visual History. Pitkethly was having lunch at a Greek restaurant near Columbia with Margot Feldman, one of Walcott's students. They were working on the *Voices and Visions* series, thirteen television programmes on American poetry from Whitman to Bishop and Plath, and Feldman suggested that Walcott be brought in for the

Hart Crane programme as he was interested in Crane. Pitkethly and Walcott first lunched together the day of Hinckley's attempted assassination of President Reagan. In 1982 Walcott officially became a consultant of the *Voices and Visions* series. Pitkethly and Walcott would work on various video projects including programmes about Hart Crane, Robert Lowell, Brodsky, and Walcott's *Ti-Jean*. Walcott can be seen in the Crane, Lowell, and Brodsky films. Richard Montgomery also worked on some of the films. Pitkethly along with MacDermot, Montgomery, and later Greg Doran were friends Walcott would call on over the years for various projects.[9]

During February and March there were readings, at the New School, at Princeton, and, 11–12 March, Walcott gave two days of workshops at Hartwick College, as part of a Visiting Writers Series, with student poets and actors. According to Bensen Walcott was meticulous and paid attention to detail. He told the students to get the moment right, find the image, let the image create its own aura, avoid mist and abstraction. One student said it was a sweatshop; they had spent ninety minutes revising one line of a poem.

The drama workshops began with loosening-up exercises; Walcott wanted the students to let their minds go blank, to help them get inside themselves, focus on their feelings and be relaxed enough to react to them. The students were paired, told to make eye contact and after a time told they should slowly lift the partner's arm and let it fall according to their own dynamic. Then they were told to do anything they wanted to the partner, but only do it when they felt like it. Actors needed to be free with each other physically on stage, but they must never violate their inner feeling of what it was right to do to others. Gestures and actions must come from deep inside. He then took a pair of students and told them to repeat a gesture and improvise some words without thinking in advance of what they were going to say. The male student used his right hand to adjust the collar of the female student's sweater and said 'Confused'. She responded by taking his hand, squeezing it, and before releasing it saying 'Yeah'. Suddenly there was a feeling of a scene being created. Now Walcott told the male student to enter from the right and repeat the scene. But before doing that all the students should loosen themselves by jumping up and down. As the scene restarted Walcott stopped it and told the male student he was obviously thinking ahead, thinking of what he was going to do.

They had to repeat the scene over and over until the pace, action, and interaction were genuine; the repetition continued towards making the actors self-absorbed and absorbed in the scene. They were not acting, it felt real; the repetition created energy that needed release. Walcott then made the pair keep the action going and tell a story, but the story did not matter, what was more important was remaining relaxed, loose, part of a scene, allowing pauses, discovering some truth in it. Walcott then took the scene and asked how to avoid its clichés becoming melodramatic. He suggested pushing emotions in the opposite direction, laughing, for instance, when mentioning that a person had broken his leg in a car accident. The male student tried that and it sounded artificial. Now Walcott said do not laugh but 'think laughter' so you are saying two things at once. The accident was terrible but it was also funny that it happened. Walcott told the students that preparation for art is hard work.[10]

The drama exercise throws light on Walcott's poetry as well as on his plays. There is often a contrary movement, a going against the grain, alternative significances worked into a line of verse, dialogue, or a scene. What had begun in his late teens as contrived Modernist word play, ambiguity, and complication had become a subtle method of enriching poetry and theatre, the creating of multiple subtexts, a method as useful for the actor as the writer.

During 1977 Walcott had proposed to Gates and the editors of the Perspectives on the Black World series, published by G. K. Hall of Boston, a book on 'The Trinidad Theatre Workshop: History of a Company, 1959–1976'. Victor Questel, a Trinidadian poet, dramatist, and critic, was writing a doctoral dissertation about Walcott at the university in Trinidad and was putting together material for a book he planned about the Workshop. In March 1981 Gates wrote from Yale to Strachan about Questel's book-length manuscript as he did not have Questel's address and wanted Walcott to know what had been decided. Gates described it as a seventy-seven page essay that needed much revision, but the bibliographies, cast lists, lists of reviews of Walcott's plays, and appendices would be valuable to students. If revised they would recommend it to Garland Press as 'Derek Walcott and The Trinidad Theatre Workshop: An Annotated Bibliography'. Questel died and his manuscript was not published. Walcott's desire for a book discussing his years with the Workshop would remain unfulfilled for a further decade and a half.

'George Campbell' was Walcott's Introductory Poem to a new edition of Campbell's 1945 *First Poems*, published in the Charles Davis – Henry Louis Gates Critical Studies on Black Life and Culture. There was the problem that Campbell not only wrote 'Holy be the white head of a Negro' and 'Jamaica Jamaicans making | Their Island their country', he also wrote 'Jesus kissed Lenin on the lips'. Walcott's poem tries to see this as the innocence of the time as Campbell tried to address the people:

> If the revolution has frozen to bas-relief postures,
> and if from the clay there emerges
> the flared nostrils of anger, in a wild stallion,
> in a boxer, in the head of a Robeson,
> behind it there was an attempt at a clear style
> plain as Blake's forehead,
> to be the first West Indian talking to people . . .
>
> .   .   .   .
>
> since Claude McKay had gone into exile . . .[11]

There were three amateur performances of *Pantomime* at Harvard mid-March. After *Pantomime* Anne Terry, a producer for the Dick Cavett television programme, telephoned Farrar, Straus and Giroux to ask where it would be possible to hear Walcott reading or see another production of the play. She was told it would be difficult as Walcott was in Chicago for a month directing a play, returning to New York in mid-April and then in May was going to Trinidad. He was reading at Lafayette College, in Pennsylvania 3–4 April, but it would probably be easiest to sit in on one of his Monday 11–1 classes at Columbia University in late April. Pat Strachan's notation on the memorandum concludes with an out-of-breath admiring 'phew!'. I suspect it could have been phewer or phewest, if she included Walcott's need to finish his new comedy, his work on 'The Little Prince', keeping an eye on the forthcoming Washington production of *Pantomime*, and other events I will soon mention.

Wole Soyinka was to direct Mustapha Matura's *Play Mas* at the Goodman Theatre, 10 April–17 May. When Soyinka had to cancel, Gregory Mosher, who was artistic director at the time, brought Walcott in as a replacement. This was only the second time Walcott had directed a major production in the United States. He was possibly suggested by Peregrine Whittlesey, Gerald Freund's wife, who worked at the Goodman. Matura, who founded London's Black Theatre, had had a success with *Play Mas* at the Royal Court Theatre in 1974; this was the first time Walcott worked with Matura who, himself a director, had different ideas. In the Goodman Theatre's 'Guide to *Play Mas*' Walcott claimed to have always been a Matura fan, although he had not read *Play Mas* previously. He described Matura as both tender and satiric, someone who could show how tenderness could also be brutal. He claimed that Matura, an Indian, was frank about Black–Indian relationships. Both whites and blacks had problems portraying the other honestly, but an Indian could be objective, an objectivity furthered by Matura's living in London. Walcott then went on to praise Trinidad for its diversity of races and cultures. Trinidad was making a national transition, from a rural to an urban society, which produced humour and satire.[12] The play was not a success with critics, but Walcott's direction was thought lively if, perhaps predictably, unable to blend scenes with the plot line.

In late April Walcott returned to Trinidad for the world première of *Beef, No Chicken* (30 April) at the Little Carib. It was directed by Cecil Gray, a Trinidadian poet, with Walcott in attendance. This was a Trinidad Theatre Workshop Production, the first of a Walcott play for five years, described in advertising as a 'Brief reunion with our respected founder'. It is a comedy about the effects of social change and accompanying political and moral corruption on a formerly sleepy small Trinidadian community, the general lethargy being indicated by Otto's Auto-Repair & Authentic Roti Shop having only beef, no chicken rotis. Trinidadian reviews thought the play lacking Walcott's usual depth, but amusing. After the opening he went, 1–3 May, to Crown Reef Hotel, Tobago.

He was brought to Trinidad by the Mucurapo School Community Project to read and discuss 'The Relevance of West Indian Poetry to the Young' in secondary schools. He read, 6–8 May, at three different schools around the island to the fifth and sixth forms as the CXC examinations included Walcott's *Malcochon, Henry Christophe*, and *Dream on Monkey Mountain*.[13]

Walcott was on a tight schedule between teaching at Columbia, directing Mustapha Matura's play at the Goodman Theatre in Chicago, working on the lyrics for 'The Little Prince' planned for Broadway, and a production of *Pantomime* in Washington. After previews, 15–19 May, *Pantomime* had its American première on 20 May in the Kreeger Theatre, Arena Stage, Washington; it ran until 7 June as part of a three-month 'Carousel' of new plays by four contemporary dramatists, and was presented by special arrangement with the Goodman Theatre. As often American reviews of Walcott's theatre were less comprehending than in, say, England. Frank Rich in the *New York Times* complained that Walcott did not bring the same artistic discipline to his plays as to his poetry and thought the play needed much reshaping and polishing. Rich thought Trewe too changeable a character, even feeble and irritating. The critic for the *Washington Star* described it as 'disheveled', a 'tangle', because of its many themes, and seemed proud that he could not follow the psychology of the resolution. The critic for the *Washington Post* felt he had seen another American play in which two people from different backgrounds 'bare their souls to each other'. *Variety* found it amusing but wordy, thought the meaning obscure but liked the production. Other reviews complained that the characters did not seem like real people, that the play examined white liberal guilt, and that there was too much talk! In *Jewish Week* Faiga Levine felt outside the emotions of the characters, but was fascinated by the wit, ideas, and theatricality. Even here praise of the writing, cleverness, and awareness of the shifting roles was followed by criticism of the rapidity of their movement and high cerebral level. If Jewish critics are going to complain about such matters how much chance does serious drama have in the United States?[14]

By 25 May Walcott was back in Port of Spain being interviewed on video and filming improvisations at Banyan Studios. He was in Trinidad during the summer and started a sequence of poems addressed to Brodsky who was in Rome.

Suddenly Walcott's life changed. He no longer had to worry as much about money or having a roof over his head. Gerald Freund, who had created the 1967–70 Rockefeller Award, was behind the new bounty. In June 1981 Walcott received a five-year John D. and Catherine T. MacArthur Foundation Fellowship of $248,000. The Foundation's press release described Walcott as a 'West Indian poet and dramatist whose works deal with man's relations with God and society'. Gerald Freund was employed by the Foundation, first as director of the Fellows Program and then as a consultant April 1980–June 1983. He was also a Foundation Vice-President. The MacArthur Fellows Program involves nomination by appointed selectors, the development of suggestions by programme staff, the choice of Fellows by a Selection Committee, and approval by the Board of Trustees. The process is conducted in great secrecy and confidentiality and in theory no one should know that he or she is under consideration. The Fellow is then contacted and asked for further information for the press release. No strings are attached to the award and even a final report after five years is voluntary.

Robert Penn Warren, A. R. Ammons, James McPherson, Leslie Marmon Silko, Henry Louis Gates, Jr. (only 30 at the time), and Brodsky were also offered MacArthur awards. The directors wanted more awards in the sciences; Freund, who knew that there was already money available for science, was responsible for bringing in literature. From a hundred nominators some 200 candidates were considered and twenty-one were recommended, six scientists, four social scientists, a social activist, and six writers. Warren, Walcott, and Brodsky were objected to by one board member, a banker, who said he wrote poetry before breakfast, why did these poets need money to write?[15] Walcott and Brodsky were lucky to have Freund behind them as the following year there was pressure to give half the awards to scientists, and, in recent years, after a long-established academic became director, the awards have appeared to seem politically correct or cautious, being given to members of minorities and the well-established avant-garde of previous generations. In the early years, however, the awards were often brilliant, including the great Indian scholar-poet-translator A. K. Ramanujan.

During July Walcott was in St Thomas for a ten-day playwrights workshop and was reported in the newspapers as attacking Carifesta, which was being held in Barbados. Walcott was reported as saying Carifesta was a waste of money and a cynical exploitation of West Indian artists by governments that did not have a cultural policy, to provide two weeks of activity for artists who were subjected to fifty weeks of indifference. Walcott said he would not take part and other artists should not.

Part VI

Boston Third Marriage, Making It

23

1981–1983 *The Fortunate Traveller, The Last Carnival*

IN the autumn Walcott continued at Columbia University and taught part-time at Harvard. In late October when he read in Boston from *The Star-Apple Kingdom* and the not yet published *The Fortunate Traveller*, he mentioned having been in Boston earlier with Lowell. Boston was still new to him, he was a New Yorker and now thought of himself as a World or International writer while remaining bitter about Trinidad. His West Indianness, and the complicated social, political, and personal contexts, meant that much of his American readership was puzzled by him. The Eastern European exiled writers could be fitted into a stereotype, but what was the available stereotype for Walcott, except the wrong ones of 'black' or 'third-world nationalist', two views of himself which he rejected— indeed he was in exile he felt because of those who held such politics. Life in the United States was, however, starting to have a pattern; during November he read once more at Hartwick College.

Although audiences were puzzled by a West Indian who did not fit American stereotypes, his plays were now being produced in the United States, England, and throughout the West Indies. *Dream* was done in Chicago. *Remembrance* had twenty performances in Denver and was broadcast on the BBC. *Pantomime* was acted in Seattle, Rochester, and there was a major production in Gainesville Florida in October as part of the fiftieth anniversary of the Centre for Latin American Studies in Gainesville. Walcott still had not given up his dream of having his plays performed in the United States with Trinidadian actors; indeed he still hoped for international productions and exchanges between the West Indies and other countries, especially the United States. Caribuste was intended for such exchanges, its seeds going back to the days when the Rockefeller Foundation tried to build links between the American and the new West Indian theatre. Walcott kept promoting West Indian actors in the United States, telling Papp about them, showing demonstration videos he made in Trinidad. No actor followed him to New York as Laveau earlier had, but Holder, who otherwise was a radio and television announcer and producer, took part in many productions outside of Trinidad. He was Jackson in the Gainesville *Pantomime* and two years later in the March 1983 *Pantomime* at the Actors' Theatre, St Paul, Minnesota, a production which later moved to the College of St Thomas as part of the Caribuste exchange programme.

The version of 'The Fortunate Traveller' that appeared in the November 1981 *London Magazine* was Walcott's last contribution for many years, although he and Ross remained friends. His relationship with Cape unravelled. In the past Cape had been regarded as Walcott's original publisher and had purchased British and Commonwealth rights independently of Farrar, Straus and Giroux. From 1982 Farrar, Straus and Giroux would be Walcott's originating publisher and Faber would purchase rights from them. Being published by Faber added to Walcott's reputation.

During 1978 Walcott had been unwilling to accept O. R. Dathorne's editorial material for the Heinemann Educational Books' *Derek Walcott Selected Poems*; he wanted Wayne Brown, a schoolteacher in Trinidad and a good poet influenced by Walcott, to write the introduction and select the poems. In return Heinemann wanted permission to include selections from all of Walcott's published work. Eleven months later, in April 1979, Cape reminded Heinemann that six years had elapsed since plans for the *Selected Poems* began. Cape asked and received an additional £100 advance and extended rights until 1983. The anthology was published during 1981 and reflects Brown's taste, attention to detail, and his seriousness as a teacher; it is well annotated. Walcott's poetry is often complex and not easy to précis. Brown includes the more difficult poems and makes few concessions to those who prefer to teach an easier Walcott. An interesting short review appeared in the Jamaican *Sunday Gleaner* suggesting that after the enthusiasm of the BBC *Caribbean Voices* programmes and the early volumes, Jamaican readers were intimidated by the length of *Another Life* and the ambiguities and many voices of the later poetry.[1] Increasingly Walcott was becoming part of the school syllabus in the West Indies and part of Commonwealth Literature courses. *Another Life* had gone out of print and Robert Hamner received permission for Three Continents Press, which published mostly books about Third World literatures, to republish it in 1982 with an introduction to be used for teaching.

After the New Year Walcott became a Visiting Assistant Professor at Boston University on a three-year appointment. Boston always had two poets in its writing programme. One, many years earlier, was Lowell who in a now famous class had

Sylvia Plath, Anne Sexton, and George Starbuck as students. After Lowell left Starbuck replaced him. Now Walcott took over the class: 'Cal's bulk haunts my classes.'[2] Walcott's previous appointments were short-term visiting professorships, which is common for writers without advanced degrees, but the Boston appointment was tenure track. Later Robert Pinsky joined the programme.

With MacArthur money Walcott purchased a largish apartment in Brookline at 71 St Mary's Street, within walking distance of Boston University. When in New York he would stay at Brodsky's apartment. Having a home once more, Walcott began reassembling a family, and married Norline Metivier on 8 May. It was an emotional relationship, they even argued about who should be invited to the wedding. Derek wanted poets, she wanted her young friends. Norline felt Derek did not want her to work, study, or to take classes. He wanted her to act in his plays or be his choreographer. She felt he was rushing her into roles. Margaret was efficient, an organizer, held a job, was a mother, and devoted herself to Derek's work. Norline wanted fun with people her own age, and wanted a career as a dancer; many of Derek's friends thought her unwilling to try to understand him and his ambitions. Yet she had given up her job and followed him to the United States. The pattern of former marriages began to be repeated, with arguments, crying, loss of control, and physical rage. Derek was in love and made Norline co-owner of his new apartment, but it was not always a love nest. Derek's children by his former marriages lived there at various times, as the girls entered Boston University, and Peter sometimes stayed with them. Norline was more their age than Derek's. The girls had taken Margaret's side, and Norline felt that Peter was disrespectful. Eventually Norline would pack her bags and in 1986 return to Trinidad. Walcott had wanted a child by her, a son. Their child miscarried. That she had a son by another man would hurt and find its way into the story of Helen and her two men in *Omeros*. Later Walcott would claim that leaving Margaret was the worst mistake of his life. That, however, was a combination of nostalgia and practical hindsight; for a decade he was deeply in love with Norline.

The Fortunate Traveller was published in 1982 by both Farrar, Straus and Giroux and Faber. There were twenty-six poems, counting the three poems in 'Map of the New World' as one. The book was in three sections: five poems in North I, eighteen poems in South II, and North III had three poems. Eight poems had first been published in the *New Yorker*, five in *Antaeus*, three in *Kenyon Review*, while several had been published in the *Trinidad and Tobago Review*. With two exceptions every poem had appeared in a magazine between 1979 and 1981 and most were autobiographical. The dedications show how much Walcott's career, especially his literary friendships in New York, had become his life. The book is dedicated to Joseph Brodsky: poems are dedicated to Mark Strand, Tony Hecht, Pat Strachan, Susan Sontag, and Robert Giroux. Other poems are for the

Trinidadian novelist Earl Lovelace, the Welsh novelist Ned Thomas, and Norline. Whereas the spine of *The Star-Apple Kingdom* was a flight from the South, *The Fortunate Traveller* reflects the division of time between the United States and the Caribbean, between North and South. Although the volume begins with appreciative poetic sketches of a new landscape and its people, the North is soon seen as brutal, inhuman, associated with colonialism, exploitation, Dachau, the Holocaust, a failed Modernism, a place where religion is only fable, myth. The South is where Walcott is personal, self-reflective.

The traveller between North and South, New World and Old, is another Odysseus travelling away from his wife and family, but the speaker in some poems appears to accept exile. Some are openly personal; 'Early Pompeian' concerns the late miscarriage of Norline's daughter in Trinidad, followed by 'Easter' addressed to 'Anna my daughter', followed by 'Store Bay', which besides mentioning his divorce, concludes:

> I envy the octopus with ink for blood,
> his dangling, disconnected wires,
> adrift, unmarried.

If the volume as a whole moves from the cheerful discovery of America in the early poems towards satire and being adrift, even disconnected, 'The Season of Phantasmal Peace', which concludes the volume, is a vision of divine love, a vision of restoration after the apocalyptic horrors of 'The Fortunate Traveller' that precedes it.

The title of *The Fortunate Traveller* derives from an Elizabethan picaresque novel by Thomas Nashe, *The Unfortunate Traveller* (1594) and Walcott, like Nashe, is wide-eyed, and ironic, and a moralist. The poems taken as a volume contrast norths and souths, show man's inhumanity to man to be universal, and allude to the conflicts in Walcott's own life. Towards the conclusion of the South section, in 'Store Bay', he is like that traditional emblem of exile the snail ('I still lug my house on my back'), and is 'quivering from sunstroke | and from my second divorce'.

The first section with its awed love of Americans and the American landscape and American literary models is the world of a naïve Fortunate Traveller, a citizen of the world, before he starts thinking of slavery, the extermination of the Jews, the history of empires, and wars in Africa. Thus the ironic title poem, a Graham Greeneish view of the fallen world. Walcott's writing about American subjects, however, gave critics a chance to point to the obvious imitation Lowellism of 'Old New-England' and question whether having worked to create an appropriate diction for the Caribbean he could start again and find one for writing about the United States. Besides intentionally writing like Lowell there was the Elizabeth Bishop title and manner of 'North and South', and the tongue-in-cheek simplicity of 'American Muse'. Many critics, including Denis Donoghue in the *New York Times Book Review*, felt 'Walcott's style is too much for its own good'. Helen Vendler, never a Walcott fan, enjoyed herself in the *New York Review of Books*. The early 'Ruins of a Great House' is not a poem but 'an essay in pentameters'. About *Another Life*, 'It seemed that his learnedness might be the death of him.' 'The degree to which Walcott is able to realize a poem still varies . . . Walcott's pentameters stubbornly retain their British cadences.' While nothing can upset some Americans more than a pentameter, *The Fortunate Traveller* made the *New York Times Book Review* list of 'Notable Books of the Year' for 1982.[3]

In England where poets still use metres the nightmare is excess. Roger Garfitt in the *TLS* praised 'The Hotel Normandie Pool' and 'The Spoiler's Return' for their fine tuning of language and use of the colloquial, but felt 'North and South' and 'The Fortunate Traveller' overwrought, a view held by many critics including Peter Porter in the *Observer*. Blake Morrison in the *London Review of Books* was more correct in calling *The Fortunate Traveller* 'an impressive collection that moves lucidly and at time brilliantly between abstract notions of power and responsibility and visual notions of landscape, cityscape and sea. But it is only the title poem that comprehensively escapes Walcott's rational grip.' Morrison accused Walcott of 'press-ganging images into the service of an idea', especially in the North American poems. Such similes as comparing a New England church spire to a 'harpoon' were too appropriate. What did Walcott really care about North America? Morrison praised poems—'North and South', 'The Fortunate Traveller', and the 'Hotel Normandie Pool'—about the guilt and regret of being away from the Caribbean. After noting Walcott's sophisticated readership and circle—as indicated by dedications to Mark Strand, Anthony Hecht, and Susan Sontag, and the MacArthur Foundation award—Morrison made what was then felt to be necessary comparisons between Walcott's 'refined' diction and the attempt of Edward Kamau Brathwaite to speak for the Caribbean, especially the Afro-Caribbean. Morrison mentioned that Brathwaite was awarded many of the same American and British literary and foundation prizes as Walcott and knew the same circles and that until recently Brathwaite's name as author did not include Kamau, but Morrison seemed to feel a greater sympathy for Brathwaite's use of dialect and 'the hubbub of living speech' in *Sun Poem*.[4]

Julian Symons, however, thought the opposite. He commented on the end of empire theme, which Walcott now applied to the United States rather than England, and said 'the whole book is marked by an unaffected eloquence which is one of the rarest qualities in modern poetry'.[5] Others agreed. 'Europa' was selected for inclusion in *The Pushcart Prize VII: The Best of Small Presses (1982–83)*, to be published by Avon. Strachan as editor gave permission, but asked that the final version from *The Fortunate Traveller* be used instead of the earlier version in *Antaeus*.

Leif Sjöberg, a professor at SUNY-Stonybrook, brought Walcott's poetry to the attention of Östen Sjöstrand who was starting a new literary journal in Sweden. Sjöstrand, who would later be on the Literature Committee for the Nobel Prize, translated four of Walcott's poems, which he published in *ARTES* I along with Sjöberg's article about, and interview with, Walcott. The interview revealed a citizen of the world. The years supposedly in exile, and a few years of being financially secure, had resulted in the manner of a world-class intellectual who sounded above rather than involved in immediate quarrels. Walcott asked, after Auschwitz, My Lai, Beirut, how was it possible to believe in human progress or heroes? There was a sense of something like Original Sin, of Mankind as fallen. 'Race . . . has meant nothing to me past early manhood. Race is ridiculous . . . I have no loyalties to one race more than another.' English was not the language of masters, but his birthright; he had the right like previous poets to fuse the language of nobles and common people. 'One's own voice is an anthology of all the sounds one has heard.' The community of any twentieth-century artist was the world. About God 'I am a believer'. Poetry was a quarrel with God that one hoped God understood. Poetry was a divine gift. 'We lose religion and we lose poetry.'[6] A few years later, during 1985, Walcott began hearing rumours he was being considered as a candidate for the Nobel Prize in Literature, rumours which would become stronger each year as his name progressed from possible candidature to an actual candidate in the final list to be discussed and voted upon. Walcott was impatient, but it normally takes at least a decade after a name is mentioned before it becomes one of a number of 'candidates' to be voted upon.

There was a major production of *Panto* (*Pantomime*) at the Goodman Theatre, Chicago, 15 January–21 February, directed by Gregory Mosher, which was to star Brian Murray and Morgan Freeman, but shortly before the opening Roscoe Lee Browne replaced Morgan Freeman as Jackson. Browne had already played in *Dream* and *Remembrance*. *Panto* was part of a series concerned with Theatricality and Identity; there were lectures on the play and its context at the Goodman Theatre, at the Chicago Public Library, and elsewhere in Chicago. In the Study Guide that the Goodman published with the production, there was a self-interview by Mosher, who was artistic director as well as director. It showed some of the problems Walcott plays had in the United States. The title *Pantomime* was changed to *Panto* as Mosher felt that Americans, unlike West Indians, were unfamiliar with the British tradition of pantomime and were likely to bring the wrong associations to 'mime'. That the play was part of a series of 'non-white-centric' plays, including *Native Son*, Soyinka's *Death and the King's Horseman*, and *Play Mas* already placed it in a context of the same conflicting white–black polarities that the play claims are mostly irrelevant to the Caribbean.

Mosher said that, bringing an American context to the script, he had originally misunderstood *Pantomime* as about racial commitments. The two men are human beings not spokesmen, there is much amusement in the racial banter. Mosher felt that Walcott was still treating political issues, but, by making them particular through human relationships, finding comedy in their expression. *Pantomime, Remembrance,* and *Beef, No Chicken* are Chekhovian. The title *Panto* indicates the relationship between acting and life, as all plays express truths through paradoxes; whether calypsonians or American naturalists you employ artifice to tell a truth. Both men share a similar background in acting, and he perceptively remarked that there are possibly twenty-five different personae in the play if you count that both Jackson and Trewe act Crusoe and Friday, Jackson's playing of a white women and the seagulls, and their lives as hotel owner, handyman, servant, cook, and ex-husband.

Although Mosher agreed that the play is not about race he ended his piece with an even more American perspective on the world, which he claims to be divided into 18 per cent whites and 82 per cent 'that is not'. Mosher's 'is nots', echoing 'have nots', assumes or at least associates all non-whites with issues of black power, race, colonialism, and otherness. This is post-colonialism as anti-white cultural imperialism. The great Western person learns that 'There is not *a* superior wisdom at all'. I doubt Walcott would be happy with the kind of American Third Worldist politics that imagines all non-Europeans to be black victims of imperialism or the kind of sloppy relativism that fails to distinguish superior wisdom even if European.[7]

During February there was a production of *Pantomime* at the Cleveland Playhouse and *Beef, No Chicken* was one of the four plays in the Yale Repertory Theatre's Winterfest. Mel Gussow in the *New York Times* called *Beef* the 'high light', a 'wry spoof'.[8] *Pantomime* remained popular and there always seemed to be a production in progress. The same cannot be said of *The Isle is Full of Noises*, an unpublished play which Walcott had been working on since 1975 and which still has not found its proper form. There was an instructive production in Hartford during the spring. According to Jim O'Quinn *The Isle is Full of Noises* started in the Virgin Islands during the mid-1970s when Walcott gave Douglas Ward fragments of a work in progress. During the 1978–9 season Ward had a grant to develop new plays and himself put together the scenes for a reading to which he added connective commentary. Walcott who was in New York working on *Remembrance* attended and they began talking about developing *The Isle is Full of Noises*. Ward said that Walcott had one basic theme, 'the culture he comes from and loves is not large enough for his aspirations. Not that it is less valuable, or less beautiful, but that it is too small, too limited in the scheme of things, and that makes him angry.' The play is an eclectic mixture of styles and moods. A lot of different plays in which it is necessary for the director to find the unity.[9]

There were previews 13–15 April; *The Isle is Full of Noises* opened 16 April and ran until 23 May at the John W. Huntington Theatre, Hartford, Connecticut. It was a joint production of the Hartford Stage Company and the Negro Ensemble Company, the director was Douglas Turner Ward, who also played Papa. Ward, a co-founder of the NEC, had directed *Malcochon* at St Mark's Playhouse.

The action takes place in a single day on Pigeon Island, which is part of the Republic of Santa Marta, itself a West Indian island. The Prologue takes place earlier on a beach when Sir Lionel Robinson, the first Prime Minister of the West Indian Federation, baptizes his godson James, the son of Achilles, and gives him a rock as symbol of the island. Sir Lionel wears his robes, symbolic of the traditions of the people belonging to both the Old and New World. The three unities, Divine, Racial, and Dramatic, are the chorus. Sir Geoffrey Thwaite, British Ambassador, explains that the West Indian Federation has collapsed and in its place Papa Henry has come to power, while Sir Lionel, suffering from a wound, lives as a hermit in a cave on Pigeon Island.

Act I opens on a tropical beach where Papa Henry holds a press conference to announce that a hotel will be built on the beach where Sir Lionel now lives. Papa respects no traditions, is only concerned with power and money, and plans to get rid of Sir Lionel. James, the editor of the party's journal, is against the corruption of the regime. This is followed by a wild party at a beach house symbolizing the present corruption and degeneracy of the Caribbean. The island is beautiful, but it is ruled by greedy, self-serving, egomaniacal politicians who create disorder. The babble of voices so far—coarse American, proper British, calypso slang, political lies, and native speech—represents a Caribbean conflicted by the attractions of identity, expansion, and various kinds of exploitation. There are two more acts, in verse and prose, heavy with symbolism alluding to Robinson Crusoe (Sir Lionel Robinson is the castaway who will return to 'civilization'), *The Tempest* (Caliban and Prospero; themes of power, usurpation, and learning the culture of others), and Sophocles' Philoctetes.

The theatre reviews rightly mentioned that the play is difficult to follow, more symbolism than plot, the plot meanders and is too convoluted, yet as theatre the play was arresting, witty, energetic. The first act was thought excellent—worth the price of the evening—but there was a lack of focus elsewhere. The mixing of various models, myths, and modes puzzled and was thought pastiche. Seeking a clear line of symbolism the reviewers puzzled how at various times Sir Lionel, Papa, and James might be considered Caliban-figures. It was baffling.

Looking back from the perspective of *Omeros*, one can see how many of the supposed postmodern ingredients of the later work were present earlier and that Walcott was still building on the idea that Caribbean art needed classical form, but this idea has become much richer as he tried to weave together a tapestry from varied materials, eras, cultures, and myths. As in *Omeros*, the main strands are Caribbean, British, Greek, and African and the form an unpredictable mixture of classical structure, Modernist complexity, and self-conscious postmodern pastiche to portray what might be considered an allegory of recent Caribbean history.

There is a possible model that might not be noticed. Wole Soyinka is the one dramatist who can write plays that appear to be topical satire, a criticism of corrupt Third Worldisms, while the action itself incarnates a sacrificial ritual. *The Isle* not only is a play which satirizes Third World tyrants, it goes beyond disillusionment in that present evil is seen as part of a redemptive pattern requiring courage and the shedding of blood. It is a vision known to Modernist writers from Fraser's *The Golden Bough* and Eliot's *The Waste Land*.

The Isle is Full of Noises is dedicated to 'my daughter Anna and her generation'. In Sir Geoffrey's opening lecture we are told that Sir Lionel was one of the many Oxford-trained nationalists of his generation, including Nehru, Barbados's Sir Grantley Adams, and Jamaica's Norman Manley, who were friends with Keynes, Sir Stafford Cripps, and other Bloomsbury liberals. Such friendships and shared values and education were part of the inheritance brought to the newly independent nations at the start of the process of decolonization as represented by the West Indian Federation. If Sir Lionel Robinson is part Grantley Adams and Norman Manley, Papa Henry is Papa Doc of Haiti and other Caribbean demagogues. The focusing of the conflict around the government's plans to build a hotel (representing money and corruption) is similar to *O Babylon!*. The attack on Americanization as the new imperial corruption occurs in *Remembrance*. Exile is also the theme of *The Star-Apple Kingdom*. There is in the play a bitterness about women—they go where there is power and excitement. They are attracted towards their opposites—white/black; élite/brute. Men, however, let women cuckold them, as it is easier than fighting, as they no longer care, as it helps their own career; they get perverse pleasure from it.

Frank Rich described *Isle* as an ambitious epic of the history of the New World, claimed Walcott had never created a fully realized play, and that this was a step backward. Characters drifted in and out of focus while the play was loaded with mythology, literary allusions, and some force-fed poetry. The production was listless, bland, at times sloppy. Everything went wrong.[10]

In March Walcott went to Trinidad where he was planning during the summer to open a new play, *The Last Carnival*, and, during April and August, film *The Rig*, a television play. The MacArthur money, he hoped, could be used to mend fences with the Trinidad Theatre Workshop. He was thinking of mounting a play or two in Trinidad each summer, working with one actor a year on mastering a great role from the classics of theatre. Walcott wanted to return to Trinidad a conquering hero.

The Fortunate Traveller was bringing Walcott's poetry before a larger readership in the United States. James Atlas had been preparing a major article on Walcott for the *New York Times Magazine* and remarked on how Walcott managed to attend some rehearsals of most American productions of his plays, while writing almost every day and flying between the Caribbean and the United States. He interviewed Walcott at the Hotel Normandie which he thought fitting for a Graham Greene novel, and was impressed by Walcott, after returning to the United States late at night, starting to write the next day. The article carried two poems (XXXIV, XXXVIII) from 'Midsummer '81', the name of the then unfinished sequence upon which Walcott was working. Atlas had visited some of Walcott's classes at Harvard. Walcott's

method was to have three or four students read out their poems . . . 'Now, what I want you to do,' he said in his lilting voice when a few poems had been read, 'is to draw a line that's a symbolic representation of the tone.' He went around the room, and the students drew their lines in the air; most of them were horizontal. 'One tone, one hum is what I hear,' Walcott noted. 'There's a terror of making music in American poetry.' He leaped up and scrawled a line from Yeats on the blackboard . . . he stared at the class. 'Where in the line does it go up?' It was that Yeatsian compound adjective that Walcott was after: rook-delighting.[11]

Walcott recited more Yeats, this time in a Bajan accent, then droned some monotonous free verse, then quoted Vaughan's 'I saw eternity the other night', and made every one in the class recite the first line of a poem, then made them recite lines of poems over and over in different orders like practising a piano.

During June, when Walcott was in Trinidad, many newspapers and magazines carried stories about a female Harvard student's claim that in November Walcott had propositioned her. It was reported that she was the only one in his class to come to his apartment for a class, she had told Walcott that she had written an erotic poem, and during the discussion of love poetry Walcott had said 'Would you make love to me if I asked you?' She claimed that after saying no Walcott was less friendly and she attributed her C in the course to the incident. After ten months of various committees, during which time Walcott was not asked about the matter and no one read her poetry, Harvard changed her grade from C to Pass. Walcott acknowledged making the comment, but said he was being misrepresented, 'The charge is unjust', as the comment concerned the interpretation of poetry and was not personal. Walcott's offer to resign from Boston University was refused. He was to be awarded an honorary degree from Lawrence University, Appleton, Wisconsin, but he cancelled it to avoid any possible embarrassment.[12]

A feminist objection to Harvard's procedures was raised by a woman writing to the *New York Times* (9 June). She objected to the student's name being kept secret. Walcott has been publicly embarrassed, but what had the woman lost in making her charges? This was special privilege not equality and Victorian in assuming that women were poor, wronged, sensitive victims that needed privacy.[13]

The publicity concerning the Harvard grade change led to Brodsky, Susan Sontag, and Roger Straus questioning Harvard's handling of the matter. What appeared to be a moment of flirtatiousness between a student and teacher—and which those who know Walcott would say is typical of the unfortunate way he 'tests' people by putting them in uncomfortable situations to study them—had turned into a public humiliation by Harvard changing his grade. Walcott did not deny that in the course of teaching a love poem to a student he had asked her how she would respond to an attempted seduction; such a remark could be neutral in the sense of trying to get the student to see that a love poem is a poem of seduction supposedly addressed to someone, or more likely such a remark could have been charged with the flirtatiousness that is often part of relations between people. American universities have no real means of handling such problems; either specialists in the area are reluctant to judge the grades given by colleagues or more often a committee of non-specialists will simply raise the grade to avoid possible controversy. The American system has no second markers and external examiners as used in England where a disputed grade is normally looked at by others in the field. Walcott had been found guilty without trial or means to defend himself.

In late October, the 29th, Joseph Brodsky wrote to Derek Bok, President of Harvard, concerning the humiliation and publicity over the changing of the grade. Susan Sontag also wrote to Bok, mentioning Brodsky's letter, and commenting that as a feminist she was of course sensitive to matters of sexual harassment. She had not discussed the details of what took place with Walcott, and could not say that there was no flirtatiousness. But by changing the student's grade Harvard was agreeing that Walcott was vindictive; Sontag found this inconceivable. Walcott was a man of integrity, decency, sensitivity, yet he had been publicly shamed without means of redress. Sontag questioned whether the real issue was Walcott; with grade inflation, American students now regarded C as the equivalent of F. Her letter was copied to Roger Straus, Brodsky, and David Rieff. By late November Brodsky and Sontag had had no reply from Bok and Roger Straus wrote (23 November) to complain that as Walcott's publisher and friend he was discontented with Harvard's failure to reply to Brodsky and Sontag. Harvard had allowed a situation to develop and was now trying to ignore it. Dean Henry Rosovsky replied (22 November) to Brodsky that the source of any information or misinformation reported was the student who was free to speak with the press. The university would not make any statement or engage in discussion of the matter. David Rieff sent a copy of Rosovsky's reply to Walcott and remarked that Bok was hiding behind his deans. While appreciating Walcott's reluctance to pursue the situation in public, Rieff wanted Walcott's permission to carry on the fight behind the scenes. Rosovsky (2 December) replied at more length to Sontag, but still refused to discuss student or faculty matters. Rosovsky did, however, argue that Walcott could have responded to the student's charges in the press if he had wished, or he could go to court if he felt he had unjustly suffered damages. He further argued that the officers of Harvard had not changed Walcott's grading. Harvard and Radcliff had an Administrative Board of deans and senior administrators who could grant exceptions to faculty rules. The Board would not challenge the judgement of an instructor, but it might change a grade from a letter to a pass–fail, or approve late withdrawal from courses. Rosovsky (22 December) sent to Straus an almost identically worded reply. Harvard University itself was not the source of any information or misinformation about the case and would not respond to inquiries.

No one could have seriously thought that Walcott would have taken a student or newspaper to court for misrepresentation, the publicity would have made the situation worse. How would he have proved in court that there was no connection between the grade he gave a student and her claim that the mark was the result of having rejected a proposition he had made while teaching a love poem? How could he have proved what he meant—the degree of seriousness and intent —in making such a remark? It is like being asked 'do you still beat your wife?'

Walcott was to suffer in the future by acting the gentleman, assuming it would blow over, and not defending himself. Perhaps he should have appeared on television and wagged his finger towards the viewers and declared 'I have not made a flirtatious joke with that woman'? From now on some students would assume that any sexual joke or flirtatiousness was sexual harassment and there were those happy to exploit such feelings for political purposes. As American law developed, any employer of such an employee could be sued with the probability of having to make an expensive out-of-court settlement.

Walcott had radically revised *In a Fine Castle* in the light of events during 1970 and 1973 and now had a play which would be acted and published as *The Last Carnival*. It incorporated much of the social history found in the many earlier versions, and basically made the claim that the Creole whites and their culture were part of the history of the region, a foundation to build upon rather than reject, and that decolonization was in part the result of a British socialist tradition brought to the islands. Walcott brought several good young American actors with him to play the parts of local white Creoles: Fran McDormand, then a young actress whom Walcott had noticed at Yale from which she had recently graduated, and Cotter Smith.

Walcott thought he had reserved the Little Carib for two plays during the summer, but an intense dispute broke out with members of the Trinidad Theatre Workshop about the Americans in the production. Walcott said that they were essential to improve local standards and as part of an exchange. The actors, who now ran the Trinidad Theatre Workshop as a production company, objected that the exchange appeared one-sided, as Equity would not allow them to work in the United States. The Workshop mounted a production at the Little Carib and Walcott's world première of *The Last Carnival* became a Warwick Production which played to often empty seats in a tent in the grounds of the Government Training College 1–17 July.

As might be expected in the circumstances the reviews were mixed. Besides the renewed conflict between Walcott and his former close friends in the Workshop, Walcott was once more challenging the now received view of local history. One reviewer objected to devoting an entire play to a Trinidad French Creole family. He wanted a play focused on the social injustice that resulted from plantations and their white owners. Judy Stone, a former Workshop actress and the best reviewer at the time, objected to a word-of-mouth campaign against the production which she said had a rare 'transcendence' and showed Walcott's 'artistry'. People had complained that it was about the death of dodos, but she agreed that Walcott was right to ask whether Trinidad would lose by being deprived of such dodos?[14]

Walcott commented in an interview that 'The whole process of civilization is cyclical. The good civilization absorbs a certain amount, like the Greeks. Empires are smart enough to steal from the people they conquer. They steal the best things. And the people who have been conquered should have enough sense to steal back.' Fran McDormand said:

I didn't think the play was about the plight of French Creoles particularly, but just about somebody, a minority group, being wiped out . . . I have felt, since I have been here, that I am at a disadvantage here because I am a white woman. The larger racial groups in this society seem to have a sense of togetherness that makes them strong.[15]

Walcott continued to have financial problems. He wrote from the Hotel Normandie (3 July) to Straus asking him to pay a $593 telephone bill in Boston as the $4,000 MacArthur Foundation cheque for June had been sent slow post to Trinidad instead of being deposited in his Cambridge account. Besides producing, directing, and revising *The Last Carnival* (for which he wrote five new pages during rehearsals), he read at Ikon Gallery for Isaiah Boodhoo's paintings based on *Star-Apple Kingdom*. He had planned a revival of *The Joker of Seville*, but when that fell through he began writing and directing *The Rig*, a one-hour television play in which he used the actors available for *Joker*. Shooting of footage began on 22 July. This was a Banyan group production and later showed on Trinidad and Tobago television.

Andrei Sergeiev (16 September) wrote from Moscow asking permission to publish his translations into Russian of Walcott's poetry. Strachan replied that Walcott granted permission provided the royalties were cleared with his publishers. Strachan needed a list of the poems so she could determine who held rights. The *Foreign Literature Monthly* intended to publish some of the poems first.

At the end of the month there was a major Stage One production of *Remembrance* in Barbados, directed by Earl Warner with the dramatist Michael Gilkes as Jordan. During 1983 Gilkes and Warner were to recreate the production at the Creative Arts Centre, University of the West Indies, Jamaica. Since the time Walcott set out to create a West Indian drama, he had become the model for others who were carrying on his ideas, often using his plays, but from Barbados and Jamaica, and usually with university or radio or television jobs to support them.

During the autumn of 1982 Walcott read at Hartwick, Oberlin, New York University, and, on 1 October at 3.15 p.m. gave a one-hour lecture at the Coffman Union at the University of Minnesota, followed by an 8 p.m. reading at the Walker Art Center, Minneapolis, for which he received $650 plus travel and expenses. The Walker Art Gallery also published a broadside series of one hundred hand-letter-pressed pamphlets with a page of unpublished writing. The pamphlets were numbered and signed by the author who was given ten copies. This was printed by Toothpaste Press for Bookslinger editions.

There was a new manuscript being prepared for publication. Strachan (22 December) wrote to Robert McCrum at Faber to say Farrar, Straus and Giroux hoped to publish it the coming July. Although Walcott would no doubt make some revisions *Midsummer* was deliberately rough in places. The volume began in the summer of 1981 when Brodsky was in Rome and Walcott in Trinidad. It now included a Puerto Rican group (Tropic Zones) and some poems from Boston, New York, and Chicago.

While poems were still being proofed for the *New Yorker* Strachan was discussing details of book publication. On 7 January there were the first galleys for 'Tropic Zone', eight poems that the *New Yorker* had to publish by June 1983, as they were to appear in *Midsummer*. Five days later Strachan sent Walcott a duplicate manuscript of *Midsummer*. She included number L with which Walcott was dissatisfied. Strachan was unhappy with XI, where she found the argument unclear. Cynthia Krupat, who was handling design, decided to have a squarish-shaped book in keeping with the form of the poems. To indicate the relationship Strachan wanted to run together the two Gauguin and the eight Puerto Rico poems rather than printing each poem on a page to itself.

Another award! The Royal Society of Literature (11 May 1983) wrote to inform Walcott that he had won the Heinemann Award for Poetry (which earlier he had won in 1966) for *The Fortunate Traveller*. The award, now worth £2,000, was to encourage contributions to literature, especially if they were unlikely to have large sales. Strachan (16 May) replied that as Walcott would be travelling in the West Indies during June he could not attend the Society's Annual General Meeting in June. She accepted the prize on his behalf.

During June (1–26) there was also another 'World Premiere production' of *The Last Carnival*, this time in Seattle, presented by The Group, at the Ethnic

Theatre directed by Ruben Sierra. It seems to have been a good production with favourable local reviews for the play, cast, and direction. The *Seattle Times* reported 'the play's complexities are enriching, not baffling; its language resonant and filled with surprises; its ideas touching and unflinching.' The doubling and changing of parts in the second act was thought interesting, and while at first confusing, made for good theatre.[16]

In a generous gesture Walcott (9 June 1983) instructed Aschenberg that in appreciation of the fine editions in which Farrar, Straus and Giroux had published his plays he would, starting with the Seattle *Last Carnival*, give 10 per cent of all his future royalties from play productions to Farrar, Straus and Giroux!

In June the Limited Editions Club published, by arrangement with Farrar, Straus and Giroux, *The Caribbean Poetry of Derek Walcott and the Art of Romare Bearden* with an Introduction by Brodsky. Two thousand copies were printed for members of the Club. Bearden created eight original lithographs, which were hand printed in editions of 250. Each book contained one lithograph. The binding was designed especially by Bearden. The copies were numbered and signed by Walcott and Bearden. Bearden, who had a home in St Maarten and was light-skinned, wrote a note at the end of the book saying that Walcott's own awareness of being comes from a West Indian locale also found in his language. Walcott's poems were, like the islands, palimpsests of the past, ruins, old houses, harbours, fishermen, British lawns, mangoes, papayas, and ancient Caribbean faces. His rhythms were Caribbean.

Bearden was the painter in the New York circle of Ralph Ellison, Albert Murray, and 'Skip' Gates. The group favoured complexity, technique, discipline, and craft, scorned the black separatists, and thought of America as black influenced —whites had assimilated to black culture. Jazz as an existential improvisation on form was their model. During the late 1970s Bearden was famous for his Jazz series of collages which combined Modernism with black American folk culture. Murray argued that the black bourgeois, the 'black Anglo-Saxons', were the real revolutionaries who learned the ways of whites and radically changed society.

The book includes selections (made by Bearden) from all of Walcott's books from *Selected Poems* to *The Fortunate Traveller*. The selections are poems about the Caribbean such as 'A Map of the Antilles', 'Lampfall', 'Homecoming: Anse LaRaye', and 'The Virgins'. Brodsky's introduction claims that at the end of empires the language as used by artists from the provinces is what keeps the empire together, a theme which in variations Walcott also sounds. Walcott is not a regional poet, not a black poet; such terms refuse to face that he has the epic descriptive powers of Homer and Lucretius, but is saved from their tedium by the quality of his ear for English. Brodsky notes how Walcott's words look like their subject, the Moon's o's for example. In a complicated argument Brodsky claims that Walcott identifies himself with the vowels of language not the colours of race. He has in his bloodstream the poetry of world culture. The essay is about poetry as sound and Walcott's ear for sound. This is the point of the Robert Graves statement—Walcott's unusual sensitivity towards words, their textures, their relationships to other words, and even their physical appearance on a page.[17]

While in Trinidad (24 June) Walcott had spoken with his old friend H. Selby Wooding about sponsorship for the Beryl McBurnie Foundation for the Arts. Walcott said that if travel and proper accommodation were provided he could bring Brodsky, Heaney, Sontag, and others to Port of Spain where there would be an auction for the Foundation of manuscripts he would get them to donate. He suggested that others such as V. S. Naipaul, C. L. R. James, Roscoe Lee Browne, Cecily Tyson, Irene Worth, Anthony Hecht, and Joe Papp be approached along with Geoffrey Holder, Romare Bearden, and Peter Minshall, who might donate paintings. Walcott kept wanting to make Port of Spain more than a southern Caribbean cultural capital, a place on the world cultural map, but it was not to be, there was neither the interest nor money.

He was writing journalism once more, this time as a freelancer for American publications; 'Native Women under Sea-Almond Trees' was for *House & Garden*. During the summer Walcott had been in St Lucia with his daughters (their first time in St Lucia) and had stayed at a hotel. He had taken an English photographer with him. The article compared the present with the past. Walcott remembered his youth before the fire, but now felt like an outsider, although the island had not really changed despite some superficial modernization, such as small airplanes and blonde Swedish tourists. The article was accompanied by a Walcott painting of small boats (1978) and another of Vendors on Choc Beach (1983).[18]

He expected payment once it was submitted; the editor wanted revisions and said Walcott would not be paid immediately. He then contacted Strachan in September saying that he had depended on the money and needed $1,200. When Strachan reminded him he had already borrowed $1,000 in February and still owed $300, Walcott shifted the conversation to a book of six new plays. Strachan suggested a book to be delivered in the autumn of 1984, with another book of two plays in 1986. They then compromised on three plays per volume. She assumed that with 10 per cent of production royalties Farrar, Straus and Giroux might earn $1,500 a year. Strachan sent a memo to Straus asking whether the $1,200 could be thought an advance on signing for the first book of three plays. Walcott wanted the advance next week.

The St Lucia trip also led to 'A Rediscovery of Islands', in the travel section of the Sunday *New York Times* based on a trip to St Lucia 'last summer' when (the story here is spelled out) he stayed at a new hotel complex, Hurricane Hole, at Marigot Bay; the trip and hotel was paid for by the magazine for which he was doing an assignment. This was a very Walcottian piece in its lack of straightforward movement, its sudden changes in direction, the return of images, the way attitudes kept changing so that opposites were encompassed without being really accepted. At times the attitudes, especially towards St Lucia and the West Indies, approached the sentimental. Walcott saw himself both as a native and a returning tourist, both resenting the rich who stayed at such places and admitting his resentment was based on envy. At the hotel he listened to the accents of others: 'But we, whose backgrounds were not posh, look for others of similar and especially of inferior origins, so we may send them a swift glare of merciful contempt. . . . This nastiness is envy, you can understand that, can't you?' 'My hostility to the privilege of the place dissolved pretty quickly once arrangements were made and I knew I could afford it, because I was on assignment for a magazine so that someone else was paying the bill. After that a diffident languor, that easy snobbery of those used to comforts was easy . . .'

Walcott amusingly admitted that when young he had wished he lived amongst jungles and rivers with crocodiles, 'that I could bluster, suncracked and grizzled through all the channels of the archipelago, and put in places called Hurricane Hole with other sailors and make heartbreaking wisecracks to the blonde behind the bar, and be well-loved by the natives until somebody told me I was one'. This macho, Hemingwayesque Walcott of his youthful imagination was based on the white man's tropics, but the article mentioned another related Walcott, who was certain he would hate the Virgin Islands as too American, too brash.

This is the Walcott of *Midsummer* in the many changes in tone, the incomplete sentences, the long sentences, the dramatic voice shifting colours and topics:

When I got up. Regardless of what time I fell asleep. And I had better be prepared for it, braced with a cup of coffee, which I would step out onto the cool floor boards of the verandah, and feel, not see, the wetness of the flowers and cool, even cold, dark green width of Marigot Bay, very dark green in the middle, and O!, annihilation of the complaining self, the first wind with the light in it! Look, this can happen to anyone. It does. And if there's no coffee or a cigarette with it, you would go crazy . . .'[19]

On the same day Walcott reviewed a thirty-eight-page children's book in the *New York Times Book Review*, *The Glorious Flight Across the Channel With Louis Blériot, July 25, 1909*, written and illustrated by Alice and Martin Provensen. Walcott mentioned its extremely poetic prose, more like aphorisms than logical exposition. 'The way back to an idealized innocence is not only a reversal of time but also a confession of time's changes and defeats.' 'Children remember long after they have matured, married, and had their own children. And what is remembered is not always registered at the time it is first known.' One feels Walcott is writing about his *Ti-Jean* and perhaps Saint-Exupéry's *The Little Prince*. 'The glory of human endeavour is not belabored, that is one of the book's delights, since there is nothing more annoying to the child than to be told to keep trying.' 'The return to innocence requires gay and brave strides; the light on the way there is direct.'[20]

Walcott continued going back and forth between Boston and Trinidad. In September he was doing video screen tests at Banyan studios for a possible television production of 'Mona', an island off the coast of Trinidad which he had often visited with the yachting crowd during the early days of his marriage to Margaret. A friend had a house there.

By September he had finished filming *The Rig*, the Caribbean's first made-for-television movie. Made-in-Trinidad television films were unlikely to earn even half their costs. There was no market abroad for them and local stations paid little. To have produced such films was a commitment to local culture by Banyan. This, however, meant that there was neither the money or planning for a professional product. Walcott wrote the script quickly and it shows. Too often when he has tried to write about contemporary life he sounds as if he were badly imitating a 1940 tough-guy film. The story explores the impact of oil discoveries off the east coast of Trinidad on the village life of the area. One strand involves a woman with a folk dance company who is faced between leaving Trinidad to remain a serious dancer or doing erotic shows at a sleazy local nightclub. Several of Walcott's works of this period involve a conflict between the opportunities abroad and the misuse of talent involved in staying in Trinidad. A significant reply in *The Rig* and some unpublished works of this period is that in the alphabet 'I' comes before 'U'.

While in Trinidad Walcott wrote an unpublished 'preface' or review for Jamaica Kincaid's *At the Bottom of the River*, a volume of autobiographical short stories about childhood in Antigua, which he compared to the writing of Naipaul and Rhys. The longest and most telling comparison is with Saint-John Perse's 'Pour Fêter Une Enfance' which 'glints' with what life in the islands is really like. Walcott further says that they are like the 'glints' in the writing of Thomas Traherne. This is not the sentimental nostalgia of someone looking back; the language creates a peace within a darkness as frightening as anything in Jacobean drama. Walcott's writing is highly metaphoric here, a series of linked private associations; basically he is claiming that one would not have expected a major writer to appear from Antigua, nor have expected a previously unknown black woman to write so well (and without tell-tale 'mistakes'), and in her own manner. What appear to be bright little sketches of her childhood are actually disturbing portraits of what life is like in the Caribbean.

After Auden died in Austria there were various tributes in New York. Brodsky asked Walcott to write the 'Eulogy to W. H. Auden' which Brodsky read on 17 October from the high pulpit at the Cathedral of St John the Divine. The American Academy of Poets had its tribute to Auden the next day. While Auden had helped Brodsky early in his exile from Russia, Walcott had only met him briefly. Although Brodsky is not mentioned in the poem, Walcott felt the need to 'translate' Brodsky's 'gratitude and love'. Walcott thought most tributes were modelled on the work of the person being commemorated. Brodsky's poem about Lowell is 'like a Lowell poem'. In seeking a form Walcott was indebted to the design, 'sound', and diction, including clever wit, of Auden's own tribute to Yeats as a model. Such impersonation is part of the homage, showing one is part of a guild of poets; the ego of the writer should not appear superior to the subject. In Section II Walcott mentions carefully reading Auden's poetry while young:

> Once, past a wooden vestry,
> down still colonial streets,
> the hoisted chords of Wesley
> were strong as miners' throats;
>
> in treachery and in union,
> despite your Empire's wrong,
> I made my first communion
> there, with the English tongue.
>
> It was such dispossession
> that made possession joy,
> when strict as Psalm or Lesson,
> I learnt your poetry.

Walcott was concerned about the poem, it was a 'burden' and 'honour' to be asked. He showed what he thought was the final draft to Brodsky who told him it should go 'up', become somewhat seraphic, above the ordinary without sounding sublime, at the conclusion:

> A barge moves, caked with rust
> in the East River wind,
> and the mouths of all the rivers
> are still, and the estuaries
> shine with the wake that gives the
> craftsman the gift of peace.

Later, commenting upon his lines

> but you, who left each feast at nine,
> knew war, like free verse, is a sign
> of awful manners.

Walcott claimed it Audenesque 'to think of war as bad manners . . . because war is based on a disrespect for another religion, culture, identity, race, whatever . . . wars begin with a kind of indiscipline . . . order is disestablished, to be reorganized aggressively . . . free verse . . . is . . . an expression of unrestrained free will'. It was to become the first poem in the 'Elsewhere' section of *The Arkansas Testament*.[21]

Greg Gatenby (24 January) had written expressing interest in Walcott for a Harbourfront Reading in Toronto. Strachan replied the following week that Walcott's fee was $700 and expenses; given enough notice he could be available any Tuesday night in the spring. They were talking at cross-purposes; Gatenby explained that the Harbourfront Readings were usually regarded as nation-wide promotions by publishers launching books in Canada. Authors were satisfied with the publicity and national interviews. Harbourfront covered expenses, it did not pay a fee. Gatenby (8 February), however, could offer a paid reading, expenses, and accommodation for a week at a Hilton hotel (Hilton was one of the sponsors) for the annual Harbourfront International Festival of Authors, 17–22 October. There would be twenty-four authors, including Ionesco, Yevtushenko, William Golding, and Angela Carter: four authors would read each night. Gatenby needed a response before 7 June. It was not until 24 August that Strachan could confirm details. Harbourfront would cover expenses and pay Walcott $700.

Walcott flew from New York to Toronto on 19 October. The next day he read along with Joseph Brodsky, the Australian Elizabeth Jolley, and the Polish Stanislaw Baranczak at the Harbourfront Centre, Toronto, as part of the Fourth Annual International Festival of Authors. Others who read during the Festival included Ted Hughes, Salman Rushdie, Ian Wedde, Mavis Gallant, Anne Beattie, and Morley Callaghan. He returned to Boston on 21 October.

Walcott was in Toronto at the time of the American invasion of Grenada. As much as he disliked the idea of the United States invading the island he approved of it. He had seen Maurice Bishop earlier at the Hilton in Trinidad and had written a poem about the corrupt and tyrannical politicians who were the region's new rulers. Bishop for him was an imitation Che, spouting revolutionary rhetoric about the people while jailing and torturing those who dissented. He had made up his mind he would never go to Grenada with such a government in power, but Bishop was popular and moderate in comparison to the small group of ideologues who had decided that he was going to betray the revolution, and had killed him and those they thought would not support them in their coup. Better to have the Americans clear up a mess before it became another nightmare. Walcott wrote two long unpublished articles about the invasion. Later he would change his mind, citing the long record of American injustice and imperialism in the New World.

The première of *A Branch of the Blue Nile*, 25 November, was at Queen's Park Theatre, Barbados, directed and designed by Earl Warner, and sponsored by Stage One and the Nation Publishing Company. The première was for invited guests, the play ran for the general public 26 November–4 December. There was an incident shortly before the opening when Walcott threatened to cancel the production unless the Trinidadian actress who had been invited to perform was replaced by Norline. He had his way and although the play had magnificent reviews the incident received much attention in Trinidad.

While Walcott no longer had his own theatre workshop, the première of *A Branch of the Blue Nile* represented another ideal. Stage One provided a cast of serious actors as good as those in Trinidad and there was sponsorship; Walcott no longer had to find the hall, pay the actors, do the advertising—it was done for him. Earl Warner was a professional director who understood Walcott as did Gilkes. Barbados society was willing to spend money for the event. The production and other Stage One Walcott productions might be thought of as international West Indian, as Gilkes was originally from Guyana and Warner now lived in Jamaica. There was Norline from Trinidad and the author from St Lucia. It might be an illusion but productions in Barbados seemed to reflect the old ideal of a West Indian Federation, a federation of West Indian artists. This was a magnificently acted production which was taken to Jamaica and at one point was to be acted at Columbia University in New York until Equity objected that it was putting minority American actors out of work.

A Branch of the Blue Nile, like *The Last Carnival* and *Beef, No Chicken*, is concerned with Trinidad, especially the troubled relations in the Trinidad Theatre Workshop, the conflicting personalities, personal affairs, and, most important, whether it is possible to have high art in the Caribbean. Can otherwise untrained actors fulfill their natural talent and become great artists through the discipline of working with European-trained directors and European plays, or is that the road to humiliation? Must the theatre of the Caribbean be dialect comedies? As in many of Walcott's writings the play involves a play within the play, rehearsals for Shakespeare's *Anthony and Cleopatra*, which might be said to mirror a love affair within the play between an actress and a married man, and it would not be absurd to see Walcott putting in some of his relationship with Norline, who took the role of Marylin Lewis in the 1983 Barbados and 1985 Trinidad productions. This is one of my favourite Walcott plays. While productions have had good reviews, friends tell me it is difficult to follow the many intersecting relationships in the published script.

Joe Papp was sent scripts for *The Last Carnival* and *A Branch of the Blue Nile*. The report about *The Last Carnival* found it impressive, complex, Chekhovian, with lovely writing, but too full, too much like a novel, especially in its language, and at times difficult to follow. It also felt too familiar, but as Walcott was an excellent poet Papp should read the script himself. This led him to writing to Walcott saying he would like to keep up with his work and meet him again.

Daniel Halpern thinks it was Christmas 1983 when he decided to buy a Walcott water-colour for his wife. He asked Walcott how much, and Walcott asked how much he would pay. Halpern offered $300 and Walcott threw in several more. Halpern compares Walcott as a painter with Elizabeth Bishop, who was also accomplished, but not a major painter.

Walcott's first appearance in a Norton anthology was in 1983, with the third edition of *The Norton Anthology of Poetry* with four poems, 'The Gulf', 'For the Altarpiece of the Roseau Valley Church, St Lucia', 'Europa', and 'The Season of Phantasmal Peace'. He was one of the few Commonwealth writers in it. Except for A. D. Hope (Australia) and James Baxter (New Zealand), the others were Canadians (where there was a market for the Norton anthologies). For American purposes Walcott had joined such authors as Adrienne Rich, Gregory Corso, Gary Snyder, and Geoffrey Hill to become part of the contemporary canon of poets born 1929–32. The 1988 fourth edition included 'A Far Cry from Africa' (which would be in most future anthologies), 'The Glory Trumpeter', 'Nights in the Gardens of Port of Spain', 'The Gulf' (four parts), 'Midsummer', and 'Adios, Carenage' from 'The Schooner *Flight*', along with Chapter XXX of *Omeros*. It also included more Commonwealth authors, such as Peter Porter, Edward Kamau Brathwaite, Fleur Adcock, Les Murray, and Wole Soyinka.

The Norton Anthology of English Literature is probably the most widely used textbook of its kind. Walcott was first included in the fifth, 1986 edition, with three poems, 'A Far Cry from Africa', 'The Glory Trumpeter', and 'Midsummer' ('Certain things here are quietly American—'). The headnotes refer to him as flamboyant yet disciplined, witty, mention his divided roots in the English literary tradition and 'a subject people', associate him with Yeats's notion that poetry expresses the quarrel of a divided self, and proclaim him the heir of Lowell in his accuracy and energy of language. The second edition of *The Norton Anthology of Modern Poetry* (1988) had a longer headnote and much more Walcott. Walcott was becoming a staple of the multicultural and post-colonial textbook industry. In the second edition of Norton's *New Worlds of Literature; Writings from America's Many Cultures* (1994), 'A Far Cry From Africa' is included under a section termed 'Language' with study questions, the last being 'Whose side is Walcott on?'. *The Norton Anthology of World Masterpieces* (expanded edition, 1995) has a longer introduction and *Dream on Monkey Mountain*.

The anthologies helped bring Walcott into the American university view of the literary canon during a time when academics were beginning to examine the cultural and social implications of expanding English to a world literature. Unfortunately, as shown by 'Whose side is Walcott on?', literary studies were becoming politicized.

This was, however, an important new large source of royalties. Publishing poetry makes little profit for publishers or authors until the poet is anthologized, especially in textbooks. Between royalties for republishing his poems and performances of his plays, Walcott was soon earning more from his writings than his university position, which was then poorly paid for someone of his stature.

There was the problem that Walcott lacked a 'terminal degree', but there was another problem; to get a 'green card' he needed to promise to stay in the United States for eighteen months while it was being processed and Walcott was unwilling to do that. The United States was a job, his exile, but even with Norline there, his real life, the source of his writing, was in the Caribbean; he had to return there several times a year. He remained Odysseus waiting to return, waiting to end his travels and exile. As much as he appreciated the support he had received in the United States and enjoyed life among New York intellectuals, the truth was that he had an older British view of Americans as uncouth, uneducated, and lacking dignity. It was a view shared by some New York intellectuals.

24

~~~~~~

1984–1986 *Midsummer,*
Collected Poems

AFTER *The Fortunate Traveller* Walcott felt overworked; he claimed he did not want to write any poems, he wanted to concentrate on painting, but lines of poetry would come into his head. Many of his poems and books have started that way, with a few lines of pure poetry. This time he wrote them down but avoided developing them. Instead of going away they kept coming, and as he began putting them together into an 'arbitrary collage' a loose shape developed, which he later tried to join together. He purposefully tried to take what he thought of as an anti-melodic approach, working against the natural melody of the lyrical impulse. By working against the poem, letting it have its rather than his personality, the vocabulary became 'challenging', the metre more 'interesting'. By his trying not to write poems they became more complex and a book began to be revealed. He then deleted what he thought unworthy and pulled the rest together.[1]

A volume of poems began to appear, first as a sequence of letters addressed by Walcott in Trinidad to Brodsky in Rome during 1981, then, as it expanded to take in other places, such as Boston, Chicago, Cape Cod, the Hamptons, New York, Puerto Rico, and Cuba, poems written in places where he had travelled and observed. *Midsummer*, 'For Elizabeth and Anna', was published early in January before Walcott's fifty-fourth birthday. It consists of a fifty-four poem sequence—each poem between seventeen to thirty lines—written during two summers in Trinidad and is meant to represent a year, from summer to summer. Mid-summer is associated with mid-career, middle age, Dante's in the middle of our life, a still point, and much else. There are recurring images of light, mirrors, and everything seems to have its double, its opposite, its contradiction. Parts of the world appear different and yet the same. Poverty requires engagement, but politics become corrupt and ideology turns tyrannical.

Midsummer avoids narrative continuity; it reads like a long soliloquy about art and social and personal realities. This needed a new sound, a new form, a new line, the creation of a longer line into which anything could be put. Such long lines allow for boredom, and can have a lack of movement, which Walcott felt was suitable for poems which often treat of the relationship of poetry to painting and which were like watercolours blurred at the edges.

While each of Walcott's volumes of poetry is different, and he consciously avoids repeating himself, the differences are mostly in form, genre, and focus, as Walcott's ideas do not radically change over the decades. Many of the same concerns recur in different ways, more complicated, nuanced, attached to other topics, even shifted from a position Walcott supports to one he opposes. One difference here is the verse itself as the lines lengthen and contract, sometimes returning to a pentameter, often expanding to a hexameter as Walcott appears to need a new basic rhythmic unit, longer than the five-foot line, for the complex associational sentences, with their elaborate puns and metaphors branching off from metaphors, that his style has been moving towards:

> Skimming over an ocher swamp like a fast cloud of egrets
> are nouns that find their branches as simply as birds.
> It comes too fast, this shelving sense of home—
> canes running the wing, a fence; a world that still stands as
> the trundling tires keep shaking and shaking the heart.[2]

Much of Walcott's poetry and verse drama from *Midsummer* to *The Bounty* uses some variation on, or experiment with, the hexameter. The alexandrines of *The Odyssey*, for example, could be thought a variation. The rhythm of the first lines of a poem establishes a pattern which the reader relies upon, the way a musician or dancer may depend on a basic beat around which to phrase over, so for practical purposes a hexameter in English might be regarded as any verse with a regular pattern of six feet, beats, stresses, or twelve syllables, around which an actual line may vary. This differs from the classical hexameters which followed a set pattern of six feet, the first dactylic or spondee, the fifth dactylic, the sixth spondee; if all four opening feet are dactylic the line has seventeen syllables. This sounds like walking on stilts and historically the hexameter has seldom been happy in English, although Walcott was to come close to the classic line in *The Bounty* and make it sound natural. He likes the challenge, of doing what has not been done well by other poets, but the main reason for his choice of the long line is that despite its technical problems it is closer to prose than the pentameter. It is a line for narrative, for verse letters, for pastorals, elegies, elaborate associations.

Free versers and other Modernists argue that metre, especially the pentameter, is unnatural, too poetic for our era. Walcott has seldom had much time for that. Poetry has to have rhythm, metre, a pattern that the reader can recognize, a background structure, a rhythmic beat, but he has always wanted to move in opposition to his natural lyricism towards something more prose-like, something more capable of carrying his own voice, his thoughts. This radical shift from his beloved pentameter was in keeping with a recent general interest in longer lines by poets, especially by C. K. Williams. In *Midsummer*, and indeed in other works, Walcott often reverts to a pentameter line. The poems are not rigid, they have form without being formal.

Midsummer was widely reviewed, but not always well. Reviewers could not make up their minds whether it was rhymed, in blank verse, willed or spontaneous, the worst or best book Walcott had written. Many recognized a debt to Lowell's *Notebooks*, but was one Lowell more than enough or had Walcott improved on his model? *Book World* suggested at times 'there's less here than meets the eye'. Terry Eagleton predictably spoke of 'literature's tendency to imitate criticism'; he thought *Midsummer* an example of 'in the age of structuralism . . . poets . . . modelling their inner and outer landscapes on language itself'. Eagleton's main concern was that the poetry did not bridge the distance between language and political engagement. The young, good, British West Indian poet Fred D'Aguiar also argued that there was no neutral space for art, it should address the oppressed; he unfavourably contrasted *Midsummer* to Brathwaite's *Third World Poems*. David Garrison correctly said Walcott 'loaded every rift of his subject with ore' and explored experience; Garrison pointed to the importance of 'juxtaposition, of how one sphere—of knowing, of feeling, of being, of creating—assimilates or is assimilated by another. . . . the sea's constant conversation with the land; the present's nearly imperceptible friction with the past; the linguistic world's ordering of the physical'. So many themes are compressed together in *Midsummer* critics were bound to be right and wrong in choosing age, political engagement, political disillusion, language, poetry, travel, death, or most anything else as a subject. It is also a volume in which light in its many meanings and significances becomes central. Walcott's methods here are not that different from those of his early Auden-influenced poetry in which there are continually shifting levels of significance within what appears a persuasive argument of some sort, except here the appearance is more ruminative.[3]

Several sides of Walcott came into play in the two essays published during March 1984. The Lowell essay is in response to biographers who concentrated on Lowell's drinking, adultery, and bouts of insanity. The essay is in Walcott's *Safe Conduct* manner; non-chronological, consisting of short scenes, small epiphanies, significant details, it ends at the beginning with a scene of Walcott late at night at the beach house listening to Lowell read from *Imitations* to the hiss of a kerosene lamp. There are nice touches like Lowell's concern with his neckware and Walcott adjusting a tie, signifying what? The aristocratic master and his young heir? The essay is like many of Walcott's major articles, close to prose poetry, a series of evocations in which plot or narrative is hidden, ignored. It is the method of many of the poems and of such volumes as *Another Life* and such plays as *Dream on Monkey Mountain*, except that the plays often have a teller, someone in whose mind or story the events occur. There are, however, two unusual flare-ups in 'On Lowell'. One occurs when Lowell, going into one of his periods of insanity, accused Walcott of using people. The other comes when, reading with Lowell in a Village apartment among other poets, one of them mocked a Walcott poem as female Lowell. It is difficult to imagine why Walcott should include scenes of humiliation except for a continuing need to reply. In both cases he argues his superiority to competitive American poets on the make. He does not forget what hurts.[4]

His review of the republication of C. L. R. James's 1963 classic *Beyond a Boundary* was one of very few in the United States. Except for Walcott there were few writers, perhaps no others, who would have known both Lowell and James, and have understood the importance of both as writers and their cultural contexts. James was for Walcott part of an older generation of West Indians with the kind of learning and broad interests that Lowell's poetry assumes. James brought such an education and values to colonial society. He understood that blacks and colonials undermined and beat the imperial tradition by joining it and making it their own. This could be seen in cricket, in the way West Indians mastered the game and the various social and racial subtexts to what was happening on the field and in committees. James discussed the changes from the time when there were separate clubs for white and coloured players to when a black captained the West Indian team. James was writing cultural criticism about cricket, about the dusk of empire and colonialism and the beginnings of independence.[5]

By now Walcott was in demand, magazines paid for his poetry and articles, and he was part of the New York literary establishment. On Monday, 23 April, he read 'Elsewhere' at a benefit for *Index on Censorship*. Strachan sent it to the *New York Review of Books*. She also sent 'Cul-de-Sac Valley', a revised 'Lighthouse' (the first poem in *The Arkansas Testament*) to the *New Yorker* and would soon send it 'Three Musicians'. *The Arkansas Testament* was starting to take shape and money was to be earned for publishing first in magazines before the book was published. Moss (15 May) unexpectedly returned 'Cul-de-Sac' saying it was rare to return a Walcott poem, but this one seemed forced, perhaps because of the analogy to carpentering. The second poem in *The Arkansas Testament*, it became a favourite of critics with its St Lucian trees *bois canot, bois campêche,*

> hissing: *What you wish*
> *from us will never be,*
> *your words in English,*
> *is a different tree.*

'The Lighthouse' recalls a friend, a photographer and actor of his youth, 'Spessy' Mondesir (brother of the current head of St Mary's College), who had no outlet for his abilities in St Lucia. A powerful but rather difficult poem, the movement is back and forth in time. Half of the new volume would have poems about St Lucia. If leaving Trinidad had made Walcott an international poet, he was already homing towards St Lucia, his original home, but more than half of his life now would be 'elsewhere'. He had hated Boston at first, joked about it being the capital of Canada, but had come to feel settled, comfortable, housed, secure, while wanting to be in the Caribbean.

At the end of May Walcott returned from Boston to Trinidad where he rented a small house in Port of Spain on Elizabeth Street near the Savannah with its mansions and race horses. He was then selecting poems for his 1986 *Collected Poems*.

Walcott first registered at Villa Beach Cottage, Choc Beach, St Lucia, on 7 July. A week later Richard Montgomery arrived; then later in the month Walcott's three children came to the cottages. The cottages were made from old American officers' quarters built during the Second World War which, after the Americans left, were somehow transported across the island and rented to tourists. The owner was an Indian Methodist who had seized his opportunity at the time. Two of the cottages are larger, face the sea, and one, Cottage 3, has an air conditioner in a window.

From that summer until the Nobel Prize, after which he needed some place more private, Walcott would stay in Cottage 3 several times a year, usually in January and for part of the summer, but also at other times such as the spring break. Between teaching and readings his year was determined by the American university schedule. Boston was where he worked and resided eight or nine months of the year; the other months were usually divided between St Lucia and Trinidad, his two 'homes', although he owned a home in neither. He would tell those who wanted to see him to come to St Lucia where he would be more relaxed than in North America. Even after 1992, when Walcott's fame made it no longer possible to stay at the cottages, the cottages would be used by such visiting Walcottians as Roderick Walcott and Andrew Tanker, and the grounds and beach would be used for tests and rehearsing a film version of *Omeros*, that never got off the ground. Many of Walcott's poems were written there in the early morning, while having coffee and smoking a cigarette, at 5.30 or 6 a.m. as the tropical sun rose.

Often after writing for hours he would then paint for several hours. He kept an easel, paints, and other materials at the Villa Beach Cottages and Cottage 3 came to be regarded as his. Walcott would come and go; during times when he was likely to come anyone renting Cottage 3 would be warned that it was already booked and it might be necessary to move at short notice. The view from the cottage of Rat Island, the cottage's palm trees, the low sea wall in front of the cottages, and the various small boats that sail in front of the cottage can be instantly recognized in Walcott's painting on the cover of *The Antilles*.

He had decided to be a painter again; he had read Walter Sickert's autobiography *A Full House* which he thought had the same 'impasto' prose as the painting. He saw himself in Sickert, an amateur professional painter. Being St Lucian Walcott should have felt French, Afro-Gallic, but he had been raised in the British public school tradition of team spirit, decency, restraint. Sickert represented English second-rateness, dullness, in comparison to the greatness of Degas. Painting was about painting, not story, not morals. Amateurs were concerned with subjects. Good painters were concerned with making, with workmanship. The painter looks on his canvas like Velásquez in *Las Meninas*. Walcott knew he lacked the wrists of a painter. His brush strokes lacked the immediate rightness. Real painters did not need to keep observing the whole. Cézanne painted thin, Van Gogh painted thick, but both painted without worry about the conclusion. Walcott felt that he was not a real painter. He thought too much, overworked the surface, and the light started to fade from the work. The more he worked the more the painting failed.[6]

If Clara Rosa de Lima's Art Creators and her sponsorship of *Marie Laveau* was the start of Walcott's professional career as a painter, it was in St Lucia that his paintings developed through constant close attention to the land and seascape, to the physical characteristics of St Lucians and especially to the changing light and colours. Walcott's landscape paintings of the 1950s, such as the one of Newcastle in the possession of Dunstan Champagnie, are not especially striking or original. The Villa Beach paintings are better structured, more technically accomplished and detailed in their treatment of light, shade, and colour. Walcott's earlier paintings, regardless of theme or subject, tended towards the abstract. The later paintings tend towards the hyper-real, a precise and sharply defined realism. Walcott watched and painted the changing colours of the water, the movement of clouds in the sky, the shades of green on a leaf, the shape of a coconut or even some debris on the beach. Walcott had earlier than most people decided that Winslow Homer was the great American watercolourist, an Adamic painter not inferior to the more widely accepted greats of Europe. Homer had also painted parts of the Caribbean and was one of the first major painters to see how its light and colours are different. Paintings made at Villa Beach Cottages would be used for the covers of many of Walcott's books including *Omeros* and

The Antilles. Moira, the maid at the cottages, became keeper of Walcott's paints, and would herself become a Walcott subject for two paintings.

Walcott was in St Lucia for the world première of his play *The Haytian Earth*, 1–5 August. While back in St Lucia Walcott read from his poetry, on 12 July, at Castries Central Library.

During recent years Walcott had not been much in St Lucia, his work and life were elsewhere, but the visit in 1983 for *House & Garden* led to his being commissioned by the Ministry of Education and Culture to prepare a play for the celebration of 150 years of emancipation since 1834 when slavery was abolished. Dunstan and other friends in the Ministry assumed he would revise *Henri Christophe*, but Walcott had for years been working on a possible film or television play about Haiti and that is what he revised.

He had at various times scouted St Lucia for a possible site for a national theatre or at least a more suitable place to produce plays than a rented Banana Shed. The old army barracks high on the Morne seemed ideal in terms of its dramatic location, the open space, and the remaining historical buildings which would contribute to the setting of his play. His friends remained in power and *The Haytian Earth* became a highly profiled large project that would have required millions elsewhere. The $80,000 St Lucia spent on it has been estimated, in terms of the proportion of the St Lucian budget, as the equivalent of the United States voting $200,000,000 to produce a play. But then this was still a time when some countries were spending large sums on experimental theatre with an international team, even with actors who shared no language; *The Haytian Earth* was comparatively small and inexpensive, although a bit international as Richard and Sally Montgomery came to do scenery, costume, and design. A few of Walcott's Trinidadian management crew were imported, and a few wealthy well-wishers came from Trinidad to view the production. The cast consisted of members of the St Lucia Arts Guild, a number of young actors who had developed in new theatre companies around workshops given by the Extra-Mural Studies, and Norline. Arthur Jacobs, a sculptor and woodcarver who appears and sounds as if he were born for the stage, acted Toussaint; Norline Metivier-Walcott had the important role of Yette, a character continued from Walcott's *Drums and Colours*, the good-natured whore whose relationship to Pompey represents the People, especially the joining of the mulatto with the black peasant against the élite.

There were the usual last-minute revisions characteristic of Walcott as director-writer. The day of the opening Walcott substituted at the end of Act I a hand-written page in which Toussaint offers a vision of Haiti with all classes and races at peace, then speaks of Dessalines's temper and how it could cause the classes and races to fight and lead to destruction. The fault, the destruction of the revolution, is personal.

The production was recorded and shown on television in St Lucia and Trinidad, but the film is poor and not clear. Walcott continued working on a film script of the play which might someday be published along with *Franklin* and *The Charlatan*, two other plays with long histories which have had major productions, but remain unpublished. While producers and directors will not première a published play, feeling it has already lost its virginal sales appeal and has become fixed in form, a major production of a play is necessary for publishers and later directors who wish to revive it, as an unproduced play could have been radically changed and the published script now only an early draft.

Most of Walcott's plays have begun with intimations of what they might look like as paintings, with the colours and shades associated with the art of some period. The actors have been chosen to fit his visualization of the characters. He would direct plays as a series of tableaux, with scenes like, even recalling, paintings. That made for their visual interest and beauty, but also tended towards static and lengthy plays. This was the last play Walcott would direct for many years. He had tried to be a director-writer-producer in the grand tradition that had existed from the Elizabethans and Molière until the early twentieth century, but times had changed and everyone was now a specialist. The close relationship he had had with the Theatre Workshop was over; now he was being told by others that he screamed rather than directed. There was little demand for him as a stage director, and his attention kept turning towards television and making films. Let others direct his plays and make money for him.

The Haytian Earth continued to keep Walcott's attention. There is a powerful painting (which was in the de Lima Collection), dated July 1985, consisting of a composite of faces from the play. Many of Walcott's paintings for *The Haytian Earth* were available for sale and this was the first time that many locals had a chance to see and buy his paintings, especially as earlier paintings had disappeared over the years. Some St Lucians say that it was with *The Haytian Earth* that Walcott started to be visible again on the island. He had regularly returned to see his mother, but had kept to himself, his family, and a few friends. The play brought him into contact with others, especially the younger generation, and afterwards Walcott would spend more time on the island, returning at Christmas, during the summer, and at Easter.

He had made many drawings and paintings to show how he visualized *The Haytian Earth* and he sold them in St Lucia and through Rosa de Lima's gallery in Port of Spain. This was the first time Walcott had sold a large number of his art works and might be considered the start of his career as a painter. During his early years in Boston Walcott had not painted much; the landscape and light were unfamiliar and his life too unsettled. Now he would begin painting in Boston as well as in the West Indies. His original dream returned of being a painter; it was in part restored by his rediscovery of St Lucia, its natural beauty coexisting with its poverty. The combination of the two would become a theme of his poetry as he began to question whether he was sentimentalizing reality.

Walcott had left St Lucia in 1950. He had lived for over two decades in Trinidad and was deeply involved in the island's life. In recent years with his life divided between Trinidad, Boston, New York, and the Virgin Islands, and as he began to think of himself as an international poet, St Lucia had been neglected, even forgotten. Now he came home as a favourite son, was treated well by former school mates who were in power, was welcomed by Dunstan and old friends in the Arts Guild, and had the attention of others. Trinidad had hurt him. He would always return there because of his children, the Trinidad Theatre Workshop, and many friends, but he would spend more time in St Lucia, write about St Lucia, and paint in St Lucia. He would buy land and begin building a house in St Lucia. It would take a decade and the Nobel Prize before he could finish the house and use St Lucia rather than Boston as his home.[7]

During *The Haytian Earth* Walcott was interviewed by Henry Mangal for the St Mary's College annual publication, a descendant of the annual Walcott had edited for a year. The interview was short but revealing. Little had changed over the decades except that nationalist chauvinism and provinciality had become the new danger, replacing the teaching of British history and culture. The early Walcott of the St Lucian folk culture revival had become wary. When questioned about youth's lack of interest in the La Rose festival, Walcott surprisingly wondered whether the festival had sufficiently deep roots to survive. People might not know it but they hungered for the arts, yet there were no true theatres, libraries, and museums in the Caribbean. They should be a natural part of cities. While artists should expect state support, artists should expect to be lonely, isolated, facing the canvas or piece of paper. All poetry is complex; even if the language is simple it should never stop reverberating, echoing. 'If people think my vocabulary is too complex for the society then that's society's fault because I'm writing in English, and I can't restrain myself in terms of limiting myself. I have never treated this society as being illiterate. If I did I would write like a moron. . . . the more the human mind takes in experience, the more complicated experience becomes.'[8]

Late September the Stage One Production of *A Branch of the Blue Nile* was supposed to move to Columbia University's Horace Mann Theatre with an eight-member cast including Michael Gilkes and Norline Metivier. It did not. In Bridgetown, Barbados, Stage One Productions picketed (22 September) the United States Embassy to protest against the New York Actor's Equity's refusal to allow the production. Equity said that because of the high unemployment of black and minority American actors the West Indians would continue to be banned. To the Barbados actors this seemed a further example of a one-way culture exchange, especially as CBS was then filming an episode of a television soap opera in Barbados with an American cast.[9]

At the end of September (27–8) Walcott read from his poetry and drama at Hardin-Simmons University, Abilene, Texas. For the university it was a coup to have Walcott and a Professor of English was quoted in the student newspaper as saying 'none of us have ever taught Walcott, so we're really quite intrigued to hear what he has to say'.[10] The visit was well prepared with the local community; the *Abilene Reporter-News* carried an intelligent review of *Midsummer*, mentioning the influence of Robert Lowell and especially of the 1973 'The Dolphin' sonnet sequence in *Midsummer*. The reviewer noted the division of the sequence into reactions to the West Indies, followed by a less tightly structured section in Boston and touring in the United States, which included an elegy for James Wright. *Midsummer* also stood for mid-life, this was a time of taking stock of life, which had become especially important to Walcott as his travels took him further from home into an always widening world. If the volume appeared meandering like life, passing reflections, or like Lowell's *Notebook* a poetic journal, it was really more like an Impressionist painting with tiny thematic details, a brilliant surface, a healthy confidence.[11]

In an interview Walcott mentioned his indebtedness to the United States for grants, opportunities, and honours. Walcott said that the effect of moving between two cultures increased each year; in Brookline he felt locked in his apartment, he could not walk in the yard without a shirt. In Brookline he was always waiting to return to the beaches and seas where swimming and re-laxation were part of his creativity. He worked all the time, and even harder in the Caribbean. Art was a challenge, every day there was room for improve-ment. As he became older he had become more conscious of the deprivation and lack of opportunities in St Lucia and his own need to respond as an artist. Walcott said that Grenadians were glad that Americans freed them from the coup. 'People were living by the gun rather than in freedom.' The ideology of the government mattered less than the violence and brutality of those who had led the coup.[12]

The reading had been arranged by Robert Hamner. Walcott told Hamner that he needed the money, and said that Norline had encouraged him to come. It was a tight schedule, a poetry reading on Thursday at 8 p.m., a forum on creative writing the next day at 3 p.m., readings from his plays at 8 p.m. followed by a public reception. Walcott went to various social engagements in the community, was exceptionally polite (as he knew it was a Baptist community), even asked permission to smoke (he had been avoiding drink for some years), but tried to have time on his own at his hotel where he worked on an early film script of *Steel*, a project that would continue until 1987, and continue as a play later. Mark Coffey came from Austin to see him about it.

Coffey, an American sound engineer and film editor, in the early 1980s formed a company to record Caribbean and African music. He attended Carnival and Pan festivals in Trinidad, hung around the pan-yards, helped produce a recording of steel band music, and was thinking of making a documentary of its social history. He was staying at the same guest house during Walcott's return to Port of Spain, played him what he had recorded, and they started talking about making a film. During April Coffey sent to Walcott in Brookline a video cassette and presentation of the 'steel drum' project, *Success Village*, which eventually evolved into Walcott's play *Steel*. Coffey saw the story as being about the evolution of steel drums and cultural development through the life of the main character. The film would show community life on the streets, in the pan-yards 'behind the bridge'. The events were based on real stories. Coffey clearly did not know Walcott well and the letter sounds a bit like a form letter.[13] A contract was signed. Between June and September Walcott worked on the script of Coffey's *Success Village*. Some of Walcott's jottings survive concerning dates, fees, and conditions (one-third of the money had to be raised) for a first draft and future costs.

Like several other projects once Walcott became involved, it would start changing into a larger, somewhat different project, which might or might not be concluded, but which would leave the originator behind. The history of *The Joker of Seville* might be taken as a model. Coffey (10 October) circulated a letter announcing Walcott's association with the film project and the change of title and aims. Walcott wanted to begin over without the previous story and to get away from a fictionalized documentary. He had already written part and wanted to finish the first draft by late November.[14]

Coffey stayed with Derek and Norline in Boston a few times; a script (with some illustrative drawings) was produced with what Coffey felt was marvellous dialogue, but with too much about individuals rather than a community. Walcott was using the situation he had earlier used in *O Babylon!* (and which was in V. S. Naipaul's 'A Flag on the Island') of someone returning from abroad to a place that had been transformed by economic 'progress', and who recalls its former poverty, energy, and ambition. Steel band had moved up socially and economically from the invented music of the unemployed, poor, thugs, and gangs to become acceptable, a national cultural symbol and export. *Steel* uses such Walcott themes of the time, found in *The Rig* and *Beef, No Chicken*, as the costs of economic progress, the destruction of the past, the possible loss of roots as the local is adapted to foreign forms, and the costs of exile and leaving home. Those who leave can never go back to what they left as it too, and those they knew, have changed. The permanence of growing apart, change, and exile, especially for the artist, were concerns already anticipated in such poems in *The Gulf* as 'Homecoming: Anse La Raye'. The art that gives form to a community's history, voices, and desires depends on alien structures and requires the artist to be different from the community to see it and give it shape. Pan music and the successful pan artist will betray their origins in poverty and violence as Walcott had to betray St Lucia to become its artist.

This contrast between subject and form once again became the source of disagreement. For Coffey the script lacked a feeling of 'the street'. He liked the way Walcott brought in conflicts between the black and Indian communities, but the ending seemed too much 'fluff' to be cinematic. There was an episode in the script concerning breaking in and thieving master tapes and records which Coffey thought a typical cliché about young independent record and film companies, but which I know was based on the history of Semp Studios in Port of Spain. I had spent weeks trying to locate the tapes and those involved. It brought me into contact with local criminals. Life in Port of Spain imitated film clichés.

Coffey circulated a proposal concerning the film, but basically there was a disagreement between his and Walcott's view. When Walcott insisted on music by Galt MacDermot the project came to a halt. Coffey was hoping they might agree on André Tanker, but Walcott's loyalty and feeling that MacDermot was what he wanted brought the project to a close. Coffey may still have rights to the film version of *Steel* and at times thinks of approaching Walcott about it once more.[15]

On Monday, 22 October 1984, Walcott read at the Poetry Center of the 92nd Street YMHA. This was Walcott's fourth reading at the Kaufmann Hall. He was paid $500 plus expenses. Like Hartwick College it was becoming a regular event.

He was, 9–10 November, at Northwestern University, outside Chicago, for the *TriQuarterly* symposium on the place of serious fiction and poetry in modern culture. Walcott lectured on 'A Colonial's Eye-View of the Empire' which was followed by a panel discussion. This was another of Walcott's digressive, off-the-cuff talks. He was one of the few speakers at the symposium not caught up in the infantile anti-American leftism and lack of familiarity with the actual world. He claimed that while empires always disappear, art offers immortality in the sense that human experience becomes legend as can be seen from Prometheus and Ulysses. Faust is emblematic of empire, including its self-destructiveness. Walcott feels like a barbarian from the distant provinces speaking to the empire. The Americans have a conscience about foreign matters, but not about their internal colonies of Puerto Ricans and blacks. When Walcott returns to the United States he suddenly must recall that he is black, something different from an alien barbarian. He had been treated generously by Americans, without American grants and other support he could not have made a living as a writer in the Caribbean. He then spoke of the need for Americans to see the New World experience as that of castaways, of the pioneer spirit, of beginning again, rather than looking back towards lost origins.[16]

Billie Pilgrim, now a long married Irma Goldstraw, had been since the late 1970s compiling a bibliography of Walcott's poetry. It had expanded into a bibliography of his published works and she was in contact with Strachan who wrote to her (1 July 1982) that as manuscripts and proofs of four Walcott books had piled up in the office, perhaps Goldstraw could sell them to the University of the West Indies library or ask the library to keep them until some arrangement could be made? Strachan's letter said that Walcott was uninterested in their fate and that she had had the idea of storing or selling them. Irma Goldstraw's 1984 *Derek Walcott: An Annotated Bibliography of his Works* was partly based on Walcott's own files which had been purchased by the University of the West Indies, St Augustine, for, it is said, TT $15,000. The materials had been kept in boxes in a utility room at Walcott's house, were damaged by rain, then were stored at Goldstraw's house, and eventually moved to the university library where they remained uncatalogued and inaccessible for over a decade. Walcott at times sent more documents to the university on the assumption that they would be available to scholars and that the West Indies was where they belonged. It is possible, however, that if an American university had made an offer the materials would now be available in Boston or Texas. Earlier Boston University had enquired about purchasing Walcott's manuscripts, and had asked for a list of what he had. The University of Texas, Austin, had been building a Caribbean collection, but decided not to approach Walcott as it was purchasing elsewhere, a decision it no doubt now regrets.[17]

Goldstraw's book included four versions of Walcott's poem 'Sea Grapes'. Walcott at times saved corrected galleys and other evidence that he was proud of having continued to make changes on his manuscripts at each stage and that he wanted scholars in the future to be aware of this and study the changes.

Although Walcott had forbidden the Theatre Workshop, which, effectively meant Errol Jones and Stanley Marshall, from producing his plays, others could. During March 1985 there was a major revival of *Dream on Monkey Mountain* at the Astor Theatre, a large cinema, by Arbee Productions in Port of Spain. Albert Laveau was director, but as Walcott and Errol Jones were still at war Arthur Jacobs was imported from St Lucia for the role of Makak. Although Laveau's directing was based on Walcott's, it lacked his vitality, and the play was said to reflect an era that had already passed when a return to Africa was thought a return to paradise. Too much had happened in Africa since then for black West Indians to regard it with nostalgia.[18]

Walcott's attention had turned towards Martinique, exploring how it differed from St Lucia, and wondering what he might have been if born in a French rather than British colony. His 'Café Martinique' in the March *House & Garden* is Walcott's only published short story. It is a supposed character sketch of Martinique and Maurice Lamartine, a brown intellectual and artist who has become decadent and instead of being creative prefers irony and holding sway at a café. He no longer makes art or women. Nothing much happens, years pass, and that is the point, as Maurice and Martinique are contrasted to St Lucia and the author. Maurice is one of Walcott's 'fictions', a projection of Walcott and what Walcott might have become if he were born on the next island. 'Café Martinique' reads like one of those chapters of Walcott's unpublished autobiographical 'American, without America' or the autobiographical essays of 'Inside the Cathedral'. Like much of Walcott art it works with stereotypes, atmosphering in a scene around a visualized face and setting. Much of the success or lack of success is as much in the touch, the amount of life, the colouring and sketching as in development. The opening paragraphs are a painter's vision, and show Walcott's own self-awareness:

Across the blue channel, from our island, we sometimes saw the haze that was Martinique. Civilization. French wines. Sidewalk cafés for disenchanted love. I went there briefly, and saw what I had imagined, so I have set him there under the blue, white, and red scalloped awning of the Café Martinique; his complexion sallow, nostrils delicate, and the posture erect, but ravaged.

Martinique was the Empress Joséphine, a liquid, golden name. Flirtatious folk music, the beguine, madras head-ties, green wine bottles with elaborate crests on their labels, and *causer*, the art of gestured conversation. There they drank wine like water. Rosé. Not those vicious punches served in our hotels, in which the waiters plant little paper parasols. The wind off the harbor braced the intellect.

All this was years ago, so there is only a blur of gendarmes in khaki shorts, who wore the hard, round caps known as *képis*; white Frenchmen who carried revolvers. It was the first time I had seen white colonial police. Our own police were local, which meant that they were black, and were not armed.

This is the prose of a painter, a painter in the manner of the School of Paris, 'the blue, white, and red scalloped awning', an Impressionist, 'the haze', a watercolourist and caricaturist, 'sallow, nostrils delicate', who can reproduce a bottle of wine in one stroke, 'Rosé.' It is also the self-conscious prose of some-one living during postmodernism and post-colonialism, 'saw what I imagined', 'white Frenchmen who carried revolvers'.

The story, what little of it there is, emerges between essays that resemble Walcott's own past, views, and writings:

He had tried to market poverty as an idea, as a poetic truth. He had seen how tourists looked for it on the pretext that they were seeking something native, real. That was the way he had tried to pay back grand-mère, and to take revenge on his illegitimate white grandfather, a khaki man with a khaki helmet on a khaki horse. He had probably tumbled her in the canes.

The young poets celebrated blackness now, but for him their devotion was another kind of Oedipal rape, or an infantile desire to hide in those skirts, away from the world, away from technology deep in matenal Africa.

At the end of the story when the author writes a letter to the Maurice of twenty-five years ago, it could be Walcott writing to his earlier self:

Did you see the whole archipelago as another Aegean? You never managed to decide what costumes we would wear. Togas. All that wonderful talk! All of that invaluable bitterness! Your muse was a black-haired, brown-skinned girl who, mentally was only visiting . . . you hoped you had pierced her heart for good. That your bitterness might send her away while your adoration needed her to remain.[19]

The story appears to have been influenced by Walcott's recent visit to Martinique, the subject of 'French Colonial. "Vers de Société" ', and by the rewriting of *The Last Carnival*. In the poem Walcott mentions his distaste of the French, of their sense of order and good taste:

> I memorize the atmosphere in Martinique
> as comfortable colonial—tobacco, awning, Peugeots, pink
> > gendarmes,
> their pride in a language that I dared not speak
> as casually as the gesticulating palms
>
> before Algeria and Dien Bien Phu—
> their nauseous sense of heritage and order

Like Samuel Johnson, who spoke Latin while visiting France, so Walcott, who speaks French Creole, and who studied French at University College and reads French, avoids speaking French for fear of mispronunciation. Martinique had become part of France and its culture remains French, whereas St Lucia is an independent nation while no longer culturally British. Martinique is more 'comfortable' than St Lucia; more and better goods are available, are flown in from France. St Lucians fly to Martinique for a day to shop, but it is also where the police, the immediate symbol of politics, government, power, and the social order, are often 'pink', unlike St Lucia where even in Walcott's youth they were brown or black. How might *Dream on Monkey Mountain* read if Lestrade and the police were the 'pink' jailers of a black Makak? Walcott's poem and story have the artist's distrust of rationality and order as repressive, 'every other frog is a Descartes', and of good taste as a superficial view of art and life which 'tainted everything with the right taste'.[20]

The Walcott who claims he could be French, having been raised around and having consciously given attention to the French Creole culture of St Lucia, and who feels part of a French Creole Caribbean, regards the French as arrogant, sees them as imperialists, and the Brown Martinican, with his or her pride in French good taste, as what he might have been, someone writing colonial, 'Vers de Société'. Then, of course, there is the joke: 'French Colonial, "Vers de Société" ' is exactly that, a satiric, malicious poem in that genre as is the following poem in *The Arkansas Testament*, 'Mimi, the Near Suicide', a short witty, vicious mockery of how women believe flattery, fall in love, and how they may handle the consequences. This Mimi, of the 'sad, interesting eyes', jumps from a bridge and survives: 'A much better | ending than plain, provincial love: | a sodden sidewalk, a soaked brown paper bag.'[21]

It is possible that Walcott's concern about the difference between himself and what he might have been if born on the next island was influenced by his friendship with Edouard Glissant. Some time after 1973 Edouard Glissant went to Trinidad to speak about 'Delirium in Martinique' (later published in his *Discours Antillais*, 1981) at a conference on mental health in the Caribbean. He already knew Walcott's name and perhaps had read a few poems, but did not know him personally until Walcott introduced himself and showed him that *Another Life* included a quotation from Glissant's novel *Le Lézarde* (first published in 1958, published in English in 1959). Walcott and Glissant next met in Jamaica during the 1976 Carifesta and in Martinique, and then after 1980 more frequently, as both were teaching in the United States and as their children studied there. Eventually Glissant's son Olivier would study music in Boston, regularly visit Walcott, become friends with Walcott's daughters, who were studying at Boston University, and Liz Walcott would start research for an advanced degree on Glissant's writing.[22]

Both writers look rather similar, although Glissant is darker and does not have green eyes; they are of a similar age, come from neighbouring islands, share the use of a French-based Creole, and have somewhat similar ideas about culture in which Caribbean assertion is mixed with a universalism and a willingness to make full use of the imperial language and its literary forms. Both men have a high regard for, and follow, the other's work. They enjoy teasing each other about the similarities in their looks, enjoy talking about women, bait each other, were then heavy smokers, and are a source of information about politics and culture in the other's part of the Caribbean, without being especially political. Both are cultural leaders who have at times been attacked by those wanting a more self-consciously African, black, or folk Caribbean culture.

Their situations are, however, different. For Glissant and those in Martinique the relationship of French to Creole is more dramatic as there has always been a French policy that French is the language of culture and must be used at the highest metropolitan standards. Martinique is legally a part of France and has a large white French population. St Lucia, besides being independent, has shared in the British casualness about language in which local forms are acceptable and often thought desirable in literature. Creole is the language of St Lucia rather than an unacceptable variant; it is the language of the market and the folk in contrast to English, the language of the city and educated. St Lucian patois might be regarded more a 'pastoral' language, something that can quietly coexist alongside English, a folk language worth retaining and developing culturally, without a strong feeling of conflict. Walcott can quietly work patois words and phrases, rhythms, transliterations, and structural elements into his writing the way an American writer will use American English without feeling this means rejecting the English language. Glissant and many Francophones, however, feel that they must choose between writing in French or in Creole, that there is no compromise. One language or the other must rule. Glissant has chosen French as his literary language while in other ways promoting cultural creolity.

During March 1985 Walcott was flown to London by Griffith Productions to be interviewed for *Tongues of Fire*, a television programme for Channel 4 about the role of religion in the lives of poets. Ian Hamilton was director and Karen Armstrong interviewed Peter Levi and Derek Walcott at Leighton House, London (25 March). There were about forty in the audience, including Anne Walmsley, Stewart Brown, John Thieme, and some students from a course Thieme was teaching at North London Poly.

Walcott was guarded during the interview as if his vagueness about religion and theology was being examined. While he spoke of poetry as spiritual in the sense that the dedication to it implied something beyond itself, he denied being inspired, claimed not to have thought about life after death and denied believing in it, and generally seemed to deny what could be found elsewhere in interviews and poems. He felt more at ease when allowed to speak of poetry as a benediction, and blessing, or when he claimed that there was a new intentional evil in the twentieth century resulting from science and calculation. The interview appeared to confirm Walcott's flight from dogma into sentiments and his metaphoric use of the language of religion. Viewing a video of the programme I mentally contrasted Walcott's imprecision with Geoffrey Hill's theological concerns. It was not a question of agreeing with one poet instead of the other, rather it was a feeling that like many writers Walcott could appear convincing on topics until someone with specialized knowledge began questioning him. That is why some critics had failed to be charmed by his poetry. It was too metaphoric. But perhaps his imprecision during this interview was a result of jet lag?

On 10 June Walcott was staying at the Villa Beach cottage. A week later Peter arrived, as did the poet Edward Hirsch who stayed a week during which time he interviewed Walcott over three days for *The Paris Review*.[23] Walcott was then waking as early as 4.30 a.m. and would work until about 9 a.m. when he would join the others. He had recently done a drawing of Norline, some watercolours for a story board for a film version of *Pantomime*, a draft of a film version of *Steel*, an essay on the invasion of Grenada ('Good Old Heart of Darkness'), and had a manuscript ready for a volume of poems, *The Arkansas Testament*. He was 'cutting' a film version of *Haytian Earth* (presumably from the television version) and *Hart Crane*. Walcott was also revising *A Branch of the Blue Nile* and working on 'The Light of the World' (an image based on the 'word' at the beginning of the Gospel of St John) which Hirsch described as a homecoming poem about Castries.

Hirsch felt that the poem explored Walcott's sense of being both guilty and of expiating his guilt for leaving St Lucia by writing his poetry about it, his being part of and yet separated from the people. Describing the beauty of a local woman he had seen in a local jitney bus, the poem contains seeds of several motifs that will later appear in *Omeros*, including the woman, the minibus, and the symbolism of the light of the world. ('Light', of course, also alludes to St Lucia, allowing Walcott to impute a theological grace to physical beauty.) Walcott described himself as a Caribbean writer, seeing his work as West Indian and not in the British tradition.

During July he was in Manhattan working on manuscript queries concerning *Collected Poems*. Strachan needed to have the galley and page proofs read in time for reviewers to have the finished volume in September; otherwise publication would be delayed until spring. This would in turn delay publication of *The Arkansas Testament*, which she was then calling 'Winter Lamps' (a poem about his failing relationship with Norline). She asked him to take the proofs from *The New Republic, Antaeus,* and *Tri-Quarterly* back to his hotel on Monday night (15 July) so that they could be picked up on Tuesday (16 July)—or perhaps let them be published as they are and revise them for the book?

Trinidad television carried interviews with Walcott during August (15, 22 August) about his Warwick Productions' *A Branch of the Blue Nile* at the Tent Theatre, on the Savannah, Port of Spain, 14–18 and 21–4 August. Earl Warner again directed, and the production included Wilbert Holder and Norline Metivier. Whether it was the continuing problems of trying to stage plays in Trinidad, the particular problems of this production, or the new personal problems that arose in 1986, but, whatever the reason, this was the last Walcott production in the West Indies. Indeed except for a revival of *Franklin* in Barbados by Michael Gilkes in 1990, Walcott stopped using the West Indies as a place to première or revise plays. This meant giving up the audiences and critics who understood what he wanted and what he was speaking about. It also meant giving up much of the warmth and companionship he had known in the theatre. He would now be an author looking on at some rehearsals.

Besides the productions of *Dream* and *Branch* in Trinidad, there was a major Stage One production (17–28 April) in Barbados of *Beef, No Chicken* directed by Earl Warner, with Errol Jones. Earlier *Pantomime* had a short run at the New Theatre of Brooklyn. It was not reviewed by any critic until after it closed, when Paul Berman in the *Nation* observed 'What the Trinidadian owns is a mixture of English and Creole; also a habit of standing aloof from language, inspecting it, making it rich, turning it into art.' Berman saw this as similar to the tension between English and Gaelic in Heaney's poetry, or between English and Yiddish in many American writers. 'Miscegenation is the key to the modern world . . . Study prosody closely enough and you arrive at anti-imperialism.'[24]

Pantomime was also produced in England by the new Temba Black Theatre Company with Albey James directing. It opened in April 1985, at the Leicester Haymarket Studio and in June moved to the Tricycle Theatre in Kilburn as part of its Black Theatre Season. It was widely reviewed and well recommended by everyone from John Barber in the *Daily Telegraph* and Francis King in the *Sunday Telegraph* to *Time Out* and Milton Shulman in the *London Standard*. Of the important critics only Michael Billington in the *Guardian* had strong reservations. Where others saw wit, subtlety, and humanity, he saw allegory, and announced his preference for the comedies of Trevor Rhone.

Walcott, Carolyn Forché, and David Ignatow were on a panel (2 November) moderated by Martin Tucker as part of an all-day conference concerning the directions taken by contemporary American poetry. The conference was at C. W. Post campus of Long Island University, and was co-sponsored by the Long Island branch of the Poetry Society of America. Ignatow, a respected poet among writers since his *Poems* (1948), had recently published his *New and Collected Poems 1970–1985*. Although Forché was the youngest on the panel, she had by then published three prize-winning volumes of poetry and a book of translations. A politically conscious poet, she had provided the text for *El Salvador: Work of Thirty Photographers*. Walcott objected to the notion of directions, saying it was common in the United States or England for a group of writers to be dominant for a couple of decades and for them to be written into literary history as the style of the period, but for those who lived in the Caribbean there was no such history. What counted for him was creativity rather than history. The discussion soon centred upon Walcott's claim that several decades of American poets were imitating the flat diction of W. C. Williams. He felt that Williams was not always successful as a poet and had worked hard to achieve his manner. Others were writing free verse without learning how to do it. The university creative writing departments were responsible. Forché admitted she had begun by sounding like Williams as that seemed what people did. Walcott returned to one of his basic arguments, that young poets should not try to be original; they should be like painters in imitating masters. Forché felt that Americans and their poets were concerned with the self, unconcerned with the world.

This led the discussion in a rather more serious direction when Walcott objected that Walt Whitman, who was a model for much American poetry, lacked any sense of guilt. Walcott felt you had to be concerned with others, their pain and grief, even if it contradicted your own. Ignatow and Walcott agreed that the widespread compassion found in Whitman came too easily; there was no confession of guilt and no engagement in a dialogue with the rest of the world. People talked about apartheid in South Africa while ignoring Mississippi. Whether planned or not America had now become an empire.[25]

In December Irving Wardle, who had favourably reviewed the Tricycle *Pantomime* in the *Sunday Times*, was brought by the Beryl McBurnie Foundation to Trinidad to be part of a symposium, concerning the role of the critic. While Wardle was invited for his reputation and experience, he was attacked by some in the audience for not having studied Caribbean drama. Achebe was spared such criticism; Wardle was being attacked as being British and white. Walcott replied that theatre communicates between cultures.[26]

Collected Poems: 1948–84 was published in January 1986, but review copies were available since the previous November. *Collected Poems* began with a suggestion by Robert Giroux that it was time for a new selected poems: the earlier British volumes were out of print and other prominent poets were already publishing selected poems for what was felt to be a new generation of readers who did not know their earlier works. The project had perhaps been suggested by Irma Goldstraw's questions for a Walcott bibliography. As there would be increased critical attention to the earlier poems, towards getting a more complete picture of Walcott, there was a need to put his writings in order. The selection was Walcott's. When the manuscript arrived, it was larger than expected, and included all of *Another Life*; a Collected Poems now appeared desirable, as this allowed large selections from over the years without necessarily republishing everything as in an edition of Complete Poems. Walcott did not insist on many revisions, but wanted the poems returned to British spelling, with which he still felt more comfortable, and Strachan, who was still at Farrar, Straus and Giroux and remained Walcott's editor, aimed for consistency. The effect of the *Collected Poems* was, however, more than a large Selected Poems. The selection provided another way of looking at Walcott.

I remember being surprised by it. I knew Walcott's poetry and plays in the context of West Indian and Commonwealth literature, I had not thought of him as an American or international poet. *The Fortunate Traveller* was not enough to have changed my perspective—I thought he was experimenting with some American poetics—and I had not read *Midsummer*. In the *Collected Poems* a number of poems I had relied on for my West Indian Walcott were not there; instead there was a poet whose imagination strode across continents, and there were many later poems. I felt a bit like Auden's British readers who one day woke up to see that there was an American Auden, and that this made the early British Auden read differently. Walcott's selection seemed to be aimed more for a global, or at least a North American, readership.

My West Indian poet had become, like Brodsky, Auden, Eliot, Yeats, Pasternak, someone addressing his time. *Another Life* looked back on his youth in St Lucia, *The Star-Apple Kingdom* seemed to end decades of trying to take West Indian culture in a direction different from its politics. The *Collected Poems* stand in triumph, superior, an exile's reflections on a troubled but creative life; they are at once a proclamation of now being able to say here is a career, I have made it as a poet, here is my world in the many dedications to other poets, writers, and editors, and yet they also speak of nostalgia, of tension, of the longing for a West Indies which has remained home, the place where those 'natives' speak his language, where he can relax and paint a familiar landscape.

Seamus Heaney's review commented upon Walcott's nineteenth-century fondness for dramatic monologue, for being in touch with nature, for subject-matter and narrative. *Collected Poems* show Walcott developing his own poetic world separate yet not orphaned from the British tradition. His titles, such as *In a Green Night*, go back to the seventeenth century; the title could be read as both an act of gratitude and ironic as could *The Castaway*, with its echo of William Cowper's poem and Defoe. Walcott, like Joyce, has an instinct for correspondence and analogy, for playing between languages and cultures, histories, mythologies, and finding parallels between himself and the time. While his autobiography becomes typical and representative, to have avoided casting himself as a victim, a voice of the people, was both a moral and artistic victory. This allowed him access to all the categories that might otherwise have stifled him, whether intelligence, sympathy, imperial, colonial, white, black, oral, written. Just as Europe provided Joyce with a further dimension than Irish/British, so North America allowed Walcott to trust his own voice, 'it is only the successful achievement of artistic form that can satisfactorily appease the contradictions which he embodies'. Walcott is intelligent and self-aware, but has a 'desire to be turned into opaque and sensual word-stuff'.[27]

Heaney's review should have been read by others. As multiculturalism and post-colonialism became the fashion and those on the Left looked for minority writers with whom to belabour the West, they had a problem with Walcott. Here was one of the best poets of the time, 'black', from a 'colony', but not the stereotype they wanted. During 1990 the British critic John Lucas reviewed the Faber edition of *Collected Poems* in *New Statesman & Society* with an erratic sense of Walcott's life and development. Lucas knows the richness of Walcott's language and how much superior his poetry is to that of a dialect poet writing West Indian poetry, but there is in the review a feeling that Walcott in the United States is becoming an unrooted international, a 'world-besotted traveller'.[28]

Collected Poems sold 2,500 copies in hardcover within a year. It was widely reviewed, and provided an opportunity to take a more serious look at Walcott's development. Rita Dove wrote a twenty-seven-page review. James Dickey seemed envious: 'he was quite literally born into a major theme—which . . . most poets of our time do not have available with such dramatic urgency as he.' Peter Balakian's eight-page review in *Poetry* concluded: 'By his fifty-fifth year Derek Walcott has made his culture, history, and sociology into a myth for our age and into an epic song that has already taken its place in the history of Western literature.' Peter

Forbes sensitively observed that 'Like Baudelaire, Walcott has a vast system of correspondences, touchstones, talismans, archetypes, and recurrent images: the surf breaking on islands, stunned stasis of midsummer, the dazzle on the sea compare to beaten metal . . . in these tortuous convolutions Walcott is searching for something that goes beyond language.' 'Walcott has become a one-man melting-pot of the great world cultures.' Many critics now realized that Walcott had developed a sacramental view of life, what McClatchy called 'a vision beyond the image'. Reed Way Dasenbrock rather contortedly said 'no contemporary English-language poet seems unquestionably greater than Walcott'. George Szirtes urged: 'If you read no other poetry this year you should read him.'[29]

There was one disappointment. Pat Strachan, his editor from *Another Life* to *Collected Poems*, left Farrar, Straus and Giroux for the *New Yorker*.

Part VII

Boston North American?, Sigrid

25

1986–1987 *The Arkansas Testament*

LIFE was falling into a pattern, taking a shape. Once teaching ended in Boston Walcott would usually go to Trinidad to see his children at Christmas, then go on to St Lucia for the New Year. He was at the Villa Beach Cottages when Coffey arrived on 10 January 1986 to discuss the steel band film. Walcott visited Robert Bensen's four-week winter term class on Caribbean Literature, which he held for Hartwick College in St Lucia, Trinidad, and sometimes Venezuela.

In 1986 Walcott was hired as a full Professor rather than Assistant Professor at Boston University. He decided to remain a Visiting Professor as tenure would have required administrative duties, committee work, and other commitments on his time which he needed for writing, readings, theatre, and travel; and he was unwilling to stay the necessary eighteen months without leaving the United States to obtain a green card, so his appointment could not be tenured. There was a tenure review, however, and the Department recommended tenure if Walcott should ever want it. He now had a regular income and a condominium. His plays had not made Broadway or repeated the success of *Dream on Monkey Mountain*, but the recent ones were often performed and earned royalties. The *New Yorker* paid well for his poems and there was a waiting list of journals that wanted more, most of which also paid. He was writing reviews and articles for the *New York Review of Books*, the *New York Times*, even *House & Garden*. Some of his expenses for visits to the West Indies were being covered by writing travel pieces. He could count on paid poetry readings most weeks, and was in demand for conferences. He was earning as much from his writings and readings as from his professorship. While living in Boston he remained part of the New York literary scene; his friends were influential in PEN, the New York Institute for the Humanities. He was accepted among the later members of 'The Family', the Jewish intellectuals who had dominated New York literary culture for decades. Early in the year Walcott was part of a panel discussing 'Alienation and the State' at the International PEN Conference in New York. Walcott said that having come from a place with no history he had created one from himself and his circumstances. An outsider, he understood American culture and ways—a 'black', he seemed white, a West Indian who could be Third World, British, St Lucian, himself.

Returning to Boston each year in mid-January for classes, Walcott would teach the first two days of the week, and use the rest of the week for work and reading elsewhere. He taught a graduate poetry seminar and a graduate practical class in drama. Both were small and advanced. He had also started to turn his graduate drama class into the Playwrights Theatre.

He was no longer someone who stayed at the Chelsea and took Trailways buses to upstate New York. He was paid more, he avoided public transport, relied on taxis, and always flew first class. He now used the Gramercy Park Hotel, a favourite of publishers looking for a place to put up writers, and therefore of writers. On 6 March 1986 he was at the Gramercy Park Hotel from which he was picked up and taken to New Jersey Institute of Technology in Newark and paid $1,000 after the reading. The next Thursday, 13 March, he read at Hartwick College as part of a series of 'black' writers, which during the semester included Earl Lovelace (who was Hartwick College's NEH Visiting Professor during 1986). On Friday and Saturday (14–15) Walcott held a two-day workshop for student actors at the college. The next week Walcott was the recipient of the first honorary degree conferred at the campus during the Twenty-Fifth Anniversary of the University of the West Indies, St Augustine. Actors from the Trinidad Theatre Workshop and other Walcott productions performed (21–2 March) extracts from *Ti-Jean and his Brothers, Dream on Monkey Mountain, The Joker of Seville, Pantomime,* and *A Branch of the Blue Nile,* under the collective title 'Let Resurrection Come'. Although two actors were conspicuously not present, this was a regrouping of the larger Trinidad Theatre Workshop which was starting to feel nostalgia about what had been lost a decade ago.

On 25 April Walcott was at the Villa Beach Cottages for the first time for some years without Norline. It was probably then that he wrote 'To Norline'. The poem is another of Walcott's early morning scenes at a beach as he wakes up and has coffee and begins to work, but:

> 'This beach will remain empty
> .   .   .   .
> a coffee mug warming his palm
> as my body once cupped yours'[1]

Returning from St Lucia ('Here' in *The Arkansas Testament*) to 'Elsewhere', he once more became a prominent international poet who read (8 May 1986) at the

World Poetry Festival at Harbourfront, in Toronto. Others who read during the Festival included Amy Clampitt, Michael Ondaatje, John Ashbery, P. K. Page, Vasko Popa, Galway Kinnell, Stanley Kunitz, and Phillis Webb. He was one of the eight non-Americans asked by the *New York Times* to remember their first impressions of the Statue of Liberty. The others included Isaac Bashevis Singer, Czeslaw Milosz (both Nobel Prize in Literature laureates), Elie Wiesel, and Yoko Ono. Walcott said that because the Statue of Liberty was a female he knew the United States would be welcoming and caring.

The August *Esquire* included a photograph of Walcott 'Dressed to Quill', superimposed over an enlarged page of 'Love after Love' from *Collected Poems*. Walcott, who normally reveals little sense of fashion and dress, is shown wearing a thousand dollar llama wrap overcoat and reverse-pleated trousers, both by Salvatore Ferragamo, a shirt by Sero, and a $245 doubleknit pullover by Jeff Sayre. During the rough years of the mid-seventies, Walcott had briefly talked with Russ Meyers, the now cult soft-pornographer who was making a film in Barbados about a black Jesus. Nothing happened, but consider one of history's might-have-beens. Walcott in the centre of *Play-Girl* covering himself with *Dream on Monkey Mountain*?²

'Love after Love' may superficially appear a Robert Gravesian lyric about the coming and going of the Muse, but it is self-punishing, doubly so because of its echoes of Divine Love and election in George Herbert's great 'Love III'. Walcott alludes to the eucharistic imagery (Walcott's 'Eat . . . Give Wine. Give Bread.') and seems more directly to be echoing Herbert's concluding 'So I did sit and eat':

> Take down the love letters from the bookshelf,
>
> the photographs, the desperate notes,
> peel your own image from the mirror.
> Sit. Feast on your life.

In June he participated for *Arena* in a BBC2 programme on Caribbean poetry with Linton Kwesi Johnson and Fred D'Aguiar with Darcus Howe in the chair. It was broadcast a few months later on BBC as part of a Caribbean Nights Special. Johnson is a highly politicized dub poet who identifies with Brixton, D'Aguiar is a more serious writer who also identifies with the oppressed. The discussion contrasted two approaches to poetry. Johnson, who admitted to having no background in poetry and to not enjoying canonical poets, championed oral poetry in Jamaican 'nation' language. His poetry was public, ideological, anti-colonialist, influenced by the lyrics of reggae music, and in the language of the folk. Walcott objected that poets do not think in dialect when alone, and that it simplified and dumbed down their intelligence and that of the public to write in such a manner. To ignore the best poetry was to become semi-literate for political reasons. D'Aguiar agreed with Walcott that the best poetry was likely

to be that of the individual in contemplation, but he also wanted social responsibility. Walcott replied that the demand for social responsibility leads directly to
censorship, banning, and the murder of poets.

During the programme clips were shown of contrasting Caribbean poets
reading; Johnson, D'Aguiar, and Walcott were asked to comment. There was an
especially hammy Brathwaite doing a public reading from the 'Negus' passage
of 'Rebellion' from *Islands*, the final part of Brathwaite's *The Arrivants: A New
World Trilogy*. In his performance the famous repetitions

> It
> it
> it
> it is not
>
> it
> it
> it is not
>
> it is not
> it is not enough . . .

were extended on and on as Brathwaite rocked slowly, loudly, on his heels like a
clock ticking. Asked his opinion of the poem Walcott replied

> It is not
> it is not
> it is not a very good poem

and quoted some remarks of Auden about the dangers of 'effects' that 'bring
down a house'.[3]

This was D'Aguiar's first meeting with Walcott who, along with Wilson
Harris, has been the major influence on his writing.

Derek's language is perhaps his greatest influence on me: his rich use of metaphor (re-
miniscent of poets like Donne and George Herbert); his ornate diction (close to Hopkins);
and the pressure of a Caribbean syntax stretching English into new expressions; giving
the poetry a verb-driven quality that is simply thrilling in terms of its narrative propulsion yet rich and allusive and meditative because he applied to those racy verbs the
brakes of metaphor. There is a tension between the two that adds to their excitement.
. . . His good ear for a voice and a tone comes I think from his playwright's side. This
tone is so assured that he can lead the reader through a thicket of the most ornate and
knotted syntax into the clearing of a precise emotion of idea. Again this gift is in part
due to the tension between his ear for creole rhythms and English diction. Sparks are
generated between the two in each Walcott line, never mind poem or book. I also think
he is a nature poet and firmly in the Romantic tradition which is edifying these days.[4]

Walcott in Boston (22 June) was quoted as saying he was devoting more time
to painting. His physical experience of the West Indies is the subject of his

paintings: 'I am talking about the physical tactile experience of the light and the weather'. . . . 'I have lived in that kind of fantastic physical environment.' Walcott felt he was limited as a painter and would be satisfied if he could paint cleanly. 'Everything you look at is framed for you. It exists in a frame.' Walcott agreed that the region was picturesque with 'beautiful poverty' and that painting it lacked political significance, but there was a deeper significance in 'spiritual gratitude'. Besides politics are not part of many lives. The elementary beauty of the Caribbean is what endures and gives people courage. He began painting again a few years earlier after he returned to St Lucia after being away for some years and was 'shocked' by the poverty of Castries, but also by its grace and endurance.[5]

In early September he was in Trinidad with his friend Lawrence Pitkethly of the Center for Visual History looking at possible locations for filming *To Die for Grenada*, a play which was opening at the Cleveland Playhouse in October. The main characters are a white American woman and a Trinidadian Indian who become lovers and the play explores how they view, and are affected by, the politics and invasion of Grenada. There was a screening of the Pitkethly *Hart Crane* film (in which Walcott appears) at the Art Creators Gallery along with his 'miniature water-colours' (story boards) for several film scripts including *To Die for Grenada*, *Pantomime*, and *Hart Crane*.

The scripting of *Hart Crane* for the *Voices and Visions* series went back to 1982. The two versions of which I have photocopies are illustrated on each page by Walcott's drawings; each script has completely different drawings. During 1985, while it was being shot in St Lucia with Nigel Scott of the Trinidad Theatre Workshop portraying Crane, Bunyan interviewed Walcott, and excerpts of the interview appeared in the *Center for Visual History Newsletter*. Walcott's attraction to Crane was partly to his energy, to the way he had modernized the pentameter. Crane proved 'that everything could be accommodated within that rhythm, including the language of bums, the language of two sailors on a boat, descriptions of Times Square . . .'. *The Waste Land* was elegiac, whereas Crane had energy. He took on the new age, machines, whereas Eliot was concerned about the death of civilization. Walcott, however, must already have been thinking of the New World epic and the difference between *The Waste Land* and *The Bridge* as possible models for *Omeros*.[6]

Walcott was in London in September as part of the promotion of his *Collected Poems*. He was interviewed by the *Voice*, then the major weekly newspaper for Black Britain. Walcott said art outlasted politics. Some younger Black British 'dialect' poets had accused him of selling out. Walcott replied, 'they have to learn to write better than they sound, if they did write better than they sounded then they would feel no urge to throw coconuts'. They do not understand that there is no natural voice in poetry, that dialect poetry is as elevated as ordinary English.

They should learn that they are English and not cut themselves off from their inheritance of the English language, a 'psychic mutilation'. The interviewer seemed stunned, and said Walcott might be right, anger was self-destructive, 'but to find the vision and courage to go beyond the castle of our skins may have to be left for [the] next generation'.[7]

There was a Caribbean Theatre Season during October at the Commonwealth Institute at which the 'St Lucian National Theatre' presented Roderick Walcott's *Banjo Man* and Derek's *Ti-Jean and His Brothers*, the latter directed by George 'Fish' Alphonse, one of the better young actors and directors. Walcott tried to attend rehearsals or at least to see productions of his plays, but now that he was so busy it was becoming uncertain whether he would appear for engagements. He was expected at a Caribbean Writers conference at the Commonwealth Institute but did not show. Besides teaching in Boston he was in Cleveland during October for *To Die for Grenada*, which opened on 24 October at the Cleveland Playhouse. It was not a success. Walcott tried it in other places, but decided that the play really should be a film. There was also a production in October of *Beef, No Chicken* by CART, the Caribbean American Repertory Theatre, at the New Theatre, on the lower East side in Manhattan. The cast was mostly West Indian. *Three Plays*, published in 1986, contains versions of *The Last Carnival*, *Beef, No Chicken*, and *A Branch of the Blue Nile*, all revised during 1985.

It was announced in late October that *Collected Poems* had won the *Los Angeles Times* $1,000 prize for poetry. There were six candidates for poetry, including John Ashbery's *Selected Poems* and Stephen Spender's *Collected Poems*. The books were nominated by more than ninety reviewers, and the prize-winners were selected by one judge in each of the categories, Fiction, Poetry, Biography, History, and Current Interest. Vikram Seth's verse novel *The Golden Gate* was included in the category Fiction along with Carlos Fuentes's *The Old Gringo* (Farrar, Straus and Giroux). Molyda Szymusiak's biography, *The Stones Cry Out* (Farrar, Straus and Giroux), was also nominated. The winners were flown to Los Angeles for the awards ceremonies on 7 November.

Although the MacArthur Fellowship was coming to an end, it was a time of many other awards, and Walcott was busy. The Institute of Jamaica awarded him the Musgrave Medal in recognition of his contribution to literature, but he was not in Jamaica to pick it up until May 1988. Something similar would happen years later with the University of Toronto, which, when I last enquired, was still waiting for Walcott to pick up his Honorary Doctorate.

By 19 November the film project for *Steel* was far beyond Coffey's original notion of a fictionalized documentary. There was a cast list of potential actors including such well-known stars as Lou Gossett, Roscoe Lee Browne, Denzel Washington, Jo-Beth Williams, and Susan Sarandon, actors from the Trinidad Theatre Workshop and St Lucia, and well-known calypsonians such as The

Mighty Sparrow and Lord Kitchener. Sets and costumes were to be done by the Montgomerys, music by André Tanker and Galt MacDermot, and there were various names listed for director, from Michael Schultz to Derek Walcott. Some actors, such as Stanley Marshall, had agreed to perform. The minimum payment for any role would be according to the Screen Actors Guild scale. Walcott was still trying to make his Trinidadian actors and musicians part of his American career and make them into American stars, but in the process of trying to combine Trinidad with Hollywood and the serious side of the musical theatre he had once more launched for the moon with a row boat and one oar.

Moreover Coffey had been having some emotional problems to which the letter of 19 November alludes. MacDermot had taped some music, Coffey wanted to hear it, but Walcott was angry that Coffey wanted examples of MacDermot's music when Coffey could not pay for it and when the question of how to treat the music for the script was still unsettled. Coffey wanted Tanker or some Trinidadian, Walcott wanted MacDermot. It is probable that Walcott had already given up on Coffey, had moved on to thinking of *Steel* as a play or a film done by others, and was telling Coffey to forget it unless he could come up with big money. By 20 April 1987, Coffey was writing formally to say that he could not pay for a second draft, would go to Trinidad looking for investors, but as this was a commissioned work for which he had paid out money he wanted the ownership of the screenplay clarified. He understood that Walcott had other investors in mind and he wanted to make clear that while he would sell his interest he had already invested nearly $50,000 in the project. Could they be co-producers?[8]

During 1986 Christopher Lydon interviewed Walcott and Seamus Heaney for the *Ten O'Clock News*, WGBH-Television, Boston. The interview was printed in *Partisan Review* the same year. The occasion was the appointment of Robert Penn Warren as the first Poet Laureate of the United States. Walcott and Heaney have a sense of tradition and of the poet as a voice of the community. Walcott spoke of the laureateship as a crowning achievement. Heaney mentioned that American poetry since Whitman had been historical and communal and that Warren had kept to this tradition in writing of history and being part of it. History is part of his subject and he has the large voice proper for it. He keeps the republic in mind in his work. Heaney several times mentioned 'Chief Joseph of the Nez Perce' for such characteristics as narrative, use of American Indian history, the roughage of prose, and the conscience and complexity of experience.

Walcott described Warren as an old hawk circling over the landscape, getting a whole image of America. Yet he had done this by keeping within his own circle. Walcott means that Warren's strength is that he is rooted in the South and sees as a southerner even when he travels. He keeps within his experience: 'it isn't that you have a huge vision, a beginning epic vision. Instead your vision is out of what you know, out of knowing where you are, where you *come* from. And that has been the strongest thing in Warren. I am from the South, I am part of the conscience of the South . . . I am part of the guilt of the South.' Walcott remarks that not being a Black American he does not feel hostile, Warren is honestly considering the situation in the South. One of the terms Walcott uses in discussing Warren is 'distance': Warren's vision of the Caribou is from a very 'high distance'. Awareness of 'distance' is characteristic of Walcott's poetry, whether in the sense of not being part of ordinary St Lucian lives or the greater distance between himself and those he observes in North America.

Walcott mentioned that he was friendly with Rosanna, Warren's daughter (who reviewed *Collected Poems* in *Partisan Review*), herself a poet, and that he had met Warren and his wife, Eleanor Clark, through Rosanna. Walcott thought Warren kind, noble, risky, amusing. Walcott had just written 'On the Indian Trail' which was 'for Eleanor Clark': 'I didn't know it was going to be a poem about Warren, all I had in mind was an old man in the middle of a stream, and there was somebody watching him, and when I began to write I realized, hey, wait a minute, these two figures are the old poet, Warren, and his daughter on the bank.'

> this young squaw and old settler by some new pines.
> I have changed this into a mottled pioneer and his daughter,
> so let Red and Rosanna Penn Warren have these lines.

The poem became a tribute to both.

> He came, carrying his things, and again, in the eyes:
> a wisdom beyond that of any parent,
> and what is the true beginning of beauty: age.

'On the Indian Trail', which Walcott said was in 'draft' appears not to have been republished since the interview was printed in *Partisan Review*.[9]

On 24 November 1986 Walcott recorded an hour of his poetry along with music for the Archive of Recorded Poetry and Literature in the Coolidge Auditorium at the Library of Congress in Washington. Robert Penn Warren introduced him as one of the best English-language poets who adds life to the tradition through his self which includes the unrestful seas, his intense, vivid imagery, and a person seeking to define himself from unsettled experience. Where was home? In 'The Schooner *Flight*' he feels rejection by both white and black worlds, and sees no hope in historical processes. When even human love fails, there is just the restless sea mirroring his own unrest and the recognition that poetry is the weapon of poets. The imagination heals and gives birth to values. Warren remarks that 'The Schooner Flight' can stand alongside Wordsworth's *Prelude* as the story of the birth of poetry for a poet. It is in style and theme the starting place for Walcott's later poetry. Walcott has rediscovered what makes dramatic poetry, the voice; he knows the interplay of vowels and their pitch, the weight of consonants, and how they can be worked against metre. He is often a poet of great eloquence.[10]

The New York revival of *Pantomime* was favourably reviewed in the *New Yorker*. 'The Hudson Guild has redeemed at one stroke all those duds of the past few years with its production of Derek Walcott's beautiful, ironic two-character comedy. . . . Mr. Walcott never loses his lightness of touch or his wit. There are flights of marvellous poetry and spurts of marvellous humour.'[11]

When Walcott left St Lucia for Jamaica he felt he was betraying those he loved, but he was bored and wanted to move on. His closest friends have suggested that he picked a quarrel with the Trinidad Theatre Workshop as he wanted to leave for North America. I have the impression something similar occurred with his marriages. Walcott the artist wanted the pain, the experience, something to write about, a chance to be by himself, move on, and start over. While reading in Pittsburgh during 1986 he met Sigrid Nama, a divorced German-Flemish-American art dealer. He invited her to a concert. She became his girl friend and after some years of a commuting relationship she moved to Boston and became his companion.

Walcott was at Hartwick College for nearly a month early in 1987. Between 13–18 January he was at Hartwick for a reading and a theatre workshop for Duncan Smith's 'reader's theatre' class as part of which there was an improvised scene about the death of Sitting Bull. As a result of the workshop Walcott was commissioned to write a play, *The Ghost Dance*, which was produced at Hartwick 9–11 November 1989. During the thirty-some months gestation of the play Walcott visited Hartwick at least twice again to work on it. Some of the material in it formed the basis of the Ghost Dance sections of *Omeros*.

Smith planned to have his students read accounts of the death of Sitting Bull and stage a confrontation between some young Sioux and farmers as a way of understanding what had become a myth of American history. He had sent Walcott copies of original documents, such as are found in Stanley Vestal's *New Sources of Indian History, 1850–1891*. Walcott watched the students without comment, then the next day himself brought in the Catherine Weldon scene and began working with the class. He worked slowly, trying to get mood and timing right, stopping to get props, and approximate lighting. He was on to something, but what was not clear and would only become clear from getting the stage details right. They did another scene and Walcott said he wanted to write a play on the topic. Smith feels Walcott had already been thinking about this before coming to Hartwick. They then took the scenes to Ithaca College for a workshop at the American College Theatre Festival Regional. The various events lasted a few weeks and Smith added some bits to the story in the theatre labs. Smith was excited by what was happening, but some of the students were not, as

Walcott seemed more involved in building up the evocative power of things and creating patterns—snow, flower, wagon wheel, lantern flame—than finding things for the students to do. Smith could see the direct connection between theatre and poetry in a way he had never experienced it before, but he also felt that Walcott was losing some of the clarity of focus on Catherine Weldon. When Smith later saw Walcott they were more concerned with practical matters like deadlines and Walcott had his own ideas about the play, based on his surprisingly wide and varied readings of Indian history. He was combining and inventing details, turning Weldon into some archetype rather than a historical person. Richard and Sally Montgomery were eventually brought in for the physical possibilities of the production.

Two undated letters from Smith to Walcott show how the project evolved. In the first, probably written December 1986, Smith was thinking of the play as a Greek tragedy in which the European expansion across the West was not evil in itself and might be seen as a sign of healthy democratic vigour, but the Indians happened to be in the way. Smith saw a parallel to the present in which continuing American power often produced tragic results and the play was a way to think about how to avoid such tragedies. This was not to be a play about victimization and white guilt, but why Western power was destructive to other people. Smith thought Walcott could work with some of the more advanced students at the Ithaca workshop.

By the time of the second letter, apparently written during the summer of 1988, the play was taking shape and Smith confessed that he was glad the main characters were white settlers, as it would be awkward to put his students into red face. Distance would also avoid sentimentalizing the Indians and retain their dignity and mystery. Walcott was finding ways to make the issues of present-day significance, and keeping to his own voice rather than historical accuracy. Classes would begin on 5 September and if the play was to be performed 17–19 November they would have about ten working weeks. Try-outs would take place the second week, and rehearsals would begin during the third, allowing only about seven weeks of rehearsals. For this they would need a full draft before the end of August and a full script by 12 September. Walcott was willing to cast the play from the students, but Smith said that if needed they could find further actors among the faculty and community.[12]

During January 1987 Walcott read and spoke at the University of Tampa and University of South Florida, St Petersburg. Steve Breslow, who then taught at the University of Tampa and was interested in Caribbean literature, contacted Walcott through Farrar, Straus and Giroux and arranged a joint programme with the University of South Florida Drama Department. Walcott gave a lecture to the honours students, a public reading from his works (mostly from *Sea Grapes*), and was part of a panel arranged with black community leaders by a local cable television station. Walcott was tired of the cold in Boston, happy to have some warm weather, and nostalgic for the Caribbean. This was early in his relationship with Sigrid, who joined him from Pittsburgh. They stayed for two nights with Breslow and his wife Kathryn Van Spanckeren and were sociable, Walcott and Breslow getting along well. Breslow had worried about whether Walcott would turn up, as a friend the previous year had some story about a missed connection. A transcript of Walcott's meeting with students was published in the first issue of the *Tampa Review*.[13]

Walcott moved from the Breslow house to a beach hotel at St Petersburg where he spent time in his room working on *Omeros*; it was new in his head and he was afraid of losing the idea. Walcott has at various times explained the genesis of the poem as watching some people on a St Lucian beach or thinking during a rainy period in St Lucia about the recent death of a friend who was an actor. The latter was associated in his mind with the Philoctetes myth, about the hero abandoned with an unhealable wound who was needed by the Greeks to conquer Troy. Although Walcott had used the myth in 'The Isle is Full of Noises', the way it is developed in *Omeros* is suggestive of the mood he was in over Norline leaving.

At the University of South Florida Walcott gave a talk and did a theatre workshop for the Drama Department in which he explained how he as director would look at the students' scripts; this was followed by stage readings of excerpts. There was great satisfaction with Walcott's readings and talks. He received little payment, perhaps not more than $500 plus his expenses for the trip to the two universities. Commonwealth and post-colonial studies were still not much appreciated at American universities and, while Walcott was highly regarded by many writers and a few critics, he was still unnoticed by most American professors of English literature.

The published Tampa conversation is a bit chaotic as students and professors interrupt Walcott with questions, and, as he often is on such occasions, he tends to be in a contradictory mood and jumps between ideas and stories without the connection being obvious. It is at such moments that he is often most revealing. At times he appears to be trying out the possibilities of opinions. In the Tampa interview Walcott tries to move on from themes of exile, bi-culturalism, an English heritage, and poets as moralists, to a further position in which he claims to have always been securely rooted in St Lucia, that the Caribbean partakes of the world's culture, that West Indians of his generation were given an especially favourable climate in which to develop as artists, and that small communities may be a better place to produce artists than the grand centres of power. Implicit is the claim that the West Indies are more like Shakespeare's London than is present-day London or New York. This is a complete inversion of Naipaul's position. It is perhaps not surprising that in April Walcott strongly criticized

Naipaul. The interview might be seen as a manifesto for the kind of poetry Walcott writes—public yet about the egotistical I. The artist is seen as a haughty rebel, isolated, alienated, a critic of those who conform whether to tyrants or democracy.

The conversation starts with Walcott denying remarks made by the introductory speaker that he is from two worlds. Walcott says he played with that view in his poetry from the age of about 18, but he did not feel it when he was younger and no longer thinks it. He always felt he was part of St Lucia, but as he explored in his writings the ambiguities of his position—such as being a lighter-skinned English speaker in St Lucia—his imagination multiplied the ambiguities while trying to resolve them. When he returns to St Lucia he is in a privileged position. He really cannot speak of being an exile the way Brodsky must, who cannot go home to Russia and see his parents. Rather Walcott is aware of an 'alienation' between himself and the impoverished St Lucian peasants and their jobs.

Walcott and Naipaul and other West Indian writers are not freaks; they were not isolated. They went to good schools with intelligent people who were being educated to be professional and who became doctors, lawyers, and journalists. Writers were also encouraged. Flowers have roots. Studying Latin in the tropics is absurd, but it fertilizes. All of the Caribbean from Florida to parts of Latin America were nourished by many cultures and the mixture was bound to produce different products. You cannot say that only one kind of cultural product is authentic. That is the New World. Once the native Indians were wiped out, it became a new start. Neruda and Whitman celebrate this cultural amnesia, this new history that is not surrounded by ruins and memories.

History is a fiction, its only value is 'plot'. The New World writer is lyrical, imaginative, in the present tense. History changes according to those in power and its use. Art is immortal, it survives. England is now of little importance, tourists visit England because of its cultural past, its Shakespeare, and Holland because of Rembrandt. Those from the New World feel that they are from an undernourished place, until they realize that any mountain is as beautiful as the Parthenon and that in their culturally great days London and Athens were smaller in size and population than Kingston, Jamaica. People romanticize being jailed, being oppressed, and such concepts are encouraged by both the oppressor and the victim who becomes dependent on them for status. The black American is treated as automatically inferior, and now receives conspicuous generosity with the result that there is either conspicuous gratitude or conspicuous ingratitude. It perpetuates a system.

It is absurd to think that power only comes from large places—England is a small island compared to what it ruled—or that genius only comes from the centre of power. Democracy is the best system, but there can be no democracy in art. There is an absolute hierarchy of imagination and achievements. An artist does not conform, but has an isolated eye, disobeys, excels, has an urge. Poetry comes to him in small blocks, maybe a line and a half. It does not start on the left of the page, it starts on the right, and he tries to fit it up somehow. He does not know where that phrase is going to be used, but works towards its incorporation. It may take a day's hard work for half a line, or it may be given by some eternal accident, but the poem heads for the phrase. In some poems the rhymes and form just happen. In others you think this looks like it is going to be a sonnet, and yes it is another sonnet.

Walcott followed Naipaul's writing with care. Naipaul would mention how he put aside a manuscript for a long time and would return to it looking for the place where the prose came alive. Walcott alludes to such an insight on one of his manuscripts and asks whether poetry came alive in the same way. He shared many of Naipaul's criticisms of the West Indies. In recent years, however, Walcott's writings were more concerned with social conditions in the region and with notions of dignity. Walcott inside the West Indies was threatened by black power, outside the West Indies he was bothered by white prejudice. His own myths of a useful colonial upbringing were damaged by the Brixton riots and changes in British immigration laws designed to keep out those with darker skins. Yes Trinidad had hurt Naipaul, but how could Naipaul complain about black prejudice in Trinidad towards Indians when there was Paki-bashing in England? 'Naipaul's repulsion towards Negroes' was becoming obscene.

Naipaul was constructing his own autobiography and history of the Caribbean through his books and it conflicted with the story Walcott was telling in interviews and poems. Naipaul's comments suggested that he was isolated, alone, that it was a miracle for him to have become a writer. This was the exact opposite of Walcott's own celebration of community, of himself as the poet of the islands, of his telling of his background as the product of a small cultured élite, of his élite public school background, and of the existing literary world into which he had moved, of Mittelholzer, Collymore, Hearne, and C. L. R. James. Naipaul and Walcott were no longer on the same side, ironizing rebels against a provincial society that did not support writers and was obsessed with past injustices. Naipaul had settled in England, praising life in the English countryside, and had become all that Walcott did not want to be. A decade earlier Walcott had been starting to be an American; now he had made it in the United States, did he really in his late fifties want to be an American, a black American with all the contradictions involved?

Naipaul was the rival writer whom Walcott admired, but Walcott felt he himself had chosen the better way. Whereas in *The Enigma of Arrival* Naipaul was celebrating his new home and taking root in England, Walcott had bought a plot of ground in St Lucia on which he planned to build a home. Naipaul claimed to be part of a diaspora from India that had left his family scattered around the world, Walcott said forget the African diaspora and make yourself at home in the New World. Naipaul wrote some of the purest prose of our age, creating a model for clarity, transparency, rationality. Walcott avoided linearity and created a world of metaphors, sounds, correspondences, allusions, a poetry often about poetry. Naipaul talked of social investigation, Walcott of art. Both were obsessed with death, both could be elegiac, but Walcott celebrated energy, vitality, the present and the future. They were two of the best living writers, both were thought to be candidates for the Nobel Prize, although Naipaul was unlikely to have enough votes as there were those who objected to his views. In *The Enigma of Arrival* Naipaul was effectively telling the history of the British Empire as a tragedy in which at the end he emerges as the heir of British literature. Walcott saw himself as part of Caribbean literature and the literature of the Americas. The two writers had a different vision and story to tell about the former colonies and Walcott was annoyed that among New York intellectuals and the *New York Review of Books* crowd Naipaul's version was being praised as honest, the real truth about the decolonized. Where did that leave him?[14]

From early March until early June 1988 Walcott was working on the play *To Die for Grenada*. He had argued earlier that the American invasion of Grenada was an act of liberation from political madness and killers, but now he was saying it was 'imperialism at its worst'. His views were changing. Not long ago he had been praising America as an imperial power that allowed freedom of speech and that the people were good hearted. America was now the new Roman Empire.[15]

He was a regular feature on the literary landscape of this new Rome. He read at a Book Fair in Miami; 2–4 April he was the keynote speaker at the Claremont College Black Studies Cross Examinations conference. He read from an advance copy of *The Arkansas Testament*. Other Caribbean writers reading were Michelle Cliffe, Maryse Condé, and Lorna Goodison; in April also he and Brodsky were at the Wheatland Conference on Literature, at the Library of Congress; he 'performed' in Seattle for what John Figueroa, writing to Alan Ross (2 May), described as an immense fee. Earlier in the year Walcott edited a special issue of *Ploughshares* (13 January 1987), a well-known 'little magazine' published by Emerson College, Boston. The idea was to have an issue consisting of verse plays or verse that could be adapted for the stage, but little was submitted and the issue mostly consisted of lyrics by Robert Bensen, Joseph Brodsky, Rita Dove, Michael S. Harper, Seamus Heaney, Dan Masterson, Lawrence Pitkethly, James Tate, Rosanna Warren, and other friends.

In May the publicity department of Farrar, Straus and Giroux submitted three books for consideration for the Leonore Marshall / *Nation* Magazine Poetry Award: Walcott's *The Arkansas Testament*, Seamus Heaney's *The Haw Lantern*, and C. K. Williams's *Flesh and Blood*. Walcott's print runs kept going up. *The Arkansas*

Testament was published on 31 August in 4,000 copies. It consisted of two parts, 'Here', seventeen poems mostly about St Lucia, and 'Elsewhere', twenty-two poems about European culture set in New York, Martinique, Central and South America, concluding with the title poem. He really does arc and soar/saw like a bird taking flight and viewing the world. 'Salsa' is about Cartagena, Colombia.

'Here' was the first large body of poetry about St Lucia that Walcott had published in a decade and a half, since *Another Life*, in fact, and that was mostly about his life twenty-five years earlier. This is Walcott's return to St Lucia, a return noticeable in the dedications—'Roseau Valley' (for George Odlum), 'A Latin Primer' (*In Memoriam*: H. D. Boxill), 'White Magic' (for Leo St Helene), 'Oceano Nox' (for the St Lucian poet Robert Lee), 'The Three Musicians' (for Hunter Francois). In 1989 Walcott would paint *The Three Musicians* (in the Alyce St Juste-Chen collection) which was later used by the Saint Lucia Cancer Society in 1993 on postcards as part of a fund-raising drive. It is a Walcott painting I especially like.

'A Letter from the Old Guard' for the actress Irene Worth is an unsent letter in verse written on Remembrance Day from a St Lucian, who served throughout the empire in the British army, to two widowed sisters who lived in St Lucia during the Second World War. The veteran who 'soldiered for my King' and 'served with Lord Alexander' in Sudan, is now a night watchman. The poem is a lovely cameo of an older social and imperial order, as nostalgic as ironic. Placed directly after the sardonic conclusion of 'White Magic' ('Our myths are ignorance, theirs are literature'), the title, 'A Letter from the Old Guard', and many of the ironies, such as the veteran's continuing respect, might seem malicious parody, but what comes through is the common humanity of people and that many people were in fact content under British imperialism. The supposed letter writer reminded me of the retired soldier who was night watchman at Villa Beach Cottages.

Many of the poems have St Lucian settings, such as Gros-Islet, or concern local social customs, such as a St Lucia First Communion. 'The Whelk Gathers' is Walcott's revisioning of Wordsworth's 'Leech Gatherers'. Both parts of the volume refer to Norline and Walcott's need for a woman to overcome his loneliness. Many poems in *The Arkansas Testament* are dedicated to poets and use quatrains. Some poems show his mastery of the hexameter, a rhythm in which he was still at times unsure in *Midsummer*. The book is dedicated to Heaney. Walcott, like Heaney, is concerned with the problem of using English without becoming English. In 'Cul-de-Sac Valley' it is Walcott as poet who writes about St Lucia and changes in the uses of English, who contributes to 'darkening English'. English darkens because the Empire is over and because it has become the inheritance of those with darker skins. It is also darkened with the oppression of the dark-skinned. His English words are seen as alien to the French and West

African 'native grain' and 'dialect' from which 'this settlement' is made. As the poem continues there is 'a mongrel | a black vowel barking'.

'The Arkansas Testament', the title poem, is set in the South; he is 'dark entering Arkansas'. He feels dark in this culture, 'a cafeteria | reminded me of my race. . . . I was still nothing'. Nothingness, what is he, what is the world, what is God, has always been a Walcott motif. What was he in the American South? In America? At the time he was faced by the problem of choosing his national passport now that St Lucia had become independent. Should it be St Lucian? That meant he could at any time be refused entry to the United States and lose the security he had in middle age worked so hard to earn. A tenured professor should be a citizen, citizenship would solve tax and other complications. Race and history in the United States suddenly seemed his problem. To become an American citizen, however, would mean accepting second-class status. Blacks in the United States are defined that way regardless of what they do. Also it would be a betrayal of St Lucia, it would mean saying he wrote about the people, but could escape to safety. He decided against it. His passport would still have two parrots.[16]

Walcott had made it but he was unhappy. His third wife had left him, Boston was not St Lucia, he was not part of a community as in Trinidad. He had a girl friend, but she lived in another city and he was lonely. *Omeros* (Chapter XXXIII) would describe this period:

> Back in a Brookline of brick and leaf-shaded lanes
> I lived like a Japanese soldier in World War
> II, on white rice and spare ribs, and just for a change,
>
> spare ribs and white rice
>
> .   .   .   .   .   .
>
> I knew they all knew
> about my abandonment in the war of love:
>
> .   .   .   .   .   .
>
> I had nowhere to go but home. Yet I was lost.
>
> Like them I could jiggle keys in purse or pocket.
> Like them I fiddled with the door, hoping a ghost
> would rise from her chair and help me to unlock it.
>
> .   .   .   .   .   .
>
> House of toothbrush, house of sin,
> of branches scratching, 'Let me in!'
>
> House where rooms echo with rain,
> Of wrinkled clouds with Onan's stain
>
> House that creaks, age fifty-seven[17]

Going to the United States had meant betrayal of the Trinidad Workshop, leaving his children, spending three-quarters of the year in a foreign land with grey skies and snow. *The Arkansas Testament* is filled with exile grumps. 'Fame' begins 'This is Fame: Sundays, | an emptiness', and concludes 'A crawling clock. | A craving for work.' The next poem, 'Tomorrow, Tomorrow', concludes:

> to stand by your bags on a cold step as dawn
> roses the brickwork and before you start regretting,
> your taxi's coming with one beep of its horn,
> sidling to the curb like a hearse—so you get in.

In 'Pentecost' he has physically and spiritually lost his way:

> Better a jungle in the head
> than rootless concrete . . .
>
> winter lamps do not show
> where the sidewalk is lost . . .

Walcott was once more feeling a castaway, he had written such poems in the tropics, but the tree had new rings. Did he really want to become part of an America that had exterminated the Indians with apparently no regret, and which in the South not long ago had laws discriminating against blacks, and which had invaded Grenada? He and Brodsky shared a vision of the United States as the new Roman Empire, it had become the imperial power. He saw the world as fallen; the German extermination of the Jews, the American extermination of Indians, the South African discrimination towards blacks, and the treatment of blacks in the American South were part of the human condition which resulted from a lack of love, a lack of charity, a lack of light. Were not his own broken marriages, relationships with women, bad temper, and vision of himself part of the fallen world, something he could not avoid whether or not in Reagan's America? If Walcott was starting to sound like an American post-colonialist looking for Western imperialism and guilt, underneath there was an older religious vision and his feelings of personal guilt. Making it was costly, he wanted to return home, the long poem he was writing was a celebration of St Lucia, but he knew that he would return changed.

His earliest poems expressed an anger at being born part-black and at white racism. This was followed by years of trying to keep a perspective in which his divided heritage was recognized, although often schizophrenically, for creative purposes. The Black Power movement of 1970, the increasing tyranny of Eric Williams's government, and his own situation made him again mulatto rather than black. Walcott was now arguing for the uniqueness of the Caribbean fusion of cultural elements in contrast to the racism of the North and Europe. He had also returned to making art of the beauty of black St Lucian women, as in 'The Light of the World':

I was deeply in love with the woman by the window.
I wanted to be going home with her this evening.
I wanted her to have the key to our small house
by the beach at Gros-Islet . . .

Not bad for hexameters, a line supposedly impossible to write naturally in English. The woman by the window is similar to the old woman earlier in the poem in being a metaphor for St Lucia.

One reviewer, while praising the volume, said it was the saddest book Walcott had published. There was something wrong. Walcott's politics were always sane, however, and he could still be sane when talking about the West Indies. During June he gave a long two-part interview to Rick Wayne for the St Lucian *Star* in which he mocked those who claimed politics were real, and poetry unreal. Walcott asked who would care in a few years about which politician crossed the aisle to join the other party, especially as there was little difference between the two major parties in St Lucia, and after twenty years they were still discussing whether to build an arts complex. Good poetry lasted, and would become how the world would see St Lucia. When talking about the United States, however, Walcott sounded hysterical. He defended his changed opinions about the invasion of Grenada by saying some Jewish intellectual (would he say black intellectual?) had claimed that the invasion of Grenada was the second worst thing to happen after the Holocaust. That sections of the American government were carrying on their own policies in Nicaragua he saw as evidence of a likely army takeover. The cynicism of the public could lead to fascism. The world might soon be governed by an unopposed American empire. Walcott had obviously been in the United States too long, especially around comfortable American intellectuals and professors who hated Reagan.

Rick Wayne said he could not recognize Walcott's St Lucia, it sounded like Fantasyland, and when he challenged Walcott's romanticization of poverty Walcott went off on an it-depends-what-you-mean-by-is reply. Poverty in St Lucia had dignity unlike in Chicago. Wayne said hunger was hunger, Walcott said that there was always fruit to eat, land to be planted. 'And anyway, if he's a drifter he should be in jail. There's no need to be hungry in the Caribbean and that's why there is so much laziness . . . Hey, I'm getting to be a real old fascist.'[18] Wayne commented on Walcott staying at a hotel with a swimming pool like a tourist.

In Boston (4 September) there was another interview, this time mostly about his painting, his return to it, and its techniques. Walcott said he had never really given up painting as he did story boards for film scripts and plays. He mostly painted watercolours, but not many oil paintings. Watercolour does not allow much abstraction, it is too fast and delicate for rhetoric, unlike oils. Walcott no longer felt he lacked the confidence and the wrists of a painter as there are other ways of painting, by layering and building. Watercolour is really for temperate climates, it is more difficult in the tropics. In the tropics the division between the horizon and the bottom of the horizon, sky and foreground, is dramatic. The incredible blue of the tropics is almost impossible, especially the 'heat' of that blue. In the tropics shadows are black, green black, colours not found in water-colours. The paints seem made for temperate climates.[19]

Two weeks later (19 September) there was a three-hour interview in Boston with Charles Rowell. Walcott had come back from St Lucia where he had seen the Governor-General, an old school friend, and Hunter Francois, then Ombudsman. Whether speaking in conversation or reciting Thomas Macaulay, Francois speaks the same, uses the same accent. One reason Walcott did not leave the Caribbean and needed to be physically there was that he thought painting and poetry were similar in not being products of memory. The real thing was for the writer to get his interior tone into the writing. From poem to poem he uses different masks and personae, but the inner voice is the same. He does not think in dialect; Shakespeare was not restricted to the provincial speech of Warwick-shire. Walcott objected to being compared to others in the kind of comparison that suggested you were meeting the standards of metropolitan writers. Colonial author, Commonwealth author, are half-way stages to a recognition of equality, that those outside can be of the same level as writers from England and the United States. It takes time to be willing to accept that former colonies are now independent and their people equal. This argument, of course, explains what is wrong with concepts like post-colonialism which are based on a sense of historical injustice.[20]

During November he was interviewed by the British poet Tony Harrison on Channel 4. While Walcott was in demand and interviews are a way to promote books and plays, the amount of Walcott interviews is staggering, especially for someone otherwise so busy. Often he contradicts himself from one interview to the next and appears to need to disagree with the interviewer. Here is a lonely man using the interviews as a way to make up for society and to express opin-ions, to shape the way he wants himself to be seen and read. It had become unwritten autobiography, and a substitute for the articles he had once written for *Public Opinion* and the *Guardian*, even for the Theatre Workshop. He was paid for most radio and television interviews, especially in England, and his fees, like those of his poetry readings, would grow along with his reputation.

Walcott began pulling together some of his published essays, to which he planned to add some new ones, for *Inside the Cathedral*, an intended book of essays. It was to include 'What the Twilight Says', 'The Muse of History', 'Robert Lowell', 'On Choosing Port-of-Spain', 'Café Martinique', and an essay on C. L. R. James. It took over a decade to evolve into *'What the Twilight Says': Essays* (1998). One would have thought that Walcott had written enough prose by now to fill several books with decent material, but his relationship to prose is often troubled as he is uncomfortable with its linearity, its reduction of significance to a narrative, to a simple argument, to history, to cause and effect. His best essays are unusually rich in style, in symbolism, in ellipses, epiphanies; they are, in fact, poetic, deep, rich. They are also unusually difficult to write well. As I look through fragments and drafts of Walcott's autobiographical pieces and essays, I am struck by the digressiveness, by the waffling about and lack of economy, as Walcott feels his way forward. The language is rich, allusive, witty, lovely, some of the best of our time, but as the structure is associational, there is hardly any forward movement or argument. It loses life. The amusing anecdotes (some of which I have borrowed) stand out. This is the opposite of Naipaul's short sentences, precision, story-telling, driving towards a conclusion. One wonders how it is possible that someone who worked as a journalist regularly filling columns with interesting reviews, news, and commentary could find it so difficult to fill a book with prose. But that is exactly why it is so hard. The poet Walcott who matches himself against the great poets also wants a prose superior to that of the journalist, he wants a prose equal to, say, Pasternak's.

'Inside the Cathedral', the essay, was apparently written during the summer of 1987 in St Lucia. Unpublished, it exists in a typescript of twenty-nine pages and concerns his childhood in St Lucia, a Protestant view of Catholics, and how he and his family felt persecuted by Catholics; it is also about painting and his friendship with Dunstan St Omer in their teens. Walcott weaves back and forth in time, bringing together various themes and symbols which are at one time in opposition and then reconciled at the end of the essay. It is instinctive to speak of 'Inside the Cathedral' as an essay, although it is autobiographical, poetic, and has a complicated structure designed on the opposite principles to the linearity and straightforwardness of modern prose. Walcott's model for autobiography at one time was *Safe Conduct*, but further back there was the wandering Jacobean prose of Sir Thomas Browne, Robert Burton, and John Donne. Some of the earlier 'American, without America' chapters are repetitive and fizzle out, but 'Inside the Cathedral' moves back and forth in time and themes with economy. The difference between the earlier essays and this one, beyond greater maturity and less self-conscious working up of the theme, is that it begins in the present and has an immediacy when speaking of the past whereas the 'American' essays feel as if Walcott was striving to recall and place half-remembered events within a sea of words he was churning up.

The essay surprises with the continuing ferocity of Walcott's anger at the Catholic Church of his youth. The troubles he and his family had with the Church remained in his mind. Walcott associates his youth with the discovery of the joys of painting, and the feeling that art, at least the art of the Old World, is Catholic, an art of abandonment whether to images or the body, whereas

Walcott is Protestant, a creature inhabiting the mind who can only look out on the world and carefully attempt to draw what he sees. Catholicism is the art of Giotto, Tiepolo, Fra Angelico. After being attacked by the Archbishop, Walcott had gone off Italian art as Catholic bigotry.

There were three important productions of Walcott's plays during 1987. Wilbert Holder died on 14 July while rehearsing *Beef, No Chicken* for a 31 July–8 August run he was to direct. Anthony Hall, one of the younger actor-directors who had been trained in Canada, and was close to Walcott, took over. This was a Trinidad Theatre Workshop co-production with the Theatre Company at the Little Carib Theatre and involved the core Trinidad Theatre Workshop members with whom Walcott had quarrelled, Errol Jones, Stanley Marshall, and Claude Reid. Lighting was by John Andrews who, angered at how Walcott had left in 1976, had taken their side. The flirtation between Walcott and the Workshop continued.

On 4–26 September, *Remembrance* was produced at the Arts Theatre, Covent Garden, to open its Black Theatre Season. Walcott went to London for the production which was widely and generally well reviewed. While in England he attended an evening of potential sponsors for a production of *O Babylon!* that Yvonne Brewster was planning. Probably because of the large West Indian community in England, Walcott was becoming a staple of Black Theatre there.

From 26 December 1987 until 9 January 1988 there was a revival of *The Joker of Seville* in Port of Spain, co-produced by Arbee Productions and the Trinidad Theatre Workshop, at the new Central Bank Auditorium. It brought together the core Trinidad Theatre Workshop members with those who had stuck by Derek since 1976.

In October Brodsky was awarded the Nobel Prize in Literature for 1987. A friend remembers Walcott around this time running to a public pay telephone, picking up the receiver, and pretending that the King of Sweden was calling— for Heaney. When Brodsky went to Stockholm in December he took many copies of books of Walcott's poems with him and showed them to publishers. Farrar, Straus and Giroux had a string of recent winners, Brodsky was widely respected, and publishers who had never heard of Walcott started to plan trans-lations on the assumption that he would be a laureate some future year.

Walcott, with Sigrid, returned to Villa Beach Cottages for the New Year.

26

~~~~~~

1988–1989 International Man of Letters

DURING January 1988 Walcott once more visited Robert Bensen's Hartwick College Caribbean Literature course in St Lucia and spoke with his students. Walcott was also in Trinidad that month where Bensen met him again. He seemed to be continually on the go moving from country to country.

He was in England in early February for rehearsals of the British première of *O Babylon!* (19 February–12 March), directed by Yvonne Brewster for the Talawa Theatre Company at Riverside Studios to mark the centenary of the birth of Marcus Garvey. *O Babylon!*, set in 1966 Jamaica during the excitement of the imminent visit of Haile Selassie, could be seen as telling of some later aspects of Garvey's back-to-Africa dream. It has a cast of twenty, thirty songs, and requires a wide stage, on a scale seldom seen for Black Theatre in England. The Talawa Theatre Company had worked hard for over a year raising funds from the Arts Council and others, including a guarantee against possible losses.

This was a different, shorter version than used in Jamaica during 1976. Walcott had considerably revised *O Babylon!* since publication; he made more revisions during the week he attended rehearsals, and Brewster made her own cuts. The new unpublished version is more a criticism of the effect of international capitalism, especially in the form of the tourist industry, on small nations and their people; an international corporation wants to take the land from the Rastas for a hotel. This is in keeping with the leftward shift in Walcott's political outlook corresponding to how the West Indies, especially St Lucia, was changing. The production was recorded for the BBC and National Sound Archive, 3 March.

world to the international traveller and friend of other famous poets, but as the home from which he was exiled and to which he hoped to return.

The Arkansas Testament was published on 7 March by Faber. A few days earlier Walcott was interviewed at a dreary London motel. He claimed that while poetry was a craft, you could only teach the craft, not the poetry. He described *Arkansas Testament* as a 'last will and testament' as there were several elegies. He talked about the crisis he felt when faced by the problem of citizenship and joked that the parrot, symbol of St Lucia, and the poet as parrot in his passport, were fading. Although he was concerned with place, here and elsewhere, poetry itself was the territory. The only valid breathing verse was the quatrain, the quatrain of his childhood, his church. People built their square houses on the hill, Walcott wanted his verse to stand like the houses.[4]

Brodsky and Walcott read again (15 April) from their poetry at Hartwick College before an audience of over 250. Among the sponsors was the New York Council for the Arts. Bensen later wrote about the evening in *The Wick*, the college magazine.[5] Whereas in 1980 Walcott and Brodsky had arrived together on a Trailways bus, now Brodsky came in his own old green, battered, diesel-fuelled Mercedes. According to Bensen what Walcott and Brodsky had in common was the rejuvenation of the language of a decaying empire through the use of metrical traditions and the redefining of its traditions.

Next came three major international conferences, in Lisbon, Jamaica, and Dublin, along with readings and conferences in the United States. In April Brodsky, Walcott, and many other Farrar, Straus and Giroux authors were at 'The Lisbon Conference on Literature: A Round Table of Central European and Russian Writers'. This was the Second Wheatland Conference on Literature sponsored by the Wheatland Foundation of New York, under the auspices of Mario Soares, the President of Portugal. The aim of the Wheatland Conferences is to bring together writers from different backgrounds and promote international cultural exchange, especially translations of literary works. Walcott and Halpern flew on a commercial airline rather than with Susan Sontag on Anne Getty's private airplane. On reaching Lisbon Walcott was given trouble about his lack of a visa. An American passport would have been better. The focus of this conference was Central Europe and among the participants were Czeslaw Milosz (Poland), Joseph Brodsky (USSR), Péter Esterházy (Hungary), Damilo Kiš (Yugoslavia), and Josef Škvorecký (Czechoslovakia). Other participants included Ian McEwan, Salman Rushdie, and Susan Sontag. Michael Scammell from England was moderator.

Besides the usual arguments about commitment, politics, and art, the discussion involved the concept of Central Europe which the Russian writers ignored and in which the Central European writers believed. Walcott objected that most of the writers assumed that civilization was European. The discussion of

European writing seemed to him provincial and lacking imagination and spirit, writers do not inherit history. Europe takes history and civilization for granted as it does a pattern of tragedy. Sontag built on Walcott's views saying that the Russians and Americans both had imperialistic visions in which the problems of other peoples were assumed to depend on their own. Brodsky, however, objected that it was myopic to disregard political and cultural realities. Writers are defined by the languages in which they write and sensibilities are affected by political systems. You cannot liberate others before you liberate yourself.[6]

Walcott was at Southern Illinois University, Carbondale, on 3 May, to read from his poetry as part of a student Honors Program series of lectures. There were over 200 in the audience. The reading started at 8 p.m.; afterwards Walcott signed books and attended a reception in his honour until 11 p.m. Walcott then spent the night talking with a small group of students until breakfast when he met with some twenty students who brought him their work for criticism. Some of the students remained in contact with him.[7]

Later in May he gave the keynote address on 'Biography/Autobiography in West Indian Literature' at a conference at the University of the West Indies, Mona, Jamaica, hosted by the English Department. Walcott attacked 'all forms of address', prose, linear thought, and especially the new theoretical criticism, as essentially political and tyrannical in contrast to 'the perpetual ignorance of poetry, the induced chaos from which a poem begins'. Walcott shocked many in the audience by praising how Auden had accepted a printer's error that resulted in an image far superior to the original. 'That is one part of the poetic process, accident as illumination, error as truth, typographical mistakes as revelation.' 'Because this is an injunction to critics; that their subject is not literature but God, or the gods, that poets should be judged by their approach towards this subject, and the source of that subject is chaos, ignorance, and its emblem is (how sweet Latin sounds in such contexts) Dominus illuminato mea, Lord, who art the light of my life.' 'I cannot think because I refuse to, unlike Descartes. I have always put Descartes behind the horse, and the horse is Pegasus.' Walcott compared recent theory to the smell of rotting fish, 'I have a horror not of that stink, but of the intellectual veneration of rot.' The lecture was published as 'Caligula's Horse'. I have heard intelligent people seriously insist that because Walcott accepts the role of chance in poetry he is a postmodernist! Like most artists Walcott has always used what came his way, just as Lowell would incorporate in his poems the odd songs and chants of his young daughter. Faye Walcott claims that if she mistyped Derek's poems he would leave some of the errors in as being more like natural speech than his own writing.[8]

Walcott was now officially given the 1986 Musgrave Medal for his contribution to West Indian literature. This was one of his few visits to Jamaica during the 1980s, his last until 1993. Walcott's world was shifting.

He was interviewed by Edward Baugh on 20 May. He told Baugh that he was glad to be at the conference as it enabled him to learn about the newer writers, such as Olive Senior. But it is significant that he mentioned that Jamaica Kincaid was at the conference. His world was increasingly that of American publishing. As much as Walcott tried to avoid sounding like the voice of a patriarch that was what he was, except in the area of theatre where he spoke favourably of the quality of Caribbean acting, and of such directors as Earl Warner who worked professionally on various islands. Easy inexpensive air travel had changed much, ending the recent nationalism in the arts. If there was no political federation there was an aesthetic federation, a federation of the artists. The older generation had to struggle to get West Indian English accepted as legitimate in literature, but now that there was a recognized West Indian literature it was too easy for a writer to do poor work and be praised. It was too easy to be melodramatic, a patriot, a blackman, a victim, and demand approval without having done the work necessary to be a poet. Instead of writing as black victims it would be more interesting to write from the perspective of the person inflicting the injury.

Walcott mentioned that he was involved in a long work which he did not want to discuss and that he had written or was working on three film scripts— *Steel*, *Pantomime*, and *To Die for Grenada*. The future for West Indian performance art was likely to be in video. It does not cost any more than to stage a production and you do not have such problems as renting a hall and touring with a set. Walcott remained furious with Trinidad, which had wasted billions of dollars during its oil boom and where there still was no building for a Little Theatre.[9]

Early in June there was the public announcement of the Queen's Gold Medal for Poetry by the Buckingham Palace Press Office and Walcott was the first Commonwealth citizen to receive the award. The poetry medal had begun in 1933 from a suggestion of John Masefield, then Poet Laureate, to King George V. The award is given for a book of verse, although exceptionally translations might be considered. Originally intended for British subjects it was decided in 1985 to extend the area to all the Queen's subjects, which included Walcott as a St Lucian. The medal itself has a crowned effigy of the Queen and a design on the reverse representing 'Truth emerging from her well and holding in her right hand the divine flame of inspiration—"Beauty is Truth and Truth Beauty"'. The medal is awarded by the Queen on the advice of a committee of eminent men and women of letters chaired by the Poet Laureate. Ted Hughes, then Poet Laureate, informed Walcott of the award. Hughes was a friend who admired Walcott's poetry, and the Earl of Gowrie had reviewed Walcott's poetry highly favourably in the newspapers; the Queen was concerned with the preservation of the Commonwealth, is thought to have disliked Margaret Thatcher's lack of interest in preserving former British connections, and made a point of reading Commonwealth authors before visiting countries abroad, a pleasure or duty that will surprise many.

In mid-June Walcott was at the First Dublin International Writers' Conference, funded by the Arts Council, at which he, Brodsky, and Les Murray enjoyed themselves with, they later bragged, 'schoolboy' jokes. Murray kindly sent me one of Walcott's jokes that he still remembered; it is, of course, unprintable. Walcott spoke on 'Literature as Celebration' the theme of the conference.

Returning to England Walcott read and participated in a poetry workshop at South Bank (18–19 June). Walcott asked Fred D'Aguiar what he was writing. D'Aguiar mentioned an idea about a long poem concerning Christopher Columbus, life in the Old World, the relevance of the classics in the New World, and the need to recast them in ways 'familiar to a sensibility made in the Caribbean'. Walcott laughed and said 'don't waste your time with that stupidness. Write what you know.' Walcott did not mention that his own *Omeros* was already in process.[10] Everyone has such a Walcott story, of Walcott writing a review saying that some theme or style was a dead end for Caribbean literature and then immediately turning to it himself, of Walcott laughing at some idea for a book that he himself was writing, of some version of leg-pulling, irony, or attempting what he claimed to be impossible.

Lisbon, Ireland, England, and now Holland. There was a production of *Pantomime* in Holland by De Nieuw Amsterdam Theatergroep, which would perform *Branch of the Blue Nile* in 1991 and *Viva Detroit* during the 1992–3 season. Except for a few anthologies of black literature Walcott had been ignored on the Continent. He was not a slogan maker, and his poetry was difficult to translate, the context unfamiliar. After 1988 interest would develop rapidly beyond the English-speaking world; a German translation by Klaus Martens of *The Star-Apple Kingdom* would be published in 1989.

Early July Walcott was again in London. He was interviewed by Waldemar Januszczak, who had last seen him at the Port of Spain Hilton being angrily heckled by those who objected that he was not black enough, nor strictly a dialect writer. Such people had contributed to Walcott's leaving Trinidad. He had now made it in the United States, and had gone through a crisis whether or not to become an American citizen, and what this might mean for him and his poetry. He had only recently decided that no matter how distant he was becoming to St Lucia that was home. Januszczak could not help comparing Walcott with D. J. Enright, the last poet to be awarded the Queen's Medal. Although Enright had widely travelled and taught abroad he has, like most British writers, 'an inviolable sense of place', which Walcott had to create. Walcott's recent poetry was filled with nights in hotels and foreign places.[11]

Walcott and Sigrid returned to St Lucia to the Villa Beach Cottages for six weeks until late August. Walcott was working on *Omeros*. He autographed copies of his books at the Sunshine Bookstore, owned by a member of the Pilgrim family—the West Indies can be like a small village. He attended a launching of

Confluences, an anthology of nine St Lucian poets, at the Central Library. As interest in West Indian literature had developed it had inevitably focused on writers in England, the United States, Jamaica, and perhaps Trinidad and Barbados. St Lucian poets were still unknown and unpublished, even in the West Indies. Conditions for a poet, or even a novelist, had not improved since 1948. If you wanted to be a poet in St Lucia, you still had to publish your own poems and try to sell them. A small amateur local theatre company, the Lighthouse Players, struggled to exist. Walcott had been right to leave. Before he left this time there was an exhibition of his new watercolours at the Artsibit Gallery in Castries.

In Washington, on 29 September, Walcott opened the Folger Library's International Voices Poetry Series as part of its twentieth anniversary season. A 4.30 p.m. seminar, 'conversation and dinner with the poet', was followed by a reading at Georgetown University. Others who read for the series included Octavio Paz, Les Murray, and Yehuda Amichai. Such readings, besides what they paid, were part of the continuing promotion of *The Arkansas Testament* and other Walcott volumes. Copies of his books would always be on sale and over a year such sales, along with reading fees, added up. He read along with poets from Iraq, Cuba, and Yugoslavia, on 21 October, as part of the International Festival of Authors at Harbourfront, Toronto. There were over forty-five authors, including Margaret Atwood, Neil Bissoondath, May Swenson, Saul Bellows, Alison Lurie, Wilson Harris, Salman Rushdie, Mordecai Richler, and A. S. Byatt.

He was interviewed for *Bill Moyers' World of Ideas*; the programme was televised on 1 November. Walcott claimed that when distinctions in language are lost a civilization withers: a culture collapses when words become interchangeable. Take-out food and taking-out (killing) are not the same and to start blurring the moral difference influences culture and ethics. Poetry is not sociology, its complaints are the 'discontent that lies at the heart of man—and how can that be redeemed?' Poets do not say there is perfection. That is why Plato banished poets. Poets are obsessed by the 'impossibility of utterly clear utterance'. 'It takes all your life to write the way you speak without faking it. It's very hard for a poet to hear his own voice without affection. I couldn't read my poetry with a British accent.'

Moyers tried to push Walcott towards the received American view that the British Empire was bad, racist, a white leprosy. Walcott once more mentioned that the empire in which he was raised seemed benign, the police were not armed, but as he has become older he has felt more 'historical responsibility' about the other results of the empire. Walcott does not mention race, but poverty. The kind of racism that produces a 'black problem' is not what he sees in the Caribbean, where there was rather a mixing and awareness of shades of skin colours than crude distinctions of black and white. Walcott praises the hybridization of Port of Spain with its many kinds of peoples and cultures. Over and over

Moyers tries to make Walcott speak for blacks. As with many who hope to do good, the potential for evil in Moyers's assumptions is frightening.[12]

During 1988 Walcott was programme consultant and an interviewer on *Joseph Brodsky—A Maddening Space*, a television film made by the New York Center for Visual History. Richard Montgomery was also involved. The programme, narrated by Jason Robards, traces Brodsky's life from his birth in 1940 Leningrad through his troubled Russian years, imprisonment, his exile in the United States, and his time at Mount Holyoke. A photograph of Walcott is noticeable above Brodsky's desk along with other close friends and then about halfway through the programme Walcott starts to interview him. They talk about what it is to live apart from one's native landscape, how the landscape is interiorized. Brodsky says W. H. Auden is the most important poet in English during this century and recites 'The Shield of Achilles'. Walcott finds in Brodsky's poetry a fixity and solidity between politics or art for art's sake. Brodsky never seems displaced, never exiled; exile is in the eye of the beholder. Brodsky replied that Walcott knew this too, that to be on the outside was to be at the core of things.

In November the *New York Review of Books* published 'Magic Industry', Walcott's review of Brodsky's *To Urania*. Besides claiming Brodsky as a poet of world standard far above others, and discussing his use of poetic genres and traditions, Walcott was concerned to demonstrate the sonorities of his verse and how they had been carried over into English. Walcott said Brodsky was as anti-American as anti-Soviet as both were against poetry that aimed so high, and was so superior to that of democracies. Walcott's poetics were becoming similar to Brodsky's, but there was something frightening in the way the failures and levelling aspects of the United States were regarded as equal to the horrors of the Soviet Union.[13]

The first broadcast of Melvyn Bragg's interview with Walcott for the *South Bank Show*, a London Weekend Television production, took place on 15 January 1989. Occasioned by Walcott's award of the Queen's Gold Medal for Poetry, the programme, filmed during 1988, surveyed Walcott's life and gave especial attention to his long poem in progress. Bragg said it looked at Homeric myth in terms of the lives of modern St Lucian fisherman. At this point Walcott did not know whether to title it Omeros or Omaros, and remarked that something was lost in translation—Homer and Virgil sound like New England farmers. Walcott talked about his Achilles being a sea-warrior, that the classical names given to the slaves were not a humiliation but a result of their showing the qualities associated with the names. The narrative was naturally West Indian as the stories had not been told before and because once you looked at the sea the distances were vast, you could be looking from St Lucia across to Africa.

By now Walcott was a star of the lecture circuit with readings, and often interviews, almost every week. He had a sabbatical from Boston University and was on the move. Interviewed at the University of Michigan in January 1989, while Hopwood Award Speaker, Walcott said he was concentrating his time in St Lucia as his mother was old. Although he had patched his quarrel with Errol Jones and Stanley Marshall, he had not spent long periods in Trinidad for a while. He felt that women writers were now of especial interest in the Caribbean, praised Olive Senior, mentioned Lorna Goodison and Velma Pollard, and said that women tended to get things done without fuss and sullenness. Walcott was not a feminist, but he was influenced by his mother. He praised the West Indian short story as being stronger than its poetry. The poets he liked were Dennis Scott, Mervyn Morris, and Tony McNeill.

Besides *Omeros* he mentioned that he was working on *Ghost Dance*, a play about the Indian absence in America. He said that America's racial problems began with the fate of the American Indians and it could not have racial reconciliation until it reconciled American history with the fate of the Indians. There is an absence at the core of the United States, a kind of psychological brutality. There was an epic story here. All epics have some beleaguered last defence, and the last days of the Sioux are like the last defences of the Israelites. His focus, however, is on a white woman, Catherine Weldon, concerned about how the Sioux are treated; it is her conscience, the conscience of women, that is the conscience of society. Men see things as political, to be solved by war. Women endure, have a domestic conscience and a sense of what is right or wrong beyond the political. There is a moral NO in which reasons are not acceptable, but which comes from a sense of right and wrong.

He said that he felt disconnected from Boston; it had never 'clicked' although it was his job, his children were near him, and he had some good friends. Home is St Lucia, but he comes from the entire Caribbean and his soul is in the Caribbean. In Boston he felt locked in. When he walked out of his house there was no grass or trees. In the Caribbean life is more open, free, you go for a walk and see and talk to people. America is becoming more racially divided. It does not affect him as he is known and treated with respect. Blacks have got to stop putting adjectives in front of their name; they must say 'I am an American. I've been here a damned long time.'

Walcott argued that you belong to a place according to how much you have loved and lived in it. Caribbean whites, blacks, browns, Asians, had to accept that the Caribbean was now home, home was not England, Africa, or India. A recent immigrant who participated fully in a community was a member of it. People had to live and work together, to see that they belonged where they lived, not to some alien place. Now black Americans and Britons were aggressively denying that they were part of the countries in which they lived, denying the continual physical and cultural cross-pollination that is part of history.[14]

On 18 January he read his poem 'The Sea is History', from *The Star-Apple Kingdom* at York University in Toronto. His remarks concerning the poem were published as an essay also called 'The Sea is History'. Walcott challenged both the notion of history as a fixed narrative of former achievements and revisionist history as seen by the oppressed. Whereas Greek art had become classical, characterized by bleached-out ruined marbles and sculptures missing parts, in its own time it was brightly painted, human, Asian, and fleshy without amputations, more like what we would consider bad Roman Catholic popular icons. Greek drama was probably more like the musical *Hair* in being noisy, danced, and full of vitality, unlike the stately, moving-statues approach we bring to Greek classical theatre. The Caribbean writer knew that every racial group in the region had much to be ashamed of. Most of the whites, for instance, were descended from convicts. It was necessary for the artist to be freed from the notion of consequential time; it was necessary to reject not only the regional burden or shame of history, but also the notion that literary history consisted of a series of discoveries similar to the history of science. Art was not like science, for a poet Dante exists the way God does, without a past or future tense. 'The Sea is History' said that history was nothing, it was like nature, the clouds, the sky, and not to be found in imperial monuments, conquests, battles, achievements. The poem also said that the worst aspect of the slave was his imitation of his master, the governing of the New World as if it were the Old.[15]

This appears to be a return to his disagreement with Naipaul. Walcott argued that a lack of a history of achievements and ruins was a liberation, a chance to build without the resentments inherited from history. During discussion time Walcott was asked whether he wanted to be the voice of his people and he said no, the voices of the people get shot. Like Joyce he wanted to make the conscience of his people, not be a political poet. Caribbean society was in fact old, but it was not written about. Although the shape of a breadfruit was beautiful, it was long thought to be amusing to write of the breadfruit.

Another ring had been added by more fully articulating an idea already long present. There is a history, but it is better to do without. Instead of seeking analogies, metaphors, which tend towards inflation and devaluation, there is reality itself which is seen as incarnating divine light. 'The Sea is History' looks forward to the deconstructive, anti-mythic last third of *Omeros* and to the Clare-like *The Bounty*. Joyce is the modern model because a realist who grounds myths in the natural world to create consciousness of his race rather than, like Yeats, romanticizing history and comparisons.

Two days later (20 January) Walcott read to an audience of perhaps one hundred at Carleton University. The local papers noticed the size of the audience, as poetry readings normally brought out between fifteen to twenty people and the weather was unusually bad, even for Ottawa. Cyril Dabydeen praised Walcott's 'even, well-modulated voice, his resisting the impulse to declaim or rhapsodize, or even to dwell on . . . incantation'. This was Walcott's first visit to Ottawa (he was to return again the next year). His reading of 'The Spoiler's Return' was commemorated by Cyril Dabydeen's poem 'Letter to Derek Walcott', 'tired as you seem now upon reading | three nights in a row, after Toronto . . . talking to the Indian girls from Guyana . . . expressing greetings to [Clyde] Hosein' (the Trinidadian short story writer who settled in Toronto).

Although there are those who complain Walcott does not make enough use of dialect or dialectics, his readings to the West Indian diaspora take on the excitement of a Hollywood star visiting the troops abroad. Most of his audience are professionals, educated, writers themselves, successful, but decades of living abroad have produced feelings of deracination and isolation. Being a separate part of a national multiracial, multicultural mosaic sounds good, but can be no better than separate and less-than-equal. Walcott melts the ice, is part of a now mythic past, feels like 'home', shows that West Indians need not be ghettoized. Cyril Dabydeen, originally from Guyana and cousin of the British writer David Dabydeen, mentioned the coming together, excitement, and pride of the local Caribbean community, especially its artists, because of Walcott's visit. Dabydeen himself is one of the younger poets who are influenced by Walcott and he remarked on the audience's surprise and pleasure with the use of dialect in 'The Spoiler's Return' in contrast to the early Walcott poems he first knew. Lloyd Stanford, who knew Walcott from his University College of the West Indies and *Drums and Colours* days, was proud that as soon as Walcott saw him he called him 'Christophe', recalling the nickname Stanford had acquired at University College after his performances in *Henri Christophe*.[16]

Two weeks later (1–3 February), Walcott was at the State University of New York, Albany, from Wednesday to Friday for a three-day residency at the New York State Writers Institute where he taught classes and gave readings. Walcott said he was not at home in the West Indies or North America, he was adrift between cultures, a cosmic castaway. He asked rhetorically why he was at Albany during Black History month, as it was not his history and said that he was unhappy with separate histories. 'There's one history and everyone knows, to the horror of some, that American cultural history is really about blacks. Look at music, dance, whatever. It would be ideal if we didn't need to have a Black History Month, that there could be a congealing of history onto one slate.' Walcott said that he would like in his sixties to have a sunlit studio in St Lucia to paint large bad sincere paintings.[17] Later in February he read from *The Arkansas Testament* at the DIA Art Foundation and was in San Francisco for a workshop on *Viva Detroit* for the American Conservatory Theatre when Gregson Davis from Barbados met him and arranged for him to read at Stanford where Davis taught Classics.

'Crocodile Dandy' in *The New Republic* is a review of Les Murray's *The Daylight Moon* and *The Vernacular Republic: Selected Poems*. Murray, an Australian who gets along well with Walcott, Heaney, and Brodsky, is a major poet, but not well known in the United States. Walcott's review is partly about his own quarrel with Whitman or what now seems the school of Whitman. Superficially Murray might be thought part of that school as he is a sprawling, vernacular poet, given to criticizing the literary and cultural establishment. Walcott, again taking up his last days of the Roman Empire image, included Murray as one of the Barbarians approaching the capital bringing vandalization of the language and their own bards. He described Murray's spiky, dark, rumbling hexameters as like a scene in Mad Max; they have power, mass, and grace, but only he can use them. They have size, are affable, even garrulous. *The Daylight Moon* is dedicated to the glory of God. Except for Dylan Thomas no one has written such dedications, rooted in the sacred, yet intimate and conversational, since the monks. Murray may seem like a patriotic eagle, a bard of open spaces, but the power of his poems is religious, holy poetry in the vernacular. They are not the poems of a hermit but praise technology as part of the development of human nature. Murray does not celebrate from a distance like Whitman, but like an engineer. His language and rhythms can batter, insist you learn his language, become jingoistic, too burly, but he has his own voice, his own accent and posture, what all major poets seek. Only major poets can be parodied, and Murray can come close to self-parody. Murray had to avoid evangelical Australianism and face the challenge of imitating Whitman, of seeing Australia as a mirror America with its energy, variety, new frontiers, modern cities, deserts, and envying of Europe. He had to wait for the light of the ordinary, and that is what the poems reveal, ordinary Australia without patriotism or guilt. Murray is not an elegiac poet. His syntax digests iron. Like Ben Jonson he is Roman, based in scholarship.[18]

In his June *New York Review of Books* review of Philip Larkin's *Collected Poems* Walcott claimed for the poet the invention of the Muse of Mediocrity. 'She lived in life itself, not as a figure beyond it.' She was a creature of average faces, habit, repetition, plainness. Larkin is a popular poet because he has a decency (which turned out to be ironic once Larkin's letters were published), an intimacy with the reader, a middle classness. Larkin used the pentametrical line, but 'shadowed it with hesitations, coarsened it with casual expletives, and compacted it with hyphens'. Larkin's hyphenated images were almost mini-poems. 'The hyphenated image is not colloquial, but Larkin's achievement is to make it sound as if it were, as if such phrasing could slip into talk.' Among such pearls of wisdom, clearly indebted to Walcott's regard for craft and his respect for a Joycean realism, were a number of rather inflated sentences common to Walcott's criticism at this time. It was like someone working himself up in the hope of saying something. There were also many inaccuracies of interpretation and fact in the review, which were pointed out in unpublished letters to the editor. Walcott had relied too much on memory and assertion.[19]

After the publication of Ted Hughes's *Wolfwatching* (1989) Walcott wrote a powerful if at times obscure essay, 'Medusa Face', for the *Weekend Telegraph*. The review was in Walcott's later prose style, weighty, profoundly intellectual, a bit rambling as each idea appears to breed its antithesis or a new direction, filled with quotable lines, obviously irritated at the shallowness of others, almost bullying in tone, rich in observations about poetry as poetry and its relationship to the history of the craft. The observations are brilliant and in a general way true, but a pedant could easily point out what is ignored or even wrong. Basically Walcott claimed that Hughes introduced to English poetry a new way to view nature, as admirable and awesome for its cold ruthless lack of sentimentality. It was a world to fear and love, not a place for nervous sensitivities. Hughes, unlike other poets, did not project himself into nature, he was not writing about himself. Rather he had become his poems, a Medusa face. Walcott saw Hughes's long lines divided by a heavy caesura as deriving from Middle English. Walcott was trying to define a tradition for Hughes, a tradition of such naturalist-based, tough poets as Clare, Hardy, and Lawrence, in contrast to the moral senti-mentalities and pastoralism often associated with Wordsworthians. He was also defending Hughes from the feminists who wanted to prove that heterosexual males destroyed their women, and that Hughes caused Plath's suicide. Walcott did not engage in the argument at that demagogic level. Instead he contrasted their art. Hughes offered awe in the face of the tragedy and fate known by the ancient Greeks; Plath was the poet of 'insomniac terror', 'the muse of aspirin', 'hysteria'. Hughes's world was impersonal, tough, unaccommodating, like the biblical prophets, exhilarating, powerful, and real.[20]

These long review essays proclaim an 'ordinary' world to be described and celebrated while recognizing it is both tragic and holy. Reality embodies, is, divine light. It is a poet's vision, contradictory, a non-sacramental sacrament-alism. Like many New World poets Walcott sees 'grace' in what he denies as transcendental, a vision that has evolved from Protestantism's inner light and Romanticism's pantheism. There is something like it in the poetry of Dylan Thomas; the Christian origins can be found in the poetry of Henry Vaughan and other religious writers of the early modern period. Walcott brings this vision to a post-Hemingway world in which many intellectuals no longer feel nostalgia for traditional sacred images. His assertion of the blessedness of the ordinary is consistent with the idea of naming and creating a local or national conscious-ness. It follows from Adam's naming of the creatures. Its enemy is the shallow, the sentimentalizing, the politicizing, of race, nation, or history, the lack of a tragic vision of the world and thus of humanity. Its ally is the writer working towards a craft that allows naming, being true to the self's inner voice. Such details as the placement of a caesura, marking the poet's breathing and speech, are essential to correct naming, to getting the ordinary into the poem.

By now an annual production of a Walcott play was expected of the black British theatre. Beyond the black British dramatists there were basically four possible imports, Walcott, Trevor Rhone, and Dennis Scott from Jamaica, and Edgar White. This year *Beef, No Chicken* was part of the Black Theatre Season at the Shaw, 9 March–1 April. *City Limits* saw that it continued the complaint against technological progress and capitalism in the previous year's *O Babylon!* and asked where were the equivalent young black British dramatists? The *Guardian* thought it a 'slapstick elegy' in which 'slick insights tickle the conscience for the price of a smile', with too many issues, not enough plot, and a lack of characterization. Not enough beef. *Time Out* found it sprawling 'but immensely likable'. Walcott was to tell Patrick Gallagher, 'Lately, I had first generation London West Indians doing a play of mine and they simply could not begin to do a Creole accent. They should not be like that.'[21]

By mid-March Walcott and Sigrid were back at Villa Beach Cottages when 'Homer in the Underground' appeared in *The New Republic* (20 March), one of the first pieces of *Omeros* to be tried in print. During April Walcott read at the Book Center, Milwaukee, on Sunday, 9 April, and at Marquette University on the Monday. As the American university year ended Walcott was made an Honorary Doctor of Humane Letters at Hartwick College (28 May) and entranced the crowd at the commencement ceremony by reading his 'The Season of Phantasmal Peace'.

He was in Europe for most of the summer. In June there was the Dublin Writers' Conference in Dun Laoghaire; the theme was 'Literature as Celebration'. A Poets' Round Table with Les Murray, Brodsky, Heaney, and Walcott, was recorded on 15 June and published in *PN Review*.[22] After Dublin there was Poetry International in Rotterdam (17–24 June). On Tuesday, 20 June, he was part of a group led by the South African Breyten Breytenback who discussed 'The Government of the Tongue'. Walcott read from his own poetry on Friday, 23 June. Others in Rotterdam included Joseph Brodsky, Natan Zach (Israel), Octavio Paz (Mexico), Les Murray (Australia), Rita Dove (United States), Alain Bosquet (France), and Lars Gustafsson (Sweden).

David Applefield, editor of the Paris-based literary journal *Frank*, was an assessor at the Rotterdam Festival and remembers Walcott as being in great form, continually partying and dining with the other poets, but quietly avoiding alcohol, although much of the hilarity was provided by Brodsky and a group of 'mad' Russian poets. Sigrid was with him. This was the third time Applefield had met Walcott and like others he was struck by how he could be distant, even haughty, at one moment and great fun the next. Brodsky and Walcott were usually together, often with Rita Dove, and Walcott and Brodsky discussed whether

Thomas Hardy or D. H. Lawrence was the better poet, with Walcott claiming that Hardy's superiority was in his use of form. It was not all jollification. Walcott was greatly disturbed by the massacre of students in Tiananmen Square and strongly took issue with some European intellectuals who thought the Chinese government was justified or had no other choice. Throughout his life Walcott has always been on the side of free speech, personal liberty, tolerance, and democracy and against those who would justify repression and tyranny in the name of some greater, abstract good or the realities of politics.

Walcott had just finished a draft of *Omeros*, which he sent by express mail to Roger Straus. He said he was feeling burnt out and loaned the manuscript, which included his line drawings, to Applefield for a few hours to read. Applefield realized he was being given a preview of a treasure and photocopied two sections which he asked Walcott's permission to publish in a forthcoming Caribbean issue of *Frank*. The double issue of *Frank* 11/12 was reviewed favourably in the *TLS*, with special praise for Walcott. Sigrid sent Applefield a note saying that Derek liked the issue and Straus sent him a fax thanking him for the advance publicity for *Omeros*.[23]

Walcott went from Rotterdam to London where, on 27 June, he was received by the Queen and presented with the poetry medal. Previous winners include Auden, Christopher Fry, Robert Graves, Philip Larkin, Stephen Spender, and R. S. Thomas. Walcott later claimed that he and the Queen talked about 'how Americans speak Shakespearean verse': ' "Ma'am," I said, "you know Sly Stallone." ' ' "Well, his version of Hamlet goes: 'To be *or what*.' " She just cracked up.'[24]

On 6 July he was once more in Dublin with Heaney. At the Dun Laoghaire DART train station he launched that summer's 'Poems on the DART' with 'To Norline'. Walcott punned 'I hope it's a moving poem.' The next day (7 July) Walcott was awarded an honorary Doctor in Letters by Trinity College, Dublin. He was interviewed by Patrick Gallagher, who was told by Heaney that Walcott did for the West Indies what Synge did for Ireland, 'finding a language woven out of dialect and literature, neither folksy nor condescending'. Brodsky and Heaney were in London the previous week. Brodsky said that the West Indies were discovered by Columbus, colonized by the British, and immortalized by Walcott. Walcott said of his friendship with Heaney and Brodsky 'We get on well, we all like corny humour. I like men who can bullshit. They can.' He was on an Irish pilgrimage with Heaney, seeing places associated with Joyce, Yeats, and Lady Gregory.[25]

The warnings in *O Babylon!* and *Beef, No Chicken* about the effects of international capitalism and tourism on the West Indies turned out to be accurate. In 1989 the government sold land for a tourist hotel between the Pitons, the two mammalian mountain peaks that, along with the parrot, have come to represent St Lucia. The Pitons near Soufriere are not only beautiful, there is something mystical about them. Visitors often spend a night sleeping on them. It was like letting a Swedish tourist agency build a swimming pool on the roof of Notre Dame in Paris. Walcott wrote angrily in the *Star* (26 August) that the sale was like selling your mother's breast. The article, titled 'Jalousie Argument Borders on Prostitution', concluded with the suggestion that if something needed to be done to earn money they could place the contractor, the foreign investors, their St Lucian associates, and their apologists, eternally in the live sulphur pits and boiling lava, which were the tourist sights of Soufriere. The government minister involved angrily replied that Walcott had become an outsider, a taunt with which the minister would be taunted after Walcott was awarded the Nobel Prize.

During August Walcott was one of the stars at the triennial Association of Commonwealth Literature and Language Studies Conference held that year at the University of Canterbury at Kent. He read from *Omeros*. Walcott, who is known to avoid public transport, does not drive a car, and expects to be chauffeured to and from readings. He arrived at Heathrow and took a taxi directly to the university, throwing the conference organizers into a panic as they had not budgeted for such a taxi bill. Walcott read on the 26th and seemed lonely and ill at ease at the conference, listening to other poets, but not attending any social functions. Such unease has often been noticeable in England where Walcott does not have the same 'feeling' of being at home as do many West Indian writers who lived in England while young, as students or as immigrants. Most of his literary friendships are also not as deep as in the United States or West Indies. John Figueroa, who often wrote about Walcott and himself a poet, was at the conference, but Figueroa was older, ill, and barely surviving. The two younger British West Indian authors, Fred D'Aguiar and Caryl Phillips, spent some time and ate with Walcott. The ACLALS reading was followed by a South Bank reading from *Omeros*.

Walcott returned to Ottawa on 6–7 October through the sponsorship of Third World Players, the Royal Commonwealth Society, the National Library of Canada, the Commonwealth Club of Ottawa, and the St Lucia–Ottawa Association. On Friday he gave two workshops at Woodroffe High School and read that night for the general public in the Auditorium of Ottawa at the National Library. The next evening there was a reception and reading at the Commonwealth Club of Ottawa. Stanford remembers how well Walcott handled the students; they stayed on for his second class. He encouraged them to read their own works, gave them information about how to publish, never read or cited his own work, and talked about the 'beat' rather than 'metre' of poetry. In one case he encouraged a student of Jamaican origin to work in Jamaican English rather than English rhyming couplets. This young man seemed intent on disrupting the class, saying he was not a poet; but he had composed a poem to his mother which Walcott helped him translate into 'patois', while providing 'the beat'. Walcott had managed to avoid an embarrassing situation, usefully taught some important lessons about poetry, while giving the student pride in himself. At the Commonwealth Club Walcott read an excerpt from *Dream on Monkey Mountain*, taking all the parts. Later Stanford would write to Walcott to ask permission for the Ottawa Third World Players to perform his plays, and as usual there was no written reply, but Roderick passed on a verbal okay.[26]

Walcott's annual readings at Hartwick College had led to his involvement in the theatre programme and eventually to his writing a play, based on events around the death of Sitting Bull, to be premièred there. In mid-October Walcott was rewriting *The Ghost Dance* for its 9–11 November première at Hartwick. Duncan Smith was director.[27] The play takes an unusual view of the events of 1890—the spread of the ghost dance, the killing of Sitting Bull, and the massacre at Wounded Knee. Although there are some Indian characters, Walcott is more interested in the variety of responses to the events by the white community. Smith sees the method as Shakespearian in its many voices and perspectives in examining history. The whites are powerful, the Indians are not, but the whites are not just villains. There is a range of sympathies and motivations, miscalculations, confusions; good people with good reasons can have evil results. Catherine Weldon, in Walcott's play, is a widow who wants to help Sitting Bull and the Indians and needs to work with James McLaughlin, the Indian agent of the Bureau of Indian Affairs.

The play is about human conduct within a political world. McLaughlin is shown as fluent in Sioux, married to a Sioux woman and the author of a book *My Friend, the Indian*. For him the ghost dance represents an inferior culture that stands in the way of Indian progress. Catherine Weldon is a rich wealthy white woman who comes close to an Indian view of the world and who sees that McLaughlin's myth of progress will end in the repression of the Indians. One of the ironies of history is that McLaughlin's attempt to stop the ghost dance as a way of preventing the United States army massacring the Indians leads to Indians killing Indians. One symbol of hope is Swift Running Deer (whose white name is Lucy or light) and her father James Eagle, who have become Christians but not lost their Indianness. Eventually rejected by the Christians, Lucy commits suicide. The play begins with a common Walcott technique of having the actors, in this case representing Indians, on the set before the performance as the audience enters, creating a contrast between the Indian world and the entering whites. If the play shows how much has been lost to progress and materialism, it also has a feeling of sadness, a sense of history as destiny which is deeper than the actual articulation of ideas in the speeches. At the end the Indian way of life is destroyed. History must include a memory of what has happened and why.

This was part of Walcott's long preoccupation with the fate of the native American Indians, which exemplified his view that all nations had a history of conquest and racial conflict. The extermination of the Caribbean Indians was perhaps too far in the past to be seen as more than a few historical facts; the conquest of the American Indians during the settling of the West was better documented and more immediate, more what he and other foreign writers living in the United States had to come to terms with. Walcott did not feel, nor wanted to be, a United States American, whether white or black. The epic tragedy of the American Indians was another matter, part of the shared history and guilt of the New World.

After the production of *The Ghost Dance*, by what were termed the Cardboard Alley Players, Bensen wrote a still unpublished review. Calling on an underlying subtext of Shakespeare's *Tempest* and tempest imagery, he described the ghost dance as itself a tempest that could bring salvation or destruction. The Federal government in ruthlessly subduing the Indians gained a land of ghosts. The ghost dance was itself a revitalization movement that turned out to be suicidal as it was viewed by the representatives of the American government as belligerent. What for the Indians was a desperate attempt to reverse the invasion of white culture precipitated a major conflict between whites and Indians. Benson suggested that Walcott used dance on stage to suggest how the cultures were alike and yet different. The Indians shared bread in the ghost dance, the Christians in the communion of the mass.[28]

I first met Walcott at the August Kent Commonwealth Literature conference. I was editing, with my wife, a series of introductory books about modern dramatists which in the preface promised coverage of Nigeria and Trinidad as well as Europe and the United States, but I was unable to find anyone who could write a book about Walcott's plays in performance. Walcott suggested that I contact him in Boston. This was the thirtieth anniversary of the founding of the Trinidad Theatre Workshop and if all went well I, Soyinka, Brodsky, and others would go to Trinidad for a production which could form the basis of a book with lots of photographs.

I am not a journalist, and, while I knew Soyinka, it sounded improbable and it was, but Walcott's visionary enthusiasm intrigued me. When he spoke about the Workshop he was in a higher gear. I knew nothing about the Workshop, hardly anyone outside West Indian theatre did, which is why I could not find an author for the book on Walcott's plays. I started to look into it, and six years later published *Derek Walcott and West Indian Drama: 'Not Only a Playwright But a Company': The Trinidad Theatre Workshop 1959–1993*, which led to this book. Walcott seemed to me guarded, introverted, explosively generous, egalitarian towards those with talent or those trying to survive, otherwise undemocratic, unhappy in the United States, and lonely (although his daughters were in Boston). Sigrid, his girl friend, was still in Pittsburgh. He assumed I was a well-paid professor at an American university that would invite him to lecture. When he learned that I was jobless and had paid my way to Boston by giving some lectures locally he wanted to know what I was paid for them, silently nodded, and said use his extra room to stay over. The next day he cooked eggs for breakfast and refried some take-away Chinese rice for lunch. He painted while talking to me, but his mind seemed to be in Trinidad in the past as he alluded to his first arrival there, workshop exercises, Albert, Errol, Stanley—people I had never heard about who were central to his life. And he had that higher gear, that poet's visionary gear.

27

1987–1989 Teacher

WALCOTT sold his car, which Norline had driven for him. He walked or took a cab to his classes; the dramatic workshop was one streetcar stop from his poetry class. Walcott was encouraging Brodsky and Heaney to write plays. At the time both Brodsky and Heaney were usually in the Boston area; later Brodsky would teach in New York at Columbia University on alternate semesters and Heaney would only teach at Harvard one semester a year. After Walcott was awarded the Nobel Prize and himself began teaching one semester a year, he taught the autumn semester while Heaney taught in the spring. Although teaching could not give him the same companionship as the Workshop, it provided him with a position as a leader, someone with skills and knowledge to impart, a teacher. It was a family tradition and he had been doing it since primary school. His drama class was turning into a small theatre, one of the by now many drama companies he had founded.

During 1982 an Indian undergraduate majoring in chemistry at Vassar had heard Walcott read before a group of ten students. Walcott had been brought to Vassar by Frank Bidart, a friend of Lowell and Bishop, and now Lowell's literary executor. Walcott read the entire 'Schooner Flight'. Reetika Vazirani had never heard a poet read in such a voice and with such an inner conviction. She knew after that she had to change her life and changed her major. The next year she travelled to India—meeting such writers as Nissim Ezekiel, Gieve Patel, and R. K. Narayan—and China, carrying with her only two books, both of Walcott's poetry. Now closely involved in non-Western matters, she took a job working for an African and Caribbean bank in Washington when she returned to the United States. She attended the reading Walcott gave at the Smithsonian during November 1986, which was not well attended, and afterwards spoke with him.

She asked where he was teaching and how she could attend his classes. He surprised her by assuming she came from Boston (her voice is American, without any regional accent but I would have guessed north-eastern), and told her to turn up on Mondays. Within a week she had quit her job and moved to Boston, found a temporary job, called Boston University which raised objections, but found out where Walcott's classes were held and began attending.

She attended the classes for three semesters, January 1987–May 1988, and afterwards remained in contact with Walcott. The poetry classes were in a small room, the same room Lowell had used long ago, and she found the lectures full of brilliancies. Walcott has a personal anthology of favourite poems and the classes were meditations on these poems, sometimes on a few lines. The students also had individual conferences. The drama workshops were held at what was then a dirty, grimy theatre on Commonwealth Avenue (since then Walcott's refurbished Boston Playwrights Theatre) and were lively. Walcott used the best actors he could get in Boston. There was an electric rapport between Walcott and the actors. Seeing Walcott's hard-working, no-nonsense approach towards revision, Vazirani started to understand what would be needed to become a writer. She was one of the many poets of the next generation who would pass through Walcott's classes and look back on them as formative.

Walcott then had his teaching on Mondays, with the poetry class in the morning; afterwards he and the students would meet for lunch, and then those interested would move on to the drama workshop. He had consultations with students on Tuesday mornings, which left the rest of the week free for his own work. After one of the classes Walcott mentioned that he needed a typist. Vazirani told him that she typed rapidly and had worked as a temporary secretary. He immediately hired her, mostly to type screenplays he was working on at the time. Walcott expected her to come to work around 7 a.m., at which time he would already be working, and to make coffee or what she needed for herself. Everyone in the Boston apartment knew to keep quiet and leave Derek undisturbed in his studio (in which he had a typewriter and easel) until about 10 a.m., when he would break and make breakfast for himself and others. Then it was back to work until early afternoon, sometimes until 4 or 5 p.m. She had to work hard and often the only sounds were of Walcott typing in one room, her typing in another room. Although she mostly typed film scripts Walcott was working on *Omeros* at the time. One day she saw and began looking at the manuscript for it, but Walcott told her not to touch it.

While he was away the summer of 1987 she stayed at his apartment and took care of his mail. She worked for Walcott until the next summer when she hoped to have the apartment again, but Peter needed it and Walcott told her to concentrate on her writing and stop being a secretary. Those whom Walcott has told to be a writer and stop trying to write on the side remember the advice—it is like having hands laid on, or being confirmed. Like others she found Walcott reluctant to edit individual poems or help her publish them, both of which he thought part of earning your own way as a writer, but he became interested when she had a book-length manuscript and a book on the way. He refused to think of his students as students; they were writers and were expected to behave as writers.

As Walcott's secretary she was part of a family as Peter or others might be living at the apartment or staying over. Sigrid came to Boston some weekends. Brodsky would come from Mount Holyoke and Heaney from Harvard. The poets would have dinner together, travel to readings together to offer support. Walcott and Brodsky showed each other their poems in manuscript and both commented upon each other's work with praise and occasional suggestions. Brodsky especially wanted the opinions of Walcott and a few other poets such as Richard Wilbur.

Vazirani thought Walcott a great teacher; she personally knows at least ten published writers who were in her classes with him including Glyn Maxwell, Kate Snodgras, George Kalogeris, and Melissa Green. Walcott considered his students younger writers learning the craft from an experienced elder and sharing in the techniques of the workshop. He had no patience with broodiness, indiscipline, the wanting of attention. Write it, send it for publication, get it published, then show it to me. He warned against rushing into print. Do not publish a book until you have a book. To have the technique to fill a book with poems is not enough. He was not happy when *Agni* did a special feature on Glyn Maxwell, it was pushing him forward too fast. (Maxwell has since said he regrets most of the poems in his first book.) Many classes were lectures in which Walcott talked about why a line or a poem interested him. Students would be expected to memorize the poem on the spot, and write exercises to improve their technique. He had them write sonnets, made them aware of the visual shape of poetry as well as the form. Lines were examined for how they looked, what visual impression the letters made, their physical as well as aural texture. Poems were compared with paintings, statues. Talking to George Kalogeris, Walcott, no doubt with the Greek name in mind, suggested trying to write in blocks with some lines at the end trailing off like a classical ruin. He told students you had to be from a place—Brodsky was Russian, Heaney Irish, Walcott St Lucian, where were their poems from? He spoke of poems as colour in motion, physically shaped. He told each student to find a painter and look at everything by that painter. He told Kalogeris to study Hooper. Learn from painting, especially learn about light. Melissa Green brought him a poem in pentameter; he said take it back and rhyme it. After she rhymed it, he said put all the vegetables of New England in it. Next time he told her to put her father into it. She learned and he came to trust her. She read *Omeros* in manuscript; Walcott and Brodsky wrote quotes for the cover of her *Squanicook Eclogues*.[1]

Walcott hated American pampering of students and the laziness it produced. He expected students to read, memorize, write, and to work hard. Writers' blocks were not an excuse. Those who said they had trouble getting up and working early were told to go to bed early. If you disliked a major writer then you were expected to read all of that writer's work and learn from it. Unlike teachers who ask what you like, really do not give a damn for their student's views, and keep their opinions to themselves, Walcott was trying to form taste, trying to make his students understand why the great were great and why many received opinions had not really been thought through. He tried to make students aware of what he saw in poetry.

He was concerned with the vernacular and showed how Shakespeare and Milton used the vulgar tongue. Walcott would say that Frost and Larkin both used the pentameter, the metric line was not anti-American; the difference was in how they modified the caesura to fit their own breath. Where others spoke of metrics versus the human voice, Walcott said you had learn how to use your breath and metre, but not regard metric forms as fixed and invariant. He was passing on what Shakespeare, Milton, and Dryden knew, and presenting it within the discourse and along with the insights that had been developed for American poetry.

He did not deny the possibility of free verse, but warned that only a very good poet could use it successfully; usually it was rhythmically weak, tonally undistinguished, and boring. He praised James Wright for his ability to move the caesura in such a way that he appeared to be breathing naturally in metre. He would tell his class that a good reader does not read metre but follows the voice. He often spoke about Hart Crane and the opening line of *The Bridge* as an example of how the printed letters might look like sound and meaning. Walcott gave special consideration to the different weight of pauses ranging from the caesura, line end-stop, stanza break, and end-stops concluding stanzas. They had different weights and had to be earned by the verse, not mechanically expected. His experience of the stage taught him that a single line in a poem by Sir Walter Raleigh or from John Webster's *The Duchess of Malfi* could have three large pauses with space for action. He would give such poems and passages to actors in his theatre workshops and seem triumphant when, without being primed of what was intended, their readings proved his point; indeed he compared the ability of actors to give emphasis and space to such pauses within a line. If his notion of poetry was informed by the visual arts it was also in part shaped by years of working with the stage.[2]

At Boston University Walcott taught the Poetry Writing seminar. Outside the seminar students could talk to him in his office, if they made appointments. George Starbuck taught the Poetry Workshop course. The Drama Workshop, however, was not a seminar; this was a practical course in which student scripts were staged, and Walcott would hire actors to perform parts. It was in this course that problems sometimes developed when Walcott disagreed with students' ideas about staging or said scripts were not ready for production. It could result in a student not getting a degree that year and quitting, so the stakes were high over what were matters of opinion. The teaching methods he used with the Trinidad Theatre Workshop and his poetry course were not always successful in this course. Some students complained about the lack of structure, about too much concentration on a few lines of text, or a scene, without any sense of a play coming together. Theatre requires co-operation. Walcott was not always co-operative and seemed in his own world. Students who felt this way quarrelled with Walcott and did not want their names mentioned in this book.

One student, William Keeney, audited Walcott's poetry seminar during 1987–9 and also attended some of the drama workshops. Keeney says Walcott guarded his time for his own work and would not attend his office on Tuesday morning unless students had made appointments, but he was helpful if you did see him. Keeney had trouble getting a recommendation from Walcott until he actually saw him in his office, and then Walcott wrote the recommendation on the spot. While Walcott avoided the campus he did at times invite his classes to lunch, and Keeney, when no longer Walcott's student, went to Walcott's apartment to show him his poems. In general the classes began with Walcott asking the students to memorize some poems; then Walcott might give them an exercise imitating the poem (one exercise involved putting prose into verse), or he might start talking about some matter of form or technique which might take up the rest of the class. Part of one class was spent on the effect of a word in the first line of Hart Crane's *The Bridge*. Part of another class concerned when to use 'a' and 'the' in poetry. Keeney had used 'illume' in a verse exercise and Walcott spent perhaps twenty minutes on the word and alternatives. The focus was often on such details. He spoke well in what appeared to be extemporary monologues, although when Keeney sat in on the course a year later he realized that Walcott had the material prepared and would circle around it to make the same points.

Whether in class or informally meeting students, Walcott liked to be in command and the centre of attention. This was the period during which Walcott was working on *Omeros* and while he never mentioned his poem he did give much attention to the American long poem. He spoke of Hart Crane's *The Bridge* and argued that Americans wanted to pretend that they did not belong to a powerful imperialistic country. Because of American democratic egalitarianism they also pretended that poetry and poets mattered little. Whitmanism had become 'ah shucks!' American poets should speak in the language of power and not be falsely modest; they should accept that they are part of an empire and use big subjects. Few American poems have large subjects.

Walcott's view of poetry was ambitious; it was challenging the best of the past, it was a desire to engage the world through poetry, and his driving force was to make his name last forever as a poet. He was unconcerned with post-modernist and post-colonialist arguments about how standards and reputations change at various times and places, that nothing lasts, and uninterested in claims that it was somehow bad to be ambitious or part of an imperial language. He would tell his classes that critics were claiming to speak for him who said the opposite of what he felt. He never felt oppressed by colonialism, the British were good. Similarly his comments on student verses were often large, general, in which he was obliquely getting at approaches towards poetry and life. Most of the students began the course writing free verse as that was published in magazines but by the time they left the course they were writing formal verse. Although they had a vague knowledge of the stanzaic forms of poetry, they never before had a teacher who taught them to understand what metre, form, and literary conventions could do. They never before had classes in which there was so much attention was paid to every word, the sounds in words, the details of poetry.

One of those of the class of 1988 who regards Walcott's seminar as having made him as a poet is Glyn Maxwell. He arrived at Boston University on a scholarship and '300 good poems' and left with 'I think, four. That is how I measure success. A good deal of waste paper, and new eyes.' Walcott told his first class that no one needs or wants poetry, that they should have all of the classics of English literature committed to memory, and asked them to put on paper a poem from memory. The prosody of the generation was wrong, most current poetry was just 'whining in a bedroom'. Eventually Walcott praised a phrase in one of Maxwell's poems and told him to throw away the other lines. Still later he told Maxwell he should never take a job if he wanted to be a poet. He introduced Maxwell to Heaney. When I interviewed Maxwell, he had no job, lived with friends, was rapidly becoming a well-known poet, and had started a theatre for verse drama.[3]

During 1989 Rei Terada began attending Walcott's poetry course at Boston University. She had come to his poetry by way of Lowell's and decided to do her dissertation on Walcott. It was later published as the *Derek Walcott's Poetry: American Mimicry*, the first book to go beyond an introductory approach. She remembers his classes as unlike any others she had, although they sound somewhat like the workshops he devised for the Trinidad Theatre Workshop. There was no textbook, assignments were seldom given in advance. Walcott would distribute a poem in class, ask the students to read it, and give attention to some particular aspect of form, sound, language, imagery, or rhythm. They might be asked to write down afterwards the phrases that stuck in their mind and discuss them, or perhaps list the allusions to English gardens they remembered in English poetry. Walcott could be sardonically dominating to students not on their toes and could be jocular in sidetracking questions that he wished to avoid. She was puzzled by his belief in formal poetry, as he had written some free verse, and that finding the right form was an illumination rather than a rational decision.[4]

Speaking with her I had the feeling of someone used to the security of highly structured American classes rather than the probing, puzzling, and questioning once common to British tutorial teaching with its use of details and practical exercises as a way to build a repertoire of analysis and methodologies. In such exercises the teacher as well as the students may be searching and the results only realized after a period of exercises. Walcott had used similar methods to train his actors in Trinidad. Judged on its own a particular class could be a frustrating experience, but how else could an actor or a poet get inside a text, investigate its many possibilities, and make them part of one's own art? Students were expected to meet Walcott for a one-to-one tutorial about their own poetry, but, as with other matters, the number of private meetings was never clear. Some students had one tutorial, others two or three, depending upon Walcott's interest, the student's interest, and chance.

Because of a schedule conflict Terada could not keep attending Walcott's classes and made use of photocopied notes taken by Bill Keeney, which she later, with Keeney's permission, passed on to me. The seminars concentrated on a variety of poems, ranging from Emily Brontë's 'Cold in the Earth' to Adam Zagajewski's 'To Go to Lvov'. Poems in other languages than English were discussed as translation—about which Walcott said try to get the sound rather than the meaning. Most comments were about the craft of poetry, especially its sound, musicality, rhythm, and memorability. Walcott's remarks elsewhere on the dictatorship of democracy come into context when they are seen as a reaction against free verse as an expression of a liberalism that says you must be free. Walcott said that it was impossible to defy tradition. Poetry was not sincerity; a poet did not write poetry; a poet remembered poetry so that *Ulysses* is Joyce's memory of the *Odyssey*, and *Paradise Lost* is Milton's memory of the Bible. The more one remembered the more the mind contained. Poetry was incantation, like the relation of music and a conductor to a score. An inward approach to metre as in modern poetry lost strength and power. A reader expected rhyme, expected a beat. The students read poems carefully discussing tones, the caesura, pitch, timbre, punctuation, timing. An analysis of 'Lycidas' might lead to comparisons with poems by Lowell, Frank O'Hara, Garcia Lorca, or the paintings of waves by Hokusai. Walcott was concerned with how the mouth makes sounds, the O of the elegy and tragedy, differences that result in speaking the same words in a different order.

During a time when academic theorists were devaluing poetry as a discourse promoting the ideology of those in power, Walcott was saying that the arts were languages in their own right, uninterested in boundaries and time, uninterested in what the artist thought or felt. You prepared yourself by learning the art as fully as possible and if you were lucky you were given something that you did not understand; you had to discover what it was by making it. This was its own reward. If you were unwilling to do this you should write prose and become a politician or go into business. What Walcott was saying sounds romantic or mystical, but is a truth known to most artists. Michelangelo would find the sculpture in the block. Walcott was also returning to the concept of the poet as bard, the tribal bard who speaks for his people rather than himself. Many of his classes were concerned with how the epic had become Eliot's fragments of memories and how Crane had by energy tried to create a modern epic of the New World. Epics were necessarily failures as they could not speak for everyone. Walcott was obviously thinking his way towards *Omeros*. Brodsky said think big, think like a real poet; Walcott was thinking big like a real poet. He was also producing the next generation of poets. While most mentioned Walcott's making them aware of poetic form, craft, and such matters as voice and place, Rafael Campo also mentioned how useful it was to study with another poet of 'colour' not obsessed with matters of race.

28

1990–1991 *Omeros*

WALCOTT returned to St Lucia for New Year 1990 and several times during the year, staying at the Village Beach Cottages where he would write, paint, and swim. A local woman was usually hired to do St Lucian cooking. He once more spoke to Robert Bensen's Hartwick College Caribbean Literature course in January. He was soon to be 60. On the 9th the Government 'honoured' him with a poetry reading by others, songs from *The Joker of Seville*, some local dances, and presented him a painting of the Pitons by Dunstan St Omer. In Barbados, on his way to the United States, he saw friends and family, watched rehearsals of *Franklin* at Queen's Park Theatre, and was interviewed by John Wickham, who used his praise of Bajan coconut bread as an example of how Walcott loved the West Indies. It would be difficult not to like West Indian coconut breads and cakes, but it is true that in recent years Walcott has often made favourable references to Caribbean food. It is part of what he misses when he is away, especially as he watches his diet because of diabetes.

Franklin (25 January–11 February) was the first major production of a Walcott play in the West Indies for two years, and it would be two more years before there was another. His plays were being performed, but he was not writing more for the region or revising older ones for new productions. *Franklin*, because of Michael Gilkes, was the exception. It was directed by Gilkes with Errol Jones as Charbon/Moses, and taken to Trinidad where it was performed 22–7 March at the Little Carib, Port of Spain, in honour of Walcott's sixtieth birthday.[1] Walcott's plays usually have a political dimension, whether nationalist in portraying peasant culture or existential in showing the paradoxes of freedom. *Franklin* evolved from an earlier play about the place of a mulatto on a small island, into a play about the problems of a white immigrant and an envious black who tries to turn

the community against him. There had been rumbles of Black Power, racial incidents, some violence, and resentment of foreigners in formerly quiet Barbados.
Gilkes, a Guyanese of Indian descent, said the play showed that the West Indies
was an ethnic quilt, a place of immigrants.

In New York, on 23 January, there was a dinner at the Players Club for his
birthday. The thirty people invited were from Farrar, Straus and Giroux along
with such friends as Heaney, Brodsky (and his new wife-to-be Maria), Roscoe
Lee Browne, Rosanna Warren, Elizabeth Hardwick, Pat Strachan, Robert Silvers
of the *New York Review of Books*, and some friends of Sigrid. Brodsky read an
affectionate poem he had written about Walcott. Next week Walcott came from
Boston for a reading (29 January) at the Poetry Center. Before the reading he
spoke to high school students who were attending as part of the YMHA Schools
Program. There was a reception afterwards. Walcott suggested Elizabeth Hardwick to introduce him, and his guest list included Brodsky, Gerald Freund,
Robert Giroux, Daniel Halpern, Jamaica Kincaid, Howard Moss, Charles McGrath
(a *New Yorker* poetry editor), David Rieff, Lloyd Richards, Robert Silvers, Irene
Worth, Patricia Storace (*New York Review of Books*)—all literary and theatre people.
After the reading from *Omeros*, which included the 'Homer in the Underground'
section, Walcott forgot and left behind his only copy of the manuscript. An
amused Karl Kirchwey delivered it the next day to Farrar, Straus and Giroux.

Edouard Glissant and Walcott had earlier given a two-man colloquium in
New York concerning the Epic as a Genre. Glissant now invited Walcott to
Louisiana State University, Baton Rouge, to share in a poetry reading. Walcott
lived in Glissant's house for a week while revising *Omeros*. Glissant's son Olivier
was studying music in Boston, and has regularly visited Walcott, becoming
friends with Walcott's daughters.[2]

Although Walcott was much in demand on the Black Studies circuit, he
was against many of the basic principles behind black separatism. They were
contrary to what a play like *Franklin* was about. Walcott had given a poetry reading at the University of Wisconsin-Milwaukee and was interviewed by Robert
Brown and Cheryl Johnson. He questioned the use of history in the Americas
and said that 'black history . . . only continues to segregate'. Applying labels to
yourself allowed others to do so. Even the usual history of slavery was the
oppressor's history, it did not include the 'cooperation of Africans in selling each
other'. 'The whole idea of slavery was that you caught people and you sold them
to the white man. Black people capturing black people and selling them to the
white man. That is the real beginning; that is what should be taught.' 'We have
to face that reality. What happened was, one tribe captured the other tribe. That
is the history of the world.' Black history continued to be a series of paren-
theses. Affirmative action was 'patronage'; it perpetuated parenthesizing people.
America would remain a second-rate civilization because of its obsession with

race. There were no other large issues in America. Unlike previous empires it was not at heart world-conquering, people did not have the same pride in domination that characterized earlier empires. America dominated culturally, not through the possession of colonies.[3]

He praised Miami as likely to be the most important city in America due to its Spanish culture. Whereas racial tensions were increasing in America, Miami was part of the Caribbean region in which, he thought, races were mixing. He noted that American blacks objected to the Spanish speakers the way people often complained at new immigrants. In America everything became vulgar, part of television. Gospel singing became part of entertainment and lost its 'faith'. The artistic creativity of the Caribbean was astonishing—Jean Rhys, Saint-John Perse, Aimé Césaire, V. S. Naipaul. They were all of different colours and races. There were also many good painters in the Caribbean. Caribbean culture was not chronological. It was fresh and simultaneous. There was not the same separation between art and life found in the north. Art was everywhere, as in the music.

Omeros showed that the Caribbean was what the Greeks were like originally. 'The Greeks were the niggers of the Mediterranean. If we looked at them now, we would say that the Greeks had Puerto Rican tastes . . . Because the stones were painted brightly. They were not these bleached stones. As time went by, and they sort of whitened and weathered, the classics began to be thought of as something bleached-out and . . . distant.' Walcott was not trying to make comparisons between Greece and the Caribbean. Comparisons reduce. Art creates significance. The physical beauty of the black people in *Omeros* is Caribbean, but you can see that as part of a classical artistic humanistic tradition in contrast to emblematic African and Indian art.

Culture was dead art; when art enters museums it becomes culture. American artists were always faced by the problem that people regarded them as marginal and the European tradition as central. You are praised for continuing the central civilization when Caribbean time is different, each day is fresh, a new beginning. Walcott objected to being told that there were echoes of T. S. Eliot in his poetry. English sentences sound like English writers. To be compared to earlier writers is to be put in a parenthesis, it is to say you sound like someone who has achieved glory. Walcott hoped by now he was beyond such patronage. If there was anyone to whom he might appreciate being compared it would be Dante, but even the images, such as the volcano in *Omeros*, that are the same as in Dante's writing are natural metaphors and a writer using them is bound to sound 'as if you were copying Dante'. Such images could just as easily come from Stephen King.

Asked about Harold Bloom's theory of 'the anxiety of influence' Walcott said it was meaningless; one could just as easily say 'the influence of anxiety'. He read poet-critics, such as Eliot and Coleridge. He also read journalism by 'people . . .

who review and appoint and crown and uncrown' although they had little to say about artists.

They next discussed craft. Why did Walcott in *Arkansas Testament* write some short-lined rhymed poems with two or three beats in a line and rhymes close together? Walcott said that the long, expansive line of *Mid-Summer* was reflective, containing 'a lot of indirection,and psychology and self-analysis and connotation', but it was also 'antagonistical'. Instead he wanted something closer to instinct and rhyme; to defend instinct is like defending breathing. He wanted the metre of someone exhaling in and out while working. He does not want rhyme bumping at the end, he wants it like breathing in and out. But he has changed once more as 'in my new book' there is a long narrative line. Pentameter would have been too heroic. Walcott thought free verse egotistical and flat-voiced; many American poets are 'so vain in their modesty', that is 'very boring.' Free verse is already dead. Eliot is a solid poet, Walcott accepted that he had been wrong to 'knock' him, but Auden is the great twentieth-century poet in his skill, deftness, scale, and subject.

American universities, he claimed, do not teach Auden because they do not believe in intelligence. Creative writers are told to be individuals and are not taught the history of poetry. Walcott liked the poetry of Mark Strand, Ted Hughes, and Thom Gunn. Brodsky translates his own poetry. He sometimes sends drafts to Walcott and Richard Wilbur who will 'put them into a certain shape'. Brodsky has the courage to change a metaphor for a rhyme. One reads Brodsky for a Russian intelligence 'entering English'.

As long ago as 'Ruins of a Great House' Walcott saw history as endless conquests of which most peoples have been guilty. More recently Naipaul's *A Bend in the River* offered a similar disillusioning history of tribes conquering and enslaving other tribes. Naipaul saw no solution beyond being prepared, saving one's self, avoiding dewy eyes, finding protection among the strongest, and keeping your bags packed. Walcott was saying that reconciliation between conquered and conquerors is possible with an acknowledgement of guilt. As someone living in the United States he was concerned how the treatment of Indians and blacks had not been acknowledged and was continuing to poison the country. While black Americans and black Britons were right to be angry, they also had to accept where they were living, see what they had contributed to the nation, and stop dreaming of homes elsewhere. American culture was black. Listen to the music, look at the dancing.

Walcott disliked comparisons between Europe and elsewhere as they usually devalued elsewhere; any comparison suggested something inferior was being honoured by being elevated as an equal to the superior. He wants himself and Caribbean art to be seen on its own for what it is, and no longer as a provincial branch of European culture that seeks acceptance. He shares Naipaul's much earlier rejection of being considered a West Indian novelist, or Salman Rushdie's rejection of being a Commonwealth writer. Such terms exist in binary opposition to some established, more valued tradition. Walcott, however, goes beyond Naipaul or Rushdie in saying look at Caribbean literature, it is a great literature, look at the range of authors, look at the many races of its authors, look at the small population that has produced such a great literature. He was saying: I do not ask to be part of or seen as equal to American or British literature. I belong to a great literature of my own region. I am part of English-language literature, but my cultural affinities are with the Spanish, French, and other Caribbean literatures.

Throughout the interview one hears Walcott's dissatisfaction with the United States and Americans. Americans have good qualities; they are far from the imperialist demons of leftist thought, but they remain obsessed with race and they trivialize the arts. The interview might be considered a declaration of Caribbean artistic independence from North American, especially Anglo-, cultural imperialism. Miami will be the new cultural capital of the United States because it is part of Caribbean culture. It is tempting to say that a decade of living in the United States has made Walcott increasingly clear-eyed or unillusioned, but much of what Walcott says he had already said and said early in his career. It is the confidence that is striking, a confidence perhaps from knowing that *Omeros* would soon be published. 'Chapter XXXIX', was published in the Spring/Autumn *Antaeus*; 'Home' in the *New Yorker* on 30 July.

Much of what Walcott published around this time concerned the United States and the relationship of the United States to the Caribbean, or asserted Caribbean uniqueness. The May *Bostonia* carried ' "Islands In The Stream", Hemingway, Winslow Homer, and the Light of the Caribbean', one of the previously unpublished chapters of 'American, without America'. Although I discussed this piece in connection with its composition in St Croix, it would be useful to return to it now as part of Walcott's vision of a Caribbean art.

The subject is the relationship between Thomas Hudson in Ernest Hemingway's *Islands in the Stream* and Winslow Homer, two artists who have influenced Walcott. The topic is, however, part of the wider issue of how modern art and painting can be used in the Caribbean, and even the relationship between the arts of the temperate to the tropical world. Hemingway was one of Walcott's early models for writing in an understated economical manner, as in the imagistic epiphanies found in the early versions of 'Tales of the Islands' with their almost Cubist montage of contrasting voices and information. But Hemingway was also the one major modern writer in English who had not only written about the Caribbean, but had, like Walcott, described it, drawing images of the water and scenery without the clichés of exoticism and tourism. It is possible to dislike Hemingway the great white father, Hemingway the wealthy sportsman, Hemingway the sentimental tough guy who pretends to speak for peasants, while still recognizing that once barriers of race and class are lowered Hemingway is someone that a West Indian writer can learn from, and can learn much more from than those who preach the clichés of race and class. Moreover, and this was of especial interest to Walcott, Hemingway's prose, a poetic prose, was influenced by the methods of painters. Walcott, over and over, would give the example of how Hemingway had learned from Cézanne to suggest the outline of a land-scape, the rocks, the almost abstract shapes, and then towards the end of the paragraph use a single word, such as 'blue', the way Cézanne would use a brush stroke of a colour. Rocks, trees, blue, green. In a way this is how Walcott often painted his watercolours, pencilling some shapes in the land- or seascape, and then adding strokes of pure colour alongside each other. There was, however, the problem that temperate colours, the actual watercolours one purchases, are temperate, suited for painting scenes in temperate climates. The sun, water, sky, and people in the tropics are of a different colour than in the north, the light and dark in the colour are different.

Just as Hemingway is the great prose writer in English of Caribbean landscapes, Winslow Homer is the great painter, the watercolourist of the Caribbean. 'Homer was no innovator of technique unless one wishes to call naturalism invention, and today many of his large oils look too literary, too rhetorical, too set-up.' Walcott observes that each of Hemingway's paragraphs in *Islands in the Stream* is a watercolour and the 'subjects . . . are the same as Winslow Homer's'. The 'melodramatics' of Hemingway and Homer are not significant because of 'the real Caribbean light' from which they are drawn, 'the nature that surrounds and engulfs the action'. (While Walcott assumes that Homer is a naturalist, I belong with those who think Homer was changed by his time in France and the influence of Japanese art on the Impressionists and returned with his own Modernism, but like Robert Frost or even W. C. Williams he kept his mouth shut about that kind of influence and pretended that he was American not a Modernist.)

Walcott's topic broadens to include *To Have and Have Not* and *The Old Man and the Sea*. 'Hemingway, like Homer, never exaggerates nature, he is always aston-ishingly exact.' Hemingway has that 'light' in his wrist that is found in Homer's watercolours. Caribbean weather is not made for tourists, the beautiful can kill or feed depending on how accurately one can see its subtle 'omens'. Several passages from this essay seem especially applicable to Walcott. About Thomas Hudson, Hemingway's Homer-like painter: 'Thomas Hudson does not paint that catalogue of degradation and disease any more than Winslow Homer would have. He paints an elegiac Eden, not a paradise of escape but one of healing.' 'Hemingway is a West Indian writer, because . . . he found this part of America new, as new as Twain found the Mississippi.'[4]

The relationship between North America and the Caribbean, and between black and white, is also part of the subject-matter of *Viva Detroit* which had its world première on 8 June at the Los Angeles Theatre Center, a theatre of 500 seats, where it ran until 29 July.

Viva Detroit is a three-character play set on an island resembling St Lucia. There are Sonny, Pat, and a Barman. Sonny, a hustler, wants to emigrate to Detroit and at first tries to pretend to Pat he is a black American millionaire. Pat, a successful white American from New York, dreams of giving up the rat race and living on the beach; she wants to purchase a house on the island and support herself by freelance photography in the United States. She falls in love with Sonny. Now that he can go to the United States, Sonny can not face what it would involve. Pat is uncertain that she really loves the island enough to give up a career in the United States. The play seems a satire on tourism and on Americans, but raises deeper issues about commitment, love and careers, dependency and independence, ease versus work. Most critics have found it too slight to carry such a weight. Sonny represents superficial Americanization and the tourist industry living off America. Walcott had in mind how the government was harming the beauty of St Lucia by giving permission to develop hotels, a funicular railway between the Pitons, and other ways of developing tourism, but the issues also touch on Walcott's personal situation—how can he remain a St Lucian while living most of the year in the United States and earning his living there?

The *Los Angeles Times* said it was not developed enough, there was really only enough for a television play. The characters were stereotyped and the symbolism vague. *Variety* thought the dialogue witty, and the play entertaining, but too limited in its concerns and making insufficient use of its social observations. This seems to me correct.⁵ *Viva Detroit* was also produced (9–19 August) by River Arts Repertory at Bearsville Theatre, Woodstock, New York. The *Woodstock Times* thought it predictable, dated, and talky.

Alix Walcott died on 13 May at the age of 96. In her later years she had lost her memory, was often ill, and had to be cared for. There is a touching portrait in *Omeros* (Chapter XXXII):

> Her days were dim as dusk. There were no more hours.
>
> From her cupped sleep, she wavered with recognition.
> I would bring my face closer to hers and catch the
> scent of her age.
>   'Who am I? Mama, I'm your son.'
> 'My son.' She nodded.
>   'You have two, and a daughter.
> And a lot of grandchildren,' I shouted. 'A lot to
> remember.'
>   'A lot.' She nodded, as she fought her
> memory. 'Sometimes I ask myself who I am.'

She was buried in the cemetery near the beach and airport. She had become one of the few fixed points of reference in Derek's world, someone he could idealize, even sentimentalize, in his poetry and interviews while perhaps leaving out some of the vitality, energy, and emotions that made her unique and which he had inherited from her, including her sense of leadership and the dramatic.

The St Lucia *Star* on 26 May carried a headline 'I'm ready to die for my country!'. Walcott had called on the government to abandon its plans to develop the Pitons into a tourist resort. Colin Tennant, the 3rd Baron Glenconner, who had made Mustique fashionable, had turned his attention to St Lucia. Jalousie was the 320-acre holiday complex with 115 bungalows he built near the Pitons. He was selling it to a Miami group while hoping to develop the adjoining estate. The government argued that the Pitons had to be treated as an economic resource and developed with tourism replacing bananas. In February, a month after being 'Honoured' Walcott called the government's claims 'the argument of whores!' And said he would do what he could to prevent it.

The government hoped Walcott had had his say; it was planning a June Arts Festival centred around Walcott and his works. Instead Walcott announced from Boston that he wanted no honours or anything to do with Compton's government which, he claimed, was going to sell the Pitons to a group of Iranians. Walcott belonged to the recently formed St Lucia Environmental and Development Association, a watchdog group threatening action over the Pitons. The government accused 'armchair politicians' in Boston and Barbados 'who have put nothing into the community' of misleading people.

The controversy was to continue as Greenpeace joined in, the Organisation of American States recommended that the Pitons be designated a World Heritage site, and, after being awarded the Nobel Prize, Walcott criticized Colin Tennant to the British press. The Pitons were the symbol of St Lucia, they are even symbolically on the St Lucian flag, designed by Dunstan St Omer; besides their natural beauty their use stood for the future of St Lucia. Walcott had seen how in other islands foreigners would own the hotels and the local people became waiters. One of the first incidents in *Omeros* is Helen quitting her job at the hotel after being humiliated by tourists.[6]

In early July Walcott surprised everyone by agreeing to participate in the annual graduation ceremony at St Mary's College. He was taking root again. One of the teachers sung his calypso 'Tribute to Derek Walcott'. Yasmin Odlum, George Odlum's daughter, who was teaching at St Mary's, introduced Walcott who was not only a celebrity poet but also a political celebrity at the time, as he had been attacked in the press by government ministers for his criticism of the Jalousie project. Walcott mocked patriotism; people were killed by patriots. Poetry had no country except conscience. That was why so many poets had been jailed, tortured, and shot. People were contradictions who would kill their brothers with one hand, while protesting against injustice with the other. He then read from *Omeros*. He stayed again at the cottage where he had written most of *Omeros* during the previous three years.

Meanwhile the Carib Theatre Company production of *Remembrance* ran 12 July–11 August at the Tricycle Theatre, Kilburn, London, directed by Anton Phillips, with Norman Beaton as Albert Perez Jordan and Barbara Assoon as Mabel. The Carib had earlier produced *Pantomime*. Pamela Beshoff in the *Weekly Gleaner* (31 July) said that Norman Beaton had at last found a role to test his talents and described *Remembrance* as complex, challenging, and stimulating. *Time Out* (25 July) said that it was a classic, but that when it was performed in 1987 it obviously needed a weighty actor, which it now had in Beaton. Charles Spencer in the *Daily Telegraph* (19 July) wrote that *Remembrance* was a 'real play, not an empty display of ethnic exuberance'. It was powerful, dense, difficult, poetic, confusing, even clumsy, with too much unwieldily crammed into a small space, but full of humour, passion, and closely argued intelligence. *City Limits* (26 July) disagreed; it was 'an extremely leaky vessel'. There were many more productions of Walcott's plays in the United States than in England, but in England they were being performed in London, had become part of the repertoire of Black British theatre, had nationally known directors and actors, and received attention in the national press.

Walcott had for several decades withdrawn himself from the British literary scene, but after the Queen's Medal and the *Arena* television interview, he was once more becoming part of its consciousness as a black, Commonwealth, and international writer. In England he was being taught as part of Commonwealth literature courses in universities and as part of the new core school syllabus. Towards the end of the year John Figueroa would give a one-day seminar (1 December) on 'The Poetry of Derek Walcott' at the Commonwealth Institute, London.

Omeros was scheduled to be published in late August for the start of the new season. Farrar, Straus and Giroux knew that they had a major work which needed publicity, reviews, and promotion. It was preceded by a letter (17 August) from Roger Straus to reviewers saying that *Omeros* was one of the most beautiful and important books published by Farrar, Straus and Giroux and should be given careful attention. A list was drawn up of people, radio and television stations, and newspapers to contact for possible reviews and interviews, including such National Public Radio programmes as *A Movable Feast, All Things Considered, Weekend All Things Considered, Morning Edition, Fresh Air*, Minnesota Public Radio, the *New York Times*, the *Washington Post*, and the *Boston Globe Magazine*. A few days later (20 August) Farrar, Straus and Giroux sent a letter to 'Dear Interviewer' saying Walcott would be in New York 12–13 September and available 'to discuss his extraordinary new poem OMEROS'. He came to New York on Sunday, 9

September. On Wednesday *Omeros* was launched at the Players Club, 16 Gramercy Park. On Thursday, 13 September, at 11.30 a.m. there was a *New York Times* photo session at Farrar, Straus and Giroux, at 12 p.m. an interview with Don Bruckner for the *New York Times* arts section, at 2.30 p.m. an interview with David Streitfield for the *Washington Post* at the Gramercy Park Hotel Restaurant, and a meeting at 4 p.m. with James Atlas of the *New York Times Magazine* to discuss an article on Seamus Heaney. Walcott agreed to do the article on Heaney by the end of October. Brodsky had married again, in Stockholm in early September; there was a Farrar, Straus and Giroux party for him for which Walcott wrote an epithalamium. Walcott was back in St Lucia for a launching of *Omeros* at the Central Library in Castries on Friday, 14 September. The St Lucian newspapers mentioned that many of the events in the book took place at Gros Ilet.

Starting 21 September, Walcott was in England, Wales, and Ireland to promote *Omeros*. Brodsky was at some of the readings with Walcott. On 29 September at 5 p.m. Walcott gave the Ronald Duncan Lecture, 'Modern Poetry and the Theatre', for the Poetry Book Society as part of the South Bank Poetry International. Ronald Duncan (1914–82) was a poet, playwright, and librettist, and a founder of the English Stage Company. The lecture was published as 'The Poet in the Theatre' by the Poetry Book Society and separately in *Poetry Review* (Winter 1990/1). Like many of Walcott's lectures, it was transcribed from tape and sent to him for corrections. It was in part a plea for the richness of verse drama in contrast to the minimalism of Beckett. At 8 p.m. Walcott read along with Brodsky also for the Poetry Book Society, which offered its members in 1990 the Faber edition of *Omeros* along with Seamus Heaney's *New Selected Poems 1966–1987*, Philip Larkin's *Collected Poems*, and a book of *Sixty Women Poets*.

The next day he read at the Watershed Media Centre, Bristol. This was the first event in a twelve-day Bristol Poetry Extra, co-ordinated by the Avon Poetry Festival. On 1 October Shaun McCarthy, chair of the Avon Poetry Festival, recorded a ninety-minute interview with Walcott which was published the next year in the special Walcott issue of *OUTPOSTS*.[7]

Walcott remarked that when he started there was no media blitz, no instant stardom, of the kind that presently surrounded the arts. It took time to learn how to write about the Caribbean. It was like American literature discovering its own voice with Twain. A writer, literature, or culture evolved to find its own voice. It is not true to say that he has merged European metrics with Caribbean speech. Much of what is called European is traditional and universal. The heartbeat, breathing, create human rhythms. You cannot be free of them. In jazz the saxophone might seem to be playing freely, but underneath there is the bass. The bass is universal. You cannot improvise without a beat behind you. Calypso is a stanzaic form with an echo at the bottom and a chorus at the end. It is in octosyllabics and pentameters. The calypso is often in couplets, eight lines to a stanza, then a chorus of a repeated last line. Or two quatrains making eight lines. This is no different from other poetry.

Such traditions are human. Metre is more of a problem as there are differences according to the 'instrument', by which Walcott means cultural conventions. West Indian rhythm is very percussive. The West Indian oral tradition is more formal and metric than much modern poetry. In all ages it is the rhythm beneath language that propels poetry and song. St Lucia is very beautiful, but there was a need to paint, record, describe, and make sense of it. The sense of the place has stayed with him. Even now he feels there is not much time left to get it right; when he paints watercolours he feels the same excitement as before since there are not many West Indians still doing watercolours.

He, Naipaul, and others of his generation are political in the sense of being always conscious of the withdrawal of the empire. Regardless of exploitation and the limits set for non-whites, it was mostly a benign neglect; there was not the same tyranny as at present. Government is now being used to intimidate and harass people. Those who talk loudest about exploitation are those who rip you off after independence. His generation continues to write about the shift of power in world history. Writers do not take sides. Rather the Caribbean is political because dramatic—too melodramatic. It was a feudal situation, with the large sugar plantations, and the racial situation, so writers had to examine it, but a writer's compassion must go to everyone and not just to one race. As soon as you write about an economic condition you are a political writer; to portray fisherman exasperated by poverty cursing God is to show political anger. Poets should not accommodate themselves to anything. Once you start saying you must reach a wider audience you can never stop. Great plays can be played anyplace. A poem is an example of the finest intelligence of the poet. You cannot say I am going to write a poem using only part of my intelligence. Once you say you must reach as many people as possible you are on the road to becoming a revolutionary or a fanatic killing those who do not think like you. Poetry is a political state outside of the actual politics of state. Because it is a state within a state it drives tyrants crazy.

Omeros is an attempt to write at a distance, so it became novelistic in scale, technically challenging. Narration, the active voice, can be heard daily in Trinidad, in calypso, the ballad singer, the political satirist. The idea of story-telling has gone out in cities where populations are too fragmented and lives are individualistic. In smaller places the writer has to be a storyteller. Too many poets write for little magazines that only poets read. Walcott said he was working on a play that is close to rap. It is in couplets, sometimes alternating rhymes. A musical. In rhyme you have to get the idea down in a line. You do not choose the best form. The structure comes from the phrases. The first phrase may reveal the shape of the poem. A simile is not an artificial device. It is part of the rhythm of natural human narration. You say something is happening and want to amplify it with 'like'. Craft requires technical admiration. Technical slackness is infuriating. Anarchy is egotistical. His friend James Tate says that contemporary free verse consists of poets writing something like 'Something hurt me'. The sound of poetry cannot be written down. Poets should know by heart what they write. They should aim at incantation. Writers should write every day. You do not try to write a poem a day, but you should practise. Writing for the theatre helps a poet because of the affinity between verse and theatre. Theatre makes poetry more colloquial, helps develop immediacy.

The next day (2 October) *Third Ear* on BBC Radio 3 broadcast Christopher Bigsby's interview with Walcott about his life and work, especially about the influence of St Lucia. On 15 October *Poetry Please!* on BBC Radio 4 broadcast Simon Rae's interview with Walcott who read 'Ruins of a Great House'. The next week's broadcast continued the interview and Walcott read from *Sea Grapes* and 'Midsummer xiv'. Walcott was in Dublin to read (3 October) from *Omeros* for the Irish launch at Peppercanister Church, sometimes used for major literary readings. He was also in Ireland to attend Seamus Heaney's *The Cure at Troy* (a version of Sophocles' *Philoctetes*) by the Field Day Theatre Company at Guildhall, Derry, Northern Ireland. It opened on 1 October. The Nobel Prize in Literature was announced the first week in October and Walcott and Gordimer were said to be finalists; it went to Octavio Paz.

The Irish trip is recalled in the unpublished article, 'Heaney's Ireland', originally intended for the *New York Times*, which was due by November. Nine months later Walcott was still labouring on it after another trip to Ireland and visit with Heaney; the seventeen-page draft that survives in the Toronto collection is dated 19 August 1991. Besides Walcott's awareness of the Irish landscape both north and south, comments on the chasteness of the translation, and a discussion of Patrick Kavanagh's poetry as a possible alternative to Joyce's internationalism, Walcott argues for Heaney as someone who remains provincial, rooted in locality, while avoiding provinciality. This is what Walcott regards as the great literary movement of our time.

Readings and promotion of *Omeros* continued between teaching assignments after he returned to the United States. He was in San Diego (8–10 November) on a panel concerning Cultural Diversity in American Theatre. The next week, 15 November, he flew from Boston to New York for an interview at WNYC Television Studios. He left Boston at 11 a.m., arrived at LaGuardia at 12.15 p.m. and had to keep receipts for reimbursement for travel to and from the airport. In New York a driver was waiting to take him directly to the studio where a 1.30 p.m. arrival would allow time for lunch and make-up before taping at 2.45 p.m. He stayed at the Gramercy Park Hotel. On Monday, 19 November, Walcott read from *Omeros*, 6.30–9.30 p.m., with a thirty-minute intermission, at the Mitzi E. Newhouse Theatre, Lincoln Center. This was a major reading, a real performance, to read from a poem for well over two hours. It was arranged by Greg Mosher, director of the Lincoln Center Theatre, who had worked with Walcott in Chicago and was one of his fans. On 5 December Walcott was reading from *Omeros* in Kansas City at the University of Missouri as part of the Midwest Poets series and for *New Letters*, which had since the 1970s expanded to a second publication, the *New Letters Review of Books*, and *New Letters On the Air*.

In the *New Letters* interview Walcott said *Omeros* was epical in the scale of the undertaking, geography, and history, but it was not an epic. It was not heroic. 'I certainly don't see myself as a hero of an epic.' Different characters had heroic elements, even Plunkett, who was wounded in a war, although he was a bit ridiculous. There were dialogue and dramatic encounters as in plays, but also elements of a scenario for a film script. There was much cinematic editing, jumping between four or five stories. As in a novel there was geography, description, action, weather. Walcott had not known what to expect as the poem proceeded. He had not had a plot in advance. He had written sequences and had needed to connect them. His main aim as a writer was to give a clear picture of life in the Caribbean, especially its beauty. In the middle passage of the book Achille the fisherman has a sunstroke and 'goes back' to Africa and sees someone he thinks is his ancestor from generations ago. But Achille is not an African. His name is Achille; he has become something else. Everyone in the Americas had come from elsewhere and had become American, and this was especially true of the Caribbean. Walcott concluded this interview like others by saying he knew exactly where he wanted to be, at a beach in the Caribbean swimming, writing, and painting.[8]

Walcott returned to Trinidad (22 December) to see his family at Christmas and then stayed at the Villa Beach Cottages in St Lucia from 28 December until the second week of January, when readings from *Omeros* continued into most of 1991. There was a production of *Pantomime* 17–19 January at Washington University, St Louis. Walcott read on the 18th. This was the first time he met William Gass; their conversation after reading led to Walcott's 1997 reading at Gass's Dual Muse symposia.

The next major reading was 30–1 January at Butler University, Indianapolis. The President of Butler University had been at Boston University and knew Walcott. The weather was bad and Walcott flew in with a bad cold, a runny nose, and a sore throat. He was still smoking cigarettes. There was a question and answer and book-signing period after the reading, after which Walcott requested to return to his hotel. The next day he conducted a workshop with poetry students, some outsiders, and members of faculty. His cold and voice were so bad that the teacher suggested cancelling the class, but Walcott wanted to do it. Normally such classes after public readings at Butler University are question and answer sessions, but Walcott asked if the students and faculty had any of their poems with them and then proceeded to discuss what they gave him. In one case he read out the first line then folded the page at the end of line as a way of visually demonstrating the sprawl and lack of form. He said that with lines of such varied length, often much longer than the first line, the reader would find it difficult to follow the rhythm. The first line creates an expectation of a rhythm and form. There were a few disciples there of Etheridge Knight, an African-American poet, who attacked Walcott for lack of racial solidity and for writing poetry filled with learned allusions over the head of the black community. This lasted five to ten minutes during which Walcott kept his cool and tried to keep the discussion at an intellectual level. After the class he let off steam by saying to the teacher that he was tired of being out-niggered by niggers. The teacher who is used to black talk and not unfamiliar with the n-word was surprised. The teacher had been at a black writer's conference in Boston with Etheridge Knight during the early 1980s; Walcott, Michael Harper, and Sam Allen were also there and he remembered Walcott and Knight seeming to get along well. Once more the disciples were less tolerant than their models.[9]

During February Walcott read in New Hampshire (6), Rochester (7–8), and at Amherst College (20). Caryl Phillips, who was now directing a creative writing programme at Amherst College, arranged for Walcott to read. Brodsky came over from Mount Holyoke College. Another old Walcott friend was the poet James Tate from the University of Massachusetts-Amherst. Phillips and Walcott were becoming close friends; both stayed at the Gramercy Park Hotel in New York, had meals together in New York and Boston, and Phillips was one of the few invited to evenings with Heaney, Walcott, and Brodsky.

The reviews of *Omeros* were exceptionally good. Walcott had been recognized for years as one of the best living poets but the recognition was not broad, not the kind that went beyond poets, some literary critics, and professors of Commonwealth literature. With *Omeros* that changed. Walcott had the kind of breakthrough in the United States and England to a wider readership that comes to novelists. The *Independent* called it 'Amazing', the *New Statesman* called it 'this great poem', 'a great poem' agreed the *Virginia Quarterly Review*. In November the Earl of Gowrie described *Omeros* as a 'masterpiece' in the *Daily Telegraph*, a view echoed by the *Harvard Book Review*, 'Only Walcott . . . could write a masterpiece like *Omeros* . . . a great poem.' Oliver Taplin said 'it may be hasty to nominate it in the same breath as *Ulysses*; yet I am far from alone in feeling that a major new work of literature has just appeared, one that will stand the test of time, of repeated rereadings and rediscovery'. The poet Sean O'Brien in the *TLS* was as impressed if more cautious: 'an extraordinarily ambitious undertaking . . . Walcott's powers of evocation seem inexhaustible.'[10] And so it went on.

Among those who declared it one of their books of the year were Marina Warner ('the most inspired poem I've read for a long time'), John Carey ('A new English epic is a rarity, and one as magnificent as . . . *Omeros* has not appeared this century'), Salman Rushdie, Hermione Lee, Adewale Maja-Pearce ('seeks to do for West Indian literature what Dante did for Italian; provide the source from which all else will flow').

The *New York Times Book Review* under 'Editor's Choice' listed *Omeros* as one of the fourteen Best Books of 1990 along with *The Complete Poems* of Anna Akhmatova, Nadine Gordimer's *My Son's Story*, A. S. Byatt's *Possession,* John Updike's *Rabbit at Rest,* Alice Munro's *Friend of My Youth,* and Martin Amis's *London Fields.* Except for the translation from Russian into English of Akhmatova, who died in 1966, *Omeros* was the only volume of poetry. Beyond the novels and books of short stories I have listed the other books were mostly biographies (T. E. Lawrence, Simone de Beauvoir, and Vladimir Nabokov) or about world politics. The short description of *Omeros* spoke of its ordinary people, richness of story, encompassing of the world's history, Walcott's humour, emotional depth, imagery, and inventive language. The Caribbean poem was seen as timeless, universal, 'history, all of it, belongs to us'. By January there was a second printing which Farrar, Straus and Giroux advertised with quotes from the *New York Times Book Review* and the *Washington Post Book World.*

Omeros consists of 2,500 stanzas, over 7,000 lines. There are seven books, sixty-four chapters, each divided into three sections of varied length. The rhythm is based on trochaic hexameter, six feet to a line, usually two-syllable feet, with a stress and unstressed syllable, or two stresses at times. The stanzas consist of three lines, basically Dante's *terza rima,* except that Walcott keeps varying the rhyme scheme and uses many unusual rhymes, half-rhymes, visual rhymes, even comic rhymes, to keep the form alive and in motion. In the *New Yorker* the poet Brad Leithauser spoke of it as 'a rhyme casebook' and devoted much space to the many kinds of rhymes.[11] Three basic strands, or kinds of material, are interwoven as its narrative. There are the lives of the poorer black St Lucians, especially Hector and Achille who compete for Helen, and Ma Kilman who is trying to cure Philoctete, a fisherman, of his wound. There are Dennis and Maude Plunkett and the other whites and their relationship to St Lucia. The third strand is the narrator, Walcott, his personality, opinions, and autobiography. *Omeros* is mostly realistic and one of Walcott's many attempts to reclaim for poetry some of the story-telling, colloquial language, social observation, varied perspectives, and invention that have become part of the novel. It also in its themes recalls some of Walcott's previous works: the wound to the black psyche caused by the Middle Passage and slavery, the impossibility of restoring what was lost, while a dream of a return to Africa can be a form of mental healing; there is the argument that all peoples of the Caribbean are equally castaways, the demonstration that the white Englishman or woman becomes native by living and loving the place.

The spine of the poem consists of specific themes governing each book. Each book has its theme. Book One starts with many epic conventions including a vision, a dedication, and the narrative beginning mid-story. Walcott's vision of Helen concludes with his taking on the vocation of poet from his father. The theme is that life consists of wounds. The characters are introduced in a state of wounded disorder. Helen, for instance, has quit her job at the restaurant after being insulted by a tourist, the Plunketts have quarrelled, Ma Kilman cannot cure Philoctete, who has been wounded in a fishing accident. Dennis was wounded in the Second World War and came to St Lucia to settle.

Book Two concerns history and the search for origins. Plunkett decides to create a history for St Lucia and researches into its past as he looks for his ancestors, as a way of justifying both the glory of the island and his being there. Maude is making a tapestry of its birds. Plunkett is like Odysseus in seeking a home and lost son, Maude is Penelope embroidering a tapestry. On the fishing boat Achille has a vision. Book Three concerns journeys. Achille imagines himself reversing the Middle Passage and returning to Africa where he finds his ancestor's village and his ancestor Afolable. In the vision he is enslaved and sent to the New World. Walcott leaves St Lucia after speaking with his now elderly mother. Books Four and Five are about empires and poetry. Walcott in Boston imagines himself at the battle of Wounded Knee, thinks about empires, Irish poetry, and the British. Book Six is about mourning and love. Walcott returns to St Lucia and on the way to his hotel he learns of the death of Hector in a motor accident. Maude also dies. Achille and Helen join Plunkett in mourning. There is love for others. Helen is pregnant with Hector's child. Helen returns to Achille, Achille and Philoctete dance. Book Seven is of cures. Omeros leads Walcott to a volcano to cure him of his vanity as a poet.

The last third of *Omeros* is deconstructive, anti-myth, anti-metaphor, as both Plunkett and the narrator are found to be wrong. Joyce is the model because he is an Irish realist and an Irish internationalist (beyond nationalism), who created his race from daily life without mythic inflation.

There is a Caribbean tradition of autobiographical epic-like works, to which *Omeros* is related, although it goes far beyond, in the sense of including more of the world, then anything by Perse, Césaire, or Wilson Harris. Like the traditional epic it makes use of a long physical journey, a discovery of previous alien parts of the world. Usually the hero's journey is that of the clan, people, or nation. Here is a double voyage, Walcott's voyage and that of foreigners to St Lucia, the colonizing and settlement of the island, whether by French, English, or through African slaves. As the background of the island's history fills in there is a new world epic, a history, although offered in bits and pieces. Then there is the epic of the narrator,

Walcott, again offered in bits and pieces, with its assumed knowledge of the author's own life, leaving St Lucia to explore the world, then returning to resettle.

The epic is usually thought of as a celebration of the nation and the building of the nation. In this sense *Omeros* is a fragmented epic of a fragmented St Lucia and perhaps of the whole Caribbean. Fragmented in the sense of a mosaic, something composed of distinct parts, something put together from bits to make a society, nation, culture, in which the bits still show, the divisions are still there, distinctive, and are likely to remain so, but this is the essence of this situation, its being together and whole despite the apparent differences of which it is made. This would correspond to the notion of creolization current in the Caribbean in contrast to the North American opposites of assimilation and separation. Creolization as the Caribbeanization of various groups that share parts of a common culture while still retaining some of their cultural differences rather than becoming a homogeneous new organism.

Omeros, like many of Walcott's long poems, appears at times to offer a parallel to such epics as the *Odyssey* and *The Divine Comedy*, but the similarities are intermittent, occasional, although there are enough to suggest some analogy. The aim is to avoid an allegorical parallel, a comparison that would say that although the West Indies appears inferior to the classics it is really as elevated a subject. Such a method would exemplify Walcott's warnings about comparisons which treat the New World as something thought to be inferior and which can only be seen as valuable if it matches up to the Old World. Instead Walcott's approach is that the West Indian experience is central, universal, and that, if you could restore the colour and original context, the world of the epics would be found little different from that of St Lucia today. The St Lucian experience is universal, timeless, classic, unlike how Europe has over the centuries imagined the world and art of the classics. Walcott started out by claiming it was necessary to treat local subject-matter within European forms, now the form itself is being challenged by the subject-matter.

Omeros is, to use the jargon of the academy, postmodern in its fragmentation, ironies, self-awareness, mixture of autobiography and fiction, and especially postmodern in the way the final third of the poem questions many illusions and assumptions of the early parts. This corresponds to Walcott's increasing concern that he was misusing and romanticizing the peasants, the past, and St Lucia as a source of his art. Needless to say *Omeros* is post-colonial in declaring its independence of comparisons to another system of valuation, in claiming the centrality of the St Lucian experience. I do not think it is post-colonial in the sense of answering back, of resisting. That would be the kind of mirror reversal Walcott tries to avoid. He is saying you are not free as long as you feel your replies reinstate dependency, the centrality and dominance of that which your oppose. Ned Thomas, Walcott's Welsh friend, put it clearly:

even the protest against this dependent condition is still controlled by that which it reacts against: no reagent is a free agent. But whatever creates a new centre of consciousness is truly liberating, and this is what love does, it endears places to us, surrounds them with an air of glory, creates a centre from which we can look outwards.[12]

One reason Walcott objects to describing *Omeros* as an epic is because of the importance of the narrator. He has in mind Joyce's distinctions of the epic as standing at a distance from the artist, the lyrical as a direct expression of the artist, and the dramatic as the genre which is Mr In-Between. *Omeros* moves back and forth between such categories, and has a strong lyric element not only in the presence of the narrator and autobiographical details, but also in its movement from Affliction to Cure. There is the obvious autobiographical source of the poem in Walcott's working himself out of the emotional depression caused by the end of his third marriage, with Helen being a representation of aspects of Norline, by undertaking a long work cure. There is also the ritual aspects of the Philoctete story, which has long fascinated Walcott, and which is also in Heaney's play. Whereas Walcott's early writings tried to keep conflict unresolved and a source of creative energy, these later works aim for resolution, curing, wholeness.

In an excellent short review Phoebe Pettingell mentions that *Omeros* is built around a love triangle (Achille, Hector, Helen) seen through the eyes of Philoctete, Ma Kilman, and Seven Seas. Major Plunkett and his wife Maude seem survivors of the colonial era; they provide an alternative triangle as Plunkett desires Helen, whom his wife (Penelope) treats harshly. Plunkett is no longer really British and could not survive there; he is part of the life of the island, even his title is a fraud. They are in part based on Walcott's parents. Walcott is Telemachus searching for his literary parentage. He is the cosmopolitan returning home as a tourist, sitting in a hotel. The central question is what is our culture, our past? No one is indigenous to the West Indies but they belong no where else. Just as Plunkett has a phoney title, so he and Walcott are uncomfortable about the use of the classical tradition. Looking for answers, Walcott takes the reader on a literary pilgrimage; the Greek revival architecture of Athens, Georgia, reminds him that Greeks also built their civilization on slavery. London is T. S. Eliot. Major writers are all exiles—Herbert, Milosz, Joyce. Throughout the world poets are making new epics of their people. All places and cultures have contributed to St Lucia. Walcott is the St Lucian Homer; most of his characters are aspects of himself as well as the island.[13]

During the summer of 1990 Walcott was interviewed by Professor Luigi Sampietro of Milan, who commented upon the lack of despair in Walcott's poetry. Walcott felt that in contrast to the European writer's burden of such recent history as the concentration camps, wartime destruction, and migrant peoples, the Caribbean landscape is bracing in its natural beauty, its lack of visible ruins, and the presence of the sea. He is always eager to return to the Caribbean where he can write and paint calmly. The composition of poetry is syllable by syllable, letter by letter. The artist is like Robinson Crusoe walking along a beach and thinking; communion is with the noise of the sea, and natural surroundings, not the noise of crowds. Being brought up as a Methodist made him self-reliant; there is a 'direct relationship to a belief in God or not'.

Walcott felt that many contemporary American and English poets were cautious and this resulted in uninteresting metres and lack of rhyme. Poetry is song. He had learned from Joyce, Hemingway, and Nabokov, but most contemporary prose is unexciting. Ideas can be expressed in poetry. 'There is no idea that Dante or John Donne couldn't express in poetry.' There is, however, the danger of ideas being topical, changing, pompous, and platitudinous. It is better to begin with the evidence of experience. Suddenly the metre or thought cracks open and you are startled by something electric, alarming and heightening, astonishing. Because of the sea Caribbean poetry has width and is ambitious. Brathwaite's poetry has an immense scope like a large mural of the Caribbean taking in aspects of Caribbean experience in England and the United States. It has many characters and voices. Neither Brathwaite nor Walcott thinks in dialect. Wilson Harris is brilliant, a genius, but his later work has become too difficult and insistent. Naipaul's early works are tragicomedies, but he is immature; he wants to astonish and shock.

Division is common to Caribbean experience—the diaspora from Africa, the division between islands, the feeling that every man is an island, the racial divisions, the sense of being of mixed blood, the realization that the black can be as cruel as the white. Man suffers from an original sin, an original fault, that requires spiritual exercise in poetry or prayer, which can provide solace although not necessarily heal the wound. Solace is a gift to others that may not help the person who gives it; a poem survives and is beautiful although it may have much pain in it. The daily life of a poet is of no consequence, the work is of value. But art is not that important, 'the real experience is really between God and yourself'.[14]

Sampietro's interview continued with a discussion of Omeros. Walcott began without a clear idea of the form, writing sections in unrhymed rough pentameter, others in couplets, but eventually, except for a few chapters, the shape became a twelve-syllable rough textured *terza rima*. Pentameter felt too conventional, predetermined, and with rhymes was likely to fall into couplets and quatrains with echoes of Milton, Tennyson, or Victorian poetry. Walcott explained that he had wanted a longer line, a hexameter line, with the feel of prose space for narrative and action. Pentameter emphasizes the beat and is difficult to use for the banal, whereas his line is flexible, leaves room for more caesuras, and can be relaxed or accelerated. This felt like a Homeric line. Quatrains are 'self-completing' and, unlike *terza rima*, do not propel into the next stanza. *Terza rima* forces the writer forward through the need to rhyme. Rhyme is propulsion, not stasis, it pushes. The chapters are of uneven length to avoid a self-conscious shape that would call attention to itself and the writer. Walcott wanted a poem for reading not for admiring its design. Near the middle of the book he allowed himself a pivotal lyric section in which the narrator summarizes his experience, but otherwise he kept with description.

A modern long poem is meant to be read, not recited. There are no more tribal bards dignifying a culture through a sense of history and the future. Such a sense of destiny and power is dangerous in the twentieth century. Even Whitman wrote in a lyrical personal manner without a story; that is democratic. *Omeros* is not the great Caribbean epic. It has epical elements, such as width, variety, and perhaps heroes, but it is not meant to redeem history or dignify a race. It celebrates 'the diurnal, day-to-day heroism of people', such as the fishermen, who do not think of expanding their power. Their relationship is to the weather, to history, and slavery.

A poem is commemorative, an act of gratitude; the greatest poetry is 'beyond the idea of mortality . . . beyond the idea of the ephemeral . . . beyond the idea of the writer's own life'. Life and death remain mysteries. To say that life consists of brutal purposeless existence is unsatisfactory. Poetry is a sacred occupation, which may be the beginning of a religion or give a 'sense beyond religion'.

There are echoes of Greek culture in *Omeros* because Caribbean culture often replicates it. 'There has never been a place that has had such a concentration in a tight space of all the cultures of the world—in places like Trinidad and Jamaica. It is actually a more interesting place than ancient Greece . . . how many cultures were fed into ancient Greece?' The Caribbean is made of various races with a multiplicity of individual possibilities. Part of the Caribbean heritage is Western education with its Greek echoes. Everybody knows the references and associations, Odysseus the Eternal Wanderer, Helen the Eternal Beauty, Achilles the Eternal Warrior. They are household names and magnify 'everybody'. Someone sailing the ocean alone or trying to get home is Odysseus; every culture, especially marine culture, has such stories of quests, people lost, returns. They are part of folklore. The simplicity of the Caribbean must be like the Greek islands; Homer's world must have been similar.[15]

In March 1991 *Omeros* won the W. H. Smith prize, unexpectedly winning instead of the usual novels and other prose, and Walcott would be awarded £10,000. Faber reprinted 5,000 copies of *Omeros*. Matthew Evans of Faber accepted the award at the Royal Festival Hall as Walcott was in Boston rehearsing *Steel*. The British press seemed upset by Walcott not himself being at the prize ceremony and carried stories about Evans pleading with Walcott to come. Walcott sent an amusing, self-mocking, acceptance speech for Evans to read, so that was all right, but Walcott was quoted as complaining that he had to pay American tax on the prize. The judges were said to have made side bets as to how long it would take for Walcott to win the Nobel Prize.

Although Walcott's poems were in most anthologies he was not often studied in the United States. Until the Nobel Prize he was seldom discussed by post-colonial theorists. With *Omeros* the situation rapidly changed; suddenly it was being taught in courses on the Epic, Long Poem, and Humanities for which Robert Hamner's *Epic of the Dispossessed: Derek Walcott's 'Omeros'* (1997) eventually provided an explicatory introduction and also included some of Walcott's drawings for the poem.

29

1991–1992 *The Odyssey*, Nobel Prize

WHILE *Omeros* was making its likely way towards Stockholm Walcott was once more becoming heavily involved in the theatre. The Trinidad Theatre Workshop had rented the Old Fire House in downtown Port of Spain, which it was slowly restoring to use as an arts centre, the dream of Walcott and others, including the Rockefeller Foundation, for almost two decades. Discussions between Walcott and the Trinidad Theatre Workshop continued like a love affair where both parties wanted to start again, but could not without either side surrendering. The Workshop was legally organized and had committees which had to meet and approve decisions, while Walcott was increasingly becoming more expensive, with famous friends he wanted to display. He still felt some bitterness—Trinidad could afford him and his work, it was a rich country, First World rather than Third, but there was not the kind of money available he wanted. He had worked hard to create theatre there, but he was not going to do it again without proper support and payment.

Meanwhile Adrian Noble (it was difficult not to title this chapter 'From Noble to the Nobel'), artistic director of the Royal Shakespeare Company, asked the bright young director Greg Doran what he might like to produce next and Doran said a play based on Homer's *Odyssey*. The epic had never been staged before as it seemed too massive for a single play. Colin Chambers, the RSC literary adviser, in the same role as Bryden had had earlier, said that Walcott might be the one to try. Doran agreed. Unlike the seventies when Walcott was unknown in the British theatre world he was now very well known, although not known personally to any members of the RSC. There were no longer any contacts or even institutional memories from the time of *The Joker of Seville*. Walcott's contacts in British theatre were now mostly with Black Theatre groups;

Doran and Chambers represented a new generation interested in the cultural results of decolonization and England's now large and settled West Indian and Asian communities. Royal Shakespeare Company actors and directors were working with black and multiracial theatre companies in South Africa. Indeed everyone was so busy no one had actually read *Omeros* although they knew of the W. H. Smith award.

Noble wrote to Walcott at Boston University (2 April) to ask whether he might be interested in exploring how Homer's *Odyssey* could be staged. This would be a collaboration between Walcott and Greg Doran. Doran wanted to have workshops for six weeks from mid-November until December, and perhaps move towards a 1992 production. Noble knew Walcott was presently in rehearsals, but suggested meeting and discussing the project in May when he understood Walcott would be in England. Noble hoped Walcott had not already had too much of Homer.

The workshops were intended for The Other Place. During the 1970s The Other Place in Stratford-upon-Avon, basically a tin hut, was famous as a studio and place for experimental theatre. It lasted until the late 1980s. Then in 1991 the Royal Shakespeare Company redeveloped the site, and planned to open a new Other Place theatre, with two rehearsal studios. Trevor Nunn would open the theatre with *Measure for Measure* and a play by Pam Gems. Beyond rehearsals the studios were intended for small works, training, and initiatives.

That April Walcott gave a short talk to a conference concerning C. L. R. James at Wellesley College, Massachusetts. James was coming into fashion as a post-Cold War generation looked at alternative forms of Marxism and as America began exploring black intellectual history. Walcott mentioned that the *Washington Post* had been after him for an article about James. He said James was a product of an older generation when the setting sun of the empire could be mistaken for the rising sun of West Indian literature. Walcott avoided the political legacy of James, which was the main preoccupation of the three-day conference. Instead he spoke about James's style as a writer, his interest in younger West Indian writers, and the unfortunate patriarchical attitude of James and other older West Indians, who even when well intended could be annoying in assuming you needed their approval. Such assurance resulted in a confident, balanced prose style and syntax. It was prose of the quality of Orwell or Nabokov, based on both Matthew Arnold and Marx. Lamming and Naipaul learned from James how to write elegantly without schizophrenic fury. James assumed he was of world class. He read widely and had a sensibility that absorbed everything. He loved great literature beyond ideas of race and politics.

Walcott then read a section of *Omeros* which he felt said something similar to what James said. This was followed by a heated, interesting discussion, in which Walcott was accused of being ahistorical and Walcott accused those who are historical of being polemical. Walcott attacked notions of historical cause and effect, placement, periodization, and similar ways of explaining and defining events. Such historicization was the way of the critic not the writer. For the artist everything was possible, life was filled with the potentiality for creation, and it was impossible to say what will or will not be creative. James's achievement was unrecognized because he was thought of as a brilliant '*black* man'.[1]

Once more Walcott argued that all such qualifications are insults, as are terms such as the Harlem Renaissance or West Indian Renaissance which suggest that this is not really significant, the real Renaissance was in Italy. Walcott's remarks carry to an extreme the tendency in his later work to dismiss discussion of cause and effect, the usual ways of explaining and historicizing events. He regarded all such contextualizations as Old Worldish, a limitation on the distinctiveness and newness of the Caribbean and the New World. The sea is real history because it is ever new, ever changing, never fixed, never predictable. It is life.

Walcott's views are sometimes said to be existential, but this is not an existentialism which depends on a context, society, Others, against which to define the Self. It is more like early Camus in its intense lyrical affirmation of the joy of being in the world, the awareness of nature, even places, rather than people as the Other to be experienced. Walcott's argument, however, is that any comparison to approved culture is likely to diminish himself, the black, the New World, since it assumes the European or something else as the standard of value. Walcott appears to be aiming at that essentializing of immediacy, individualization, and thing-in-itself-ness that has been characteristic of many New World writers.

In making such comparisons I am doing just what Walcott warns against. He becomes a regional offshoot of a North American tradition rather than unique and part of the Caribbean. We, however, normally work in metaphor, in contexts, by explaining cause and effect. He began his talk by explaining that James was a product of a particular class and time. So there will always be this conflict between metaphorizing and an absolute clarity, a conflict which represents a failure to achieve the pure poetry of John Clare and Dante, to use two very different poets offered by Walcott as praiseworthy.

As Walcott's views have become clearer they have also become more difficult to explain because they require realization in works of art. They are mystical or religious as they assume the divine in light, in the bounty of creation, and the created. But that is Walcott's own vision of what has been a common problem of modern secular art, how to write about the relationship of the experienced world to the Self. In these later works Walcott is concerned with the problems raised by Emerson's essay on 'Nature' or Wallace Stevens's *Notes Towards a Supreme Fiction* (more comparisons!), but the question of the perceiver's relationship to the natural world is in Walcott's work placed within a discussion of Caribbean culture and New versus Old World rather than Transcendentalism or Cubism.

He always was someone whose thought went beyond the superficialities of political arguments. Just as his poetry moved far beyond any influence, so his ideas had become his own, which was part of what he was claiming. Using the Holocaust and himself as subjects he had decided there was indeed something like an original fall whatever it was called. There was no question whether people are evil, it is obvious that they can be: the miracle was that they can be good, can love. In everything there is God, God expressed as light, the divine light that shines in each person or thing.

That is why a portrait of a coconut shell, part of a larger painting, can be used for the cover of *Collected Poems: 1948–1984* or why the landscape on the cover of *The Bounty* has energy, light, and life. And that is why Walcott's paintings need to be reproduced in colour, to bring out the light, and why watercolour is natural for his art, although his way of approaching it is not natural to watercolour. The seeds of his philosophy derive from his early Methodism, his father's approach to details in draughtmanship, his belief in a divine gift of poetry.

Margaret Walcott originally brought *Steel* to the attention of Robert Brustein, whom Derek knew from Yale Drama School. It was co-directed by Walcott and Robert Scanlan, under MacDermot's musical direction, with Richard Montgomery doing the scenery. The production was part of Harvard's American Repertory Theatre New Stages. It was originally intended for the Loeb Theatre but because of some delay was performed at the Hasty Pudding in Cambridge and scheduled to run 3–21 April, after which it moved to the Plays and Players Theatre, Philadelphia, in conjunction with the American Music Theatre Festival 26 April–11 May.

The rehearsals for *Steel* had not gone well. A leading actor was replaced, lines rewritten and redistributed, and critics asked not to review previews, but to wait as long as possible please. Colley's docudrama about the Desperados Steelband was long left behind, as Walcott and MacDermot turned the core notion of the history of steel band into a story about a Trinidadian musician who gives up a career in London to play 'pan', who falls in love with the daughter of a prostitute, who works for an unscrupulous Arab in a New York nightclub, who is tainted by success, and too much else, including the corruption of Trinidad by Arabs during the oil boom. There is a story about a shady land development deal based on events in Trinidad. Much of what Walcott included was historically true, the play could be seen as an allegory about Trinidad, even allegorical of Walcott's own career and its temptations, but like many Walcott plays it has never found its form. It is too much an oratorio with voice over.

Walcott and MacDermot had since *The Charlatan* been determined to make the American musical into a serious musical form and while doing so have a hit on Broadway, or at least in a New York theatre. It was not impossible, Stephen Sondheim and Harold Prince had renewed the musical while having immense successes, but Walcott and MacDermot were unable to put the pieces together correctly. *The Joker of Seville* is marvellous, a neglected theatre classic, but the other plays have too much plot, uninteresting characters, and music that sounds familiar. MacDermot had two Broadway hit plays, but since then there had been three Broadway flops. He and Walcott claimed not to be interested in Broadway, but they were not running from it. Too often the plays repeated themselves. Telling a musical's story through lyrics was already a Broadway cliché. Here there is a narrator, the *conteur*, a calypsonian, Growler, who acts like a master of revels, and who is supposed to know everything and pull the many narrative strands together. It is a device also found in many of Ben Jonson's comedies. Walcott and MacDermot have continued to revise *Steel*, workshopping bits when they have a chance.

Critics were divided about everything. Those who liked the play liked the direction and scenery; those who disliked the play disliked everything, and complained that it was too ambitious, sprawling, had too many stories and themes, and mixed too many forms. There was melodrama, politics, and documentary in a musical. The plot was explained in the programme, but one critic observed that the 'Cliff Notes for *Steel* would be as thick as *War and Peace*'. The *Boston Globe* said it started badly and became worse. Critics complained that there were thirty-three short musical numbers, one critic said more than forty, and little development of character.[2]

Walcott was 9–11 May at the 16th Annual Sandhills Writers' Conference at Augusta College, Augusta, Georgia, directed by Anthony Kellman (whose poetry is Walcott-influenced in its form and subjects) from Barbados. On Thursday, 9 May, Walcott gave a 'conference' at 1 p.m. and read that evening along with two other poets. On Friday morning he taught a poetry workshop and after lunch was on a panel discussing poetry. On Saturday morning he gave another conference. The conferences were individual tutorials based on writing sent in previously by the students. Perhaps sensing that he was still unknown to many of those who attended the conference, Walcott won over the participants by giving a brilliant explication of an Allen Tate poem which he had memorized. Walcott was in good form, kidding Kellman for having just had a novel accepted for publication. 'A Barbadian who can write novels?'[3]

During May he was in England and read from *Omeros* as part of the Readers' and Writers' Festival at the Midland Arts Centre in Birmingham. On 16 May he read from *Omeros* at the Royal Albion Hotel as part of the Brighton Festival, where he described Plunkett as 'spiritually native', implying that the white half of his own origins belonged in the West Indies if it loved it.[4] On 24 May he read from *Omeros* at the Hay-on-Wye Festival of Literature in Wales and discussed his work with Ned Thomas. Walcott was at a reading in London by Seamus Heaney when *Seeing Things* was launched. Afterwards they and Ted Hughes supped at the flat of Matthew Evans, a managing director of Faber.

Walcott was at Durrants Hotel, George Street, London, from 22 May. Doran spoke with Walcott, who wanted to come to Stratford-upon-Avon in early June. He wanted a self-catering flat for himself and Sigrid for two weeks, 4–16 June, and to spend three or four afternoons having a small group of actors read what he was writing. Walcott wanted a per diem and advance and reminded Doran that he needed a place himself in Stratford for the period. Doran saw him at the National Theatre on the 24th, after which Walcott was in Stockholm until early June.

The newspapers noted that Paul Simon was at Walcott's reading at the National Theatre and mentioned that they were great friends and that Walcott attended Simon's concerts. A few years previously Simon had asked a mutual friend on the *New Yorker* to introduce him to Walcott. They had met, got along, and Walcott introduced Simon to his classes at Boston and took him to a meeting at Farrar, Straus and Giroux. He played some drums at Simon's studio in New York and when Simon's *The Rhythm of the Saints* album (Phonodisc 3334) was released in 1990, 'The Coast' was dedicated 'For Anna, Elizabeth and Derek Walcott'. The *New York Times*, Sunday, 14 October 1990, reported that for lyrical inspiration Simon relied heavily on the words of Derek Walcott, the noted poet from St Vincent (*sic*) and quoted Simon, 'He's an extraordinary poet whose Caribbean settings seemed to fit what was going on . . . I would start out by using his words, then gradually wean myself from them and put in my own. I would come up with phrases that I thought sounded nice, although I had no idea what they meant.' This was the period of World Music and Simon had been using the world's cultures in his music. He also had another long-term project in mind which he was keeping to himself for the present. Walcott was interested in Simon as a popular poet with an immense following; there was a time when his 'Sound of Silence' was an anthem for poets, part of the American surrealist-lite, indicating areas of true poetry beyond speech from which poems were born. He was also part of that Hollywood stardom which Walcott wanted to enter. They got along, appreciated each other's work, and they seemed to enjoy being publicly identified with each other.[5]

Walcott had been asked to workshop one of his plays at the Royal Dramatic Theatre in Stockholm for a possible future production. They tried *Viva Detroit*, 30–1 May, but it seemed too small; instead *The Last Carnival* was decided upon as a production for 1992.

Using E. V. Rieu's Penguin prose translation published by Penguin for the story, Walcott worked rapidly on *The Odyssey*. He tried to reduce the epic to the essential story and find a form in which to put it. He approached the problem by seeing ancient Greece and the modern Caribbean as similar, both being societies that lived by and on the sea; they were societies affected by the rhythms of the sea and its weather; they were societies that produce wanderers and exiles, people who long for home, women who await the return of their men. Walcott saw Homer as a dialect poet, part of an oral tradition, someone who could range from the solemn to the vulgar. He found a form, the classical alexandrine line arranged in quatrains, a twelve-syllable line in quartets with alternating rhyme, which had the classicism of Corneille and Racine and allowed a rapid give and take from line to line. After twenty pages he knew it was possible and forged ahead as he had with projects in the past that others thought were still in the discussion phase.

Doran wrote to Adrian Noble (3 June) that the twenty pages and Walcott's enthusiasm were already moving events ahead of the exploratory two-week November workshop that was planned. Walcott was going to have a rough draft by the end of the summer, so instead of exploring an idea as an exercise they had to think about preparing for a production, timing, the actors, and much else. This would be the first RSC production by a 'black' author, and it would be an opportunity for integrated casting, having a truly multiracial company. Would it go on tour? Walcott was arriving soon, he would be with them for a few days, they would start reading the twenty pages, and there was much to discuss.

On 9 June Walcott was the 'castaway' on the popular BBC Radio 4 *Desert Island Discs* programme. The usual formula was followed of playing the celebrity's favourite records, asking which one book and luxury he wanted on a desert island. Walcott, still a heavy smoker (he did not give up until the summer of 1994), chose a carton of cigarettes, James Joyce's *Ulysses*, two tracks from Paul Simon's album *Born at the Right Time*, two numbers by Bob Marley ('Redemption Song' and 'No Woman No Cry'), a track from *Hair*, 'Ten to One is Murder' by The Mighty Sparrow, 'O Paradiso' from Meyerbeer's *L'Africana*, and the music for 'Les Sylphides'. In November 1992 the programme was rebroadcast after the publication of *The Odyssey* in connection with the Nobel Prize. Knowing Walcott's friendship with Galt MacDermot and Paul Simon, his interest in Caribbean music, in treatments of Africa, in ballet, and his continuing interest in Joyce along with Homeric epics, the selections are not surprising. 'O Paradiso' was background music for *In a Fine Castle* and Walcott had in 1977 explicated 'Ten to One is Murder' as an example of drama in calypso.

Walcott was in Stratford-upon-Avon 5–19 June and was paid £500 a week along with a per diem and accommodation, a distinct improvement on the years after he left Trinidad and was trying to get producers to pay for a hotel room or per diem. The Royal Shakespeare Company thought it was worth it; the project was already at the phase they had hoped to reach by the end of November. The script had grown from twenty to ninety pages. Walcott and Doran balanced each other. Walcott was wildly inventive, Doran was disciplined, trying to keep to the Homer story. The many manuscript drafts show Doran's active involvement as he questioned why this bit of Homer was left out, was this allusion too obscure, why not try it this way? Few people have been as willing to challenge Walcott, and those who have done so seldom know their art better than he does. Doran understood how to turn scripts into good yet serious theatre. Walcott could not dismiss him as American or Broadway; Doran was becoming famous for his productions of Shakespeare's more difficult plays. He had his own mind. The RSC now decided to commission the play, and Walcott with his usual enthusiasm wanted to know when a production would be mounted. The RSC needed a draft script, had to make a decision whether to stage it, and fit the play into its schedule. It would take at least nine months. They were thinking of a commission of £6,500.

In 1991 Dublin was the European City of Culture and those participating in the Second Dublin International Writers' Conference (18–21 June) included Louis Simpson, Marina Warner, Mario Vargas Llosa, Edmund White, Nuruddin Farah, and Miroslav Holub. On the 21st there was a 'Gala Reading' at the Great Hall of the Royal Hospital, by John Ashbery, James Berry, Tony Harrison, Louis Simpson, C. H. Sisson, Anne Stevenson, R. S. Thomas, and Walcott. Marina Warner and Walcott exchanged family histories; she is descended from a family of Caribbean landowners, has speculated on some racial mixing in the past, and feels that she has a relationship to colonial and post-colonial history. Walcott once more visited Heaney.

He returned to Trinidad and for two days in July gave a poetry workshop for twelve people, selected from sixty, at the Central Bank Towers in Port of Spain. He gave an informal lecture on metaphors and talked about discipline and great poetry. After Walcott returned to St Lucia Doran came for a week. Walcott finished (19 August) writing the unpublished 'Heaney's Ireland' concerning his 1990 and 1991 trips to Ireland and then worked on *The Odyssey* until early August. Some of his paintings were on display at the Artsibits Gallery in Castries and there were plans to display more at a new gallery in Cap Estate near Gros Islet. During August the well-known St Lucian painter Llewellyn Xavier had his first showing at Silver Point, his home studio. Walcott, Sigrid, and Dunstan were at the opening.

It seems to have been during this summer that Glissant and Walcott were at a FESTAG Colloquium in Guadeloupe, by invitation of Maryse Condé, who organized a lunch in Walcott's honour at Fort Royal, a tourist resort on the Leeward Coast of Guadeloupe. Before the 1992 Nobel Prize Walcott was unknown on Guadeloupe.

Back in the United States Walcott gave a poetry course with Brodsky at Columbia during the autumn. Harold Blumenfeld's musical composition 'Mythologies', based on three Walcott poems—'The Dream', 'Europa', and 'Archipelagoes'—premièred in Dallas on 30 September. Walcott read at Yale University (9 October), and was the featured speaker (24 October) when the

Mrs Giles Whiting Foundation in New York, with the guidance of Gerry Freund, gave ten young writers each $30,000. Walcott called such awards twice bounties. The authors were receiving a 'bounty', but there was the larger bounty of giving to 'the idea and the necessity of your true calling'.[6]

Walcott decided that now was the time to develop his drama classes into the Playwrights Theatre at Boston University, something more permanent. The building he was using had space for two small theatres and a few extra rooms. He hoped to put in seating, proper lighting, a sound and video taping system, dressing rooms, and administrative offices. He wanted to use the theatre for verse or poetic plays.

As usual his notion of poetry was less specific than might be expected as Walcott claimed that the use of common language by Mamet, Shepard, and Guare showed how it would be possible to create with the vigour of Elizabethan theatre. He spoke about the fusion of the lyric and the dramatic in the work of Philip Levine, Mark Strand, Michael Harper, Amy Clampitt, Brodsky, and Heaney. He saw this as having started with the confessional poetry of Lowell, Berryman, and Plath and said that American poetry had become dramatic, it could be put on stage. It was a matter of having space and commissioning the plays. He wanted to use professional Equity actors for staged readings.

Among those with whom he had spoken who agreed to assist were Strand, Heaney, Brodsky, Clampitt, C. K. Williams, and John Guare. Walcott mentioned Heaney's *The Cure at Troy*, and two plays by Brodsky. He even hoped for musicals. He wanted the poet present though the initial reading, casting, and rehearsals. While he hoped the theatre might lead to a revival of verse plays, the idea resembles some of the ideas that had previously gone into his own work, the modern verse play using contemporary language performed by excellent actors on a bare stage. He planned to commission and develop at least three verse plays a year which would become a series perhaps published through Boston University. He had a summary of estimated costs totalling over $225,000 of which $85,000 would be recurring to go into the commissioning, developing, and production of plays. In mid-September Walcott asked those he contacted for $5,000 to be patrons and invited them to a buffet dinner followed by an evening of poetry, music, and dance at the Tsai Performance Center at Boston University. This became a reading, 1 November, with Clampitt, August Wilson, Strand, Soyinka, and Brodsky for the benefit of the Playwrights Theatre and an expensive dinner afterwards with the performers.

Brodsky and Robert Pinsky also gave a poetry reading to a packed paying crowd at Boston Auditorium during November. Brodsky was not at his best and kept muddling his pages and stopping his reading. Les Murray came to Boston, read at MIT, and had dinner with Walcott in New York. From 19 November for ten days Walcott and Sigrid were at the Villa Beach Cottages.

Between 26 December and 25 January 1992, *Pantomime* was produced by the Arbee Company and directed in Port of Spain by Brenda Hughes, who told part of the story through a video sequence. Nigel Scott, the white Trinidadian, who had starred in the Trinidad Theatre Workshop *Joker* and in the video of Hart Crane, took the role of Harry Trewe. Walcott was in Trinidad, attended, and approved.

During 1991 the National Trust of St Lucia had begun Project Helen. Because of what was felt to be changes in the appearance of St Lucia with tourism and modernization, St Lucian painters were commissioned to travel around the island and paint landscapes. As there was no national art gallery this might be thought the basis for a collection. There were twelve Walcott paintings, including *Winter, Boston* which contrasts the perspective of looking out from the warm brightly coloured book-lined study of his Brookline apartment to the contrasting white snow outside. This was later used as a cover for *'What the Twilight Says'* *Essays* (1998). The other eleven were *Red Snapper, Braiding, Marina Channel—Gros Islet, Workman under Trees—Choc Bay, Reduit Bay, Garden—Rodney Bay, Causeway —Pigeon Island, The Holy Family, Musicians, Portrait of Thesbia,* and *Mooring— Reduit.* Four of the paintings—*The Holy Family, Reduit Bay, Causeway—Pigeon Island,* and *Musicians*—were later used on postcards by the National Trust and *The Holy Family* was one of the two used by the St Lucian government for telephone cards!

During the year Walcott wrote his most important article about art; it was about Jackie Hinkson, the Trinidadian watercolourist whom he admires. The article was indirectly a response to the recent fashion for deconstructive sculpture in Trinidad. Hinkson and the kind of art Walcott did was now thought old-fashioned. Walcott's reply shows what he is aiming for as a painter. 'A painter is known for his devotion to light.' Light 'catches' life and is 'that innate, organic radiance, however muted' found in Manet and Bacon. 'There is only one way to praise art, and that is through technique. That is what other artists admire, not subjects, themes, or novelty.' 'Masterful' artists were devourers, which meant energy, even possession, a power of 'reductions'. Hinkson's reductions were more than swift economy of drawing, 'in which mass is indicated without detail, but . . . the instant weight of water in copious brush-strokes, strokes which contain not only form but light and not merely light, but the precise time of day, if possible to the very half hour'.

In this compressed, packed, essay Walcott explained how the tropical land- sea- and skyscape differed from that in northern lands and contrasted Turner with Winslow Homer: 'our astonishment at Winslow Homer's tropical water-colours is for their glare, a brilliance rapidly indicated by not using more than two washes, one for colour, the other for action.'

This question of weight and accuracy of balance, this finesse of knowing how to load the brush in open-air painting, is of course admirable because it is made simple, and demands a concentration on the instant, one that must adapt to the speed and betrayal of changing clouds and the shadows made by these clouds . . . so that three o'clock in the afternoon does not look like five o'clock in another, later corner of the surface.

In poor painting nature 'out-paced the painter' and false details were added. Time was a 'condition' of all paintings including abstractions and action paintings where the response was supposedly to the subconscious instant. But the watercolour painter was 'under a stiff sentence' as the medium required a much swifter attack than an oil painting. 'Great water-colours are not merely superb sketches but awesome witness of time, to transience and a depth of mood.'

'Hinkson's best paintings are close to Homer's. In our time, and particularly in countries far from the metropolis of taste, any such indebtedness is looked on as imitation, but the history of great painting is a history of succession . . . Real painters are not afraid to learn.' The essay was about all art. 'Getting the light right has been the hope of saints as well as of painters, of poets, from Augustine to Turner, to Wordsworth and Dante . . .'[7]

Besides focusing on the technique of art in relation to the medium and representation of life (of any kind) and explaining the difficulties of mastery and accuracy, Walcott was offering a theory of art and religion, both of which were concerned about getting the light right. Light was life, nature, art, god, the life within the self. Too often literary critics and those mostly concerned with literature assume that Walcott's interest in painting is that of a dilettante. But in fact the discussion of technique, the comparison of Homer with Turner, the analysis of time and light, the explanation of why watercolours can be a greater art form than oil painting, are at the highest level and have much of the compression and rapid movement of Walcott's poetry. Moreover, as can be seen from passages of the essay I have not cited, the appreciation of Hinkson is also a position being taken within still another West Indian quarrel about authenticity and art in which older artistic styles and forms are being called colonial, passé, copies, and newer extensions of the recent American and European avant-garde are being offered as authentic, native, better. Walcott's defence of Hinkson is also a poetics for *Omeros* and much of his later work. On the surface a defence of the past and imitation, it is also a subtle discussion of what makes an artist unique, contemporary, of his time and place. The biblical 'let there be light' is the obvious source of a powerful theory of art and life in contrast to the parroting of whatever were that year's slogans.

For several decades Walcott had been commuting between his jobs in the United States and his homes in the West Indies, and in more recent years he had been commuting as well between England and the United States. Now

Continental Europe became part of his market, requiring frequent trips. Besides promoting his books and the international poetry readings and various international literary conferences, he was becoming recognized in Europe as a dramatist. During 1992 he had three plays in production in England, a play in Holland, and a play in Sweden. For a time he was working on *The Odyssey* in England while commuting to Sweden to direct a production in Swedish of *The Last Carnival* at the Royal Dramatic Theatre (Kunglia Dramatiska Teatern).

The Odyssey was rapidly moving through drafts; the *New York Times*, 1 January 1992, published an extract, 'Homeric Chorus'.[8] After the New Year Doran (8 January) wrote to Walcott about the recent Stratford-upon-Avon readings. The characters, invented events, and realization were excellent, but the audience following the play needed more information. There were various comments and Doran was looking forward to seeing Walcott in February when Walcott was coming again to England, this time in connection with a production of *Viva Detroit*.

The next week Doran wrote once more to Walcott sending the drafts as now printed. He added more points to discuss. Doran wanted to start rehearsals on 4 May and wanted to come to Boston to do a rehearsed reading, which he could pay for with workshops. Doran's notes suggested that Walcott was overdoing the analogy between the Cyclops and Orwell's police state. It needed more Errol Flynn. There was too much suggestive of Eastern Europe, which was becoming dated since the fall of the Berlin Wall; the symbol of the Iraqi secret service, however, was a giant's eye! Doran suggested a sequence of events for the Cyclops scene.

Malcolm Frederick directed the Black Theatre Co-operative's production of *Viva Detroit*, which tried out in Leeds, where the *Yorkshire Evening Post* (6 February) found it weak and unconvincing, before it moved on to the Tricycle Theatre in London, 11 February–7 March, after which it went on a national tour 11 March–13 June, starting with Bracknell and Chipping Norton and ending in Birmingham and Manchester. Norman Beaton, a leading black actor who has been in Shakespearian plays at the National Theatre and regularly on television serials, was the philosophizing bartender and stole the show when on stage.

The production was widely reviewed although the reviewers appear to have witnessed several different plays. Where Michael Billington, the *International Herald Tribune* (19 February), saw a 'highly engaging comedy' told 'with wit, grace and good deal of sympathy for the individuals involved', the *Standard* heard clichés from a 'banal and pretentious' play. The reviews were revealing. *The Times* reviewer explained that he had lived in Los Angeles during the later 1980s, the *Financial Times* critic suggested (15 February) that as Walcott taught at Boston University he preferred 'American sentimentality to old world scepticism' and predicted that *The Odyssey* 'will be a sentimental journey', while the *Observer*'s critic (16 February) had once been on holiday in St Lucia.

Those who disliked *Viva Detroit* said that although the comedy was good the characters and plot were thin and undeveloped. The play was said to start slowly, and the second half seemed contrived. *Stage* (27 February), however, thought 'More poets should write plays . . . Walcott's highly charged lines have a rhythmic buoyancy that makes them irresistible.' Michael Billington (14 February), this time in the *Guardian*, interpreted *Viva* as about the clash between American possessiveness and Caribbean fantasy and found the play stylish. Giles Foden (21 February) in the *TLS* recognized the larger themes, the price of respect, and the human desire to be elsewhere and different.

Roger Pringle, director of the Shakespeare Birthplace Trust, approached Walcott during May rehearsals for *The Odyssey* about the possibility of his reading for the annual Stratford-upon-Avon Poetry Festival, which Pringle also directs. After Walcott agreed to give a reading, Pringle asked if he would like to share the session.

Walcott, Seamus Heaney, and Ted Hughes read their own work on 5 July at the 1992 Stratford-upon-Avon Poetry Festival in the Swan Theatre. All three authors are published by Faber. Hughes, who was the same age as Walcott, shared his interests in landscape, environment, adaptation of myth, and theatre. Heaney was Professor of Poetry at Oxford in 1989 and wanted to nominate Walcott for the professorship, but Walcott was not interested. The 400-seat auditorium was sold out, and the press mentioned that Paul Simon was in the audience. This was an occasion when Walcott was relaxed, effective, and responsive to the audience during the reading and afterwards. Although in recent years Walcott often gives the impression of being in a hurry, rushing between continents, and being engaged in endless new creative tasks, at Stratford he was sociable, friendly, and took pleasure in meeting and listening to people. Roger Pringle commented 'Not all great poets are also sociable.'[9]

This one was at his most sociable when unsociably busy. Besides the *Odyssey* opening, there was *The Last Carnival* in Birmingham, the rehearsals of which Walcott tried to attend, and the Stockholm *The Last Carnival* performed in Swedish that he was directing. Somehow in the midst of this he and Martin Carter of Guyana read from their works during July at the Central Bank Auditorium, in Port of Spain.

As the opening approached Walcott and Doran disagreed more and more about the play, until Doran declared that he was the director and had the final word and Walcott angrily threatened legal action. *The Odyssey* opened on 2 July and ran until January 1993. In many ways The Other Place is a superior, larger, version of The Basement Theatre, seating about 200 on three sides. Although lasting over three hours, the play received critical praise as 'busy like the mackerel-crowded seas around Ithaca: attractive and lively fare'. Michael Billington called it 'total theatre with strong Shakespearean overtones: a story of homecoming, reconciliation and rebirth'. Billington praised the muscular language, metaphor-filled text, and the way Walcott unified the action by suggesting that the monsters Odysseus meets on his way home are 'projections of his own private fears, fantasies and inner demons'. Other critics mentioned Walcott's 'extraordinary retelling of this classic tale' as 'magnificently visual' with 'the spectacular hues and rhythms of a West Indian carnival'. Oliver Taplin said it 'tries to be too many things at once; and it shamelessly succeeds'. Walcott set the epic 'in an archipelago that is at once Caribbean and Mediterranean, and in a sense universalized beyond locality. The scope of Homer is still here, yet all the speeches and narrative links are "reduced" to dialogue, nearly all in quick-fire stichomythia.' 'This production is a cyclopean feat of poetry. Its text, which rhymes (or half- or quarter-rhymes) in quatrains, is encrusted with metaphors and similes as thick as quartz —or at least barnacles. The sea seems never to have had so many images so fleetingly lavished on it.'[10]

Paula Burnett commented upon the Caribbean and non-Greek characteristics. The narrator, Blind Billy Blue, was an Egyptian praise singer, based on the blues and calypso traditions. Odysseus was less a Greek hero than an Anansi trickster who lived by his wits. Walcott had told her, and would keep saying over the years, that he would like to stage the play on a Caribbean beach.[11]

Anna and Liz Walcott were in England, along with Sigrid, during the rehearsals, and Anna was to write about it in the *Sunday Guardian*, seeing the autobiographical in the dramatized epic:

'They've sprung up like two pliant saplings, my daughters'—at the sound of these lines from a home sick sailor on board Odysseus's ill-fated ship, my father squeezes both our hands.

In the final scene on stage stands Odysseus's lost son, Telemachus, the ghost of his mother still dressed in a mournful black and his wife the faithful Penelope who bathes Odysseus's feet.

The ghosts haunt not only the cunning Odysseus but also his recreator, Derek Walcott . . . . At times the story is painful to watch, the memory of his mother, known in St Lucia as teacher Alix, seems reincarnated in the character of Odysseus's mother, Anticleia . . . The second change introduced by Walcott is the way in which characters return as corrupted doubles of themselves.[12]

Anna also mentioned driving on 10 July through Warwickshire 'my grandfather's namesake', to the première of *The Last Carnival* in Birmingham.

This was a production of *The Last Carnival*, directed by John Adams, at the Birmingham Repertory Theatre, 10 July–1 August, to coincide with Birmingham's own Carnival. Adams had known nothing about Walcott, purchased a copy of *Three Plays*, liked *The Last Carnival*, and contacted Walcott's publishers about producing it. This, the European première, was a new, radically different, version that Walcott finished on 25 March in Boston. Steve Toussaint, who played Brown, had taken the role of Sonny in the Black Theatre Co-op first tour of Walcott's *Viva Detroit*, which had also played in Birmingham and was well liked. Walcott came to Birmingham whenever possible to see what Adams was doing with his play. He said little. It was a curious situation as Walcott was himself directing the play in Stockholm using the same new version. The situations were radically different. The Birmingham Rep is an immense theatre, one of the largest in which a Walcott play has been performed. The production had to be cast and rehearsed rapidly. There were black actors. In Stockholm the play was performed in a small intimate theatre, there was a long time to rehearse with the resources of one of the best companies in the world, and Walcott directed a play which had been translated into Swedish; his new version would only be published in Swedish, *Sista Karnevalen*. Adams wished that he could read Swedish to see how Walcott had changed the script and wondered if any of the changes might resemble his own. Walcott was in Birmingham for the opening. The *Guardian* (17 July) praised Walcott's power of language and the way the play showed the complexities of colonialism, but some reviewers found *The Last Carnival* too complex, plodding, filled with monologues, and undramatic.

Sista Karnevalen rehearsals began on 3 April, and the play opened 5 September. If the RSC production offered a chance to used mixed casts, white and black, the Stockholm production, besides being in Swedish, had only white actors. The company was uncomfortable at first with the idea of whites being made up as black, but Walcott told them that they were leading the way towards colour-neutral casting. Another problem was the lack of a Swedish equivalent to Creole or a dialect. Apparently Sweden does not have regional accents that could be used for the purpose. Walcott kept changing the text. The changes had to be written in a master English copy, then translated into Swedish and added to the scripts. This became a standing joke among the company. Eventually at the cast party at the last performance there was a spoof 'The Very Last Carnival', supposedly a rehearsal for 'the absolutely, irrevocably final version . . . that cannot be changed . . . ever!!!'

The cast loved Walcott. He was warm, charming, full of humour. Some of the cast even travelled to St Lucia. Brodsky, who was often in Sweden, read with Walcott on 15 August. The production, however, was too long, three hours and twenty-five minutes. Even for an audience used to Bergman it seemed a slow production. For Swedes it could have been a play about the moon, although it gave the audience a taste of Trinidad. Reviews were mixed.

On Sunday, 4 October, Elizabeth Walcott was given away in marriage by her father. Walcott came to Trinidad from St Lucia for the wedding and returned to Boston. Paul Simon and his wife also attended.

The 1992 Nobel Prize in Literature was announced on Thursday, 8 October: 250 writers had been considered and this time Walcott won 'for a poetic œuvre of great luminosity, sustained by a historical vision, the outcome of a multicultural commitment'. The Swedish Academy said 'In him West Indian Culture has found its great poet.' *Omeros* 'is a work of incomparable ambitiousness . . . deriving from the poet's wide-ranging contacts with literature, history, and reality'. Walcott, who had been hoping for the award for decades, supposedly asked Sture Allén, the Permanent Secretary of the Nobel Academy, 'Why me?' and said that he was 'honoured and shocked'. Which is possibly correct. Walcott thought that if he did not get it in 1990 when *Omeros* appeared he probably would not. He led journalists from his apartment in Brookline to a Dunkin' Donuts near where he lived and had breakfast while being interviewed. News came through during the London production of *The Odyssey*. The audience was told about it and treated the performance like a sermon.

The selection of Walcott came about four days before the quincentenary of Columbus's arrival in the West Indies, which possibly might have influenced some votes on the Committee which decides the award, but in any case his name had come up seriously from about 1985 onwards and it was time for the award. The production of *The Last Carnival* in Sweden and *The Odyssey* in England no doubt also helped make it this year. Usually awards of the Nobel Prize in Literature are marked by charges of playing cultural or real politics, such as when Soyinka was chosen ahead of Gordimer, or earlier when the award to Pasternak seemed to require a pro-Stalinist Russian next time around. The committee itself had been short of members since some resigned after Allén was unwilling to issue a declaration supporting Rushdie. As appointment to the committee was for life, resignation was treated as impossible and the members merely absent for the vote each year. This year the response was, however, muted about the possible symbolism of the award and mostly devoid of the usual quibbling about who really deserved the prize. Literary critics and newspaper editorials accepted that Walcott was perhaps the best poet in English, maybe in any language, who deserved the honour. Some might have given the nod to Naipaul, but it was thought that his views meant it was unlikely he would ever receive a majority of votes. Only the French seemed surprised, asked who was Walcott, and as Michel Fabre was away, could find no one to discuss him and his works. They did rediscover St Lucia which immediately became part of Francophonie along with Rumania! They also began looking hard at their own possible candidates for a Nobel Prize in Literature among writers in the French Caribbean. Those of us who follow the new literatures had long felt that Césaire and L. S. Senghor deserved the award, but their time and politics had passed and the new hopes were Glissant and more likely Chamoiseau.

Walcott has always been private about his life and the newspapers were often misinformed about matters Caribbean. They were filled with misinformation.

He was a citizen of St Lucia not Trinidad. He had been married three times not twice. Sigrid was his friend not his wife. He was not the first Caribbean writer to win the Nobel Prize in Literature, Perse was. An article by a well-known magazine known for its fact checking managed to get almost every fact wrong. It did not take long, however, for a British newspaper to quote an unidentified student supposedly from his 1981 Harvard class and a recent one from Boston University, who both claimed that Walcott had propositioned them.[13]

On the day Walcott received news of the Nobel Prize for Literature he flew to Charlottesville; New World Studies at the University of Virginia had a colloquium, 8–10 October, on 'Stories of American Identities 500 Years After the Columbian Encounter', at which Walcott was the keynote speaker on the 8th. Professor James Arnold had been organizing the conference for two years and was afraid that Walcott would not turn up that night to avoid being mobbed by reporters. Farrar, Straus and Giroux telephoned to say that Walcott was coming, but would need to be put on an early airplane the next day. The British West Indian poet David Dabydeen was in the car that met Walcott at the airport. Dabydeen was in awe until Walcott began asking about many of the younger West Indian and British West Indian writers. He had read them and mentioned various poems he liked. He was in a joking mood and told Dabydeen to give up poetry, at which David's heart sank until after a pause he heard, 'it does not pay'. He told Dabydeen that for $120 he would mention him in his address, but it would cost a couple of thousand if he wanted his poetry quoted. They were two West Indians among the serious Americans. The 150 seats at the auditorium were overflowing for Walcott's speech. Afterwards Walcott read from *Dream on Monkey Mountain* and talked about narrative in a hybrid Caribbean culture. There were reporters present from American, British, Swedish, and German news organizations.[14]

This was Walcott's first talk after the announcement of the Nobel award. Other speakers included Dabydeen and Maryse Condé. The emphasis of the symposium was on story-telling ('Werewolves of the Franco-Americans', 'Animal Figures among the West Indian Hindus'). The *Washington Post* (9 October) mentioned that the award was announced four days before the 500th anniversary of Columbus's arrival in the West Indies and quoted James Arnold, Director of New World Studies at the University of Virginia, as saying that 'of all the writers in the Western world, he's the one who ties us together best. From the Native Americans through the Europeans and the descendants of Africans, he moves apparently effortlessly but with great art from his small island across space and time. He gives enormous breadth and depth to our experience in the Americas.'

Walcott's impromptu remarks were edited by Arnold from an audio tape and published as 'Afterword: Animals, Elemental Tales, and the Theatre' in Arnold's *Monsters, Tricksters, and Sacred Cows: Stories of American Identities*. Walcott said that one source of West Indian theatre is in the folk imagination and memory. He spoke of the figure of Odysseus as the first humanist, called *The Odyssey* the first modern novel, but claimed that Odysseus is also someone out of folklore and has the kind of characteristics ascribed to animals in folklore. Odysseus confronting Cyclops is like a small and large animal; emblems have their source in animalization. Defining what is folk is risky as politicians and academics patronize and use the folk. To anthropologize is to make people into specimens, representatives. The real distinction for drama is naturalism in contrast to the mythical or folk. Much of Western drama wastes time and money on pretending to be real. The real power of theatre narrative is in the folk imagination, the power of the poor, as represented by the storyteller and dancers, rather than by expensive attempts to recreate reality.[15]

Walcott and the Arnolds had first met at the 1987 Claremont conference. Walcott discussed being raised a Methodist with Jim who also was. Walcott told Jo that he too is a type 2 diabetic who treats his condition through diet rather than insulin. This undoubtedly contributes to Walcott's moodiness and times of anger. It means he gets depressed and angry before needing meals because of low blood sugar. When a meal time is delayed he will need a lift by having something sweet.

There was a press conference at the Farrar, Straus and Giroux office on Friday, 9 October. Walcott was the eighteenth winner of the Nobel Prize in Literature for Farrar, Straus and Giroux, who had published six of the last ten literature laureates.

West Indian responses to the Nobel Prize were ecstatic. The poet Lorna Goodison said that he was the best poet writing in English. Edward Baugh praised Walcott's having received international recognition by writing from and about his society, its concerns, and contradictions, rather than attempting to transcend it.

Faber was also ecstatic. It produced a poster, set up a hot line for telephone orders, and planned to publish *The Odyssey* during November when Walcott was expected in England and scheduled to read at the South Bank. He did not get there. Walcott cancelled his participation in the Poetry Society of America's meeting (23 October) of Caribbean poets. He also cancelled the flight to England for his reading at South Bank on 7 November for Poetry International. I spoke with Walcott shortly after the Nobel award and he said that he was tired and on doctor's orders he was cancelling engagements.

For months there were tributes throughout the West Indies. The last Sunday in October, at its monthly Sunday Morning of Theatre and Coffee, The Company Limited (TCL) paid tribute to Walcott at the Creative Arts Centre, Mona. The TCL had begun with its reading of *Branch of the Blue Nile* and in August had presented *Pantomime*. Sheila Graham said Walcott had been a friend and mentor of the company and called the Nobel award 'the most exciting thing that has happened in the Caribbean for a long time'. The director Earl Warner described Walcott as 'the most generous Caribbean artist'. There were readings of Walcott's poems by Professor Edward Baugh, the businessman and poet Ralph Thompson called on business to help fund the arts, and the audience tried to listen to a taped interview with Walcott, of rather poor sound quality, provided by FM station KLAS.[16]

On Friday, 13 November, at the University of the West Indies Creative Arts Centre, there was an evening of reading from Walcott's poems, scenes from his plays, and tributes by friends. Edward Baugh read from *Another Life* and 'The Spoiler's Return'.[17] Walcott was invited to attend many different West Indian conferences, meetings of regional politicians, and was appointed to the newly formed UNESCO World Commission on Culture and Development. He was even invited to Carifesta (the Caribbean Festival of the Arts which he had often criticized, and which had at times pointedly not invited him), which was this year to be held in Port of Spain, but he was told he had to find himself a place to stay. He did not attend. Two weeks before Carifesta, he was staying at Kapok Hotel, which he increasingly liked as it had a good Chinese restaurant favoured by those who could afford it. He was annoyed that nothing had changed, he complained to the *Trinidad Guardian* that even a Nobel Prize winner was expected to make plans for himself when invited to Carifesta.

Walcott continued teaching, but the prize for a time played havoc with his courses, which never had been highly structured American classes. A reporter, who observed his teaching, attended his poetry class in which nine students recited some of Dylan Thomas's poetry. Whereas some critics claimed that the colonies were colonized by making students learn poetry by heart(!), Walcott said that memorization and recitation was how poets learnt poetry—art was cannibalistic, writers grew on the writing that they consumed. He continually quoted passages to his students, especially from Shakespeare. This led to questions and advice, such as how much perfection of sound might be sacrificed for clarity. Using an example from Thomas Hardy he showed that great poetry could sound meaningless, that it might be difficult to understand it without reading it on a page. He discussed how Shakespeare mixed the languages of different classes within a speech. Walcott made comparisons between poetry and other arts. Poetry was visual, it compressed the narrative expected of a novel. The class read Hardy's 'During wind and rain' line by line. He made them read it slowly, and showed that the first line of a poem set the tone, tempo, and metre for the rest of a poem. He offered to give two dollars to any student who could correctly finish a couplet he recited, not mentioning that it was from an Auden poem which they did not recognize. No one suggested the right final word. Walcott said that great writers were regionalists, that there was regionalism within any individual. He announced that two of the next three classes would need to be cancelled as Walcott was going to St Lucia for a documentary and then to Sweden for the award. It appeared a class or two had already been cancelled because Walcott had attended to some legal matters concerning his green card. He told the students to continue reading Hardy and Thomas along with Elizabeth Bishop and James Wright.[18]

He left Boston on 11 November for Miami, where he had some business during the afternoon, then to Trinidad to see his family. On the 16th he went on to St Lucia where he stayed at the luxury St Lucian Hotel while a Swedish Television film crew interviewed him, between 18–20 November, at various locations, for, Farrar, Straus and Giroux and his doctors demanded, no more than $2\frac{1}{2}$ hours a day. The film crew left on the 21st, and Walcott returned to Boston on the 22nd. Swedish Television had been doing similar Nobel Prize documentaries for more than thirty years; they are shown in all Nordic countries around the time of the Nobel festivities in December.

A tired Walcott, who also had to prepare an impressive publishable Nobel Lecture, could not avoid the celebrations that followed. On 17 November the government rapidly put together a celebration at Columbus Square, filled with singing schoolchildren, which was followed by another celebration at St Mary's College in his honour. St Lucia had gone wild. The *Weekend Voice* (21 November) reported on the first page 'Walcott Feted at the Mall'. There had been a party at new Gablewoods Mall. Walcott was given a Dunstan St Omer painting of what will eventually become a mural to be located at the Mall, representing the island's two Nobel Laureates. His sister Pam and his two daughters were there as was Sigrid who flew in from Pittsburgh and returned with him to Boston.

Walcott's long-running battle with Bridget Aschenberg was coming to an end. Walcott had thought that the Stockholm production of *The Last Carnival* might be the final push for a laureateship, but Aschenberg had wanted Stockholm to pay the normal fee, which might have put the production in doubt. Roger Straus telephoned Aschenberg (24 November 1992) who sent him copies of outstanding contracts. Among them there was a dramatic adaptation of *Omeros* being read in Rotterdam throughout the year. The Dutch seemed addicted to Walcott's later work whereas the Germans and Italians seemed more inclined towards the earlier writings. During September 1992 an all-night production by De Nieuw Amsterdam Theatergroep of 'readings' from *Omeros* was broadcast by a radio station. Between 13 November–21 December 1991, De Nieuw Amsterdam Theatergroep had toured with a Dutch translation of *A Branch of the Blue Nile* (*Een Tak Van de Blauwe Nijl*) to Utrecht, the Hague, Arnheim, Bruges, Rotterdam, Amsterdam, Leiden, and other cities. A Dutch translation of *Viva Detroit* was performed in Holland 28 October 1992–7 February 1993 by DNA in Amsterdam for twenty-one days and toured Rotterdam, Arnheim,

Groningen, and other cities. A major revivial of *Dream* was in the works. There would soon be productions of plays in Denmark and Italy. Walcott was becoming internationally known as a dramatist. His new agent for lectures and plays would be Howard Rosenstone of Rosenstone & Wender, MacDermot's agency.

After having lunch with Walcott (2 December) Straus faxed Faber that Walcott wanted to make changes in *The Odyssey* and could not have them ready until mid-January. He complained of typos in the Faber galleys which Walcott and Farrar, Straus and Giroux would work with. It was decided to produce a small hardback of the Nobel speech. How many copies should they print for Faber?

When Walcott arrived in Stockholm on 5 December he spoke to reporters about the wave of attacks on immigrants and revival of anti-Semitism in Europe. That evening he attended a production of *Sista Karnevalen* at the Kungliga Dramatiska Teatern at which he was expected to give a small talk. On Sunday the 6th there was a get-together with the other laureates and family members. On Monday at 5.30 p.m., dressed in formal clothes, he gave his Nobel lecture, *The Antilles*, followed by a private dinner hosted by the Swedish Academy. On Tuesday his publishers Wahlström & Widstrand hosted a lunch, at 5 p.m. There was an official presentation of the 1992 Nobel stamps of Derek Walcott, followed at 8 by a Nobel Concert conducted by Vladimir Ashkenazy.

Wednesday, the 9th, was a very busy day starting in the morning with a special showing of the exhibition 'Rembrandt and His Age' at the National Museum for the Fine Arts, a tour of Stockholm, a buffet lunch at the English Department of Stockholm University, an informal meeting with its students, and at 4 p.m. a reception by the Nobel Foundation from which he and others were taken to the Royal Dramatic Theatre at which there was a reading sponsored by Swedish PEN and the Royal Theatre; Walcott read 'Blues', 'Sunday in the Old Republic', 'My Double, Tired of Morning, Closes the Door' (from *Midsummer*), and a passage from *Omeros*. The other poems were read in Swedish.

The morning of the 10th all the laureates rehearsed for the Prize Award Ceremony at the Concert Hall at 4.30 p.m. for which formal dress was required, white tie and tails for men, long evening gowns for ladies, or national costumes. Long gowns meant long gowns. The same attire was required for the banquet that evening at the City Hall. Like most of the events this was highly structured. The guests were seated at 6.45 p.m., then students bearing the standards of the Stockholm Student Union paraded through the Blue Hall to music. At 7 p.m. the guests of honour entered in a procession to a fanfare. At 7.05 p.m. the Chairman of the Board of the Nobel Foundation proposed a toast to the King. Two minutes later the King proposed a toast to the memory of Alfred Nobel. There was a procession before each of the three courses of the banquet. The first two, presented by male and female dancers, were garlands of pine branches and floral decorations, before a terrine of minted salmon and sole with a caviar sauce ('sauce aux oeufs d'ablette'), and the 'exterior' fillet of roast lamb with a cider sauce accompanied by mushrooms, carrots, and black salsify glazed in honey. The third, before a dessert of mixed white chocolate and redcurrant ice-cream included a solo dance inspired by Loïe Fuller. The wines included a Brut Imperial champagne, a 1984 Château Mouton, and a 1983 Johannisberger, Riesling. After speeches by the laureates, the Royal Family received the laureates, and dancing began, an hour of 'hot and swing', a half-hour of a steel band playing calypso and soca, and then a final half-hour, until midnight, of 'hot and swing'.

The schedule for Friday included a visit to the Office of the Nobel Foundation, a lunch with theatre people at the Royal Theatre, and a banquet in the evening given by the King and Queen at the Royal Palace, for which the most formal attire was necessary. Saturday the 12th there was a round-table discussion for Swedish Television. Sunday, 13 December, is St Lucia Day, which is traditionally celebrated in Sweden with candle-lit crowns. That Walcott is from St Lucia meant that he would be the centre of much attention and photograph taking. The local and Caribbean press carried a photogragh of him lighting the candles on the crown of a tall blonde St Lucie. Sunday began with the opening of the 'Derek Walcott' exhibition at Uppsala University Library, a reception, a luncheon at the Castle given by the University of Uppsala, the crowning of St Lucie at Skansen, Stockholm, and a St Lucie dinner given by the Student Union of the University of Stockholm at which formal attire was once more necessary.

The next few days included a visit to a UNESCO seminar outside Stockholm concerning 'Coexistence of Communities with Diversified Cultural Identities', a supper hosted by the Minister of Culture, a trip to, and programme at, the University of Göteborg. On Wednesday, the 16th, it was over, he was free to leave.

Walcott did not have tails and a white tie. Native costume in St Lucia ranged from swimming briefs to English suits, so he rapidly had to rent some formal wear in Stockholm. Black patent leather shoes presented a problem and in some photographs he can be seen wearing what appear to be untied combat boots; when receiving the award there was fear he might trip on his too long trousers. Those poets! He was, however, among friends. Sigrid, Roderick, and some friends from St Lucia, including Odlum, were there either as family paid for by the Nobel Foundation or at their own expense to share in the joy of Derek's achievement. Helen Television sent Alva Clarke and John Robert Lee to broadcast directly home.

While Walcott's Nobel lecture was a celebration of the joy of being part of the birth of a new literature, it began by describing an Indian ritual drama in Trinidad and saying that he would be a better writer if he had also shared in such a culture. Among the significances of *The Antilles* is Walcott's recognition that he had ignored the vitality and continuity of Indian culture in Trinidad. The links between Africa and the New World black had been broken except in small ways and, Walcott knew, talk of African roots was usually little more than sentimentality. What had been brought from Africa and survived, survived as something new, a blend of various tribes, cultures, and had become New World Creole. Indeed it was often part of the blend and change of European cultures in the New World as they adapted and mutated. Indian culture in Trinidad had, however unexpectedly, managed to survive without (as V. S. Naipaul felt it was doing in the 1940s) ossifying. Moreover it had in recent years been invigorating the black Creole culture of Trinidadian popular music and dance. Walcott had been discovering that even he, the writer who had argued for the Caribbean as multiracial, multicultural, a mixture of all its people, had missed out on one of the major events, the Indians taking their place in east Caribbean society. He had been obsessed with white–black relations, he had attacked black tyrannies, but he had not spoken up against the racial persecution committed by black governments against Indians. He had some Indian actors in the Trinidad Theatre Workshop, indeed some of his best Trinidadian actors in recent decades were Indians, but he had few parts for them as his mythology, politics, and sociology were about whites, blacks, and mulattos, not Indians. It was not prejudice, Walcott had written plays such as *Franklin* about the Indians, Indians were prominent in the Methodist community in St Lucia, but he had not shared in, or really seen, what had become the largest ethnic group of Trinidad and Guyana. The discussion with the Trinidad Theatre Workshop about producing *Othello* in 1989 was significant; Walcott continued to see a white Desdemona and black Othello whereas Errol Jones and others thought an Indian Desdemona would transform the play into something closer to present-day Trinidadian racial tensions.

Stage One, in association with the National Cultural Foundations of Barbados, had *A Derek Walcott Evening*, on 19 December, at the Frank Collymore Hall with parts of the plays, readings of poems, and video tapes. Michael Gilkes portrayed Walcott. The evening traced Walcott's career from his early dedication to being the artist who discovered the West Indies through his feelings of alienation and disillusionment, his responses to Black Power politics, to his mastery and remaking of European cultural forms, especially in his later works where, rather than just the empire writing back, Walcott is being a kind of Columbus showing a region for what it is in its complexity, its fishermen, taxi cab drivers, and changes.

Walcott returned to Trinidad to be with his family at Christmas. Sigrid and Margaret had learned to accept each other, unlike the terrible and continuing clash between Norline and Margaret. Even now Walcott was alert for new local artists. At a musical production he discovered Glenda Thomas, an extremely talented singer, and recommended her to the Trinidad Theatre Workshop as a new member. Within days she was working with them.

There was a tribute to him at the university on 13 December, then, 28–9 December at the Old Fire Station, the Trinidad Theatre Workshop reformed to perform *Celebration*, a long evening of music, songs, and dramatized poems, and parts of plays. This developed into a production called *Celebration* which was taken on tour internationally. At the first *Celebration* many of the local poets, such as Wayne Brown, and critics, including Ken Ramchand and Pat Ismond, participated along with Walcott and members of the Trinidad Theatre Workshop. Walcott read from *Omeros* and there were excerpts from *Sea at Dauphin*, *Pantomime*, *Dream on Monkey Mountain*, *Ti-Jean and His Brothers*, and *Joker of Seville*, and music by André Tanker and the reunion of the Trinidad Theatre Workshop Dancers, followed by a Trinidadian 'lime' in which a phrase was taken up and everyone had to improvise a comic sketch using it. It was a long Trinidad evening and party, the kind that Walcott loved and which partly explains why his plays often seem long by North American tastes. Proceeds from the celebrations were for the Save the Old Fire Station Fund. The next day the Trinidad Theatre Workshop showed *Derek*, the forty-minute Swedish Television documentary made after the announcement of the Nobel Prize. The event was advertised as Walcott reading from *Omeros* on Monday and Tuesday, 28 and 29, at TT $50, to go towards restoring the Old Fire Station. Walcott and the Trinidad Theatre Workshop would now work together after a separation of sixteen years and Walcott was once again the boss!

Suddenly all those translations of Walcott which publishers had encouraged were appearing. There were various approaches. In Sweden different translators contributed to the same volume. The Danish translator, Bo Green Jensen, was a well-known Danish poet, novelist, film and music critic, and television celebrity, who had lived in the United States and translated many volumes of American poetry. Not familiar with the Caribbean, and afraid that West Indian idioms could not be put into Danish without sounding like provincial dialects, Jensen translated the verse as if it were American. In most languages there was the problem of what to do about dialect and Creole as there were few acceptable regional varieties that did not sound oafish, limited, misleading. Many translators also took the easy way by using free verse as highly structured poetry was out of fashion in most of Europe. By general agreement the best translations, starting with *Le Royaume du fruit-étoile* (1992), were by the poet Claire Malroux, who published poetry in French under the name Claire Sara Roux and who has won several prizes for her translations. Her translations were themselves works of art, sensitive towards language, hesitantly using some French Caribbean patois.

The prize money was less than expected as the kroner had recently been devalued, the million dollars becoming $700,000. Then Walcott had to pay the

United States 40 per cent tax on the prize. The remaining money was soon to disappear in various ways as Walcott finished his house in St Lucia, paid for operations for his son Peter, helped out Roderick, settled his divorce with Norline, and contributed towards various artists and artistic organizations, including the Trinidad Theatre Workshop and his Rat Island Foundation which he was hoping to establish on St Lucia. As friends became aware of how rapidly the award money was going and how Walcott seemed to be pushing his self-demands to still another level, there were amused comments about how he was working towards a second Nobel Prize to pay his debts.

The Minister of Education in Trinidad told students in Arima Girls' Roman Catholic School that Walcott's Nobel Prize was a lesson in working hard for achievement. Walcott had not sat back with his talent. Students should become well-rounded citizens fit for society and 'not deviants and misfits, as we already have enough of them'.[19]

Part VIII

~~~~~~

St Lucia, New York, London
Laureate

30

~~~~~~

1993 Celebrations

AFTER the Nobel Prize it took a few years to catch up with the celebrations, invitations, other awards, and such immediate effects as the renewal of Walcott's leadership of the Trinidad Theatre Workshop. Norline's wish for a divorce had been held up by Derek having given her half-ownership of the Boston apartment; he now settled that. He had money towards building his new house in St Lucia. Besides the main house decorated with works of art, many from Sigrid's days as a gallery owner, there would be a guest house, plus a studio on a half-acre reaching down to the water's edge between Pigeon Point and Gros Islet from which Walcott could swim daily. His studio would come to be filled with local scenes and sketches for plays. The house was in a newly developed section of Cap Estate of other architect-designed houses for the wealthy, including wealthy foreigners.

The early years of genteel poverty, of making do, of occasional dependency on others (such as the family had known after Warwick's death), of feeling humiliated by family history, of looking enviously on those civil servants who after the 1948 Castries fire could afford to have houses on Vigie, had been symbolically put to rest. He had followed his destiny as a poet, he had used his talent and worked very hard to make his place in modern literature; he had returned from exile, from journeying through the world, as a conqueror. His house was being built, it would restore the place of the Walcotts on St Lucia, he would no longer need to rent cottages, live in hotels—he was among the wealthy, he was famous. He also now only had to teach one semester a year at Boston for a full salary. Even at that some of his American students I spoke with had not heard of him when they registered for their MA course in poetry or drama.

He was back in St Lucia in early January with a BBC film crew for *Arena*'s 'Derek Walcott: Poet of the Island', produced and directed by Julian Henriques. Henriques is the son of the Jamaican Fernando Henriques, who, as Professor of Anthropology at Leeds University, helped bring Walcott to the attention of British publishers and academics. Julian, who has been described as one of 'the cinema's great black hopes', has often made documentaries about the Caribbean and England's multicultural arts. The programme was broadcast on 26 February with Professor Stuart Hall of the Open University doing the interviewing.

Walcott made a day trip to Martinique on 6 January to meet Césaire, Chamoiseau, Bernabé, and especially Glissant, and there was a press conference. The photographers took pictures of Walcott holding a book by Césaire and of Césaire holding one of Walcott's books. While Walcott and Glissant have a warm friendship, follow each other's writings, share each other's general outlook, and trust each other, they differ about the relationship of their local culture to Europe. Glissant feels that Walcott does not trust the French, and does not understand the social and cultural complexities that would be involved in using Creole for writing in the Francophonic Caribbean. Glissant, who has chosen French as the language of writing, thinks that Walcott is always conscious of Brathwaite's nativism and wary of being thought too British. The final question reporters asked Walcott was what advice would he give to a young writer. Walcott replied 'never speak with Edouard Glissant'. Walcott was invited by the Cercle Frantz Fanon and the Municipalité de Rivière-Pilote for a second, longer, visit to Martinique at the end of the month. He met the lawyer Marcel Manville, who was the 1992 Frantz Fanon laureate; the headline in *France-Antilles* (29 January) was 'Walcott et Manville, deux hommes de combat'. Walcott spoke about the diversity of people in the Caribbean and once more said that the next major author could be Chinese.[1]

Like many returning heroes Walcott's achievements, fame, and opinions attracted local controversy. On Tuesday, 5 January, he was interviewed on local television and once more claimed that the West Indies were wealthy enough to support the arts. Now he suggested that culture should be linked to tourism. Painting and sculpture should be displayed and purchased by hotels. There should be scholarships for those in the theatre. Walcott was still claiming that cultural independence was what mattered, political independence had proved disillusioning, and economically the region still remained a colony with tourism replacing plantations.

As if to prove him right about West Indian politicians the Culture Minister in Trinidad announced (12 January) that the Trinidad Theatre Workshop's five-year tenancy at the Old Fire Station would not be extended, despite appeals from Walcott and protests in the press. Walcott had offered to donate some of his Nobel Prize money to the theatre if it became a permanent home for the

Trinidad Theatre Workshop and said he would return regularly to work with the company. The government plans for the space were, to be polite, not very convincing. The government claimed it would eventually build a large arts centre, a promise that had been made by previous ministers of culture under Walcott's old enemy Eric Williams; now Williams's party was back in power. No one wanted promises of a large Stalinist arts centre staffed by a large, inefficient bureaucracy for occasional grand productions; they needed a decent little theatre with rooms for teaching, rehearsals, art classes, something over which the artists had some control and for which they were willing to work. Besides, the Old Fire Station was a monument, a real tourist attraction in a part of Port of Spain which still had buildings of historical and architectural interest. To level it for a modern building would in itself be a crime.[2]

There was a dramatized reading (22–4 January) of *Henri Christophe* at the University of the West Indies, Cave Hill, Barbados, directed by Leonard St Hill, Derek's brother-in-law. St Hill claimed that the play was still as valid as it had been forty years before; the enemy of the formerly colonized was within. Colonial servitude had been exchanged for another slavery, the tyranny of the liberators. Part of the proceeds were to be sent to the fund for the Propagation of Democracy in Haiti.[3]

In contrast to Trinidad where Walcott and the government appeared to be returning to the same feud that had led to Walcott's leaving for Boston, St Lucia was active with its Nobel Laureates week which included an exhibition of fifty local paintings that were part of Project Helen for which the St Lucia National Trust had commissioned painting by Walcott, Dunstan St Omer, and Llewellyn Xavier. Walcott was present at the opening as was George Lamming. Both Walcott and Sir Arthur Lewis were born on 23 January and both were awarded the St Lucia Cross, St Lucia's highest honour. The guitarist Ronald 'Boo' Hinkson was awarded a Les Piton Medal for his contribution to music. In Castries, Columbus Square, which was given that name in 1893, was renamed Derek Walcott Square.

Nobel Laureate week lasted 21–8 January, and has become an annual event in St Lucia. It celebrates Derek Walcott and Arthur Lewis, who in 1979 had been awarded the Nobel Prize in Economics. On the 21st Project Helen officially opened; that evening the Walcott Studies Association was launched with a public lecture by Patricia Ismond, the critic from St Lucia who taught at the University of the West Indies in Trinidad. On the Friday there was a symposium, 'Columbus—Impact and Aftermath'. The speakers were the famous University of West Indies, Jamaica, historian Professor Roy Augier who was himself a St Lucian, the novelist George Lamming, Monseigneur Patrick Anthony (a black St Lucian who was writing a dissertation about Walcott), and Roderick Walcott. On Saturday, 23 January, Walcott 'arrived' in the presence of the Prime Minister and Governor-General. There were welcoming remarks by Hunter Francois, who was chairman of the celebrations committee, and whose one and only book of poems had been published in 1950 with Walcott's cover and introduction. Marie 'Sessene' Descartes, whose magnificent folk songs in Creole Walcott had praised, was followed by addresses, proclamations, music by Luther Francois (the saxophonist son of Hunter Francois), Ronald 'Boo' Hinkson (St Lucia's other best-known jazz musician), the Diamond Steel Orchestra, and Citations on Lewis and Walcott, the latter by his old school chum George Odlum who, besides editing the *Crusader*, was St Lucian representative at the UN in New York.

Odlum, recommending the award of the St Lucia Cross, spoke of Walcott as representing the spirit of the age and nation as had Shakespeare and James Joyce. Walcott 'infused our country with the heroic dimensions of Homer's Greece', he had 'described . . . the psyche of the St Lucian people . . . the elemental dignity and pride of Afa the fisherman and Makak the Charcoal-burner'. Walcott embraced G. K. Chesterton's 'only the local is real'. He observed the flowers, animals, hills, and omnipresent sea. He found his stories in the island's tales. He explored the exuberance of the French Romantics, G. M. Hopkins, and Dylan Thomas. He imbibed the formalism and classicism of such poets as Yeats, Eliot, and Auden. He crossed continents to feed from the sensibility of Robert Lowell, Brodsky, and Heaney. Walcott had moved West Indian poetry away from 'the sterility of racial hegemony' and quests of racial identity, away from the past to embrace other cultures and forge unity from diversity. Odlum then quoted a passage from *Antilles*, the point of which is that in the putting together of such a unity the pain of diasporas will remain in the pieces as they are assembled in a new Caribbean wholeness.

Odlum, like most of the circle in which Walcott was raised and moves, is very intelligent and a good literary critic. Even in the conciseness of such a speech he had pointed to the way Walcott's poetry expanded in concentric circles, without losing its inner core, from attention to the local, through various romanticisms, formalisms, and foreign cultures, to embrace the world beyond St Lucia, the British tradition, North America, and Western Europe. Odlum saw this as a model for St Lucia itself which, like most of the Caribbean, risked social and racial divisions, especially as it was becoming part of the world's economic system and in the process was welcoming new, wealthy, foreign investors and residents. Odlum ignored Walcott's reminder that the Caribbean would not be a place of easy general assimilation, but of a painful coming together, and that the parts would continue to feel that they were once part of other cultures and had other homes.

Walcott was then presented with an anthology of St Lucian writings by the younger poet and dramatist, Kendall Hippolyte. He was also given a painting by Cedric George, whose style Simmons and Walcott had reacted against, but who was now seen as part of the line of St Lucian painting that was being traced from Warwick Walcott to the present. Warwick, Derek, Rodney, Dunstan St Omer, Simmons, and Cedric George were most of what there was of interest until the new, younger generation. That night there was a reception. Sunday consisted of such public events as a picnic with local arts at Pigeon Island. Roderick Walcott's public lecture on 'The History of Drama in St Lucia' was on Monday, Tuesday evening was devoted to poetry, folk music, and folk dancing at the National Cultural Centre (a beautiful great house which the Deveau family, one of the few remaining old white French families, had recently given as a home for the Centre), and on Thursday and Friday, 28–9 January, the dramatist Allan Weekes directed a production of Derek Walcott's *Malcochon* and the Trinidad Theatre Workshop (28–30 January) performed *Celebration*.[4] The actual presentation of the Cross would not occur until August.

The white Walcotts of Barbados, who had rejected making Warwick part of the family, now offered to include Warwick and Derek in their official genealogy. Derek refused. The St Lucia government would offer him a knighthood. He thought more about that, but also refused. He tried to prevent others from knowing about the Walcott offer, but he did not seem to mind their hearing about the rejected knighthood.

On 23 January Walcott was interviewed on radio about Kweyol (Creole). The programme occurred the day after the launching of a Kweyol dictionary by Jones Mondesir. Walcott objected to the kind of phonetic spelling that was becoming common for teaching. Why write the childlike and barbarous 'dlo' when 'deleau' was what was said? Such an orthography diminished the elegance of Kweyol and made the written form appear like graffiti. To politicize a living language was to wither it. Others soon joined in the fray. Hunter Francois pointed out that he, Walcott, and others had written poems in Creole without needing such a grotesque system of writing it. Moreover the dictionary was at times wrong. While there were differences between the Creole of Castries and the country, nowhere in St Lucia were certain words pronounced as recommended in the dictionary, which had relied on a standardized form for the Francophonic Caribbean; in other words the supposed St Lucian dictionary was really closer to usage found in such places as Martinique and Guadeloupe. Dunstan St Omer romantically but perceptively objected that putting a still developing language into a standardized written form would harm its development. Comments made to me include that the dictionary is Victorian in its definitions and misses the vigorous expression of Creole in St Lucia. The main argument for the dictionary was educational. Some form of Creole needed to be agreed upon and taught especially as English became increasingly more important in the life of the island. In other words this was a nationalist attempt to preserve and teach a language, something Simmons and Walcott had started four decades previously.[5]

A later more rigorous nationalism was in conflict with an earlier more cosmopolitan humanistic nationalism. For Walcott Creole was French, a local national language, that also shared in the history, metropolitan and Caribbean, of French literature and culture. The new way of writing it was separatist, making it inaccessible to those who know French or even those unfamiliar with the new phonetic spelling. Those using it would lose their window to French culture. In Martinique and elsewhere in the Caribbean the publication of literary and cultural magazines written in such phonetic Creoles had often resulted in rigidity, stridency, and a lack of subtlety. Underneath the quarrel was the question whether Creole was to be seen as part of an evolving modern world, a developing language related to European languages and cultures, or as something unique, inaccessible to others, yet, somehow, African. The Creole poems that Walcott had written assumed that the Martinicans and Haitians were also heirs of French literature and that Creole culture would become part of world culture. The new UNESCO-approved Kweyol was like breaking up the Federation, it gave power to local cultural politicians. It was like Trinidadian cultural politics all over again. There were many forms of Creole in St Lucia, that of Castries was different from that of rural areas; instead of letting a modern national form develop naturally as a result of improved communications, a nationally approved form was being imposed to teach the folk their own language.

James Rodway, the Guyanese-born teacher who influenced Walcott in his youth by lending him books of modern poetry, had recently died and Walcott announced (28 January) that part of his Nobel Prize money would be used to create a James Rodway Memorial Prize for poetry open to all Caricom citizens. It was to be both a cash prize, United States $1,200, and a semester's free tuition at Boston University studying with Walcott.[6]

Later in Boston Walcott (28 February) announced he was forming an international centre for the arts on Rat Island in St Lucia. He hoped to raise funds for it from corporations and successful artists. It would be used for poets, playwrights, even economists. This scheme and the basis of its finances kept changing. Walcott was also to suggest that the Rat Island centre be used as part of a three-way exchange between his Boston University students, the Trinidad Theatre Workshop, and St Lucian artists. During the year Walcott gave a talk, 'Flight of the Pelican', at the Folk Research Centre to raise funds for Rat Island. The Folk Research Centre issued a tape of it. At various times he was to bring famous writers to St Lucia to help him raise money, seek help among his former contacts in American foundation circles, and expect the St Lucian government or Boston University to come up with the money. Paul Simon and Arthur Miller were at a benefit for Rat Island late in January 1994. Rat Island itself is tiny; it faces the cottage on Choc Bay where Walcott used to stay, and has a large house which was abandoned after a hurricane and allowed to deteriorate. A good swimmer can reach it from the beach.

Prizes always bring complaints. While there were some West Indians who wanted a more committed 'black' writer, such as Brathwaite, the main lament was from Indians who favoured V. S. Naipaul and who felt that antagonism towards Naipaul's analysis of West Indian black politics would always keep the novelist from the top literary prize. Sasemarine Persaud, in *Caricom Perspective*, noted that Walcott had probably mistakenly called dholak drums tablas in his Nobel lecture and saw this as typical of his lack of attention to the Indian community and its culture. While Walcott had acknowledged the Indian presence and Indian writers in the West Indies, he had offered a vision of a mongrelized Creole melting pot, whereas the Indians were concerned to keep a heritage they had never lost and which they kept renewing through contact with India. Persaud claimed that except for George Lamming the black writers had not actively spoken out against the repression of Indians and Indian culture in Burnham's tyrannical Guyana.[7]

At the end of January Walcott returned to Boston. If he had flown on USAir he could have listened to himself read on Channel 4 or 11 as part of the Inflight Audio Entertainment. The *Poetry in Paradise* programme was produced in conjunction with the International Poetry Forum of Pittsburgh.[8]

Annuska Pamle Sanavio (of OSI and Ellepi Film) had translated *Ti-Jean* into Italian and had in Sweden discussed with Walcott a possible July production at the famous San Miniato Festival. Walcott wanted to direct it and to bring musicians from Trinidad. The production was progressing. Sanavio sent a fax (12 January) saying a singer of Somali origin had been found for the Mother. It was hoped to have an exhibition of Walcott's painting. Could Sigrid send colour slides? There would also be the problem of translating the music into Italian styles and rhythms which required time and meetings. She was now translating *The Last Carnival* from Swedish to Italian as she was thinking of producing that as well. Could she be sent the final English stage version? Sanavio wrote again on 21 January to Straus as she had had no reply from Walcott and nothing could be done without something more than what she assumed was a verbal agreement.

Karl Kirchwey had been sent a photocopy of *The Odyssey* and wrote (2 February) asking whether Walcott might do a reading at the Poetry Center, at the YMHA in New York, during 1993–4. The Poetry Center's history of presenting verse drama had started in 1953 with the first public reading of Dylan Thomas's *Under Milkwood*, had included some of Yeats's plays over the years, and had scheduled Heaney's *The Cure at Troy* for March 1993. Kirchwey was hoping for a presentation that could be rehearsed during a weekend for a Monday night show, perhaps using James Earl Jones as Odysseus. He suggested that the YMHA might schedule the play either to open the year or perhaps to mark Martin Luther King day. They could pay $1,000 plus transportation and accommodation.

Walcott wanted his poet friends to write for the stage and had invited Heaney to write a play for a thousand dollars for the Boston Playwrights theatre. Nothing came of it as Heaney was not ready to write another verse play. Now (15 February) Walcott, on Heaney's suggestion, was asked to direct the reading of Heaney's *The Cure at Troy* at the Y on Monday, 15 March 1993. Rehearsals were to start on Friday, 12 March, but as Walcott was unlikely to be at the Friday rehearsal Heaney agreed to take the first rehearsal. The Poetry Center could pay $500 for directing plus up to $800 for transportation, accommodation, and expenses. Walcott agreed.

Heaney's version of Sophocles' *Philoctetes*, *The Cure at Troy*, was acted at the Unterberg Poetry Center of the 92nd Street Y with Roscoe Lee Browne as Philoctetes. There were three actors, a small chorus of three, and two musicians, and, as Walcott prefers, the casting was colour neutral. There were various problems, including storms and airplane delays, in getting everyone to the rehearsals on time. Walcott, familiar with emergencies, was at his best. Although the reading lacked polish the acting was felt to have more life than the 1997–8 professional production in New York. Walcott had ambitious ideas and used the rehearsals more as a workshop trying out ideas in movement, dance, and music (there was an Irish pipe and drum). His approach to directing was improvisation. Kirchwey has often found Walcott generous with his time (he was later to visit Kirchwey's classes at Columbia). Walcott, now a celebrity, was quoted in the May 1993 *Vanity Fair* as asking 'Is Paul here?' at the interval of *The Cure at Troy*. According to *Vanity Fair*, Stephen Rea and Courtney Kennedy were there, but not Simon.

During the second half of March there were two notable productions of Walcott's plays. Richard Montgomery, who now taught at Villa Julie College in Maryland, had decided to produce *Pantomime* with his students and as the production developed hired two professional actors. Montgomery invited Walcott and soon the production became an event with old friends flying in. Walcott gave a talk on 19 March followed by lunch, a steel band, and a panel, as well as *Pantomime*. Although Montgomery had worked with Walcott since 1970 and had a good idea of what he wanted, this production was thought pessimistic about racial relations between the two characters. Perhaps that was to be expected with American actors. The other production was *The Sea at Dauphin*, directed by Earl Warner which opened on 26 March in Barbados.[9]

Kirchwey (1 April) wrote to Walcott in Boston thanking him for his energy and resourcefulness in managing to get a coherent reading of *The Cure at Troy*. He said he was contacting Roscoe Lee Browne, Faye Dunaway, and Al Pacino for *The Odyssey*. Kirchwey thought Dunaway and Pacino unlikely to commit themselves in advance and suggested Irene Worth, who was both a friend of his and an admirer of Walcott's work. The Royal Shakespeare Company's *The Odyssey* had lasted three hours and Walcott had spoken of a two-and-a-half hour version. What would it be like? The schedule would start with a Saturday, 18 September, rehearsal leading to a Monday reading.

Walcott was briefly back in New York and then on 2 April he returned to Hartwick College. An attractive announcement of the reading contained reproductions of a Swedish stamp issued with Walcott's portrait at the time of the Nobel Prize and a stamp from St Lucia.

Awards continued. On Monday, 12 April, Walcott arrived in Jamaica. On the 14th he was awarded the Order of Merit, Jamaica's third highest honour, for his contribution to Caribbean literature. (The OM is outranked by the National Hero award and the Order of the Nation, the latter being reserved for Governors-General.) Walcott was in Jamaica to give the main address at the two-day 'Gathering of Graduates' at the University of the West Indies where, instead of the annual Pelican award, he received the first ever Golden Pelican from the Guild of Graduates of the University of the West Indies. This was his first visit to Jamaica since 1988.

'The Land of Look Behind', the title of his talk to the graduates, is taken from the story of Lot's Wife who looked back and was turned into salt. It is an unusual address, as much angry as joking, celebratory, and revealing. Walcott had been unhappy at UCWI, had avoided his classes, and thought the University College was British or West Indian British. He did not object to studying English or Latin literature, but rather that the university wanted to produce a scholar and he wanted to be an artist.

The talk is notable for Walcott's sense of sadness concerning those of his friends who had since died, his willingness still to brag about student pranks (such as barking back at a watch dog at night) and excessive drinking, his sense of Jamaica as a place different from St Lucia and therefore frightening and requiring being distanced from himself and put down, and his present anger at having to prepare something suitable for the occasion when such a stance and rhetoric was far from his own. The talk for all its looseness of structure is held together by various recurring symbols and motifs, by metaphoric analogies, by the methods of poetry rather than the linearity and clarity of prose. It concludes with Walcott recognizing that for all his discontent University College was part of what had made him. He seemed embarrassed at his earlier discontent.

Walcott still lamented the loss of the West Indian Federation. Part of Walcott's embarrassment is that the UCWI and those he knew there represented the ideal of the Federation. He and those of his generation in the audience were allowed the privilege of discontent with what soon afterwards, once lost, could only be nostalgia. Walcott's discontent was also homesickness; indeed the basic theme of West Indian novels of the period and most university novels is the betrayal of a first love for the sake of higher education. This is the start of exile, of division, you return home at various times but you can no longer be part of that original unity. The West Indian novel was a product of exile, of memory, and such exile is the muse of autobiographical prose. The writers who went abroad were published in real books, bound, printed, and paid for by a publisher, unlike Walcott's own self-published poetry. Walcott complains that the university should have helped publish local literature, but it was too much concerned with stocking the library with the works of minor British authors even to purchase Hemingway, Faulkner, or Steinbeck. Now Walcott worries that the official recognition of West Indian literature, of writers of his generation, and of himself, will create pride, pride that deadens the real love of literature, the real rebellion of scholarship. His mother's conviction that he was a poet and her willingness to help him publish is more the spirit in which a West Indian literature should be created than concern for the authority of recognized publishers in other countries.[10]

The talk, like many of Walcott's addresses, is as much about poetry and being an artist as it is about its supposed topic. His instincts about creativity made him a rebel to the ways of a university and scholarship; this was a kind of conceit, but conceit is also an important part of poetry as metaphor, so that in trying to look backward he sees a series of mirrors offering contrasting, fragmented images, which is the way of poetry unlike autobiographical prose with its connected narrative. Such conceits suggestive of the infinite are terrifying as can be looking back at one's self. Poetry like history has no plot since plots require the Third Person. Like many of Walcott's poems the speech becomes a metaphoric discussion of language, its parts and organization, as the base upon which, according to generic conventions, superstructures of kinds of feeling, story, and argument can be built.

While he was in Jamaica Walcott gave a Gala Poetry Reading at the Ward Theatre. The Company Limited was presenting a Season of Walcott, who attended the special gala opening performance of *Pantomime* on Saturday, 17 April, directed by Alwin Bully. (*Pantomime* had been produced by the Jamaican School of Drama a few years previously and by Alwin Bully during September 1992.) Walcott autographed copies of his books for The Bookshop so that they could be sold at the theatre during the run of the play and he was promised a donation for the Rat Island Foundation by West Indian Publishing Limited which owned The Bookshop. He returned to Boston on 18 April.

Decades earlier Walcott had dreamed of the Trinidad Theatre Workshop performing in the United States, even touring internationally. It had been too expensive to bring the troupe to the United States and Equity had guarded jobs for Americans. Now with the Nobel Prize there were people who would listen and help. Walcott had never learned how to apply for grants, had never learned the correct terms for university committees and administrations, but Tom McClellan, his assistant at the Playwrights Theatre, had. Funds were found to bring the Trinidad Theatre Workshop to Boston to celebrate the Nobel Prize and for a production of *Pantomime* to open the season of the Playwrights Theatre, into which Walcott and the university were putting money for lights, sound, and other basics that it had previously lacked during the decade Walcott had taught practical theatre at Boston. Any profits from the two productions would go to the Theatre, the Trinidad Theatre Workshop, and the Rat Island Foundation.

Walcott held both his poetry and drama classes on Wednesday, 21 April, and began rehearsing singers and others for the *Nobel Celebration* that night. The Trinidad Theatre Workshop and André Tanker arrived in Boston on 22 April. Tanker came from New York where he had been doing the music for a West Indian play at the Lincoln Center. Rehearsals for the *Nobel Celebration* began at the Playwrights Theatre on Friday, 23 April. Saturday night after rehearsals there was a large party with Tanker's band playing music for dancing. As there was a show already at the large Charles Playhouse, it was only possible to begin set construction on the evening of 25 April for the *Nobel Celebration* the next night. Walcott had his poetry class at 9 a.m. on Monday. Starting at noon his poetry and drama classes attended rehearsals at the Charles which had been going on since morning. At 5 p.m. Walcott dined with John Silber, the President of Boston University, and the King and Queen of Spain.

Celebration was at 8 p.m. Tickets were $50, but patrons were sold tickets for $250 which entitled them to the play and a reception afterwards. *Celebration* consisted of a Welcome by John Silber, then Walcott read from his poetry; and the Trinidad Theatre Workshop performed selections from *Dream on Monkey Mountain*, *Pantomime*, *Ti-Jean and His Brothers*, and *The Joker of Seville*. The Workshop was once again together. The cast included Errol Jones, Stanley Marshall, Claude Reid, Nigel Scott, Albert Laveau, Carol La Chapelle, Adele Bynoe, Charles Applewhaite, along with new members Glenda Thomas and Sonja Dumas. For me the highlights were the intensity of Errol Jones in *Dream*'s healing scene, the comedy of Nigel Scott and Claude Reid in *Pantomime*, and the amusing double entendres, acting, and singing of Glenda Thomas in *The Joker of Seville*.

At the party afterwards Galt MacDermot played the piano and Paul Simon, who had flown in from California for the occasion, performed with a tall South African singer to prerecorded music. Heaney, Henry Louis Gates, and many others were enjoying themselves. The patrons had their money's worth.

The next day the set of *Celebration* had to be dismantled, rehearsals began for *Pantomime*, and there was a farewell dinner for the Workshop which turned into a Trinidadian 'lime', with each person expected to perform, usually saying, singing, or rhyming something insulting about the others. Such parties, dances, and other communal events, which all members of the Workshop were expected to attend, had contributed to the closeness of the company and their loyalty to Walcott.

The Boston Playwrights Theatre opened its season with a production of *Pantomime*, 29 April–2 May, which was supposed to have been rehearsed in Trinidad before the actors came to Boston. Nigel Scott had admirably taken the role of Trewe in earlier productions; this was Claude Reid's first time as Jackson. Perhaps critics were right that Walcott became too obsessed with details during rehearsals to direct plays, but he brought out a range of subtleties I had not seen in the lines. It was a great play for actors. Reid, who had been magnificent in the *Celebration*, did not know his lines for *Pantomime* during rehearsals. Everyone was certain that Scott would pull him along, but on opening night Scott made the first error, which sent Reid to another part of the play; what followed was a disaster. For a great company the Workshop was notorious for sloppy first nights, but this was a shambles. It was so mixed up, it was almost funny. The *Boston Globe*'s reviewer mercifully left at the interval. Walcott surprisingly was philosophical about it. He said it would improve.

The next day Walcott (30 April) flew to Chicago to read from *Omeros* at the Art Institute. The reading lasted forty-five minutes and was described by a local critic as magical, subtly energetic. Walcott spoke of poetry as an act of grace and redemption, of a poem as a benediction. He then returned to Boston.[11]

Walcott was in Amsterdam at the John Adams Institute 9–15 May. He gave a press conference on 9 May, some interviews, another press conference, and then met with Queen Beatrix, and attended a reception given by the American Ambassador on 10 May. An interview, a theatre workshop, and a dinner with questions followed on the 11th, another interview, book signing, and reading in Amsterdam on the 12th, an interview for a television programme and a poetry workshop on the 13th, and an interview and a reading in Rotterdam on the 14th. The readings were in conjunction with the publication of the Dutch translation of *Omeros*. He returned to Boston on 15 May where on the 16th he was given an honorary degree by Boston University. Farrar, Straus and Giroux suggested to Carl Hanser Verlag that this would be a good time for Walcott to visit Germany in connection with the publication of the second book of his works to be translated into German by Klaus Martens. A reading was arranged for Monday, 17 May, at the large Prinzregenten Theater, Munich, as part of an End of the Century lecture series, and on 18 May to reopen a famous bookshop in Hamburg after its renovation. The latter was regarded as a high society event. Wherever Walcott went in Western Europe there were translations of his poems being published.

To fill in the time before going to England, Walcott accepted an invitation to the fourth St Malo International Festival of Literature and Voyages, 20–3 May.

The trip was later recalled in *The Bounty*'s 'I cannot remember the name of that seacoast city . . . a town with hyphens, I believe in Normandy | or Brittany' in which he painted 'a good watercolour'. He was part of a panel (20 May) on world fiction, nomads, and the literature of mulattos and was scheduled to speak (21 May) as part of the 'Café littéraire'. There was also a press conference. He spoke of his own poetry and its connection with French and French Creole literature, and said that Aimé Césaire deserved the Nobel Prize in Literature. He also met two French African writers, Tierno Monénembo and Abdourahman Waberi, at the conference cafeteria who thought him kind, calm, and casual. He talked to them about poetry, and African literature, and spoke favourably about Nuruddin Farah as a person and author.

Farah is from Somali, Waberi is from Djibouti, both former colonies where the main native language and cultures are Somali. For both writers nationalism and traditionalism are fake, reactionary; both authors have become exiles, Farah a writer in English, Waberi, in French. Walcott's claim that he and Brodsky share a similar exile and that the poets who are dedicated to poetry are the opponents and judges of the tyranny of politicians was increasingly making sense to post-colonial African writers, few of whom could remain in Africa and survive. The writers knew that they had to keep up with the modern European and American world and that they shared an international culture of the arts.

Tierno Monénembo, an exiled Guinean novelist who has lived in Normandy since 1985, remembers that although he spoke little English, he needed to speak English with Walcott. In St Malo and Paris Walcott avoided speaking French, although he had studied it in school and university and reads it fluently and understands it when spoken. In the same way as many writers who are careful with language, Walcott avoids what he thinks he may mispronounce. His spoken French is mainly St Lucian Creole, a version of the Creole spoken in Martinique and Guadeloupe.

The St Malo conference was really the introduction of the French to Walcott. Unlike many other Anglophone writers, such as Soyinka, he had not been much translated into French and his works were seldom taught in French universities (which still too often think of African literature as Sartre's introduction to the Black Orpheus anthology along with a bit of Césaire and Senghor). Despite France's close neo-colonial relationship with Francophonie, the exile of many French African writers in Paris, and the growth of a new black culture in France, as represented by Monénembo and Waberi, French intellectuals still think in terms of the negritude period.

Walcott was expected in London on 24 May for *The Odyssey* at the Barbican. There were several weeks of rehearsals in London for *The Odyssey*, which opened on 22 June at the Pit Theatre at the Barbican. This was basically the 1992 pro-duction with some cast changes. Most London reviewers liked the imaginative staging, the merging of the Aegean with the Caribbean Sea, and the mixtures of dictions. The *Daily Express* (26 June) praised a 'beguiling combination of the homely and the epic as Walcott veers between witty jive-talk and wondrous imagery to bring the ancient story alive'. The *Jewish Chronicle* felt 'Three hours devoted to the 20-year wandering of Odysseus . . . does not seem a moment too long.' The *Guardian* spoke of a 'user-friendly adaptation'. The run was sold out before opening.

Walcott seemed to be every place except at his play. He read (30 May) along with Edna O'Brien at the Hay-on-Wye Festival in Wales. On Friday, 4 June, he read from *Omeros* for two and a half hours at the Purcell Room, South Bank, for the fortieth birthday of the Poetry Library. The readings and opening coincided with the British, Faber, publication of *The Antilles: Fragments of Epic Memory*. He read (11 June) at Durham Castle for Colpitts Poetry and Durham LitFest.

On 17 June in Rotterdam the RO Theatre offered a seven-hour, all-night, 'narration' in Dutch, translated by Jan Eijkelboom, and directed by Pieter Vrijman, of the complete *Omeros* at the Rotterdamse Schouwburg. This was considered a continuation of the Afro-Caribe Festival at which the Trinidad Theatre Workshop performed in 1992 and publicity for 'The Night of Omeros' claimed that 'We might have to revert to Shakespeare to find an equal to Walcott's lavish use of the English language' and called the poem a 'thrilling tale'. Thirteen actors took part in the event which started at 11.30 p.m. on the 17th and concluded at 7 a.m. on the 18th. The narration was divided into seven sections, each lasting about an hour, which began with a brief introduction to the story so far, allowing the audience, as in traditional oral epic performances, to come and go. Food and drink were also available. Unlike traditional oral presentations of epics, the narration was broadcast live on radio station VPRO.

Walcott was in London (19 June) discussing a television version of *Ti-Jean* which two companies, one of them Tony Hall's Lord Street Communications, planned to produce for the BBC. Walcott was to write the script and be executive producer with creative control. The provisional budget was a million dollars, and Walcott was to earn $15,000 for the first draft. If the first-choice director did not accept, Walcott wanted to direct. This was another *Ti-Jean* film that has not materialized.

Returning to Trinidad, Walcott (2 July) spoke to the press at the Old Fire Station to announce the association of the Neal and Massey group of companies with the forthcoming production of *The Odyssey* and to criticize the government's plans to move the Trinidad Theatre Workshop from its theatre. He noted how the suicide of West Indian artists might have been influenced by the lack of support and he suggested that some large company should sponsor the Trinidad Theatre Workshop. Walcott's press conference produced a response in which it was claimed that the Old Fire Station at present was worth TT $23 million; if

Walcott wanted the Trinidad Theatre Workshop to continue he should seriously offer to invest TT $3 million in it and the Minister of Culture and the government would provide an alternative property and space.[12] Walcott began directing the rehearsals for *The Odyssey* in July and then went away when Doran arrived and took over.

On 17 July Kirchwey wrote to Walcott in St Lucia through his new agent, Howard Rosentone, about the 20 September *The Odyssey* at the Y. Morgan Freeman and Faye Dunaway were busy at the time, but James Earl Jones was now considering it. He would call Browne again in August to check his commitments. Walcott had been shooting for the stars and was having trouble getting them.

Ti-Jean, translated into Italian by Annuska Palme Sanavio, was produced 16–22 July at the Festa del Teatro at San Miniato. It was directed, using Tanker's original music, and staged by Sylvano Bussotti (a well-known composer as well as a director of operas), for the Teatro Dello Spirito of the Istituto del Dramma Popolare di Miniato (Pisa). *Ti-Jean* and *Dream* were published in Italian translations to coincide with the production. Walcott provided new watercolours to illustrate the programme which mentioned the universality of the Ti-Jean story, explaining that versions can be found in Africa and France. The programme noted the play's similarity to George Peele's *The Old Wives Tale* as well as Brechtian theatre. While Walcott and Tanker were present, Bussotti shaped the production to his artistic vision, designing the scenes, costumes, and lighting; he alluded to operas, comics, and recent news. The mother's hut was shown as a protective nest with eggs in the foreground.[13]

William Baer, editor of *The Formalist*, a magazine of metric verse, interviewed Walcott (1 August) during the Sewanee Writers' Conference at the University of the South. Baer was introduced to Walcott through Arthur Miller. The discussion with Walcott mostly concerned the 1983 'Eulogy to W. H. Auden' along with *The Arkansas Testament*. Walcott claimed that Auden's seemingly contradictory remarks in 'In Memory of W. B. Yeats' about poetry making 'nothing happen', yet teaching the 'free man how to praise' should be seen in relationship to images of nature—a poem is like a river or cloud, sacred, like prayer, which makes things happen by touching them. The politics of a poet's life is irrelevant to poetry in so far as great poetry remains pure of prejudices; 'It's a kind of grace that's bestowed on the serious and talented poet.' But real hate and bitterness cannot be made into poetry as poetry must 'achieve a supreme compassion and tenderness'. It is patronizing to be told by a British critic that you are doing well and wrong to be accused by local critics of betrayal. Writers feel such complications which adds to the dramatic and historical interest of their work. For a nation with a great consciousness of, and responsibility for, justice, the contemporary poetry of America is small, provincial, and muted, without large egos, without

Pity or Love. There is no exaltation or daring. American poets are embarrassed to be happy. Auden was a great poet who could write of Pity and Justice. Baer later edited *Conversations with Derek Walcott* for the University Press of Mississippi (1996).

There was a dramatized reading of *The Odyssey* by the Trinidad Theatre Workshop, 5–11 August, at the Old Fire House in Port of Spain. Gregory Doran considerably changed the production, getting rid of the masks Walcott had started with. The opening night was a Gala with tickets at TT $125 (United States $25) to raise funds for the Trinidad Theatre Workshop. The ticket collectors and ushers wore floral-print wrappers and there was a lounge with music from a steel pan, and such snacks as mini-roti and baked chicken drumsticks. Television was invited and those in attendance included Beryl McBurnie, Peter Minshall, the theatre director Ralph Maraj, who was now Minister for External Affairs, the former Prime Minister A. N. R. Robinson, the Mayor of Port of Spain, and the Chairman of the Airports Authority.

The *Trinidad Guardian* described what people wore and carried pictures of what was clearly a social as well as a cultural event, while commenting on the absence of 'those multifunctional shirtjack suits made famous by the PNM'. The PNM had governed for most of the time Walcott had been in Trinidad. They had never supported him and he had learned to seek his support elsewhere, but both seemed engaged in a continuing quarrel which erupted even in such remarks as how people were dressed on opening night and which concerned the history and future of the Trinidad Theatre Workshop. Reviews described *The Odyssey* as the best production in Trinidad for years. Ramcharitar commented that Walcott added a contemporary Caribbean flavour to Homer's story—the Gods and Underworld no longer exist, 'soldiers goose step over philosophers'. The production was sold out and could have continued, but the Workshop had to prepare *Dream on Monkey Mountain* for its trip to Holland in September.[14]

Meanwhile in Trinidad the newspapers wondered who would receive the Trinity Cross, Trinidad's highest honour, on Independence Day, Tuesday, 31 August. A petition supposedly signed by 10,000 recommended 'Kitch', the popular calypsonian Lord Kitchener. Walcott was the only recipient of the top award and he was one of the four that night who had sent apologies saying that they had alternative plans and would receive their medals at a later date. The second highest award went to the calypsonian singer Mighty Sparrow.

Although Walcott chose to receive the Trinity Cross privately in December rather than along with other honours awarded at the President's house, the newspapers made a point of mentioning that Sparrow returned to Trinidad especially for the ceremony while Walcott attended a musical show at the Moon Over Bourbon Street club in the West Mall about six miles away. The newspapers implied that Walcott was angry at the government; his conduct was said to be an insult to the nation which conferred the award rather than to the party in power. Although Walcott had a right to accept the award later and had notified the President of his plans for that night, there were many letters in the newspapers calling his behaviour arrogant. As Walcott left on Thursday, Albert Laveau was left to calm the storm. Laveau claimed that officials from the White House and Her Majesty the Queen of England had telephoned to ask when it would be convenient for Walcott to meet the President and the Queen; only in Trinidad was there a 'big bacchanal'. Laveau denied that Walcott was protesting against the government's treatment of the Trinidad Theatre Workshop and said that discussions were still being held with the government. Later it turned out that Lord Kitchener had turned down the Chaconia award as he felt he deserved the Trinity Cross, while one reason Walcott probably did not attend the ceremony was that Manning, Prime Minister and head of the PNM, was on the platform and had regularly used such public occasions to promote his party. So what should have been a national event indeed had become a Trinidadian bacchanal.[15]

Independence Day brought many comments about Walcott and his role as a West Indian intellectual and artist. The *Sunday Guardian Magazine* reprinted from 1963 Walcott's Independence perspective on the arts, 'The Future of Art Promising', along with pieces by C. L. R. James and others. Wayne Brown lamented James's corruption by power, but praised him for seeing that Trinidad's relationship to England was similar to Ireland's in being capable of using British traditions and forms without being imprisoned by them, a characteristic as much of West Indian cricket as of Walcott's poetry. If James's mind was seminal, Walcott's article foresaw how the recent collapse of the Federation would hurt the growing community of West Indian artists. Nations would become isolated; politics seldom helped the arts, but helped to breed amateurism. Amateurism was more of a danger than imperialism and the colonial mentality. There were too many banks and business houses in Port of Spain that had on their nice new walls cheap reproductions of foreign landscapes.[16]

Early in September Walcott was in St Lucia assisting with plans to film *Ti-Jean* during 1994; he and Brodsky then read at several places in Sweden including at the Gothenburg Bookfair; on 30–1 September Walcott, Ashbery, and Tomas Tranströmer read at the Nordic Poetry Festival in New York.

At the Unterberg Poetry Center of the 92nd Street Y, New York, Greg Doran directed the semi-dramatized reading of *The Odyssey* (20 September) with Walcott as Menelaus, Irene Worth as Athena and Anticlea, Roscoe Lee Browne as Billy Blue, Tiresias, and the Cyclops, and, from Trinidad, Eunice Alleyne as Eurycleia, and Cecilia Salazar as Nausicaa. Walcott had previously refused to act in plays, but from now on he started to appear in staged readings; actors and directors have told me he is good. Kirchwey (21 September) wrote thanking Walcott for his work on *The Odyssey*, and remarked how well he had worked with Greg

Doran, whom Kirchwey hoped to use again in future. Walcott had surprised Kirchwey with his drumming and suggestions about adding various blues, calypsos, and shango songs.

The Trinidad Theatre Workshop and Walcott were already in Rotterdam for the fifth Afro-Caribe Festival. *Dream* was performed 21–2 September and *Celebration* the next two nights. The casts included two new young stars, Wendell Manwarren and Glenda Thomas. *Dream* was performed again in October in Port of Spain and once more became part of the regular repertory of the Workshop.

For the autumn term 1993 Walcott was Northrop Frye Visiting Professor in Literary Theory (!) at the University of Toronto's Centre for Comparative Literature. This was arranged by Ted Chamberlin, a scholar in Canadian and West Indian literature, who was a professor in New College. Between September and December Walcott gave twelve graduate seminars on 'The Language of Poetry' (two every alternate Friday at 10 a.m.–12 p.m. and 2–4 p.m.) for the Centre for Comparative Literature and Department of English, read with Michael Ondaatje on 30 September, and gave a public lecture, 11 November, on 'Europe' which consisted of brief opening remarks followed by readings from his own work. Roderick Walcott attended the lecture as did Sir Alister McIntyre, the Vice-Chancellor of the University of the West Indies, and the Jamaican writer Louise Bennett. Chamberlin, introducing both Ondaatje's and Walcott's readings, mentioned that when he first met Ondaatje, Michael had asked him for a copy of Walcott's recently published *The Star-Apple Kingdom*. Chamberlin, himself a Canadian nationalist, praised Walcott for 'bringing new visions in new voices to create a new literary tradition', for 'locating sources of inspiration in the everyday', and for showing 'that the imaginative power and literary authority of the English language is something too important to be left solely in the hands of the English'. Chamberlin cited a Cornish proverb, 'the tongueless man gets his land took'.[17]

Walcott still taught at Boston University on Monday and Tuesday, and was busy with other readings or meetings mid-week and weekends, so Toronto was mostly an overnight stop on a circuit of professional activities. On 22 October he read at San Diego State University.

I remember one weekend when he had just returned from Amsterdam; he did his teaching in Boston, and the next day flew to Chicago, for a reading Wednesday night and a lecture the next morning at the University of Valparaiso in Indiana (10–11 November). He was picked up at the airport in Chicago, taken to his hotel to sign in just before the reading, then taken to the lecture hall where he read from *Omeros*. At Valparaiso there was the usual party after the reading to meet the staff and community at which Walcott sat on a sofa in a corner, obviously tired, quietly answering questions from various well-wishers. When I asked him what he was now working on, he mentioned four plays, including *The*

Capeman with Paul Simon and the revision of *Steel*. He said he was once more writing short poems. The next morning, Thursday, he gave a poetry class and there was an open question and answer session.

Most of the English Department at Valparaiso, a good liberal arts college, had not read Walcott's poetry or plays. He was not their speciality, not part of the American or their Black literature canon. The students, who had been given some poems to study, kept asking Walcott embarrassing questions that belonged to the current discourse of politically correct racial victimization and separatism. They seemed unwilling to accept that Walcott was saying anything else. At one point, annoyed, he said he did not believe in multiculturalism as it now meant separatism. While copies of his books were on sale before and after the reading and lecture, Walcott hurriedly left for Chicago immediately after the question and answer session to fly to Toronto for his 'Europe' lecture that night. He was going on to New York for the weekend as he had some business concerning the theatre and with his editor; Monday and Tuesday he would be back in Boston. Apparently this Toronto trip was the start of a plan for the University of Toronto and the University of the West Indies to share Walcott's papers and manuscripts. Toronto would in a few years purchase his post-1984 papers.

He read at Queens College, in New York, on 23 November, then, on 30 November, he, Brodsky, Arthur Miller, Wendy Wasserstein, Tony Kushner, Don DeLillo, Jamaica Kincaid, and Susan Sontag were brought together by the PEN American Center in New York to raise money to help Bosnian writers endure another winter of the war. Sontag, who had recently produced Beckett's *Waiting for Godot* in Sarajevo, read a 1983 essay by the Yugoslav writer Danilo Kiš who died in 1989. Kiš was a poet Brodsky and Walcott admired. Later that week, on Saturday, 4 December, he read along with Czeslaw Milosz, Octavio Paz, Brodsky, and Rita Dove at the Cathedral of St John the Divine in New York for the Academy of American Poets.

The next week, 10 December, there was a reading of 'Walker' a one-act unpublished opera at the Athenaeum, a Boston library that sometimes has musical events. The libretto was by Walcott, the music by T. J. Anderson, who was then Austin Fletcher Professor in the Department of Music at Tufts University. 'Walker' is based on the life of David Walker a black abolitionist active in Boston after 1825. David Kelley, a former project director of the Athenaeum, had in 1984 'worked with' Walcott on a performance of *The Last Carnival* at the Athenaeum. In 1988 he decided to bring together Walcott and Anderson, a well-known African-American composer and conductor. Walcott said that he did not know opera, it was not his kind of music, but he agreed to look at the lives of various abolitionists which were presented to him. Quickly, within a few weeks, he made an outline and notes on the character of Walker. Walcott became interested in the story, which was self-contained; he sent Anderson material, which the composer cut until there was a libretto. During February 1992 he asked for more songs for arias. Walcott provided more than could be used. Anderson cut out two hours of a three-hour libretto. They worked separately, as Anderson had trouble contacting Walcott who was never at home when he telephoned.

The unpublished libretto is a poem of about seventy-five minutes. Walcott added to the facts, including a break between Walker and William Lloyd Garrison. Walker becomes a Malcolm X, a Martin Luther King, a poet haunted by language. Walcott did not hear the music until December. Anderson used a chamber orchestra of nine musicians along with six singers, three black and three white. Anderson only saw the production after it was assembled as he had retired and was living in North Carolina. It was performed as a concert and videotaped in a small packed room before perhaps a hundred patrons of the Athenaeum. 'Walker' was supposed to be done again in 1994 at Longy Music School but was cancelled as Walcott and Donna Roll, a singer who taught at the school, wanted a longer version. Walcott apparently wanted 'Walker' expanded to a full-length opera and did not appreciate the problems in expanding a chamber opera to a larger work.[18]

Around 1993 Walcott started painting in oils again. The decision whether to use watercolour or oil has been largely determined by the time available, as oils require more time, but the effect and technique are also different. Just as I find Walcott's drawings for the theatre often more spontaneous and free-flowing in appearance than the highly structured land- and seascapes, so I find that the use of detailed contrasts of shade and light in the oil paintings results in a hyperrealism, a realism that is so closely observed and worked as to seem a bit surreal. There have been so many badly done amateur paintings in this mode that to see an artist with great technique handling similar subjects in what may seem at first a similar manner is unsettling. Part of Walcott's success and trouble as a painter is the highly structured nature of his compositions.

Rhona Pilgrim has the original watercolour used for the cover of *Omeros*, a watercolour of a canoe on a beach painted near the Villa Beach Cottages at around that time, and an oil painting of Pigeon Point done in 1993. Each of the three paintings uses a similar compositional design, and outlines could be transferred from one painting to another. In two of the paintings, done five years apart and at two different places, vertical and curving framing lines are made by trees and vegetation at the same places in the canvas. The scenes are very much St Lucian, but the composition belongs to a tradition deriving from Nicolas Poussin and later French painters. This is Walcott's limitation and strength as a painter.

In March it was announced that Colonial Life Insurance's 1994 calendar would feature Walcott's watercolours for the theatre along with texts from his poems and plays. The year ended with the distribution of the 1994 calendar, which used thirteen Walcott paintings as illustrations, sold for TT $55, and soon became a collector's item. This was the third, and the most successful, illustrated Colonial Life Insurance (Clico) annual calendar, the previous two having used Jackie Hinkson paintings. The idea for a Walcott calendar began after the announcement of the 1992 Nobel Prize and was first intended to contain only extracts from his poetry. Soon it was remembered that Walcott had exhibited at the Art Creators gallery and Clara de Lima showed some of his work to Clico. Walcott suggested simplifying the appearance of the calendar to emphasize the paintings, and by March 1993 had prepared rough drawings and chosen the texts to illustrate. Some of the painting was done during the August–September fuss over Walcott not attending the award ceremony. There are fifteen paintings in total on the calendar, thirteen new ones and two loaned by Lizzie Walcott. While many of the paintings are of expected scenes, such as from *Omeros* (January), *Steel* (February), *Ti-Jean* (March and April), some are surprising, such as the Edwardian *Sulphur* (November), a play Walcott was working on then about which little is known. The calendar won Colonial Life Insurance Company a 1994 calendar design award for creativity.[19]

The Nobel Award was celebrated on at least eleven stamps and two souvenir sheets of stamps. Sweden began in 1992 with two 5.50 krona stamps, in September 1993 Walcott was pictured on a $7.60 stamp from Guyana, while Trinidad issued in four denominations an unusual stamp depicting the first three recipients of the Order of the Caribbean Community: Walcott, the Secretary-General of the Commonwealth Shridath Rampal from Guyana, and the Trinidadian economist William Demas. Bahamas and St Kitts had souvenir sheets commemorating the three men. Walcott was also on a Barbados stamp. For Walcott the most important was the 75 cent stamp issued on 25 October 1993 by St Lucia in its Carib Art series. This shows Walcott's painting of Reduit Bay.[20] Walcott is not a great painter, but how many painters have had their work on a calendar, on stamps, and on St Lucia telephone cards? There are unexpected advantages to be had from winning a Nobel Prize.

31

1994–1996 More Journeys and Homecomings

WALCOTT views life as a journey, a voyage outward, but increasingly the theme was the voyage home, the hero's return. His conversation was a mixture of letting the listener know of new projects, plays that famous directors wanted to commission, plans to make films of *Ti-Jean* and *Omeros*, pride in the success in England of some younger Trinidadian actors, and talk of retiring from Boston to St Lucia and painting full time. The latter seemed unlikely, especially as so many famous writers were coming to St Lucia to visit Walcott that there were amused comments to the effect that he needed his private international airport before he could retire. During 1994 Walcott's wanderings or at least his promotion of books included visits to Spain and Japan. For a few years the Trinidad Theatre Workshop had a second lease on life, partly because it began teaching in Port of Spain, but mostly as an extension of Walcott's new fame.

At the New Year Walcott was in his partly built new home between Gros Islet and Pigeon Point. He attended the now annual international jazz festival which has become one of St Lucia's tourist attractions. (It has since been moved to later in the year.) He was scheduled to read at Michigan State University, East Lansing, on 19 January. I planned to attend, but there was a terrible winter storm and radio stations warned that roads were impassable and airplane flights were cancelled or badly delayed. The journey from St Lucia to a small Michigan airport for a one-night stand seemed improbable, with Walcott likely to be delayed in Miami or, if he got that far, Chicago. I was certain the reading would be cancelled. Later a friend sent me a taped copy of the reading. I asked Walcott how he got to East Lansing; there was the usual half-smile and deep nicotine-stained half-grunt.

The Workshop was once more active and took *Dream on Monkey Mountain* to St Lucia (25–9 January) as part of Laureate Week. The next month the Workshop travelled to St Croix and St Thomas. *Celebration* was at the Island Center for the Performing Arts, St Croix (21 February). Walcott's participation was now a 'Special Appearance'. They moved on to the Reichhold Center for the Arts, St Thomas, performing *Celebration* (23 February), and *Dream on Monkey Mountain* (25–6 February).

Rehearsals began in early January in Minneapolis for the Guthrie Theatre's production of *Dream on Monkey Mountain*, directed by dancer-choreographer Bill T. Jones. The production included eight dancers from Jones's Dance Company. *Dream on Monkey Mountain* was now a classic of black theatre, associated in the American mind with decolonization, nationalism, the sixties, and the civil rights movement; Jones's production was a nineties deconstruction, concretizing Walcott's images, contrasting Walcott's St Lucia with urban black America, ironizing the hopes of the past. Whereas the paradoxes and possible tyranny of a return to Africa in Walcott's text are shown by the verbal destruction of white literature, culture, and history, in Jones's version an immense white book is brought on stage and page by page white history is torn out and held up to ridicule. Jones suggests the passing of time, racial continuities, and cultural contrasts by beginning with a barefoot West Indian listening to music from a small, hard-cased portable record player, and ended the show with ten inner-city blacks dressed in Nikes, baggy clothes, with a boom box. Two worlds, two times, supposedly the same people. Jones's images and music were also very boom-boxy reinterpretations of Walcott's vision, but that is what happens to classics, although it is rare that they are being rewritten by later generations while the author is still alive, very active, and still trying to get his own version seen.

I wish some famous American theatre such as the Guthrie had made the Trinidad Theatre Workshop's great production of *Dream* part of its schedule. The Guthrie was trying to be multicultural, and Jones is certainly not a black separatist, rather the contrary, but somehow Walcott's plays do not translate into white or black-American English. Instead of the beheading of the white apparition in Makak's dream, intended as a means of freeing oneself from feelings of inferiority to whiteness, Jones substituted a beam of light for the woman as 'Maya Angelou convinced him that ritually sacrificing white women onstage in African-American theatre has been done so often it is now cliché'.[1]

Glyn Maxwell had returned to England from his year at Boston University and was now on his way to Port of Spain to see Carnival on a travel award for young writers. On the same airplane was Greg Doran, who had been invited by Walcott to direct the Trinidad Theatre Workshop's *The Joker of Seville* for a forthcoming tour. Three decades earlier Walcott had pleaded with the Rockefeller Foundation to send him a professional director to give his company further training and the experience of a different director. Walcott and Doran had fought during the final days of *The Odyssey*, but the results showed what a professional director could do. Walcott was also returning to Port of Spain as he wanted to see, and wanted Doran to see, Peter Minshall's 'The Odyssey' presentation at Carnival. Doran and Maxwell stayed with Margaret Walcott, who elected to be one of Circe's swine in Minshall's Carnival band. Maxwell and Doran, unused to getting up at 2 a.m. to begin a day's drunken dancing, decided to forgo mas' and watch. Once he and Doran had cast *Joker*, Derek, not himself someone to 'jump-up' and join the Carnival frenzy, left for the peace of St Lucia.

In March the poet, performance artist, and journalist Patricia Smith also came to stay with Margaret. Patricia Smith was to perform six days of her 'Life After Motown' under the sponsorship of the Trinidad Theatre Workshop. She had first performed it under Derek's direction in Boston. Walcott returned to Port of Spain.

During April he was usually on the road. He was at the Roethke Humanities Festival at Lafayette College, Eaton, Pennsylvania, 18–19 April, where he gave the keynote speech on 'Earth: Matter and Metaphor', and the next day talked to a drama course about his work in the context of 'the Euro-American tradition'. He flew to Ireland for the A. T. Cross Cúirt Festival of Literature in Galway, where he read from *Omeros* to conclude the festival (25 April), then returned to the United States the next day. Tom Kilroy introduced Walcott by comparing his poetry to the sea, as powerful, full of life and mythology, and linking continents.

Eileen Battersby in the *Irish Times* wrote of the powerful images, various political and cultural currents, and many forms of exile in *Omeros*. Earlier Paddy Woodworth in the *Irish Times* had said that Walcott was the most sought-after poet in the English-speaking world, that he was now paid up to $25,000 a reading in the United States, and that after some bargaining the Cúirt Festival had managed to get him to come for less, but for what was still the largest fee they had paid. Walcott had not answered their letters, but they had contacted him through mutual friends. Walcott had earlier visited Galway with Seamus Heaney 'to taste the oysters'.[2]

At this point, with all the comings and goings, I need a split-screen book. Doran was quoted by local press (23 April) as saying that coming to Trinidad to direct *The Joker of Seville* was like directing *Le Malade imaginaire* at the Comédie Française or *Mother Courage* with the Berliner Ensemble. Doran especially praised the new members of the cast, Wendell Manwarren, Cecilia Salazar, Leah Gordon, Michael Cherrie, and John Isaacs. (When I interviewed Doran a year later he said that Walcott was reluctant to accept that Jones, Marshall, and the older members of the Workshop were past it, while some of the younger actors were international star calibre.) MacDermot also came to rehearsals as there were six new songs. When Walcott returned there were some workshops with a local pan band and a vocal group for a revised *Steel*.

A camera crew and Walcott came from Boston (29 May) to shoot footage for a documentary concerning Walcott and the Trinidad Theatre Workshop. They also went to St Lucia. Boston University was hoping to sell the documentary and a record of the forthcoming tour to Public Broadcasting System television. Nigel Scott, Claude Reid, with Brenda Hughes as director, left Trinidad (30 May) for Singapore where (4–6 June) the Workshop's *Pantomime* was part of the Singapore Festival of Arts. The Central Bank of Trinidad and Tobago announced (2 June) a partial scholarship in creative writing, United States $4000, to study with Walcott at Boston University. The university would waive tuition fees for the scholar. Applications had to include fifteen pages of poetry which Walcott would read. Even with Walcott out of the country he remained in the news. The *Sunday Guardian Magazine* (12 June) had an article about rehearsals of *Joker* at the Old Fire Station. There was a photograph of MacDermot at the piano, Walcott at drums, and Doran directing.

With Doran directing *Joker* Walcott could go to Spain (3–16 June). This, his first trip to Spain, was to accept the award of an honorary degree by the University of Alcalá de Henares (Madrid). The Vice-President of the university wanted a non-canonical writer and Walcott was suggested by José Anonito Gurpegui of the Department of Modern Philology, who knew him from Boston where he goes to do research every year. From 5–8 June Walcott was the guest of the Mayoress of Calahorra, in the province of La Rioja, and spent time at San Adrián (Navarre) with José Antonio Gurpegui, who was his guide in Spain (and to whom the 'Spain' sequence in *The Bounty* is dedicated). On 10 June he was invested as 'Doctor Honoris Causa' for the Department of Modern Philology at the University of Alcalá. After the ceremony he went to Granada, 11–13 June, where he read from his poetry at the university and visited the Alhambra. *Omeros* had been translated into Catalan as well as Castilian. The Catalan publisher, Edicions Alfons el Magnànim, had written several letters to Straus inviting Walcott to come to Valencia for a 'presentation' of the book. Walcott postponed his return to the United States to travel to Valencia (13–15 June), where Canal 9 taped a television programme for 'La esfera de la cultura'. Indeed the national and local university television stations filmed most of his public appearances; interviews appeared in many local and national newspapers.

Walcott loved Spain, its food, the bull fights (he called himself El Walcotto), and talked about returning. He called Velásquez's *Las Meninas* the masterpiece of art history and said it was worth coming to Spain just to see it. During his days in Granada he had to change his hotel several times; Joyce Carol Oates had previously moved from one of the same hotels and Walcott joked that in the future there might be a notice saying 'Joyce Carol Oates left here, Derek Walcott left here.' In *The Bounty* there are several poems based on this trip, including 'Granada. Red earth and raw, the olive clumps olive and silver'. One supposed reason Walcott stayed on in Spain was to have a paella, which he loved, but which my Spanish informant says was terrible, the worst he ever ate.[3]

Omeros was translated into Spanish by the Mexican poet José Luis Rivas, with the assistance of an American, Norman Glass. It was published in 1994 by Anagrama (Barcelona) and had by the end of the year sold nearly 3,000 copies. Although Walcott was not known in Spain before the Nobel Prize he received much attention; my impression is that because of Latin American literature there was an understanding of what he had written in *Omeros*. The reviewer for *El Pais* started with the examples of Carpentier, Neruda, and Lezama to discuss the negation of European civilization and colonial history that is needed to bring out the many voices of the Antilles.

On 9 June 'At Alcalá', Walcott started a poem of over 140 lines, a mixture of alexandrines, trisyllabic quatrameters, and iambic pentameters, to be read the next day as his 'Discurso de Aceptación' for the 'Doctor Honoris Causa'. The manuscript, published by the university, in Walcott's own script, was finished the next morning, before the afternoon's ceremony. An unusual example of a contemporary poet discoursing in verse, the poem is remarkable for the way Walcott writes easily in metre, creates a harmony of end rhymes, and moves through various topics. The autobiographical, recent events from his Spanish trip, the relationship of Spain and the Spanish language to the West Indies, comments on Spanish art, culture, and politics, become part of an apology for offering no wisdom beyond the richness of life itself to which art must give form and permanence. The poem is self-consciously aware of the Spanish tradition of the baroque, of the greatness of Spanish oratory, of the expected touristy clichés, and of the ways in which Spanish culture both soars above and is rooted in the elemental.

The poem is an example of how art illuminates by naming, fixing, associating, and celebrating. The metaphorizing of reality is the poem, 'every rock-pile a poem, every clear stream the metre'. The rapid but fine movement between the commonplace and poetic is described ironically as catching 'as I have the influenza of your rhetoric'. Walcott contrasts his Anglophone New World reading of Spanish history (the Armada, Conquistadors, butchered Indians) with the 'honourable doctors' of the past (Loyola, Savanarola, Erasmus) who could provide the university with a 'discourse'. But poetry at its best, like San Juan de la Cruz, offers only 'radiance and silence'. Beyond allusions to Spanish literature, and to Walcott currently reading a novel by Cela, the poem also pays tribute to Spanish art; *Las Meninas* 'is worth crossing the ocean-sea for'. Walcott also pays tribute to his hosts, 'the incredible roasted lamb of José Antonio's uncle, | the laugh of Carmel, the real taste of olives, | they are the real history, those events of the senses'. After mocking himself as having become a fourth-rate Hemingway, Walcott claims the true honour is in being able to share experiences with people, and that this is love. The poem then rapidly returns to themes that were broached earlier. Other languages, histories, and cultures are a burden, but the truths echo in translation, just as part of Spain and Spanish can be found in the West Indies. The light and geography of the New World may differ, but the sins remain similar. Poetry offers no solutions to the horrors of history, nor does it pretend to have found paradise.

The Audenesque echoes, especially to the poem on the death of Yeats, make me feel that 'At Alcalá' is more than an occasion piece, more than a verse 'discourse' on many familiar Walcott topics. Is it not a reply or indirect comment on Auden's famous '1939', the ultimate poem of commitment, engagement, of making politics happen at the expense of ordinary life? Walcott knew how Auden had later repudiated and revised 'September 1939', and that the poem on the death of Yeats is often cited as part of Auden's recantation. Expected to offer a learned 'discourse' at a university in post-Franco Spain, and expected to be representative of the non-canonical New World, Walcott's mind turned to the various contradictions of history, the way life and poetry continue regardless of the need for 'continual revolution | against cruel empires or banal dictatorships'. There are no 'Islands of the Blest remote from confusion'. Walcott like Auden sees a fallen world, a world of evils, which can only be rescued by love, a version of Christian charity, the love of God through his creation and creatures as well as himself. You can love God by loving others.[4]

After the 1993 Boston production of *Nobel Celebration* John Silber wrote to Walcott (28 April 1993) saying that it was a memorable evening and Silber hoped that in future there would be more co-operation between the university and the Workshop as well as with the Rat Island Foundation. He would explore whether the Huntington Theatre might be used for a Workshop production. In fact there were to be three plays, two at the Huntington and one at the Playwrights Theatre, although at a time of the year when most Bostonians were at the beach and a large theatre like the Huntington was difficult to fill. This was to be the longest and best prepared Trinidad Theatre Workshop tour of North America; it was recorded on video by Boston University. It was also the celebration of the thirty-fifth anniversary of the Trinidad Theatre Workshop.

On 3 July a cast of thirty left Port of Spain for Boston. *The Joker of Seville*, directed by Doran, had ten performances at the Huntington Theatre starting 7 July. Richard Montgomery created the very inventive costumes and design which were similar to his 1975 Jamaican production except, following Walcott's wishes, it was in places based on Goya's paintings. Wendell Manwarren now had the role of the Don Juan, the Joker, instead of Nigel Scott who although still handsome was older and heavier. *Dream on Monkey Mountain*, directed by Albert Laveau, opened on 21 July for ten performances. John Andrews's lighting scheme was the most complex I and local professionals have seen. It was a work of art in itself. Andrews learned his art using painted and coloured cellophane in the days when the Workshop had little lighting equipment. A painter and dancer in his youth he was now a very upper-level administrator who kept the Trinidad government running regardless of the politicians in power, one of those who run the country during a crisis. Both plays were videotaped by Boston University. There was also a private showing of *Pantomime* for Silber and friends, and four days of workshops on *Steel*, both at the Playwrights Theatre. Boston University invested a quarter of a million dollars on the tour, filming, and other events.

As usual on Trinidad Theatre Workshop tours there were a number of social events designed to keep the group together, to keep up morale. Even free time was planned with suggested group shopping trips or jazz clubs. One evening there was a boat ride in Boston Harbour, and there were several parties. These were Trinidadians, even the boat ride was an opportunity for dancing. Another night there was a dinner and dance. Afterwards Walcott spoke to the company about the inhospitality of the Trinidadian national government, and how Laveau had kept the company going, even having to clean up dog shit. The resources available in Boston were what they should have had thirty-five years ago; they should not have needed to find their own costumes. No ensemble in the world had such a sense of family love. Boston University had agreed to offer Glenda Thomas a singing scholarship. After Derek spoke Glenda started the cast singing.

The tour was notable for the number of young actors, actresses, and technicians. Many of the young were of star quality and had been developed by other Trinidadian theatre groups during the years Walcott and the Trinidad Theatre Workshop were quarrelling. Jones and Marshall were marvellous actors, but clearly ageing—within a few years this would become even more obvious. The resurrection of the Trinidad Theatre Workshop as a vital company could only last a few years. It was an uneven but brilliant company and those who witnessed the Boston tour understood what Walcott had been aiming at all those years when he hoped to create a West Indian troupe to perform his plays. There was talk of bringing *Joker* to the London International Festival of Theatre, but Doran, a white Englishman, was director, thus making the play open to charges of 'ventriloquism'. Another victory for the politically correct and post-colonialists who knew what minorities and victims and the formerly colonized must say. For those who knew a bit about Doran it was especially ironic; he was himself from a minority and also more genuinely engaged than most of the killjoy 'sensitive' wannabees ever would be.

Kevin Kelly in the *Boston Globe* described *Dream* as a great play, dense, demanding, an anthem about freedom, difficult to absorb all at once, but powerful. He thought the production wonderfully directed, with powerhouse performances by Errol Jones and Wendell Manwarren. The *Boston Herald* called the Workshop a 'talented ensemble', praised Walcott's 'brilliant drama' and spoke of the 'visceral impact of his images'. Bill Marx in the *Boston Phoenix* saw *Dream* as meditating on the 1960s romanticization of black power, and thought that while the play was far above contemporary American theatre it was not quite up to Marlowe and Shakespeare. The Brechtian distancing of *Joker* and the complications of getting a large amateur company up to professional level were reflected in some of the reviews. Carolyn Clay in the *Boston Phoenix* thought the Trinidad Theatre Workshop an ebullient troupe of varying abilities ranging from the irresistible to the amateurish. There were certainly some mistakes. I remember at one performance Errol Jones joining a crowd mid-scene, and the singing could have been improved, but, taken to a European drama festival, this would have been a hit covered by the international press. Instead American drama critics were concerned about the dangers of seduction in an era of Aids. They would have been happier with a lecture on safe sex.[5] In Trinidad *The Joker* had a twelve-performance run at the large Queen's Hall in Port of Spain, 8–18 September, and then was taken to San Fernando, 30 September–2 October.

Walcott was in St Lucia during August doing some preliminary shooting of *Omeros* when his many years of chain-smoking caught up with him; he found it difficult to get rid of a cough. He was advised to give up smoking, advice seconded by his daughter Lizzie. He enjoyed one more day of cigarettes and in a display of will gave up immediately. As with many ex-smokers his voice developed a somewhat raspy quality, and many friends thought he became constantly irritable and likely to lose his temper. Some thought his personality had changed, or perhaps that his less attractive characteristics showed more often. It is impossible to know how much was overwork and worry about his work, especially the seemingly never ending *Capeman* project with Paul Simon, how much was an intensification of a long obsession about death and judgement, how much was a decrease in energy as he became older, but Walcott often was rude to friends, quarrelled, and seemed increasingly hypersensitive. He no longer began work absurdly early in the morning, and claimed that he no longer cared whether his plays were performed in London and New York, was silent for long periods, complained of fatigue, and distrusted others. A year previously the Nobel Prize appeared to have brought him great joy and a sense of accomplishment that he wanted to share. Now he seemed walled in the fortress of his fame, a mighty monarch annoyed that he could no longer keep up his former schedule, although he still remained extremely active.

'Odysseen af Derek Walcott efter Homer' was performed 23 September–5 November 1994 at the Aarhus Theater Scala in Bo Green Jensen's translation into Danish directed by Hans Rosenquist. *The Odyssey* had been performed in Stratford-upon-Avon and London by the RSC, in Aarhus in Danish, given a dramatized reading by the Trinidad Theatre Workshop in Port of Spain, read in New York at the YMHA, and now there was to be a major production in Washington, DC.

Rehearsals for *The Odyssey* at the Arena stage began in late August. The play opened for previews on 30 September, 5 October was press night, and the play ran until 6 November. This production was directed by Douglas Wager; MacDermot was commissioned to write the vocal music, and Carol LaChapelle was brought in from Trinidad as a movement and cultural consultant. *The Odyssey* was done in the round with the audience sitting on four sides. There was a cast of twenty to perform more than forty characters; there were 150 costumes. As with most plays the final script for the production was different from that used in the printed version. The rehearsal script is filled with the usual comments about cutting, clarifying, but here there are also notes to add another quatrain to allow time for an actor to do something. Was this how Shakespeare wrote?

Walcott was expected to attend rehearsals and generally joined in the play's promotion as a part of a reassessment of the epic journey in an age of post-colonial multiculturalism. He spoke with high school teachers for three hours on how to teach Homer's *Odyssey*. On 3 October he read at the Annual Literary Festival, Old Dominion University, Virginia, where, as for many of these literary festivals, his reading was now the star event.

The Washington *Odyssey* was thought good but slow. Vincent Canby in the *New York Times* claimed that the fancy production worked against the text; Walcott's words described enough without all the machinery. There were too many spectacular effects dropping from the ceiling or rising through trap doors. Richard Corliss in *Time* said that the play started slowly and treated heroics in a stilted fashion, but as it progressed it was fun, 'sassy', and a 'playroom filled with spritely wonder'. The review gave more attention to the machinery than to the text, which might be regarded as the critic's taste or Walcott's increasing ability to write plays for theatrical spectacle. The *Georgetown Voice* praised the 'constant kaleidoscope of movement, colour, and dramatic images'. Amy E. Schwartz in the *Washington Post* pointed to a cultural significance. While the National Endowment for the Humanities sponsored a debate between historians and writers concerning 'Who Owns History' (by which was meant should it be rewritten from the perspective of minorities), Walcott laid claim to a literature some would argue was not his own 'since Walcott is usually identified as black'. Schwartz thought the play 'a surprisingly faithful rendition of Homer' and seemed to think that it had started as an invitation from the Arena. Maybe she might have caught up on some recent theatre history, but she was correct that *The Odyssey* took a different perspective on history from the assumptions that governed discussion in the United States. It neither defended an older view nor was it black or minority history.[6]

Walcott, Glissant, and Condé were now being asked to comment on American policy in the Caribbean. Glissant came to Boston to talk about Haiti and was introduced by Walcott. Later Condé and Walcott would speak at Howard University and in Washington. Walcott was interviewed on 20 September by Nathan Gardels about the American occupation of Haiti. Walcott praised it as benign, something had to be done to save the people from their rulers, but Walcott criticized American policy towards Cuba. Why tolerate one dictator and be aggressive towards another? The United States should be consistent. The Americas should all be democratic from Canada to Chile; the United States supported some tyrants. The United States had an amazingly democratic imperialism in which the public discussed and debated issues, unlike England, France, or Russia which did not allow public scrutiny of policies.[7]

On 22 October, Walcott was part of the International Festival of Authors at Harbourfront Toronto. During a tightly packed festival when events were often taking place in three different rooms, he shared the evening with Ursula LeGuin, Frank Moorhouse, and David Malouf. By now Harbourfront had become a nine-day marathon including Kamau Brathwaite, Nadine Gordimer, Amitav Ghosh, Alison Lurie, Mordecai Richler, Philippe Sollers, Tony Harrison, Brodsky, Malcolm Bradbury, Robert Bly, and many others. Walcott read from his poetry and Fred D'Aguiar read from his new novel *The Longest Memory*. As often, Walcott gravitated towards other West Indian writers. D'Aguiar and Walcott had lunch together with Sigrid and D'Aguiar gave Walcott a copy of *British Subjects*, which Derek looked at during the meal while they talked about who was writing what.[8]

I keep mentioning D'Aguiar, Phillips, and David Dabydeen as it seems to me that while other West Indian poets, such as Wayne Brown and Tony Kellman, were directly influenced by Walcott's writings, his most important influence was indirect, on this group of university-educated West Indian writers in England who had in their own ways thought through their relationship to his example. He had become their anxiety of influence. Each is a productive, prize-winning writer, part of a new generation trying to balance knowledge of Milton and Walcott with dub poetry and Brathwaite. Dabydeen liked putting dialect on top of canonical models, claimed a relationship between the language of the medieval lyric and Caribbean speech, had a Walcottian sense of humour, and in *Turner* (1993) demonstrated some of Walcott's lyricism along with his interest in British art, although Dabydeen was more concerned with finding a black cultural presence in England through the history of its art. Such writers had spent most of their life in England and were in the process of rediscovering the West Indies and negotiating their relationship to such influences as black America and West Indian popular culture. Walcott had already been there.

Walcott's name headed a letter sent to the press from Toronto protesting against the detention of Ken Saro-Wiwa in Nigeria by the government. This was part of an international campaign to save Saro-Wiwa, led by writers, Amnesty, Greenpeace, and PEN, and later taken up by Commonwealth and European university circles and shamefully ignored by most of the American left, black America, and most Nigerians in the United States, who regarded it, as a famous black American intellectual expressed it to me, as a Nigerian affair. Without a humanist universalism intellectuals had no basis to join others in defence of basic freedoms against tyranny, indeed any shift in focus from criticism of Western imperialism and social injustices was regarded as intolerable. Good writers were now more likely to be suspect as élitists than defended, a task left to the writers themselves. Soyinka, Walcott, and other writers kept up a campaign for free speech and freeing writers, while many intellectuals looked the other way and said it was a shame how the West used Rushdie or Saro-Wiwa to criticize the culture of Others. On 5 December, Walcott read with two others at Harvard for the New England Poetry Club as part of a benefit for the Armenian Writers Union.

During mid-November Walcott was in Japan with sponsorship from the Tsudajukukai Institute and a major newspaper. On 13 November he recited one of his poems to a small gathering including Empress Michiko (who had published a volume of her poems in the past and was known from her student days to be a fan of Robert Frost). The next day he read at Tsude Hall, Tokyo. He also read at Konan Women's University, Kensai (16 November). Interest in Walcott had risen rapidly after the Nobel Prize. The Japanese journal *Herumes* (Hermes) in 1993 devoted a section to Walcott: translations of poems, the David Montenegro (1987) *Partisan Review* interview, and some photographs of St Lucia. There was a group of Japanese publishers, art administrators, and an academic at the Boston Trinidad Theatre Workshop tour and Walcott tried to persuade them to bring the Trinidad Theatre Workshop to Japan. His visit to Japan coincided with the publication of a book of his works selected and translated by Shozo Tokunaga. A few years later, in 1998, Shozo Tokunaga published a critical study of Walcott and Heaney, and had a translation of *The Odyssey* in progress.[9]

In his youth Walcott had hoped to become part of the canon, to have his name in anthologies, and to be seen as an heir of Marlowe and Shakespeare. In his sixties he was suddenly becoming a classic. Mid-September Ted Chamberlain wrote to Walcott to initiate a possible purchase by the University of Toronto of some of Walcott's papers and manuscripts for their library with the idea of building up a West Indian research collection. With *Omeros* and the Nobel Prize Walcott began to become the subject of conferences and seminars. He, however, did not fit into the prevailing politics. On Thursday, 8 December, he read at San Jose State College; this was followed the next day with a seminar on his work. He was presented as someone trying to integrate the black culture of the Caribbean into the mainstream of European literature(!); a local interviewer seemed obsessed by his not being politically correct and not exactly being a black writer about race. Walcott retained his same concern with West Indian and personal uniqueness, the same arrogance, the same sense of self-promotion, and of being amusing. He told the interviewer that he had turned down an invitation to the White House as he had another engagement at the time and also because he was expected to pay for his own transportation.[10]

Six months later, during July 1995, *New Statesman & Society* published 'The Commonwealth: Pedestal or Pyre?' in which Walcott told Marina Benjamin 'Compared to the experiences of other colonies . . . the experience was a benign one: there was no sense of being politically persecuted or repressed . . . It was certainly not the kind of experience we read about . . . If any repression occurred, it did not come politically or culturally from Britain, it came from the Catholic church, whose sources in the case of St Lucia were particularly French.' There was one-way cultural traffic, but that did not make him an Englishman, it was something added to being St Lucian. The cultural presence of all the religions and races in present-day Trinidad was 'being continually adapted', not like the idealized image of different races holding hands in a poster, but as a day-to-day reality. The English empire encompassed and extended rights to so many races that the Commonwealth became something one was proud to belong to, yet in England there was prejudice. The British still have not understood how much they have been changed by immigration. The idea of the Commonwealth has to endure. Commonwealth nations can fight each other and have civil wars, but the idea of the Commonwealth is peace and the shared experience represented by the Queen. Commonwealth nations can be more powerful and richer than England, but the idea includes the possibility of a world at peace sharing such experiences as cricket, immigration, and literature. The millions of people who share the idea of a Commonwealth of nations in which big and small are equal is more important than England's search for identity. Rushdie, Soyinka, Ondaatje share an experience that has developed from the idea of the empire. Commonwealth writers are as good as any in England, but the days are over of talking about Commonwealth or black writers, they are part of 'literature in English'. England has never been part of Europe, and will not be as the British do not want it. England can be stronger culturally and economically through the Commonwealth. It will only be a minor power in Europe.[11]

After Walcott moved to Boston his poetry took on a different emphasis, which might be considered more political while being opposed to the basic assumptions of post-colonial theory. He became more outspoken about racism in North America and England and about the economic poverty of blacks, but he and the Caribbean had earned the right to be valued on their own and not as part of, reaction to, or in relation to others. Post-colonial theory really means anti-colonial, but Walcott was indicating something different. To regard people, art, or a culture as essentially anti-colonial was to continue the humiliations and power relationships of colonialism. The task remained the essential American naming of the new, seeing, describing, and thus celebrating what is there; it is Adamic, divine. This Walcott continued to have more in common with Whitman or W. C. Williams than with Edward Said or even Homi Bhabha.

Ronald Bryden's January 1995 visit to St Lucia was the first private conversation that he had had with Walcott in many years, since the fiasco over the Royal Shakespeare Company *Joker*. Walcott talked about wanting to finish building his house and about *The Capeman*. Carlos Fuentes also visited. Laureate Week included an exhibition of Walcott's paintings, Michael Gilkes's illustrated lecture about Walcott's 'Art', and the presentation of the James Rodway Memorial Prize for Poetry to Jane King, niece of the Derek King who won the scholarship to England in 1948 and studied dentistry. Walcott was interviewed in his studio by Rose Styron for *Voice of America*. As part of the interview he read a draft version 'Oedipus at Colonus', which became the concluding poem of *The Bounty* (1997). He said that in Trinidad he first became aware of the variety of races in the Caribbean. In Trinidad there were Chinese, Indians, Arabs, Spanish. The mixture and numbers kept increasing with more Indians and Syrians. Walcott claimed he was still a small town boy who was scared of and found every city in Europe a shock. He still had not been to Greece. He spoke about films he admired, such as Ford's *My Darling Clementine*, which he saw over and over. Kurosawa's *Seven Samurai* and Huston's *Treasure of Sierra Madre* were economical, short in terms of their content, width, volume, and the amount that happens.[12]

In mid-April he did a series of readings in the American South followed by a talk in England. He went to Duke University at the invitation of Gregson Davis, a West Indian from Barbados who is Professor of Classics. Walcott was reluctant to fit Duke into a tight schedule, but he was well paid and so came. There was a public reading, 19 April, with an off-the-cuff commentary and what was meant as a reading from and discussion of *Omeros* to a small group. This was held in a room exhibiting Romare Bearden paintings, which led Walcott into reminiscing about Bearden and his contacts in the late 1970s. Gregson Davis later edited the taped talk under the title of 'Reflections on Omeros' for a special Walcott issue of *South Atlantic Quarterly*. Davis also telephoned Wayne Pond who recorded an interview with Walcott for *Soundings*, a thirty-minute programme on National Public Radio from the National Humanities Center. Pond remembers that this was the day of the bomb blast in Oklahoma. When they began discussing the relationship of poetry to public events Walcott mentioned the bombing. They talked for two hours, recording perhaps forty-five minutes. The interview was broadcast on 23 July and concerned threats to literature by contemporary culture. *Soundings* was later cancelled by NHC and the master disc mislaid, but Davis turned out to have a copy of the broadcast.[13]

Walcott was honoured by Kennesaw State College (about twenty-five miles from Atlanta) as part of its Contemporary Literature and Writing Conference, which lasted 19–21 April, and focused on the literature of the Caribbean. Participants included the Jamaican poet Lorna Goodison, and the Jamaican Anthony Winkler, author of three novels, including an amusing small classic *The Lunatic*. Walcott read on the 21st and there were panels about his writings. He was not at his best, the strain of continual travel was showing; he seemed tired, ageing, aloof, and faltered during his reading.

He then went to Atlanta for the Literary Olympics, a convocation of Nobel Prize laureates for a Cultural Olympiad (23–5 April), mostly notable for Wole Soyinka's initial refusal to appear on stage with Jimmy Carter because of Carter's softness towards the tyranny in Nigeria, which gave it the appearance of international support. Walcott was on Panel II along with Czeslaw Milosz, Octavio Paz, and Claude Simon, moderated by Ted Koppel. Asked how the prize had changed his life, Walcott replied that for a few years laureates were in such demand that they made enemies by turning down worthwhile invitations. It was true that I was hearing complaints that Walcott was so busy that he did not seem to have time for old friends. The next night Soyinka and Walcott were at Emory University.[14]

Walcott arrived in London on 30 April, apparently contacted no one, and showed up at the Beautiful Translations Conference held in the Clore Gallery Auditorium of the Tate. The organizers were, to say the least, relieved. They had advertised Walcott's appearance, but had never received a signed confirmation until at the last moment someone named Sigrid sent them a note.

After a highly theoretical opening address and a subsequent absurdly theoretical presentation of themes by members of the Kent Institute of Art and Design, which, along with *Rear Window*, had organized the conference, Walcott and George Steiner spoke, and a short question period followed. Walcott and Steiner appeared out of place among what were basically philosophers concerned with the problem of the misfit between feelings and their verbal and pictorial representation in the arts. Although Walcott came with some notes for his talk he appeared to improvise out of a contradictory spirit. The general assumption behind the conference was not only that poetry is what is lost in translation, but the reality of a thought or emotion is lost in language and art. Walcott said that the problem of language did not concern him. Translation was imitation. An artist entered into the spirit of the work and had to find means to convey the tone of the original across languages. Walcott spoke of problems of technique such as line length, voice, and diction. Was the line heavy enough, the tone similar, the words dialect, archaic? He spoke of art as illumination, light, a quality of personal touch and genius that distinguished one painter or writer from another. During the question period Walcott dismissed Steiner's backward-looking concern with dying languages. In St Lucia the Creole popular songs were now beginning to approach poetry. There was a contrast of views, Steiner lamenting a past of European high culture being killed by television, Americanization, and computers, Walcott celebrating the evolution of a New World language and culture.

The Turners upstairs at the Tate were Walcott's main interest. As soon as he could he went to see them and said he would return the next day. Seeing the paintings appeared to be his purpose for being at the conference. That night he had dinner with the conference organizers and invited some friends from Trinidad, including the novelist Lawrence Scott, a young British-Trinidadian poet who had sent him an 'epic' in verse (which Walcott liked), an actress who had been in one of his plays, and Paula Burnett, editor of *The Penguin Book of Caribbean Verse*, who was writing a dissertation about his works. A few days before the conference Burnett had given a lecture at the Tate on Walcott's use of paintings in his poetry. Anne Walmsley and Paula Burnett seemed puzzled why Walcott had come to London for such a short trip, but thought that Walcott was becoming more interested in England. Earlier he seemed to avoid London for Wales and Ireland where he felt more at home and where he saw a parallel to the literary and cultural situation in the West Indies. Burnett said that Walcott had always been helpful to her, and Walmsley remembered with affection her early meetings with Walcott in Trinidad when he had been very hospitable, although afterwards he had never replied to her letters. I imagine that, besides the Turners, he had some business, probably about those television films.

He left London on 3 May and returned to St Lucia for a new production of *Ti-Jean*, 4–9 May, directed by John Isaacs with additional music by Tanker. The Trinidad Theatre Workshop was a curtain raiser to the St Lucia annual jazz festival which had been moved to May. This was a younger, different *Ti-Jean*, with the new stars Michael Cherrie, Wendell Manwarren, Cecilia Salazar, and Leah Gordon. Although St Lucia still did not have a proper arts centre there were now several tourist restaurants with small stages and spectacular settings. There was a gala night at the Great House's Moonlight Theatre and a performance, 9 May, at La Sikwi Sugar Mill, Anse La Raye. Proceeds were to benefit the Rat Island Foundation.

During May the newspapers in Paris, where I was living at the time, frequently had short articles on *The Capeman*, the musical play on which Walcott and Paul Simon were working. Simon was sponsoring auditions of young singing groups for possible use in the show, which was intended for Broadway. The articles all spoke of it as Simon's play, although one or two mentioned Walcott's involvement.

Walcott, along with Rita Dove, was presented with an honorary degree by Dartmouth College on 11 June; President Clinton was Commencement speaker. In Trinidad Walcott was one of the nine artists honoured by the Symposia/

Book Fair Committee of Carifesta (24 August). The others were Rex Nettleford, V. S. Naipaul, Kamau Brathwaite, Martin Carter, George Lamming, Earl Lovelace, and Sylvia Wynter. The ceremony included the dramatization of a poem and a scene from *Dream*.

Walcott had always disliked the term 'black writer' as limiting and made a point of reminding people that he was a West Indian not a black American. He was interested in West Indian writing and quietly kept up with what was published. He had not, however, shown much interest in black American writers except for his friend Michael Harper and the dramatist August Wilson. Occasionally he would see the possibilities of black performance poetry as theatre, as he did with Patricia Smith, but white or black or green writers needed to be good and have technique. He had met Rita Dove at a Poetry International, they got along well, and he thought her work interesting. She was one of the poets he was pushing for his verse theatre revival. He agreed (26 July) to direct a staged reading of Dove's *The Darker Face of the Earth* (a black/white version of *Oedipus Rex*) on Monday, 20 November, at the Kaufmann Concert Hall at the Unterberg Poetry Center. Rehearsals would start at 10 a.m. on Saturday, 18 November, and continue until shortly before the 8 p.m. performance. Walcott, who would be in New York at the time, was offered $500 plus $300 expenses and a hotel for the period. Walcott did not sign and return the letter until late, on 15 September. Kirchwey wrote to Walcott in Trinidad (23 August), jokingly calling him his favourite neo-colonialist poet (a reference to a recent *New York Times Magazine* article). He enclosed a revised version of *The Darker Face of the Earth* for Walcott and for Wendell Manwarren, who was going to take the role of Augustus. The play was too long and needed cutting, but it was looser and more imaginative with better symbolism than the previous draft. After the performance in November Kirchwey wrote (27 November) to thank Walcott for directing the reading. He thought it the best of Walcott's three directoral stints at the YMHA. Walcott had seen the play as melodrama and put emphasis on communal action and stagecraft, especially movement. There was not, however, time to get through the complete play in rehearsals. As so often Walcott had aimed at perfection in the early part of the text. He was excellent with the actors, but somehow he never had time for the whole work. Admittedly the Y readings leave little time, but Walcott's habits tend to recur.

He was in New York during October and November to work on *Capeman* with Simon. Rehearsals were now planned for the coming summer and the idea was to open in Chicago the following September. On 5 October he was once more at Hartwick College for a reading when it was announced that Seamus Heaney had been awarded the Nobel Prize in Literature. Just as Brodsky was one of the former prize winners who had written in support of Walcott, so Walcott, along with Brodsky, had supported Heaney. When Heaney retired from being

Professor of Poetry at Oxford University in 1994 he had asked Walcott if the latter wanted to be nominated at Oxford, but Walcott had said that he would be too busy with his teaching at Boston, plays, and time in the West Indies. Roger Straus was soon often quoted as saying 'It is extraordinary, and a rare and beautiful thing, this respectful and admiring friendship shared by the three greatest poets alive today.'

Because of the hurricanes Walcott returned (8 October) to look after his house. Caryl Phillips was in St Lucia for the filming of one of his novels and dined with him. Phillips, who knows the ways of publishing and the literary market, has at times discussed Walcott's career with him and they discussed it this Sunday. As I talked to Phillips I had the feeling that he was one of the few people I had interviewed who understood how far and wisely Walcott had travelled from self-publication in St Lucia to Nobel Prize circles and the conflicts and traps he had faced on his way towards an international literary career while remaining true to some notion of 'home', even if the home was often more disillusioning for a writer than one liked to admit. Listening to Phillips talk about Walcott was at times hearing Phillips talking about himself. Phillips thought part of his relationship with Walcott was because there was no real competition involved; they were of different generations, had different personal histories, and wrote in different genres. Most of Walcott's inner circle consisted of poets or those involved with the theatre. Phillips and Jamaica Kincaid were the two West Indians who mainly wrote prose to whom Walcott seemed close.

Walcott, we agreed, seemed obsessive about Naipaul. He was the one competitor, the rival, the one writer whose career Walcott had compared with his own decade by decade. The one writer he felt to be his equal. By his forties, during the late 1970s, Naipaul had won literary prize after prize and was being considered for the Nobel Prize, but his lack of identification with any one place, whether the West Indies or England, meant that the Nobel Prize would probably never be his. The lack of identification also led to Naipaul's work being 'fragmented'; there were excellent books but no single vision. Walcott remained in the Caribbean until he was a mature person and a mature writer. His early works were good but he was still learning and they did not add up. When he did enter the international market he had already found his voice, themes, technique, manner, and was creating major works. He had a strong relationship to the Caribbean before he left it to work in the United States. His time with the Trinidad Theatre Workshop was essential. He needed it as part of his career and to remain rooted in the region.

Walcott, Phillips said, was already 'savy' in the ways of the literary and publishing world by the time he went to Mona. He was always practical and knew when to take chances and when to move on. He knew his career as a writer had to be abroad, but unlike the other writers of his generation he would remain in the West Indies and try to work the foreign market from there. The big break was when Roger Straus took him on, as there were few important publishing houses for poets and Farrar, Straus and Giroux had many of the best in the United States. Straus also led to his being taken on at Faber, which is the number one publishing house for English-language poets. Until then Walcott was internationally known, but only to a small group of poets and critics, most of whom saw him as part of the West Indies or Commonwealth; now he had a much larger public profile and he was seen as part of a tradition that included Eliot and Auden. Farrar, Straus and Giroux had brought him into contact with Heaney and other well-known poets. Walcott entered the 'Western' literary world with finesse. He did not want to become an American; he was not challenged by a different culture. He felt at ease in the intellectual and artistic milieu of New York. It also helped free him from watching Naipaul's success. He had his own circle. A major break was when he moved to Boston. This solidified his career by giving him a regular university position and salary, but at first he felt out of place in Boston and did not respond to it. It took some time before he began to feel at ease there and he was probably already bored with it. Phillips mentioned Brodsky's active role in bringing Walcott to the attention of others, and said that Brodsky had recently put Walcott forward for a major Italian award.[15]

There was a time two decades ago when a trip to Ohio was so new to Walcott that it would result in his writing a poem; now, on Sunday, 5 November, Walcott read at Idaho State University, Pocatello. Three days later, 8 November 1995, Walcott read the part of Virgil in a staged reading of Robert Pinsky's translation and adaptation of *The Inferno of Dante* for the Poets Theatre, Harvard. The other three voices were Wallace Shawn, Katherine Walker, and Pinsky. David Wheeler of the American Repertory Theatre directed. Pinsky's recent translation of Dante was selling well and Robert Scanlan of the ART and the Poets Theatre invited him to write a stage version. Walcott talked about directing it in New York at the Y preferably using Trinidad Theatre Workshop actors, which would be followed by the Trinidad Theatre Workshop taking the play on tour in the United States and the West Indies. This proved impossible and Pinsky took the play on tour himself during 1999.

I wondered about Walcott and Pinsky as colleagues at Boston University. When I spoke with Pinsky he said that while they worked together with no problems it was a distanced relationship. Pinsky gave me a view of Walcott I had not expected. Walcott was not the sort to volunteer for committees, but always did his professional work co-operatively, without complaint or trouble. They discussed graduate students, went together to see the deans and others about departmental or other needs, and both were on the board of the literary magazine *Agni*, for which they had to seek support within the administration. There was an annual reading for faculty and students in which they both participated. They had over the years done a number of readings together, after which at times they would have a meal. Walcott was always agreeable, professionally considerate, but the relationship remained cordial but distant.[16]

There was just such an annual faculty reading at Boston University on 14 November, with Walcott, Pinsky, Rosanna Warren, Leslie Epstein, and others, at the Boston Playwrights Theatre. Walcott read in December at Sarah Lawrence College where *Omeros* was now being taught—rather a change of circumstances from the early eighties when he was interviewed for a job there.

Since 1987 the *New Republic* had become, along with the *New York Review of Books*, one of Walcott's preferred places to publish criticism. The literary editor seemed to know what he might want to review and gave him space. During November the *New Republic* published his essay review of the Library of America's *Robert Frost: Collected Poems, Prose, & Plays*, edited by Richard Poirier and Mark Richardson. Walcott saw Frost as the Poet Laureate of the new Roman Empire at a time, under Kennedy, when it was still not troubled by a history of slavery and the dispossession of the American Indians. Frost had become an emblem of dry, wise Yankee values, an autocratic, tight-lipped, distant ironist, more full of surly warnings than invitations. Frost's world was threatened, besieged, not the open community of work found in Whitman.[17]

Much of Walcott's review was based on his own experience and problems as a poet, as when he praised Frost's ambitious adaptation and seizure of Hardy or the way Frost's metrical line, or use of such details as a parenthesis, was related to tone and significance. He noticed Wordsworth, Keats, and Clare in Frost's early verse, but Walcott was more concerned with such matters of craft as 'the syntactical variety in Frost's verse' and Frost's 'mastery of stress'. Frost was a modern and regional poet, not by following fashions or using rustic vocabulary and dialect, but by directness, vigour, a 'vernacular elation in tone'. The dialogue in Frost's verse plays, however, was more metrically rigid than the narration, because they were being thought of as poetry rather than part of action in the theatre. There was one voice and tone—more complaint and elegy than conflict —rather than those of many characters. Frost's theatre was private, not vulgar and oral, his dialogues were one voice, his own. Whereas Yeats in *Purgatory* broke with the pentameter to use pub and street talk, bringing lyric and dramatic together, in Frost's theatre the high diction worked against the accent.

The change in Frost's verse from British Georgian occurred with *North of Boston* when he began to write 'free or syllabic' verse within the pentameter. He began writing American. Walcott quoted 'Something there is that doesn't love a wall' and said that while in British English the line would probably be pronounced in six units, in Frost's new American sense of scansion, there was only a rapid caesura after 'is' which, occurring within the pentameter and being part of a personal regional voice, was as radical a breakthrough as anything by W. C. Williams or cummings. Frost along with Yeats thus became one of the 'most memorable poets of the century'. Yeats had a tradition, Frost was alone; 'many of the poems dramatize his own singularity'. Frost did not pretend to be a romantic neglected by a crass society, but instead he took over the American myth of the practical tinkerer, the fusion of art with commerce. Walcott saw this in Frost's technique; why change the pentameter if it was not broken, metrical composition was carpentry. Instead of the open road of Whitman's vagabonds, Frost wanted walls, mowed grass, a formal republic.

Frost's rhymes were ordinary, banal, yet they shine in part because there was danger in treating the supposedly worn out with such calm confidence as natural. There was black humour and terror within an inflexible morality and metronomic rhythm, but the pinched narrow lives could become tiring; there was 'something mean, sour and embittered'. Frost could come close to sing-along, greeting-card wisdom leaving out 'turmoil, contradiction', and anguish, but there was terror not far away when he was read with attention. Walcott noted the colour prejudice in Frost's letters, finding them a product of their time and place, yet disturbing. Still 'poetry is its own realm'. 'Poetry pronounces benediction not on the poet but the reader. A great poem is a state of raceless, sexless, timeless grace.'

Roger Straus wrote to Walcott in Brookline (20 November), although he did not know where Derek was at the time. Brodsky had telephoned him about Walcott's Frost essay and suggested that Straus make a book of it. There was an essay on Frost by Brodsky and an essay on Frost by Heaney. Straus thought it a great idea and wrote to Matthew Evans at Faber to ask about the Heaney essay. It was a lecture that had appeared in *Salmagundi*. Straus then went to Stockholm for Heaney's Nobel award.

Walcott was at the time (16–17 November) in Port of Spain where a group called Partners for America wanted to develop investment between the United States and the Caribbean. Walcott, Peter Minshall, and Paul Keens-Douglas talked about the possibilities of working with Caribbean art and culture. It was part of the same vision Walcott had argued for during the 1960s when he felt West Indian theatre needed outside professionalism and the American market. It had taken him to the United States and within two decades had put him at the centre of the literary and intellectual world. He was still arguing it for Trinidad.

Walcott, who now only taught one semester each year, had the spring semester free and, as the next academic year would be a sabbatical year, would not be returning to teach at Boston University until September 1997. He was thinking of leaving Boston after that semester. Before returning to the West Indies, he attended the closing night of *Pantomime* at the Nantucket Theatre Workshop on 2 December. He left for St Lucia in mid-December.

The Moonlight Theatre behind the Great House, near where Walcott has his house in St Lucia, was renamed the Derek Walcott Theatre and, 16–17 December, there was supposed to be a Derek Walcott week there featuring the Trinidad Theatre Workshop Dance Company directed by Carol La Chapelle, music by Luther Francois, with Walcott present as the guest of honour. Walcott had thought about using this theatre as a second home for his Workshop, a place to perform in St Lucia. It was not to be. Time, personalities, even moodiness, were adding to the lack of Trinidadian support for the Workshop. There was a disagreement between Laveau and La Chapelle over this tour, which led to Walcott banishing La Chapelle from the Workshop for indiscipline—two decades of friendship and working together down the drain. Besides paintings of the St Lucian landscape in watercolour and oil, Walcott was working for a filmed version of *Omeros*. Some of the watercolours and ink drawings would be reproduced in Robert Hamner's *Epic of the Dispossessed*.

Now other writers were dedicating books to Walcott. Jamaica Kincaid's latest book was dedicated to him. The year ended with evidence that Walcott's fame remained fragile even in the best circles. The *New York Times* (31 December) claimed that a Walcott born in Trinidad had been awarded the 1992 Nobel Prize in Literature. The mistake was corrected the next day.

Walcott was in Trinidad over the New Year's holiday to see his family and to discuss with the Trinidad Theatre Workshop an American tour of *O Babylon!*. He was reluctant to revise the play without a firm contract and fee. He was also scouting and casting for the projected television film of *Ti-Jean* for England and the video version of *Omeros* for Pitkethly. Walcott returned to St Lucia before his house was ready, only to learn that his Swedish publishers were arriving immediately. An apartment needed to be found for them at Rodney Bay while work was done on the Cap Estate House and as furniture sent from abroad was unpacked and put into place. Walcott relaxed by doing some painting at Gros Islet and going to the beach at Pigeon Point. He then went to Trinidad to see his family and returned when Paul Simon arrived to work on *Capeman*. One problem that had held up the play was the lack of availability of a suitable director at the times needed; Walcott and Simon flew in directors to St Lucia to interview them.

The focus of the 1996 Nobel Laureates Week was the recent publication of Sir Arthur Lewis's collected writings. Walcott gave a reading at Folklore Centre on the evening of 25 January. Also on the programme was the poet Jane King, music by Luther Francois and Boo Hinkson, and a showing of a video made by Hinkson, *Chausee Road to Stockholm*. This was a St Lucian get-together. Walcott appeared more relaxed and joking than I had seen him at readings in the United States and England where, according to those who had known him for years, he often appeared to have lost his enjoyment of reading and being a poet in public.

He read some St Lucian poems from the 'Here' section of the *Arkansas Testament*, and I suddenly realized that I had never really understood those poems as the allusions were local, even private. I asked Jane King and she said that because she knew the people and events they were clear to her. I had mentioned in reviews that Walcott's poems were at times addressed to the Caribbean and at other times to the wider world, but I had not seen before just how local the allusions could be. There was also an exhibition of St Lucian art at the Point, featuring Walcott's watercolours, many of which belonged to Patricia Charles.

The home on Cap Estate was finished. The furniture arrived at the New Year and there were the usual problems of moving into a new house with this and that not working and already needing repairs. After moving from Villa Beach Cottages Walcott had rented an apartment from a friend on Rodney Bay and had then lived in the guest house of his new 'house' while the rest was being built. There are four buildings, a large central house, a studio for Walcott, the guest house, and a small house for use by others, such as a night watchman. There is also a small swimming pool. The houses are attractive, modern, landscaped on a terrace above the water overlooking Pigeon Point. The tranquil, clear skies and water, marked by puffy white clouds and the silhouettes of small distant yachts in transit, can become dramatic at sunset and especially during a storm when it becomes a seascape by Turner. Walcott, who has mostly been a painter of the structured and who seems at times uncomfortable at trying to capture motion, appears not to have tried his hand at Turneresque landscapes.

One characteristic of the landscape on the terrace is the dark, almost black, shadows and shades among the trees and shrubs. This probably accounts for the hyper-realism of Walcott's recent paintings in which green and black are in sharp contrast. But the recent paintings are also extremely structured, very detailed, static. Many are in oil rather than water. Oil by its nature creates a sense of the static and of sharp contrast. One can see Walcott trying to get more and more light into the pigment of the oils. It is technically interesting and represents a new period, but I like it less. There are some good paintings in each decade, but I like best the ink and charcoal drawings, costume sketches, theatre posters, story boards, and some of the loose watercolours of the sixties, seventies, and early eighties. They attempt less, have spontaneity and an attractive use of colour.

32

1996-1997 *The Bounty*

WITH Walcott settled in St Lucia, on leave for eighteen months, thinking of retiring, and generally on the top of the world, there was bound to be a new agon and there was. The *Boston Globe* (20 January) reported that Walcott had been accused of sexual harassment. A former student in the play-writing programme claimed that during November 1993 Walcott had threatened to fail her if she did not have sex with him and had said that he would not produce her play. After February 1994 three professors had read the students' plays to decide which ones should be produced and hers was not one of them. She withdrew from the course and filed a complaint in April 1994 and later in May 1995. This was the third complaint by a student, once at Harvard and apparently now twice at Boston University. Under a recent ruling employers were responsible for providing an unthreatening climate for women and other protected groups. That Walcott had been previously accused made Boston University liable for employing him. Eventually, in November 1996, the matter was settled out of court by Boston University, but not before, in pre-Bill-and-Monica days, Walcott had become another target in the American cultural wars.

An April 1996 issue of the *Chronicle of Higher Education* carried a two-page article headed 'When a Faculty Star Faces Harassment Charges' with the subheading 'Suit accuses Boston U. of ignoring complaints against winner of Nobel Prize'. The article was accompanied by a large photograph of Walcott and various quotations from the former student, and included claims that since 1981 Walcott had been the subject of such charges and had been protected by universities—there was even a quotation from a novelist who had written a book about sexual harassment in universities. As many feel that the *Chronicle* is an instrument of political correction, it is perhaps not surprising that the article's presentation was unevenly balanced. Her lawyer was asking for over half a million dollars and Walcott was being promoted as the season's unfavourite flavour. Just as he was entering the canon the cannons had been trained on him.[1]

By current North American standards Walcott was careless; humour, irony, sarcasm, teasing, and *double entendres* can be seen as insensitive and indeed Americans have seldom liked irony. It was not straightforward. Walcott enjoyed obscene humour, had a reputation for persistent *double entendres*, but was also said to lay off once it was clear attentions were unwanted. The student's complaint looked like sour grapes. If offended by remarks sensitive people do not take a taxi with the offender and risk further offence; if really threatened one might not wait months until the results of a competition are announced to withdraw from a course and complain. Walcott said something, he maybe made a joke which included some element of 'testing'; after all he is a master of multiple significances with words, and the student may have been unsure of the tone. What happened beyond that can only be conjecture, but Walcott's own mental calm, work, and perhaps career, were to be affected by having such charges aired. Previously he had turned down offers of positions in New York; he had begun to think that it might be the time to make such a move, but now this seemed unlikely.

A later issue of the *Chronicle of Higher Education* produced another example of the defamations of the cultural wars; the *Chronicle* quoted an anonymous source who said that Walcott was acting like a traditional St Lucian male. Far from following the new cultural relativism advocated by the sensitive, this implied that West Indian men were macho-patriarchal beasts. Several St Lucian males complained to the *Chronicle* that such national and racial stereotyping would harm their chances of employment in the United States.

Unlike earlier accusations of sexual misconduct this one was reported abroad in England, France, and the West Indies, and is said later to have lost him the Poet Laureateship of England. It caused much distress to Walcott's immediate family and something approaching a paranoiac distrust of whites, especially Americans. The French may not necessarily do things better, but they see them differently; an article in *Le Monde* was headlined 'Le poète Derek Walcott, "harceleur" ou "harcelé"?' This period was reflected in both the 'Homecoming' and the 'Six Fictions' sequences of *The Bounty*:

> . . . The true faith is Job's poised curse
> on a lost reputation, my name and the envy that steals it
> and stuffs it between her thighs, and its mouldering purse.[2]

North America now felt a foreign land, the people strangers,

> . . . He moved through its crowds like a criminal,
> summoning what grace he could find in a lightest
> gesture, the casual phrase, holding a cup, eating
> without hanging his head . . .[3]

Life outside of St Lucia was Purgatory, the pains he was now suffering were examples of the vanity of human wishes and a preparation for greater Purgatory after death:

> O leaves, multiply the days of my absence and subtract them
> from the humiliation of punishment, the ambush of disgrace
> for what they are: excrement not worthy of any theme,
> not the burl and stance of a cedar or the pliant grass,
> only the scorn of indifference, of weathering out abuse . . .[4]

There was another, more important, reason for Walcott to be melancholic, even angry; Brodsky had died of a heart attack on 28 January. For two decades Brodsky had been his closest friend, the person he most admired, his model. He had stayed at his apartment in the Village when he first moved to the United States, they shared the teaching of courses, had similar tastes, and enjoyed each other's company. Brodsky had a similar belief in the importance of poetry and had led Walcott's way towards fame in Europe. At the Brodsky Memorial Service at the Cathedral of St John the Divine in New York (8 March), Walcott, Strand, Heaney, Anthony Hecht, and others read from Brodsky's poetry in English and Russian and read poems by Frost, Auden, Osip Mandelstam, and Akhmatova. The newspapers mentioned that Paul Simon was also there.

Walcott returned to the West Indies where Lawrence Pitkethly spent a week with him on St Lucia as they worked on another version of the *Omeros* film script. Later in March the newspapers mentioned that Walcott had sponsored the United States residency of Karen Zacarias, a Mexican who in 1991 as a student at Stanford University had won a play-writing prize and who since has had plays produced throughout the United States, including Massachusetts. She was one of the many foreign artists finding it difficult to remain in the United States under a new regulation.[5]

He was on the road again in April, reading on the 10th with two other Nobel Poets Laureate, Czeslaw Milosz (1980) and Octavia Paz (1990), at the Miami Book Fair International, co-sponsored by the *New York Review of Books*. This was the first National Poetry month in the United States. Walcott was introduced by the poet Edward Hirsch. He read a new long poem, a tribute to Brodsky, the 'Italian Eclogues', which would be published during August in the *New York Review of Books*, and later in *The Bounty*. When asked what he was reading he replied, 'I always read Ovidly'. He next read in New York at Fordham University (11 April), the DIA Foundation (12 April) with Seamus Heaney, and then travelled to Swarthmore College (19 April). In New York he now stayed at the Mayflower Hotel where he had a small suite with cooking facilities; Capeman Productions contributed. He saw Farrar, Straus and Giroux about his new book of poems. In Wilmington, Delaware, he was honoured (28 April) with the Common Wealth

Award for outstanding achievement (initiated by Ralph Hayes of Coca Cola), along with the actor Jason Robards, the film maker Ken Burns, the mathematician Andrew Wiles, and Eunice Kennedy Shriver. He planned to leave Boston on 30 April for the Canary Islands for an Arts Festival at which he was to be awarded still another prize and honoured, but the Festival was cancelled and he returned to St Lucia.

Karl Kirchwey faxed Walcott (24 April) at the Mayflower about plans for readings in November. Kirchwey's comments in the fax on Walcott's reading at the DIA Foundation are an excellent critical introduction to what was to become *The Bounty*. He mentioned the way Walcott interpreted himself and his mortality directly through nature without a middle ground. He thought the immediacy of the sensual and the detail of the language was breathtaking, beyond even Walcott's former subtle balance of the formal and colloquial. The poems seemed spontaneous. The use of rhyme was so unobtrusive as to be unnoticeable. The belief in the craft of poetry counterbalanced resignation.[6]

The Bounty was coming together rapidly. The 'Black in America' double issue of the *New Yorker* (29 April–6 May 1996) published a sequence of four poems, 'The Bounty I, II, III, IV'. These were from among the short poems Walcott had been mentioning since *Omeros*. They were unlike his other recent poems, more bare, more plain, more open, less a labyrinth of elaborated metaphors and oblique angles and entries, less playful and amusing. Meditations using the landscape as a point of departure, they were inward, low keyed, almost depressed. Besides the fear of death there was a fear of an unknown future. Infinite nothingness, infinite hell, whatever it would be it would be the cessation of a life of meditating on the landscape and writing poetry.

The long lines, the sentences often as long as six lines of verse, the regular but varied and at times distant rhymes, the approximate three-part division into which the poems appeared to fall, the lack of stanzaic breaks, the fact that the first three poems are twenty-two lines and the fourth twenty-four lines, make the poems, like those in *Midsummer*, appear Walcott's own blend of the classics, the sonnet, and at times feel like an approximation of a Romance language such as Spanish. American poets had preached a free verse based on one's own speech rhythms, Walcott had through years of practice created what seemed a classical, yet natural, metric—formal yet flexible, using a mixture of voices that were very much his own. There seem to be fewer metaphors breeding metaphors, but *The Bounty* makes clear Walcott's continuing relationship to Dylan Thomas's verse, the Thomas who endowed the Welsh seaside with hallowing bird calls and other suggestions of a Christian transcendental order in the physical world. Here it is stripped, made more a distant world that the poet had once been offered by the muse and perhaps God—which made his vision, for which he was thankful, and which he would soon lose forever, which he dreaded.

It would be possible to read these poems differently, indeed they could say the opposite, they could be read as quiet celebrations of having lived. To speak of change, with its implication of inconstancy or difference, is misleading. The transcendence, the universalism, is 'The Bounty'. 'The Bounty' metaphorizes, associates, links, enlightens, transforms. 'The Bounty I' begins 'Never get used to this'; and within a few lines moves on the paradoxical 'at your age | and its coming serene extinction'. 'The Bounty IV' concludes with Walcott thinking of a boy he knew as a child 'who made death a gift that we quietly envied'. The space in between might be said to be a demonstration of how the mind creates art from trying to find words and thoughts that might pacify fears. Whatever Walcott intended, or whatever illnesses or private sorrows were behind the poems, this was going to be a new phase, a later period with its manner, metric, and vision, yet it was all potentially there in those poems he wrote in his teens.

Walcott was in Trinidad and St Lucia in early May 1996, then flew through London to Italy where his schedule took him to Milan (21–2 May), Venice (24 May), Reggio Calabria (27 May, where he was awarded the Regium Julid), Rome (29 May), and the Festival of Nervi, near Rome. The Caribana Milano Convegno di Studi sulle Letterature dei Caraibi concerned 'La Musa Paradisiaca' (Paradise, but also palm-tree!) where on the 21st he was part of a round table chaired by Paula Burnett with the writers James Berry, Wilson Harris, David Dabydeen, George Lamming, Alecia McKenzie, Olive Senior, and Mayra Montero (Cuba). The 'Incontro con Derek Walcott' began with Derek asking Lamming to read 'Sea-Chantey'. Walcott said it brought back memories of listening to Lamming read his poems on *Caribbean Voices* in the 1950s. Then Walcott introduced and read some poems selected by Professor Luigi Sampietro. The next day Walcott read at his Italian publisher, Adelphi Edizioni. He was, along with Soyinka (29–31 May), at the Ulisse Archeologia Dell'uoma moderno Conference in Rome. He was awarded a large financial prize, Premio Internationale dello Stretto, which Brodsky had arranged for him.[7] He also toured Messina and Taormina. At an interview after the Milan conference Walcott said that one of the greatest moments of theatre he had seen was a demonstration of Japanese acting; he reaffirmed his belief that theatre is body and movement, not words.

In June he was in the United States for meetings, and late in June gave Farrar, Straus and Giroux the manuscript of *The Bounty*. Walcott and Sigrid Nama also signed a contract with Farrar, Straus and Giroux for a book of about a hundred Walcott paintings and drawings which Walcott said he would introduce with a ten-page essay. This later became 'Tiepolo's Hound', a long poem about Camille Pissarro, the Jewish Impressionist painter born in St Thomas. He sold the Brookline apartment to a neighbour in the house. His papers were packed and sold to the University of Toronto. Ted Chamberlain and a librarian came to get them. Sigrid packed so quickly that some manuscripts were included that Walcott had hoped to revise in the future.

He arrived in St Lucia on 3 July, went to Trinidad for a week, and returned to work on an article for *Architectural Digest* and on *The Capeman*. Paul Simon arrived and stayed until 23 June. By now they had decided that Mark Morris was to do the choreography. It was still intended to open in Chicago before moving to New York. They were still discussing directors and Simon wanted to complete the soundtrack first, before rehearsing a production. That would be part of the problem; he thought of the play as a staged album and it was his money, agent, and fame driving the project. He and Walcott worked together on the book and lyrics (whereas MacDermot and Walcott worked separately with MacDermot setting Derek's lyrics). Walcott surprised me by seeming nervous when he was meeting Simon, like someone going on a date. This was Simon's project that Walcott had been invited to join, and possibly enter into the really big money and commercial fame that Walcott still desired. Friends asked for Simon's autograph; he had already signed photographs they could give out.

This stunned me. Some of Simon's songs were good in a barbershop quartet sort of way; I had my period of being fascinated by the possibilities of 'The Sound of Silence', but plenty of blues lyrics, Lorenzo Hart, and Cole Porter songs were better. Five minutes of Simon a year would be enough. I was more interested that in July some California firm was making a CD-ROM about Walcott for schools and the National Theatre of Martinique was supposed to stage Walcott's early version of the Trojan War, *Ione*.

Walcott read (18 September) along with John Ashbery, James Fenton, Thom Gunn, Seamus Heaney, Muldoon, C. K. Williams, Zagajewski, and Robert Pinsky at the Town Hall in New York as part of Farrar, Straus and Giroux's fiftieth birthday celebrations. The next night there were readings by the prose writers, including Grace Paley, Susan Sontag, and Jamaica Kincaid. There was a party afterwards at the New York Public Library. The Farrar, Straus and Giroux celebrations were a major event mentioned in the *New Yorker* and the *New York Times*. Farrar, Straus and Giroux was founded by Roger Straus in 1946 and by 1996 had become perhaps the most famous publishing house for serious literature. Nobel Prize winning authors Farrar, Straus and Giroux published included Heaney (1995), Walcott (1992), Gordimer (1991), Camilo José Cela (1989), Joseph Brodsky (1987), Wole Soyinka (1986), William Golding (1983), Elias Canetti (1981), Czeslaw Milosz (1980), Isaac B. Singer (1978), Pablo Neruda (1971), and Solzhenitsyn (1970). Pulitzer and National Book Award winners included John Berryman, Bernard Malamud, Jean Stafford, Robert Lowell, Susan Sontag, Philip Roth, C. K. Williams, Arthur Danto, William Steig, Tom Wolfe, Flannery O'Connor, and Elizabeth Bishop.

Part of Walcott's amusing, otherwise unpublished 'Epithalamium for Brodsky' was included in the Farrar, Straus and Giroux promotional material for the celebrations and was reprinted in *Poets & Writers Magazine* for March/April 1997 along with an article on Farrar, Straus and Giroux. It read like one of those annual *New Yorker* verse letters which mentioned all the celebrities of the year. Here the celebrities and in-jokes were Farrar, Straus and Giroux authors and their books.

The birthday celebrations were followed by *Homage to Robert Frost*, with republished essays by Brodsky, Heaney, and Walcott. Three Nobel Prize winners from different countries were commenting on the American poet. Each poet had resided in recent years in the United States for at least part of the year, each was a metricalist and rhymer rather than a free verser, and each, like Frost, was a poet regarded as part of his national culture. Brodsky offered a close reading of a few poems, 'Come In' and 'Home Burial', and showed how the poems were less about story than a revelation of someone isolated with a chilly vision of life as terror, a New England Conrad in the Heart of Frozen Whiteness. Heaney argued that Frost was neither the nice old grandfather of American literary nationalists nor an alienated Modernist. There was a creative joy, a personality, someone who went from withdrawal to self-projection and then to silence in the poems. The silence itself could be full and enjoyable. Walcott was concerned with Frost the artist, Frost's voice, ear, and metre as his poetry turned to an American vernacular between 'A Boy's Will' and 'North of Boston', but also Frost's biography in relationship to his art, Frost's debt to Hardy, the touch of racism, the shadows within his mind. Walcott's Frost at times seemed to have faced problems similar to those of Walcott; at times he was a warning against looking too closely at the person who gave birth to the poetry. This tightening down of the hatch against revelations and emotional storms found in Frost's verse is now Walcott's. While Walcott's poetry seems more open and confessional with bits of his private life displayed, his life has been private, guarded, and kept from general sight.

Walcott made New York his base for months while working on *Capeman*. Indeed he was once more becoming a New Yorker, living in a high-rise rented apartment with a view of the river. He was revising *The Bounty*; in early October he made a quick trip to Las Palmas for the prize and the money. The same month the American Academy of Achievement, whose Awards Council included Maya Angelou, Jimmy Carter, Robert de Niro, Rita Dove, William Gates III, Colin Powell, Barbra Streisand, and Oprah Winfrey, invited Walcott to be one of the twenty-five new honorees at its June 1996 weekend in Sun Valley, Idaho. There was to be a television programme bringing role models directly into the classroom and the Academy's Museum of the American Dream was to include the life stories of the century's most extraordinary achievers.

He returned from California for a Tribute to Joseph Brodsky at Columbia University (29 October). Susan Sontag read one of Brodsky's early poems. Walcott read 'Letters from the Ming Dynasty' and explained that he and others such as Richard Wilbur had tried to put Brodsky's own translations into a new idiom. Mark Strand and Tatyana Tolstaya also read. A normally sceptical friend told me that Walcott's dignity and seriousness were outstanding.

He was working with Simon almost on a daily basis when, on 18 November, he read from *The Bounty* at the Poetry Center of the 92nd St YMHA and afterwards told a friend that he could feel death coming off the page. This was part of a three-day reading schedule. At the Y on Monday he was paid $1,000. At Queens College on Tuesday (19 November) he was in the afternoon to participate in a memorial for Brodsky and read that night, for which he would be paid $3,000. He would earn another $3,000 for reading at Seton Hall University in New Jersey on 20 November. The three organizations combined to pay for his hotel costs and had been willing to pay a round trip airfare from St Lucia if he had not already been in New York.

There was another production of a Walcott play in London. *Beef, No Chicken* was produced, 18 December 1996–1 February 1997, at the Tricycle Theatre by Yvonne Brewster's Talawa Company. This was mostly a restaging of the 1989 London production. Michael Billington thought *Beef* wobbly in structure, amiably ramshackle, but lacking narrative, and running off in various directions. It was a comic elegy to a disappearing Trinidad. Sarah Hemming in the *Financial Times* found the characters enjoyable, the dialogue peppery, but the plot saggy; Brewster's production was loud, almost hysterical, which accentuated the play's shortcomings. *Time Out* thought Brewster had no choice; the play was hopelessly stuffed with too much to make anything of. *Stage* thought it a Caribbean equivalent of an Ealing comedy. All the critics mentioned the relevance of the question of progress versus tradition, but most thought it required a serious play rather than a farce. I see it more like a Gogol farce.

The January 1997 *Architectural Digest* carried Walcott's 'Where I Live', one of the many contracted pieces he had written about St Lucia for American magazines. This version in very poetic prose seems written from within the mind and moves by association rather than clear narrative. The reasons for thinking that way, however, remain clear. 'The less history one is forced to remember, the better for Art—better the name of a painter than a general's, a poet's than a pope's'; 'the Atlantic with the invisible but always subliminal shores of Africa'; 'All our literature is based on that expanse that does not permit bases or structures: slavery, white convict labor, Indian indenture.'

The prose is built around images. He is now living in north (image) St Lucia in contrast to the beach and city of his youth. This has changed his 'palette' from brighter colours to the 'ochers, siennas and umbers of a Braque reproduction'. In his youth Cap Estate, where he now lives, was thorns and dry although Castries was wet. It was white with well-tended gardens, at which when he was young he was angry, as the rich ignored the poor in the villages, but which he now accepts as part of his inheritance. In the essay there are long sentences, prose as complex as any of Walcott's poetry, moving from colours, to references to imperial and black history, and what he did and does, and tourism and what is offered tourists.

This is prose in which metaphor builds on metaphor:

For the rest of the week the village reverts to its primal, original simplicity, which, for a visitor, may simply mean its degradations of drunkenness and unemployment, to a small industry of fishing that could fade out of existence because of the insatiable maw of the growing hotels, and it hurts to think of the fisherman fading, because his individuality was his independence, his obedience to the sea an elemental devotion, his rising before dawn and his return with his catch at the end of the day as much an emblem of writing, sending the line out, hauling in, with any luck, wriggling rhyme, learning to keep his humility on that expanse that is his home, his pasture with its ruled troughs cresting, as the farmer was to Virgil or the ploughman to Crabbe.

In youth he imagined himself on Cap Estate because of social status and because he loved its colours and imagined himself painting and commemorating the fishermen, fruit sellers, the cathedral, beach, the birds, roads, music.[8]

The *New Yorker*, November 1996, published 'Reading Machado' and, January 1997, 'Granada', two more poems from that 1994 visit; they would become part of the 'Spain' sequence in *The Bounty*. I was taking notes on Walcott's poems as they appeared and my notes usually concerned their musicality and form. It was the sound rather than the meaning that communicated. So much of the meaning was that of a tourist abroad. While Walcott was a short-term tourist in Spain, a land he knew mostly before from art and literature, there has always been this tendency towards representational stereotypes in his writings.

The St Lucian Nobel Laureates' week was opened by Rex Nettleford's lecture on Walcott, who returned from Trinidad the next day (21 January 1997) and read at the Folk Research Centre the next evening. He was supposed to read again, with local poets, at the Derek Walcott Theatre at the Great House, on Saturday night (25 January), but did not show up after some dispute. The audience had paid $40 each and were not happy. There was an exhibition at Pointe Seraphine (21–5 January) of portraits of Walcott by Ross Wilson, for a work commissioned by the National Portrait Gallery, London. Ross Wilson is Irish and a friend of Seamus Heaney. That week Cable and Wireless celebrated St Lucia's two Nobel Laureates with a limited edition of 10,000 phone cards in EC $53/United States $20 denomination. Pictures of Sir Arthur Lewis and Walcott are on the phone cards.

For the first week of April Walcott was 1997 Eugene McDermott Lecturer at the University of Dallas, a Catholic conservative university with a traditional liberal arts great books core curriculum. On 2 April he gave a lecture before an overflowing audience at Lynch Auditorium, during which he read from *Omeros*. The ground for the lecture had been prepared by one of the teachers offering a summary of the long poem's narrative and themes along with some commentary in the *University News*. Walcott attended dinners, and gave poetry seminars and a five-hour theatre workshop to a group of actors who performed a scene from *Odyssey* on the 4th. His *Omeros* was added to the 'core curriculum' replacing T. S. Eliot, although Walcott commented that it was inconceivable to study modern poetry without Eliot. As usual Walcott charmed the students with his sense of humour. When a student said they were reading his work that semester Walcott said 'Sorry'. He spent hours on two sentences. A drama student said that he taught them to see the colour and flavour of each word, and that as actors they would need to bring it to life. During the week Walcott spoke often about living in the present, of not knowing there would be a future, of living among poets rather than being at the end of an epic tradition. When Robert Hamner spoke with him Walcott said he felt tired, and wanted to retire to writing and painting.[9]

In an interview Walcott spoke of himself as a West Indian playwright who, in the United States, was only thought of as a black playwright. The West Indies was a mixture of African, Spanish, and French influences. He praised Martinican Patrick Chamoiseau's *Texaco*. Chamoiseau combined a fusion of elements that would not be found in New York or Paris. Walcott was going back to St Lucia after the week, then to Washington. Someone had asked him to talk in Washington about Asia in the twenty-first century! Because his mind is erratic, uncontrolled, impulsive, and does not follow arguments, he said that he finds giving speeches, like writing prose, difficult. Poetry does not aim for resolution, it aims for contradiction, denial, subversion.[10]

Carol Moldaw for the *New Mexican* interviewed Walcott, in St Lucia, over the telephone (23 April) in preparation for his 8 May SITE reading in Santa Fe. This was one of a series of 'multicultural' poetry readings during the year funded in part by the Lannan Foundation, the first year of poetry readings at this performance space in Santa Fe, a renovated 18,000 square foot warehouse. Walcott would be followed on 15 May by Moldaw, a poet who lives in New Mexico, and who had published *Taken from the River* (1993). She was also a former student of Walcott and in her article remembered being interviewed by him for his class. He had played at burning her packet of poems, 'playing chicken with her'. The tension had ended in laughter. She praised his ability to enter into each word and metaphor of her poems, visualizing possibilities she had not seen. The workshops were really Walcott's close explications of poems or Walcott meditating and lecturing on poetics.

For part of the summer Walcott was in St Lucia. He read with Chamoiseau (28 June); his 'A Letter to Chamoiseau' would appear in the *New York Review of Books* on 14 August 1997. Walcott signed copies of *The Bounty* at Sunshine Books, 1 July, then left for New York and Spain. He was in Nantucket, 20 July, for two weeks with Simon working on what had become, perhaps always was, Paul Simon's musical *The Capeman*, which was now scheduled to begin previews at the Marquis Theatre, New York, on 1 December, and then open on 8 January. Mark Morris was to be the director as well as choreographer after the first two directors were fired.

In late May copies of *The Bounty* were available for June publication although in March the *New York Review of Books*, to Walcott's annoyance, surprisingly reviewed it long before publication. The cover, by Walcott, signed December 1994, looked a bit like a more structured Van Gogh in Trinidad. It had a lot of light, especially in its yellows which dominated the landscape. The clouds, distant hills, and the title of the book were in a white light grey blue. The cover introduces one of the main themes of the book, light as a divine bounty. 'Light' is an encompassing term for the light of the creation, the light that illuminates the world, the light that illuminates art (especially painting) and the inner light of the divine in the artist and all humans. Here the 'Bounty' includes all gifts from God: daybreak, each day, light, the natural world and its creatures, the beauty of St Lucia and Trinidad, being a writer, the gift of poetry, even Walcott having been taught by his mother to respect the bounty and being taught to work to use it. The bounty is the gift of life in its varied aspects, including the ship the *Bounty*, which brought the breadfruit from the Pacific to the Caribbean; the breadfruit itself becomes a surprising analogy to the tree of life and the biblical manna.

These poems are filled with unexpected analogies, the making of analogies being part of the bounty as all creation is linked, as can be seen by the ant that will eventually help turn the dead into bread. Walcott is at times Jacobean in that the ingenuity of analogy can be sardonic. The acknowledged model is John Clare, the supposedly mad Clare whose poetry, like Adam, names the natural world as good unto itself. Walcott has found in Clare a predecessor to his own attempts to praise by describing. Walcott, however, is not simple Clare; the effect is different. His painter's eye for the exact colour of a detail can result, like a brush stroke, in patches of abstraction. In a way this can be seen as a further development of the notion of poetry as naming, as homage, as celebration, of Walcott's personal view of poetry as religious, the word—here the light—expressing something beyond itself in itself within people and things.

The volume begins with 'Between the vision of the Tourist Board and the true | Paradise,' which suggests a this-worldly realism, but the vision Walcott offers is of his mother, Alix, buried near the beach in St Lucia, a rose in the desert, an analogy to Dante's vision that concludes the *Paradiso*. There is complexity and density, even hermeticism, in *The Bounty*. The contrasting pulls of clarity and of regarding poetry as the making of metaphors, of a religious vision and of wanting each thing to shine forth with its own inner essence, have always been there in his writing, but seldom as fully. Here there is insistent pressure throughout the volume—each of its parts seems almost of equal weight. It is easy to lose sight of themes and even the subject in a poem when each long line may have several shifts in focus. Although very different from those Dylan Thomas-ish poems of Walcott's early volumes, the new ones also expand the range of material and allusion by a rapid accumulation of analogies.

The Bounty is also a sequence of seven poems, an elegy commemorating Alix Walcott, which comprises the first part of the volume. It is followed by a second part divided into thirty-seven poems, several of which are themselves numbered sequences of poems. Each poem is twenty-one to twenty-five lines, often closely rhymed, hexameters of variable line length (twelve to seventeen being the possible range) according to the syllables in each foot. The volume covers the years after the publication of *Omeros*, during which time Walcott made trips to Spain and Italy as well as moving between Boston, Trinidad, and St Lucia. Many of the poems have a twilight feel as if he were awaiting death. There are elegies to Joseph Brodsky and other recently dead friends such as Charles Applewhaite of the Trinidad Theatre Workshop. The 'Bounty' must be praised because it is necessary to be thankful, even to confess. At times Walcott seems in purgatory, life in Boston being exile from the Paradise of St Lucia where he now has built a home. His odyssey has concluded after years of wandering, but there are also confessions of continuing restlessness and desire. He is Oedipus at Colonus, Lear, and Yeats in old age. These are not welcoming or always accessible poems; their complicated numbering and untitled presentation are confusing.

Andrew Frisardi described *The Bounty* as energetically and artfully exploring such themes of old age as the passing of self and the self's world, the re-evaluation of life and works. Walcott confronts mortality and mourning as the consolation for death. *Time* published a short, highly favourable review which mentions Walcott's gift of mixing ease, eloquence, private moments, and 'burnished diction of a sunlit Shakespeare'. Walcott struggled to blend the world of sun and rain with autumn leaves and opera houses. 'Images keep recurring, crisscrossing, gaining new associations, in verses that have the noble radiance of stained glasses.' These are poems of thanksgiving and affirmation. Walcott is the most serious and sonorous living writer.[11]

William Logan disagreed. He claimed that Walcott's poetry is filled with charm and concerned with self-display. Walcott's verbal gift is unmatched since Lowell; the imagery is rich, but *Omeros* broke down about half-way through becoming a poet's reading tour and sentimental revision of *Roots*. Walcott has written few memorable poems. You remember Walcott's texture, not the poems. *The Bounty* is badly organized and diffuse, it is rhyming prose. Walcott revisits the past, he nurses wounds, and wishes to merge with the paradise he lost. Logan found the volume 'romantic blather'. There is 'never one image when half a dozen will do'. There is a 'surfeit of the visual', an 'impressionistic blur'. *The Bounty* is airless, self-indulgent, tedious, grandiloquence.[12]

John Bayley described Walcott as a poet of nostalgia, 'singular honesty', and earthiness, with an Ovidian wryness aware of the self-protective and incongruous, along with the complexity and even helplessness of modern life. Bayley mentions the phantom homecoming, the evocation of what is lost, the fantasies of what Walcott might have been in 'Six Fictions', the attractions of the colonial past. An elegiac sense of what has been lost, of ghosts that are still alive, is common to Walcott's book. The review that struck me was a few comments by Robert Hass in his *Washington Post* 'Poet's Choice' column introducing one of the poems: 'His task was to make a Caribbean poetry: an American poetry of the tropics, a region which might include in its literature, if you can imagine the map in your mind, William Faulkner and Garcia Marquéz.' That was so right, if not really about these poems.[13]

British reviews of *The Bounty* were fulsome, respectful, and penetrating, at times sceptical. Richard Sanger saw *The Bounty* as fulfilling the promise in 'As John to Patmos' to 'praise lovelong, the living and the brown dead'. The language is gorgeous, the elegies unconventionally move in unexpected directions. Attention will shift to red ants, the contents of his refrigerator; all are part of nature's, life's and God's bounty. In the past Walcott used the beauty of St Lucia in reply to Europe's monuments, here it is nature that provides the tombs. The seven-part title poem is the most impressive. It is reticent and traces the stages of grief. In the second half of the book there are long hexametric and heptametric lines with alternating often feminine rhymes. The page-length poems follow on from *Midsummer*, a form in which to improvise and meditate. They are modelled on Robert Lowell's *Notebook* sonnets, in containing the minutiae and dross of life. Walcott, however, is more polished, more distanced. 'Walcott has written some of the best polemic and invective in English poetry since Yeats.' He has a fear of God; faith and soul are used without apology. Walcott is 'one of the two or three most important poets in English of the half-century' and 'has produced most of his best work since his mid-forties, and much of it . . . in late middle age'.[14]

Sean O'Brien said that there is a grandeur in Walcott's contemplation on time and death, but his writing can be clotting, as he piles up motionless clauses, overly detailed and vivid, then jumps to the symbolic. 'The Schooner *Flight*' is his masterpiece in free-running clarity. John Burnside in the *Scotsman* thought *The Bounty* one of Walcott's finest books, rich and complex. Walcott seems only able to enjoy or express his bounty through metaphor and mediation. Being on the move, an exile, places merge, sensations run together, names cannot be remembered. In the *Observer* it was 'Paperback of the Week'. Kate Kellaway thought the title of the volume appropriate for the abundance of places, themes, exoticism, at times 'too much of a good thing' which, like O'Brien, she felt slowed up the motion of the poems. Even when Walcott contemplates the sea there is adventure in the blood, a desire for 'a sail'.[15]

David Dabydeen saw Walcott trying to lay the ghosts of his life and career while elegizing his mother and reminiscing about the world, art, and the Caribbean. *The Bounty* begins with the death of his mother, moves on to Europe, its culture, sins, French Impressionism, classical Rome, and ends with Oedipus at Colonus whose fate was passed on to his daughter. Walcott compresses his life into the book. He writes the best verse in the world, does not cease to amaze.[16]

Interviewed in his house in St Lucia, Walcott told Maya Jaggi that *The Bounty* reflected waking up to the sound of the sea at his new home. There was an elegiac sadness tinged with the sense of nature's abundance. Walcott said 'the book has the confrontation and acceptance and bafflement of death. It's elegiac, but I don't think it's tragic.' The interview contained many of the themes of Walcott's recent interviews, lectures, and poems: an almost-New Age romanticism that the Amerindians were at one with the earth and their universe, whereas the white settlers conquered and fenced off land for personal possession. The rejection of the I, the individual, was also now found in Walcott's romantic claim that the artist's duty was to something beyond himself, that he was a vessel. Walcott still was unhappy about the government; there was not even a museum in which he could hang his paintings. Walcott said he had had great friends, especially Brodsky and Heaney. His elegies to Brodsky entered into Brodsky's voice. Every good elegy used the voice of the dead. This was his period of preparation, of acknowledgement, of gratitude. The creation of a continuity.[17]

On 19 August Walcott returned to St Lucia from New York for two weeks. *Capeman* rehearsals were to start in September and Walcott was planning to commute from New York to Boston to teach. He was worried about leaving the Village apartment after December, as it was expensive and partly paid for by the producers of *Capeman*. He was working on a long poem to introduce his book of paintings. He was also trying to finish his book of essays while working on the film scripts of *Ti-Jean* and *Omeros*.

Robert Hamner's *Epic of the Dispossessed: Derek Walcott's 'Omeros'* was published in September with five illustrations, watercolours and ink drawings, by Walcott. There was also a reproduction of *Gulf Stream*, an oil painting by Winslow Homer (at the Metropolitan Museum of Art) to which Walcott refers in *Omeros* and which he has used as a model for paintings. (There is a closely imitated Walcott version in the John Gillespie Collection in Trinidad, an interesting example of seeing, catching, and balancing tensions where others might miss them.)

Walcott, on 10 September, gave the keynote address at the President's convocation at Illinois Wesleyan University, and was awarded an honorary doctorate of the Humanities. For someone who failed to obtain a Dip.Ed. he was collecting many doctorates. Thursday, 9 October, he read at the Elizabeth Bishop Poetry Festival, Worcester Polytechnical Institute, at Clark University.

On Monday, 29 September, there was an evening with Paul Simon and Derek Walcott, previewing parts of *The Capeman* as a benefit for the Academy of American Poets. The actor and playwright Wallace Shawn participated in the evening, interviewing Walcott, Simon, and Morris. The co-chairs included Walcott's editor Jonathan Galassi; the Benefit Committee included Mark and Julie Strand and Roger Straus. Gerald Mosher was also there. Walcott read, followed by a half-hour of songs from *Capeman* performed by the stars, and then Walcott took questions about the production. Galassi asked Walcott to do the benefit and Simon agreed. Walcott was now claiming that he had never seen Broadway as a goal and would not have done the musical except for Simon. The benefit was held at John Jay College followed by a dinner at the Copacabana. Tickets were $500 and $350.[18]

During 1991 Walcott had been in St Louis for a production of *Pantomime* (31 January–17 February 1991) and had read from *Omeros* at the International Writers Center of Washington University (18 February). The novelist William Gass, Director of the Center, had followed Walcott's poetry, was aware that Walcott's paintings were on the jackets of the books, and thought the chance to exhibit might tempt him to return as part of The Dual Muse: The Writer as Artist, the Artist as Writer (7–9 November 1997). Besides the symposium there was an exhibition of paintings in the Gallery of Art and of books and manuscripts in the libraries. Walcott read from his new poem in progress about painting which was to introduce his own art work; his poem and book would eventually be called *Tiepolo's Hound*. The book of the exhibition included some of Walcott's paintings. Walcott's reading was treated as a lecture or essay and moderated by William Gass; the panel included Breyten Breytenback, who also paints and exhibits as well as being a writer. The next day, Sunday, Walcott was on a panel when Breytenback spoke. The conference concluded with readings and book-signing by Derek Walcott and Thom Phillips (who does illustrated translations and an unusual form of 'book-art', 'treating' pages from earlier works), introduced by Caryl Phillips and Kevin Ray.

William Gass spoke to me about the similarities between Walcott and Elizabeth Bishop, how, in the poetry of both, their visual, painterly eye for the tropical landscape found expression in strongly detailed observations of a lush, sensuous environment. Whereas Bishop was limited to the beach, seeing the world from the shore, Walcott also painted and wrote about water, seeing the world from the sea. Walcott's poems on nature became meditations; Gass used the phrase forlorn meditations, in which Walcott reflected upon himself. During our short telephone conversation I had the impression that although Gass did not know Walcott well he had thought about why, beyond earning money, Walcott spent so much time in the United States, a culture in which though at home he still felt alien, and how marginalized he must be in the West Indies.

Walcott had enjoyed the museum at the university and had spoken of Cézanne and Velásquez in his poem, which Gass thought would be a major work of literature, and which he thought might be the place to end this book about Walcott. Unfortunately it would not be published until 2000.[19]

33

1997–1999 *The Capeman, Essays, Crowned Again?*

LIKE most people Walcott is a tangle of contradictions, although in his case they are often extreme. There is the arrogant Walcott who feels he has no equal, that he is a second Shakespeare, and the insecure Walcott who worries whether any of his writings will survive. There is the sociable, amusing, generous, manipulative leader, and the distanced, depressed, self-protective paranoiac. He can be 'red', 'black', St Lucian, Trinidadian, West Indian, American, Commonwealth, even British. He can claim to be part of French culture, refuse to speak French, and dislike the French because of their rationalism and their continuing colonialism in the Caribbean. He is one of the few contemporary writers who would let friends know that a book such as this has his permission, but there are times when I felt he would have killed me if that would have stopped my research. Like many talented, ambitious people he uses others, and has bragged about it, but he can also deny to himself that he does. He likes to clown, but becomes enraged at anything that subtracts from his dignity. His poetry often is made of metaphor built on metaphor, yet he keeps claiming to aim at a prose-like clarity. Sometimes the more prose-like the poetry appears, the denser and more compressed the metaphors are, and the more difficult it is to interpret. Having a great natural talent for poetry he at times seems to want to become a master of, and earn his living from, every art except poetry. An excellent journalist, and a master of prose, he can aim so high in trying to write great prose that he has seldom finished what he regards as his serious prose writings. Instead of accepting his real abilities with design, line, colour, and atmosphere in ink drawings, charcoal sketches, small watercolours, and posters, he worries to death larger paintings. An uneven but serious dramatist, with a few real classic plays to his credit, whose natural home is the Little Theatre and off-Broadway, he has long wanted a hit on Broadway with its fame and riches.

During 1993 Walcott became a partner on the book and lyrics of *The Capeman*, a musical Paul Simon had been working on since 1988, the story of which goes back to 1959. *The Capeman* was Paul Simon's reply to *West Side Story* (now seen as a politically incorrect story of New York Puerto Rican gang violence), the 1957 classic by Leonard Bernstein, Stephen Sondheim, and Arthur Laurents, which had transformed the Broadway musical into an indigenous art form before Sondheim led it towards the affectations of light opera. After Sondheim musicals began being 'composed through; like operas, and seemed to have less and less plot. *The Capeman* was composed through; indeed it consisted almost totally of singing, but it had a plot, too much of the wrong one.

In the summer of 1959 a 16-year-old immigrant Puerto Rican wore a cape while killing two white teenagers. Sentenced to death Salvador Agrón became one of those 1960s progressive 'causes'. Youth, broken family, lack of education, ethnicity, and repugnance against the death penalty were on his side. His trial prefigured many of the class and racial tensions of present-day America. He was convicted by an all-white jury; those who made him a cause included Eleanor Roosevelt and Governor Nelson Rockefeller. After his execution was commuted, Agrón read widely, became a Marxist, and wrote poems and a memoir. He corresponded with admiring radicals, and became a model prisoner to a warden whose own cause was rehabilitation. Several months before he would have been freed for good conduct Agrón escaped from jail in the hope of joining a female admirer in Arizona. He was once more imprisoned, but pardoned and released in 1979. He died in hospital in 1986.

Paul Simon had followed the case and thought it could be the basis of a play, a pop-opera in the musical styles of the period. A decade later the play had an eleven million dollar budget (trimmed down from thirteen million), a more than all-star cast of actors and collaborators, and was to open at a Broadway theatre that seats 1,500. On 10 August 1997, the Sunday *New York Times* carried a full-page advertisement in colour for *The Capeman* by Paul Simon, starring Ruben Blades, Marc Anthony, and Ednita Nazario. Music, book, and lyrics by Paul Simon. Book and lyrics by Derek Walcott. Director and choreographer Mark Morris. Sets and costumes by Bob Crowley. Lighting Natasha Katz. Previews to begin Monday, 1 December, opening 8 January. Preview price scale $67.50–$50; regular $75–$55. Marquis Theatre Broadway and 46th St. As the previews approached there were numerous television appearances by Simon and the play's cast. The *New Yorker* and the *New York Times* seemed unable to get enough of *The Capeman*.

The original Capeman story was uninspiring, as there was no provocation for the knife attack which killed two teenagers. The Vampires normally preyed upon homosexuals, but this night they were looking for a fight and hoped to find an Irish gang that had supposedly insulted a Puerto Rican who tried to peddle drugs to someone's mother. Instead the Vampires happened across some other teenagers. That night Agrón borrowed a red satin cape to give himself style. A fellow Vampire gang member was Luis Hernandez, the Umbrella Man. Agrón, who had a history of mental problems, purposefully murdered two innocents and wounded another. After he was caught he was unrepentant and bragged to reporters 'I don't care if I burn'.

American identity politics turned Agrón into a cause, and identity politics continued to rear its many heads. Parents of Murdered Children said the play made a hero of a young killer from an approved 'minority' group at the expense of the two whites for whose death he expressed no remorse. The survivor of the 1959 Vampire attack told *New York Magazine*, 'The Capeman killed them kids, and stabbed me. He done it because we were white, and I don't guess that is anything to fucking sing and dance about.' Before the play had opened its politics were being questioned, especially by those it appeared to romanticize. A former gang member criticized Simon as coming from a comfortable community far from the actual violence. Agrón was no different from present-day members of the Crips, Bloods, and other violent gangs. Luis Hernandez, the Umbrella Man, was discovered to be alive, and unlike Agrón very repentant for the killings. A father of eight he was now a supporter of the death penalty and feared that his children would be recruited by the new gangs. He did not believe in the social explanations about the cause of gang wars. His gang had gone looking for trouble, but Agrón surprised them by using a knife to kill. Agrón's tough-guy act made the public hate them and led to Hernandez's imprisonment. Paul Simon now added a further song to the play, 'You Fucked Up My Life'.[1]

The Agrón of Simon and Walcott was more fiction than reality. His poem from the late 1970s about his dead father showed neither repentance nor talent:

> But you murdered him
> With vain promises
> Of progress
> While you ravished and stole
> His land, his house
> And put him on welfare—
> American capitalism,
> Yankee colonialism,
> Uncle Sam imperialism.

Walcott and Simon, however, claimed it was a story of someone 'rehumanized'.

What began as a collaboration in which Simon wrote the songs and Simon and Walcott co-authored the lyrics and the book had become Paul Simon's play in advertisements and newspaper stories. In magazines and television interviews it was Simon who always spoke. Simon denied that he had turned to World Music (South African, Brazilian, and now Puerto Rican) because people were becoming bored with the 1960s Simon.

The Capeman had a long strange history before rehearsals began. Unlike most plays it did not begin with a script. Simon started by recording rhythm tracks, then added music, then lyrics. The play script came last. Simon spent years recording the songs and assumed he would hire a director and choreographer to stage what was essentially a concept album. The first two directors were unable to stand up to Simon, who fired them and most of the cast. Mark Morris, famous as a dancer and avant-garde choreographer, was the third director. He has his own company, the Mark Morris Dance Group, and he has a busy international schedule. While working on *The Capeman* he also directed Rameau's 1745 opera *Platée* for the Royal Opera in England, and his group performed in Boston.[2]

I saw an early preview. The singing and orchestra were better than any musical I can remember; otherwise it was embarrassing. It had to be radically revised quickly, but Walcott was hyper-sensitive to criticism, saying that it was like an opera and meant to be boring; if they allowed any dancing it would be Morris's show. It was shoot-the-messenger time. After I tried to explain why the second act needed simplification, I was later chewed out by Sigrid for not giving Derek support. Soon after the New Year, the opening of *The Capeman* was postponed from 8 January until 29 January as veteran Broadway directors were being asked to save *The Capeman*.

I saw *The Capeman* again on 10 January and it had improved over the past month. There was more dance and movement (although still not enough). Everything seemed faster, even the tempi of the music. At least three songs and a scene change had been eliminated from Act I; the play's length was reduced to the normal two and a half hours. The Puerto Rican nationalism was accentuated and an offensive anti-white song was no longer there. Agrón's repentance was emphasized by remarks throughout the play, as were the interracial gang tensions that led up to the killings. Act II remained too complicated and overloaded by Walcott's own interest in 'fate' and Agrón's trip to Arizona during his escape from imprisonment. Advertisements for *The Capeman* now mentioned 'Good seats still available for week night previews'.

The afternoon before the Thursday, 29 January, opening of *The Capeman* National Public Radio stations discussed the claim that Simon should have used a Puerto Rican writer. Pedro Pietri, himself one, was savage about Simon turning to Walcott. Could not Simon tell one part of the Caribbean from another? That night as Julia Roberts, Barbara Walters, and other stars attended the opening, television crews were once more recording a demonstration outside the theatre by the Parents of Murdered Children. Because of picket lines Walcott did not go to the opening (29 January). The *New York Times* treated the opening night party at the Marriott Marquis as one of the two most important social events of the week. There was paella to eat and Tito Puente played for the dancers. Aurea Agrón, Sal's sister, and some of her children were at the party. She said that 'Salvador would have loved this'. Her youngest son claimed that 'he died of a broken heart'.[3]

I saw *The Capeman* again, two days after the opening. Jerry Zaks, the fourth director, had even replaced Morris as choreographer with a Broadway veteran. Simon had agreed to let Zaks make changes that he was unwilling to grant Morris. Many scenes had been compressed and rearranged. The dancing was more showy. The ethnic tensions of New York were exaggerated to make it appear that youths, especially Puerto Ricans, were in danger if they left their neighbourhood. By now I was tired of Paul Simon's music, which is too limited to sustain a show, and I thought many of the play's problems derived from the contrast between his sentimentality and Walcott's Shakespearian objectivity. A friend's teenage daughter suggested, unironically, that Disney would have been a better partner for Simon than Walcott. The critics passed the death sentence on *The Capeman*.

Reviews in the *New York Times* can make or break a play. There was a vicious review that Friday: 'it would take a hard-core sadist to derive pleasure from the sad, benumbed spectacle that finally opened Thursday night . . . three weeks behind schedule. Although it may be unparalleled in its wholesale squandering of illustrious talents . . . *The Capeman* is no fun even as a target . . . It's like watching a mortally wounded animal. You're only sorry that it has to suffer and that there's nothing you can do about it.' *Newsday* punned that *Capeman* had a strong beat but a weak pulse. The *New Yorker* questioned how *The Capeman* could go on and on about Agrón as a victim of prejudice; the show was a 'prison of stale ideas' including 'the old poetry defense'; 'there should a Monopoly card that says "Write a book—get out of jail free." '[4]

The *Village Voice* asked 'what Paul Simon saw in this story' or why in the middle of his life he should decide to dramatize it. John Peters in the London *Sunday Times* described *The Capeman* as 'heavy with half-digested ideas and oozing with an uninviting mixture of sanctimonious sentimentality and naive political clichés'. Agrón was 'repeatedly compared to Jesus . . . pseudo-religious hocus-pocus'.

There is certainly such an allegory in the play, which leads towards the mother's vision of Agrón in heaven. Although this may accurately express Agrón's mother's view of her dead son, there is no reason given in the play to accept such a valuation beyond the blaming of society as evil and the claim that Agrón has somehow remade himself through reading and writing. Redemption has long been a Walcott theme, but nothing appeared redeemed about this killer. Instead we were given the usual excuses about a broken home, and the pressures of being from a minority group. If there was anything individual or redeemable about Agrón it was not in the play. The last three decades have had more than enough killer punks who picked up a radical ideology in prison, wrote books, even best sellers, and became a cause. The play's politics were mainstream, but the vision belonged to the past.

Walcott, smelling disaster and angry that his writing had been cut by the last director, now claimed that *The Capeman* had nothing to do with him. The show was Simon's album set to lights and scenery. Most of what he had done had been cut or somehow changed. He felt four years had been wasted.

I agreed with the fourth director. The Arizona sequence in Act II was digressive (although based on truth) and the symbolism absurd and heavy. However, when I saw the play in late January the cuts speeded up and made clear what was previously long-winded and uninteresting. I wondered whether Walcott's strong interest in the relationship between Agrón and the radical Indian female correspondent was not another transposition of the Catherine Weldon story from *The Ghost Dance* and *Omeros*, or his attraction to the suffering of Amerindians. If, symbolically, you mixed someone from the Spanish Caribbean with an American Indian you would be making a large claim about the rightful possession of the continent to the disfavour of Anglos.

The Capeman closed on 28 March 1998, the biggest flop in Broadway history as both New York's tabloids proclaimed loudly in immense front-page headlines. Simon, continuing to pick fights, thanked Latino audiences for coming. The *New York Times* seemed almost gloating—Simon had criticized Broadway and its ways so often that he had put many backs up. His claim that he was going to bring Salsa from the margins to the mainstream showed how out of touch he was. In Indianapolis on a week night I can find hotter Salsa dancing than in his play. Commentators mentioned that towards the end Walcott had also contributed to his share of risen backs. He had resisted efforts to rewrite the musical's book, which many felt was static and unclear, and had effectively left the production in the weeks before the opening. Towards the end Walcott was less open to suggestions than Simon. *The Capeman* was barely breaking even and future sales were weak. The producers were still claiming that the show was ahead of its time and would be seen as historically important. There were still plans for a cast album, and possibly for a national concert tour including Simon.

I could not help mentally contrasting *The Capeman* disaster, indeed all the energy Walcott had wasted for two decades trying to get musicals staged in the United States, with Roscoe Lee Browne then touring nationally in a one-man show which included a scene from *Dream on Monkey Mountain* or, in January 1998, the Denver Sidewalk Theatre producing *Dream*. That play never had the immense publicity of *The Capeman*, never got to Broadway, but was a classic, and is still often produced. I know that you cannot stand still, that one must always accept new challenges, and that *The Capeman* was such a challenge, but like many others with great talents Walcott has often misdirected them. He knew he was a poet so wanted to be a painter instead. He created a fantasy of living off the theatre in the Caribbean, a place where there was no professional serious theatre, and instead lived off his poetry, his wife, journalism, and American grants. He hoped to make it on Broadway and Hollywood with verse plays and giant musicals, whereas his plays were constantly being produced and earning him money in small theatres, on college campuses, wherever there was serious drama. His poetry had taken him to the Nobel Prize while he had wasted immense energy trying for Hollywood or Broadway. There was always the fantasy of making it big commercially, making it in mass culture, when his art, whether in poetry, the theatre, directing, or even his prose, was the essence of high culture. That was its greatness. And then there was the surprising insecurity behind the arrogance, an insecurity that led him into the collaboration with Simon and which made him unable to see that he had to give up his favourite ideas for the play if it were to survive. *The Capeman* brought to my mind 'Heavenly Peace'; on a larger scale and more crudely Walcott had tried to piggy-back his own vision on to that of progressive North America and it did not work artistically or bring the financial rewards he wanted.

Perhaps I was seeing it wrong? In November 1997 Warner Brothers released Paul Simon's 'Songs from *The Capeman*', thirteen songs from the play, sung mostly by Simon. The reviews said it sounded like any Simon album, and no one could tell what was Walcott's, but Walcott would be earning money on some of the songs. A full-cast album was still planned. Walcott had once more returned to New York, and was living well in the Village. After pretending for a time that *The Capeman* had little to do with him, he started featuring it prominently among lists of his works. Walcott had reached the ultimate of New York literary celebrity-hood; he was on the cover of the 1998 David Levine Calendar.

Walcott's use of classics had attracted the attention of academics. The American Philological Association at its annual meeting in December had a panel session 'From Homer to *Omeros*: Approaches to Derek Walcott's *Omeros* and the *Odyssey*'. Topics included 'The Design' of *Omeros*, Walcott's post-colonial Homer, *Omeros* as a version of the pastoral, and the Ithacan-Antillean metaphor. Gregson Davis was one of the organizers. After a long period which saw the collapse of the Classics as a discipline, *Omeros* was part of a renewal of interest in the heritage of Greek and Roman literature. There seemed to be numerous new translations, anthologies, selections. George Steiner's *Homer in English* (1993), Robert Fagles's translation of *The Odyssey* (Penguin/Viking), and Stanley Lombardo's translation of *The Iliad* were being reviewed and cited.

It was probably just as well Walcott was not in St Lucia during the 1998 Laureates week. There was a revolt by a new generation of dub and rap poets against what they called the local élite poets, such as Jane King and Robert Lee, and they staged their people's poetry and art week in a disused factory, but, as their supporters in the local press complained, the people for whom their art was intended did not come, and there were complaints at the lack of government subsidies for those trying to bring people's art to the people. Walcott did go to St Lucia in mid-February for two weeks and then was in Jamaica during part of March when there was a staged reading of *Omeros* at the university. He was visiting Distinguished Professor at the University of North Carolina, Chapel Hill, 2–8 April 1998. He lectured on Literature and the Classics and on Contemporary Caribbean Literature, and gave various classes. The next week, 14 April, he was in Austin, Texas.

He left for Germany where he was expected in Saarbrücken (3–8 May). Because of flight delays he arrived twenty hours late, on Monday the 4th, the day of his 'poetics' lecture. The next two days there were drama workshops leading to a performance of *Ti-Jean* in German. Friday, 8 May, he read at the Art Gallery. There was a trip to Metz to see the Chagalls there, which did not seem to interest him. While he was in Germany, a trip for later in the year, in late October, was planned. He would spend a few days in Paris, then return to New York and St Lucia. He had arranged to continue in the Village apartment and would commute to Boston for teaching in future.

Onlookers were sceptical about the Rat Island Writers Workshop. Everyone had a story about Walcott being involved in too many other matters for it to succeed. However, there it was, the first Rat Island workshop took place for three weeks, late July until mid-August 1998, sponsored by Boston University. Richard Montgomery, eight Trinidad Theatre Workshop actors, some Boston Playwrights Theatre actors, and some from Dallas University, workshopped scenes from *The Odyssey* which Walcott was still hoping to produce on the beach in St Lucia. He was hoping to have another workshop the following summer, but that depended on funding. The government of Trinidad, however, showed its usual contempt for Walcott and the arts during 1999 by evicting the Workshop from the Old Fire House, effectively destroying forty years of work by Walcott, Errol Jones, Stanley Marshall, Albert Laveau, and others to build a little theatre, arts centre, and school for teaching the performing arts. Left to the government of Trinidad no one will know a few decades from now where Walcott, Naipaul, Samuel Selvon, or any of the great West Indian artists lived and worked or what they did. The burden of history is not solely the past with its slavery and illegitimacy; perhaps as bad or worse are the politicians since independence, which is why West Indian artists continue to leave the region for places more interested in their art.

What Walcott especially liked now was the opportunity to exhibit his paintings for sale along with giving a reading. At the State University New York-Albany he shared an exhibition with Jackie Hinkson. 'Island Light: Oil and Watercolors by Derek Walcott and Donald Hinkson' was at the University Art Museum, 2 October–15 November 1998. The official opening was on 7 October. Thursday afternoon (8 October) there was a seminar and that evening Walcott read from his poetry. The Albany trip was sponsored by the New York State Writers Institute, for its Visiting Writers series. Ten days later (19 October) he read at Carnegie Music Hall in Oakland, Pittsburgh.

To coincide with the publication of 'What the Twilight Says': Essays there was a rapid tour of four European nations, Spain, Germany, France, and England, in two weeks. Readings in Spain included Madrid and the Lorca Festival in Granada; in Germany there was Hanover and Heidelberg, and then he and Sigrid went to Cannes where on 27 October he read at La Napoulle, an artists' residence. He read from his poetry and prose, including some translations, and said he spoke patois, not French. He had a small audience of forty. There was a quick visit to the Perse house. His time in England included a reading at Poetry International, South Bank, were he read (31 October) at the Royal Festival Hall Purcell Room. The reading was sold out several weeks in advance. He had a bad cold and was hoarse.

There was a Walcott Day, 3 November, at the University of Warwick, where the Centre for Caribbean Studies held a conference on the Life and Works of Derek Walcott. Speakers included Edward Baugh, who came from Jamaica, Philip Nanton, Paula Burnett, Louis James, the Trinidadian novelist Lawrence Scott, Stewart Brown, and John Figueroa. There was a reading by Eddie Baugh, David Dabydeen, John Figueroa, Ron Kwabena, and Amryl Johnson, and that evening a reading by Walcott. There was such a demand for tickets that the reading was moved from a conference room to a larger hall and 600–700 were in the audience, the largest audience at Warwick for a reading. Walcott read from a range of his poetry from 1948 to the present, including, from Sea Grapes, 'Sea Canes':

> Half my friends are dead.
> I will make you new ones, said earth.
> No, give them back, as they were, instead,
> with faults and all, I cried.[5]

He criticized the way the British press had treated Ted Hughes during his life. The next day Walcott was awarded an honorary doctorate by the university. The oration was given by David Dabydeen, who had for years been trying to get Walcott to come to Warwick University. Dabydeen spoke of how writing of the sea made one part of a body of literature dating back to the Bible and Homer. Walcott was in good form, enjoying himself, relaxed.

He could not attend the funeral of Ted Hughes as it coincided with the events at Warwick. His name almost immediately started to be mentioned as a possible

Poet Laureate to follow Hughes. After England Walcott went to Bermuda for a production of *Remembrance*.

Advance copies of *'What the Twilight Says': Essays* were sent out in late October. After years of talk about a book of autobiographical prose works, 'American, without America', 'Inside the Cathedral', of attempts by Farrar, Straus and Giroux editors to locate the essays Walcott had published, this was a bit of a letdown. There was nothing new; Walcott had republished some of his essays, and the selection was smallish. There were three general essays about the Caribbean, 'What the Twilight Says' (1970), 'The Muse of History' (1974), and the Nobel lecture, *The Antilles: Fragments of Epic Memory*. The second section consisted of eleven republished essays starting with 'On Robert Lowell' (1984) and concluding with the recent 'A Letter to Chamoiseau' (1997), which led into the third section, 'Café Martinique' (1985), his one published story. The book jacket includes Walcott's painting of looking through his window in Boston from a book-lined, warm-coloured room on to the snowy white outside. Unfortunately the cover is in brown, distorting the contrast between the clear white of the snow and the tropical warm bright colours inside the room. A pity as it is a witty painting saying much about Walcott in Boston and the North and South, and is one of his successful paintings. Walcott had arranged the essays to offer a kind of autobiography, but you would need to read a biography such as this to see the hidden stories. Each of the essays and reviews swirled and twirled, dances of veils with occasional revelations of brilliant jewels and desired information.

Late autumn 1998 everyone was talking about Paul Theroux's *Sir Vidia's Shadow*. Walcott was happy to see that he was treated well, as the one author Naipaul respected and someone whose early poems Naipaul would recite. Theroux cited some of Walcott's criticism of Naipaul, especially of the later novels. Not so indirectly Theroux used Walcott as a means of skewering Naipaul. Literary fashion had changed. Walcott had become a model for the new culture of our time, someone global, highly accomplished and successful, yet still authentic, 'black', and, perhaps most important, not imitation British. (Later Naipaul would get his own back by telling a talkative editor that Walcott's poetry had gone wrong after 1965.)

Walcott (19 November) lectured at the San Francisco Public Library, then, for a week beginning the end of November, he was writer in residence at the University of Michigan, Ann Arbor, where he read (2 December) from his new poem about art. He left New York for Trinidad (17 December), and then went to St Lucia for the New Year. He would return to the United States in late March 1999. He was still leasing the apartment in Greenwich Village rented by Paul Simon's company, although because of a quarrel he and Simon were no longer talking. *The Capeman* cast album was now supposed to appear in the spring of 1999; there was still talk of publishing *The Capeman* as a book. Walcott was painting self-portraits.

He left New York in mid-December for what was supposed to be four months in St Lucia. Although he was likely to go to sleep early and miss the wild dancing at Gros Islet or the large crowds at the beach, it had become his tradition to spend the New Year there. Pam, Peter, and others of the family were to assemble for a gathering of the Derek-now-headed clan. Those not invited were annoyed. Derek had replaced his lost father, replaced Alix, had established a family, re-established a home, overcome the humiliations of his youth, the lack of money, the not being white enough, and such anxieties as illegitimacy in the family past. Peter now had a house on the island. Michael St Hill, Pam's son, also practised there as an architect. Derek had become a painter once more. Everyone seemed to be writing books and dissertations about him, but people knew little about his life. The return home by the conquering hero had taken place during 1992–3, but traditionally the hero finds home changed and cannot really settle. Walcott was more tired than in the past, but he had become an international commuter to the world's literary markets and that was unlikely to change. He still taught at Boston University and he still loved life in New York and the Village. He could be as ambitious, amusing, and irascible as ever.

He was due to be reading in Indianapolis at Butler University again in late March 1999, during a time I would be in England. I had a list of other readings scheduled for April and May, including a star-studded celebration in Boston of the hundredth anniversary of Ernest Hemingway's birth. Walcott intended to remain busy. Perhaps more busy than at any time in his life. Meantime the newspapers continued to speculate on who would be appointed Poet Laureate of England and Walcott was said to be the first choice. Could you have a Laureate residing outside England, and if it were offered would Walcott accept? My wild guess was that the Queen would be favourable to a Laureate from within the Commonwealth. Would he accept? Walcott knew all the proper genres, was an heir to the Classics, Dryden, Johnson, and perhaps might even revitalize the laureateship.

When Larkin declined it the laureateship had gone to Ted Hughes, and among Brodsky, Walcott, and Heaney there had been jokes at Hughes's official poetry for royal occasions. I assumed that Walcott would say no, as he is St Lucian, but when I enquired if it were true that he had declined being considered, I was told he had not been asked, which was a way to keep his options open. Walcott liked publicity, and knew it was good for sales and the value of his readings if his name were being mentioned. He had mocked Naipaul's settling in England, and his acceptance of a knighthood, and Walcott had rejected being made a knight in St Lucia, but the laureateship might be seen as the final reversal of British cultural imperialism, the conquest of England by its former colonies, a symbol for a new hybridity, a real equality, even a sign to the younger black British writers and the British that England had changed to a land where a young Albert Perez

Jordan could marry an Esther Hope and feel at home. It would temporarily solve the problem of what peak to conquer after the Nobel Prize, and perhaps needle Sir Vidia; besides the British had the money and resources to sponsor those films he always wanted to make. He had agreed to be at the London Festival of Literature in late March. Peter Florence had been after him to agree, but perhaps it might influence a committee if that was what he wanted. It would also help promote the forthcoming book of his paintings introduced by his long poem about art.

An article in *The Times* claimed Walcott was the favourite in a four-horse final, along with Tony Harrison, Wendy Cope, and U. A. Fanthorpe.[6] The Prime Minister had short lists from the Society of Authors, the Royal Literary Fund, the Poetry Society, and the Royal Society of Literature. A list was awaited from the Arts Council. Andrew Motion and James Fenton also had been favourites, but there was a feeling that it was time for an outsider, a black, woman, gay, maybe a writer from the Commonwealth. The committee supposedly was keen on Walcott. Seamus Heaney had ruled himself out as Irish. Harrison reminded the press that he was an anti-monarchist interested in celebrating royal beheadings; the laureateship was unlikely to be his scene. This appeared to leave Cope, Motion, and Walcott. Whatever happened the laureateship and Walcott were in the news. A friend of mine supposedly in the know said not to bet that was going to be my final paragraph. Another friend in the know said that Walcott would be a certainty after the report about the Stephen Lawrence murder and police racism in England. It seemed to me obvious that Walcott would be appointed unless there was some problem negotiating the terms. He is the best poet, he would help mend England's links to the Commonwealth, and he would help make England a model of a multicultural Europe. English literature would suddenly appear different. Maybe the French would stop listing as 'African' black French writers born and bred in France. Walcott, however, was capable of deciding that the terms were not good enough, or it would take too much of his time, and rejecting the laureateship.

A few weeks later both the *Sunday Times* and *Observer* carried interviews with Walcott in St Lucia in which he said he would be flattered to be asked to be Poet Laureate and mentioned his new poem, 'Tiepolo's Hound', about the divided heritage of the Impressionist painter Camille Pissaro, who was born in St Thomas and lived and worked in France.[7] It was widely assumed that this was Walcott saying he wanted the post. I thought it Walcott finding a way to publicize his next book, which because of the illustrations would be expensive and needed much promotion. Two long-time friends of Walcott said I was wrong. Walcott had told them he wanted to be Laureate and a knight, Sir Derek. One of them told me a story about Derek looking up the Walcott family in Scotland, and of being rejected, and it still hurting. It sounded like a mixed-up version of the story about Warwick being rejected by the Walcotts of Barbados, but was possible. So much of his life has been influenced by a desire to compensate for those early humiliations. Pressure to appoint Walcott was building up. David Dabydeen was asked by the BBC to travel to St Lucia to interview him. After his return Dabydeen wrote to the Prime Minister's office to recommend Walcott be made Laureate. The *Sunday Times* carried a large extract from the new poem.

The London Festival of Literature was a new event, over two weeks packed with readings, discussions, even films by poets, spread over the thirty-two boroughs. Throughout the days and evenings there were many overlapping events, the writers ranging from Nobel Laureates to the latest dub and rap poets. Walcott had a packed schedule, including two events after he had left. There were so many readings and panels that some mix-ups and failures of communication were to be expected. Walcott arrived on Monday, 22 March, and shared the programme with Soyinka and Achebe at the immense Hackney Empire, where he read parts of *Omeros*, but was tired and unimpressive. Wednesday noon (24 March) he was supposed to read at the British Museum, but this was cancelled due to an industrial dispute by part of the staff. That night he was interviewed by Radio 4 during which he said it was unlikely he would be Poet Laureate as he would not live in England. A friend told me that there were unexpected legal difficulties in having a Laureate living outside England and the matter was still being looked into; that is why no decision had been made. Walcott found time to visit the National Portrait Gallery, where a portrait of him was now part of the collection. As he looked closely at the details Sigrid wondered whether others saw the resemblance, that he was the man in the painting.

Thursday (25 March) he read at more length from *Omeros* and talked about poetry for over two hours for New Peckham Varieties in a small theatre, seating perhaps 150, in Southwark, south-east London. The hall was difficult to find and a grumbling Walcott arrived late without time to compose himself for the reading. Once inside he obviously liked the size of the theatre and the setting; it was a brilliant reading and a brilliant discussion of the sound of poetry in which Walcott analysed some lines in great detail, explaining rhythm, structure, harmonization, contrasts, pitch, even the visual appearance of letters. He showed how words that at first seemed to have no musical relationship to each other were in fact part of patterns of sound, with subtle harmonic relationships and hidden part-rhymes; it was obvious why Walcott was a great poet, one whom other poets respected. Anyone present that evening was lucky.

During Friday (26 March) he gave a master class for twenty-five poets at the Poetry Café, for the Poetry Society. This was also brilliant, although at times rambling and confusing. The poets ranged from unpublished beginners to at least three established writers whose names I recognized, one of whom had already published three volumes of verse and herself taught poetry workshops. Walcott seemed particularly interested in the views of a woman who had a play at the Birmingham Rep, where his own *The Last Carnival* had been performed during 1992. She had a good ear for the sound of language and what worked. There were two observers from Korea who were scouting for writers to invite to some event. There was a well-published Chinese poet who lived in London and translated some of his poetry into English. Several of the poets were housewives or trying to raise a family and write, and Walcott told them that it was necessary to find time to be a poet; poetry could not be done in odd hours. It was an occupation, but it was better to stay at home and have someone pay the rent than try to write poetry while being a journalist or writing prose in ways that conflicted with a poet's way of thinking.

All of the poets had brought two of their own poems with them, and Walcott apparently at random chose one to discuss in detail. It was by a performance poet, in free verse, and already had been the subject of a poetry workshop with another teacher. It seemed a rather romantic, even dreamy, lyric about exile and alienation as the sources of the poem itself. The author was originally from the Spanish Caribbean, had lived in France, and spoke mid-Atlantic English. Walcott mentioned the advantages of a writer having several languages as he does—English, St Lucian English, French Creole, and French. He said that language was racial, and it was important to find your own voice, although this could take decades. The author was then asked to read her poem to the group. She was used to public reading and quickly fell into a rehearsed tone like an incantation; this picked up speed so by line 5 I was only hearing sounds and not words. Walcott stopped her, asked the class what they were hearing, and, after some prodding to get people to speak honestly, was told that no one was paying much attention after line 3. He said that this was normal. For some reason people only listen to about three lines at a time. He told the poet to start by dividing the poem into stanzas of three lines; she should leave a blank space after each stanza as the mind and eye count time and will treat it as a fourth line. The poem needed breath, needed the changes of rhythm that come from space, whether within lines or at the end of stanzas.

She then reread what had become the first stanza of a stanzaic poem. Walcott slowed her down; this poem should be slow not fast. He then asked the class about the rhythm of a line. We assumed that it had an iambic feel, but he showed that it was divided into two equal heavy beats. The lines were then reread with attention to the caesura, punctuation, and small groups of words. Just by giving attention to what was already there, the poem was changing from a chant to a carefully crafted work of art. Walcott proceeded to show how one finds a poem in what had now become a body of material to be shaped. The next six lines were discussed as to whether they were two three-line stanzas or whether it was better to compress them into one stanza as the three middle lines were not needed. This was left to the judgement of the poet. Lines 10 and 11 appeared to form a complete unit, an unrhymed couplet. Walcott became interested in a parallelism of sound and a reversal of meaning between two clusters of words that no one had noticed and this led to a meandering conversation about the precise meaning of 'olivades' and whether it should remain in Spanish or be translated into olive trees.

For me as a writer of prose there was no excuse to have one word in Spanish. This required an unnatural shift in the speaking voice, but Walcott was interested in the sound and possible associations of the word. Where did the woman imagine the line was set? What were the rivers of that region of Spain? Instead of seeking the economy and transparency of English prose, he was looking at the possibilities of associations, of building images on images. Mentally I deleted several words and saw that by doing so I had changed the rhythm of the poem, broken the flow, made it prose. I was not a poet. At one point we were being asked to repeat the sounds in a Chinese language for some tree. I could see people fidgeting, feet trying to shuffle without challenging Walcott's dominance over the class. What appeared at first a friendly conversation about poetry had become Walcott's revision of a poem along with attempts to bring the class into what was becoming his own world of imagined possible associations.

Walcott said that the couplet needed a third line, and the way to find that was by way of a half-rhyme which would challenge the imagination. First we had to find a line-end sound in the couplet with which to half-rhyme as a full rhyme would be too strong and obvious. This confounded everyone as various rhymes were offered for 'quietness', but no one could think of a half-rhyme until Walcott suggested 'noise' which also could be linked to the associations of wind and leaves in the 'olivades'. This was an example of how the writer finds the poem in the given material. A poem is not what the author wants to say, not an idea imposed on a form, it potentially exists in those first lines heard. There is no poet, instead there is a poem that needs to be discovered and shaped like a sculpture found in the grains and patterns of a block of material. The poet is a vessel and craftsman not a person; the poem is formed in the process of finding it. Walcott asserted that finding the correct half-rhyme was more important than the day's political issues. Political issues would pass, the half-rhyme would last.

After two hours we had discussed eleven lines of a thirty-line poem. While I had an appointment I was reluctant to leave as I had witnessed magic. What I thought was just another lyric about unhappiness and exile was becoming a surprisingly good poem. Walcott had the eye, craft, experience, and genius, to have seen possibilities where I at first saw clichés. Remarkably, not much had been actually changed; rather Walcott had seen the material differently from the author, had seen it was a slower poem, had seen that its parts needed clear distinct articulation. It needed a stanzaic form, it needed love, care, and attention for itself and not as a projection of the poet's ego. I was, however, also glad to leave, I wanted fresh air, needed to clear my head. The class was to continue for at least another hour and I had already forgotten the pronunciation of that Chinese tree.

That evening Walcott was listed as reading along with Doris Lessing, Peter Carey, and Chinua Achebe at the Commonwealth Institute in Kensington, but he was already flying to New York where he would spend a day before starting a reading tour in Ohio, Illinois, and Indiana; one of the readings, he proudly told another writer, was to earn him $10,000. He then had to be tested for a possible cataract operation and was hoping to return to St Lucia for a rest, but he had also promised to appear at literary festivals in Italy, Holland, and Israel. Then there was a production of *Remembrance* for four nights in St Lucia in July. His continually being on the road meant that those who needed replies from him were unhappy. The Swiss publisher of a new volume of his poems translated into French was holding up printing for final approval and, not having had a reply from Walcott, asked me if I could locate him and get an answer. All I could do was pass on telephone numbers and say keep trying until you find him there.

Meantime the National Endowment for the Humanities 1999 summer seminars for schoolteachers included, at Sarah Lawrence College, 'The Classical and the Modern Epic: Homer's *Iliad* and Walcott's *Omeros*', 28 June–30 July. This would be the second time the seminar had been given. American schools would now be teaching *Omeros* as a post-colonial, postmodern, classic, perhaps allowing some teachers to sneak Homer's epics into the syllabus in those schools where reading and literature still survived. Culture does not stand still; in these days Homer could have a worse buddy. He had already appeared as 'Blind' Billy Blue in Walcott's *The Odyssey*. During that poetry master class in London Walcott had muttered some half-joking comment that those educated in previous decades would have known how to find a half-rhyme. He had become the tradition; the small self-culturing group around Alix and Warwick Walcott, the St Lucian Methodists, generations of West Indian schoolteachers, the former colonials of the Empire, had recreated English literature and were now changing British and American culture. They had become the heirs to the estate; whether or not Walcott officially became Poet Laureate (Andrew Motion was eventually appointed) was only a matter of form, a legality. The many streams of the Western cultural tradition, including its awareness of other cultures, flowed into his work, as did what was now being termed the Black Atlantic. I had been wondering what to call my book. I thought of titling it *The Making of a Laureate*, but that was too much like carrying on an argument. Several people said that the British would never have appointed a Caribbean writer; I was writing about a Caribbean life in its many complexities.

I had started working on a biography of Derek Walcott in part because I had become bored with writing books of literary criticism. I wrote a few theoretical articles in the new style and found words generated words without reference or even meaning. You could rant if you used the correct jargon, a few easy-to-learn ideas, and implied the correct politics. I wanted the opposite, something concrete, real, that told me how culture was actually produced, something with real people (those 'agents' that theorists said were an illusion), their desires, friendships, writings, finances, choices, particular advantages and disadvantages, the complexities of class, social position, education, family, personality, luck. While working on *Derek Walcott and West Indian Drama* I had seen that his life was so active, varied, and full of surprises, that trying to research and write about it would be the opposite of boring. I would learn much about the arts and culture in our time. After all these years what did I know about how poets support themselves, what a literary career meant, how great publishing houses become great, how Nobel Laureates are chosen, what it would mean to try to live in the West Indies as a poet or dramatist? I had in mind something like the commentary that accompanies major art exhibitions.

The more I thought about it the more I wanted to write a biography of Derek Walcott that would be ready for his seventieth anniversary. It would be a small repayment for my enjoyment of his work and, indeed, of West Indian literature and the many other new literatures and cultures of our time. The history of how European culture was taken to foreign lands and returned changed from former colonies is one of the great stories of the past five hundred years. I knew that Walcott's life and work was a representative part of that story, but it would be an impossible book to write as Walcott had done so much and there was so much to learn and put into order. He would not be very co-operative, he had his own life to lead and it was in full swing. I would need to depend mostly on the paper trail and interviews with others. At least I could make a start.

34

1999–2000 Tiepolo's Hound

WILLIAM GASS was prophetic in saying that this book should conclude with
'Tiepolo's Hound'. What had started as an idea that Sigrid would write an introduction to a book of Walcott's paintings had somehow evolved into a long
poem which would be accompanied by the paintings. Preparation of the plates
was taking time, time which Walcott was using for further revisions. During
August 1999, while my manuscript was being copy-edited, Walcott sent me a
near final draft provided that I did not quote from it. Farrar, Straus and Giroux
wanted it in September and he was still revising.

I had expected a Popean essay on art and painting; even the newspaper interviews saying it was about the nineteenth-century painter Camille Pissarro had
not prepared me for the poem itself. It was long, ninety-seven printed pages in
the version I had, over 2,500 couplets, and the first half of the poem was mostly
a verse biography of Pissarro. It was much more; it was autobiographical, about
the relationship of memory to art, about the life of the artist, exile, the nature of
modern art, and about the relationship of Caribbean and other New World arts
to Europe and other cultures. It was about Walcott. Walcott was reading himself
and Caribbean art into Pissarro. That Pissarro's family were Jews who had fled
to France from the Inquisition and then later fled an outburst of French anti-
Semitism to settle in St Thomas, illustrated Walcott's claim that the Caribbean
was a mosaic of peoples, arts, and cultures, outcast from their origins, and that
the region's cultural heritage included the French along with the African. That
was the theme of the many versions of *In a Fine Castle* or *The Last Carnival*.

The poem was also a discussion of the relationship of art to reality, and of
the Caribbean artist to his region; it alluded to many of Walcott's usual themes,
but went beyond them by taking a different perspective, treating, for example,

history as decaying or false memory. Even the title of the volume was illustrative as Walcott confesses in the poem that he is uncertain whether he has in mind a painting by Paolo Veronese or Giambattista Tiepolo. Epiphanies, obsessions, ideas, and symbols, the materials of art, belief, discourse, history, and self, may be based on wrongly remembered facts. I thought this strange so started looking at art books about the painting of *A Feast in the House of Levi* and discovered its history was indeed strange. It was originally a painting of the *Last Supper*, but after the Inquisition objected to its festive aspects, Veronese made some minor changes and retitled it *A Feast in the House of Levi* (about a wealthy Jewish family). Another art book, however, titles the same Veronese painting *The Feast in the House of Simon* and reproduces it along with (what is thought to be) Domenico Tiepolo's *A Feast in the House of Simon*, an almost identical imitation.

Why Tiepolo? Walcott suggests that he might have chosen it for the sound, but there is a better reason. Walcott's concern is with the dog in the painting, which for him becomes a symbol of making great art from the ordinary world, and which throughout his poem is echoed by and contrasted to actual dogs until eventually in the Caribbean he comes across a sick starving mongrel that he realizes should be the object of his love rather than the white hound (or muse) of the painting. The painted dog, however, might not have been by Veronese, as Tiepolo imitated Veronese's dogs and also included them in the scenes he painted. I could attempt to straighten out this confusion by consulting more studies, but why? The symbol and what it stands for have come loose from its source and are being used creatively by Walcott. From the perspective of the artist the *Last Supper*, *The Feast in the House of Simon*, or *A Feast in the House of Levi* are equally valid, the purpose of the painting being in the painting itself not in its interpretation. And why care if Walcott's source is Veronese or one of the Tiepolos since rather than remembering an actual painting he remembers his impressions of a part of the painting, impressions which themselves are later shown to be misleading in the sense of standing for European rather than West Indian life and culture.

I am making the poem sound nationalistic. It is not, although the conclusion moves in that direction, implying a contrast between Pissarro the exile who remained in Europe and Walcott who although exiled in Boston returned to the Caribbean. A Walcott poem, however, is not a message, is more like, although more sensuous and lyrical, one of those long Wallace Stevens poems in which various ways of looking at life are examined and contrasted. It might be thought a series of Impressionist paintings done in different lights at various times and places.

In contrast to the lyricism, impressionism, and unpredictable changes in the focus and subject of the poem there is an elaborate formal structure. The couplets are rhymed ab ab cd cd, and might be thought of as quatrains with breathing and visual space every two lines, so that Walcott's voice and the reader's eye and mind can move along with the story without being cramped into tightly rhymed aa couplets or blocked into abab rhymed quatrains. Space does make a difference. The poem imitates the art of Pissarro and his time in providing a frame (made of fours) within which there is a large portrait of apparently spontaneous impressions of life. 'Tiepolo's Hound' consists of four books, twenty-three chapters given Arabic numerals, each chapter having four sections given Roman numerals. The books are of slightly varied lengths, Book 1 consisting of six chapters, Book 2 of four chapters, Book 3 of six chapters, Book 4 of seven chapters. The sections are of varied lengths ranging from twelve to seventy-two lines. The elaborate numbering acts like a frame and grid, providing structural support to the otherwise impressionistic poetry with its shifting time, place, and focus.

After the Nobel Prize Walcott appeared a bit directionless. Many poems in *The Bounty* were excellent, some startling, but it was a difficult volume to like if only because of its obsession with death; it would take time to get used to. The essays, while excellent in themselves and impressive as a volume, were still a selection of reprinted writings, alluding to a larger autobiographical story. Much time had been wasted with *The Capeman*. Throughout the past seven years Walcott's talk of retiring to St Lucia and concentrating on his paintings has been a more financially secure version of that beachcomber painter of his earlier dreams. Now, unexpectedly, there was a long major poem, an important piece in his career, a poem which like his other recent works touched on his autobiography, brought together many themes from the past, but was in itself a sign of renewal, creativity, joy. Rather than the high art of poetry becoming a dying species appreciated by only the few, this was a poem to be enjoyed by any person with a general education; it did not need a classroom and critical guide to be understood and give pleasure.

My initial impression was that while it was not as great as *Another Life* or *Omeros*, it deserved similar attention. The brooding over death, over the pains of the sexual harassment case, was no longer dominant. This poem was a celebration of life; towards its conclusion it alluded to many of the people mentioned in my book (which curiously began to seem like annotations to Walcott's poem).

Like many of Walcott's poems 'Tiepolo's Hound' begins halfway through to change its focus, during chapter 12, from a biography of Pissarro to Walcott, concluding with his many travels in recent years and the new friends he has made. Here are the Spanish trip, the quick trip to the Canaries, the Italian trip, Coventry, a reading in Albany, Jose Antonio, Luigi, Walcott once more back in the Village eyeing a blonde on Christopher Street, taking a taxi to the airport. Like Naipaul, Walcott has for years been circling around an autobiography, alluding to his life, yet avoiding it. He has been collecting photographs and has often spoken of a possible photographic autobiography, but he is unlikely to write one. He is too busy with the present, and 'Tiepolo's Hound' concerns how the past crystallizes into images which become more and more distant from their origins and take on a life of their own, and become less and less like their source, which in itself keeps changing, so that history, narrative, memories, are bound to deceive, yet are the sources of art, the way memories of 1948 in St Lucia were a source of *Another Life*.

Walcott imagines Pissarro as like himself, from a minority in the West Indies, someone who discovered his interests and talents were in an art for which there was little local interest and from which he could not support himself. As Walcott had his Harry Simmons and Dunstan St Omer, so Pissarro had his Georg Melbye, a bohemian Dane who travelled through the Caribbean and who helped Pissarro decide to become an artist. Pissarro had to leave for France and compete with the best; he was often poor, often in debt, at times homeless, his daughter died. He thought of the Caribbean as a lost paradise, learned the colours, sky, and landscape of Europe, and he was part of a major change in the world's art, a movement away from well-defined outlines, narratives, and polished finish, to spontaneity, impressions, the bringing to the viewer's attention the actual materials of the art, the scientific analysis of colour into small dots. In England, fleeing a German invasion of France, Pissarro saw that the British watercolourists had gone even further in making a new art capturing the experience of a moment's perception.

These are some of the origins of Walcott's own paintings, the paintings which will accompany his long poem in *Tiepolo's Hound*, even the origins of his way of approaching drama and poetry in which the epiphany, the image, the impression, the scene, is more important than the narrative or argument. That is why he makes poems of sequences. A Walcott poem is discovered while writing, and is filled with contradictions, different voices, tones, perspectives. It has no designs on you, except perhaps to celebrate, to celebrate the West Indies, to celebrate life. It is often unexpected. There are parts of 'Tiepolo's Hound' which could refer to Walcott or Pissarro and occur any place, France, St Lucia, or Trinidad. They are small verbal paintings, lyrical descriptions, watercolours, even pure paint like those brush strokes of Cézanne, and they illustrate how a syllable is like a brush stroke.

Walcott wanted to write fiction and he has kept returning to notions of a clear prose-like verse while his poetry is heavily metaphoric. Parts of 'Tiepolo's Hound' are as close as he has come to a clear verse style, a poetry with the clarity of prose. There are few of those accumulated metaphors building on metaphors. At the start even the parallels between Pissarro and Walcott are shown by, say, a section concerning Pissarro being followed by a section focusing on Walcott. Similarly Walcott establishes the rhythm for the reader with couplets that are clearly iambic pentameters with close rhymes, although later there will be much substitution with trisyllabic feet, lengthening lines to thirteen and fourteen syllables as Walcott draws on the lessons he learned with his hexametric poetry. The lines here are prose-like yet more concise than in *The Bounty*. This is not to say that the poem is unmetaphoric. Rather it works by direct leaps, jump-cut metaphors from one realm to another, as when verse couplets are said to be stairs, or the sounds of poetry are treated as the brush strokes of painters. The couplets are a staircase through the scenes exhibited in his poem and towards the art works which accompany the poem in the book. The poem and book are his museum, his church, his monument in contrast to those of the Old World and the North.

Walcott in his teens and twenties had worried about drying up, losing the freshness of experiencing reality and the intensity of poetry. Yet here he is approaching his seventieth birthday as lively, self-renewing, inventive, surprising, and as hard-working as ever. I knew that Walcott had an exhibition of his paintings scheduled along with a reading at Hartwick College, and no doubt other places, but *Tiepolo's Hound* would bring what until now had been his secret desire to be a painter to public attention and risk public criticism and rejection. This was different from friends, other poets and some literary critics knowing that you painted. His painting along with his poem would be reviewed in major newspapers and magazines. He had conquered the world of poetry, and done well in the world of theatre, but now here he was at 70 launching a new public career in a different art form. The celebrations being planned in the West Indies for this birthday were less significant than his trying to start again what he had abandoned earlier, a career as a painter. A few years back Walcott was telling me I could not use his paintings in my book and Robert Hamner had only with great difficulty managed to get some of Walcott's drawings for *Omeros* for his study of the poem. Walcott was, however, pleased at how the drawings had appeared in the Hamner book, and his mood was much more cheerful, happier than a few years earlier now that the trial and *The Capeman* were out of the way. He offered Claire Malroux drawings for her translation of *The Dream on Monkey Mountain* into French and gave me permission to reproduce his work in my book.

In 'Tiepolo's Hound' Walcott mentions his mother teaching the need to triumph over affliction. Pissarro's life and Derek's own life might be regarded as illustrations. This poem, like much of Walcott's writing, is about living in the present, creating, seeing life as a bounty to be used now, and working towards the future without looking back, without allowing yourself to be burdened by history. What would he do next? He would spend his mornings and afternoons in St Lucia painting and swimming, he would visit family and friends in Trinidad, he would continue teaching in Boston, but perhaps six months after the publication of *Tiepolo's Hound* another poem or play would start coming to him. He might try to resist it, try to concentrate on painting, but eventually he would wake up early and begin writing again.

Endnotes

Notes Chapter 1

1 Derek Walcott, *Omeros* (New York: Farrar, Straus and Giroux, 1990), 69–70.
2 Derek Walcott, 'Midsummer L', *Midsummer* (New York: Farrar, Straus and Giroux, 1984), 70.
3 *Omeros*, XII, 68.
4 Derek Walcott, 'Veranda', *The Castaway and Other Poems* (London: Jonathan Cape, 1965; pb 1969), 38–9.
5 Derek Walcott, 'A Letter from Brooklyn', *In a Green Night* (London: Jonathan Cape, 1962), 53–4.
6 Patrick Leigh Fermor, *The Traveller's Tree: A Journey through the Caribbean Islands* (London: John Murray, 1950).
7 *Omeros*, XII, 67.
8 'Death of Mr. Warwick Walcott', *Voice of St Lucia*, 25 Apr. 1931, 5; 'Moving Tribute to Late W. Walcott: One of Nature's Gentlemen', *Voice of St Lucia*, 25 Apr. 1931, 5.
9 Derek Walcott, 'The Bounty', *The Bounty* (New York: Farrar, Straus and Giroux, 1997), 4.
10 'XVII', *Midsummer*, 27; Will Johnson, 'The Van Romondt Family', *For the Love of St Maarten* (London: Macmillan, 1987; 1994), 55–66.
11 'Methodist School Honours Ex-Principal', *Voice of St Lucia*, 11 Feb. 1989, 2.
12 George Odlum, 'Alix Walcott—A Catalyst for Genius', *Crusader*, 19 May 1990, 5.
13 Roderick Walcott, 'In Good Company', *Trinidad and Tobago Review*, Apr. 1993, 28–31.
14 'Dogstar', *Castaway*, 13.
15 'The Glory Trumpeter', *Castaway*, 25–6.
16 Derek Walcott, 'D'Aubaignan', *The Gulf and Other Poems* (London: Jonathan Cape, 1969), 52.
17 'The Prince', *Castaway*, 29.

Notes Chapter 2

1 J. P. White, 'An Interview with Derek Walcott', *Green Mountains Review*, NS 4: 1 (Spring/Summer 1990), 14–37 at 15.
2 Unpublished MS, 'Inside the Cathedral', 13.
3 Derek Walcott, 'D'Aubaignan', *The Gulf and Other Poems* (London: Jonathan Cape, 1969), 52.

4 Patrick Leigh Fermor's *The Traveller's Tree: A Journey through the Caribbean Islands* (London: John Murray, 1950), 202–3.

5 Thomas Craven (ed.), *A Treasury of Arts Masterpieces: From the Renaissance to the Present Day* (New York: Simon and Schuster, 1939).

6 Derek Walcott, 'The Sea is History', in Frank Birbalsingh (ed.), *Frontiers of Caribbean Literature in English* (New York: St Martin's Press, 1996), 22–8 at 26.

7 Derek Walcott, 'XIV', *Midsummer* (New York: Farrar, Straus and Giroux, 1984), 24.

8 Derek Walcott, 'Afterword: Animals, Elemental Tales, and the Theatre', in James Arnold (ed.), *Monsters, Tricksters, and Sacred Cows: Stories of American Identities* (Charlottesville, Va.: University Press of Virginia, 1996), 269–77; 274–5.

9 Robert Brown and Cheryl Johnson, 'Thinking Poetry: An Interview with Derek Walcott', *Cream City Review*, 14: 2 (Winter 1990), 208–23 at 209; J. P. White, 'An Interview with Derek Walcott', *Green Mountains Review*, NS 4: 1 (Spring/Summer 1990), 14–37 at 15.

10 Edward Hirsch, 'The Art of Poetry XXXVII', *The Paris Review* (Winter 1986), 196–230 at 222.

11 Derek Walcott, 'To Nigel', *Poems* (Kingston: City Printery, 1951), 34.

Notes Chapter 3

1 Derek Walcott, '1944', *Voice of St Lucia*, 2 Aug. 1944, 3.

2 Father Jesse, FMI, 'Reflections on Reading the Poem "1944" ', *Voice of St Lucia*, 5 Aug. 1944.

3 A. Seeker, 'The Offending Poem', *Voice of St Lucia*, 9 Aug. 1944, 3.

4 C. Jesse, FMI, 'The Agreed Syllabus', *Voice of St Lucia*, 2 Sept. 1944.

5 Revd C. Jesse, FMI, MBE, *Outlines of St Lucia's History* (The St Lucia Archaeological and Historical Society, 1956; 5th edn., 1994).

6 'The Art Exhibition', *Voice of St Lucia*, 20 Dec. 1944.

7 *Voice of St Lucia*, 15 Dec. 1944, 1, 3.

8 Harold Simmons, 'The Need for an Arts and Crafts Society', *Voice of St Lucia*, 21 Apr. 1945, 3, 4.

9 Harold Simmons, 'First Poems by George Campbell', *Voice of St Lucia*, 27 Mar. 1946, 2, 3.

10 Joseph Auslander, *Cyclops Eye* (New York: Harper and Brothers, 1926), 118.

11 Robert Brown and Cheryl Johnson, 'Thinking Poetry: An Interview with Derek Walcott', *Cream City Review*, 14: 2 (Winter 1990), 208–23 at 210.

12 William Baer, 'An Interview with Derek Walcott', *The Formalist*, 5: 1 (1994), 12–25; rpt. in William Baer, *Conversations* (Jackson, Miss.: University Press of Mississippi, 1996), 194–206.

13 'Mr Rodway Gets British Council Scholarship', *Voice of St Lucia*, 22 June 1946, 4; letter from John Figueroa to author, 11 May 1996.

14 'Literary Enterprise', *Voice of St Lucia*, 7 Nov. 1946, 2.

15 D.W., 'Two Poems', *Voice of St Lucia*, 12 Sept. 1946, 3 ('Pardon me Muse, I am a humble man,' and 'Once, long ago I made two world [*sic*] be one').

16 Derek Walcott, 'Epitaph for the Young', *Voice of St Lucia*, 21 Dec. 1946, 8 ('Yes, yes it had rained nearly two weeks now, . . .').

17 D.W., 'One Poem', *Voice of St Lucia*, 28 June 1947, 5.

18 D. A. Walcott, 'As John to Patmos', *25 Poems* (Port of Spain, Trinidad: Guardian, 1948 [1949]; rpt. Bridgetown, Barbados: Advocate, 1949), 6.

Notes Chapter 4

1 *West Indian Crusader*, 7 Apr. 1948, 1, 2, 3.

2 Derek Walcott, 'I With Legs Crossed Along the Daylight Watch', *25 Poems* (Port of Spain, Trinidad: Guardian, 1958), 23–4.

3 'West Indian Aspirations', *West Indian Crusader*, 7 Feb. 1948, 4.

4 Unpublished MS, 'Inside the Cathedral', 7.

5 Derek Walcott, 'Native Women under Sea-Almond Trees: Musings on Art, Life and the Island of St Lucia', *House & Garden*, 156: 8 (Aug. 1984), 114–15, 161–3; at 115.

6 *West Indian Crusader*, 10 July 1948, 7; P.J.M.S., 'Castries Fire 1948', *Voice of St Lucia*, 18 June 1949, Special Weekend Section, 1.

7 'A City's Death by Fire', *25 Poems*, 23.

8 'A Latin Primer (in Memoriam: H. D. Boxill)', *The Arkansas Testament* (New York: Farrar, Straus and Giroux, 1987), 22–3.

9 Derek Walcott, 'Brise Marine', *In a Green Night: Poems 1948–1960* (London: Jonathan Cape, 1962; pb 1969), 56.

10 'Inspire Modesty By Means of Nightly Verses', *25 Poems*, 5.

11 'Letter to a Painter in England', *25 Poems*, 7–8.

12 Based on unpublished MS 'Influences'.

13 'Private Journal', *25 Poems*, 15–16; Wayne Brown, 'The Singer in his Prime', *Sunday Guardian*, 11 Oct. 1992, 5.

14 Pat Strachan interviewed in New York, Nov. 1995.

15 Simmons to Collymore, 17 Jan. 1949; Frank Collymore, 'An Introduction to the Poetry of Derek Walcott', *Bim*, 3: 10 (June 1949), 125–32.

16 Revd E. C. Maclaren Mural, MB, PI, 'Derek Walcott's 25 Poems', *Voice of St Lucia*, 22 Jan. 1949, 7.

17 Republished as Wayne Baxter, 'D. Walcott's 25 Poems', *Voice of St Lucia*, 7 May 1949, 4.

18 V. S. Naipaul's 'Foreword' to *The Adventures of Gurudeva and Other Stories* by Seepersad Naipaul (London: André Deutsch, 1976).

19 Erika J. Waters, 'Interview with John J. M. Figueroa', *The Caribbean Writer*, 6 (1992), 69–76 at 73; author's telephone conversation with Figueroa, 23 Apr. 1996; John Figueroa, 'The Flaming Faith of These First Years: Caribbean Voices', in Maggie Butcher (ed.), *Tibisiri: Caribbean Writers and Critics* (Sydney: Dangaroo Press, 1989), 59–80 at 59.

20 *West Indian Crusader*, 12 Mar. 1949, 5.

21 Roy Fuller, 'The Poetry of D. A. Walcott', *Voice of St Lucia*, 9 June 1949, 5–7; 'The Poetry of Derek Walcott', *Public Opinion*, 4 June 1949, 6.

22 Hunter Francois, *First and Last Poems* (Bridgetown: Self, 1949).

23 H[unter]. J. F[rancois], 'Latin in Schools Should Be Compulsory', *Voice of St Lucia*, 20 June, 1978, 5–6.

24 Derek Walcott, 'Letter to Margaret', *Bim*, 3: 12 (June 1950), 342–3; 'Letter for Broodhagen', *Bim*, 3: 11 (Dec. 1949), 238.

25 Derek Walcott, *Epitaph for the Young: XII Cantos* (Barbados: Advocate, 1949); Keith Alleyne, '*Epitaph for the Young*', *Bim*, 3: 11 (1949), 267–72.

26 A. L. Hendriks, 'Epitaph for the Young', *Public Opinion*, 31 Dec. 1949, 6.

27 L.M.D., 'Derek A. Walcott—Poet', *St Mary's Annual 1948–1949* (Castries, 1949), 20.

28 *Another Life* (New York: Farrar, Straus and Giroux, 1973), 106–7.

Notes Chapter 5

1 'Arts Guild Formed', *Voice of St Lucia*, 11 Mar. 1950, 8.

2 For a list of early unpublished plays see Irma E. Goldstraw, *Derek Walcott: An Annotated Bibliography of His Works* (New York: Garland, 1984), 199–202.

3 P. Bledman, 'Introducing Dunstan St Omer', *Voice of St Lucia*, 10 May 1950, 5.

4 Dunstan St Omer, 'Vulgarity in Art', *Voice of St Lucia*, 20 May 1950, 8.

5 Derek Walcott, 'Introduction to The Work of Dunstan St Omer', *Voice of St Lucia*, 28 July 1950, 5, 6.

6 BBC Box 41336–475; and Fuller estate.

7 Umberto Bonsignori, *Derek Walcott: Contemporary West Indian Poet and Playwright*, Ph.D. diss., University of California, Los Angeles, 1972 (Ann Arbor: University Microfilms, 1977), 102.

8 Derek Walcott, 'The New Verse Drama', *Voice of St Lucia*, 17 June 1950, 2.

9 Maurice M. Mason, 'Derek Walcott's *Henri Christophe*', *Voice of St Lucia*, 10 Aug. 1950, 3, 4. Paper read by Mason to the Arts Guild on 3 Aug.

10 Harold Simmons, 'A Critique of the Art Exhibition of Dunstan St Omer & Derek Walcott', *Voice of St Lucia*, 9 Sept. 1950, 2, 8.

11 'Eavesdropper', 'Candid Comments of "Henri Christophe" ', *Voice of St Lucia*, 8 Sept. 1950, 3.

12 'The Arts Guild present Henri Christophe by DEREK WALCOTT', *West Indian Crusader*, 16 Sept. 1950, 5.

13 Lucille Mathurin, ' "Henri Christophe"—a Review', *Voice of St Lucia*, 16 Sept. 1950, 4, 5.

14 Photocopy of typescript dated 8.9.50, at University of West Indies, Mona. Issue not located.

15 Anon. review, *Kyk-Over-Al*, 3: 11 (Oct. 1950), 73–4.

16 Eric Williams, 'The Significance of the Haitian Revolution', *Voice of St Lucia*, 6 Jan. 1951, 4, 5, 8.

17 *Voice of St Lucia*, 4 May 1950, 1; Barbara Gloudon, 'Go deh . . . You-Wee', *Sunday Gleaner Magazine*, 7 May 1985, 11.

18 Philip Sherlock, 'Young Derek Walcott', *Sunday Gleaner*, 18 Oct. 1992, 22C; and interview.

19 'Walcott For W. I. University', *Voice of St Lucia*, 23 Sept. 1950, 4.

Notes Chapter 6

1 'The Problem Facing W. I. Leaders: Through the Eyes of Derek Walcott in His Poems "The Star-apple Kingdom"', *Voice of St Lucia*, 18 June 1978, 10, 11, 15 at 10.

2 Derek Walcott, 'The Land of Look Behind', *The Money Index* [Jamaica], 366 (27 Apr. 1993), D; transcript at UWI, Mona.

3 *The Gulf: Poems* (New York: Farrar, Straus and Giroux, 1970), 116.

4 All of Us, 'Three Evenings with Six Poets', *Kyk-Over-Al*, 3: 13 (1951), 214–20.

5 'Sambo Agonistes', *Bim*, 4: 15 (1951), 209–11.

6 G. A. Holder, 'BBC's Broadcast of Henri Christophe', *Bim*, 4: 14 (Jan–June 1951), 141–2.

7 5 Aug. 1951, *Caribbean Voices*, Box 60464. 638, 639. Recorded 12 July 1951.

8 B.M., 'A Review: *Poems*: By Derek Walcott', *Public Opinion*, 6 Oct. 1951, 5, 6.

9 B. L. Auguste, 'A Triumph', *St Mary's College, Annual Magazine 1950–1951* (Castries, 1951), 9–10.

10 'Derek Walcott Praised in London', *Voice of St Lucia*, 1 Feb. 1952, 1.

11 'New Methodist School Opened', *Voice of St Lucia*, 19 Apr. 1952, 1, 2.

12 Derek Walcott, *Harry Dernier: A Play for Radio Production* (Barbados Advocate, 1952); reviewed in *Bim*, 5: 17 (1952), 79–80.

13 'New Walcott Play For Production During September', *Voice of St Lucia*, 8 Aug. 1953, 1.

14 Vernon Cooper, 'St Lucian Greats: Derek & Roddy Walcott', *Voice of St Lucia*, 7 Nov. 1981, 2. I was often told this about Boxill in St Lucia; Roderick Walcott confirmed the probability.

15 Letters from Hill to King 17, 31 Oct. 1995.

16 'Ruins of a Great House' was first published in *New World Writing*, Tenth Mentor Selection (New York: American Library, 1956), 159–60; Erika J. Waters, 'Interview with John J. M. Figueroa', *The Caribbean Writer*, 6 (1992), 69–76; conversations between author and Figueroa.

17 'A Far Cry from Africa', *Public Opinion*, 15 Dec. 1956, 7; *In a Green Night* (London: Jonathan Cape, 1962), 18.

18 'A Leave Taking', *Bim*, 5: 18 (June 1953), 110–11.

19 'Annual Ceremony of Presentation of Graduates Takes Place March 19: Derek Walcott Among Those in Bachelor of Arts Group', *Voice of St Lucia*, 17 Mar. 1954, 2.

20 'Derek Walcott', *Pelican Annual*, 1955?, 142.

21 'New Walcott Play for UCWI Staging', *Voice of St Lucia*, 13 June 1954, 11.

22 *The Sea at Dauphin* in *Dream on Monkey Mountain and Other Plays* (New York: Farrar, Straus and Giroux, 1970), 73–4.

23 Waters, 'Interview', 73.

Notes Chapter 7

1 'Extra-Mural Director Sect'y Here', *Voice of St Lucia*, 6 July 1954, 3.

2 'St Lucian U.C.W.I. Arts Graduate Weds Jamaican Extra-Mural Secretary', *Voice of St Lucia*, 27 Aug. 1954, 3.

3 Telephone interview with Faye Walcott Chin, 1 May 1996.

4 Dated Mar. 1954 UCWI, in E. Hill's personal collection; published by UCWI Extra-Mural series of West Indian plays; J. S. Barker, 'Not the Stuff for a West Indian Theatre', *Trinidad Guardian*, 15 Aug. 1954, 4.

5 'A Far Cry from Africa', *Public Opinion*, 15 Dec. 1956, 7; *In a Green Night* (London: Jonathan Cape, 1962), 18.

6 Walcott to Roy Fuller, 8 Oct. and 30 Oct. 1954, Roy Fuller Estate.

7 Box 16648. Goldstraw lists this as 1953, which may have been when it was written. The BBC MS lists it as recorded and broadcast in 1954.

8 'Folk Dance at Friday's Production', *Voice of St Lucia*, 12 Dec. 1954, 2; 'Patois Phrases in Walcott's Sea at Dauphin', *Voice of St Lucia*, 15 Dec. 1954, 1; 'Walcott Arrive [*sic*] from Grenada', *Voice of St Lucia*, 15 Dec. 1954, 3; 'Walcott Play Staging Again on Monday', *Voice of St Lucia*, 18 Dec. 1954, 1; 'Arts Guild Play Being Repeated Tomorrow Night', *Voice of St Lucia*, 19 Dec. 1954, 1.

9 Anon., ' "Sea at Dauphin" Vignette of Life and its Struggles', *Voice of St Lucia*, 19 Dec. 1954, 1; C. H. Stugeon, ' " The Sea at Dauphin" Reflected Great Credit to All Concerned', *Voice of St Lucia*, 21 Dec. 1954, 4, 6.

10 Catholicus, 'The Message of "The Sea at Dauphin"—a Message of Morbid Fatalism', *Voice of St Lucia*, 22 Dec. 1954, 4.

11 Letter from Shirley Gordon, 26 Sept. 1994; Barbara Gloudon, 'Go deh . . . You-Wee', *Sunday Gleaner Magazine*, 7 May 1985, 11.

12 'Words for Rent', *Caribbean Quarterly*, 5: 2 (Feb. 1958), 99–102; rpt. *Caribbean Quarterly*, 38: 4 (Dec. 1992), 9–13.

13 *Kyk-Over-Al*, 6: 20 (1955), 139–40.

14 Derek Walcott, 'Soufriere "a manor of thy friends" ', *Voice of St Lucia*, 22 June 1955, 4.

15 John Wickham, 'A Look at Ourselves', *Bim*, 6: 22 (June 1955), 128–30; Basil McFarlane, 'Drama Festival Awards', *Public Opinion*, 28 July 1956.

16 'U. C. W. I Newsletter', *Voice of St Lucia*, 12 Aug. 1956, 5; *The Wine of the Country* exists in a duplicated typescript published by the Extra-Mural Department.

17 Roderick Walcott, 'A Federated West Indian Theatre', *Voice of St Lucia*, 11 Mar. 1956, 6, 11.

18 'St Lucia Arts Guild Puts Another Writer on West Indian Drama Field', *Voice of St Lucia*, 8 May 1956, 3; Harry Simmons, 'New West Indian Playwright Makes Debut', *Voice of St Lucia*, 8 July 1956, 3.

19 'The Poetry of George Campbell', *Public Opinion*, 20 July 1957, 7.

20 *Bim*, 6: 24 (Jan.–June 1957), 231–2.

21 Derek Walcott, *Ione: A Play with Music* (Kingston: printed by the Gleaner: Extra-Mural Department, University College of the West Indies, 1957), Caribbean Plays No. 8.

22 Travis Weekes, 'Walcott's IONE: Where OMEROS Began', *Weekend Voice*, 13 July 1996, 3.

23 Derek Walcott, 'Modern Theatre', *Daily Gleaner*, 25 Mar. 1957; Derek Walcott, 'Christianity and Tragedy', *Public Opinion*, 30 Mar. 1957, 4.

24 Roderick Walcott, ' "A Mirror up to Nature", Reflections on the Creative Arts Summer School, Jamaica', *Voice of St Lucia*, 22 Sept. 1957, 4; Roderick Walcott, 'A Mirror up to Nature', *Voice of St Lucia*, 29 Sept. 1957, 7.

25 'Mainly Personal', *Voice of St Lucia*, 17 Nov. 1957, 2.

26 Roderick Walcott, 'A Creole Folk Tale: A Preview of "Ti-Jean and His Brothers"', *Voice of St Lucia*, 1 Dec. 1957, 5; Slade Hopkinson, 'So the Sun Went Down', *Sunday Gleaner*, 15 Apr. 1956, 17.

27 Harold Simmons, '"Ti Jean and His Brothers" A Creole Tale', *Voice of St Lucia*, 29 Dec. 1957, 2?.

28 See Lawrence H. Schwartz, *Creating Faulkner's Reputation: The Politics of Literary Criticism* (Knoxville, Tenn: University of Tennessee Press, 1988).

Notes Chapter 8

1 Harold Simmons, 'The Flower Festivals of St Lucia', *Voice of St Lucia*, 27 Aug. 1953, 2.

2 '"Arts" Guild Withdraws Plays', *Voice of St Lucia*, 15 Mar. 1958, 1.

3 Harold Simmons, '"Spotlight" On the Dungeon of Culture: *The Banjo Man*', *Voice of St Lucia*, 15 Mar. 1958, 4.

4 'Statement by His Lordship the Bishop of Castries on the Incident of the "Banjo Man" etc.', *Voice of St Lucia*, 22 Mar. 1958, 8.

5 *Voice of St Lucia*, 22 Mar. 1958, 3.

6 B. H. Easter, 'Banjo Man', *Voice of St Lucia*, 22 Mar. 1958, 4, 7.

7 Kenneth Monplaisir, 'The Arts Guild and Its Struggle', *Voice of St Lucia*, 22 Mar. 1958, 4, 7.

8 'Catholicus Says—"Plays Profane"', *Voice of St Lucia*, 22 Mar. 1958, 4; La Rose, 'Vive La Rose', 5.

9 Roderick Walcott, 'The Candle In the Bushel of Art and Immorality', *Voice of St Lucia*, 29 Mar. 1958, 4, 5.

10 Dunstan St Omer, 'The Crown of Glory', *Voice of Saint Lucia*, 5 Apr. 1958, 1, lithograph with a short commentary below.

11 'Who's Who in the Festival', Central Committee of the West Indian Festival of Arts, Trinidad 1958; rpt. *Voice of St Lucia*, 22 Mar. 1958, 3.

12 Roderick Walcott, 'Raising the Colours: The West Indian Festival of Arts in Retrospect', *Voice of St Lucia*, 17 May 1958, 4, 8; 24 May 1958, 6, 8.

13 Noel Vaz, 'The Stage', *West Indies Festival of Arts 1958*, 33; Derek Walcott, *Drums and Colours*, *Caribbean Quarterly*, 7: 1–2 (Mar. 1961), 8–9.

14 Noel Vaz, 'Original Foreword', *Caribbean Quarterly*, 38: 4 (Dec. 1992), 22–3.

15 Umberto Bonsignori, *Derek Walcott: Contemporary West Indian Poet and Playwright*, Ph.D. diss., University of California, Los Angeles, 1972 (Ann Arbor: University Microfilms, 1977), 9.

16 Adrian Espinet, '*Drums and Colours* Seeks to Trace Evolution of West Indian Consciousness', *Sunday Guardian*, 27 Apr. 1958, 7; Tony Swann, '*Drums and Colours*— Guts at Least', *Public Opinion*, 10 May 1958, 57; Veronica Jenkin, *Bim*, 7: 27 (July–Dec. 1958), 183–4.

17 'Suggestions For An English-Based Orthography for Creole', *Voice of St Lucia*, 19 Apr. 1958, 6.

18 Derek Walcott, 'Ballades Creole pour Harry Simmons par Derek Walcott', *Voice of St Lucia*, 8 Feb. 1958, 2.

19 Irvin Gray, 'Il Faut Paller', *Voice of St Lucia*, 8 Mar. 1958, 7.

20 Gordon Lewis, 'The West Indies Middle Class & the Future', *Voice of St Lucia*, 6 Sept. 1958, 4, 5.

21 'Arts Guild Plays Impress D'Ca Audience', *Voice of St Lucia*, 9 Aug. 1958, 1; 'A Farewell to a Patriot', *Voice of St Lucia*, 20 Dec. 1958, 6, 11.

22 Robertson interviewed by Harrison, 9 July 1958. Harrison's diaries, Rockefeller Foundation archives.

23 Robertson interviewed by Harrison, 3 Sept. 1958.

24 'Derek Walcott Gets Fellowship', *Voice of St Lucia*, 4 Oct. 1958, 1.

Notes Chapter 9

1 Here and elsewhere I have made use of Walcott's unpublished MS 'American, without America' which exists in several versions at the University of the West Indies, Trinidad.

2 'Soso's Wake' information from Roderick Walcott; *Jourmard or A Comedy Till the Last Minute* was published in an undated duplicated typescript during the 1960s by the Extra-Mural Department.

3 Umberto Bonsignori, *Derek Walcott: Contemporary West Indian Poet and Playwright*, Ph.D. diss., University of California, Los Angeles, 1972 (Ann Arbor: University Microfilms, 1977), 135.

4 MS, 'American, without America'.

5 'A Village Life', *The Castaway and Other Poems* (London: Jonathan Cape, 1965; pb 1969), 16.

6 Ibid.

7 'Greenwich Village, Winter', and 'A Statue, Overlooking Central Park', *In a Green Night: Poems 1948–1960* (London: Jonathan Cape, 1962; pb 1969), 50.

8 'God Rest Ye Merry Gentlemen', *The Castaway and Other Poems*, 44.

9 'Spring Street '58', *Sea Grapes* (London: Jonathan Cape, 1976), 51–2.

10 Bonsignori, *Derek Walcott*, 143.

11 Ibid. 145–6.

12 *Malchochon* in *Dream on Monkey Mountain and Other Plays* (New York: Farrar, Straus and Giroux, 1970), 188.

13 Ibid. 190.

14 'Afterword: Animals, Elemental Tales, and the Theatre', in James Arnold (ed.), *Monsters, Tricksters, and Sacred Cows: Stories of American Identities* (Charlottesuille, Va.: University Press of Virginia, 1996), 269–77 at 276–7.

15 Bonsignori, *Derek Walcott*, 141.

16 'Bleecker Street, Summer', *In a Green Night: Poems 1948–1960*, 52.

17 'Blues', *The Gulf and Other Poems* (London: Jonathan Cape, 1969), 34.

18 Slade Hopkinson, ' "Public Opinion" To Back Walcott Play', *Public Opinion*, 29 Nov. 1958, 7.

19 'Time's Surprise', *In a Green Night: Poems 1948–1960*, 50.

Notes Chapter 10

1 Umberto Bonsignori, *Derek Walcott: Contemporary West Indian Poet and Playwright*, Ph.D. diss., University of California, Los Angeles, 1972 (Ann Arbor: University Microfilms, 1977), 157.

2 Derek Walcott, 'Reflections on the November Exhibition', *Sunday Guardian*, 13 Nov. 1960, 7.

3 *Opus: A Review* (Feb. 1960), 30, 31–2; *Opus: A Review* (Dec. 1960), 27–8.

4 Published in *Caribbean Quarterly*, 7: 1–2 (1961).

5 Derek Walcott, 'Jose Limon Highlighted Indifferent Theatre Year', *Sunday Guardian*, 1 Jan. 1961, 7.

6 *London Magazine*, NS 35: 5 (Aug. 1995), 61; the story is described more fully in Ross's *Through the Caribbean: The M.C.C. Tour of the West Indies 1959–1960* (London: Hamish Hamilton, 1960), 79–82.

7 Derek Walcott, 'Orient and Immortal Wheat', *In a Green Night: Poems 1948–1960* (London: Jonathan Cape, 1962; pb 1969), 48.

8 Kenneth Young, 'Black Actors in Two Plays', unidentified newspaper clipping, 11 July 1960; K.J., 'New Day Theatre Company, at the Tower', *New Statesman*, 1960.

9 Derek Walcott, 'On Choosing Port of Spain', in *David Frost Introduces Trinidad and Tobago*, ed. Michael Anthony and Andrew Carr (London: André Deutsch, 1975), 14–23 at 14.

10 *New Statesman*, 10 Sept. 1960, 341; *In a Green Night: Poems 1948–1960*, 73–4.

11 Derek Walcott, *Trinidad Guardian*, 20 Aug. 1961, 7.

12 Derek Walcott, *Trinidad Guardian*, 30 Aug. 1961, 5.

13 Plomer's In-letters 228/1, Durham University.

14 Derek Walcott, 'A Sea-Chantey', *In a Green Night: Poems 1948–1960*, 64.

15 Derek Walcott, 'Man O' War Bird', in *Bim*, 5: 19 (Dec. 1953), 233–4; 'A Latin Primer', *The Arkansas Testament* (New York: Farrar, Straus and Giroux, 1987), 21, 23–4.

16 Bryden letter to author 17 July 1995; telephone interview 19 Mar. 1996.

17 Derek Walcott, 'Chapter VI', *In a Green Night*, 28.

18 John Figueroa (ed.), *Caribbean Voices* (London: Evans, 1966–72), 2 vols. ii. 225; John Figueroa, 'Creole in Literature: Beyond Verisimilitude', *Yearbook of English Studies*, 25 (1995), 156–62.

19 Marian Stewart, 'Walcott & Painting', *Jamaica Journal*, 45 (May 1981), 56–68.

20 Cyril Connolly, 'The Professor and the Others', *Sunday Times*, 29 Apr. 1962.

21 F. N. Furbank, 'New Poetry', *Listener*, 5 July 1962, 33.

22 Hugo Williams, *London Magazine*, July 1962, 77–9; John Montague, 'Fluent Muse', *Spectator*, 19 June 1962, 864.

23 'Edward Brathwaite Looks at Walcott's *In a Green Night*', *Voice of St Lucia*, 13 Apr. 1963, 4; John Figueroa, 'In a Green Night', *Caribbean Quarterly* (Dec. 1962), 67–9.

24 C. L. R. James, 'Here's A Poet Who Sees The Real West Indies', *Sunday Guardian*, 6 May 1962, 5.

25 A. N. Forde, *Bim*, 9: 36 (Jan.–June 1963), 288–90.

26 W. I. Carr 'The Clear-Eyed Muse', *Sunday Gleaner* [Jamaica], 20 Jan. 1963, 14, 20; Bill Carr, 'The Significance of Derek Walcott', *Public Opinion*, 28 Feb. 1964, 8.

27 Gordon Rohlehr, 'Derek Walcott's The Gulf and Other Poems', *Black Images*, 1: 1 (1972), 66–9 at 66.

Notes Chapter 11

1 'O Trees of Life, What are your Signs of Winter?', *Selected Poems* (New York: Farrar, Straus, 1964), 76.

2 Elizabeth Hardwick to author, 16 Jan. 1995; Edward Hirsch, *Paris Review*, 28: 101 (Winter 1986), 225–7; Derek Walcott, 'Poet From the Land of Bean and The Cod', *Sunday Guardian*, 10 June 1962; Derek Walcott, 'On Robert Lowell', *New York Review of Books*, 1 Mar. 1984, 25, 28–31.

3 'Derek Walcott Looks at off-Broadway Theatre', *Trinidad Guardian*, 20 Oct. 1963, 7.

4 Derek Walcott, 'An Artist Interprets Cricket', *Trinidad Guardian*, 1 Jan. 1964, 5.

5 Derek Walcott, 'Spiritual Purpose Lacking', *Sunday Guardian*, 5 Jan. 1964, 3.

6 Derek Walcott, 'Bewildered and betwixt am I', *Trinidad Guardian*, 2 Sept. 1964, 5.

7 A scene was published as 'Robin and Andrea' in *Bim*, 4: 13 (Dec. 1950), 19–23.

8 Derek Walcott, 'On the Beat in Trinidad', *New York Times Magazine*, 5 Oct. 1986, 38, 40, 41, 43, 44.

9 Derek Walcott, 'A Great New Novel of the West Indies: The Man who was Born Unlucky', *Sunday Guardian*, 5 Nov. 1961, 17; 'History and Picong in *The Middle Passage*', *Sunday Guardian*, 30 Sept. 1962, 9; 'The Achievement of V. S. Naipaul', *Sunday Guardian*, 12 Apr. 1964, 15.

10 Derek Walcott, 'Mr Naipaul's Passage to India', *Sunday Guardian*, 20 Sept. 1964, 2, 4.

11 'A Great Russian Novel', *Sunday Guardian*, 19 Apr. 1964, 15.

12 'Origins', *Selected Poems*, 51–5.

13 *15 Poems for William Shakespeare*, ed. E. W. White, (Stratford-upon-Avon: The Trustees and Guardians of Shakespeare's Birthplace). See BM 52594, The Arts Council Collection of Modern Literary Manuscripts 1963–1972, Catalogue by Jenny Stratford (London: Turret Books, 1974), 24–25. *The Castaway and Other Poems* (London: Jonethan Cape, 1965; pb 1969), 27–8.

14 Derek Walcott, 'Necessity of Negritude', *Trinidad Guardian*, 28 Sept. 1964, 8; 'Berlin: The ABC of Negritude', *Sunday Guardian*, 18 Oct. 1964, 11; 'Drama: East Side, West Side', *Sunday Guardian*, 25 Oct. 1964, 11.

15 Derek Walcott, 'Conversations with a General', *Trinidad Guardian*, 18 Nov. 1964, 5; Derek Walcott, 'Spate of Anthologies Coming Up', *Trinidad Guardian*, 11 Nov. 1964, 5.

16 'Robert Lowell Introduces Derek Walcott at the Solomon R. Guggenheim Museum, October 15, 1964', *Envoy*, 46 (1985), 2–3.

17 The recording of the 'Guggenheim Reading' is at Harvard Houghton Library.

18 Raphael Lennox, 'The Poet Read with a Twinkle in his Eyes', *Trinidad Guardian*, 26 Oct. 1964, 7.

19 Derek Walcott, 'S. Grande Tonight', *Trinidad Guardian*, 27 Jan. 1965, 5.

20 'Lines in New England', *The Castaway and Other Poems*, 48–9.

21 'November Sun', *The Castaway and Other Poems*, 45–6.

22 Edward Hirsch, 'The Art of Poetry', *The Paris Review* (Winter 1986), 213–14.

23 Josephine Jacobsen, 'Books in Review', *Evening Sun* [Baltimore], 30 July 1964; Robert Mazzocco, 'Three Poets', *New York Review of Books*, 31 Dec. 1964, 18–19.

Notes Chapter 12

1 Derek Walcott, 'S. Grande Tonight; Broadway Next', *Trinidad Guardian*, 7 Jan. 1965, 5.

2 Errol Hill, 'Is "Man Better Man", Mr. Walcott', *Trinidad Guardian*, 3 Feb. 1965, 5.

3 Errol Hill, 'No Tears for Narcissus', *Sunday Guardian*, 7 Mar. 1965, 7.

4 Derek Walcott, 'Efficient "Birdie", Minus the Feather-Ruffling', *Trinidad Guardian*, 6 Jan. 1965, 6; 'Mighty Terror—A Great Matador', *Trinidad Guardian*, 17 Jan. 1965, 13; 'The Spoiler's Return', *The Fortunate Traveller* (New York: Farrar, Straus and Giroux, 1981), 53–60.

5 Derek Walcott, 'A Tribute to C. L. R. James', in *C. L. R. James: His Intellectual Legacies*, ed. Selwyn R. Cudjoe and William E. Cain (Amherst, Mass.: University of Massachusetts Press, 1995), 34–48 at 34.

6 Derek Walcott, 'Interview with V. S. Naipaul', *Sunday Guardian*, 7 Mar. 1965, 5, 7.

7 Mervyn Morris, 'Walcott and the Audience for Poetry', *Caribbean Quarterly*, 14 (1968), 10–11.

8 Derek Walcott, 'Return to Jamaica: Remembered Mountains', *Sunday Guardian Magazine*, 4 Apr. 1965, 6, 7; 'Return to Jamaica: Struggle for a New Outlook in the Arts', *Sunday Guardian Magazine*, 11 Apr. 1965, 7, 8.

9 Derek Walcott, 'A Journey into the Interior', *Sunday Guardian*, 11 Apr. 1965, 6; 'Analysing Wilson Harris', *Sunday Guardian Magazine*, 30 May 1965, 8, 14.

10 Anson Gonzalez, 'Walcott's "Laventille"', *New Voices* (Mar. 1982), 39–44.

11 Derek Walcott, 'Rogosin's Effort Could Compensate', *Trinidad Guardian*, 25 Aug. 1965, 5; interview with Walcott, Boston, May 1994; telephone interview with Lionel Rogosin, London, 1 July 1995.

12 Derek Walcott, 'Migrants' Lot', *Trinidad Guardian*, 29 Oct. 1966, 8.

13 Derek Walcott, 'Crisis of Conscience: Ban, Ban Caliban is the Cry', *Sunday Guardian*, 22 Aug. 1965, 11; 'What Do You Want, Mama? Caiso Men Don't Whisper', *Trinidad Guardian*, 29 Sept. 1965, 5; 'Commonwealth Literature', *Sunday Guardian*, 17 Oct. 1965, 14; 'Chairman's Report in Colour', *Sunday Guardian*, 14 Nov. 1965, 21.

14 *London Magazine*, 5: 6 (Sept. 1965), 15–30, 59.

15 Gerald Freund diaries, 10 Feb. 1965, Rockefeller Foundation Archives.

16 Bernard Taper, 'Letter from Port of Spain', *New Yorker*, 23 Oct. 1965, 203–6.

17 Derek Walcott, 'Theatre in Guyana', *Sunday Guardian Magazine*, 21 Nov. 1965, 6.

18 Derek Walcott, 'The Figure of Crusoe', in Robert D. Hamner (ed.), *Critical Perspectives on Derek Walcott* (Washington: Three Continents Press, 1993), 33–40.

19 Stewart Brown, ' "Between me and thee is a great gulf fixed": The Crusoe Presence in Walcott's Early Poetry', in Lieve Spaas and Brian Stimpson (eds.), *Robinson Crusoe: Myths and Metamorphoses* (Basingstoke: Macmillan, 1996), 210–24.

20 No. 30, *The Bounty* (New York: Farrar, Straus and Giroux, 1997), 63.

21 Saint-John Perse, 'Ecrit sur la Porte', 'Images à Crusoé', *Éloges*, 1911 (written 1904, first published 1909), in Saint-John Perse [Léger, Aléxis Saint-Léger], *Éloges and Other Poems*, bilingual edn., trans. Louise Varèse (New York: Pantheon Books, 1944, 1956, Bollingen Series LV), 50–63.

22 'Crusoe's Island', *The Castaway and Other Poems* (London: Jonathan Cape, 1965; pb 1969), 54–7.

23 A. Alvarez, *Observer*, 24 Oct. 1965, 27; Maurice Wiggin, 'Tropical Glory', *Sunday Times*, 21 Nov. 1965; Richard Kell, 'Books of the Day', *Guardian*, 10 Dec. 1965; Graham Martin, 'New Poetry', *Listener*, 10 Mar. 1966; 'Movement's Wake', *TLS*, 10 Feb. 1966, 104.

24 Alan Ross, *London Magazine*, NS 6: 10 (Jan. 1966), 88–91.

25 Gordon Rohlehr, 'Derek Walcott's The Gulf', *Black Images*, 1: 1 (1972), 66–9.

26 Derek Walcott, 'The Prospect of a National Theatre', *Sunday Guardian*, 6 Mar. 1966, 6; 'Problems of Exile', 13 July 1966, 6.

27 Karen Phelps, 'Where Actors and Audience Share the Same Level', *Trinidad Guardian*, 12 Jan. 1966, 3; Earl Lovelace, 'Theatre and Audiences', *Sunday Guardian*, 1 May 1966, 6.

28 'An Appreciation', *Voice of St Lucia*, 18 May 1966; Derek Walcott, 'Tribute to a Master', *Trinidad Guardian*, 15 May 1966, 9.

29 Derek Walcott, 'Tracking Mr. Wilson Harris', *Sunday Guardian*, 24 Apr. 1966: Derek Walcott, 'Time to Separate Politics from Good Verse', *Trinidad Guardian*, 17 Mar. 1966, 5; R. G. Coulthard, 'Defence of an Anthology', *Trinidad Guardian*, 17 Mar. 1966, 8.

30 Margaret Ramsay to Maschler, Cape files (Reading University).

31 Derek Walcott, 'The Theatre of Abuse', *Sunday Guardian*, 2 Jan. 1965, 4; 'T. S. Eliot—Master of an Age', *Trinidad Guardian*, 10 Jan. 1965, 3.

32 Derek Walcott, 'The Great Irony', *Sunday Guardian*, 25 Sept. 1966, 6.

33 Derek Walcott, 'Patterns of Existence', *Trinidad Guardian*, 24 Mar. 1966, 7; 'Contemplative is Word for his Genius', *Trinidad Guardian*, 5 Oct. 1966, 5.

Notes Chapter 13

1 Derek Walcott, 'Is V. S. Naipaul an Angry Young Man?', *Trinidad Guardian*, 6 Aug. 1967, 8–9.

2 Derek Walcott, 'Another Kind of Sentimentality', *Sunday Guardian Magazine*, 12 Feb. 1967, 8.

3 *London Magazine*, 8: 2 (May 1968), 5–11.

4 'Elegy', *The Gulf and Other Poems* (London: Jonathan Cape, 1969), 31.

5 'Che', 'Negatives', *The Gulf and Other Poems*, 47, 48.

6 'Homecoming: Anse La Raye', *The Gulf and Other Poems*, 50.

7 Mervyn Morris, 'Walcott and the Audience for Poetry', *Caribbean Quarterly*, 14 (1968), 1–24.

8 Library of Congress Archives, Poetry Office and Literary Programs 1966–1979, Container 20.

9 Collections of the Manuscript Division, Library of Congress.

10 Leif Sjöberg, 'On Derek Walcott', *The Greenfield Review*, 12: 1–2 (1984), 7, 10.

11 'Postcards 1. Washington', *The Gulf and Other Poems*, 32.

12 'Cold Spring Harbour', *The Gulf and Other Poems*, 61.

Notes Chapter 14

1 John Melser, 'A Similar Quality Could Be Achieved', *Trinidad Guardian*, 25 Apr. 1969.

2 Samuel Hirsch, 'Trinidad Workshop: Ensemble of Extraordinary Power', *Sunday Herald Tribune*, 10 Aug. 1969, 1, 9; Raymond Bordner, 'Allegorical Folk Play Produced in Waterford', *Day*, 2 Aug. 1969, 15; 'Trinidad Group Does Folk Play at O'Neill Meet', *Variety*, 13 Aug. 1969.

3 Roy Fuller, 'Poetry', *London Magazine*, 9: 8 (Nov. 1969), 89–90.

4 Clyde Hosein, 'The New Walcott: Sweeping, Involved, Audacious', *Express*, 9 Nov. 1969, 25.

5 Gordon Rohlehr, 'Making Love Look More Like Despair', *Trinidad Guardian*, 13 Dec. 1969, 8.

6 *Another Life* (New York: Farrar, Straus and Giroux, 1973), 123, 78.

7 Lawrence Laurent, 'An Experiment on a Dream', *Washington Post*, 16 Feb. 1970, C4; Daku, 'Telepic Review: Dream on Monkey Mountain', *Variety*, 17 Feb. 1970.

8 'Letter From Trinidad', Whit Weekend, 1970, MSS UWI Trinidad.

9 *Another Life*.

10 Dan Sullivan, 'Language Weds Heartbeat in "Mountain"', *Los Angeles Times*, 28 Aug. 1970, Part IV, 1, 11.

11 Polly Warfield, 'West Indies Fantasy is Brilliant Mosaic', *Gardena Valley News*, 3 Sept. 1970, 6; Tom Tugend, 'Taper Forum "Dream" Is Almost Too Good', *Heritage*, 11 Sept. 1970; Hazel La Marre, ' "Dream on Monkey Mountain"—Stunning, Exciting Theatre', *Southwest News*, 3 Sept. 1970.

12 Jim Guthrie, ' "Dream on Monkey Mountain": Poem's The Thing', *Star Free Press*, 3 Sept. 1970; Jeanne Pieper, 'Meanderings in Malibu', *Malibu Times*, 18 Sept. 1970, 2; Kimmis Hendrick, 'Walcott's Poetic Play in L.A.', *Christian Science Monitor*, 9 Sept. 1970; Richard Vale, ' " Monkey Mountain" Provides Thrilling West Indian Fare', *Evening Outlook*, 3 Sept. 1970.

13 Selden Rodman, 'Caribbean Poet of Elizabethan Richness', *New York Times Book Review*, 11 Oct. 1970, 24; Chad Walsh, 'A Life of Contradictions, a Poetry of Unities', *Book World*, 13 Dec. 1970, 3.

14 Anne Walmsley, 'Dimensions of Song', *Bim*, 13: 5 (July–Dec. 1970), 152–67.

Notes Chapter 15

1 Clive Barnes, 'Racial Allegory: The "Dream on Monkey Mountain" Presented', *New York Times*, 15 Mar. 1971, 52; Edith Oliver, 'Off Broadway: Once Upon a Full Moon', *New Yorker*, 27 Mar. 1971, 83–4.

2 John Lahr, 'On-Stage', *Village Voice*, 18 Mar. 1971, 57–8.

3 Derek Walcott, 'The Muse of History', *Is Massa Day Dead?*, ed. Orde Coombs (Garden City, NY: Anchor/Doubleday, 1974), 1–27; Edward Brathwaite, 'Timehri', in *Is Massa Day Dead?*, 35; Bill Moyers, 'The Leprosy of Empire', *Sunday Guardian Magazine*, 6 Dec. 1992, 6–7.

4 Published in the *New Yorker*, 28 Oct. 1972, 36–7, and ch. 22, i–vi, of *Another Life* (New York: Farrar, Straus and Giroux, 1973).

5 Derek Walcott, 'Superfluous Defence of a Revolutionary', *Express*, 20 Aug. 1971, 4.

6 'Poem', *Tapia*, 17 (27 June 1971).

7 'Man of the Theatre', *New Yorker*, 26 June 1971, 30–1.

8 Umberto Bonsignori, 'Derek Walcott: Contemporary West Indian Poet and Playwright', Ph.D. diss., University of California, 1972. This has useful information, but as Bonsignori used his transcripts without checking facts and by guessing at Walcott's pronunciation there are also many errors.

9 'That Bill Hit the Press, Says Lawyers', *Express*, 30 Oct. 1971; Therese Mills, 'Conversation with Derek Walcott', *Sunday Guardian*, 20 June 1971, 10, 17.

10 *Haggis/Baggis*, 9 (Spring 1972), 28–9. Miss Porter's School, Farmington, Connecticut 06032.

Notes Chapter 16

1 Umberto Bonsignori, 'Derek Walcott: Contemporary West Indian Poet and Playwright', Ph.D. diss., University of California, Los Angeles, 1972 (Ann Arbor: University Microfilms, 1977), 231.

2 Ibid.

3 Ibid.

4 Letter from G. M. Papp to author, 22 Sept. 1997.

5 Clive Barnes, 'Walcott's "Ti-Jean" Opens in Park', *New York Times*, 28 July 1972, 20; Douglas Watt, ' "Ti-Jean & Brothers" Comes to Central Park', *Daily News*, 28 July 1972, 57.

6 'The Silent Woman', *Trinidad Guardian*, 14 Dec. 1972, 2; *Express*, 14 Dec. 1972, 25.

7 'To the Actors', in Daniel Berrigan, *Poetry, Drama, Prose*, ed. Michael True (Maryknoll, NY: Orbis Books, 1988), 266–86.

Notes Chapter 17

1 Selden Rodman, 'Derek Walcott: Redefinitions', *The American Way*, 6: 2 (Feb. 1973), 26–32; the article was republished in Rodman's *Tongues of Fallen Angels* (New York: Dutton, 1973).

2 'Ohio, Winter (for James Wright)', *Sea Grapes* (London: Jonathan Cape, 1976), 59.

3 *Journal of Interamerican Studies and World Affairs*, 16: 1 (Feb. 1974), 3–13.

4 *New Letters* (Feb. 1974), 3–13; Dr Robert Farnsworth Papers, KC: 3/13/4; University of Missouri-Kansas City Archives.

5 'Revolution Rhetoric Clouds Writer's Search for Truth', *Kansas City Times*, 13 June 1973, 18A.

6 Michel Fabre, ' "Adam's Task of Giving Things Their Name": The Poetry of Derek Walcott', *New Letters*, 41: 1 (Fall 1974), 91–107.

7 *New Letters*, 40: 1 (Oct. 1973), 67–8.

8 Raoul Pantin, 'We Are Still Being Betrayed', *Caribbean Contact*, 1: 7 (July 1973), 14, 16; 'Any Revolution Based on Race is Suicidal', *Caribbean Contact*, 1: 8 (Aug. 1973), 14, 16.

9 'Commune', *Tapia*, 17 Dec. 1972, 6; 'Volcano', 9 Sept. 1973, 9; 'Non Serviam', 9 Sept. 1973, 9.

10 Derek Walcott, 'Magic Industry', *New York Review of Books*, 24 Nov. 1988, 35–9 at 38; rpt. '*Twilight*'.

11 Elizabeth Jennings, 'A Poet of Power', *Scotsman*, 29 Sept. 1973; Kildare Dobbs, 'An Outstanding Poet of this Generation', *Toronto Star*, 19 May 1973.

12 Ned Thomas, 'Loud World of the Mind', *Times Educational Supplement*, 5 Apr. 1974.

13 Edward Baugh, 'Painters and Painting in Another Life', *Caribbean Quarterly*, 26 (Mar.–June 1980), 83–93.

14 Alice Walker, 'Another Life', *Village Voice*, 11 Apr. 1974, 26.

15 Claire Tomalin, 'Derek Walcott's *Another Life*', *New Statesman*, 20 Dec. 1974, 904.

Notes Chapter 18

1 Charles Hawes, 'Crucian Comment', *St Croix Avis*, 23 Mar. 1974, 10.

2 Henry Goodman, 'Carnival With a Calypso Beat', *Wall Street Journal*, 4 June 1974, 20.

3 'Walcott Presents New Play', *Weekly Journal* [St Croix], 10–16 Oct. 1974, 3A, 14A.

4 Reviews are discussed in my *Derek Walcott and West Indian Drama* (Oxford: Oxford University Press, 1995), 213–16, 224–9.

Notes Chapter 19

1 *Co-operation Canada*, 19 (Mar./Apr. 1975), 31–5.

2 'Sea-Grapes', *Sea Grapes* (London: Jonathan Cape, 1976), 3. The Farrar, Straus and Giroux 1976 edition has a few variants.

3 'The Snow Queen, A Television Play', *People* (Apr. 1977), 39–42. Goldstraw says this derives from the 1954 'A Sound of Hunting' written in Jamaica, based on the earlier 'A Georgian House'.

4 'Harvest', *Sea Grapes*, 71.

Notes Chapter 20

1 14 Feb. 1977. Walcott (POS) to Halpern. Ecco Press Records New York Public Library.

2 *Remembrance & Pantomime* (New York: Farrar, Straus and Giroux, 1980), 7, 8.

3 'Princess Elizabeth's Scholarship Proposed', *West Indian Crusader*, 24 Jan. 1948, 4.

4 Carrol Fleming, 'Talking with Derek Walcott', *The Caribbean Writer*, 7 (1993), 52–61; *St Croix Avis*, 21 Apr. 1977.

5 MS version; 'On Hemingway', *Bostonia*, May/June 1990; rpt. *'What the Twilight Says':
Essays* (New York: Farrar, Straus and Giroux, 1998).

6 'From the Schooner Flight', *Massachusetts Review*, 18: 4 (Winter 1977), 795–800;
'Reflections Before and After Carnival: An Interview with Derek Walcott', in Michael
Harper and Robert Stepho (eds.), *Chant of Saints: A Gathering of Afro-American Literature,
Arts and Scholarship* (Urbana, Ill.: University of Illinois Press, 1979), 296–309.

7 Edward Hirsch, 'An Interview with Derek Walcott', *Contemporary Literature*, 20: 3
(Summer 1979), 279–92.

8 RAP[antin], 'Poet Walcott Blasts Trinidad on Freedom', *Caribbean Contact*, 5: 10
(Feb. 1978), 1.

9 MS, 'Essay on Soyinka's The Road', 12 Feb. 1978.

10 'Forest of Europe', *The Star-Apple Kingdom* (New York: Farrar, Straus and Giroux,
1979), 38–41 at 38, 40.

11 Maya Jaggi, 'No Trouble in Paradise', *Guardian* [UK], 12 July 1997.

12 Derek Walcott, 'Reflections on *Omeros*', *The Poetics of Derek Walcott*, ed. Gregson
Davis, *South Atlantic Quarterly*, 96: 2 (Spring 1997), 229–46.

13 Derek Walcott, 'Pinache', *Sunday Guardian*, 18 Dec. 1966, 6.

14 'The Leprosy of Empire', *Sunday Guardian Magazine*, 6 Dec. 1992, 6–7.

15 'The Problem Facing W. I. Leaders: Through the Eyes of Derek Walcott in His
Poems "The Star-apple Kingdom"', *Voice of St Lucia*, 18 June 1978, 10, 11, 15.

16 Valerie Trueblood, 'On Derek Walcott', *American Poetry Review*, 7: 8 (May/June
1978), 3–6.

17 Carl Little, 'Celebrating a Nobel Laureate: Derek Walcott', *Maine in Print*, 7: 11 (Dec.
1992), 1, 3.

18 Carrol Fleming, 'Talking With Derek Walcott', *The Caribbean Writer*, 7 (1993), 52–61.

19 David Pryce-Jones, 'Island Fling', 'A Caribbean Evening', Thursday 7.30 Radio 3,
Radio Times, 25 Jan. 1979, 71–3; BBC Sound Archive Index: Derek Walcott author
and speaker: Caribbean Evening a sequence of programmes. SP T061504–11.

Notes Chapter 21

1 Arnold Highfield, telephone interview, 24 Apr. 1996.

2 Edith Oliver, 'Displaced Person', *New Yorker*, 21 May 1979, 105–6.

3 In 1983 Bensen edited *One People's Grief: Recent Caribbean Literature* for Outriggers
Publications, New Zealand, to which Walcott contributed. Bensen later wrote some
essays on Walcott's poetry including the often republished 'The Poet as Painter:
Derek Walcott's *Midsummer*', *The Literary Review*, 29: 3 (Spring 1986), 257–68.

4 'The Schooner Flight', *The Star-Apple Kingdom* (New York: Farrar, Straus and
Giroux, 1979), 3–20 at 4.

5 Benjamin DeMott, 'Poems of Caribbean Wounds', *New York Times Book Review*, 13
May 1979, 11, 30; Vicki Feaver, 'An Island and its Noises', *TLS*, 8 Aug. 1980, 903.

6 Letter from Seamus Heaney to author, 13 Feb. 1995; Edward Hirsch, 'The Art of
Poetry XXXVII', *The Paris Review* (Winter 1986), 196–230 at 228; Seamus Heaney,
'The Language of Exile', *Parnassus*, 8: 1 (Fall–Winter 1979), 5–11.

7 'Cantina Music', *The Fortunate Traveller* (New York: Farrar, Straus and Giroux, 1981), 48–50.
8 Jo Thomas, 'For a Caribbean Poet, Inner Tension and Foreign Support', *New York Times*, 21 Aug. 1979, 2.
9 Dennis Parker, telephone interview, 29 Apr. 1996.
10 Edmund White, telephone interview, Paris, 8 June 1997.
11 Irving Wardle, 'Brilliant Portrayal of Changed Roles', *The Times*, 19 Dec. 1979.
12 The four video tapes are held by Banyan, POS.
13 *The Fortunate Traveller*, 63–70 at 63, 64, and 65.

Notes Chapter 22

1 *Caribbean Quarterly*, 26: 1 and 2 (1980).
2 Joseph Brodsky, 'Letters from the Ming Dynasty', trans. Derek Walcott, *New Yorker*, 28 Jan. 1980, 32; *Part of Speech* (New York: Farrar, Straus and Giroux, 1980), 132–3.
3 'The Insulted Landscape', Poetry Audio PR9216.W35x1980. This and some other taped readings are at the Harvard College Library.
4 *The Fortunate Traveller* (New York: Farrar, Straus and Giroux, 1981), 11–16 at 14–15.
5 Ibid. 54–60 at 55.
6 Ned Thomas, *Derek Walcott: Poet of the Islands* (Cardiff: Welsh Arts Council, 1980).
7 Fiona McKenzie, 'A Borrowed Language', *Art Link: A Commonwealth Arts Review*, 3 (Dec. 1980), 27.
8 The four tapes are available through Banyan Studios, POS, as is 'Scrapbook' (8 Jan.).
9 Lawrence Pitkethly's 8 Feb. 1994 letter to author; Mar. 1996 telephone interview.
10 Robert Bensen, 'Getting the Moment Right', *The Wick* (Spring 1981), 9–11.
11 'George Campbell', in George Campbell's *First Poems* (New York: Garland, 1981), pp. vii–viii.
12 'Celebration: An Interview with Derek Walcott', *Play Mas*, The Goodman Theatre [Study] Guide (Chicago, 1981), 31–3.
13 'Derek Walcott Goes Back to School to Read Poetry', *Express*, 4 May 1981.
14 Frank Rich, 'Stage: Derek Walcott's "Pantomime" in Washington', *New York Times*, 30 May 1981; David Richards, 'A Tangle of Masks in "Pantomime"', *Washington Star*, 21 May 1981; James Larder, 'Troubled Island' and '"Pantomime" in Trinidad', *Washington Post*, 21 May 1981, D1 and 2; 'Paul', *Variety*, 17 June 1981, 90; Faiga Levine, 'Theatre Lines', *Jewish Week*, 4–10 June 1981.
15 Gerald Freund, *Narcissim & Philanthropy* (New York, Viking, 1996), 62.

Notes Chapter 23

1 Wayne Brown (ed.), *Derek Walcott Selected Poetry* (London: Heinemann, 1981); 'Walcott—for Schools', *Sunday Gleaner*, 7 May 1982.
2 'XXXII', *Midsummer* (New York: Farrar, Straus and Giroux, 1984), 45.
3 Helen Vendler, 'Poet of Two Worlds', *New York Review of Books*, 4 Mar. 1982, 23, 26–7 at 23.

4 Roger Garfitt, *TLS*, 24 Sept. 1982, 1041; Blake Morrison, 'Beach Poets', *London Review of Books*, 16 Sept. 1982, 16.

5 Julian Symons, *Sunday Times*, 18 Apr. 1982.

6 Leif Sjöberg article on, and interview with, Walcott in *ARTES*, 1 (1983), 23–37; rpt. as 'On Derek Walcott' and 'Interview', *Greenfield Review*, 12: 1 and 2 (1984), 1–25. Östen Sjöstrand's translations are in the same issue of *ARTES*.

7 Gregory Mosher, 'The Director Speaks: A Dialogue', *Panto*, The Goodman Theatre [Study] Guide (Chicago, 1982), 31–7.

8 Mel Gussow, 'Dinner is Served at Times in a Barroom', *New York Times*, 25 Feb. 1982.

9 Jim O'Quinn, 'Hartford Hosts Ward, Walcott and a New Idea', *Theatre Communications*, 4: 2 (May 1982), 1–3.

10 Frank Rich, 'Theatre: Douglas Turner Ward Directs Premiere', *New York Times*, 2 May 1982, 63.

11 James Atlas, 'Derek Walcott: Poet of Two Worlds', *New York Times Magazine*, 23 May 1982, Section 6, 32–4, 38–51 at 50.

12 'Teacher to Offer to Leave His Post', *New York Times*, 1 June 1981; 'Love and the Poet', *Express*, 13 June 1982; 'Coed Accuses Teacher', *Time*, 14 June 1982, 56.

13 Ruth C. Baldwin, 'Women Lose a Round', *New York Times*, 9 June 1982.

14 RAP, 'The Last Carnival Disappointing', *Express*, 6 July 1982, 16; Judy Stone, 'Death of our Dodos in "The Last Carnival"', *Trinidad Guardian*, 15 July 1982, 18–19.

15 Derek Walcott, 'This Country is a Very Small Place', *Sunday Express*, 14 Mar. 1982, 18–19; Anthony Milne, 'Fran McDormand's Trinidad Adventure', *Express*, 25 July 1982.

16 Wayne Johnson, 'Gaiety and Tragedy Coexist in "Carnival"', *Seattle Times*, 2 June 1983, D13.

17 *The Caribbean Poetry of Derek Walcott and the Art of Romare Bearden* (New York: Limited Editions Club, 1983), selected poems by Derek Walcott, illustrations by Romare Bearden, introduction by Joseph Brodsky.

18 Derek Walcott, 'Native Women Under Sea-Almond Trees: Musing on Art, Life and the Island of St Lucia', *House & Garden*, 156: 8 (Aug. 1984), 114–15, 161–3.

19 Derek Walcott, 'A Rediscovery of Islands', *New York Times*, 13 Nov. 1983, XX, 21.

20 Derek Walcott, 'Papa's Flying Machines', *New York Times Book Review*, 13 Nov. 1983, 37, 51.

21 'Eulogy to W. H. Auden', *New Republic*, 21 Nov. 1983; *The Arkansas Testament* (New York: Farrar, Straus and Giroux, 1987), 61–5; William Baer, 'An Interview with Derek Walcott', *The Formalist*, 5: 1 (1994), 12–25; rpt. William Baer, *Conversations* (Jackson, Miss.: University of Mississippi Press, 1996), 194–206.

Notes Chapter 24

1 Edward Hirsch, 'The Art of Poetry XXXVII', *The Paris Review* (Winter 1986), 196–230.

2 'I', *Midsummer* (New York: Farrar, Straus and Giroux, 1984), 11.

3 'Midsummer', *Book World*, 4 Mar. 1984; Terry Eagleton, *TLS*, 9 Nov. 1984, 1290; Fred D'Aguiar, *Wasafiri*, 1: 2 (Spring, 1985), 37–8; David Garrison, '*Midsummer*', *Minnesota Daily*, 17–19 Sept. 1984, 20, 'Welcome Week Section'.

4 'On Robert Lowell', *New York Review of Books*, 1 Mar. 1984, 25, 28–31; rpt. *'What the Twilight Says': Essays* (New York: Farrar, Straus and Giroux, 1998).

5 'A Classic of Cricket', *New York Times Book Review*, 25 Mar. 1984, 1, 36–7; rpt. *Twilight*.

6 Unpublished MS 'Inside the Cathedral', 7.

7 William Doyle-Marshall, 'Derek Walcott Speaks Through a New Medium', *Sunday Gleaner*, 23 June 1986, 8–9.

8 Henry Mangal, 'Interview with Derek Walcott', *St Mary's College Annual*, 1984, 29–30.

9 'Walcott's Play Runs Into a Picket Storm in the U.S.', *Express*, 23 Sept. 1984.

10 Thomas Graham, 'West Indian Poet Derek Walcott to Speak at HSU', Abilene Christian University *Optimist*, 18 Sept. 1984.

11 Mike Ditmore, 'Walcott's Poetry Demands Rereading', *Abilene Reporter-News*, 23 Sept. 1984, 6E.

12 Jim Conley, 'Poet is Willing Captive of Society', *Abilene Reporter-News*, 23 Sept. 1984, Books, 6.

13 Mark Coffey to Walcott, 12 Apr. 1984; Coffey's files.

14 Coffey files.

15 Telephone interview with Mark Coffey, 7 May 1996.

16 'A Colonial's Eye-View of the Empire', *TriQuarterly* (Winter 1986), 73–84. American Audio Prose Library, AAPL 510.

17 Irma Goldstraw, *Derek Walcott: An Annotated Bibliography of his Works* (New York: Garland, 1984).

18 Wayne Brown, 'Chow Time, King Kong', *Express*, 21 Mar. 1985, 10.

19 Derek Walcott, 'Café Martinique', *House & Garden*, 157: 3 (Mar. 1985), 140, 222, 224, 226, 228; rpt. *'Twilight'*.

20 Derek Walcott, 'French Colonial, "Vers de Société"', *The Arkansas Testament* (New York: Farrar, Straus and Giroux, 1987), 75–6.

21 'Mimi, the Near Suicide', *The Arkansas Testament*, 77.

22 Interview with Edouard Glissant, Paris, 4 Aug. 1995.

23 Edward Hirsch, 'The Art of Poetry XXXVII', *The Paris Review*, (Winter 1986), 196–230.

24 Paul Berman, 'Theatre', *Nation*, 13 Apr. 1985, 443–4.

25 Martin Tucker *et al.*, 'Education by Poetry', *Confrontation*, 33 (1986), 295–306.

26 Judy Stone, 'We Can Gain From Outside Experience', *Trinidad Guardian*, 1 Dec. 1985, 17.

27 Seamus Heaney, 'An Authentic Poetic Voice', *Boston Globe* 9 Feb. 1986, A27–8.

28 John Lucas, 'In Multitudinous Dialects', *New Statesman & Society*, 2 Feb. 1990, 33–4.

29 Rita Dove, '"Either I'm Nobody, or I'm a Nation"', *Parnassus: Poetry in Review*, 14: 1 (1987), 49–76; James Dickey, 'The Worlds of a Cosmic Castaway', *New York Times Book Review*, 2 Feb. 1986, 8; Peter Balakian, 'The Poetry of Derek Walcott', *Poetry*,

148: 3 (June 1986), 169–77; Peter Forbes, 'Far and Feverish', *Poetry Review*, 76: 3 (1986), 14–16; J. D. McClatchy, 'Divided Child', *The New Republic*, 194: 12 (24 Mar. 1986), 36–8; Reed Way Dasenbrock, *World Literature Today*, 60: 3 (Summer 1988), 512–13; George Szirtes, 'Sculptor of Light', *Literary Review* (Feb. 1987).

Notes Chapter 25

1 'To Norline', *Arkansas Testament* (New York: Farrar, Straus and Giroux, 1987), 57.

2 John Berger, 'At First Sight', *New York Times*, 18 May 1986, 102; 'Love after Love', *Esquire*, Aug. 1986, 97. 'Love after Love' in *Collected Poems* (New York: Farrar, Straus and Giroux, 1986), 328.

3 Edward Brathwaite, 'Negus', *The Arrivants* (London: Oxford University Press, 1973), 222–4.

4 Fred D'Aguiar's letter, 25 Sept. 1995, to author.

5 William Doyle-Marshall, 'Walcott Speaks Through a New Medium', *Sunday Gleaner*, 22 June 1986, 8–9.

6 'Derek Walcott on Hart Crane: Interview Excerpts', *Center for Visual History Newsletter*, 1: 2 (Fall 1985).

7 Tony Sewell, 'The Human Factor', *Voice* [UK], week ending 20 Sept. 1986, 31.

8 Coffey to Walcott, 19 Nov. 1986 and 20 Apr. 1987. Coffey files.

9 Derek Walcott, Seamus Heaney, and Christopher Lydon, 'Robert Penn Warren', *Partisan Review*, 53: 4 (1986), 606–12; 'On the Indian Trail', ibid. 612.

10 Robert Penn Warren collection, Beinecke Rare Book and Manuscript Library, Yale University.

11 Edith Oliver, *New Yorker*, 29 Dec. 1986, 78–9.

12 Undated letters from Duncan Smith to Walcott in the possession of Robert Bensen.

13 'A Conversation with Derek Walcott', *Tampa Review*, 1 (1984), 39–49.

14 Derek Walcott, 'The Garden Path', *The New Republic*, 13 Apr. 1987, 27–31; rpt. *'Twilight'* (New York: Farrar, Straus and Giroux, 1998), 121–33.

15 Frederick C. Stern, 'The Formal Poetry Reading', *The Drama Review*, 35: 3 (Fall 1991), 67–84 at 71–2.

16 Caryl Phillips, 'Derek Walcott', *Bomb* (Summer 1992), 46–9.

17 Derek Walcott, *Omeros* (New York: Farrar, Straus and Giroux, 1990), 170–1, 173.

18 Rick Wayne, 'Monkey-Mountain Man Dreams On', *Star* [St Lucia], 13 June 1987, 6–7, 19; 20 June 1987, 12–13.

19 David Montenegro, 'An Interview with Derek Walcott', *Partisan Review* (Spring 1990), 202–14.

20 Charles Rowell, 'An Interview with Derek Walcott Part I', *Callaloo*, 34 (Winter 1988), 80–8.

Notes Chapter 26

1 Telephone interview with Caryl Phillips, 15 Oct. 1995.

2 Irving Wardle, 'A Rum Do in Jamaica', *The Times*, 9 Feb. 1988.

3 'History in E. K. Brathwaite and Derek Walcott', *The Commonwealth of Letters*, 1: 1 (June 1989), 5–12.

4 Kate Kellaway, 'Caribbean Son', *Observer*, 6 Mar. 1988.

5 Robert Bensen, 'Poets of Two Worlds', *The Wick*, 2: 3 (Dec. 1988) 14–16.

6 'The Lisbon Conference on Literature: A Round Table of Central European and Russian Writers', *Cross Currents: A Yearbook of Central Europe Culture*, 9 (1990), 75–124.

7 E-mail communication from Rick Williams, Director of University Honors Program, 19 Sept. 1995.

8 Derek Walcott, 'Caligula's Horse', *Kunapipi*, 11: 1 (1989), 138–42.

9 Edward Baugh, 'Derek Walcott on West Indian Literature', *Jamaica Journal*, 21: 2 (May 1988), 50–2.

10 Fred D'Aguiar's letter to author, 25 Sept. 1995.

11 Waldemar Januszczak, 'The Longing on St Lucia', *Guardian*, 9 July 1988.

12 'The Leprosy of Empire', *Sunday Guardian Magazine*, 6 Dec. 1992, 6–7.

13 Derek Walcott, 'Magic Industry', *New York Review of Books*, 24 Nov. 1988, 35–9; rpt. '*Twilight*' (New York: Farrar, Straus and Giroux, 1998).

14 Brenda Flanagan, 'An Interview with Derek Walcott', *Voices of the African Diaspora: CAAS*, 7 (1991), 16–20.

15 Derek Walcott, 'The Sea is History', in Frank Birbalsingh (ed.), *Frontiers of Caribbean Literature in English* (New York: St Martin's Press, 1996), 15–21.

16 Cyril Dabydeen, 'Derek Walcott in Ottawa', *The Spectrum*, 6: 2 (7 Feb. 1989), 1–2; Cyril Dabydeen, 'Letter to Derek Walcott', *Ariel*, 22: 2 (Apr. 1991), 21–2; telephone interview with Cyril Dabydeen, 5 Aug. 1997.

17 Paul Grondahi, 'West Indian Poet At Ease in Albany', *Times Union*, 2 Feb. 1989, B6.

18 Derek Walcott, 'Crocodile Dandy', *The New Republic*, 200: 6 (5 Feb. 1989), 25–8; rpt. '*Twilight*'.

19 Derek Walcott, 'The Master of the Ordinary', *New York Review of Books*, 1 June 1989, 37–9; rpt. '*Twilight*'.

20 Derek Walcott, 'Medusa Face', *Weekend Telegraph*, 21 Oct. 1989; rpt. '*Twilight*'.

21 *London Theatre Record*, 26 Feb.–11 Mar. 1989, 305–6.

22 'Poets' Round Table "A Common Language"', *PN Review*, 15: 4 (1989), 39–47.

23 Interview with David Applefield, Paris, 27 July 1995.

24 Geordie Greig, 'On the Crest of a Wave', *Sunday Times*, 14 Feb. 1999, 8.

25 Patrick Gallagher, 'Homer to Windward', *Sunday Independent*, 16 July 1989, 18.

26 Telephone interview with, and subsequent fax from, Lloyd Stanford, 15 Aug. 1997.

27 Letter from Robert Bensen to author, 15 Sept. 1995.

28 Unpublished review by Robert Bensen.

Notes Chapter 27

1 Melissa Green, *Squanicook Eclogues* (New York: Norton, 1987).

2 Reetika Vazirani, telephone interview, 21 Mar. 1996, plus letters to author.

3 Glyn Maxwell, 'Mr Malleable Meets the Spoiler', *Poetry Review*, 78: 3 (1988), 23–5; interview with Glyn Maxwell, Jan. 1995, London.

4 Telephone interview with Rei Terada, 26 Sept. 1995; telephone interview with William Keeney.

Notes Chapter 28

1 John Wickham, 'Now That the Poet is 60', *Daily Nation*, 29 Jan. 1990, 7.
2 Author's interview with Edouard Glissant in Paris, 4 Aug. 1995.
3 Robert Brown and Cheryl Johnson, 'Thinking Poetry: An Interview with Derek Walcott', *Cream City Review*, 14: 2 (Winter 1990), 208–23.
4 Derek Walcott, ' "Islands in the Stream", Hemingway, Winslow Homer, and the Light of the Caribbean', *Bostonia* (May/June, 1990) 20–2; rpt. *'Twilight'* (New York: Farrar, Straus and Giroux, 1998).
5 Sylvie Drake, 'Walcott: He Sells Sarcasm by the Seashore', *Los Angeles Times*, 11 June 1990, F1, 3; Daws, *Variety*, 12 June 1990.
6 Rick Wayne, 'Says Derek Walcott "I'm ready to die for my country!" ', *Star*, 26 May 1990, 3; Jeremy Bacon, 'Baron and Nobel Laureate Do Battle Over Island Idyll', *Sunday Telegraph*, 11 Oct. 1992.
7 Shaun McCarthy, *OUTPOSTS*, 171 (Winter 1991), 4–24.
8 Rebekah Presson, 'The Man Who Keeps the English Language Alive: An Interview with Derek Walcott', *New Letters*, 59: 1 (1992), 8–15.
9 Telephone interview with Fran Quinn, 13 Mar. 1996.
10 Oliver Taplin, 'Derek Walcott's *Omeros* and Derek Walcott's Homer', *Arion* (Spring 1991), 213–25; Sean O'Brien, 'In Terms of the Ocean', *TLS*, 14 Sept. 1990, 977–8.
11 Brad Leithauser, 'Ancestral Rhyme', *New Yorker*, 11 Feb. 1991, 91–5.
12 Ned Thomas, *Derek Walcott: Poet of the Island* (Cardiff: Welsh Arts Council, 1980), 21.
13 Phoebe Pettingell, 'Making Epic Connections', *New Leader*, 11–25 Mar. 1991, 15–16.
14 Luigi Sampietro, 'An Object Beyond One's Own Life', *Caribana*, 2 (1991), 25–36.
15 Luigi Sampietro, 'On *Omeros*', *Caribana*, 3 (1992–3), 31–44.

Notes Chapter 29

1 See 'A Tribute to C. L. R. James', in *C. L. R. James: His Intellectual Legacies*, ed. Selwyn R. Cudjoe and William E. Cain (Amherst, Mass.: University of Massachusetts Press, 1995), 34–48.
2 Bill Marx, '*Steel* Lite', *Boston Phoenix*, 19 Apr. 1991, sect. 3, 10.
3 Letter from Tony Kellman to author, 3 July 1995.
4 Paula Burnett, 'Omeros', *Wasafiri*, 14 (1991), 32–3.
5 'Paul Simon's Journey to Brazil and Beyond', *New York Times*, 14 Oct. 1990, 1, 32–3.
6 Derek Walcott, 'Take the Money—and Write', *New York Times*, 3 Nov. 1991, sect. 4, E15.
7 Derek Walcott, 'Jackie Hinkson', *Galerie* (Trinidad), ed. Geoff McLean, 1: 2 (1992); rpt. *The Massachusetts Review* (Autumn–Winter 1994), 413–17.
8 Derek Walcott, 'Homeric Chorus', *New York Times*, 1 Jan. 1992, 15.

9 Letter from Marian Pringle to author, 8 Mar. 1995.

10 Andrew St George, 'A Caribbean Odyssey', *Financial Times*, 4 July 1992; Michael Billington, 'The Odyssey', *Guardian*, 6 July 1992; Peter McGarry, 'Grandeur of Greece goes Caribbean', *Coventry Telegraph*, 3 July 1992, 20; Oliver Taplin, 'Hustling Homer', *TLS*, 17 July 1992, 19.

11 Paula Burnett, 'Walcott's Spellbinding Drama', *Caribbean Times*, 7 July 1992.

12 Anna Walcott, 'Walcott on Walcott', *Sunday Guardian*, 19 July 1992, 5.

13 'Students Say Nobel Winner is Sex Pest', *Evening Standard*, 12 Oct. 1992.

14 Jeanne Nicholson Siler, 'Nobel Countenance: A Prized Writer Keeps His Commitment', *UVA Alumni News*, Jan. 1993, 31.

15 Derek Walcott, 'Afterword: Animals, Elemental Tales, and the Theatre', in James Arnold (ed.), *Monsters, Tricksters, and Sacred Cows: Stories of American Identities* (Charlottesville, Va.: University Press of Virginia, 1996), 269–77.

16 Michael Reckford, 'The Company Pays Tribute to Derek Walcott', *Sunday Gleaner*, 1 Nov. 1992, 5D.

17 Keith Noel, 'The Many Sides of Derek Walcott', *Sunday Gleaner*, 22 Nov. 1992, 19D, 24D.

18 Staci D. Kramer, 'Tropical Bard', *Chicago Tribune*, 25 Nov. 25 1992, C1, 5.

19 'Walcott's Success a Lesson in Achievement', *Express*, 12 Oct. 1992, 3.

Notes Chapter 30

1 Interview with Edouard Glissant, Paris, 4 Aug. 1995.

2 Judy Raymond, 'Enter a New Set of Strolling Players', *Sunday Express*, 17 Jan. 1993.

3 Albert Brandford, 'A Sample of Walcott's Drama', *Weekend Nation*, 15 Jan. 1993, 19.

4 *Programme, Citations and Proclamation for Nobel Laureate Week January 21st to 28th 1993 Saint Lucia*, compiled by The Crusader Publishing Co., printed by the Lithographic Press, Castries, St Lucia, 1993.

5 Barnard Fanis, 'What Walcott Really Said', and David Vitalis, 'An Attack on the "Kweyol Laureate"', both in *Weekend Voice*, 6 Feb. 1993, 14. A file about this controversy can be found at the Folk Research Center, Castries.

6 'Walcott's Award for the Young', *Daily Gleaner*, 29 Jan. 1993, 4.

7 Sasemarine Persaud, 'Whose Image?', *Caricom Perspective*, 61–2 (July–Dec. 1993), 38–9; also Raymond Ramcharitar, 'And What for Naipaul?', *Trinidad Guardian*, 11 Oct. 1992.

8 *USAir Magazine*, 15: 2 (Feb. 1993), 112.

9 *The Villager* (Villa Julie College), 19 Mar. 1993, is devoted to Walcott.

10 Derek Walcott, 'The Land of Look Behind', *Money Index*, 27 Apr. 1993, c–f.

11 Rohan Preston, 'Walcott Gives Life to Caribbean Epic', *Chicago Tribune*, 2 May 1993, sec. 5, tempo 5.

12 Kay Baldeosingh, 'Walcott: Immoral to Move Workshop', *Daily Express*, 5 July 1993, 1, 4; Trevor Smith, 'Walcott in Dream World', *Sunday Guardian*, 18 July 1993.

13 Christina Scaglia, 'The Teatro Nationale of Milan goes Caribbean . . . *Ti-Jean*', *Caribana*, 4 (1994–5), 35–41.

14 'Journey with Walcott', *Trinidad Guardian*, 10 Aug. 1993; Raymond Ramcharitar, 'Odyssey Best Production to Hit TT Theatre in Years', *Trinidad Guardian*, 10 Aug. 1993.

15 'Walcott Fails to Show', *Trinidad Guardian*, 1 Sept. 1993; 'Ire of the Laureate', *Trinidad Guardian*, 2 Sept. 1993; 'Walcott May Meet Clinton, Queen', *Trinidad Guardian*, 2 Sept. 93; 'Walcott Insulted Us', *Sunday Guardian*, 5 Sept. 1993; 'Walcott to Receive Award in December', *Express*, 2 Sept. 1993.

16 Wayne Brown, 'Glimpses of the Past', *Sunday Guardian*, 5 Sept. 1993.

17 Letter and copies of introductions from J. Edward Chamberlin to author, 19 June 1995.

18 Anderson said it was an hour work, but a newspaper says ninety minutes. Linda Matchan, 'Making History Sing', *Boston Sunday Globe*, 5 Dec. 1993, B13, B18; telephone interview with Anderson on 29 July 1997.

19 Kim Johnson, 'Double Vision: Derek Walcott as Painter', *Express*, 5 Dec. 1993, 1, 3.

20 'Nobel Prize Winner on 11 Stamps', *Linn's Stamp News*, 12 Sept. 1994, 8.

Notes Chapter 31

1 Tad Simmons, 'Bill T. Jones Sets Walcott's *Mountain* in Motion', *American Theatre*, May/June 1994, 48–51.

2 Eileen Battersby, *The Irish Times*, 28 Apr. 1994.

3 Letter from José Antonio Gurpegui to author, 6 June 1995.

4 The five pages written in ink and signed by Derek Walcott are dated 'Weds. June 9 94 11:05 and Thurs. 9 to [illegible]' and have various corrections and insertions.

5 Kevin Kelly, 'The Poetic Power of Walcott's "Dream"', *Boston Globe*, 26 July 1994, 57, 60; Terry Byne, 'Nobel Laureate's Drama Casts a Spell', *Boston Herald*, 27 July 1994, 41; Bill Marx, 'Right Dream: Derek Walcott takes on Marlowe and Shakespeare', *Boston Phoenix*, 29 July 1994, 10–11; Carolyn Clay, 'Don Wanders', *Boston Phoenix*, 15 July 1994, 7.

6 Vincent Canby, 'The Caribbean Flavors a Homeric "Odyssey"', *New York Times*, 30 Oct. 1994, 35–6; Richard Corliss, 'Club Adriatic', *Time*, 21 Nov. 1994, 61; Rebecca Humphries, 'Walcott goes on a Caribbean *Odyssey*', *Georgetown Voice*, 13 Oct. 1994, 13; Amy E. Schwartz, 'Who Owns History', *Washington Post*, 19 Oct. 1994, A23.

7 Nathan Gardels, 'Occupation Is an "Act of Salvation"', *Los Angeles Times*, 22 Sept. 1994: also published as 'The Salvation of Haiti', in *New Perspectives*, 11: 4 (Fall 1994), 24–5.

8 Letter from Fred D'Aguiar to author, 25 Sept. 1994.

9 Information mostly from Shozo Tokunaga's letter of 12 Feb. 1998 to author.

10 Mark Smoyer, 'Far from "Omeros"', *Metro*, 8–14 Dec. 1994, 24.

11 Derek Walcott, 'The Commonwealth: Pedestal or Pyre?', *New Statesman & Society*, 21 July 1995, 30–1.

12 'Derek Walcott: An Interview by Rose Styron', *American Poetry Review*, 26: 3 (May/June 1997), 41–6.

13 Derek Walcott, 'Reflections on Omeros', *South Atlantic Quarterly*, 96: 2 (Spring 1997), 229–46.

14 'Panel II', *The Georgia Review* (Winter 1995), 861–84.

15 Telephone interview with Caryl Phillips, 15 Oct. 1995.

16 Telephone interview with Robert Pinsky, 18 Nov. 1995.

17 Derek Walcott, 'The Road Taken', *New Republic*, 213 (27 Nov. 1995), 29–36; rept. *'Twilight'* (New York: Farrar, Straus and Giroux, 1998).

Notes Chapter 32

1 Patrick Healy, 'When a Faculty Star Faces Harassment Charges', *Chronicle of Higher Education*, 19 Apr. 1996, A23–4; Catherine Pepinster, 'Nobel Laureate Accused of Sexual Harassment', *Independent on Sunday*, 5 May 1996, 1.

2 Derek Walcott, *The Bounty* (New York: Farrar, Straus and Giroux, 1997), 34.

3 Ibid. 52.

4 Ibid. 53.

5 *International Herald Tribune*, 21 Mar. 1996, 6.

6 Copies of the fax and other letters from Kirchwey and the Unterberg Center that I mention are in the files at the Poetry Center.

7 Walter Mauro, 'Derek Walcott: "Io vivo in un Paradiso rubato" ', *Il Giorno*, 31 May 1996.

8 Derek Walcott, 'Guest Speaker: Derek Walcott: Where I Live', *Architectural Digest* (Jan. 1997), 30, 32, 34, 36.

9 Scott Crier, 'What Does it Takes [*sic*] to Appreciate Walcott?', *University News*, 2 Apr. 1997, 4; Lisa Makson, 'Walcott Activities Enlighten Campus', *University News*, 9 Apr. 1997, 1, 4.

10 Jerome Weeks, 'Across the Great Divide', *Dallas Morning News*, 3 Apr. 1997, 1C and 'back page'.

11 Andrew Frisardi, 'Verses of Things Past', *Boston Globe*, 12 Oct. 1997, E1, 4; Pico Iyer, 'Hymns for the Indigo Hour', *Time*, 14 July 1997, 85.

12 William Logan, 'The Fatal Lure of Home', *New York Times Book Review*, 29 June 1997, 11.

13 John Bayley, 'Living Ghosts', *New York Review of Books*, 27 Mar. 1997, 18–21; Robert Hass, 'Poet's Choice', *Washington Post*, 5 Oct. 1997.

14 Richard Sanger, 'The Apples of this Second Eden', *TLS*, 19 Sept. 1997, 10–11.

15 Sean O'Brien, 'Unexpected Grandeur', *Sunday Times*, 13 July 1997; John Burnside, 'Imagining a Body's Language', *Scotsman*, 19 July 1997; Kate Kellaway, 'Paperback of the Week', *Observer*, 27 July 1997.

16 David Dabydeen, 'Its Food to Exorcise', *Times*, 17 July 1997, 8.

17 Maya Jaggi, 'No Trouble in Paradise', *Guardian*, 12 July 1997; also 'Enjoying the Fruits of Life's Bounty', *Guardian Weekly*, 27 July 1997, 27.

18 Rick Lyman, 'On Stage and Off', *New York Times*, 26 Sept. 1997, E2.

19 William Gass, telephone interview by author, 26 Mar. 1998.

Notes Chapter 33

1 Walter Scanlon, 'Simon Says Capeman', *New York Press*, 26 Nov.–2 Dec. 1997, 32; Mike McAlary, 'Cape Fear', *New York*, 10 Nov. 1997, 38–44, 81.

2 The backstage history is told in Stephen J. Dubner, 'The Pop Perfectionist On a Crowded Stage', *New York Times Magazine*, 9 Nov. 1997, sect. 6, 42–9, 56, 63–6, 83.

3 Phoebe Hoban, 'Sharing Capeman Memories', *New York Times*, 1 Feb. 1998, sect. 6.

4 Ben Brantley, '"The Capeman": The Lure of Gang Violence to a Latin Beat', *New York Times*, 30 Jan. 1998; also Brantley, '"Capeman": A Sad Spectacle', *International Herald Tribune*, 31 Jan. 1998.

5 'Sea Canes', *Sea Grapes* (London: Jonathan Cape, 1976), 81.

6 Dalya Alberge and Mark Henderson, 'Hard Lines for Poet Laureate Favourites', *The Times*, 9 Jan. 1999.

7 Geordie Greig, 'On the Crest of a Wave', *Sunday Times*, 14 Feb, 1999.

Acknowledgements

A TWO year grant from the National Endowment for the Humanities: Interpretive Research Division (which is not responsible for my opinions) made possible a major portion of the research, especially in the West Indies. I owe a special debt to Irma E. Goldstraw, *Derek Walcott: An Annotated Bibliography of His Works* (1984), and to Goldstraw's *Derek Walcott Collection List* for the West Indian Collection at the University of the West Indies, St Augustine, 'detailed' by Patrick Anthony. The two notebooks (University of the West Indies, Mona) containing a prose draft for *Another Life* and Walcott's various manuscript drafts for the unfinished 'American, without America' (Walcott Collection at St Augustine), an aborted prose continuation of *Another Life*, provided me with many facts, starting-places for my research, and insights into Walcott's feelings and ideas. It is difficult to acknowledge the precise nature of such debts or where and how they have been used, but they often have. Gordon Collier saved me much work by supplying me with computer disks containing most of Walcott's Trinidadian and Jamaican journalism that he and Christopher Balme were collecting. Robert Hamner has always been helpful. Roderick Walcott, Faye Walcott Chin, and Richard Montgomery commented on parts of my manuscript. Adele King and James Harris (in the Ball State Honours program) helped me with revisons and checking facts.

This book would have been impossible without information, documents, and help from the following individuals, libraries, publishers, foundations, festival organizations, theatre companies, and radio and television companies:

Australia: Anne Collett, Les Murray.

Barbados: Ellice Collymore, Leonard and Pamela St Hill, George Lamming, Christine Matthews, Monica Henry Procope, John Wickham, David Williams, Cynthia Wilson. Department of Archives, *Nation* library.

Belgium: Chantal Zabus.

Canada: Ronald Bryden, Ted Chamberlin, Cyril Dabydeen, Greg Gatenby, Edna Hajnal, Janette Turner Hospital, Doris Hambuch, Luella Massey, D. C. Emerson Mathurin, Norline Metivier, Michael Millgate, Victor Ramraj, Paula Sperdakos, Lloyd Stanford, Roderick Walcott. Harbourfront (Toronto); University of Toronto, Thomas Fisher Rare Book Library.

Denmark: Bruce Clunes-Ross, Pia Hansen, Bo Green Jensen, Ib Lauritzen, Benedicta Pécseli, Johannes Riis. Gyldendal (Copenhagen); Aarhus Teater.

England: John Adams, Philippa Bassett, Janet Birkett, Debra Blackwood, David Blake, Michael Bott, Antonia Bradford, Yvonne Brewster, David Brierley, Stewart Brown,

Paula Burnett, Antonia Byatt, Burt Caesar, Colin Chambers, David Cohen, Ros Cranston, David Dabydeen, Marjorie Davies, Greg Doran, Mary Enright, Jane Feaver, John Figueroa, Peter Forbes, Malcolm Frederick, John Fuller, John Gilmore, Simon Gimson, Shirley Gordon, Roger Green, Terry Hands, Anna Harries, Julian Henriques, Chris Hill, Judith Hillmore, Charlotte Howard, Michael Horovitz, Claire Hudson, Pat and Peter Ireson, Lyn Innes, Veronica Jenkin, Ruth Vaughn Jones, Peter Kampados, Jacqueline Kavanagh, Christiane Keane, Liz Kirby, Andrew Kirk, Paola Marchionni, E. Archie Markham, Tom Maschler, Mustapha Matura, Glyn Maxwell, Joan-Ann Maynard, Sylvia Morris, Alastair Niven, Charles Osborne, Bruce Palling, Anton Phillips, Marian and Roger Pringle, E. M. Rainey, Chris Rice, Lionel Rogosin, Alan Ross, Lawrence Scott, Sudeep Sen, Christopher Sheppard, F. M. Smith, Neil Somerville, Martha Smart, Max Stafford-Clark, Jackie Tuckey, John Thieme, Eva Tucker, Jeff Walden, Anne Walmsley. The Secretary and the Deputy Treasurer to The Queen; and Press Office, Buckingham Palace. BBC Information & Archives (Reading); British Film Institute, National Film and Television Archive; British Library, National Sound Archive; Commonwealth Institute (London); Poetry Library, South Bank Centre (London); British Library, Reference Division; Shakespeare Birthplace Trust (Stratford-upon-Avon, England); University of Birmingham, Special Collections; University of Durham, Special Collections; University of Leeds, Brotherton Collection; University of Reading, Archives; University of Warwick, Centre for Caribbean Studies; Theatre Museum (London); Jonathan Cape; Faber and Faber; London Festival of Literature; South Bank Show, London Television Centre; BBC Radio 4 (*Desert Island Discs*, created by Roy Plomley); BBC South (for *Poetry Please*); Birmingham Repertory Theatre; Black Theatre Co-operative (London); The Black Theatre Forum (London); Royal Shakespeare Company (London and Stratford-upon-Avon); Talawa Theatre Company (London); Tower Theatre (London); Poetry Book Society; Poetry Society; Tate Gallery, BWIA (for *Caribbean Beat*); London Festival of Literature.

France: David Applefield, Jacqueline Bardolph, Tirthankar Chanda, Arnaud Dornon, Jean-Pierre Durix, Geneviève and Michel Fabre, Michelle Lapautre, Claire Malroux, Tierno Monénembo, José Turpin, Abdourahman Wabéri, Edmund White.

Germany: Christopher Balme, Eckhard Breitinger, Gordon Collier, Hölger Ehling, Klaus Martens, Bettina Schrewe, Mark Stein. Carl Hanser Verlag (Munich).

Guadeloupe: Maryse Condé.

Holland: Ricardo Burgzorg, Rufus Collins, Martin Mooij, Anne Wertheim. De Nieuw Amsterdam Theatergroep, DNA; Poetry International Rotterdam; Stichting John Adams Instituut West-Indisch Huis (Amsterdam).

Isle of Wight: Les Sklaroff.

Italy: Simonetta Mazza, Luigi Sampietro, Francesca Zannese, Susanna Zevi. Adelphi edizioni (Milan).

Ireland: Laurence Cassidy, Michael Diskin, Theo Dorgan, Seamus Heaney, Bob Welch. *Irish Times* Library; Arts Council; Cúirt Festival (Galway).

Acknowledgements 661

Jamaica: Roy Augier, Edward Baugh, Dunstan Champagnie, Cheryl Dash, J. Michael Dash, Patricia Dunn, Allan Kirton, Lucille Mair, Alma Mock Yen, Mary Morgan, Mervyn Morris, Archie Hudson-Phillips, Velma Pollard, Frances Salmon, Sir Philip Sherlock, Jean Small, Gloria Thompson, Ralph Thompson. University of West Indies, West Indian Collection; University of the West Indies, Radio Education Unit and UWI Library of the Spoken Word; University of the West Indies, Public Relations.

Japan: Shozo Tokunaga.

Martinique: Edouard Glissant.

Mexico: Norman Glass, José Luis Rivas.

St Croix: Arnold Highfield, Lorraine Joseph, Erika Waters. *The Caribbean Writer*.

St Lucia: Nancy Atkinson, Father Patrick Anthony, Victoria Augustin, Emma Clarke Bernez, Oliver Cadet, Helen Camps, Cuthbert Charles, Pat Charles, Frances Clauzel, Sonia Elliot, Moira Flavius, André Francis, June Frederick, Hunter Francois, Luther Francois, Patrick Freeman, Michael Gilkes, Kendel Hipolyte, Ria Hodgson, Colin Hunte, Arthur Jacobs, Carleen Jules, Ann King, Brigid King, Derek King, Jane King, Owen King, Winville King, John Robert Lee, Michael Mondesir, Sigrid Nama, George Odlum, Rhona Pilgrim, Father St Rose, Dunstan St Omer, Daphne St Helene, Lady Simmons, Wanda Bernez-Sutherland, Randall Sutherland, Ruth Theobolds, Margot Thomas, Francis Tobias, Derek Walcott, O. A. Walker, Chester Williams, Deidre Williams, Gregor Williams. Central Library (Castries); *Crusader*; Folklore Research Centre; Sir Arthur Lewis Community College Library (St Lucia); National Archives; National Trust; Pastoral Centre; Radio St Lucia; Cadet Photos.

St Maarten: Catherine Benoît.

St Thomas: Winifred Heftell Honigfort, Dennis Parker.

Scotland: Robert Crawford, A. N. Jeffares.

Spain: Kathleen Firth, José Antonio Gurpegui, Pilar Barrero Garcia (Ministerio de Cultura- Directora del Centro del Libro y de la Lectura), Jorge Herralde, Isabel Santaolalla. Anagrama (Barcelona).

South Africa: Nuruddin Farah. South African Library (Capetown).

Sweden: Äke Erlandsson, Magnus Florin, Gabi Gleichmann, Baroness Carola Hermelin, Seppo Laukkanen, Lars Löfgren, Maria Kristoferson, Anita Molander, Östen Sjöstrand, Ena Strandmark. Nobelbibliotek, Svenska Akademiens (Stockholm); Wahlström & Widstrand (Stockholm); Kungliga Dramatiska Teatern (Stockholm).

Trinidad: Gloria Baptiste, Stella Beaubrun, Lloyd Best, Sookdeo Bhagwandeen, Carol La Chapelle, Colvin Chen, Mary-Alyce St Juste-Chen, Margaret Chow, Karen De Lima Foster, Fay Gillespie, John Gillespie, Anson Gonzales, Rachael Hope, Winston James, Errol Jones, Jackie Hinkson, Annette Knight, Vere Knight, Colin Laird, Albert Laveau, Earl Lovelace, Mark Lyndersay, Stanley Marshall, Therese Mills, Sonya Moze, Marilyn Patrick, Grace Phelps, Ken Ramchand, Rabia Ramlogan, Nigel Scott, André Tanker,

Margaret Walcott. Art Creators; Colonial Life Insurance; Library, *Daily Express*; Library, *Trinidad Guardian*; University of the West Indies, West Indiana Collection.

United States: Donald Allen, T. J. Anderson, James Arnold, Jo Arnold, Bridget Aschenberg, William Baer, Linda Jane Barnette, Frederick W. Bauman, Jr., Steven Benedict, Robert Bensen, Pat Boone, Bernie Boxill, Sarah Breckenridge, Laurence Breiner, Paul Breslin, Stephen Breslow, Eloise Brière, Lisa Browar, Marilyn Burlingame, Rafael Campo, John Chernoff, Faye Walcott Chin, Mark Coffy, George Core, Ann Patrice Corrigan, Lorin Cuoco, Fred D'Aguiar, Gregson Davis, Surjit Dulai, Carrol B. Fleming, Gerald Freund, Jonathan Galassi, William Gass, Anne Gefell, Robert Giroux, Eliahus Glasser, Russ Greer, Eileen Gregory, Ronald Gwiazda, Oscar Haac, Marilyn Hacker, Daniel Halpern, Robert Hamner, Elizabeth Hardwick, James Harris, Errol Hill, Edward Hirsch, Cathy Henderson, George Houston, Pam Jordan, Paul Kane, Bill Keeney, Tony Kellman, Karl Kirchwey, Valerie Komor, Keri Kotler, Dirk Kuyk Jr., Diana Lachatanere, Joanne Lafler, Amy K. Leimkuhler, Harald Leusman, Jonathan Levi, Bernth Lindfors, Nancy Lyon, Tom McClellan, Andrea Mark, Nina Marshall, Peggy Miller, Richard Montgomery, Ruth Moore, Rose Marie Morse, Kent Mullikin, James Najarian, Harold Orlans, Lee Oser, Lisa Paddock, Gail Merrifield Papp, Basil Paquet, Sandra Pouchet Paquet, Tara Parmiter, Marny Payne, Ellen Pearson, Richard Pettengill, Caryl Phillips, Robert Pinsky, Lawrence Pithkethly, Mary Donna Pond, Wayne Pond, Kemp Powers, Carolyn Prager, Fran Quinn, Sara Qureshi, David Ray, William Riggan, Carl Rollyson, Ken Rose, Barney Rosset, Rhonda Cobham Sander, Joan Sandler, A. Vincent Scarano, Stephen Scott, Rock Schulfer, Kendra Schwartz, Jeff Seroy, Brenda Shaugnhessy, William Schullenberger, Amelia Silvestri, Michael Simpson, Edward Skipworth, Duncan Smith, William Jay Smith, Amy Stevens, Catharine R. Stimpson, William Stingone, John D. Stinson, Pat Strachan, Roger W. Straus, G. Thomas Tanselle, Rei Terada, Kathryn Van Spanckeren, Reetika Vazirani, Alan R. Velie, George White, Peregrine Whittlesey, Rick Williams, David Wise, Nisma Zaman. Rockefeller Archive Center; John Simon Guggenheim Memorial Foundation; John D. and Catherine T. MacArthur Foundation; Chicago Public Library (Goodman Archives, Special Collections); Cornell University, Rare Books and Manuscript Collections; Oral History Research, Columbia University; Houghton Library, Harvard University; Lamont Poetry Room, Harvard University; Library of Congress, Manuscript Division; University of Dallas, English Department; Lilly Library, University of Indiana; University of Missouri, Kansas City (Rare Books); Harry Ranson Humanities Research Center, University of Texas at Austin; Institute of Latin American Studies, University of Texas, Austin; New York Public Library for the Performing Arts, Billy Rose Theatre Collection; New York Public Library Center for the Humanities (Rare Books and Manuscripts); New York Public Library, Schomburg Center for Research in Black Culture; Rockefeller Archive (Tarrytown, New York); International Writers Center (Washington University, St Louis); Yale Drama School Library; Yale University Library, Beinecke Rare Book and Manuscript Library; Farrar, Straus and Giroux (New York); New York Center for Visual History; Arena Stage (Washington); Boston Playwrights Theatre; Goodman Theatre (Chicago); Guthrie Theatre (Minneapolis); Hartford Stage Company; New York Shakespeare Festival; SITE Santa Fe; *World Literature Today*; Boneau/Bryan-Brown; livetreichard; 92nd Street Y, Unterberg Poetry Center; Ball State University.

Wales: Eirionedd Baskerville, Tony Bianchi, Peter Florence, Ned Thomas. National Library of Wales (Aberystwyth); Hay-on-Wye Festival (Wales); Arts Council of Wales.

I apologize to those I have forgotten. My *Derek Walcott and West Indian Drama* offers a more detailed history of the Trinidad Theatre Workshop, productions of Walcott's plays in the West Indies, and their reception. It should be consulted for reviews of the plays and information about the actors.

My thanks to Paul Breslin for helping with the proof-reading.

Sources

PROPER scholarly documentation of this book would itself require a book, as many paragraphs would need long lists of citations. To avoid a Variorum *Walcottiad* I have kept documentation to a minimum. My Acknowledgements includes sources, but the following might be a useful guide.

Bound copies of the *Voice of St Lucia* and the *West Indian Crusader* can be found in the National Archives, St Lucia. The West Indiana Collection at the University of the West Indies, St Augustine, Trinidad, holds the largest body of Walcott's letters, manuscripts, and notes, especially until 1976. The University of the West Indies, Mona, Jamaica, holds the notebooks for *Another Life*, Jamaican publications, and photocopies of Walcott materials destroyed in a fire in St Lucia. Walcott's recent manuscripts, letters, and other materials are in the Thomas Fisher Rare Book Library, University of Toronto. Materials concerning BBC *Caribbean Voices* and Swanzy are at BBC Information in Reading and the Rare Books Collection, Birmingham University. Collymore material not at the University of the West Indies, St Augustine, can be found at the National Archives, Barbados. Most Harrison and Freund materials can be found in the Rockefeller Foundation Archives, Tarrytown, NY. Letters between Ross and Walcott and other *London Magazine* material can be found at the University of Texas and Brotherton Library, Leeds University. Cape and Tom Maschler correspondence is held by the University of Reading. John Fuller owns letters and other material concerning his father. A few William Plomer letters are at Durham University. Lowell letters are at Harvard, Texas, Trinidad, and the Rockefeller Archives. The New York Public Library holds *New Yorker* and Farrar, Straus and Giroux materials until 1980 and Ecco Press correspondence. Farrar, Straus and Giroux made files after 1980 available to me, and allowed me to photocopy its publicity files including copies of reviews. Jane Feaver supplied me with many reviews from Faber files. Pat Strachan has a selection of copies of letters during the time she was Walcott's editor. The New York Public Library of Performing Arts holds Joseph Papp and New York Shakespeare Festival materials. Berrigan material is at Cornell University and St Augustine. British theatre reviews can be found at the Theatre Museum; *London Theatre Record* is the place to start. Gordon Collier supplied me with computer disks of photocopies he and Chris Balme made of articles from *Public Opinion* and the *Trinidad Guardian* which filled many gaps between copies I made in Trinidad and Jamaica. They supplemented broken runs at the University of the West Indies, Jamaica, and the Jamaican Library with newspaper files at the British Museum. Banyan Studios, Port of Spain, has useful video tapes.

Select Bibliography

As a bibliography of Walcott's writing, manuscripts, and letters, together with other relevant materials, would take many volumes, this select bibliography is mostly based on what is mentioned in the book. Previously unrecorded early writings are marked*; those entries marked tt are to be found in the Walcott Archives, West Indian Collection, University of the West Indies, St Augustine. The entries are listed under the following headings:

I. Primary Sources

A. 1. Collected Poems
A. 2. Some Uncollected Poems
A. 3. Translation
B. 1. Published Plays
B. 2. Unpublished Plays for which Scripts Exist
B. 3. Unpublished Plays for which No Scripts Exist
B. 4. Film Scripts
B. 5. Film Scripts Unmade
C. 1. Prose
C. 2. Edited Lectures
C. 3. Some Unpublished Prose
D. Interviews
E. Introductions to Anthologies
F. Panels

II. Secondary Sources

A. 1. Books
A. 2. Special Issues of Journals
A. 3. Reviews and Articles
B. 1. Unattributed Background Material
B. 2. Attributed Background Material

III. Personal Communications with the Author

A. 1. Letters
A. 2. Interviews
A. 3. Telephone Interviews
A. 4. E-mails

I. Primary Sources

A. 1. Collected Poems

25 Poems (Port of Spain, Trinidad: Guardian, 1948 [1949]; rpt. Bridgetown, Barbados: Advocate, 1949).

Epitaph for the Young: XII Cantos (Barbados: Advocate, 1949).

Poems (Kingston: City Printery, 1951).

'Ruins of a Great House', *New World Writing*, Tenth Mentor Selection (New York: American Library, Nov. 1956), 159–60.

'A Far Cry from Africa', *Public Opinion*, 15 Dec. 1956, 7.

In a Green Night: Poems 1948–1960 (London: Jonathan Cape, 1962).

'Goats and Monkeys', in *15 Poems for William Shakespeare*, ed. E. W. White (Stratford-upon-Avon: The Trustees and Guardians of Shakespeare's Birthplace, 1964), 5–6.

Selected Poems (New York: Farrar, Straus, 1964).

The Castaway and Other Poems (London: Jonathan Cape, 1965; pb 1969).

The Gulf and Other Poems (London: Jonathan Cape, 1969).

The Gulf: Poems (New York: Farrar, Straus and Giroux, 1970).

'The Silent Woman', *Trinidad Guardian*, 14 Dec. 1972, 2; *Express*, 14 Dec. 1972, 25.

Another Life (New York: Farrar, Straus and Giroux, 1973).

Sea Grapes (London: Jonathan Cape, 1976.) Farrar, Straus and Giroux, 1976 has a few variants.

'From the Schooner Flight', *Massachusetts Review*, 18: 4 (Winter 1977), 795–800.

The Star-Apple Kingdom (New York: Farrar, Straus and Giroux, 1979).

'The Insulted Landscape' [revised from 'Star-Apple Kingdom'], 1980 Poetry Audio PR9216. W35x1980. This and some other taped readings are at the Harvard College Library.

The Fortunate Traveller (New York: Farrar, Straus and Giroux, 1981).

Selected Poetry, ed. Wayne Brown (London: Heinemann, 1981).

The Caribbean Poetry of Derek Walcott and the Art of Romare Bearden, selected poems by Walcott, illustrations by Bearden, introduction by Brodsky (New York: Limited Editions Club, 1983).

Midsummer (New York: Farrar, Straus and Giroux, 1984).

'Love after Love', *Esquire*, Aug. 1986, 97.

Collected Poems 1948–1984 (New York: Farrar, Straus and Giroux, 1986).

The Arkansas Testament (New York: Farrar, Straus and Giroux, 1987).

Omeros (New York: Farrar, Straus and Giroux, 1990).

Poems 1965–1980 (London: Jonathan Cape, 1992). Republishes Cape editions of *The Castaway and Other Poems* (1965), *The Gulf and Other Poems* (1969), *Sea Grapes* (1976), and *The Star-Apple Kingdom* (1980).

The Bounty (New York: Farrar, Straus and Giroux, 1997).

A. 2. Some Uncollected Poems

Derek Walcott, '1944', *Voice of St Lucia*, 2 Aug. 1944, 3.

*D.W., 'Two Poems', *Voice of St Lucia*, 12 Sept. 1946, 3 ('Pardon me Muse, I am a humble man, . . .' and 'Once, long ago I made two world [*sic*] be one, . . .').

*Derek Walcott, 'Epitaph for the Young', *Voice of St Lucia*, 21 Dec. 1946, 8 ('Yes, yes it had rained nearly two weeks now, . . .').

*D.W., 'One Poem' *Voice of St Lucia*, 28 June 1947, 5 ('Each bird throating down to the ripening year's').

*'As the Dying Water' by D. A. W., *St Mary's Annual 1948–49*, Castries, 1949, 22.

'Letter for Broodhagen', *Bim*, 3: 11 (Dec. 1949), 238.

'A Packet for Eros', BBC *Caribbean Voices*, 5 Aug. 1951.

'Sambo Agonistes', *Bim*, 4: 15 (Dec. 1951), 209–11.

'A Leave Taking', *Bim*, 5: 18 (June 1953), 110–11.

'Man O' War Bird', *Bim* 5: 19 (Dec. 1953), 233–4.

'A Fragment from Mantegna', BBC *Caribbean Voices*, 5 Apr. 1953.

'The Well of Being', BBC *Caribbean Voices*, 20 Sept. 1953.

'Hatred by Moonlight', BBC *Caribbean Voices*, 14 Nov. 1954.

'He who fears the scattered seed', *Kyk-over-al*, 6: 20 (Mid-Year 1955), 140.

'Though suns burn still, remembering pyres', *Kyk-over-al*, 6: 20 (Mid-Year 1955), 139.

'When I dreamed I found', *Kyk-over-al*, 6: 20 (Mid-Year 1955), 139–40.

'Go, Lovely Worm', *Bim*, 6: 24 (Jan.–June 1957), 231.

'A Lost Age', *Bim*, 6: 24 (Jan.–June 1957), 231–2.

'Ballades Creole pour Harry Simmons par Derek Walcott', *Voice of St Lucia*, 8 Feb. 1958, 2.

'Words for Rent', *Caribbean Quarterly*, 5: 2 (Feb. 1958), 99–102; rpt. *Caribbean Quarterly*, 38: 4 (Dec. 1992), 9–13.

'A Missile of Devotions from Her Faith', *Opus* (Feb. 1960), 30.

'Commune', *Tapia* (17 Dec. 1972), 6.

'A Patriot to Patriots', *New Writing in the Caribbean*, ed. A. J. Seymour (Georgetown, Guyana, 1972), 112–13.

'Non Serviam', *Tapia* (9 Sep. 1973), 9.

'O. S. Moses; The Man and the Myth', *New Letters*, 40: 1 (Oct. 1973), 65–7.

'Rider', *New Letters*, 40: 1 (Oct. 1973), 67–8.

'For Mildred', *David Frost Introduces Trinidad and Tobago*, ed. Michael Anthony and Andrew Carr (London: André Deutsch, 1975), 14.

'Interior', *Co-operation Canada*, 19 (Mar./Apr. 1975), 32–3.

'The Little Nations', *Co-operation Canada*, 19 (Mar./Apr. 1975), 31.

'Martial Law', *Co-operation Canada*, 19 (Mar./Apr. 1975), 31–2.

'George Campbell', in George Campbell's *First Poems* (New York: Garland, 1981), pp. vii–viii.

'On the Indian Trail', *Partisan Review*, 53: 4 (1986), 612.

A. 3. Translation

Joseph Brodsky, 'Letters from the Ming Dynasty', trans. Derek Walcott, *New Yorker*, 28 Jan. 1980, 32; in Brodsky's *Part of Speech* (New York: Farrar, Straus and Giroux, 1980), 132–3.

B. 1. Published Plays

Henri Christophe: A Chronicle in Seven Scenes (Bridgetown, Barbados: Advocate, 1950).

'Robin and Andrea', *Bim*, 4: 13 (Dec. 1950), 19–23.

Harry Dernier: A Play for Radio Production (Bridgetown, Barbados: Advocate, 1952).

The Sea at Dauphin (Port-of-Spain: Extra-Mural Department, 1954).

The Wine of the Country (University of the West Indies: Extra-Mural Department, Caribbean Plays, Duplicated typescript, n.d. [1956?]).

Ione: A Play with Music (Kingston: printed by the Gleaner: Extra-Mural Department, University College of the West Indies, 1957), Caribbean Plays No. 8.

Ti-Jean: A Play in One Act (Jamaica: Extra-Mural Department, 1957).

Drums and Colours: An Epic Drama, Caribbean Quarterly, 7: 1–2 (Mar. 1961), 1–104.

Jourmard or A Comedy to the Last Minute (University of the West Indies: Extra-Mural Department, Duplicated typescript, n.d. [early 1960s]).

Dream on Monkey Mountain and Other Plays (New York: Farrar, Straus and Giroux, 1970).

The Joker of Seville & O Babylon! (New York: Farrar, Straus, and Giroux, 1978).

Remembrance & Pantomime (New York: Farrar, Straus and Giroux, 1980).

Three Plays. The Last Carnival, Beef No Chicken, A Branch of the Blue Nile (New York: Farrar, Straus and Company, 1986).

Sista karnevalen (Stockholm: Wahlström & Widstrand, 1992). The Swedish 1992 version is different from *The Last Carnival* published in *Three Plays*.

The Odyssey: A Stage Version (New York: Farrar, Straus and Giroux, 1993).

B. 2. Unpublished Plays for which Scripts Exist

Paolo and Francesca (Senza Alcan Sospetto), 1950.

The Charlatan, 1962, 1973, 1974.

Batai, 1965.

Franklin, 1969, 1973, 1990.

Heavenly Peace (unperformed, 1973).

Solo to the Hudson (unperformed, 1979).

Marie Laveau, 1979–80.

Wind, Sand and Stars: The Little Prince (unperformed, 1980).

The Isle is Full of Noises, 1982.

Haytian Earth, 1984.

To Die for Grenada, 1986.

The Ghost Dance, 1989.

Viva Detroit, 1990.

Steel, 1991.

The Capeman (with Paul Simon), 1994.

B. 3. Unpublished Plays for which no Scripts Found

Another World for the Lost, 1946.

Simple Cornada.

So-So's Wake.

Cry for a Leader, 1950.

The Dying Gods, 1953.

Crossroads, 1954.

The Golden Lions, 1956.

B. 4. Film Scripts
'The Snow Queen, A Television Play', *People*, Apr. 1977, 39–42.
'The Rig', 1982–3.
'Hart Crane'.

B. 5. Film Scripts Unmade
'Un Voyage A Cythère' (27-page short story).
Vangelo Nero, 1972.

C. 1. Prose
*'Note' prefacing Hunter François, *First and Last Poems* (Bridgetown, 1949), n.p.
*'The New Verse Drama', *Voice of St Lucia*, 17 June 1950, 2.
*'Introduction to The Work of Dunstan St Omer', *Voice of St Lucia*, 28 July 1950, 5, 6.
*'Soufriere "a manor of thy friends"', *Daily Gleaner*, 15 June 1955, 8; *Voice of St Lucia*, 22 June 1955, 4.
'Modern Theatre', *Daily Gleaner*, 25 Mar. 1957, 12.
'Christianity and Tragedy', *Public Opinion*, 30 Mar. 1957, 4.
'The Poetry of George Campbell', *Public Opinion*, 20 July 1957, 7.
'*Drums and Colours*', *West Indies Festival of Arts 1958*, 8–9.
[?] 'The Little Carib Theatre Workshop', *Opus A Review* (Feb. 1960), 31–2 [unsigned].
'Reflections on the November Exhibition', *Sunday Guardian*, 13 Nov. 1960, 7.
'Jose Limon Highlighted Indifferent Theatre Year', *Sunday Guardian*, 1 Jan. 1961, 7.
'Unique Lighting Equipment Offered', *Trinidad Guardian*, 20 Aug. 1961, 7.
'United States Director Takes a Look at Queen's Hall', *Trinidad Guardian*, 30 Aug. 1961, 5.
'A Great New Novel of the West Indies/ The man who was born unlucky', *Sunday Guardian*, 5 Nov. 1961, 17.
'Poet From the Land of Bean and The Cod', *Sunday Guardian*, 10 June 1962, 9.
'History and Picong in *The Middle Passage*', *Sunday Guardian*, 30 Sept. 1962, 9.
'Derek Walcott Looks at off-Broadway Theatre', *Trinidad Guardian*, 20 Oct. 1963, 7.
'An Artist Interprets Cricket', *Trinidad Guardian*, 1 Jan. 1964, 5.
'Spiritual Purpose Lacking', *Sunday Guardian*, 5 Jan. 1964, 3.
'The Achievement of V. S. Naipaul', *Sunday Guardian*, 12 Apr. 1964, 15.
'A Great Russian Novel', *Sunday Guardian*, 19 Apr. 1964, 15.
'Bewildered and Betwixt am I', *Trinidad Guardian*, 2 Sept. 1964, 5.
'Mr Naipaul's Passage to India', *Sunday Guardian*, 20 Sept. 1964, 2, 4.
'Necessity of Negritude', *Trinidad Guardian*, 28 Sept. 1964, 8.
'Berlin: The ABC of Negritude', *Sunday Guardian*, 18 Oct. 1964, 11.
'Drama: East Side, West Side', *Sunday Guardian*, 25 Oct. 1964, 11.
'Spate of Anthologies Coming Up', *Trinidad Guardian*, 11 Nov. 1964, 5.
'Conversations with a General', *Trinidad Guardian*, 18 Nov. 1964, 5.
'The Figure of Crusoe' [1965], *Critical Perspectives on Derek Walcott*, ed. Robert D. Hamner (Washington: Three Continents Press, 1993), 33–40.
'Leaving School', *London Magazine*, 5: 6 (1965), 4–14.
'The Theatre of Abuse', *Sunday Guardian*, 2 Jan. 1965, 4.

'Efficient "Birdie", Minus the Feather-Ruffling', *Trinidad Guardian*, 6 Jan. 1965, 6.

'T. S. Eliot—Master of an Age', *Sunday Guardian*, 10 Jan. 1965, 3.

'Mighty Terror—A Great Matador', *Trinidad Guardian*, 17 Jan. 1965, 13.

'S. Grande Tonight; Broadway Next' *Trinidad Guardian*, 27 Jan. 1965, 5.

'Interview with V. S. Naipaul', *Sunday Guardian*, 7 Mar. 1965, 5, 7.

'Return to Jamaica: Remembered Mountains', *Sunday Guardian Magazine*, 4 Apr. 1965, 6, 7.

'Return to Jamaica: Struggle for a New Outlook in the Arts, *Sunday Guardian*, 11 Apr. 1965, 7, 8.

'A Journey into the Interior', *Sunday Guardian*, 11 Apr. 1965, 6.

'Analysing Wilson Harris', *Sunday Guardian Magazine*, 30 May 1965, 8, 14.

'Crisis of Conscience: Ban, Ban Caliban is the Cry', *Sunday Guardian*, 22 Aug. 1965, 11.

'Rogosin's Effort Could Compensate', *Trinidad Guardian*, 25 Aug. 1965, 5.

'Theatre in Guyana', *Sunday Guardian Magazine*, 21 Nov. 1965, 6.

'What Do You Want, Mama? Caiso Men Don't Whisper', *Trinidad Guardian*, 29 Sept. 1965, 5.

'Commonwealth Literature, *Sunday Guardian*, 17 Oct. 1965, 14.

'Chairman's Report in Colour', *Sunday Guardian*, 14 Nov. 1965, 21.

'The Prospect of a National Theatre', *Sunday Guardian*, 6 Mar. 1966, 6.

'Time to Separate Politics from Good Verse', *Trinidad Guardian*, 17 Mar. 1966, 8.

'Patterns of Existence', *Trinidad Guardian*, 24 Mar. 1966, 7.

'Tracking Mr. Wilson Harris', *Sunday Guardian*, 24 Apr. 1966.

'Tribute to a Master', *Trinidad Guardian*, 15 May 1966, 9.

'An Appreciation', *Voice of St Lucia*, 18 May 1966.

'Problems of Exile', *Sunday Guardian*, 13 July 1966, 6.

'The Great Irony', *Sunday Guardian*, 25 Sept. 1966, 6.

'Contemplative is Word for His Genius', *Trinidad Guardian*, 5 Oct. 1966, 5.

'Migrants' Lot', *Trinidad Guardian*, 29 Oct. 1966, 8.

'Pinache', *Sunday Guardian*, 18 Dec. 1966, 6.

'Another Kind of Sentimentality', *Sunday Guardian Magazine*, 12 Feb. 1967, 8.

'Is V. S. Naipaul an Angry Young Man?', *Sunday Guardian Magazine*, 6 Aug. 1967, 8–9.

'What the Twilight Says: An Overture', *Dream on Monkey Mountain and Other Plays*, 3–40; rpt. '*Twilight*'.

'Meanings', *Savacou*, 2 (Sept. 1970), 45–51.

'Superfluous Defence of a Revolutionary', *Express*, 20 Aug. 1971, 4.

'The Caribbean: Culture or Mimicry?', *Journal of Interamerican Studies and World Affairs*, 16: 1 (Feb. 1974), 3–13.

'The Muse of History', in *Is Massa Day Dead?*, ed. Orde Coombs (Garden City, NY: Anchor/Doubleday, 1974), 1–27; rpt. '*Twilight*'.

'On Choosing Port of Spain', in *David Frost Introduces Trinidad and Tobago*, ed. Michael Anthony and Andrew Carr (London: André Deutsch, 1975), 14–23.

'A Rediscovery of Islands', *New York Times*, 13 Nov. 1983, XX, 21.

'Papa's Flying Machines', *New York Times Book Review*, 13 Nov. 1983, 37, 51.

'On Robert Lowell', *New York Review of Books*, 1 Mar. 1984, 25, 28–31; rpt. '*Twilight*'.

'A Classic of Cricket', *New York Times Book Review*, 25 Mar. 1984, 1, 36–7; rpt. '*Twilight*'.

'Native Women under Sea-Almond Trees: Musings on Art, Life and the Island of St Lucia', *House & Garden*, 156: 8 (Aug. 1984), 114–15, 161–3.

'Café Martinique', *House & Garden*, 157: 3 (Mar. 1985), 140, 222, 224, 226, 228; rpt. '*Twilight*'.

'A Colonial's Eye-View of the Empire', *TriQuarterly*, Winter 1986, 73–84. American Audio Prose Library. AAPL 510.

'On the Beat in Trinidad', *New York Times Magazine*, 5 Oct. 1986, 38, 40–1, 43–4.

'The Garden Path', *The New Republic*, 13 Apr. 1987, 27–31; rpt. '*Twilight*'.

'Magic Industry', *New York Review of Books*, 24 Nov. 1988, 35–9; rpt. '*Twilight*'.

'Caligula's Horse', *Kunapipi*, 11: 1 (1989), 138–42.

'Crocodile Dandy', *The New Republic*, 200: 6 (5 Feb. 1989), 25–8; rpt. '*Twilight*'.

'Master of the Ordinary', *New York Review of Books*, 1 June 1989, 37–9; rpt. '*Twilight*'.

'Medusa Face', *Weekend Telegraph*, 21 Oct. 1989; rpt. '*Twilight*'.

'"Islands In The Stream", Hemingway, Winslow Homer, and the Light of the Caribbean', *Bostonia* (May/June 1990), 20–2; rpt. '*Twilight*'.

'Jackie Hinkson', *Galerie* [Trinidad, ed. Geoff McLean], 1: 2 (1992); rpt. in *The Massachusetts Review* (Autumn–Winter 1994), 413–17.

The Antilles: Fragments of Epic Memory (New York: Farrar, Straus and Giroux, 1993). The Nobel Lecture; rpt. in '*Twilight*'.

'The Road Taken', *The New Republic*, 213 (27 Nov. 1995), 29–36; rpt. in Joseph Brodsky, Seamus Heaney, and Derek Walcott, *Homage to Robert Frost* (New York: Farrar, Straus and Giroux, 1996), and '*Twilight*'.

'Guest Speaker: Derek Walcott: Where I Live', *Architectural Digest* (Jan. 1997), 30, 32, 34, 36.

'A Letter to Chamoiseau', *New York Review of Books*, 14 Aug. 1997, rpt. '*Twilight*'.

'What the Twilight Says': Essays (New York: Farrar, Straus and Giroux, 1998).

C. 2. Edited Lectures

'Take the Money—and Write', *New York Times*, 3 Nov. 1991, sect. 4, E15.

'The Land of Look Behind', *Money Index* [Jamaica], 366 (27 Apr. 1993), c–f.

'A Tribute to C. L. R. James', in *C. L. R. James: His Intellectual Legacies*, ed. Selwyn R. Cudjoe and William E. Cain (Amherst, Mass.: University of Massachusetts Press, 1995), 34–48.

'The Sea is History', in Frank Birbalsingh (ed.), *Frontiers of Caribbean Literature in English* (New York: St Martin's Press, 1996), 22–8.

'Afterword: Animals, Elemental Tales, and the Theatre', in James Arnold (ed.), *Monsters, Tricksters, and Sacred Cows: Stories of American Identities* (Charlottesville, Va.: University Press of Virginia, 1996), 269–77.

'Reflections on *Omeros*', *The Poetics of Derek Walcott*, ed. Gregson Davis, *South Atlantic Quarterly*, 96: 2 (Spring 1997), 229–46.

C. 3. Some Unpublished Prose

'Passage to Paradise', 1952 (lost novel).

'Notes: The Road', partly from Oct. 1966? (4 pages) [tt].

'Forward', Trinidad, Aug. 1969 [to Dream on Monkey Mountain and Other Plays, tt].

'Letter from Trinidad', May 1970 [tt].

'Influences', n.d. [tt].

'American, without America'. While part of this was published as 'The Caribbean: Culture or Mimicry' there are over a hundred pages including:

(*a*) 'The Shouting in the Square' (5 pages), [tt].

(*b*) 'The Chelsea' [tt].

(*c*) 'A third through this book's guessed length', 1974 [tt].

(*d*) 'Isla Incognita', 1973 [tt].

'Calypso as theatre', 1977 (6 pages).

'Essay on Soyinka's *The Road*', 12 Feb. 1978 (draft, 9 pages) [tt].

'The Grenadian Revolution' (47 pages) [tt].

'The One Moutain Road', Toronto, 1984? (45 pages about Grenada and the American invasion).

'Good Old Heart of Darkness', Toronto, 1984 (about Grenada).

'Inside the Cathedral', 1987 (29 pages) [tt].

'Heaney's Ireland', Toronto, 1991.

D. Interviews

'Man of the Theatre', *New Yorker*, 26 June 1971, 30–1.

'Revolution Rhetoric Clouds Writer's Search for Truth', *Kansas City Times*, 13 June 1973, 18A.

'Celebration: An Interview with Derek Walcott', *Play Mas*, The Goodman Theatre [Study] Guide, Chicago, 1981, 31–3.

'This Country is a Very Small Place', *Sunday Express*, 14 Mar. 1982, 18–19.

'Derek Walcott on Hart Crane: Interview Excerpts', *Center for Visual History Newsletter*, 1: 2 (Fall 1985).

'A Conversation with Derek Walcott', *Tampa Review*, 1 (1984), 39–49.

ATLAS, JAMES, 'Derek Walcott: Poet of Two Worlds', *New York Times Magazine*, 23 May 1982, sect. 6, 32–4, 38–51.

BACON, JEREMY, 'Baron and Nobel Laureate Do Battle Over Island Idyll', *Sunday Telegraph*, 11 Oct. 1992.

BAER, WILLIAM, 'An Interview with Derek Walcott', *The Formalist*, 5: 1 (1994), 12–25; rpt. in William Baer, *Conversations* (Jackson, Miss.: University Press of Mississippi, 1996).

——(ed.), *Conversations with Derek Walcott* (Jackson, Miss.: University Press of Mississippi, 1996).

BATTERSBY, EILEEN, *Irish Times*, 28 Apr. 1994.

BAUGH, EDWARD, 'Derek Walcott on West Indian Literature and Theatre', *Jamaican Journal*, 21: 2 (May 1988), 50–2.

BENJAMIN, MARINA, 'The Commonwealth: Pedestal or Pyre?', *New Statesman & Society*, 21 July 1995, 30–1.

BENSEN, ROBERT, 'Poets of Two Worlds', *The Wick* [Hartwick College] 2: 3 (Dec. 1988), 14–16.

BROWN, ROBERT, and JOHNSON, CHERYL, 'Thinking Poetry: An Interview with Derek Walcott', *Cream City Review*, 14: 2 (Winter 1990), 208–23.

CICCARELLI, SHARON L., 'Reflections Before and After Carnival: An Interview with Derek Walcott', in Michael Harper and Robert Stepho (eds.), *Chant of Saints: A Gathering of Afro-American Literature, Arts and Scholarship* (Urbana, Ill.: University of Illinois Press, 1979), 296–309.

CARTY, CLARAN, 'Nobel for a Brothers Boy', *Sunday Tribune* [Ireland], 8 May 1994, B5.

CHRISTON, LAWRENCE, 'Island Son', *Los Angeles Times*, 7 June 1990, sect. F, 1, 6.

CONLEY, JIM, 'Poet is Willing Captive of Society', *Abilene Reporter News*, 23 Sept. 1984, Books 6.

DOYLE-MARSHALL, WILLIAM, 'Walcott Speaks Through a New Medium', *Sunday Gleaner*, 22 June 1986, 8–9.

FLANAGAN, BRENDA, 'An Interview with Derek Walcott', *Voices of the African Diaspora: CAAS*, 7 (1991), 16–20.

FLEMING, CARROL, 'Talking With Derek Walcott', *The Caribbean Writer*, 7 (1993), 52–61.

GALLAGHER, PATRICK, 'Homer to Windward', *Sunday Independent* [Dublin], 16 July 1989, 18.

GARDELS, NATHAN, 'Occupation Is an "Act of Salvation"', *Los Angeles Times*, 22 Sept. 1994; also published as 'The Salvation of Haiti' in *New Perspectives*, 11: 4 (Fall 1994), 24–5.

GREIG, GEORDIE, 'On the Crest of a Wave', *Sunday Times*, 14 Feb. 1999, 8–9.

GRONDAHI, PAUL, 'West Indian Poet at Ease in Albany', *The Times Union*, 2 Feb. 1989, B-6.

HALL, STUART, *Derek Walcott: The Poet on the Island*, BBC, producer, Julian Henriques, *Arena*, 26 Feb. 1993.

HARTIGAN, PATTI, 'The Passions of Derek Walcott', *Boston Sunday Globe*, 25 Apr. 1993, B25–6.

HIRSCH, EDWARD, 'An Interview with Derek Walcott', *Contemporary Literature*, 20: 3 (Summer 1979), 279–92.

—— 'The Art of Poetry XXXVII', *The Paris Review* (Winter 1986), 196–230.

JAGGI, MAYA, 'No Trouble in Paradise', *Guardian*, 12 July 1997; also 'Enjoying the Fruits of Life's Bounty', *Guardian Weekly*, 27 July 1997, 27.

JANUSZCZAK, WALDEMAR, 'The Longing on St Lucia', *Guardian*, 9 July 1988.

KELLAWAY, KATE, 'Caribbean Son', *Observer*, 6 Mar. 1988.

LYDON, CHRISTOPHER (with Walcott and Seamus Heaney), 'Robert Penn Warren', *Partisan Review*, 53: 4 (1986), 606–12.

McCARTHY, SHAUN, 'Interviewed By', *Outposts*, 171 (Winter 1991), 4–24.

McKENZIE, FIONA, 'A Borrowed Language', *Art Link: A Commonwealth Arts Review*, (Dec. 1980), 27.

MANGAL, HENRY, 'Interview with Derek Walcott', *St Mary's College St Lucia: Annual College Magazine* (Oct. 1984), 29–30.

MAURO, WALTER, 'Derek Walcott: "Io vivo in un Paradiso rubato"', *Il Giorno*, 31 May 1996.

MILLS, THERESE, 'Conversation with Derek Walcott', *Sunday Guardian*, 20 June 1971, 10, 17.

MONTENEGRO, DAVID, 'An Interview with Derek Walcott', *Partisan Review* (Spring 1990), 202–14.

MOYERS, BILL, 'The Leprosy of Empire', *Sunday Guardian Magazine*, 6 Dec. 1992, 6–7.

PANTIN, RAOUL, 'We Are Still Being Betrayed', *Caribbean Contact*, 1: 7 (July 1973), 14, 16.

—— 'Any Revolution Based on Race is Suicidal', *Caribbean Contact*, 1: 8 (Aug. 1973), 14, 16.

RAP[antin], 'Poet Walcott Blasts Trinidad on Freedom', *Caribbean Contact*, 5: 10 (Feb. 1978), 1.

PHILLIPS, CARYL, 'Derek Walcott', *Bomb* (Summer 1992), 46–9.

PRESSON, REBEKAH, 'The Man Who Keeps the English Language Alive: An Interview with Derek Walcott', *New Letters*, 59: 1 (1992), 8–15.

PRYCE-JONES, DAVID, 'Island Fling—A Caribbean Evening', *Radio Times*, 25 Jan. 1979, 71–3; BBC Sound Archive Index, 'Derek Walcott Author and Speaker: Caribbean Evening a Sequence of Programmes', SP T061504–11.

Victor Questel interviews Walcott about drama and the Trinidad Theatre Workshop, 5 Jan. 1980, Banyan, Port of Spain, 4 video tapes.

Kenneth Ramchand interviews Walcott about his poetry, 7 Jan. 1981, Banyan, Port of Spain, 4 video tapes.

RODMAN, SELDEN, 'Derek Walcott: Redefinitions', *The American Way* (Feb. 1972), 27–32 [American Airlines]. Also in Rodman's *Tongues of Fallen Angels* (New York: New Directions, 1974), 232–59.

ROWELL, CHARLES, 'An Interview with Derek Walcott Part I', *Callaloo*, 34 (Winter 1988), 80–9.

SAMPIETRO, LUIGI, 'An Object Beyond One's Own Life', *Caribana*, 2 (Rome: Bulzoni Editore, 1991), 25–36.

—— 'On *Omeros*', *Caribana*, 3 (Rome: Bulzoni Editore, 1992–3) 31–44.

SJÖBERG, LEIF, 'An Interview with Derek Walcott', *ARTES*, 1 (1983), 23–37.

STONE, JUDY, 'We Can Gain from Outside Experience', *Trinidad Guardian*, 1 Dec. 1985, 17.

STYRON, ROSE, 'Derek Walcott: An Interview by Rose Styron', *American Poetry Review*, 26: 3 (May/June, 1997), 41–6.

THOMAS, JO, 'For a Caribbean Poet, Inner Tension and Foreign Support', *New York Times*, 21 Aug. 1979, 2.

WALCOTT, DEREK, 'The Commonwealth: Pedestal or Pyre?', *New Statesman & Society*, 21 July 1995, 30–1.

WARDLE, IRVING, 'Brilliant Portrayal of Changed Roles', *The Times*, 19 Dec. 1979.

WAYNE, RICK, 'Monkey-Mountain Man Dreams On', *Star* [St Lucia], 13 June 1987, 6–7, 19; Part II, 20 June 1987, 12–13.

—— 'Says Derek Walcott "I'm ready to die for my country!"', *Star*, 26 May 1990, 3.

WEEKS, JEROME, 'Across the Great Divide', *Dallas Morning News*, 3 Apr. 1997, 1C, and 'back page'.

WHITE, J. P., 'An Interview with Derek Walcott', *Green Mountains Review*, NS 4: 1 (Spring/Summer 1990), 14–37.

E. Introductions to Anthologies

'Some West Indian Poets: Selected by Derek Walcott', *London Magazine* (Sept. 1965), 15–30.

F. Panels

TUCKER, MARTIN, 'Education by Poetry', *Confrontation*, 33 (1986), 295–306.
'Poets' Round Table "A Common Language"', *PN Review*, 15: 4 (1989), 39–47.
'The Lisbon Conference on Literature: A Round Table of Central European and Russian
  Writers', *Cross Currents: A Yearbook of Central Europe Culture*, 9 (1990), 75–124.
'Panel II', *The Georgia Review* (Winter 1995), 861–84.

II. Secondary Sources

A. 1. Books

ALLIS, JEANNETTE B., *West Indian Literature: An Index to Criticism, 1930–1975* (Boston:
  G. K. Hall, n.d. [1980?]).
BAUGH, EDWARD, *Derek Walcott: Memory as Vision: Another Life* (Harlow: Longman, 1978).
BONSIGNORI, UMBERTO, *Derek Walcott: Contemporary West Indian Poet and Playwright*, Ph.D.
  diss., University of California, Los Angeles, 1972 (Ann Arbor: University Microfilms,
  1977).
BROWN, LLYOD, *West Indian Poetry* (Boston: Twayne, 1978).
BROWN, STEWART (ed.), *The Art of Derek Walcott* (Poetry Wales Press: Seren Books, 1991).
GOLDSTRAW, IRMA E., *Derek Walcott: An Annotated Bibliography of His Works* (New York:
  Garland, 1984).
HAMNER, ROBERT D., *Derek Walcott* (New York: Twayne, 1981; 1993).
—— (ed.), *Critical Perspectives on Derek Walcott* (Washington: Three Continents Press, 1993).
—— *Epic of the Dispossessed: Derek Walcott's 'Omeros'* (Columbia, Mo., and London:
  University of Missouri Press, 1997).
KING, BRUCE, *Derek Walcott and West Indian Drama: 'Not Only a Playwright But a Company':
  The Trinidad Theatre Workshop 1959–1993* (Oxford: Clarendon Press, 1995).
STONE, JUDY S. J., *Theatre: Studies in West Indian Literature* (London: Macmillan Caribbean,
  1994).
TERADA, REI, *Derek Walcott's Poetry: American Mimicry* (Boston: Northeastern University
  Press, 1992).
THIEME, JOHN, *Derek Walcott* (Manchester: Manchester University Press, 1999).
THOMAS, NED, *Derek Walcott: Poet of the Islands* (Cardiff: Welsh Arts Council, 1980).

A. 2. Special Issues of Journals

The Literary Half-Yearly, 26: 1 (Jan. 1985), guest editor, Samuel Asein.
OUTPOSTS, 171 (Winter 1991), 1–49.
The Villager, 19 Mar. 1993, Villa Julie College.
Verse, 11: 2 (Summer 1994), 91–170.
The South Atlantic Quarterly, 96: 2 (Spring 1997), special issue, ed. Gregson Davis, 'The
  Poetics of Derek Walcott: Intertextual Perspective'.

A. 3. Reviews and Articles

Review of *Harry Dernier: A Play for Radio Production*, *Bim*, 5: 17 (1952), 79–80.
Anon., ' "Sea at Dauphin": Vignette Of Life and its Struggles', *Voice of St Lucia*, 19 Dec.
  1954, 1.

'Movement's Wake', *Times Literary Supplement*, 10 Feb. 1966, 104.

'Trinidad Group Does Folk Play at O'Neill Meet', *Variety*, 13 Aug. 1969.

'The Problem Facing W. I. Leaders: Through the Eyes of Derek Walcott in His Poems "The Star-apple Kingdom"', *Voice of St Lucia*, 18 June 1978, 10, 11, 15.

ALLEYNE, KEITH, 'Epitaph for the Young', *Bim*, 3: 11 (1949), 267–72.

ALVAREZ, A., *Sunday Observer*, 24 Oct. 1965, 27.

ANTHONY, PATRICK, 'Derek Walcott's "Easter"', *Pastoral Bulletin* [St Lucia], 7: 4 (1992), 3–10.

ASEIN, S. O., 'Walcott's Jamaica Years', *The Literary Half-Yearly*, 21: 2 (July 1980), 23–41.

AUGUSTE, B. L., 'A Triumph', *St Mary's College, Annual Magazine 1950–51*, 9–10.

BALAKIAN, PETER, 'The Poetry of Derek Walcott', *Poetry*, 148: 3 (June 1986), 169–77.

BARKER, J. S., 'Not the Stuff for a West Indian Theatre', *Guardian*, 15 Aug. 1954, 4.

BARNES, CLIVE, 'Racial Allegory: The "Dream on Monkey Mountain" Presented', *New York Times*, 15 Mar. 1971, 52.

—— 'Walcott's "Ti-Jean" Opens in Park', *New York Times*, 28 July 1972, 20.

BATTERSBY, EILEEN, 'Cúirt in Fine Sessions', *Irish Times*, 28 Apr. 1994.

BAXTER, WAYNE, 'D. Walcott's 25 Poems', *Voice of St Lucia*, 7 May 1949, 4.

BAUGH, EDWARD, 'Painters and Painting in Another Life', *Caribbean QuerFerly*, 26 (Mar.–June 1980), 83–93.

BAYLEY, JOHN, 'Living Ghosts', *New York Review of Books*, 27 Mar. 1997, 18–21.

BENSEN, ROBERT, 'Getting the Moment Right', *The Wick* (Spring 1981), 9–11.

—— 'The New World Poetry of Derek Walcott', *Concerning Poetry*, 16: 2 (1983), 29–42.

—— 'The Poet as Painter: Derek Walcott's *Midsummer*', *The Literary Review*, 29: 3 (Spring 1986), 257–68.

—— 'Poets of Two Worlds', *The Wick*, 2: 3 (Dec. 1988), 14–16.

—— 'Catherine Weldon in *Omeros* and *The Ghost Dance*', *Verse*, 11: 2 (Summer 1994), 119–25.

BERGER, JOHN, 'At First Sight', *New York Times*, 18 May 1986, 102.

BERMAN, PAUL, 'Theatre', *Nation*, 13 Apr. 1985, 443–4.

BHABHA, HOMI K., 'How Newness Enters the World: Postmodern Space, Postcolonial Times and the Trials of Cultural Translation', *The Location of Culture* (London: Routledge, 1994), 212–35.

BILLINGTON, MICHAEL, 'The Odyssey', *Guardian*, 6 July 1992.

BORDNER, RAYMOND, 'Allegorical Folk Play Produced in Waterford', *Day*, 2 Aug. 1969, 15.

'Edward Brathwaite looks at Walcott's *In a Green Night*', *Voice of St Lucia*, 13 Apr. 1963, 4.

BROWN, BOB, ' "The Isle is Full of Noises" Failure', *Bristol Press*, 30 Apr. 1982.

BROWN, STEWART, ' "Between me and thee is a great gulf fixed": The Crusoe Presence in Walcott's Early Poetry', in Lieve Spaas and Brian Stimpson (eds.), *Robinson Crusoe: Myths and Metamorphoses*, (Basingstoke: Macmillan, 1996), 210–24.

BROWN, WAYNE, 'Chow Time, King Kong', *Express*, 21 Mar. 1985, 10.

—— 'Caribbean Booktalk: Derek Walcott—His Poetry and His People', *Caribbean Affairs*, 1: 3 (July 1988), 174–93.

—— 'The Singer in his Prime', *Sunday Guardian*, 11 Oct. 1992, 5.

—— 'Glimpses of the Past', *Sunday Guardian*, 5 Sept. 1993.

BURNETT, PAULA, 'Omeros', *Wasafiri*, 14 (1991), 32–4.

—— 'Walcott's Spellbinding Drama', *Caribbean Times* (July 1992).

BURNSIDE, JOHN, 'Imagining a Body's Language', *Scotsman*, 19 July 1997.

BYNE, TERRY, 'Nobel Laureate's Drama Casts a Spell', *Boston Herald*, 27 July 1994, 41.

CARR, W. I., 'The Clear-Eyed Muse', *Sunday Gleaner* [Jamaica], 20 Jan. 1963, 14, 20.

—— 'The Significance of Derek Walcott', *Public Opinion*, 28 Feb. 1964, 8.

CATHOLICUS [C. JESSE], 'The Message of "The Sea at Dauphin": A Message of Morbid Fatalism', *Voice of St Lucia*, 22 Dec. 1954, 4.

CLAY, CAROLYN, 'Don Wanders', *Boston Phoenix*, 15 July 1994, 7.

COLLYMORE, FRANK, 'An Introduction to the Poetry of Derek Walcott', *Bim*, 3: 10 (June 1949), 125–32.

CONLEY, JIM, 'Poet is Willing Captive of Society', *Abilene Reporter-News*, 23 Sept. 1984, Books, 6.

CONNOLLY, CYRIL, 'The Professor and the Others', *Sunday Times*, 29 Apr. 1962.

DABYDEEN, DAVID, 'Its Food to Exorcise', *The Times*, 17 July 1997, 8.

L.M.D., 'Derek A. Walcott—Poet', *St Mary's Annual 1948–1949* (Castries, 1949), 20.

D'AGUIAR, FRED, *Wasafiri*, 1: 2 (Spring 1985), 37–8.

—— 'Adam's Other Garden: Derek Walcott's Exploration of the Creative Imagination', *Caribana*, 3 (Rome: Bulzoni Editore, 1992–93), 67–77.

DAKU, 'Telepic Review: Dream on Monkey Mountain', *Variety*, 17 Feb. 1970.

DASENBROCK, REED WAY, *World Literature Today*, 60: 3 (Summer 1988), 512–13.

DAWS, *Variety*, 12 June 1990.

DAY, RICHARD, ' "The Isle is Full": Finely Honed Satire', *Bridgeport Telegram*, 27 Apr. 1982.

DE DITMORE, MIKE, 'Walcott's Poetry Demands Rereading', *Abilene Reporter-News*, 23 Sept. 1984, 6E.

DeMOTT, BENJAMIN, 'Poems of Caribbean Wounds', *New York Times Book Review*, 13 May 1979, 11, 30.

DICKEY, JAMES, 'The Worlds of a Cosmic Castaway', *New York Times Book Review*, 2 Feb. 1986, 8.

DOBBS, KILDARE, 'An Outstanding Poet of This Generation', *Toronto Star*, 19 May 1973.

DONOGHUE, DENIS, 'Themes from Derek Walcott', *Parnassus: Poetry in Review* (Fall/ Winter 1977), 88–100.

DOVE, RITA, ' "Either I'm Nobody, or I'm a Nation" ', *Parnassus: Poetry in Review*, 14.1 (1987), 49–76.

DRAKE, SYLVIE, 'Walcott: He Sells Sarcasm by the Seashore', *Los Angeles Times*, 11 June 1990, F1, 3.

EAGLETON, TERRY, 'Plenty of Life', *Times Literary Supplement*, 9 Nov. 1984, 1290.

ESPINET, ADRIAN, '*Drums and Colours* Seeks to Trace Evolution of West Indian Consciousness', *Sunday Guardian*, 27 Apr. 1958, 7.

FABRE, MICHEL, ' "Adam's Task of Giving Things Their Name": The Poetry of Derek Walcott', *New Letters*, 41: 1 (Fall 1974), 91–107.

FEAVER, VICKI, 'An Island and its Noises', *Times Literary Supplement*, 8 Aug. 1980, 903.

FIGUEROA, JOHN, 'In a Green Night', *Caribbean Quarterly* (Dec. 1962), 67–9.

FORBES, PETER, 'Far and Feverish', *Poetry Review*, 76: 3 (1986), 14–16.

FORDE, A. N., *Bim*, 9: 36 (Jan.–June 1963), 288–90.

FRANCIS, WILLIAM V., Jr., 'Revolution Rhetoric Clouds Writer's Search for Truth', *Kansas City Times*, 13 June 1973, 18A.

FRISARDI, ANDREW, 'Verses of Things Past', *Boston Globe*, 12 Oct. 1997, E1, 4.

FULLER, ROY, 'The Poetry of D. A. Walcott', *Voice of St Lucia*, 9 June 1949, 5–7; 'The Poetry of Derek Walcott', *Public Opinion*, 4 June 1949, 6.

—— 'Poetry', *London Magazine*, 9: 8 (Nov. 1969), 89–90.

FURBANK, F. N., 'New Poetry', *Listener*, 5 July 1962, 33.

GARFITT, ROGER, *Times Literary Supplement*, 24 Sept. 1982, 1041.

GARRISON, DAVID, '*Midsummer*', *Minnesota Daily*, 17–19 Sept. 1984, 20 'Welcome Week Section'.

GONZALEZ, ANSON, 'Walcott's "Laventille"', *New Voices* (Mar. 1982), 39–44.

GOODMAN, HENRY, 'Carnival With a Calypso Beat', *Wall Street Journal*, 4 June 1974.

GRAY, IRVIN, 'Il Faut Paller', *Voice of St Lucia*, 8 Mar. 1958, 7 (poem in Creole praising Derek Walcott).

GUSSOW, MEL, 'Dinner is Served at Times in a Barroom', *New York Times*, 25 Feb. 1982.

GUTHRIE, JIM, ' "Dream on Monkey Mountain": Poem's The Thing', *Star Free Press*, 3 Sept. 1970.

HAMMERICH, R. C., 'Powerful Opening Act Highlights Play at Hartford Stage', *Morning Union* [Springfield, Conn.], 23 Apr. 1982.

HAMNER, ROBERT (ed.), 'Bibliography', in *Critical Perspectives on Derek Walcott* (Washington: Three Continents Press, 1993), 409–78.

HASS, ROBERT, 'Poet's Choice', *Washington Post*, 5 Oct. 1997, X02.

HEANEY, SEAMUS, 'The Language of Exile', *Parnassus*, 8.1 (Fall–Winter 1979), 5–11.

—— 'An Authentic Poetic Voice', *Boston Globe*, 9 Feb. 1986, A27–8.

HENDRICK, KIMMIS, 'Walcott's Poetic Play in L. A.', *Christian Science Monitor*, 9 Sept. 1970.

HENDRIKS, A. L., 'Epitaph for the Young', *Public Opinion*, 31 Dec. 1949, 6.

HILL, ERROL, 'Is "Man Better Man", Mr. Walcott', *Trinidad Guardian*, 3 Feb. 1965, 5.

—— 'No Tears for Narcissus', *Sunday Guardian*, 7 Mar. 1965, 7.

HIRSCH, SAMUEL, 'Trinidad Workshop: Ensemble of Extraordinary Power', *Sunday Herald Tribune*, 10 Aug. 1969, 1, 9.

HOLDER, G. A., 'BBC's Broadcast of Henri Christophe', *Bim*, 4: 14 (Jan.–June 1951), 141–2.

HOPKINSON, SLADE, 'So the Sun West Down', *Sunday Gleaner*, 15 Apr. 1956, 17.

HOSEIN, CLYDE, 'The New Walcott: Sweeping, Involved, Audacious', *Express* 9 Nov. 1969, 25.

ISAACS, ROBERT M., ' "Isle Full of Noises": Better Poetry than Play', *Waterbury Republican*, 30 Apr. 1982.

ISMOND, PATRICIA, 'Walcott's "Omeros"—A Complex, Ambitious Work', *Caribbean Contact*, 18: 5 (Mar.–Apr. 1991), 10–11.

IYER, PICO, 'Hymns for the Indigo Hour', *Time*, 14 July 1997, 85.

K. J., 'New Day Theatre Company, at the Tower', *New Statesman*, 1960.

JACOBSEN, JOSEPHINE, 'Books in Review', *Evening Sun* [Baltimore], 30 July 1964.

JAMES, C. L. R., 'Here's A Poet Who Sees The Real West Indies', *Sunday Guardian*, 6 May 1962, 5.

JENKIN, VERONICA, 'Drums and Colours', *Bim*, 7: 27 (July–Dec. 1958), 183–4.

JENNINGS, ELIZABETH, 'A Poet of Power', *Scotsman*, 29 Sept. 1973.

JOHNSON, WAYNE, 'Gaiety and Tragedy Coexist in "Carnival"', *Seattle Times*, 2 June 1983, D13.

JONES, BRIDGET, '"With Crusoe the Slave and Friday the Boss": Derek Walcott's *Pantomime*', in Lieve Spaas and Brian Stimpson (eds.), *Robinson Crusoe: Myths and Metamorphoses* (Basingstoke: Macmillan, 1996), 225–38.

JONES, KATIE, 'The Mulatto of Style', *Planet*, 62 (Apr.–May 1987), 97–9.

KELL, RICHARD, 'Books of the Day', *Guardian*, 10 Dec. 1965.

KELLAWAY, KATE, 'Paperback of the Week', *Observer*, 27 July 1997.

KRAMER, STACI D., 'Tropical Bard', *Chicago Tribune*, 25 Nov. 1992, C 1, 5.

LA MARRE, HAZEL, '"Dream on Monkey Mountain"—Stunning, Exciting Theatre', *Southwest News*, 3 Sept. 1970.

LAHR, JOHN, 'On-Stage', *Village Voice*, 18 Mar. 1971, 57–8.

LARDER, JAMES, 'Troubled Island' and '"Pantomime" in Trinidad', *Washington Post*, 21 May 1981, D1 and 2.

LAURENT, LAWRENCE, 'An Experiment on a Dream', *Washington Post*, 16 Feb. 1970, C4.

LEITHAUSER, BRAD, 'Ancestral Rhyme', *New Yorker*, 11 Feb. 1991, 91–5.

LENNOX, RAPHAEL, 'The Poet Read with a Twinkle in His Eyes', *Trinidad Guardian*, 26 Oct. 1964, 7.

LEVINE, FAIGA, 'Theatre Lines', *Jewish Week*, 4–10 June 1981.

LOGAN, WILLIAM, 'The Fatal Lure of Home', *New York Times Book Review*, 29 June 1997, 11.

LOVELACE, EARL, 'Theatre and Audiences', *Sunday Guardian*, 1 May 1966, 6.

LOWELL, ROBERT, 'Robert Lowell Introduces Derek Walcott at the Solomon R. Guggenheim Museum, October 15, 1964', *Envoy*, 46 (1985), 2–3. The recording of the 'Guggenheim Reading' is at Harvard Houghton Library.

LUCAS, JOHN, 'In Multitudinous Dialects', *New Statesman & Society*, 2 Feb. 1990, 33–4.

B.M., 'A Review: *Poems*: By Derek Walcott', *Public Opinion*, 6 Oct. 1951, 5, 6.

MACLAREN MURAL, REVD E. C., MB, PI, 'Derek Walcott's 25 Poems', *Voice of St Lucia*, 22 Jan. 1949, 7.

McCLATCHY, J. D., 'Divided Child', *The New Republic*, 194: 12 (24 Mar. 1986), 36–8.

McFARLANE, BASIL, 'Drama Festival Awards', *Public Opinion*, 28 July 1956.

McGARRY, PETER, 'Grandeur of Greece goes Caribbean', *Coventry Telegraph*, 3 July 1992, 20.

MARTIN, GRAHAM, 'New Poetry', *Listener*, 10 Mar. 1966.

MASON, MAURICE M., 'Derek Walcott's *Henri Christophe*', *Voice of St Lucia*, 10 Aug. 1950, 3, 4.

MATCHAN, LINDA, 'Making History Sing', *Boston Globe*, 5 Dec. 1993, B13, B18.

MATHURIN, LUCILLE, '"Henri Christophe"—a Review', *Voice of St Lucia*, 16 Sept. 1950, 4, 5.

MARX, BILL, 'Steel Lite', *Boston Phoenix*, 19 Apr. 1991, sect. 3, 10.

—— 'Right Dream: Derek Walcott takes on Marlowe and Shakespeare', *Boston Phoenix*, 29 July 1994, 10–11.

MAZZOCCO, ROBERT, 'Three Poets', *New York Review of Books*, 31 Dec. 1964, 18–19.

MELSER, JOHN, 'A Similar Quality Could be Achieved', *Trinidad Guardian*, 25 Apr. 1969.

MONTAGUE, JOHN, 'Fluent Muse', *Spectator*, 19 June 1962, 864.

MORRIS, MERVYN, 'Walcott and the Audience for Poetry', *Canbbeen Querterly*, 14 (1968), 1–24.

MORRISON, BLAKE, 'Beach Poets', *London Review of Books*, 4 (16 Sept. 1982), 16–17.

MOSHER, GREGORY, 'The Director Speaks: A Dialogue', *Panto*, The Goodman Theatre [Study] Guide (Chicago, 1982), 31–7.

O'BRIEN, SEAN, 'In Terms of the Ocean', *Times Literary Supplement*, 14 Sept. 1990, 977–8.

—— 'Unexpected Grandeur', *Sunday Times*, 13 July 1997.

OLIVER, EDITH, 'Off Broadway: Once Upon a Full Moon', *New Yorker*, 27 Mar. 1971, 83–4.

—— 'Displaced Person', *New Yorker*, 21 May 1979, 105–6.

—— 'Pantomime', *New Yorker*, 29 Dec. 1986, 78–9.

O'QUINN, JIM, 'Hartford Hosts Ward, Walcott and a New Idea', *Theatre Communications*, 4: 2 (May 1982), 1–3.

RAP[antin], 'The Last Carnival Disappointing', *Express*, 6 July 1982, 16.

'Paul', *Variety* 17 June 1981, 90.

PETTINGELL, PHOEBE, 'Making Epic Connections', *New Leader*, 11–25 Mar. 1991, 15–16.

PHELPS, KAREN, 'Where Actors and Audience Share the Same Level, *Trinidad Guardian*, 12 Jan. 1966, 3.

PIEPER, JEANNE, 'Meanderings in Malibu', *Malibu Times*, 18 Sept. 1970, 2.

PRESTON, ROHAN, 'Walcott Gives Life to Caribbean Epic', *Chicago Tribune*, 2 May 1993, sect. 5, tempo 5.

RICH, FRANK, 'Stage: Derek Walcott's "Pantomime" in Washington', *New York Times*, 30 May 1981.

—— 'Theatre: Douglas Turner Ward Directs Premiere', *New York Times*, 2 May 1982, 63.

RICHARDS, DAVID, 'A Tangle of Masks in "Pantomime"', *Washington Star*, 21 May 1981.

RODMAN, SELDEN, 'Caribbean Poet of Elizabethan Richness', *New York Times Book Review*, 11 Oct. 1970, 24.

—— 'Derek Walcott: Redefinitions', *The American Way*, 6: 2 (Feb. 1973), 26–32; rpt. in Selden Rodman, *Tongues of Fallen Angels* (London: Dutton, 1973).

—— 'Books in Brief: "The Star Apple Kingdom"', *National Review*, 31: 21 (May 1979), 694.

ROHLEHR, GORDON, 'Making Love Look More Like Despair', *Trinidad Guardian*, 13 Dec. 1969, 8.

—— 'Derek Walcott's The Gulf and Other Poems', *Black Images*, 1: 1 (1972), 66–9.

ROSS, ALAN, *Through the Caribbean: The M.C.C. Tour of the West Indies 1959–1960* (London: Hamish Hamilton, 1960).

—— 'The Castaway', *London Magazine*, NS 6: 10 (Jan. 1966), 88–91.

—— 'Derek Walcott & St Lucia', *London Magazine*, NS 35: 5 and 6 (Aug. 1995), 61–6.

ST GEORGE, ANDREW, 'A Caribbean Odyssey', *Financial Times*, 4 July 1992.

SANGER, RICHARD, 'The Apples of this Second Eden', *Times Literary Supplement*, 19 Sept. 1997, 10–11.

SEWELL, TONY, 'The Human Factor', *Voice* [UK], 20 Sept. 1986, 31.

SHERLOCK, PHILLIP, 'Young Derek Walcott', *Sunday Gleaner*, 18 Oct. 1992, 22C.

SIMMONS, HAROLD, 'An Appreciation of 25 Poems', *West Indian Crusader*, 29 Jan. 1949, 4–5; 'Appreciation of 25 Poems (Derek Walcott)', *Voice of St Lucia*, 5 Feb. 1949, 7, 9; '25 Poems by Derek Walcott . . . An Appreciation', *Guardian Weekly*, ? Feb., 1949, 14; 'An Appreciation of Twenty-Five Poems', *Public Opinion*, 5 Feb. 1949, 10, 11; 'A West Indian Poet Fulfills His Promise', *Sunday Gleaner*, 27 Feb. 1949.

—— 'A Critique of the Art Exhibition of Dunstan St Omer & Derek Walcott', *Voice of St Lucia*, 9 Sept. 1950, 2, 8.

—— ' "Ti Jean and His Brothers" A Creole Tale', *Voice of St Lucia*, 29 Dec. 1957, 2.

SJÖBERG, LEIF, 'On Derek Walcott' and 'Interview', *Greenfield Review*, 12: 1 and 2 (1984), 1–25. Translated from *ARTES*, 1 [Sweden] (1983), 23–37; Östen Sjöstrand's translations are in the same issue of *ARTES*.

STERN, FREDERICK C., 'The Formal Poetry Reading', *The Drama Review*, 35: 3 (Fall 1991), 67–84, 71–2.

STEWART, MARIAN, 'Walcott & Painting', *Jamaica Journal*, 45 (May 1981), 56–68.

STONE, JUDY, 'Death of our Dodos in "The Last Carnival" ', *Trinidad Guardian*, 15 July 1982, 18–19.

STUGEON, C. H., ' "The Sea at Dauphin" Reflected Great Credit to All Concerned', *Voice of St Lucia*, 21 Dec. 1954, 4, 6.

SULLIVAN, DAN, 'Language Weds Heartbeat in "Mountain" ', *Los Angeles Times*, 28 Aug. 1970, part IV, 1, 11.

SWANN, TONY, '*Drums and Colours*—Guts at Least', *Public Opinion*, 10 May 1958, 57.

SYMONS, JULIAN, 'Poetry', *Sunday Times*, 18 Apr. 1982.

SZIRTES, GEORGE, 'Sculptor of Light', *Literary Review* (Feb. 1987).

TAPLIN, OLIVER, 'Derek Walcott's *Omeros* and Derek Walcott's Homer', *Arion* (Spring 1991), 213–25.

—— 'Hustling Homer', *Times Literary Supplement*, 17 July 1992, 19.

THIEME, JOHN, 'Derek Walcott and "The Spoiler's Return" ', *The Yearbook of English Studies*, 25 (1995), 163–72.

THOMAS, NED, 'Loud World of the Mind', *Times Educational Supplement*, 5 Apr. 1974.

TOMALIN, CLAIRE, 'Derek Walcott's *Another Life*', *New Statesman*, 20 Dec. 1974, 904.

TRUEBLOOD, VALERIE, 'On Derek Walcott', *American Poetry Review*, 7: 8 (May/June 1978), 3–6.

TUGEND, TOM, 'Taper Forum "Dream" Is Almost Too Good', *Heritage*, 11 Sept. 1970.

VALE, RICHARD, ' "Monkey Mountain" Provides Thrilling West Indian Fare', *Evening Outlook*, 3 Sept. 1970.

VAZ, NOEL, 'Original Foreword', *Drums and Colours, Caribbean Quarterly*, 38: 4 (Dec. 1992), 22–3.

VENDLER, HELEN, 'Poet of Two Worlds', *New York Review of Books*, 4 Mar. 1982, 23, 26–7.

WALKER, ALICE, 'Another Life', *Village Voice*, 11 Apr. 1974, 26.

WALMSLEY, ANNE, 'Dimensions of Song', *Bim*, 13: 5 (July–Dec. 1970), 152–67.

WALSH, CHAD, 'A Life of Contradictions, A Poetry of Unities', *Book World*, 13 Dec. 1970, 3.

WARFIELD, POLLY, 'West Indies Fantasy is Brilliant Mosaic', *Gardena Valley News*, 3 Sept, 1970, 6.

WATT, DOUGLAS, ' "Ti-Jean & Brothers" Comes to Central Park', *Daily News*, 28 July 1972, 57.

WEDDE, IAN, 'Total Immersion: Derek Walcott's OMEROS', *Landfall*, 46: 4 (Dec. 1992), 483–9.

WICKHAM, JOHN, 'A Look at Ourselves', *Bim*, 6: 22 (June 1955), 128–30.

WIGGIN, MAURICE, 'Tropical Glory', *Sunday Times*, 21 Nov. 1965.

WILLIAMS, HUGO, *The London Magazine* (July 1962), 77–9.

B. 1. Unattributed Background Material

'Death of Mr. Warwick Walcott', *Voice of St Lucia*, 25 Apr. 1931, 5.

'Moving Tribute to Late W. Walcott: One of Nature's Gentlemen', *Voice of St Lucia*, 25 Apr. 1931, 5.

'Cards', *Voice of St Lucia*, 25 Apr. 1931, 5.

'The Art Exhibition', *Voice of St Lucia*, 20 Dec. 1944.

'St Lucia Arts and Crafts Society', *Voice of St Lucia*, 26 Apr. 1945, 2.

'Arts and Crafts Society Inaugurated', *Voice of St Lucia*, 27 Apr. 1945, 1–4 (probably by H. Simmons).

'Major and Mrs. Plunkett Leave To-morrow', *Voice of St Lucia*, 28 Aug. 1947, 1, 4.

'Mr Rodway Gets British Council Scholarship', *Voice of St Lucia*, 22 June 1946, 4.

'Literary Enterprise', *Voice of St Lucia*, 7 Nov. 1946, 2.

'Mrs. Christiana Walcott, 81', *Voice of St Lucia*, 1 Oct. 1947, 2.

'Princess Elizabeth's Scholarship Proposed', *West Indian Crusader*, 24 Jan. 1948, 4.

'West Indian Aspirations', *West Indian Crusader*, 7 Feb. 1948, 4.

'Arts Guild Formed', *Voice of St Lucia*, 11 Mar. 1950, 8.

'Eavesdropper', 'Candid Comments of "Henri Christophe" ', *Voice of St Lucia*, 8 Sept. 1950, 3.

'The Arts Guild present Henri Christophe by DEREK WALCOTT', *West Indian Crusader*, 16 Sept. 1950, 5.

'Walcott For W. I. University', *Voice of St Lucia*, 23 Sept. 1950, 4.

'Derek Walcott Praised in London', *Voice of St Lucia*, 1 Feb. 1952, 1.

'New Methodist School Opened', *Voice of St Lucia*, 19 Apr. 1952, 1, 2.

'New Walcott Play For Production During September', *Voice of St Lucia*, 8 Aug. 1953, 1.

'Annual Ceremony of Presentation of Graduates Takes Place March 19: Derek Walcott Among Those in Bachelor of Arts Group', *Voice of St Lucia*, 17 Mar. 1954, 2.

'New Walcott Play for UCWI Staging', *Voice of St Lucia*, 13 June 1954, 11.

'Extra-Mural Director Sect'y Here', *Voice of St Lucia*, 6 July 1954, 3.

'St Lucian U.C.W.I. Arts Graduate Weds Jamaican Extra-Mural Secretary', *Voice of St Lucia*, 27 Aug. 1954, 3.

'D. Walcott For Acting Post at GBSS', *Voice of St Lucia*, 20 Aug. 1954, 1.

'Folk Dance at Friday's Production', *Voice of St Lucia*, 12 Dec. 1954, 2.

'Patois Phrases in Walcott's Sea at Dauphin', *Voice of St Lucia*, 15 Dec. 1954, 1.

'Walcott Arrive [sic] from Grenada', *Voice of St Lucia*, 15 Dec. 1954, 3.

'Walcott Play Staging Again on Monday', *Voice of St Lucia*, 18 Dec. 1954, 1.

'Arts Guild Play Being Repeated Tomorrow Night', *Voice of St Lucia*, 19 Dec. 1954, 1.

'Derek Walcott', *Pelican Annual*, 1955?, 142.

'St Lucia Arts Guild Puts Another Writer on West Indian Drama Field', *Voice of St Lucia*, 8 May 1956, 3.

'U. C. W. I Newsletter', *Voice of St Lucia*, 12 Aug. 1956, 5.

'Mainly Personal', *Voice of St Lucia*, 17 Nov. 1957, 2.

'Arts' Guild Withdraws Plays', *Voice of St Lucia*, 15 Mar. 1958, 1.

'Who's Who in the Festival', *Voice of St Lucia*, 22 Mar. 1958, 3.

'Statement by His Lordship the Bishop of Castries on the Incident of the "Banjo Man" etc.', *Voice of St Lucia*, 22 Mar. 1958, 8.

'Suggestions For An English-Based Orthography for Creole', *Voice of St Lucia*, 19 Apr. 1958, 6.

'Arts Guild Plays Impress D'Ca Audience', *Voice of St Lucia*, 9 Aug. 1958, 1.

'Derek Walcott Gets Fellowship', *Voice of St Lucia*, 4 Oct. 1958, 1.

'A Farewell to a Patriot', *Voice of St Lucia*, 20 Dec. 1958, 6, 11.

'That Bill Hit the Press, Says Lawyers', *Express*, 30 Oct. 1971.

Haggis/Baggis, 9 (Spring 1972), 28–9. Miss Porter's School, Farmington, Connecticut 06032.

'Walcott Presents New Play', *Weekly Journal* [St Croix], 10–16 Oct. 1974, 3A, 14A.

'Derek Walcott Goes Back to School to Read Poetry', *Express*, 4 May 1981.

'Walcott—for Schools', *Sunday Gleaner*, 7 May 1982.

'Teacher to Offer to Leave His Post', *New York Times*, 1 June 1982.

'Love and the Poet', *Express*, 13 June 1982.

'Coed Accuses Teacher', *Time*, 14 June 1982, 56.

'Walcott's Play Run into a Picket Storm in the U.S.', *Express*, 23 Sept. 1984.

'Methodist School Honours Ex-Principal', *Voice of St Lucia*, 11 Feb. 1989, 2.

'Paul Simon's Journey to Brazil and Beyond', *New York Times*, 14 Oct. 1990, 1, 32–3.

'Walcott's Success a Lesson in Achievement', *Express*, 12 Oct. 1992, 3.

'Walcott's Award for the Young', *Daily Gleaner*, 29 Jan. 1993, 4.

'Journey with Walcott', *Trinidad Guardian*, 10 Aug. 1993.

'Walcott Fails to Show', *Trinidad Guardian*, 1 Sept. 1993.

'Ire of the Laureate', *Trinidad Guardian*, 2 Sept. 1993.

'Walcott may meet Clinton, Queen', *Trinidad Guardian*, 2 Sept. 1993.

'Walcott to Receive Award in December', *Express*, 2 Sept. 1993.

'Walcott Insulted Us', *Sunday Guardian*, 5 Sept. 1993.

'Nobel Prize Winner on 11 Stamps', *Linn's Stamp News*, 12 Sept. 1994, 8.

B. 2. Attributed Background Material

A Seeker, 'The Offending Poem', *Voice of St Lucia*, 9 Aug. 1944, 3.

All of Us, 'Three Evenings with Six Poets', *Kyk-over-al*, 3: 13 (1951), 214–20.

ALBERGE, DALYA, and HENDERSON, MARK, 'Hard Lines for Poet Laureate Favourites', *The Times*, 9 June 1999.

ANTHONY, FR. PATRICK, 'The Silent Revolution', *Caribbean Contact* (Aug. 1977), 10–11.

AUSLANDER, JOSEPH, *Cyclops Eye* (New York: Harper and Brothers, 1926), 118.

BALDEOSINGH, KAY, 'Walcott: Immoral to Move Workshop', *Daily Express*, 5 July 1993, 1, 4.

BALDWIN, RUTH C., 'Women Lose a Round', *New York Times*, 9 June 1982.

BERRIGAN, DANIEL, *The Trial of the Catonsville Nine* (Boston: Beacon Press, 1970).

—— *The Dark Night of Resistance* (Garden City, NY: Doubleday, 1971).

—— *Poetry, Drama, Poetry*, edited with an introduction by Michael True (Maryknoll, NY: Orbis Books, 1988).

BLEDMAN, P., 'Introducing Dunstan St Omer', *Voice of St Lucia*, 10 May 1950, 5.

BRANDFORD, ALBERT, 'A Sample of Walcott's Drama', *Weekend Nation*, 15 Jan. 1993, 19.

BRANTLEY, BEN, ' "The Capeman": The Lure of Gang Violence to a Latin Beat', *New York Times*, 30 Jan. 1998; also Brantley, ' "Capeman": A Sad Spectacle', *International Herald Tribune*, 31 Jan. 1998.

BRATHWAITE, EDWARD KAMAU, 'Timehri', in Orde Coombs (ed.), *Is Massa Day Dead?* (Garden City, NY: Anchor/Doubleday, 1974).

CANBY, VINCENT, 'The Caribbean Flavors a Homeric "Odyssey" ', *New York Times*, 30 Oct. 1994, 35–6.

'Catholicus Says—"Plays Profane" ' [C. Jesse], *Voice of St Lucia*, 22 Mar. 1958, 4.

COOPER, VERNON, 'St Lucian Greats: Derek & Roddy Walcott', *Voice of St Lucia*, 7 Nov. 1981, 2.

CORLISS, RICHARD, 'Club Adriatic', *Time*, 21 Nov. 1994, 61.

COULTHARD, R. G., 'Defence of an Anthology', *Trinidad Guardian*, 17 Mar. 1966, 8.

CRAVEN, THOMAS (ed.), *A Treasury of Arts Masterpieces: From the Renaissance to the Present Day* (New York: Simon and Schuster, 1939).

CRIER, SCOTT, 'What Does It Takes [*sic*] to Appreciate Walcott?', *University News* [Dallas], 2 Apr. 1997, 4.

CROWLEY, DAN, 'Painting in St Lucia', *Voice of St Lucia*, 6 Jan. 1956, 3, 4.

DABYDEEN, CYRIL, 'Derek Walcott in Ottawa', *The Spectrum*, 6: 2 (7 Feb. 1989), 1–2.

—— 'Letter to Derek Walcott', *Ariel*, 22: 2 (Apr. 1991), 21–2.

DUBNER, STEPHEN J., 'The Pop Perfectionist On a Crowded Stage', *New York Times Magazine*, 9 Nov. 1997, sect. 6, 42–9, 56, 63–6, 83.

EASTER, B. H., 'Banjo Man', *Voice of St Lucia*, 22 Mar. 1958, 4, 7.

FANIS, BARNARD, 'What Walcott Really Said', *Weekend Voice*, 6 Feb. 1993, 14.

FERMOR, PATRICK LEIGH, *The Traveller's Tree: A Journey through the Caribbean Islands* (London: John Murray, 1950).

FIGUEROA, JOHN (ed.), *Caribbean Voices* (London: Evans, 1966–72), 2 vols.

—— 'The Flaming Faith of These First Years: Caribbean Voices', in Maggie Butcher (ed.), *Tibisiri: Caribbean Writers and Critics* (Sydney: Dangeroo Press, 1989), 59–80.

—— 'Creole in Literature: Beyond Verisimilitude', *The Yearbook of English Studies*, 25 (1995), 156–62.

FLEMING, CARROL B., 'Poet Not Taken', *The Caribbean Writer*, 9 (1995), 58–9.

FRANCOIS, HUNTER J., *First and Last Poems* (Bridgetown: Self, 1949).

—— 'Latin in Schools Should Be Compulsory', *Voice of St Lucia*, 20 June 1978, 5–6.

FREUND, GERALD, *Narcissim & Philanthropy* (New York, Viking, 1996).

GLOUDON, BARBARA, 'Go deh . . . You-Wee', *Sunday Gleaner Magazine*, 7 May 1985, 11.

GRAHAM, THOMAS, 'West Indian Poet Derek Walcott to speak at HSU', Abilene Christian University *Optimist*, 18 Sept. 1984.

GRONDAHI, PAUL, 'West Indian Poet at Ease in Albany', *Times Union*, 2 Feb. 1989, B-6.

HARRISON, J. P., meeeting with Robertson, 9 July 1958. Harrison's diaries, Rockefeller Foundation Archives.

—— meeting with Robertson, 3 Sept. 1958. Harrison's diaries, Rockefeller Foundation Archives.

HAWES, CHARLES, 'Crucian Comment', *St Croix Avis*, 23 Mar. 1974, 10.

HEALY, PATRICK, 'When a Faculty Star Faces Harassment Charges', *Chronicle of Higher Education*, 19 Apr. 1996, A 23–4.

HOBAN, PHOEBE, 'Sharing Capeman Memories', *New York Times*, 1 Feb. 1998, sect. 6.

HOPKINSON, SLADE, ' "Public Opinion" To Back Walcott Play', *Public Opinion*, 29 Nov. 1958, 7.

HUMPHRIES, REBECCA, 'Walcott Goes On a Caribbean *Odyssey*', *Georgetown Voice*, 13 Oct. 1994, 13.

JESSE, FATHER CHARLES, FMI, 'Reflections on Reading the Poem "1944" ', *Voice of St Lucia*, 5 Aug. 1944.

—— 'The Agreed Syllabus', *Voice of St Lucia*, 2 Sept. 1944.

—— *Warblings from St Lucia* (Portus Hispaniac: Finbar, 1954).

—— *Outlines of St Lucia's History* (The St Lucia Archaeological and Historical Society, 1956; 5th edn., 1994).

JOHNSON, KIM, 'Double Vision: Derek Walcott as Painter', *Express*, 5 Dec. 1993, 1, 3.

JOHNSON, WILL, 'The Van Romondt Family', *For the Love of St Maarten* (London: Macmillan, 1987; 1994), 55–66.

JULES, DIDACUS, 'Patois Folk's Cry for Justice', *Caribbean Contact* (Mar. 1979), 9–10.

KELLY, KEVIN, 'The Poetic Power of Walcott's "Dream" ', *Boston Globe*, 26 July 1994, 57, 60.

LEWIS, GORDON, 'The West Indies Middle Class & the Future', *Voice of St Lucia*, 6 Sept. 1958, 4, 5.

LIEBERMAN, LAURENCE, *The Mural of Wakeful Sleep* (New York and London: Macmillan Publishing and Collier Macmillan, 1985).

LITTLE, CARL, 'Celebrating a Nobel Laureate: Derek Walcott', *Maine in Print*, 7: 11 (Dec. 1992), 1, 3.

LYMAN, RICK, 'On Stage and Off', *New York Times*, 26 Sept. 1997, E 2.

MCALARY, MIKE, 'Cape Fear', *New York*, 10 Nov. 1997, 38–44, 81.

MAKSON, LISA, 'Walcott Activities Enlighten Campus', *The University News* [Dallas], 15: 9 (9 Apr. 1997), 1, 4.

MARIANI, PAUL, *Lost Puritan: A Life of Robert Lowell* (New York: Norton, 1994).

MILNE, ANTHONY, 'Fran McDormand's Trinidad Adventure', *Express*, 25 July 1982.

MONPLAISIR, KENNETH, 'The Arts Guild and Its Struggle', *Voice of St Lucia*, 22 Mar. 1958, 4, 7.

NAIPAUL, V. S., 'Foreword' to *The Adventures of Gurudeva and Other Stories* by Seepersad Naipaul (London: André Deutsch, 1976).

NOEL, KEITH, 'The Many Sides of Derek Walcott', *Sunday Gleaner*, 22 Nov. 1992, 19D, 24D.

ODLUM, GEORGE, 'Alix Walcott—A Catalyst for Genius', *Crusader*, 19 May 1990, 5.

PEPINSTER, CATHERINE, 'Nobel Laureate Accused of Sexual Harassment', *Independent on Sunday*, 5 May 1996, 1.

PERSAUD, SASEMARINE, 'Whose Image?', *Caricom Perspective*, 61–2 (July–Dec. 1993), 38–9.

PICKERING, DAVID, *International Dictionary of Theatre, iii. Actors, Directors and Designers* (New York: St James Press, 1996).

Programme, Citations and Proclamation for Nobel Laureate Week January 21st to 28th 1993 Saint Lucia, compiled by The Crusader Publishing Co., printed by the Lithographic Press, Castries, St Lucia, 1993.

RAMCHARITAR, RAYMOND, 'And What for Naipaul?', *Trinidad Guardian*, 11 Oct. 1992.

—— 'Odyssey Best Production to Hit TT Theatre in Years', *Trinidad Guardian*, 10 Aug. 1993.

Margaret Ramsay letter to Tom Maschler, Reading Cape files.

RAYMOND, JUDY, 'Enter a New Set of Strolling Players', *Sunday Express*, 17 Jan. 1993.

RECKFORD, MICHAEL, 'The Company Pays Tribute to Derek Walcott', *Sunday Gleaner*, 1 Nov. 1992, 5D.

LA ROSE, 'Vive La Rose', *Voice of St Lucia*, 22 Mar. 1958, 5.

[Saint-Léger, Aléxis], 'Images a Crusoé', *Éloges*, 1911 (written 1904, first published 1909), in St John Perse [Léger, Aléxis Saint-Léger], *Éloges and Other Poems*, bilingual edition, translation by Louise Varèse (New York: Pantheon Books, 1944; 1956), Bollingen Series LV, 50–63.

ST OMER, DUNSTAN, 'Vulgarity in Art', *Voice of St Lucia*, 20 May 1950, 8.

—— 'The Crown of Glory', *Voice of Saint Lucia*, 5 Apr. 1958, 1. Lithograph with a short commentary below.

SCAGLIA, CHRISTINA, 'The Teatro Nationale of Milan goes Caribbean ... *Ti-Jean*', *Caribana*, 4 (1994–5), 35–41.

SCANLON, WALTER, 'Simon Says Capeman', *New York Press*, 26 Nov.–2 Dec. 1997, 32.

SCHWARTZ, AMY E., 'Who Owns History', *Washington Post*, 19 Oct. 1994, A23.

SCHWARTZ, LAWRENCE H., *Creating Faulkner's Reputation: The Politics of Literary Criticism* (Knoxville, Tenn.: University of Tennessee Press, 1988).

P.J.M.S. [herlock?], 'Castries Fire 1948', *Voice of St Lucia*, 18 June 1949, Special Weekend Section, 1.

SHERLOCK, PHILIP, 'Young Derek Walcott', *Sunday Gleaner*, 18 Oct. 1992, 22C.

SILER, JEANNE NICHOLSON, 'Nobel Countenance: A Prized Writer Keeps His Commitment', *UVA Alumni News*, Jan. 1993, 31.

SIMMONS, HAROLD, 'The Need for an Arts and Crafts Society', *Voice of St Lucia*, 21 Apr. 1945, 3, 4.

—— 'First Poems by George Campbell', *Voice of St Lucia*, 27 Mar. 1946, 2, 3.

—— 'The Flower Festivals of St Lucia', *Voice of St Lucia*, 27 Aug. 1953, 2.

—— 'New West Indian Playwright Makes Debut', *Voice of St Lucia*, 8 July 1956, 3.

—— ' "Spotlight" On the Dungeon of Culture: *The Banjo Man*', *Voice of St Lucia*, 15 Mar. 1958, 4.

—— 'Suggestions For An English-Based Orthography for Creole', *Voice of St Lucia*, 19 Apr. 1958, 6.

SIMMONS, TAD, 'Bill T. Jones Sets Walcott's *Mountain* in Motion', *American Theatre* (May/June 1994), 48–51.

SMITH, TREVER, 'Walcott in Dream World', *Sunday Guardian*, 18 July 1993.

SMOYER, MARK, 'Far from "Omeros"', *Metro*, 8–14 Dec. 1994, 24.

TAPER, BERNARD, 'Letter from Port of Spain', *New Yorker*, 23 Oct. 1965, 203–6.

VAN SERTIMA, IVAN, *Caribbean Writers: Critical Essays* (London: New Beacon Books, 1968).

VAZ, NOEL, 'The Stage', *West Indies Festival of Arts 1958*.

VITALIS, DAVID, 'An Attack on the "Kweyol Laureate"', *Weekend Voice*, 6 Feb. 1993, 14.

WALCOTT, ANNA, 'Walcott on Walcott', *Sunday Guardian*, 19 July 1992, 5.

WALCOTT, RODERICK, 'A Federated West Indian Theatre', *Voice of St Lucia*, 11 Mar. 1956, 6, 11.

—— '"A Mirror up to Nature": Reflections on the Creative Arts Summer School, Jamaica', *Voice of St Lucia*, 22 Sept. 1957, 4.

—— 'A Mirror up to Nature', *Voice of St Lucia*, 29 Sept. 1957, 7.

—— 'A Creole Folk Tale: A Preview of "Ti-Jean and His Brothers"', *Voice of St Lucia*, 1 Dec. 1957, 5.

—— 'The Candle In the Bushel of Art and Immorality', *Voice of St Lucia*, 29 Mar. 1958, 4, 5.

—— 'Raising the Colours: The West Indian Festival of Arts in Retrospect', *Voice of St Lucia*, 17 May 1958, 4, 8; 24 May 1958, 6, 8.

—— 'In Good Company', *Trinidad and Tobago Review*, Apr. 1993, 28–31.

WATERS, ERIKA J., 'Interview with John M. Figueroa', *The Caribbean Writer*, 6 (1992), 69–76.

WEEKES, TRAVIS, 'Walcott's IONE: Where OMEROS Began', *Weekend Voice*, 13 July 1996, 3.

WICKHAM, JOHN, 'Now That the Poet is 60', *Daily Nation*, 29 Jan. 1990, 7.

WILLIAMS, ERIC, 'The Significance of the Haitian Revolution', *Voice of St Lucia*, 6 Jan. 1951, 4, 5, 8.

III. Personal Communications with the Author

A. 1. Letters

Fred D'Aguiar, 25 Sept. 1995.

Robert Bensen, 15 Sept. 1995.

Ronald Bryden, 17 July 1995.

J. Edward Chamberlin, 19 June 1995.

John Figueroa, 11 May 1996.

Shirley Gordon, 26 Sept. 1994.

José Antonio Gurpegui, 6 June 1995.

Elizabeth Hardwick, 16 Jan. 1995.

Seamus Heaney, 13 Feb. 1995.

Errol Hill, 17 Oct. 1995; 31 Oct. 1995.
Tony Kellman, 3 July 1995.
G. M. Papp, 22 Sept. 1997.
Lawrence Pitkethly, 8 Feb. 1994.
Marian Pringle, 8 Mar. 1995.
Shozo Tokunaga, 12 Feb. 1998.

A. 2. Interviews

David Applefield, 27 July 1995.
Edouard Glissant, 4 Aug. 1995.
Glyn Maxwell, Jan. 1995.
Pat Strachan, Nov. 1995.
Derek Walcott, May 1994.

A. 3. Telephone Interviews

T. J. Anderson, 29 July 1997.
Ronald Bryden, 19 Mar. 1996.
Faye Walcott Chin, 1 May 1996.
Mark Coffey, 7 May 1996.
Cyril Dabydeen, 5 Aug. 1997.
John Figueroa, 23 Apr. 1996.
William Gass, 26 Mar. 1998.
Arnold Highfield, 24 Apr. 1996.
Dennis Parker, 29 Apr. 1996.
Caryl Phillips, 15 Oct. 1995.
Robert Pinsky, 18 Nov. 1995.
Lawrence Pitkethly, Mar. 1996.
Fran Quinn, 13 Mar. 1996.
Lionel Rogosin, 1 July 1995.
Lloyd Stanford, 15 Aug. 1997.
Rei Terada, 26 Sept. 1995.
Reetika Vaziani, 21 Mar. 1996.
Edmund White, 8 June 1997.

A. 4. E-mails

Rick Williams, 19 Sept. 1995.
William Schullenberger, Jan. 1999.
Nuruddin Farah, 7 Feb. 1999.

General Index

Index to Walcott's Works

Note: * indicates an unpublished text and ** indicates that a play was produced but was unpublished.